Mastering™ AutoCAD® 14

George Omura

SYBEX®

San Francisco • Paris • Düsseldorf • Soest

Associate Publisher: Amy Romanoff
Acquisitions Manager: Kristine Plachy
Acquisitions & Developmental Editor: Melanie Spiller
Editor: Maureen Adams
Technical Editor: Robin Hansen
Book Designer: Catalin Dulfu
Graphic Illustrator: Steve Brooks
Electronic Publishing Specialist: Nathan Johanson
Production Coordinator: Theresa Gonzalez
Proofreaders: Charles Mathews, Duncan J. Watson,
    Katherine Cooley
Indexer: Ted Laux
Cover Designer: Design Site
Cover Photographer: Mark Johann

Screen reproductions produced with Collage Complete.
Collage Complete is a trademark of Inner Media Inc.

SYBEX is a registered trademark of SYBEX Inc.
Mastering is a trademark of SYBEX Inc.

TRADEMARKS: SYBEX has attempted throughout this book to
distinguish proprietary trademarks from descriptive terms by following the capitalization style used by the manufacturer.

Netscape Communications, the Netscape Communications logo,
Netscape, and Netscape Navigator are trademarks of Netscape
Communications Corporation.

The CD interface music is from GIRA Sound AURIA Music
Library ©℗ GIRA Sound 1996.

The New San Francisco Library was designed by Pei Cobb Freed
& Partners and Simon Martin-Vegue Winkelstein Moris
Associated Architects. Floor plans prepared by SMWM and
Technical Publications. Exterior elevations prepared by PCF & P.

The author and publisher have made their best efforts to prepare
this book, and the content is based upon final release software
whenever possible. Portions of the manuscript may be based upon
pre-release versions supplied by software manufacturer(s). The
author and the publisher make no representation or warranties of
any kind with regard to the completeness or accuracy of the contents herein and accept no liability of any kind including but not
limited to performance, merchantability, fitness for any particular
purpose, or any losses or damages of any kind caused or alleged
to be caused directly or indirectly from this book.

Library of Congress Card Number: 97-67593
ISBN: 0-7821-2109-8

Manufactured in the United States of America

10 9 8

To my family and my teachers

ACKNOWLEDGMENTS

Book production is a complicated process, so I'm always amazed at how quickly *Mastering AutoCAD* evolves from manuscript to finished product. In many ways, it's quite magical; but behind the magic, there are many hardworking people giving their best effort. I'd like to thank those people who helped bring this book to you.

Heartfelt thanks go to the editorial and production teams at Sybex for their efforts in getting this book to press on an incredible schedule. Developmental Editor Melanie Spiller got things going and offered many great suggestions. Editor Maureen Adams made the frantic schedule bearable with humor and encouragement. Robin Hansen, technical editor, provided helpful suggestions as she carefully reviewed the book. Nathan Johanson, electronic publishing specialist, created the pages you see before you, and Theresa Gonzalez, production coordinator, steadfastly proofread every one of those pages. Finally, Molly Sharp and Dale Wright compiled our CD and made it easy and fun to use.

Thanks also go to the people at Autodesk for their support. Jim Quanci was always willing to give a helping hand. Kathy Koepke cheerfully provided the materials we needed and was always quick to respond to my questions.

I also wish to thank the many contributors to this book. First, a big thanks to Mike Gunderloy for his great work on ActiveX Automation in Chapter 20. Many thanks to my friend and colleague Robert B. Callori for his work on the *AutoCAD Instant Reference* on the CD-ROM. And thanks to Paul Richardson and Christine Merredith of Technical Publications for their work on the appendices and the *ABCs of AutoLISP*, which is also on the CD.

The handiwork of CAD specialists Technical Publications can also be seen in the sidebars that discuss the San Francisco Main Library. Thanks for the use of your wonderful drawings. And while we are on the subject, thanks also go to architectural firms of Pei Cobb Freed & Partners and Simon Martin-Vegue Winkelstein Moris Associated Architects for generously granting permission to reproduce drawings from their design of the San Francisco Main Library.

And finally, a great big thanks to my wife and sons who are always behind my work 100 percent.

CONTENTS AT A GLANCE

TABLE OF CONTENTS

7 Printing and Plotting 319

8 Adding Text to Drawings 359

Part III   Becoming an Expert   459

10   Storing and Linking Data with Graphics   461

INTRODUCTION

Welcome to *Mastering AutoCAD 14*. As many readers have already discovered, *Mastering AutoCAD* offers a unique blend of tutorial and source book that offers everything you need to get started and stay ahead with AutoCAD.

How to Use This Book

Rather than just showing you how each command works, *Mastering AutoCAD 14* shows you AutoCAD in the context of a meaningful activity. You will learn how to use commands while working on an actual project and progressing toward a goal. It also provides a foundation on which you can build your own methods for using AutoCAD, and become an AutoCAD expert yourself. For this reason, I haven't covered every single command or every permutation of a command response. The *AutoCAD 14 Instant Reference*, which we've included on the companion CD-ROM, will fill that purpose nicely. This online resource will help you quickly locate the commands you need. You should think of *Mastering AutoCAD 14* as a way to get a detailed look at AutoCAD as it is used on a real project. As you follow the exercises, I encourage you to also explore AutoCAD on your own, applying the techniques you learn to your own work.

Both the experienced and beginning AutoCAD user will find this book useful. However, if you are not an experienced user, the way to get the most out of this book is to approach it as a tutorial—chapter by chapter. You'll find that each chapter builds on the skills and information you learned in the previous one. To help you navigate, the exercises are shown in numbered steps. This book can also be used as a ready reference for your day-to-day problems and questions about commands. Optional exercises at the end of each chapter will help you review what you have learned and look at different ways to apply the information you've learned. In addition to the tutorial, experienced users will also find this book to be a handy reference tool.

Getting Information Fast

I've also included plenty of *Notes*, *Tips*, and *Warnings*. Notes supplement the main text, Tips are designed to make practice easier, and Warnings steer you away from pitfalls. Also, in each chapter you will find more extensive tips and discussions in the form of specially screened *sidebars*. To help encourage you along the way, some of the sidebars show you how topics in a chapter were applied to a real-world project, the San Francisco Main Library. Together the notes, tips, warnings, and sidebars provide a wealth of information I have gathered over years of using AutoCAD on a variety of projects in different office environments. You may want to browse through the book, just reading the margin notes and sidebars, to get an idea of how they might be useful to you.

Another quick reference you'll find yourself turning to often is Appendix D. This appendix is composed of tables of all the system settings with comments on their use.

What to Expect

Mastering AutoCAD 14 is divided into five parts, each representing a milestone in your progress toward becoming an expert AutoCAD user. Here is a description of those parts and what they will show you.

Part I: The Basics

As with any major endeavor, you must begin by tackling small, manageable tasks. In this first part, you will get familiar with the way AutoCAD looks and feels. Chapter 1, *This Is AutoCAD*, shows you how to get around in AutoCAD. In Chapter 2, *Creating Your First Drawing*, you will learn how to start and exit the program and how to respond to AutoCAD commands. Chapter 3, *Learning the Tools of the Trade*, tells you how to set up a work area, edit objects, and lay out a drawing. In Chapter 4, *Organizing Your Work*, you will explore some tools unique to CAD: symbols, blocks, and layers. As you are introduced to AutoCAD, you will also get a chance to make some drawings that you can use later in the book and perhaps even in future projects of your own.

Part II: Building on the Basics

Once you have the basics down, you will begin to explore some of AutoCAD's more subtle qualities. Chapter 5, *Editing for Productivity*, tells you how to reuse drawing setup information and parts of an existing drawing. In Chapter 6, *Enhancing Your Drawing Skills*, you will learn how to assemble and edit a large drawing file. Chapter 7, *Printing and Plotting*, shows you how to get your drawing onto hard copy. Chapter 8, *Adding Text to Drawings*, tells you how to annotate your drawing and edit your notes. Chapter 9, *Using Dimensions*, gives you practice in using automatic dimensioning, another unique CAD capability. Along the way, I will be giving you tips on editing and problems you may encounter as you begin to use AutoCAD for more complex tasks.

Part III: Becoming an Expert

At this point, you will be on the verge of becoming a real expert. Part 3 is designed to help you polish your existing skills and give you a few new ones. Chapter 10, *Storing and Linking Data with Graphics*, tells you how to attach information to drawing objects and how to link your drawing to database files. In Chapter 11, *Working with Preexisting Drawings and Raster Images*, you will learn techniques for transferring paper drawings to AutoCAD. In Chapter 12, *Advanced Editing Methods*, you will complete the apartment building tutorial. During this process you will learn how to integrate what you've learned so far and gain some tips on working in groups. Chapter 13, *Drawing Curves and Solid Fills*, gives you an in-depth look at some special drawing objects, such as spline and fitted curves. Chapter 14, *Getting and Exchanging Data from Drawings*, you will practice getting information about a drawing and learn how AutoCAD can interact with other applications, such as spreadsheets and desktop-publishing programs. You'll also learn how to copy and paste data.

Part IV: Modeling and Imaging in 3D

While 2D drafting is AutoCAD's workhorse application, AutoCAD's 3D capabilities give you a chance to expand your ideas and look at them in a new light. - Chapter 15, *Introducing 3D*, covers AutoCAD's basic features for creating three-dimensional drawings. Chapter 16, *Using Advanced 3D Features*, introduces you to some of the program's more powerful 3D capabilities. Chapter 17, *3D Rendering in AutoCAD*, shows how you can use the AutoCAD Renderer to produce lifelike views of your 3D drawings. Chapter 18, *Mastering 3D Solids*, is a guided tour of AutoCAD Release 14's solid-modeling feature.

Part V: Customization: Taking AutoCAD to the Limit

In the last part of the book, you will learn how you can take full control of AutoCAD. Chapter 19, *Introduction to Customization*, gives you a gentle introduction to the world of AutoCAD customization. You'll learn how to load and use existing utilities that come with AutoCAD and find out how you can publish high-resolution drawings on the Web. Chapter 20, *Using ActiveX Automation with AutoCAD*, shows you how you can tap the power of Automation to add new functions to AutoCAD and link AutoCAD to other applications. Chapter 21, *Integrating AutoCAD into Your Projects and Organization*, shows you how you can adapt AutoCAD to your own work style. Customizing menus, line types, and screens are only three of the many topics.

The Appendices

Finally, this book has four appendices. Appendix A, *Hardware and Software Tips*, offers information on hardware related to AutoCAD. It also provides tips on improving AutoCAD's performance and troubleshooting. Appendix B, *Installing and Setting Up AutoCAD*, contains an installation and configuration tutorial. If AutoCAD is not already installed on your system, you should follow this tutorial before starting Chapter 1. Appendix C, *What's on the Companion CD-ROM*, describes the utilities available on the companion CD-ROM. Appendix D, *System and Dimension Variables*, will illuminate the references to the system variables scattered throughout the book. Appendix D also discusses the many dimension settings and system features AutoCAD has to offer.

The Minimum System Requirements

This book assumes you have an IBM-compatible Pentium computer that will run AutoCAD and support a mouse. Your computer should have at least one CD-ROM drive, and a hard disk with 100 MB or more free space after AutoCAD is installed (about 70 MB for the AutoCAD to work with and another 30 MB available for drawing files). In addition to these requirements, you should also have enough free disk space to allow for a Windows virtual memory page file of at least 60 MB. Consult your Windows manual or Appendix A of this book for more on virtual memory.

AutoCAD Release 14 runs best on systems with at least 32 MB or more of RAM, though you can get by with 16 MB for Windows 95 and 24 for Windows NT. Your computer should also have a high-resolution monitor and a color display card. The current standard is the Super Video Graphics Array or SVGA display. This is quite adequate for most AutoCAD work. The computer should also have at least one serial port. If you have only one, you may want to consider having another one installed. I also assume you are using a mouse and have the use of a printer or a plotter. Most computers come equipped with a sound card, though you won't necessarily need one to use this book.

If you want a more detailed explanation of hardware options with AutoCAD, see Appendix A. You will find a general description of the available hardware options and their significance to AutoCAD.

Doing Things in Style

Much care has been taken to see that the stylistic conventions in this book—the use of upper- or lowercase letters, italic or boldface type, and so on—will be the ones most likely to help you learn AutoCAD. On the whole, their effect should be subliminal. However, you may find it useful to be conscious of the following rules that we have followed:

1. Pull-down selections are shown by a series of menu options separated by the ➤ symbol (e.g., Choose File ➤ New).

2. Keyboard entries are shown in boldface (e.g., enter **Rotate** ↵).

3. Command line prompts are also shown in a different font (e.g., Select object).

For most functions, we describe how to select options from toolbars and the menu bar. In addition, where applicable, we include related keyboard shortcuts and command names in parentheses. By providing command names, we have provided continuity for those readers already familiar with earlier releases of AutoCAD.

All This, and Software Too

Finally, we have included a CD-ROM containing a wealth of utilities, symbols libraries, and sample programs that can greatly enhance your use of AutoCAD. We have also included two online books: The *AutoCAD 14 Instant Reference* and the *ABCs of AutoLISP*. These easy-to-use online references compliment *Mastering AutoCAD 14* and will prove invaluable for quick command searches and customization tips. Appendix C gives you detailed information about the CD-ROM, but here's a brief rundown of what's available. Check it out!

Software You Can Use Right Away

An AEC add-on to AutoCAD offers the typical symbols and wall and door utilities needed to construct architectural drawings. It is a simple, straightforward add-on to AutoCAD that won't take you months to master.

Eye2eye is a utility that makes perspective viewing of your 3D work a simple matter of moving camera and target objects. This utility lets you easily fine-tune your Perspective views so you can in turn use them to create rendered images using AutoCAD 14's enhanced rendering tools.

Online Resources

If you just need to find information about a command quickly, the online version of the *AutoCAD 14 Instant Reference* is here to help you. It is a comprehensive guidebook that walks you through every feature and command of AutoCAD Release 14. *Mastering AutoCAD* and the *AutoCAD Instant Reference* have always been a great combination. We have included an electronic version of this best-selling reference so you can have the best AutoCAD resources in one place.

And if you want in-depth coverage of AutoLISP, AutoCAD's macro programming language, you can delve into the *ABCs of AutoLISP*. This book is an AutoLISP online reference and tutorial. AutoCAD users and developers alike have found the original *ABCs of AutoLISP* book an indispensable resource in their customization efforts. Now in its new HTML format, it's even easier to use.

Drawing Files for the Exercises

We have also included drawing files from all the exercises throughout this book. These are provided so that you can pick up an exercise anywhere in the book, without having to work through the book from front to back. You can also use these sample files to repeat exercises or to just explore how files are organized and put together.

New Features of Release 14

AutoCAD Release 14 offers a higher level of speed, accuracy, and ease of use. It has always provided drawing accuracy to 16 decimal places. With this kind of accuracy, you can create a computer model of the earth and include details down to submicron levels. It also means that no matter how often you edit an AutoCAD drawing, its dimensions will remain true. And AutoCAD Release 14 has greatly improved its overall speed. The interface is more consistent than in prior releases, so learning and using AutoCAD is easier than ever.

Other new features include:

- Improved layer and display controls
- Solid fills for irregular shapes
- Improved hatch patterns that require much less memory
- New raster image tools
- Expanded keyboard shortcuts
- External reference and raster image clipping to show just the portion of a drawing you want
- Full rendering capabilities including Ray Tracing
- Simplified configuration
- Internet tools to allow full Web and FTP access for reading and posting drawings
- Support for ActiveX automation
- Full TrueType support for improved text quality

- A more consistent, easier-to-use interface

Finally, perhaps the most important feature is what AutoCAD doesn't offer. You will not see a Release 14 version for DOS, Macintosh, SGI, or UNIX. By eliminating these other platforms, and concentrating on Windows 95 and NT, Autodesk is able to produce a leaner, meaner AutoCAD. It uses less memory than its previous Windows version, and is faster than the previous DOS version. In many ways, this is the AutoCAD you've been waiting for.

The AutoCAD Package

This book assumes you are using AutoCAD Release 14. If you are using an earlier version of AutoCAD, you will want to refer to *Mastering AutoCAD 13 for Windows 95 and NT*.

When you purchase AutoCAD Release 14, you receive a set of manuals in both hard copy and electronic formats. They are:

- The *AutoCAD Command Reference*

- The *AutoCAD User's Guide*

- The *Installation Guide*

- The *Customization Guide*

In addition, the AutoCAD package contains the AutoCAD Learning Assistant. This is a CD-ROM-based multimedia training and reference tool designed for those users who are upgrading from earlier versions of AutoCAD. It offers animated video clips, tips, and tutorials on a variety of topics. You'll need a sound card to take full advantage of the Learning Assistant.

You'll probably want to read the installation guide for Windows first, and then browse through the *Command Reference* and *User's Guide* to get a feel for the kind of information available there. You may want to save the *Customization Guide* for when you've become more familiar with AutoCAD.

AutoCAD comes on a CD-ROM and offers several levels of installation. This books assumes that you will use the full installation, which includes the Internet and Bonus Tools. You'll also want to install the ActiveX Automation software, also included on the AutoCAD CD-ROM, if you plan to explore this new feature.

The Digitizer Template

If you intend to use a digitizer tablet in place of a mouse, Autodesk also provides you with a digitizer template. Commands can be selected directly from the template by pointing at the command on the template and pressing the pick button. Each command is shown clearly by name and a simple icon. Commands are grouped on the template by the type of operation the command performs. Before you can use the digitizer template, you must configure the digitizer. See Appendix A, *Hardware and Software Tips*, for a more detailed description of digitizing tablets and Appendix B for instructions on configuring the digitizer.

> **NOTE** I won't specifically discuss the use of the digitizer for selecting commands because the process is straightforward. If you are using a digitizer, you can use its puck like a mouse for the all of exercises in this book.

I hope that *Mastering AutoCAD 14* will be of benefit to you and that, once you have completed the tutorials, you will continue to use the book as a reference. If you have comments, criticisms, or ideas about how the book can be improved, you can write to me or send e-mail to me at the address below. And thanks for choosing *Mastering AutoCAD 14*.

George Omura
P.O. Box 6357
Albany, CA 94706-0357
Gomura@sirius.com

PART I

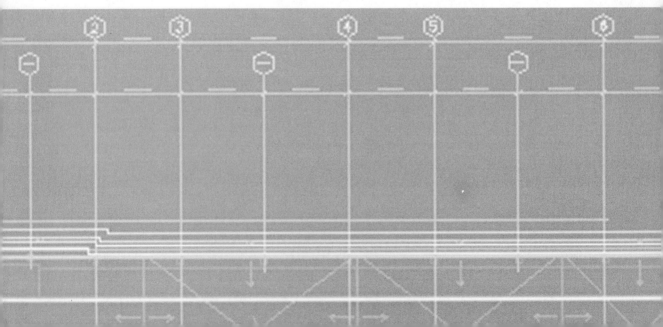

THE BASICS

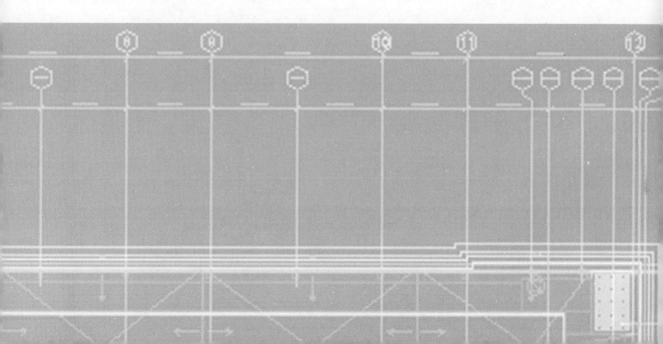

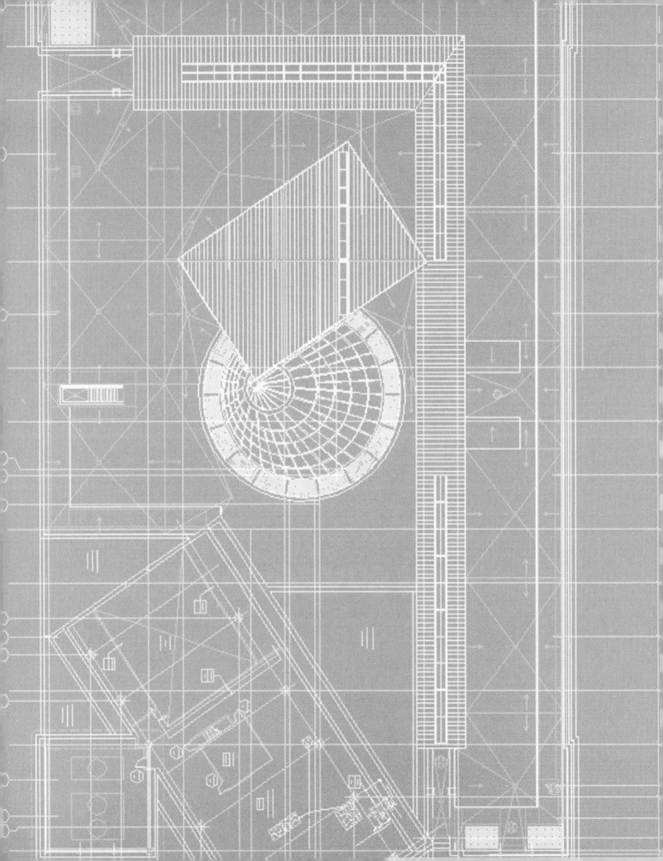

CHAPTER

ONE

This Is AutoCAD

- Taking a Guided Tour

- Working with AutoCAD

Over the last few years, AutoCAD has evolved from a DOS-based, command line-driven program, to a full-fledged Windows 95/NT application. With Auto-CAD Release 14, Autodesk is making a complete break from the DOS world. Neither DOS nor UNIX is supported with AutoCAD Release 14.

By concentrating on a single operating system, Autodesk is able to create a more efficient, faster AutoCAD. As an added benefit, Release 14 offers smaller file sizes than Release 13 and reduced memory requirements. Its speed matches—and in many cases, exceeds—those found in earlier DOS versions of AutoCAD. If you're a DOS AutoCAD user who has been waiting for a faster Windows-based AutoCAD, your wait is over. AutoCAD Release 14 offers the speed you demand with the convenience of a windows multitasking environment. You'll also find that AutoCAD makes great use of the Windows environment. For example, you can use Windows' OLE features to paste documents directly into AutoCAD from Excel, Windows Paint, or any other programs that support OLE as a server application. And, as in Releases 12 and 13, you can export AutoCAD drawings directly to other OLE clients. This means no more messy conversions and reworking to get spreadsheet, database, text, or other data into AutoCAD. It also means that if you want to include a photograph in your AutoCAD drawing, all you have to do is cut and paste. Text-based data can also be cut and pasted, saving you time in transferring data, such as layer or block names.

NOTE   OLE stands for *Object Linking and Embedding*—a Windows feature that lets different applications share documents. See Chapter 14 for a more detailed discussion of OLE.

With Windows, you have the freedom to arrange AutoCAD's screen by clicking and dragging its components. AutoCAD 14 offers many time-saving tools not found in the older DOS-based version, such as a drop-down list for layer settings and line types, and toolbars for easy access to all of AutoCAD's commands. There's even an expanded Help system, with online tutorials and full documentation.

If you are new to AutoCAD, this is the version you may have been waiting for. Even with its many new features, the programmers at Autodesk have managed to make AutoCAD easier to use than previous releases. AutoCAD's interface has been trimmed down and is more consistent than prior versions. Release 14 is fully compliant with the Windows interface guidelines, and is especially designed to conform to the Microsoft Office standard interface. So if you are familiar with the Microsoft Office suite of programs, you will feel right at home with AutoCAD Release 14.

In this first chapter, we will look at many of AutoCAD's basic operations, such as opening and closing files, getting a close-up look at part of a drawing, and making changes to a drawing.

Taking a Guided Tour

First, you will get a chance to familiarize yourself with the AutoCAD screen and how you communicate with AutoCAD. Along the way, you will also get a feel for how to work with this book. Don't worry about understanding or remembering everything that you see in this chapter. You will get plenty of opportunities to probe the finer details of the program as you work through the later chapters. If you are already familiar with earlier versions of AutoCAD, you may want to read through this chapter anyway, to get acquainted with new features and the graphical interface. To help you remember the material, you will find a brief exercise at the end of each chapter. For now, just enjoy your first excursion into AutoCAD.

NOTE   You might also consider purchasing *Mastering Windows 95* by Bob Cowart or *The ABCs of Windows 95* by Sharon Crawford, both published by Sybex.

If you already installed AutoCAD, and you are ready to jump in and take a look, then proceed with the following steps to launch the program.

1. Click on the Start button in the lower-left corner of the Windows 95 or NT 4.0 screen. Then choose Program ➢ AutoCAD R14 ➢ AutoCAD R14. You can also double-click on the AutoCAD R14 icon on your Windows Desktop.

2. You will see an opening greeting, called a splash screen, telling you which version of AutoCAD you are using, to whom the program is registered, and the AutoCAD dealer's name and phone number should you need help.

3. Next, you will see the Create New Drawing dialog box. This dialog is a convenient tool for setting up new drawings. You'll learn more about this tool in later chapters. For now, click Cancel in the Create New Drawing dialog box.

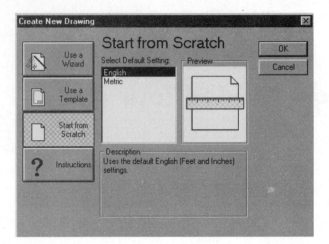

Message to Veteran AutoCAD Users

Autodesk is committed to the Windows operating environment. The result is a graphical user interface that is easier on the AutoCAD neophyte, but perhaps a bit foreign to a veteran AutoCAD user.

If you've been using AutoCAD for a while, and you prefer the older interface, you can still enter AutoCAD commands through the keyboard, and you can still mold AutoCAD's interface into one that is more familiar to you.

You can, for example, restore the side menu that appears in the DOS version of AutoCAD. Here's how it's done:

1. Select Tools ➣ Preferences.

2. At the Preferences dialog box, click on the Display tab.

3. Click on the checkbox labeled Display AutoCAD Screen Menu in Drawing Window.

4. Finally, click on OK. The side menu will appear.

A word of caution: If you are accustomed to pressing Ctrl + C to cancel an operation, you must now retrain yourself to press the Esc (Escape) key. Ctrl + C now conforms to the Windows standard, making this key combination a shortcut for saving marked items to the Clipboard. Similarly, instead of using F1 to view the full text window, you must use F2. F1 is most commonly reserved for the Help function in Windows applications.

If you prefer entering commands through the keyboard, you'll also want to know about some changes to specific commands in Release 14. Several commands that usually invoke dialog boxes can be used through the Command window prompt. Here is a list of those commands:

Bhatch	Boundary	Group	Hatchedit	Image
Layer	Linetype	Mtext	Pan	
XBind	Style	Osnap	XRef	

When you enter these commands through the keyboard, you will normally see a dialog box. In the case of Pan, you will see the Realtime Pan hand graphic. To utilize these commands from the command prompt, add a minus sign (-) to the beginning of the command name. For example, to use the Layer command in the older command line method, enter **–layer** at the command prompt. To use the old Pan command, enter **–pan** at the command prompt.

Even if you don't care to enter commands through the keyboard, knowing about the use of the minus sign can help you create custom macros. See Chapter 21 for more on AutoCAD customization.

The AutoCAD Window

The AutoCAD program window is divided into five parts:

- Pull-down menu bar

- Docked and floating toolbars

- Drawing area

- Command window

- Status bar

NOTE

A sixth hidden component, the Aerial View window, displays your entire drawing and lets you select close-up views of parts of your drawing. After you've gotten more familiar with AutoCAD, consult Appendix B for more on this feature.

Figure 1.1 shows a typical layout of the AutoCAD program window. Along the top is the *menu bar,* and at the bottom are the *Command window* and the *status bar.* Just below the menu bar and to the left of the window are the *toolbars.* The rest of the screen is occupied by the *drawing area.*

Many of the elements within the AutoCAD window can be easily moved and reshaped. Figure 1.2 demonstrates how different AutoCAD can look after some simple rearranging of window components. Toolbars can be moved from their default locations to any location on the screen. When they are in their default location, they are in their *docked* position. When they are moved to a location where they are free-floating, they are *floating.*

FIGURE 1.1:

A typical arrangement of the elements of the AutoCAD window

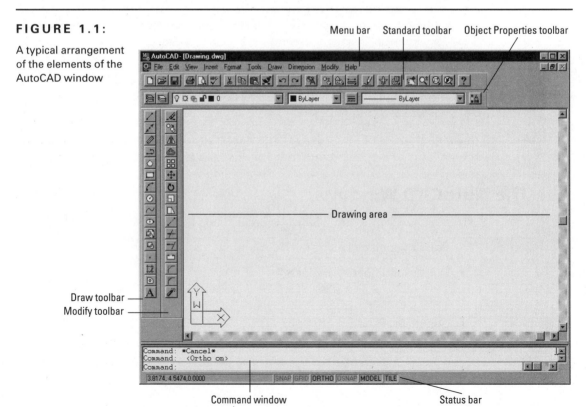

FIGURE 1.2:

An alternative arrangement of the elements of the AutoCAD window

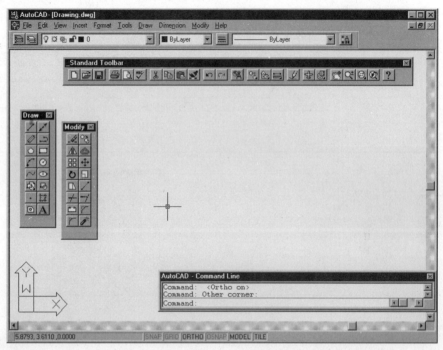

The menu bar at the top of the drawing area (as shown in Figure 1.3) offers pull-down menus from which you select commands in a typical Windows fashion. The toolbars offer a variety of commands through tool buttons and drop-down lists. For example, the *layer* name or number you are presently working on is displayed in a drop-down list in the Object Properties toolbar. The layer name is preceded by tools that inform you of the status of the layer. The tools and lists on the toolbar are plentiful, and you'll learn more about all of them later in this chapter and as you work through this book.

NOTE A *layer* is like an overlay that allows you to separate different types of information. AutoCAD allows an unlimited number of layers. On new drawings, the default layer is 0. You'll get a detailed look at layers and the meaning of the Layer tools in Chapter 4.

The Draw and Modify toolbars (Figure 1.4) offer commands that create new objects and edit existing ones. These are just two of many toolbars available to you.

FIGURE 1.3:

The components of the menu bar and toolbar

Standard Microsoft Office functions

Pan and Zoom tools

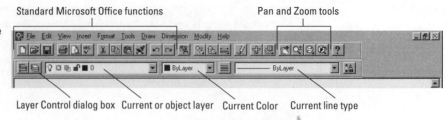

Layer Control dialog box   Current or object layer   Current Color   Current line type

FIGURE 1.4:

Here are the Draw and Modify toolbars as they appear when they are *floating*.

The drawing area—your workspace—occupies most of the screen. Everything you draw appears in this area. As you move your mouse around, you will see crosshairs appear to move within the drawing area. This is your drawing cursor that lets you point to locations in the drawing area. At the bottom of the drawing area, the status bar (see Figure 1.5) gives you information at a glance about the drawing. For example, the coordinate readout toward the far left of the status line tells you the location of your cursor. The Command window can be moved and resized in a manner similar to toolbars. By default, the Command window is in its docked position, shown here. Let's practice using the coordinate readout and drawing cursor.

FIGURE 1.5:

The status bar and Command window

Command prompt   Command window

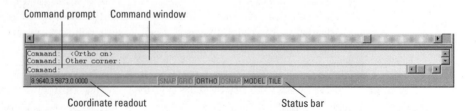

Coordinate readout   Status bar

Picking Points

1. Move the cursor around in the drawing area. As you move, note how the coordinate readout changes to tell you the cursor's location. It shows the coordinates in an X,Y format.

2. Now place the cursor in the middle of the drawing area and press and immediately release the left mouse button. You have just picked a point. Move the cursor, and a rectangle follows. This is a *Selection window*; you'll learn more about this window in Chapter 2.

3. Move the cursor a bit in any direction; then press and let go of the left mouse button again. Notice that the rectangle disappears.

4. Try picking several more points in the drawing area.

> **NOTE**
>
> **Terminology to Remember:** The operation you performed in steps 1 and 2—placing the cursor on a specific point and pressing the left mouse button—is referred to as *clicking* or *clicking on* a point.

UCS Icon

In the lower-left corner of the drawing area, you see a thick, L-shaped arrow outline. This is the *User Coordinate System* (UCS) icon, which tells you your orientation in the drawing. This icon becomes helpful as you start to work with complex 2D drawings and 3D models. The X and Y inside the icon indicate the x- and y-axes of your drawing. The W tells you that you are in what is called the *World Coordinate System*. We will discuss this icon in detail in Chapter 16. For now, you can use it as a reference to tell you the direction of the axes.

> **NOTE**
>
> **If you can't find the UCS icon...** The UCS icon can be turned on and off, so if you are on someone else's system and you don't see the icon, don't panic. It also changes shape depending on whether you are in Paper Space or Model Space mode! If you don't see the icon or it doesn't look like it does in this chapter, see *Switching to Paper Space* in Chapter 12 for more on Paper Space and Model Space. Also see Chapter 16 for more on the UCS icon.

The Command Window

At the bottom of the screen, just above the status bar, is a small horizontal window, which is the *Command window*. Here AutoCAD displays responses to your input. It shows three lines of text. The bottom shows the current messages while the top two show messages that have scrolled by, or in some cases, components of the current message that do not fit in a single line. Right now, the bottom line displays the message "Command" (see Figure 1.5). This tells you that AutoCAD is waiting for your instructions. As you click on a point in the drawing area, you'll see the message "Other corner." At the same time, the cursor starts to draw a Selection window that disappears when you click on another point.

As a new user, it is important to pay special attention to messages displayed in the Command window because this is how AutoCAD communicates with you. Besides giving you messages, the Command window records your activity in AutoCAD. You can use the scroll bar to the right of the Command window to review previous messages. You can also enlarge the window for a better view. (We'll discuss this in more detail in Chapter 2.)

NOTE
As you become more familiar with AutoCAD, you may find you don't need to rely on the Command window as much. For new users, however, it can be quite helpful in understanding what steps to take as you work.

Now let's look at AutoCAD's window components in detail.

The Pull-Down Menus

Like many Windows programs, the pull-down menus available on the menu bar offer an easy-to-understand way to access the general controls and settings for AutoCAD. Within these menus you'll find the commands and functions that are the heart of AutoCAD. By clicking menu items, you can cut and paste items to and from AutoCAD, change the settings that make AutoCAD work the way you want it to, set up the measurement system you want to use, access the help system, and much more.

TIP
To close a pull-down menu without selecting anything, press the Esc (Escape) key. You can also click on any other part of the AutoCAD window or on another pull-down menu.

The pull-down menu options perform three basic functions:

- Display additional menu choices.

- Display a dialog box that contains settings you can change.

- Issue a command that requires keyboard or drawing input.

- Offer an expanded set of the same tools found in the Draw and Modify toolbars.

As you point to commands and options in the menus or toolbars, AutoCAD provides additional help for you in the form of brief descriptions of each menu option, which appear in the status bar.

Here's an exercise to let you practice with the pull-down menus and get acquainted with AutoCAD's interface:

1. Click on View in the menu bar. The list of items that appear are the commands and settings that let you control the way AutoCAD displays your drawings. Don't worry if you don't understand them; you'll get to know them in later chapters.

2. Move the highlight cursor slowly down the list of menu items. As you high-light each item, notice that a description of it appears in the status line at the bottom of the AutoCAD window. These descriptions help you choose the menu option you need.

3. Some of the menu items have triangular pointers to their right. This means the command has additional choices. For instance, highlight the Zoom item, and you'll see another set of options appear to the right of the menu.

NOTE If you look carefully at the command descriptions in the status bar, you'll see an odd word at the end. This is the keyboard command equivalent to the highlighted option in the menu or toolbar. You can actually type in these keyboard commands to start the tool or menu item that you are pointing to. You don't have to memorize these command names, but knowing them will be helpful to you later if you want to customize AutoCAD.

This second set of options is called a *cascading menu*. Whenever you see a pull-down menu item with the triangular pointer, you know that this item opens a cascading menu offering a more detailed set of options.

You might have noticed that other pull-down menu options are followed by an ellipsis (...). This indicates that the option brings up a dialog box, as the following exercise demonstrates:

1. Move the highlight cursor to the Tools option in the menu bar.

NOTE If you prefer, you can click and drag the highlight cursor over the pull-down menu to select an option.

2. Click on the Preferences... item. The Preferences dialog box appears.

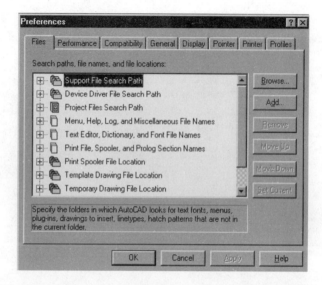

NOTE

If you're familiar with the Windows 95 Explorer, you should feel at home with the Files tab of the Preferences dialog box. The plus sign to the left of the items in the list expand the option to display more detail.

This dialog box contains several "pages," indicated by the tabs across the top, that contain settings for controlling what AutoCAD shows you on its screens, where you want it to look for special files, and other "housekeeping" settings. You needn't worry about what these options mean at this point. Appendix B describes this dialog box in more detail.

3. In the Preferences dialog box, click on the tab labeled General. The options change to reveal new options.

    In the upper-left corner of the dialog box, you'll see a checkbox labeled Automatic Save, with the Minutes between Saves setting placed on every 120 minutes. This setting controls how frequently AutoCAD performs an automatic save.

4. Change the 120 to 20, and then click OK. You have just changed AutoCAD's automatic save feature to automatically save files every 20 minutes instead of every two hours. (Let this be a reminder to give your eyes a rest!)

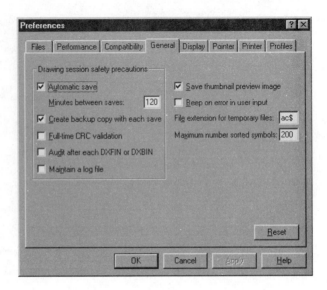

The third type of item you'll find on pull-down menus is a command that directly executes an AutoCAD operation. Let's try an exercise to explore these.

1. Click on the Draw option from the menu bar, and then click on the Rectangle command. Notice that the Command window now shows the comment:

   First corner:

   AutoCAD is asking you to select the first corner for the rectangle.

2. Click on a point roughly in the lower-left corner of the drawing area, as shown in Figure 1.6. Now as you move your mouse, you'll see a rectangle follow the cursor with one corner fixed at the position you just selected. You'll also see the following message in the Command window:

   Other corner:

3. Click on another point anywhere in the upper-right region of the drawing area. A rectangle appears (see Figure 1.7). You'll learn more about the different cursor shapes and what they mean in Chapter 2.

At this point you've seen how most of AutoCAD's commands work. You'll find that dialog boxes are offered when you want to change settings, while many drawing and editing functions present messages in the Command window. Also, be aware that many of the pull-down menu items are duplicated in the toolbars that you will explore next.

FIGURE 1.6:

Selecting points to define a Zoom window

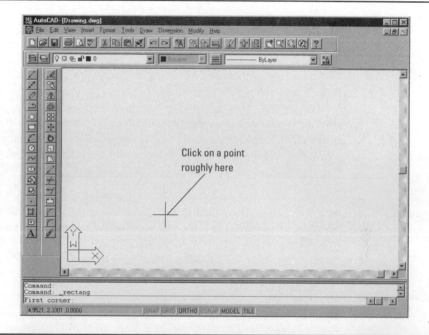

FIGURE 1.7:

Once you've selected your first point in a Zoom window, the cursor disappears and you see a rectangle follow the motion of your mouse.

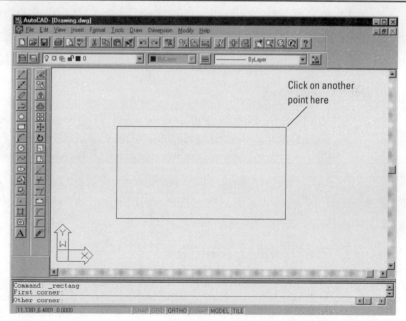

Communicating with AutoCAD

AutoCAD is the perfect servant: It does everything you tell it to, and no more. You communicate with AutoCAD using the pull-down menus and the tools on tool-bars. These devices invoke AutoCAD commands. A command is a single-word instruction you give to AutoCAD telling it to do something, such as draw a line (the Line tool in the Draw toolbar) or erase an object (the Erase tool in the Modify toolbar). Whenever you invoke a command, by either typing it in or selecting a menu or toolbar item, AutoCAD responds by presenting messages to you in the Command window, or by displaying a dialog box.

The messages in the Command window often tell you what to do next, or they offer a list of options. A single command will often present several messages, which you answer to complete the command. These messages serve as an aid to new users who need a little help. If you ever get lost while using a command, or forget what you are supposed to do, look at the Command window for clues. As you become more comfortable with AutoCAD, you will find that you won't need to refer to these messages as frequently.

A dialog box is like a form you fill out on the computer screen. It lets you adjust settings or make selections from a set of options pertaining to a command. You'll get a chance to work with commands and dialog boxes later in this chapter.

The Toolbars

While the pull-down menus offer a full range of easy-to-understand options, they require some effort to navigate. The toolbars, on the other hand, offer quick, single-click access to the most commonly used AutoCAD features.

The tools in the toolbars perform three types of actions, just like the pull-down menu commands: They display further options, open dialog boxes, and issue commands that require keyboard or cursor input.

The Toolbar Tool Tips

AutoCAD's toolbars contain tools that represent commands. To help you under-stand each tool, a *tool tip* appears just below the arrow cursor when you rest the cursor on a tool. Each tool tip helps you identify the tool with its function. A tool tip appears when you follow these steps.

1. Move the arrow cursor onto one of the toolbar tools and leave it there for a second or two. Notice that the command's name appears nearby—this is the tool tip. In the status bar, a brief description of the button's purpose appears (see Figure 1.8).

2. Move the cursor across the toolbar. As you do, notice that the tool tips and status bar descriptions change to describe each tool. The keyboard command equivalent of the tool is also shown in the status bar at the end of the description.

FIGURE 1.8:

Tool tips show you the function of each tool in the toolbar. AutoCAD also displays a description of the tool in the status bar.

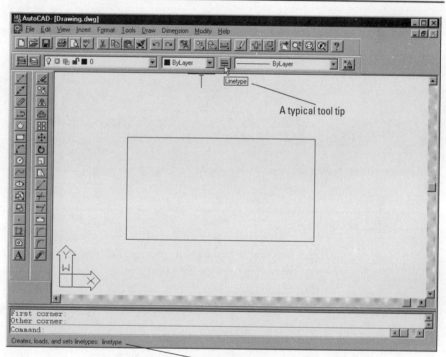

A typical tool tip

Tool description in the status bar

Flyouts

Most toolbar tools start a command as soon as you click on them, but other tools will display a set of additional tools (similar to the cascading menus) that are related to the tool you have selected. This set of additional tools is called a toolbar *flyout*. If you've used other Windows graphics programs, chances are you've seen flyouts. Look closely at the tools just below the Help pull-down menu option on your screen or in Figure 1.8. You'll be able to identify which toolbar tools have flyouts; they'll have a small right-pointing arrow in the lower-right corner of the tool.

NOTE Remember: When an instruction says "click on," you should lightly press the left mouse button until you hear a click; then immediately let it go. Don't hold it down.

The following steps show you how a flyout works.

1. Move the cursor to the Zoom window tool in the Standard toolbar. Click and hold the left mouse button to display the flyout. Don't release the mouse button.

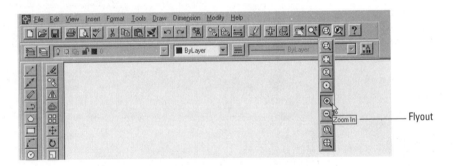

Flyout

2. Still holding down the left mouse button down, move the cursor over the flyout; notice that the tool tips appear here as well. Also, notice the description in the status bar.

3. Move the cursor to the Zoom window tool at the top of the flyout and release the mouse button.

4. You won't need to use this tool yet, so press the Esc key to cancel this tool.

As you can see from this exercise, you get a lot of feedback from AutoCAD!

Moving the Toolbars

One unique characteristic of AutoCAD's toolbars is their mobility. They can either be floating anywhere on the AutoCAD window or in a *docked* position. Docked means it is placed against the top and side borders of the AutoCAD window, so that the toolbar occupies a minimal amount of space. If you want to, you can move the toolbar to any location on your desktop, thus turning it into a floating toolbar.

Later in this section you'll find descriptions of all AutoCAD's toolbars, but first try the following exercise to move the Object Properties toolbar away from its current position in the AutoCAD window.

1. Move the arrow cursor so that it points to the border of the Object Properties toolbar, as shown here:

2. Press and hold down the left mouse button. Notice that a gray rectangle appears by the cursor.

3. Still holding down the mouse button, move the mouse downward. The gray box follows the cursor.

4. When the gray box is over the drawing area, release the mouse button and the Object Properties toolbar—now a floating toolbar—moves to its new location.

NOTE

Terminology to Remember: The action you perform in steps 2 and 3 of this exercise—holding down the mouse/pick button while simultaneously moving the mouse—is called *click and drag*. (If you have used other Windows applications, you already know this.) From now on, we will use "click and drag" to describe this type of action.

You can now move the Object Properties toolbar to any location on the screen that suits you. You can also change the shape of the toolbar; try the following.

5. Place the cursor on the bottom-edge border of the Object Properties toolbar. The cursor becomes a double-headed arrow, as shown here:

6. Click and drag the border downward. The gray rectangle jumps to a new, taller rectangle as you move the cursor.

7. When the gray rectangle changes to the shape you want, release the mouse button to reshape the toolbar.

8. To move the toolbar back into its docked position, place the arrow cursor on (point to) the toolbar's title bar and slowly click and drag the toolbar so the cursor is in position in the upper-left corner of the AutoCAD window. Notice how the gray outline of the toolbar changes as it approaches its docked position.

9. When the outline of the Object Properties toolbar is near its docked position, release the mouse button. The toolbar moves back into its previous position in the AutoCAD window.

You can move and reshape any of AutoCAD's toolbars to place them out of the way, yet still have them at the ready to give you quick access to commands. You can also put them away altogether when you don't need them and bring them back at will, as shown in these next steps.

10. Click and drag the Draw toolbar from its position at the left of the AutoCAD window to a point near the center of the drawing area.

11. Click on the Close button in the upper-left corner of the Draw floating toolbar. This is the small square button with the rectangle in it. The toolbar disappears.

NOTE **Terminology to remember:** When we ask you to select an option from the pull-down menu, we will use the notation *Menu* ➤ *Option.* For cascading menus, we will use the notation *Menu* ➤ *Option* ➤ *Option;* the second ➤ *Option* is in a cascading menu. In either case, the selected menu option issues a command that performs the function being discussed. As mentioned earlier, the actual command name appears in the status bar when you point to a menu option or toolbar tool.

NEW! 12. To recover the toolbar, click on the View pull-down menu and then on Toolbars (View ➤ Toolbars). The Toolbars dialog box appears.

TIP You can also right-click on any toolbar to open the Toolbar's dialog box.

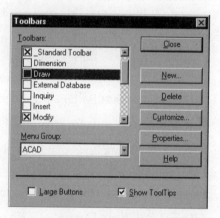

13. Locate Draw in the list of toolbars shown in this dialog box, and then click in the checkbox next to the Draw item so that an X appears in the box.

14. Click the Close button in the upper-right corner of the dialog box. The Draw toolbar reappears.

15. Click and drag the Draw toolbar back to its docked position in the far-left side of the AutoCAD window.

AutoCAD will remember your toolbar arrangement between sessions. When you exit and then reopen AutoCAD later, the AutoCAD window will appear just as you left it.

You may have noticed several other toolbars listed in the Toolbar's dialog box that don't appear in the AutoCAD window. To keep the screen from becoming cluttered, many of the toolbars are not placed on the screen. The toolbars you'll be using most are displayed first; others that are less frequently used are kept out of sight until they are needed. Here are brief descriptions of all the toolbars available from the Toolbar's dialog box:

Draw: Commands for creating common objects, including lines, arcs, circles, curves, ellipses, and text. This toolbar appears in the AutoCAD window by default. Many of these commands are duplicated in the Draw pull-down menu.

Modify: Commands for editing existing objects. You can Move, Copy, Rotate, Erase, Trim, Extend, and so on. Many of these commands are duplicated in the Modify pull-down menu.

Modify II: Commands for editing special complex objects such as polylines, multilines, 3D solids, and hatches.

Dimension: Commands that help you dimension your drawings. See Chapter 9. Many of these commands are duplicated in the Dimension pull-down menu.

Solids: Commands for creating 3D solids. See Chapter 18.

Surfaces: Commands for creating 3D surfaces. See Chapters 15 and 16.

References: Commands that control cross-referencing of drawings. See Chapters 6 and 12.

Render: Commands to operate AutoCAD's rendering feature. See Chapter 17.

External Database: Commands for linking objects to external databases. See Chapter 10.

Select Objects: Tools for modifying the method used to select objects on the screen. See Chapter 2.

Object Snap: Tools to help you select specific points on objects, such as endpoints and midpoints. See Chapter 3.

UCS: Tools for setting up a plane on which to work. This is most useful for 3D modeling, but it can be helpful in 2D drafting, as well. See Chapter 16.

Object Properties: Commands for manipulating the properties of objects. This toolbar is normally docked below the pull-down menu bar.

Standard Toolbar: The most frequently used commands for view control, file management, and editing. This toolbar is normally docked below the pull-down menu bar.

Inquiry: Commands for finding distances, point coordinates, object properties, mass properties, and areas.

Insert: Commands for importing other drawings, raster images, and OLE objects.

Viewpoint: Tools for viewing 3D models.

Zoom: Commands that allow you to navigate your drawing.

You'll get a chance to work with all of the toolbars as you work through this book. Or, if you plan to use the book as a reference rather than working through it as a chapter-by-chapter tutorial, any exercise you try will tell you which toolbar to use for performing a specific operation.

Menus versus the Keyboard

Throughout this book, you will be told to select commands and command options from the pull-down menus and toolbars. For new and experienced users alike, menus and toolbars offer an easy-to-remember method for accessing commands. If you are familiar with the DOS version of AutoCAD, you still have the option of entering commands directly through the keyboard. Most of the commands you know and love still work as they did from the keyboard.

Another method for accessing commands is to use accelerator keys, which are special keystrokes that open and activate pull-down menu options. You might have noticed that the commands in the menu bar and the items in the pull-down menus all have an underlined character. By pressing the Alt key followed by the key corresponding to the underlined character, you activate that command or option, without having to engage the mouse. For example, to issue File ➤ Open, press Alt, then F, then finally O (Alt+F+O).

Continued on next page

Many tools and commands have keyboard shortcuts; one or two letter abbreviations of a command name. As you become more proficient with AutoCAD you may find these shortcuts helpful. As you work through this book, we'll point out the shortcuts for your reference.

Finally, if you are feeling adventurous, you can create your own accelerator keys and keyboard shortcuts for executing commands by adding them to the AutoCAD support files. We'll discuss customization of the menus, toolbars, and keyboard shortcuts in Chapters 19 and 21.

Working with AutoCAD

Now that you've been introduced to the AutoCAD Window, let's try using a few of AutoCAD's commands. First, you'll open a sample file and make a few simple modifications to it. In the process, you'll get familiar with some common methods of operation in AutoCAD.

Opening an Existing File

In this exercise, you will get a chance to see and use a typical Select File dialog box. To start with, you will open an existing file.

1. From the menu bar, choose File ➤ Open. A message appears asking you if you want to save the changes you've made to the current drawing. Click No.

2. Next, a Select File dialog box appears. This is a typical Windows file dialog box, with an added twist. The large Preview box on the right allows you to preview a drawing before you open it, thereby saving time while searching for files.

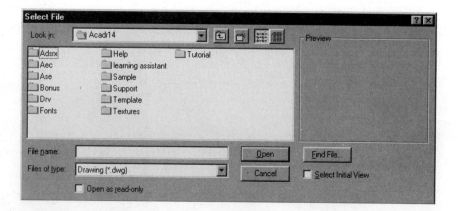

3. In the Select File dialog box, go to the Directories list and locate the directory named Figures (you may need to scroll down the list to find it). Point to it and then double-click (press the mouse/pick button twice in rapid succession). (If you're having trouble opening files with a double-click, here's another way to do it until you are more proficient with the mouse: Click on the file once to highlight it, and then click the OK button.) The file list on the left changes to show the contents of the Sample directory.

4. Move the arrow to the file named Nozzle3d, and click on it. Notice that the name now appears in the File Name input box above the file list. Also, the Preview box now shows a thumbnail image of the file.

NOTE   The Nozzle3D drawing is included on the companion CD-ROM. If you cannot find this file, be sure you have installed the sample drawings from the companion CD-ROM. See Appendix C for installation instructions.

5. Click on the OK button at the bottom of the dialog box. AutoCAD opens the Nozzle3d file, as shown in Figure 1.9.

FIGURE 1.9:

In the early days, this Nozzle drawing became the unofficial symbol of AutoCAD, frequently appearing in ads for AutoCAD third-party products.

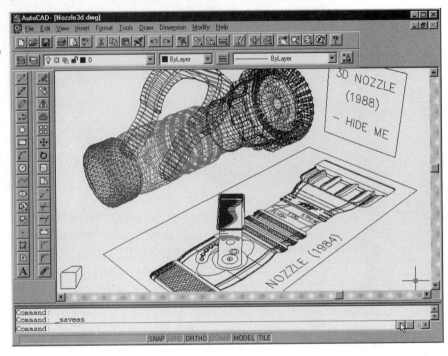

The Nozzle3d file opens to display the entire drawing. Also, the AutoCAD window's title bar displays the name of the drawing. This offers easy identification of the file. This particular file contains both a 2D and 3D model of a fire hose nozzle. The opening view is actually a 3D view.

Getting a Closer Look

One of the most frequently used commands is the Zoom command. Zoom lets you get a closer look at a part of your drawing. It offers a variety of ways to control your view. Now you'll enlarge a portion of the Nozzle drawing to get a more detailed look. To tell AutoCAD what area you wish to enlarge, you will use what is called a *window*.

1. Choose View ➤ 3D Viewpoint ➤ Plan View ➤ World UCS. Your view changes to display a two-dimensional view looking down on the drawing.

2. Click on the Zoom Window button on the Standard toolbar.

You can also Choose View ≻ Zoom ≻ Window from the pull-down menu.

3. The Command window displays First corner:. Look at the top image of Figure 1.10. Move the crosshair cursor to a location similar to the one shown in the figure; then press the left-click on the mouse. Move the cursor and you see the rectangle appear, one corner fixed on the point you just picked, while the other corner follows the cursor.

4. The Command window now displays First corner: Other corner:. Position the other corner of the window so it encloses the handle of the nozzle, as shown in the figure, and press the mouse/pick button. The handle enlarges to fill the screen (See the bottom image of Figure 1.10).

NOTE   You will notice that tiny crosses appear where you picked points. These are called *blips*—markers that show where you've selected points. They do not become a permanent part of your drawing, nor do they print onto hard copy output.

In this exercise, you used the Window option of the Zoom command to define an area to enlarge for your close-up view. You saw how AutoCAD prompts you to indicate first one corner of the window, and then the other. These messages are helpful for first-time users of AutoCAD. You will be using the Window option frequently—not just to define views, but also to select objects for editing.

Getting a close-up view of your drawing is crucial to working accurately with a drawing, but you'll often want to return to a previous view to get the overall picture. To do so, click on the Zoom Previous button on the Standard toolbar.

FIGURE 1.10:

Placing the Zoom window around the nozzle handle. After clicking on the Zoom Window button in the Standard toolbar, select the two points shown in this figure.

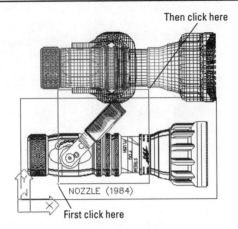

Then click here

NOZZLE (1984)

First click here

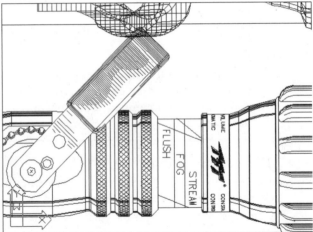

Do this now, and the previous view—one showing the entire nozzle—returns to the screen. You can also get there by choosing View ➢ Zoom ➢ Previous.

You can quickly enlarge or reduce your view using the Zoom Realtime button on the Standard toolbar.

NOTE

You can also zoom in and out using the Zoom In and Zoom Out buttons in the Zoom Window flyout of the Standard toolbar. The Zoom In button shows a magnifying glass with a plus sign; Zoom Out shows a minus sign.

1. Click on the Zoom Realtime button on the Standard Toolbar.

The cursor changes into a magnifying glass.

2. Place the Zoom Realtime cursor slightly above the center of the drawing area, and then click and drag downward. Your view zooms out to show more of the drawing.

3. While still holding the left mouse button, move the cursor upward. Your view zooms in to enlarge your view. When you have a view similar to the one shown in Figure 1.11, release the mouse button. (Don't worry if you don't get the *exact* same view as the figure. This is just for practice.)

4. You are still in Zoom Realtime mode. Click and drag the mouse again to see how you can further adjust your view. To exit, you can select another command besides a Zoom or Pan command, press the Escape key, or right-click on your mouse.

5. Go ahead and right-click now. A pop-up menu appears.

This menu lets you select other display-related options.

6. Click on Exit from the pop-up menu to exit the Zoom Realtime command.

As you can see from this exercise, you have a wide range of options for viewing your drawing, just by using a few buttons. In fact, these three buttons, along with the scroll bars at the right side and bottom of the AutoCAD window are all you need to control the display of your 2D drawings.

FIGURE 1.11:

The final view you want to achieve in step 3 of the exercise.

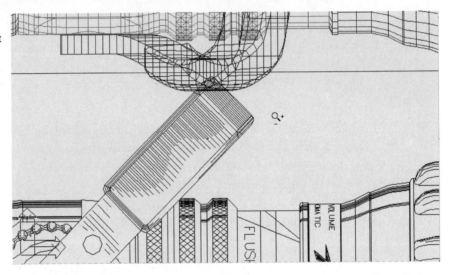

The Arial View Window

The *Aerial View* window is an optional AutoCAD display tool. It gives you an overall view of your drawing, no matter how much magnification you may be using for the drawing editor. Aerial View also makes it easier to get around in a large-scale drawing. You'll find that this feature is best suited to more complex drawings that cover great areas, such as site plans, topographical maps, or city planning documents.

We won't discuss this view much in the first chapter, as it can be a bit confusing for the first-time AutoCAD user. However, as you become more comfortable with AutoCAD, you may want to try it out. You'll find a detailed description of the Arial View window in Chapter 6.

Saving a File as You Work

It is a good idea to periodically save your file as you work on it. You can save it under its original name (with File ➤ Save) or under a different name (with File ➤ Save As), thereby creating a new file.

By default, AutoCAD automatically saves your work at 120-minute intervals under the name AUTO.SV$; this is known as the *autosave* feature. Using system variables, you can change the name of the autosaved file and control the time between autosaves. See the *Using AutoCAD's Automatic Save Feature* sidebar in Chapter 3 for details.

Let's first try the Save command. This quickly saves the drawing in its current state without exiting the program.

Choose File ➤ Save. You will notice some disk activity while AutoCAD saves the file to the hard disk. As an alternative to picking File ➤ Save from the menus, you can type **Alt+F+S**. This is the accelerator key, also called *hotkey*, for the File ➤ Save command.

Now try the Save As command. This command brings up a dialog box that allows you to save the current file under a new name.

1. Choose File ➤ Save As, or type **Saveas** ⏎ at the command prompt. The Select File dialog box appears. Note that the current file name, Nozzle3d.dwg, is highlighted in the File Name input box at the bottom of the dialog box.

2. Type **Myfirst**. As you type, the name "Nozzle3d" disappears from the input box and is replaced by "Myfirst." You don't need to enter the .dwg file name extension. AutoCAD adds it to the file name automatically when it saves the file.

3. Click on the Save button. The dialog box disappears, and you will notice some disk activity.

You now have a copy of the nozzle file under the name Myfirst.dwg, and the name of the file displayed in the AutoCAD window's title bar has changed to Myfirst. From now on, when you use the File ➤ Save option, your drawing will be saved under its new name. Saving files under a different name can be useful when you are creating alternatives or when you just want to save one of several ideas you are trying out.

If you are working with a monitor that is on the small side, you may want to consider closing the Draw and Modify toolbars. The Draw and Modify pull-down menus offer the same commands, so you won't lose any functionality by closing these toolbars. If you really want to maximize your drawing area, you can also turn off the scroll bars and reduce the Command window to a single line. See *Setting Preferences* in Appendix B for details on how to do this.

Making Changes

You will be making frequent changes to your drawings. In fact, one of the AutoCAD's chief advantages is the ease with which you can make changes. The following exercise shows you a typical sequence of operations involved in making a change to a drawing.

1. From the Modify toolbar, click on the Erase tool (the one with a pencil eraser touching paper). This activates the Erase command. You can also choose Modify ➣ Erase from the pull-down menu.

Notice that the cursor has turned into a small square; this square is called the *pickbox*. You also see `Select object:` in the command prompt area. This message helps remind new users what to do.

2. Place the pickbox on the diagonal pattern of the nozzle handle (see Figure 1.12) and click on it. The 2D image of the nozzle becomes highlighted. The pickbox and the `Select object` prompt remain, telling you that you can continue to select objects.

3. Now press ↵. The nozzle and the rectangle disappear. You have just erased a part of the drawing.

FIGURE 1.12:

Erasing a portion of the
Nozzle handle

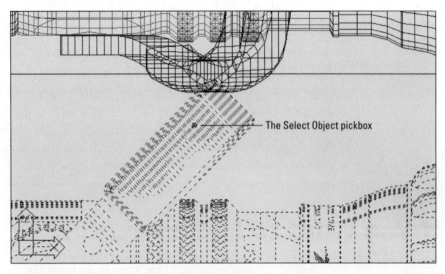

The Select Object pickbox

In this exercise, you first issued the Erase command, and then selected an object by clicking on it using a pickbox. The pickbox tells you that you must select items on the screen. Once you've done that, you press ⏎ to move on to the next step. This sequence of steps is common to many of the commands you will work with in AutoCAD.

Closing AutoCAD

When you are done with your work on one drawing, you can open another drawing, temporarily leave AutoCAD, or close AutoCAD entirely. To close a file and exit AutoCAD, you use the Exit option on the File menu.

1. Choose File ➤ Exit, which is the last item in the menu. A dialog box appears, asking you if you want to "Save Changes to Myfirst.dwg?" and offering three buttons labeled Yes, No, and Cancel.

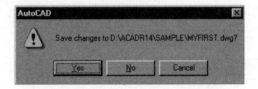

2. Click the No button. AutoCAD exits the nozzle drawing and closes without saving your changes.

Whenever you attempt to exit a drawing that has been changed, you will get this same inquiry box. This request for confirmation is a safety feature that lets you change your mind and save your changes before you exit AutoCAD. In the previous exercise, you discarded the changes you made, so the nozzle drawing reverts back to its state before you erased the handle.

If you only want to exit AutoCAD temporarily, you can minimize it so it appears as a button on the Windows 95 or NT 4 toolbar. You do this by clicking on the Minimize button in the upper-right corner of the AutoCAD window; this is the button with the underline sign. Alternatively, you can use the Alt+Tab key combination to switch to another program.

If You Want to Experiment ...

Try opening and closing some of the sample drawing files.

1. Start AutoCAD by choosing Start ➢ Programs ➢ AutoCAD R14 ➢ AutoCAD R14.

2. Click on File ➢ Open.

3. Use the dialog box to open the Myfirst file again. Notice that the drawing appears on the screen with the handle enlarged. This is the view you had on screen when you used the Save command in the earlier exercise.

4. Erase the handle, as you did in the earlier exercise.

5. Click on File ➢ Open again. This time, open the Dhouse file from the companion CD-ROM. Notice that you get the Save Changes inquiry box you saw when you used the Exit option earlier. File ➢ Open acts just like Exit, but instead of exiting AutoCAD altogether, it closes the current file and then opens a different one.

6. Click on the No button. The 3D Dhouse drawing opens.

7. Click on File ➢ Exit. Notice that you exit AutoCAD without getting the Save Changes dialog box. This is because you didn't make any changes to the Dhouse file.

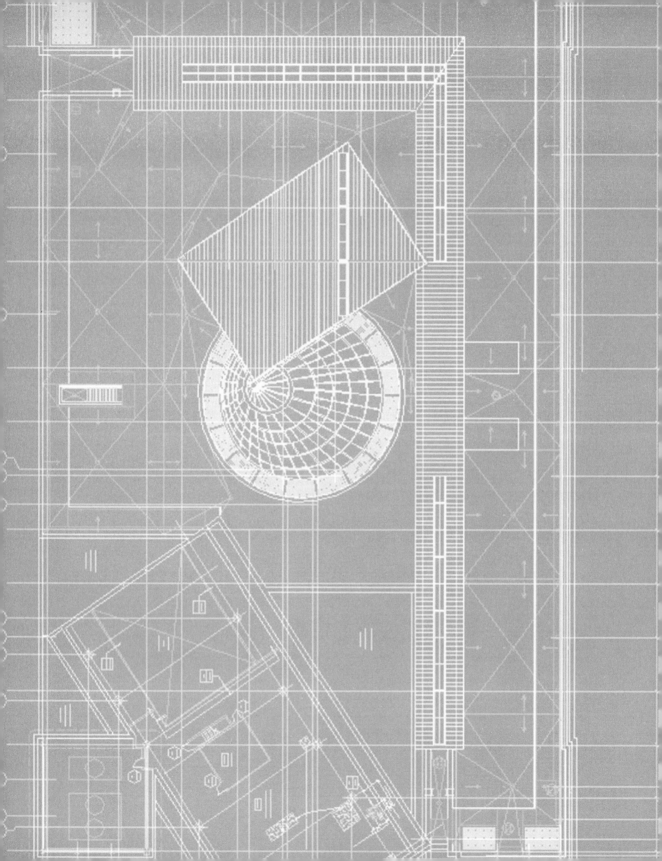

CHAPTER
TWO

Creating Your First Drawing

In this chapter we'll examine some of AutoCAD's basic functions and practice with the drawing editor by building a simple drawing to use in later exercises. We'll discuss giving input to AutoCAD, interpreting prompts, and getting help when you need it. We'll also cover the use of coordinate systems to give Auto-CAD exact measurements for objects. You'll see how to select objects you've drawn, and how to specify base points for moving and copying.

If you're not a beginning AutoCAD user, you might want to move on to the more complex material in Chapter 3. You can use the files supplied on the companion CD-ROM of this book to continue the tutorials at that point.

Getting to Know the Draw Toolbar

Your first task in learning how to draw in AutoCAD is to try and draw a line. But before you begin drawing, take a moment to familiarize yourself with the toolbar you'll be using more than any other to create objects with AutoCAD: the Draw toolbar.

1. Start AutoCAD just as you did in the first chapter, by clicking on Start ➤ Programs ➤ AutoCAD R14 ➤ AutoCAD R14.

2. In the AutoCAD window, move the arrow cursor to the top icon in the Draw toolbar, and rest it there so that the tool tip appears.

3. Slowly move the arrow cursor downward over the other tools in the Draw toolbar, and read each tool tip.

NOTE   Moving the arrow cursor onto an element on the screen is also referred to as "pointing to" that element.

In most cases, you'll be able to guess what each tool does by looking at its icon. The icon with an arc, for instance, indicates that the tool draws arcs; the one with the ellipse shows that the tool draws ellipses; and so on. For further clarification, the tool tip gives you the name of the tool. For further help, you can look to the status bar at the bottom of the AutoCAD Window. For example, if you point to the Arc icon just below the Rectangle icon, the status bar reads "Creates an Arc." It also shows you the actual AutoCAD command name: Arc. This name is what you would type in the Command window to invoke the Arc tool. You would also use this word if you are writing a macro or creating your own custom tools.

Figure and Table 2.1 will aid you in navigating the two main toolbars (Draw and Modify). You'll get experience with many of AutoCAD's tools as you work through this book.

FIGURE 2.1:

The tools available on the Draw and Modify toolbars are listed by number in Table 2.1.

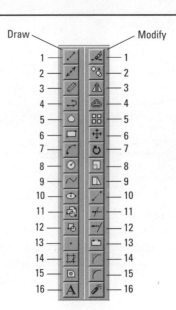

TABLE 2.1: The options that appear on the Draw and Modify toolbars and flyouts

Draw Toolbar

1	Line
2	Construction Line (Xline)
3	Multiline (Mline)
4	Polyline (Pline)
5	Polygon
6	Rectangle
7	Arc
8	Circle
9	Spline
10	Ellipse
11	Insert Block
12	Make Block
13	Point
14	Hatch
15	Region
16	Multiline Text

Modify Toolbar

1	Erase
2	Copy Object
3	Mirror
4	Offset
5	Array
6	Move
7	Rotate
8	Scale

TABLE 2.1 CONTINUED: The options that appear on the Draw and Modify toolbars and flyouts

Modify Toolbar

9	Stretch
10	Lengthen
11	Trim
12	Extend
13	Break
14	Chamfer
15	Fillet
16	Explode

As you saw in Chapter 1, clicking on a tool issues a command. Some tools allow clicking *and dragging*, which opens a flyout. A flyout offers further options for that tool. You can identify flyout tools by a small triangle located in the lower-right corner of the tool.

1. Click and drag the Distance tool on the Standard toolbar. A flyout appears with a set of tools. As you can see, there are a number of additional tools for gathering information about your drawing.

2. Move the cursor down the flyout to the second to last tool, until the tool tip reads "List"; then let go of the mouse button. Notice that the icon representing the Distance tool now changes and becomes the icon from the flyout that represents List. By releasing the mouse you've also issued the List command. This command lists the properties of an object.

3.   Press Escape twice to exit the List command.

TIP   If you find you are working a lot with one particular flyout, you can easily turn that flyout into a floating toolbar, so all the flyout options are readily available with a single click. See Chapter 21 for details on how to do this.

By making the most recently selected option on a flyout the default option for the toolbar tool, AutoCAD gives you quick access to frequently used commands. A word of caution, however: This feature can confuse the first-time AutoCAD user. Also, the grouping of options on the flyout menus are not always self-explanatory—even to a veteran AutoCAD user.

NOTE   Release 13 offered flyout menus on nearly every toolbar. Release 14 has reduced the number of flyouts so that on a typical screen they only appear on the Standard toolbar.

Working with Toolbars

As you work through the exercises, this book will show you graphics of the tools to choose, along with the toolbar or flyout that contains the tool. Don't be alarmed, however, if the toolbars you see in the examples don't look exactly like those on your screen. To save page space, I have horizontally oriented the toolbars and flyouts for the illustrations; the ones on your screen may be oriented vertically, like the Draw and Modify toolbars to the left of the AutoCAD Window. Although the shape of your toolbars and flyouts may differ from the ones you see in this book, the contents are the same. So when you see a graphic showing a tool, focus on the tool icon itself with its tool tip name, along with the name of the toolbar in which it is shown.

Starting Your First Drawing

In Chapter 1, you looked at a preexisting sample drawing. This time you will begin to draw on your own, by creating a door that will be used in later exercises. First, though, you must learn how to tell AutoCAD what you want and, even more important, to understand what AutoCAD wants from you.

1. Choose File ➤ New.

2. When the Create New Drawing dialog box appears, click on the Start from Scratch button, click on English from the Select Default Settings list box, and then click OK. This creates a new drawing using the standard AutoCAD default settings for the English (inches) system of measurement. You'll get a chance to use other options in this dialog box later. For now, you'll explore some basic AutoCAD options.

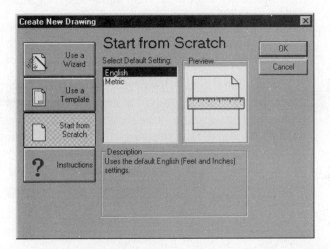

3. To give your new file a unique name, choose File Save ➤ As.

4. At the Save Drawing As dialog box, type **Door**. As you type, the name appears in the File Name input box.

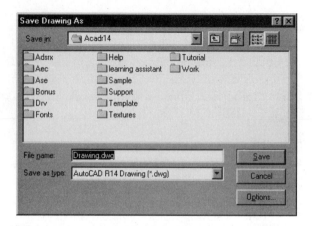

5. Double-click on the Sample folder shown in the main file list of the dialog box. By doing this, you open the Samples subdirectory.

6. Click Save. You now have a file called Door.dwg, located in the Samples subdirectory of your AutoCAD R14 directory. Of course, your drawing doesn't contain anything yet. You'll take care of that next.

The new file shows a drawing area roughly 16 inches wide by 9 inches high. To check this for yourself, move the crosshair cursor to the upper-right corner of the screen, and observe the value shown in the coordinate readout. This is the standard AutoCAD default drawing area for new drawings.

To begin a drawing, follow these steps:

1. Click on the Line tool on the Draw toolbar, or type **L** ↵. You've just issued the Line command. AutoCAD responds in two ways. First, you see the message:

    ```
    From point:
    ```

    in the command prompt, asking you to select a point to begin your line. Also, the cursor has changed its appearance; it no longer has a square in the crosshairs. This is a clue telling you to pick a point to start a line.

NOTE You can also type **Line** ↵ in the Command window to start the Line command.

2. Using the left mouse button, select a point on the screen near the center. As you select the point, AutoCAD changes the prompt to:

    `To point:`

    Now as you move the mouse around, you will notice a line with one end fixed on the point you just selected, and the other end following the cursor (see the top image of Figure 2.2). This action is called *rubber-banding*.

FIGURE 2.2:

Two rubber-banding lines

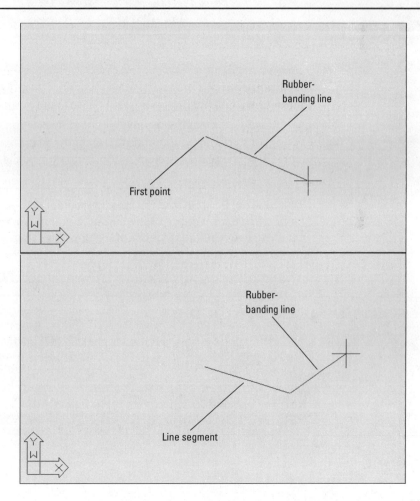

Now continue with the Line command:

3. Move the cursor to a point to the right of the first point you selected, and press the left mouse button again. The first rubber-banding line is now fixed between the two points you selected, and a second rubber-banding line appears (see the bottom image of Figure 2.2).

4. If the line you drew isn't the exact length you want, you can back up during the Line command and change it. To do this, click on Undo in the Standard toolbar, or type **U**↵ from the keyboard. Now the line you drew previously will rubber-band as if you hadn't selected the second point to fix its length.

You've just drawn, and then undrawn, a line at an arbitrary length. The Line command is still active. There are two things that tell you that you are in the middle of a command, as mentioned above. If you don't see the word "Command" in the bottom of the Command window, you know a command is still active. Also, the cursor will be the plain crosshair without the little box at its intersection.

NOTE   From now on, I will refer to the crosshair cursor without the small box as the *point selection mode* of the cursor. If you look ahead to Figure 2.8, you'll see all the different modes of the drawing cursor.

Getting Out of Trouble

Beginners and experts alike are bound to make a few mistakes. Before you get too far into the tutorial, here are some powerful yet easy-to-use tools to help you recover from accidents.

Backspace [←]   If you make a typing error, you can use the Backspace key to back up to your error, and then retype your command or response. Backspace is located in the upper-right corner of the main keyboard area.

Escape [Esc]   This is perhaps the single most important key on your keyboard. When you need to quickly exit a command or dialog box without making changes, just press the Esc key in the upper-left corner of your keyboard. Press it twice if you want to cancel a selection set of objects or to make absolutely sure you've canceled a command.

Tip: Use the Esc key before editing with grips or issuing commands through the keyboard. You can also press Esc twice to clear grip selections.

U ⏎   If you accidentally change something in the drawing and want to reverse that change, click on the Undo tool in the Standard toolbar (the left-pointing curved arrow). You can also type **U** ⏎ at the Command prompt. Each time you do this, AutoCAD will undo one operation at a time, in reverse order—so the last command performed will be undone first, then the next to last, and so on. The prompt will display the name of the command being undone, and the drawing will revert to its state prior to that command. If you need to, you can undo everything back to the beginning of an editing session.

Redo   If you accidentally Undo one too many commands, you can redo the last undone command by clicking on the Redo tool (the right-pointing curved arrow) in the Standard toolbar. Or type **Redo** ⏎. Unfortunately, Redo only restores one command and it can only be invoked immediately after an Undo.

Specifying Distances with Coordinates

Next, you will continue with the Line command to draw a *plan view* (an overhead view) of a door, to no particular scale. Later, you will resize the drawing to use in future exercises. The door will be 3.0 units long and 0.15 units thick. To specify these exact distances in AutoCAD, you can use either *relative polar coordinates* or *Cartesian coordinates*.

Specifying Polar Coordinates

To enter the exact distance of 3 units to the right of the last point you selected, do the following:

1.   Type **@3<0**. As you type, the letters appear in the command prompt.

2. Press ↵. A line appears, starting from the first point you picked and ending 3 units to the right of it (see Figure 2.3). You have just entered a relative polar coordinate.

FIGURE 2.3:

Notice that the rubber-banding line now starts from the last point selected. This tells you that you can continue to add more line segments.

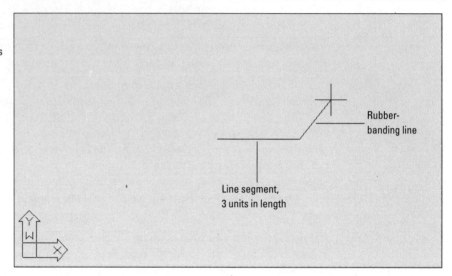

The at sign (@) you entered tells AutoCAD that the distance you are specifying is from the last point you selected. The 3 is the distance, and the less-than symbol (<) tells AutoCAD that you are designating the angle at which the line is to be drawn. The last part is the value for the angle, which in this case is 0. This is how to use *polar coordinates* to communicate distances and direction to AutoCAD.

NOTE If you are accustomed to a different method for describing directions, you can set AutoCAD to use a vertical direction or downward direction as 0°. See Chapter 3 for details.

Angles are given based on the system shown in Figure 2.4, where 0° is a horizontal direction from left to right, 90° is straight up, 180° is horizontal from right to left, and so on. You can specify degrees, minutes, and seconds of arc if you want to be that exact. We'll discuss angle formats in more detail in Chapter 3.

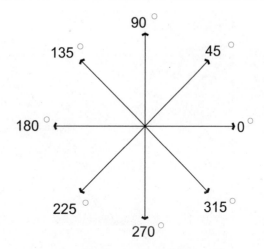

Specifying Relative Cartesian Coordinates

For the next line segment, let's try another method of specifying exact distances.

1. Enter **@0,.15** ↵. A short line appears above the endpoint of the last line.

Once again, the @ tells AutoCAD that the distance you specify is from the last point picked. But in this example, you give the distance in x and y values. The x distance, 0, is given first, followed by a comma, and then the y distance, 0.15. This is how to specify distances in relative Cartesian coordinates.

2. Enter **@-3,0** ↵. The result is a drawing that looks like Figure 2.5.

The distance you entered in step 2 was also in x,y values, but here you used a negative value to specify the x distance. Positive values in the Cartesian coordinate system are from left to right and from bottom to top (see Figure 2.6). (You may remember this from your high school geometry class!) If you want to draw a line from right to left, you must designate a negative value.

FIGURE 2.5:

These three sides of the door were drawn using the Line tool. Points are specified using either relative Cartesian or polar coordinates.

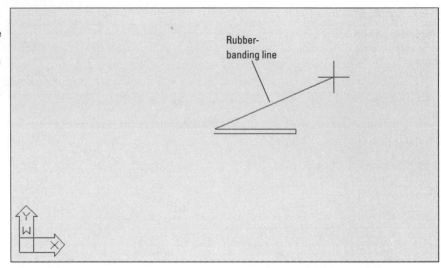

FIGURE 2.6:

Positive and negative Cartesian coordinate directions

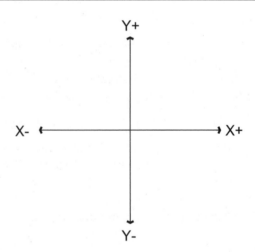

TIP　　To finish drawing a series of lines without closing them, you can press Esc, ↵, or the spacebar.

3. Now type **C** ↵. This C stands for Close. It closes a sequence of line segments. A line connecting the first and last points of a sequence of lines is drawn (see Figure 2.7), and the Line command terminates. The rubber-banding line also disappears, telling you that AutoCAD has finished drawing line segments. You can also use the rubber-banding line to indicate direction while simultaneously entering the distance through the keyboard. See the *A Fast Way to Enter Distances* sidebar in this chapter.

FIGURE 2.7:

Distance and direction input for the door

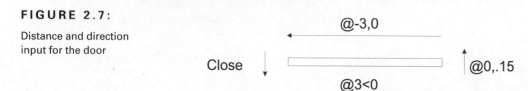

A Fast Way to Enter Distances

A third method for entering distances is to simply point in a direction with a rubber-banding line, and then enter the distance through the keyboard. For example, to draw a line 3-units long from left to right, click on the line tool from the draw toolbar, click on a start point, and then move the cursor so the rubber-banding line points to the right at some arbitrary distance. While holding the cursor in the direction you want, type **3** ↵. The rubber-banding line becomes a fixed line 3-units long.

Using this method, called the *Direct Distance* method, along with the Ortho mode described in Chapter 3, can be a fast way to draw objects of specific lengths. Use the standard Cartesian or Polar coordinate methods when you need to enter exact distances at angles other than those that are exactly horizontal or vertical.

Cleaning Up the Screen

On some systems, the AutoCAD Blipmode setting may be turned on. This will cause tiny cross-shaped markers, called *blips*, to appear where you've selected points. These blips can be helpful to keep track of the points you've selected on the screen. You can also enter **R** ↵ .

Continued on next page

Blips aren't actually part of your drawing and will not print. Still, they can be annoying. To clear the screen of blips, click on the Redraw tool in the toolbar (it's the one that looks like a pencil point drawing an arc), or type **R** ↵. The screen quickly redraws the objects, clearing the screen of the blips. You can also choose View ➤ Redraw View to accomplish the same thing. As you will see later in this book, Redraw can also clear up other display problems.

Another command, Regen, does the same thing as Redraw, but also updates the drawing display database—which means it takes a bit longer to restore the drawing. In general, you will want to avoid Regen, though at times using it is unavoidable. You will examine Regen in Chapter 7.

To turn Blipmode on and off, type **blipmode** ↵ at the Command prompt, and then enter **on** ↵ or **off** ↵.

Interpreting the Cursor Modes and Understanding Prompts

The key to working with AutoCAD successfully is understanding the way it interacts with you. In this section you will become familiar with some of the ways AutoCAD prompts you for input. Understanding the format of the messages in the Command window and recognizing other events on the screen will help you learn the program more easily.

As the Command window aids you with messages, the cursor also gives you clues about what to do. Figure 2.8 illustrates the various modes of the cursor and gives a brief description of the role of each mode. Take a moment to study this figure.

The Standard cursor tells you that AutoCAD is waiting for instructions. You can also edit objects using grips when you see this cursor. The Point Selection cursor appears whenever AutoCAD expects point input. It can also appear in conjunction with a rubber-banding line. You can either click on a point or enter a coordinate through the keyboard. The Object Selection cursor tells you that you must select objects—either by clicking on them or by using any of the object selection options available. The Osnap marker appears along with the Point Selection cursor when you invoke an Osnap. Osnaps let you select specific points on an object, such as endpoints or midpoints.

FIGURE 2.8:

The drawing cursor's modes

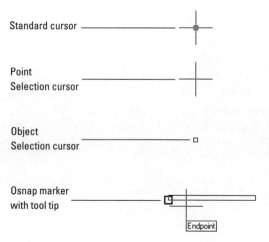

Standard cursor

Point
Selection cursor

Object
Selection cursor

Osnap marker
with tool tip

Endpoint

TIP

If you are an experienced AutoCAD user and would prefer to use the older style crosshair cursor that crosses the entire screen, you use the Pointer tab of the Preferences dialog box (Tools ➤ Preferences...) to set the cursor size. Set the Percent of Screen Size option near the bottom of the dialog box to 100. The cursor will then appear as it did in prior versions of AutoCAD. As the option implies, you can set the cursor size to any percentage of the screen you want. The default is 5 %.

Choosing Command Options

Many commands in AutoCAD offer several options, which are often presented to you in the Command window in the form of a prompt. Here, we'll use the Arc command to illustrate the format of AutoCAD's prompts.

Usually, in a floor-plan drawing, an arc is drawn to indicate the direction of a door swing. Figure 2.9 shows some of the other standard symbols used in architectural style drawings. This is a small sampling of the symbols available on the CD-ROM included with this book. See Appendix C for more information.

FIGURE 2.9:

Samples of standard symbols used in architectural drawings

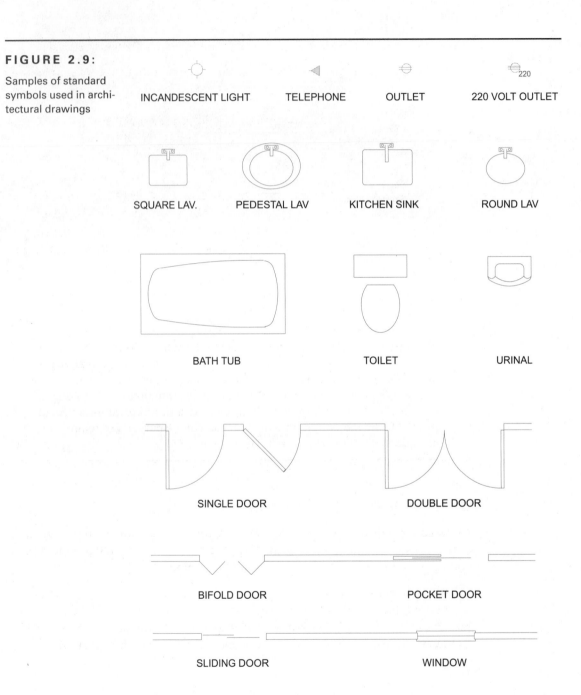

INCANDESCENT LIGHT   TELEPHONE   OUTLET   220 VOLT OUTLET

SQUARE LAV.   PEDESTAL LAV   KITCHEN SINK   ROUND LAV

BATH TUB   TOILET   URINAL

SINGLE DOOR   DOUBLE DOOR

BIFOLD DOOR   POCKET DOOR

SLIDING DOOR   WINDOW

Next, you'll draw the arc for the door you started in the previous exercise.

1. Click on the Arc tool in the Draw toolbar. The prompt `Center/<Start point>` appears, and the cursor changes to point selection mode.

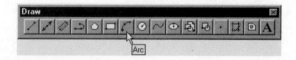

Let's examine this `Center/<Start point>` prompt. It contains two options. The *default* option always appears between angle brackets (< >), and all other options are separated by slashes (/). If you choose to take the `Start point` default, you can input a point by clicking on a location on the screen or by entering a coordinate.

NOTE   The *default* is the option AutoCAD assumes you intend to use unless you tell it otherwise.

---

2. Type **C** ↵ to select the Center option. The prompt `Center` appears. Notice that you only had to type in the C and not the whole word "Center."

NOTE   When you see a set of options in the Command window, note their capitalization. If you choose to respond to prompts using the keyboard, these capitalized letters are all you need to enter to select that option. In some cases, the first two letters are capitalized to differentiate two options that begin with the same letter, such as LAyer and LType.

---

3. Now pick a point representing the center of the arc near the upper-left corner of the door (see the first image of Figure 2.10). The prompt `Start point` appears.

4. Type **@3<0**. The prompt `Angle/Length of chord/<End point>` appears.

5. Move the mouse and you will see a temporary arc originating from a point 3 units to the right of the center point you selected and rotating about that center, as in the top continued image of Figure 2.10.

As the prompt indicates, you now have three options. You can enter an angle, length of chord, or the endpoint of the arc. The default, indicated by <End point> in the prompt, is to pick the arc's endpoint. Again, the cursor is in a point selection mode, telling you it is waiting for point input. To select this default option, you only need to pick a point on the screen indicating where you want the endpoint.

6. Pick a point directly vertical from the center of the arc. The arc is now fixed in place, as in the bottom continued image of Figure 2.10.

This exercise has given you some practice working with AutoCAD's Command window prompts and entering keyboard commands—a skill you will need when you start to use some of the more advanced AutoCAD functions.

As you can see, AutoCAD has a distinct structure in its prompt messages. You first issue a command, which in turn offers options in the form of a prompt. Depending on the option you select, you will get another set of options or you will be prompted to take some action, such as picking a point, selecting objects, or entering a value.

As shown in Figure 2.11, the sequence is something like a tree. As you work through the exercises, you will become intimately familiar with this routine. Once you understand the workings of the toolbars, Command window prompts, and dialog boxes, you can almost teach yourself the rest of the program!

FIGURE 2.10:

Using the Arc command

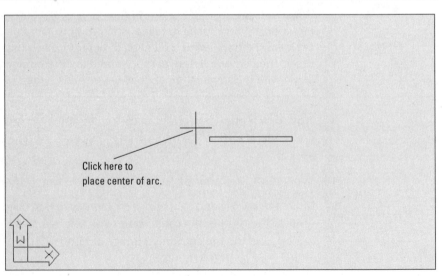

Click here to
place center of arc.

**FIGURE 2.10:
CONTINUED**

Using the Arc command

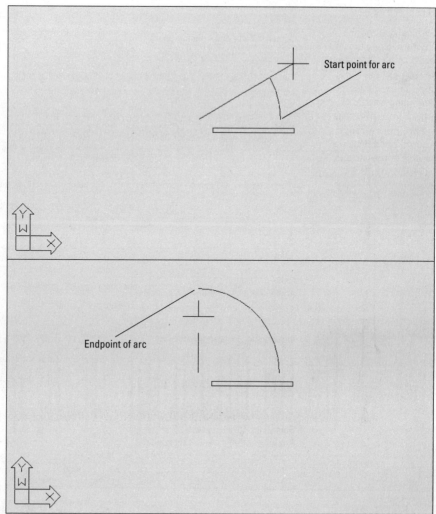

Start point for arc

Endpoint of arc

FIGURE 2.11:

A typical command structure, using the Arc command as an example. You will see different messages depending on the options you choose as you progress through the command. This figure shows the various pathways to creating an arc.

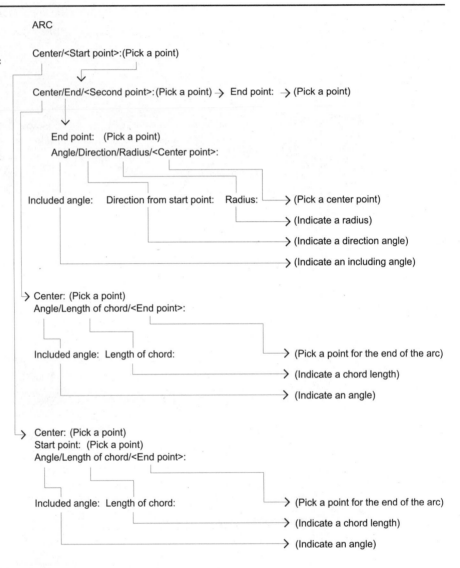

ARC

Center/<Start point>:(Pick a point)

Center/End/<Second point>:(Pick a point) → End point: → (Pick a point)

End point: (Pick a point)
Angle/Direction/Radius/<Center point>:

Included angle: Direction from start point: Radius: → (Pick a center point)

→ (Indicate a radius)

→ (Indicate a direction angle)

→ (Indicate an including angle)

→ Center: (Pick a point)
Angle/Length of chord/<End point>:

Included angle: Length of chord: → (Pick a point for the end of the arc)

→ (Indicate a chord length)

→ (Indicate an angle)

→ Center: (Pick a point)
Start point: (Pick a point)
Angle/Length of chord/<End point>:

Included angle: Length of chord: → (Pick a point for the end of the arc)

→ (Indicate a chord length)

→ (Indicate an angle)

Selecting Objects

AutoCAD provides many options for selecting objects. This section has two parts: The first part deals with object selection methods unique to AutoCAD, and the second part deals with the more common selection method used in most popular graphic programs, the *Noun/Verb* method. Because these two methods play a major role in working with AutoCAD, it's a good idea to familiarize yourself with them early on.

Selecting Objects in AutoCAD

Many AutoCAD commands prompt you to `Select objects`. Along with this prompt, the cursor will change from crosshairs to a small square (look back at Figure 2.8). Whenever you see this Object Selection prompt and the square cursor, you have several options while making your selection. Often, as you select objects on the screen, you will change your mind about a selection or accidentally pick an object you do not want. Let's take a look at most of the selection options available in AutoCAD, and learn what to do when you make the wrong selection.

1. Choose Move from the Modify toolbar.

2. At the `Select objects` prompt, click on the two horizontal lines that compose the door. As you saw in the last chapter, whenever AutoCAD wants you to select objects, the cursor turns into the small square pickbox. This tells you that you are in *Object Selection mode*. As you pick an object, it is *highlighted*, as shown in Figure 2.12.

FIGURE 2.12:

Selecting the lines of
the door and seeing
them highlighted

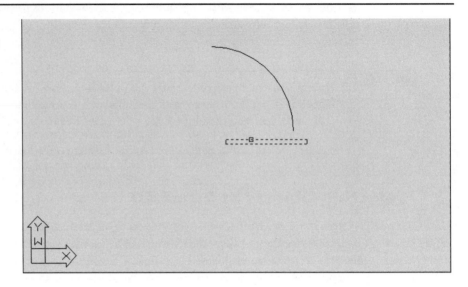

3. After making your selections, you may decide to deselect some items. Click
   on Undo in the Standard toolbar, or enter **U** ↵ from the keyboard.

Notice that one line is no longer highlighted. The Undo option deselects
objects, one at a time, in reverse order of selection.

4. There is another way to deselect objects: Hold down the Shift key and click
   on the remaining highlighted line. It reverts to a solid line, showing you that
   it is no longer selected for editing.

By now you have deselected both lines. Let's try using another method for
selecting groups of objects.

5. Another option for selecting objects is to *window* them. Type **W** ↵. The cursor changes to a Point Selection cursor, and the prompt changes to:

   First corner:

6. Click on a point below and to the left of the rectangle representing the door. As you move your cursor across the screen, the window appears and stretches across the drawing area.

7. Once the window completely encloses the door but not the arc, click on this location and all of the door will be highlighted. This window selects only objects that are completely enclosed by the window, as shown in Figure 2.13.

NOTE   You might remember that you used a window with the Zoom command in Chapter 1. That window option under the Zoom command does not select objects. Rather, it defines an area of the drawing you want to enlarge. Remember that the window option works differently under the Zoom command than it does for other editing commands.

WARNING   If you are using a mouse you're not familiar with, it's quite easy to accidentally click the right mouse button, which is the button that triggers the ↵ action, when you really wanted to click the left mouse button, and vice versa. If you click the wrong button, you'll get the wrong results. On a two-button mouse, the right button acts like the ↵ key. On a three-button mouse, it's the center button.

8. Now that you have selected the entire door but not the arc, press ↵. *It is important to remember to press ↵ as soon as you have finished selecting the objects you want to edit.* Pressing ↵ tells AutoCAD when you have finished selecting objects. A new prompt, Base point or displacement, appears. The cursor changes to its Point Selection mode.

Now you have seen how the selection process works in AutoCAD—but we've left you in the middle of the Move command. In the next section, we'll discuss the prompt that's now on your screen, and see how to input base points and displacement distances.

FIGURE 2.13

Selecting the door within a window

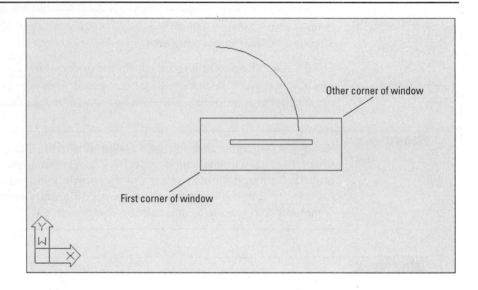

Providing Base Points

When you move or copy objects, AutoCAD prompts you for a *base point*, which is a difficult concept to grasp. AutoCAD must be told specifically *from* where and *to* where the move occurs. The base point is the exact location from which you determine the distance and direction of the move. Once the base point is determined, you can tell AutoCAD where to move the object in relation to that point.

1. To select a base point, hold down the Shift key and press the right mouse button. A menu pops up on the screen. This is the *Object Snap (Osnap)* menu.

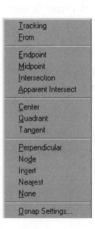

WARNING When right-clicking the mouse, make sure the cursor is within the AutoCAD drawing area, otherwise you will not get the results described in this book.

2. Pick Intersection from the Osnap menu. The Osnap menu disappears.

3. Move the cursor to the lower-right corner of the door. Notice that as you approach the corner, a small X-shaped graphic appears on the corner. This is called an Osnap marker.

4. After the X-shaped marker appears, hold the mouse motionless for a second or two. A tool tip appears telling you the current Osnap point AutoCAD has selected.

5. Now press the left mouse button to select the intersection indicated by the Osnap marker. Whenever you see the Osnap marker at the point you wish to select, you don't have to point exactly at the location with your cursor. Just left click on the mouse and the exact Osnap point is selected (see Figure 2.14). In this case, you selected the exact intersection of two lines.

6. At the Second point of displacement prompt, hold down the Shift key and press the right mouse button again. You'll use the Endpoint Osnap this time, but instead of clicking on the option with the mouse, type the letter "E."

7. Now pick the lower-right end of the arc you drew earlier. (Remember that you only need to move your cursor close to the endpoint until the Osnap marker appears.) The door moves so that the corner of the door connects exactly with the endpoint of the arc (see Figure 2.15).

As you can see, the Osnap options allow you to select specific points on an object. You used Endpoint and Intersect in this exercise, but other options are available. We will look at some of the other options later in Chapter 3. You may have also noticed that the Osnap marker is different for each of the options you used. You'll learn more about Osnaps in Chapter 3. Now let's continue with our look at point selection.

FIGURE 2.14:

Using the Osnap cursor

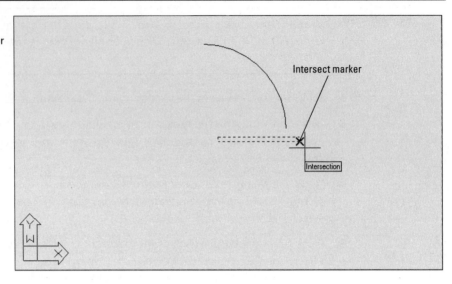

FIGURE 2.15:

The rectangle in its new position after using the Endpoint Osnap

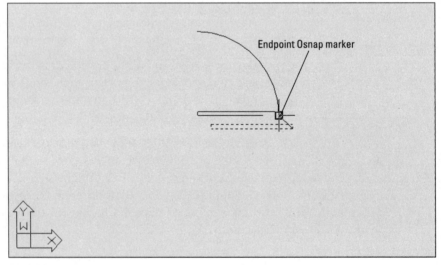

If you want to specify an exact distance and direction by typing in a value, you can select any point on the screen as a base point. Or you can just type @ followed by ↵ at the base point prompt; then enter the second point's location in relative coordinates. Remember that @ means the last point selected. In this next exercise, you'll try moving the entire door an exact distance of 1 unit in a 45° angle.

1. Click on the Move tool from the Modify toolbar.

2. Type **P** ↵. The set of objects you selected in the previous command is highlighted. "P" is a selection option that selects the previously selected set of objects.

3. You're still in the Object Selection mode, so click on the arc to include it in the set of selected objects. Now the entire door, including the arc, is highlighted, as shown in Figure 2.16.

4. Now press ↵ to tell AutoCAD you have finished your selection. The cursor changes to Point Selection mode.

5. At the Base point or displacement prompt, pick a point on the screen between the door and the left side of the screen (see Figure 2.16).

6. Move the cursor around slowly and notice that the door moves as if the base point you selected were attached to the door. The door moves with the cursor, at a fixed distance from it. This demonstrates how the base point relates to the objects you select.

7. Now type **@1<45** ↵. The door will move to a new location on the screen at a distance of 1 unit from its previous location and at an angle of 45°.

TIP

If AutoCAD is waiting for a command, you can repeat the last command used by pressing the right mouse button, the Spacebar key, or the ↵ key.

FIGURE 2.16:

The highlighted door and the base point just left of the door. Note that the base point does not need to be on the object you are moving.

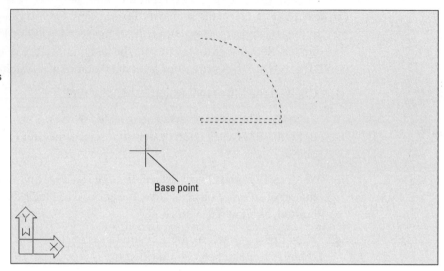

Base point

This exercise illustrates that the base point does not have to be on the object you are manipulating. The base point can be virtually anywhere on your drawing. You also saw how you can reselect a group of objects that were selected previously, without having to duplicate the selection process.

Other Selection Options

There are several other selection options you haven't tried yet. This sidebar describes these other options. You'll see how these options work in exercises later in this book. Or if you are adventurous, try them out now on your own. To use these options, type their keyboard abbreviations (shown in brackets in the following list) at any Select Object prompt.

All [all ↵]   selects all the objects in a drawing except those in frozen or locked layers (see Chapter 4 for more on layers).

Crossing [c ↵]   is similar to the Select Window option but will select anything that crosses through the window you define.

Crossing Polygon [cp ↵] acts exactly like WPolygon (see below) but, like the Select Crossing option, will select anything that crosses through a polygon boundary.

Fence [f ↵] selects objects that are crossed over by a temporary line called a fence. The operation is like crossing out the objects you want to select with a line. When you invoke this option, you can then pick points, as when you are drawing a series of line segments. When you are done drawing the fence, press ↵, then go on to select other objects, or press ↵ again to finish your selection.

Last [l ↵] selects the last object you input.

Multiple [m ↵] lets you select several objects first, before AutoCAD highlights them. In a very large file, picking objects individually can cause AutoCAD to pause after each pick, while it locates and highlights each object. The Multiple option can speed things up by letting you first pick all the objects quickly, and then highlight them all by pressing ↵. This has no menu equivalent.

Previous [p ↵] selects the last object or set of objects that was edited or changed.

Window [w ↵] forces a standard selection window. This option is useful when your drawing area is too crowded to use the Autoselect feature to place a window around a set of objects (see the Auto entry in this sidebar). It prevents you from accidentally selecting an object with a single pick when you are placing your window.

Window Polygon [wp ↵] lets you select objects by enclosing them in an irregularly shaped polygon boundary. When you use this option, you see the prompt First polygon point. You then pick points to define the polygon boundary. As you pick points, the prompt Undo/<Endpoint of line> appears. Select as many points as you need to define the boundary. You can Undo boundary line segments as you go by clicking on the Undo tool on the Standard toolbar, or by pressing the U key. With the boundary defined, press ↵. The bounded objects are highlighted and the Select object prompt returns, allowing you to use more selection options.

The following two selection options are also available, but seldom ever used. They are intended for use in creating custom menu options or custom toolbar tools.

Continued on next page

Auto [au ⏎]   forces the standard automatic window or crossing window when a point is picked and no object is found (see *Using Autoselect* later in this chapter). A standard window is produced when the two window corners are picked from left to right. A crossing window is produced when the two corners are picked from right to left. Once this option is selected, it remains active for the duration of the current command. Auto is intended for use on systems where the Automatic Selection feature has been turned off.

Single [si ⏎]   forces the current command to select only a single object. If you use this option, you can pick a single object; then the current command will act on that object as if you had pressed ⏎ immediately after selecting the object. This has no menu equivalent.

Selecting Objects before the Command: Noun/Verb

Nearly all graphics programs today have tacitly acknowledged the *noun/verb* method for selecting objects. This method requires you to select objects *before* you issue a command to edit them. The next set of exercises shows you how to use the noun/verb method in AutoCAD.

You have seen that when AutoCAD is waiting for a command, it displays the crosshair cursor with the small square. This square is actually a pickbox superimposed on the cursor. It tells you that you can select objects, even while the command prompt appears at the bottom of the screen and no command is currently active. The square momentarily disappears when you are in a command that asks you to select points. From now on, we'll refer to this crosshair cursor with the small box as the *standard cursor.*

TIP   This chapter presents the standard AutoCAD method for object selection. AutoCAD also offers selection methods with which you may be more familiar. Refer to the section on the Object Selection Settings dialog box in Appendix B to learn how you can control object selection methods. This appendix also describes how you can change the size of the pickbox cursor.

Now try moving objects by first selecting them and then using the Move command.

1.   First, press Esc twice to make sure AutoCAD isn't in the middle of a command you may have accidentally issued. Then click on the arc. The arc is

highlighted, and you may also see squares appear at its endpoints and midpoint. These squares are called *grips*. You may know them as workpoints from other graphics programs. You'll get a chance to work with them a bit later.

2. Choose Move from the Modify toolbar. The cursor changes to Point Selection mode.

3. At the Base point prompt, pick any point on the screen. The prompt To point appears.

4. Type @1<0 ↵. The arc moves to a new location 1 unit to the right.

WARNING If you find that this exercise does not work as described here, chances are the Noun/Verb setting has been turned off on your copy of AutoCAD. Refer to Appendix B to find out how to activate this setting.

In this exercise, you picked the arc *before* issuing the Move command. Then, when you clicked the Move tool, you didn't see the object selection prompt. Instead, AutoCAD assumed you wanted to move the arc you had selected and went directly to the base point prompt.

Using Autoselect

Next you will move the rest of the door in the same direction by using the Autoselect feature.

1. Pick a point just above and to the left of the rectangle representing the door. Be sure not to pick the door itself. Now a window appears that you can drag across the screen as you move the cursor. If you move the cursor to the left of the last point selected, the window appears dotted (see the top image of Figure 2.17). If you move the cursor to the right of that point, it appears solid (see the bottom image of Figure 2.17).

2. Now pick a point below and to the right of the door, so that the door is completely enclosed by the window, as shown in panel 2 of Figure 2.17. The door is highlighted (and again, you may see small squares appear at the line's endpoints and midpoints).

3. Click the Move tool again. Just as in the last exercise, the base point prompt appears.

4. Pick any point on the screen; then enter @1<0 ↵. The door joins with the arc.

The two different windows you have just seen—the solid one and the dotted one—represent a *standard window* and a *crossing window*. If you use a standard window, anything that is completely contained within the window will be selected. If you use a crossing window, anything that crosses through the window will be selected. These two types of windows start automatically when you click on any blank portion of the drawing area with a standard cursor or point selection cursor; hence the name Autoselect.

FIGURE 2.17:

The dotted window (top image) indicates a crossing selection; the solid window (bottom image) indicates a standard selection window.

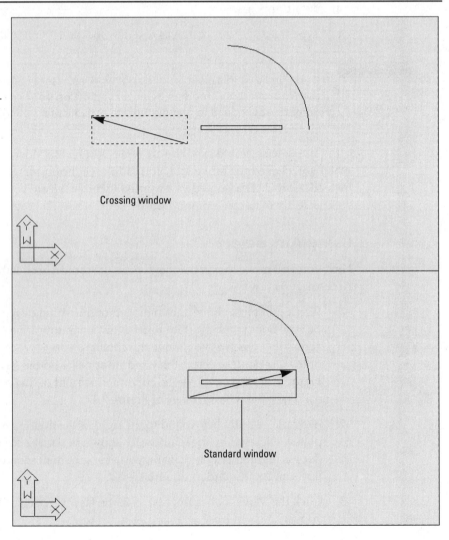

Next, you will select objects with an automatic crossing window.

1. Pick a point below and to the right of the door. As you move the cursor to the left, the crossing (dotted) window appears.

2. Select the next point so that the window encloses the door and part of the arc (see Figure 2.18). The entire door, including the arc, highlights.

3. Click on the Move tool.

4. Pick any point on the screen; then enter @1<180. The door moves back to its original location.

FIGURE 2.18:

The door enclosed by a crossing window

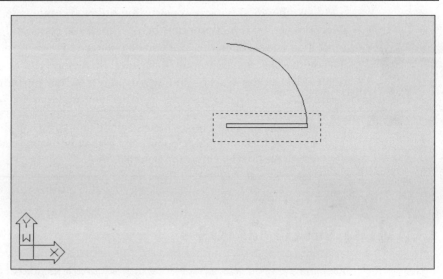

You'll find that in most cases, the Autoselect standard and crossing windows are all you need when selecting objects. They will really save you time, so you'll want to get familiar with these features.

Before we continue, you need to use File ➤ Save to save the Door file. You won't want to save the changes you make in the next section, so saving now will store the current condition of the file on your hard disk for safekeeping.

Restrictions on Noun/Verb Object Selection

If you prefer to work with the Noun/Verb selection feature, you should know that its use is limited to the following subset of AutoCAD commands, listed here in no particular order.

Array	Mirror	Wblock	Block
Dview	Move	Erase	Explode
Change	Rotate	Chprop	Hatch
Scale	Copy	List	Stretch

For all other modifying or construction-oriented commands, the Noun/Verb selection method is inappropriate because for those commands you must select more than one set of objects. But you do not need to remember this list. You'll know if a command accepts the noun/verb selection method right away. Commands that don't will clear the selection and then display a `Select object` prompt.

NOTE   If you want to take a break, now is a good time to do it. If you wish, you can exit AutoCAD and return to this point in the tutorial later. When you return, start AutoCAD and open the Door file.

Editing with Grips

Earlier, when you selected the door, little squares appeared at the endpoints and midpoints of the lines and arcs. These squares are called *grips*. Grips can be used to make direct changes to the shape of objects, or to quickly move and copy them.

WARNING   If you did not see small squares appear on the door in the previous exercise, your version of AutoCAD may have the Grips feature turned off. Before continuing with this section, refer to the information on grips in Appendix B.

So far, you have seen how operations in AutoCAD have a discrete beginning and ending. For example, to draw an arc, you first issue the Arc command and then go through a series of operations, including answering prompts and picking points. When you are done, you have an arc and AutoCAD is ready for the next command.

The Grips feature, on the other hand, plays by a different set of rules. Grips offer a small yet powerful set of editing functions that don't conform to the lock-step command/prompt/input routine you have seen so far. As you work through the following exercises, it will be helpful to think of the Grips feature as a "subset" to the standard method of operation within AutoCAD.

To practice using the grips feature, you'll make some temporary modifications to the door drawing.

Stretching Lines Using Grips

In this exercise, you'll stretch one corner of the door by grabbing the grip points of two lines.

1. Press Esc to make sure AutoCAD has your attention and you're not in the middle of a command. Click on a point below and to the left of the door to start a selection window.

2. Click above and to the right of the rectangular part of the door to select it.

3. Place the cursor on the lower-left corner grip of the rectangle, *but don't press the pick button yet.* Notice that cursor jumps to the grip point.

4. Move the cursor to another grip point. Notice again how the cursor jumps to it. When the cursor is placed on a grip, the cursor moves to the exact center of the grip point. This means, for example, that if the cursor is placed on an endpoint grip, it is on the exact endpoint of the object.

5. Move the cursor to the upper-left corner grip of the rectangle and click on it. The grip becomes a solid color, and is now a *hot grip.* The prompt displays the following message:

    ```
    **STRETCH**
    <Stretch to point>/Base point/Copy/Undo/eXit:
    ```

    This prompt tells you that the Stretch mode is active. Notice the options shown in the prompt. As you move the cursor, the corner follows and the lines of the rectangle stretch (see Figure 2.19).

When you select a grip by clicking on it, it turns a solid color and is known as a *hot grip*. You can control the size and color of grips using the Grips dialog box (see Appendix B).

6. Move the cursor upward toward the top end of the arc and click on that point. The rectangle deforms, with the corner placed at your pick point (see Figure 2.19).

FIGURE 2.19:

Stretching lines using hot grips. The top image shows the rectangle's corner being stretched upward. The bottom image shows the new location of the corner at the top of the arc.

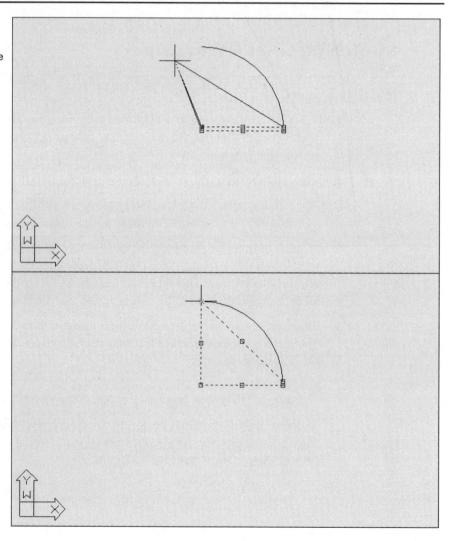

NOTE   When you click on the corner grip point, AutoCAD selects the overlapping grips of two lines. When you stretch the corner away from its original location, the endpoints of both lines follow.

Here you saw that a command called **STRETCH** is issued simply by clicking on a grip point. As you will see, a handful of other hot grip commands are also available.

1. Notice that the grips are still active. Click on the grip point that you moved before to make it a hot grip again.

2. Right click on the mouse. A pop-up list of grip edit options appears.

3. Select Base Point from the list, and then click on a point to the right of the hot grip. Now as you move the cursor, the hot grip moves relative to the cursor.

4. Right click again, and then select the Copy option from the pop-up list and enter @1<-30. Instead of moving the hot grip and changing the lines, copies of the two lines are made, with their endpoints 1 unit below and to the right of the first set of endpoints.

5. Pick another point just below the last. More copies are made.

6. Press ↵ or enter **X** ↵ to exit the Stretch mode. You can also right click again and select Exit from the pop-up list.

In this exercise, you were shown that you can select a base point other than the hot grip. You also saw how you can specify relative coordinates to move or copy a hot grip. Finally, with grips selected on an object, a right click of the mouse opens a pop-up list showing grip edit options.

Moving and Rotating with Grips

As you've just seen, the Grips feature offers an alternative method of editing your drawings. You've already seen how you can stretch endpoints, but there is much more you can do with grips. The next exercise demonstrates some other options. You will start by undoing the modifications you made in the last exercise.

1. Click on the Undo tool in the Standard toolbar, or type **U** ↵. The copies of the stretched lines disappear.

2. Press ↵ again. The deformed door snaps back to its original form.

TIP   Pressing ↵ at the command prompt causes AutoCAD to repeat the last command entered—in this case, **U**.

---

3. Select the entire door by first clicking on a blank area below and to the right of the door.

4. Move the cursor to a location above and to the left of the rectangular portion of the door, and click. Since you went from right to left, you created a crossing window. Recall that this selects anything enclosed and crossing through the window.

5. Click on the lower-left grip of the rectangle to turn it into a hot grip. Just as before, as you move your cursor, the corner stretches.

6. Right click on the mouse. Then at the grip edit pop-up list, select Move. The Command window shows:

   ```
   **MOVE**
   <Move to point>/Base point/Copy/Undo/eXit:
   ```

   Now as you move the cursor, the entire door moves with it.

7. Position the door near the center of the screen and click there. The door moves to the center of the screen. Notice that the command prompt returns, yet the door remains highlighted, telling you that it is still selected for the next operation.

8. Click on the lower-left grip again, and right click on the mouse. This time, select Rotate from the pop-up list. The Command window shows:

   ROTATE <Rotation angle>/Base point/copy/Undo/Reference/eXit:

   As you move the cursor, the door rotates about the grip point.

9. Position the cursor so that the door rotates approximately 180° (see Figure 2.20). Then, while holding down the Shift key, press the mouse/pick button. A copy of the door appears in the new rotated position, leaving the original door in place.

10. Press ø to exit the grip edit mode.

> **NOTE** You've seen how the Move command is duplicated in a modified way as a hot grip command. Other hot grip commands (**Stretch**, **Rotate**, **Scale**, and **Mirror**) also have similar counterparts in the standard set of AutoCAD commands. You'll see how those work later in this book in Chapters 9 and 12.

After you've completed any operation using grips, the objects are still highlighted with their grips still active. To clear the grip selection, press Esc twice.

FIGURE 2.20:

Rotating and copying the door using a hot grip. Notice that more than one object is being affected by the grip edit, even though only one grip is "hot."

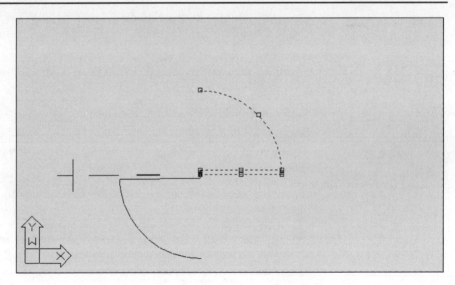

In this exercise, you saw how hot grip options appear in a pop-up list. Several other options are available in that list, including Exit, Base Point, Copy, and Undo. You can also make adjustments to an object's properties using the Properties option.

Many of these grip edit options are also available by pressing the spacebar or ↵ key while a grip is selected. With each press, the next option becomes active. The commands then repeat if you continue to press ↵. The Shift key acts as a shortcut to the Copy option. You only have to use it once; then each time you click on a point thereafter, a copy is made.

A Quick Summary of the Grip Feature

The exercises in this chapter using hot grips include only a few of the Grips options. You'll get a chance to use other hot grip commands in later chapters. Meanwhile, here is a summary of Grips:

- Clicking on endpoint grips causes those endpoints to stretch.

- Clicking on midpoint grips of lines causes the entire line to move.

- If two objects meet end to end and you click on their overlapping grips, both grips are selected simultaneously.

- You can select multiple grips by holding down the Shift key and clicking on the desired grips.

- When a hot grip is selected, the Stretch, Move, Rotate, Scale, and Mirror commands are available to you by right-clicking on the mouse.

- Or you can cycle through the Stretch, Move, Rotate, Scale, and Mirror commands by pressing ↵ while a hot grip is selected.

- All the hot grip commands allow you to make copies of the selected objects by either using the copy option or by holding down the shift key while selecting points.

- All the hot grip commands allow you to select a base point other than the originally selected hot grip.

Getting Help

Eventually, you will find yourself somewhere without documentation and you will have a question about an AutoCAD feature. AutoCAD provides an online help facility that will give you information on nearly any topic related to AutoCAD. Here's how to find help:

1. Click on Help in the menu bar and choose AutoCAD Help Topics. A Help window appears.

2. If it isn't already selected, click on the Contents tab. This window shows a table of contents. There are two more tabs labeled Index and Find, and each offers assistance in finding specific topics.

NOTE You can also press F1 to open the AutoCAD Help window.

3. Scan down the screen until you see the topic named Command References, and double-click on it. The list expands to show more topics.

4. Double-click on the item labeled Commands. The Help window expands to show a list of command names.

5. At the top of the list is a set of alphabet buttons. In the main window, you see a list of commands beginning with 3D. You can click on the alphabetical button to go to a listing of commands that start with a specific letter. For now, scroll down the list and click on the word Copy shown in green. A detailed description of the Copy command appears.

6. Click on the Help Topics button at the top of the window. The Help Topics dialog box appears.

7. Click on the Find tab. If this is the first time you've selected the Find tab, you will see the Find Setup Wizard. This dialog box offers options for the search database that Find uses to locate specific words.

8. Accept the default option by pressing the Next button at the bottom of the dialog box. Find options appear with a list of topics in alphabetical order. You can enter a word to search for in the drop-down list at the top of the dialog, or you can choose a topic in the list box.

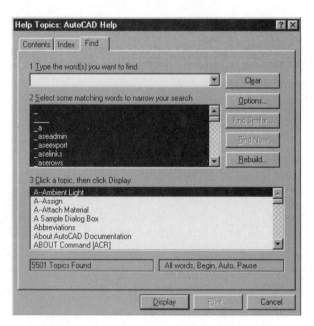

9. Type the word **Change.** The list box immediately goes to the word Change in the list.

10. Click on the word "CHANGE" in all capital letters. Notice that the list box at the bottom of the dialog box changes to show some options.

11. Double-click on Change Command [ACR] in the list. A description of the Change command appears.

AutoCAD also provides *context-sensitive help* to give you information related to the command you are currently using. To see how this works, try the following:

1. Close or minimize the Help window and return to the AutoCAD window.

2. Click on the Move tool in the Modify toolbar to start the Move command.

3. Press the F1 function key, or choose Help ➣ AutoCAD help topics. The Help window appears, with a description of the Move command.

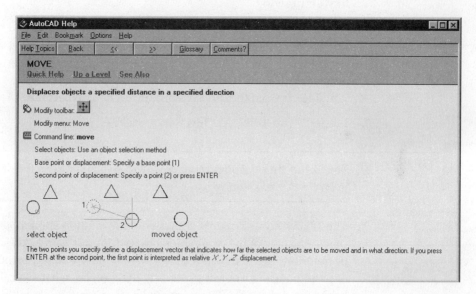

4. Click on the Close button or press Esc.

5. Press Esc to exit the Move command.

If you are already familiar with the basics of AutoCAD, you may want to install the AutoCAD Learning Assistant. This tool offers quick tips and brief tutorials on a wide variety of topics, including working in collaborative groups, and making the most of the Windows environment. The Learning Assistant is on its own CD-ROM as part of the AutoCAD R14 package. See Appendix B for more on its installation and use.

Displaying Data in a Text Window

Some commands produce information that requires a Text window. This frequently happens when you are trying to get information about your drawing. The following exercise shows how you can get an enlarged view of messages in a Text window.

1. Click on the List tool in the Standard toolbar (it's the icon that looks like a piece of paper with writing on it). This tool offers information about objects in your drawing.

2. At the Select objects prompt, click on one of the arcs and press ↵. Information about the arc is displayed in the AutoCAD Text window (see Figure 2.21). Toward the bottom is the list of the arc's properties. Don't worry if you don't understand this listing. As you work through this book, you'll learn what the different properties of an object mean.

3. Press F2. The AutoCAD Text window closes.

TIP   The F2 function key offers a quick way to switch between the drawing editor and the Text window.

The Text window not only shows you information about objects, it also displays a history of the command activity for your AutoCAD session. This can be helpful for remembering data you may have entered earlier in a session, or to help recall an object's property that you have listed earlier. The scroll bar to the right of the Text window lets you scroll to earlier events. You can even set the number of lines AutoCAD will retain in this text window using the Preferences dialog box, or you can have AutoCAD record the Text window information in a text file.

4. Now you are done with the door drawing, so choose File ➤ Exit.

5. At the Save Changes? dialog box, click on the No button. (You've already saved this file in the condition you want it in, so you do not need to save it again.)

The AutoCAD text screen showing the data displayed by the List tool

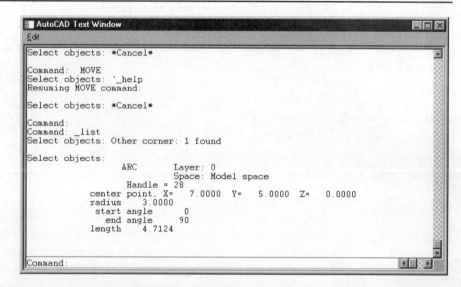

```
AutoCAD Text Window                                          _ □ ×
Edit
Select objects: *Cancel*

Command:  MOVE
Select objects: '_help
Resuming MOVE command.

Select objects: *Cancel*

Command:
Command: _list
Select objects: Other corner: 1 found

Select objects:
                     ARC         Layer: 0
                                 Space: Model space
                          Handle = 28
          center point, X=    7.0000  Y=    5.0000  Z=    0.0000
          radius     3.0000
           start angle       0
             end angle      90
          length     4.7124


Command:
```

If You Want to Experiment...

Try drawing the latch shown in Figure 2.22.

1. Start AutoCAD, open a new file, and name it **Latch**.

2. When you get to the drawing editor, use the Line command to draw the straight portions of the latch. Start a line as indicated in the figure; then enter relative coordinates from the keyboard. For example, for the first line segment, enter **@4<180** to draw a line segment 4 units long from right to left.

3. Draw an arc for the curved part. To do this, click on the Arc tool from the Draw toolbar.

4. Use the Endpoint Osnap to pick the endpoint indicated in the figure to start your arc.

5. Type **E ⏎** to issue the End option of the Arc command.

6. Using the Endpoint Osnap again, click on the endpoint above where you started your line. A rubber-banding line and a temporary arc appear.

7. Type **D**⏎ to issue the Direction option for the Arc command.

8. Position your cursor so the ghosted arc looks like the one in the figure, and then press the mouse/pick button to draw in the arc.

FIGURE 2.22:

Try drawing this latch. Dimensions are provided for your reference.

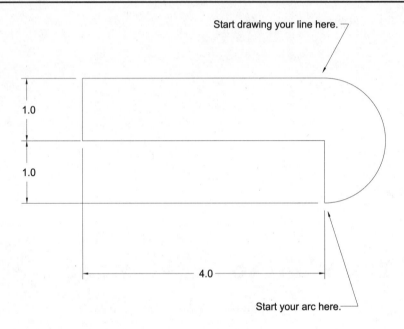

Start drawing your line here.

1.0

1.0

4.0

Start your arc here.

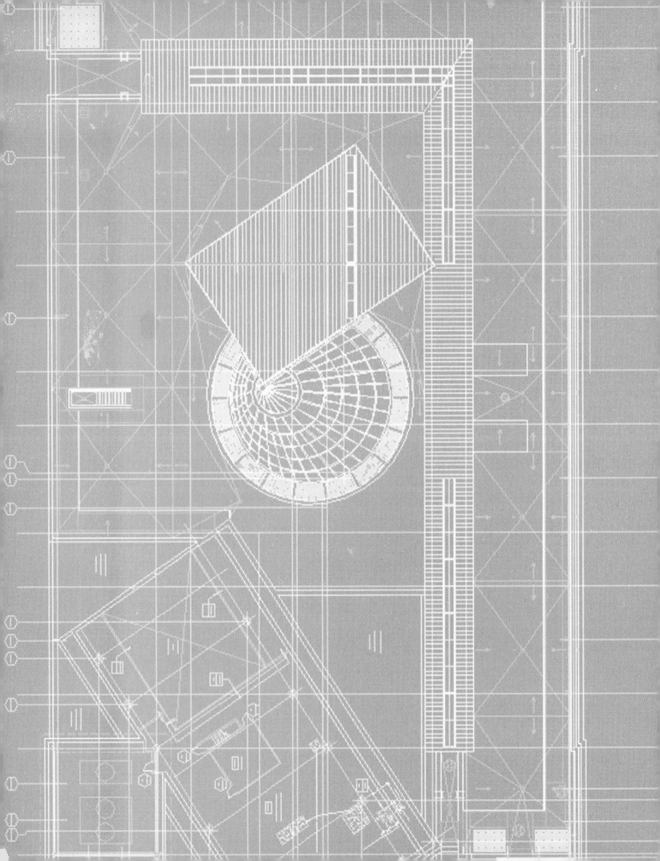

CHAPTER

THREE

Learning the Tools of the Trade

3

- Setting Up a Work Area

- Using the AutoCAD Modes as Drafting Tools

- Exploring the Drawing Process

- Planning and Laying Out a Drawing

So far we have covered the most basic information you need to understand the workings of AutoCAD. Now you will put your knowledge to work. In this architectural tutorial, which begins here and continues through Chapter 12, you will draw an apartment building composed of studios. The tutorial illustrates how to use AutoCAD commands and will give you a solid understanding of the basic AutoCAD package. With these fundamentals, you can use AutoCAD to its fullest potential, regardless of the kinds of drawings you intend to create or the enhancement products you may use in the future.

In this chapter you will start drawing an apartment's bathroom fixtures. In the process, you will learn how to use AutoCAD's basic tools.

Setting Up a Work Area

Before beginning most drawings, you will want to set up your work area. To do this you must determine the *measurement system*, the *drawing sheet size*, and the *scale* you want to use. The default work area is roughly 9"×16" at full scale, given a decimal measurement system where 1 unit equals 1 inch. If these are appropriate settings for your drawing, then you don't have to do any setting up. It is more likely, however, you will be doing drawings of various sizes and scales. For example, you may want to create a drawing in a measurement system where you can specify feet, inches, and fractions of inches at 1"=1' scale, and print the drawing on an 8½×11" sheet of paper. In this section, you will learn how to set up a drawing the way you want.

Specifying Units

Start by creating a new file called **Bath**.

1. Start up AutoCAD; then pick File ➢ New.

2. In the Create New Drawing dialog box, click on the Start from Scratch button and select English from the Select Default Setting list.

3. Click OK to open the new file.

4. Choose File ➢ Save As.

5. At the Save Drawing As dialog box, enter **Bath** for the file name.

6. Check to make sure you are saving the drawing in the Samples subdirectory, or the directory you have chosen to store your exercise files, and then click Save.

Although you could start drawing in the AutoCAD Window immediately after starting up AutoCAD, and then save the file later under the name Bath, use File ➢ New for this exercise—in case you are using a system that has an altered default setup for new files. We'll discuss default setups in Chapter 5.

The first thing you will want to tell AutoCAD is the *unit style* you intend to use. So far, you've been using the default, which is decimal inches. In this style, whole units represent inches, and decimal units are decimal inches. If you want to be able to enter distances in feet, then you must change the unit style to one that accepts feet as input. This is done through the Units Control dialog box.

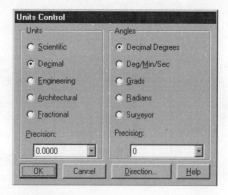

If you are a civil engineer, you will want to know that the Engineering unit style allows you to enter feet and decimal feet for distances. For example, the equivalent of 12"-6" would be 12.5'. Earlier versions of AutoCAD did not have this feature, so engineers had to resort to using the Decimal unit style and feet as the base unit instead of inches. This caused problems when Architectural drawings were combined with Civil drawings. The scales of each type of drawing did not match. Even though this feature has existed since Release 12, old habits die hard. If you use the Engineering unit style, you will ensure that your drawings will conform to the scale of drawings created by your architectural colleagues. And you will have the ability to enter decimal feet.

1. Choose Formats ➤ Units …, or type **Un** ↵. The Units Control dialog box appears. Let's look at a few of the options available.

2. Notice the unit styles listed in the Units group. Click on the Architectural button.

TIP

The Units Control settings can also be controlled using several system variables. To set the unit style, you can type **'lunits** ↵ at the command prompt. (The apostrophe lets you enter this command while in the middle of other commands.) At the New value for Lunits <2> prompt, enter **4** for Architectural. See Appendix D for other settings.

---

3. Click on the down-pointing arrow in the Precision drop-down list at the bottom of the Units group. Notice the options available. You can set the smallest unit AutoCAD will display in this drawing. For now, leave this setting at its default value of 1/16".

4. Close the drop-down list and then click on the Direction… button at the bottom of the dialog box. The Direction Control dialog box appears. This dialog box lets you set the direction for the 0° angle and the direction for positive degrees. For now, don't change these settings—you'll read more about them in a moment.

5. Click on the Cancel button.

6. Click on OK in the main Units Control dialog box to return to the drawing.

NOTE Remember that the status bar displays a description of the tool or pull-down menu option including the command name. If you prefer entering commands through the keyboard, look at the tool description in the status bar during the exercises. The command name will be listed last. You can type in the command name to issue the command instead of clicking on the tool during any of these exercises. Command names are also useful when you want to create your own custom macros. You'll get a chance to create some macros in Chapter 19.

You picked Architectural measurement units for this tutorial, but your own work may require a different unit style. You saw the unit styles available in the Units Control dialog box. Table 3.1 shows examples of how the distance 15.5 is entered in each of these styles.

TABLE 3.1: Measurement systems available in AutoCAD

Measurement System	AutoCAD's Display of Measurement
Scientific	1.55E+01 (inches)
Decimal	15.5000 (inches)
Engineering	1'-3.5" (input as 1'3.5")
Architectural	1'-3 1/2" (input as 1'3-1/2")
Metric	15.5000 (mm, cm, or meters)
Fractional	15 1/2" (input as 15-1/2")

In the previous exercise, you needed to change only one setting. Let's take a look at the other Units Control settings in more detail. As you read, you may want to refer to the illustration of the Units Control dialog box.

Fine-Tuning the Measurement System

Most of the time, you will be concerned only with the Units and Angles setting groups of the Units Control dialog box. But as you saw from the last exercise, you can control many other settings related to the input and display of units.

TIP
To find the distance between two points, choose Distance from the Standard toolbar, or type **Di** ↵ and then click on the two points (Di is the shortcut for entering **Dist** ↵). But if you find that this command doesn't give you an accurate distance measurement, examine the Units/Precision option in the Units Control dialog box. If it is set too high, the value returned by Dist may be rounded to a value greater than your tolerances allow, even though the distance is drawn accurately.

The Precision drop-down list in the Units group lets you specify the smallest unit value that you want AutoCAD to display in the status line and in the prompts. If you choose a measurement system that uses fractions, the Precision list will include fractional units. This setting can also be controlled with Buprec system variables.

The Angles group lets you set the style for displaying angles. You have a choice of five angle styles: decimal degrees, degrees/minutes/seconds, grads, radians, and surveyor's units. In the Angles group's Precision drop-down list, you can determine the degree of accuracy you want AutoCAD to display for angles. These settings can also be controlled with the Aunits and Auprec system variables.

NOTE
You can find out more about system variables in Appendix D.

The Direction Control dialog box lets you set the direction of the 0° base angle. The default base angle (and the one used throughout this book) is a direction from left to right. However, there may be times when you will want to designate another direction as the 0° base angle. You can also tell AutoCAD which direction is positive, either clockwise or counterclockwise. In this book we use the default, which is counterclockwise. These settings can also be controlled with the Angbase and Angdir system variables (see Appendix D for more on the AutoCAD System Variables).

Things to Watch Out For When Entering Distances

When you are using Architectural units, there are two points you should be aware of:

- Hyphens are used only to distinguish fractions from whole inches.

- You cannot use spaces while giving a dimension. For example, you can specify eight feet, four and one-half inches as 8' 4-1/2 " or 8'4.5, but not as 8'-4 1/2 ".

These idiosyncrasies are a source of confusion to many architects and engineers new to AutoCAD because the program often displays architectural dimensions in the standard architectural format but does not allow you to enter dimensions that way.

When inputting distances and angles in unusual situations, here are some tips:

- When entering distances in inches and feet, you can omit the inch (") sign. If you are using the Engineer unit style, you can enter decimal feet and forego the inch sign entirely.

- You can enter fractional distances and angles in any format you like, regardless of the current unit system. For example, you can enter a distance as **@1/2<1.5708r** even if your current unit system is set for decimal units and decimal degrees (**1.5708r** is the radian equivalent of 90°).

- If you have your angle units set to degrees, grads, or radians, you do not need to specify g, r, or d after the angle. You do have to specify g, r, or d, however, if you want to use these units when they are not the current default angle system.

- If your current angle system is set to something other than degrees, but you want to input angles in degrees, you can use a double less-than symbol (<<) in place of the single less-than symbol (<) to override the current angle system of measure. The << also assumes the base angle of 0° to be a direction from left to right and the positive direction to be counterclockwise.

- If your current angle system uses a different base angle and direction (other than left to right for 0° and a counterclockwise direction for positive angles), and you want to specify an angle in the standard base direction, you can use a triple less-than symbol (<<<) to indicate angle.

- You can specify a denominator of any size when specifying fractions. However, you should be aware that the value you have set for the maximum

Continued on next page

number of digits to the right of decimal points (under the Units setting) will restrict the actual fractional value AutoCAD will use. For example, if your units are set for a maximum of 2 digits of decimals and you give a fractional value of 5/32, AutoCAD will round it out to 3/16 or 0.16.

- You are allowed to enter decimal feet for distances in the Architectural unit style.

Setting Up the Drawing Limits

One of the big advantages in using AutoCAD is that you can draw at full scale; you aren't limited to the edges of a piece of paper the way you are in manual drawing. But you still have to consider what will happen when you want a printout of your drawing. If you're not careful, you may create a drawing that won't fit on the paper size you want at the scale you want. When you start a new drawing, it helps to limit your drawing area to one that can be scaled down to fit on a standard sheet size. While this is not absolutely necessary with AutoCAD, the limits will give you a frame of reference between your work in AutoCAD and the final printed output.

In order to set up the drawing work area, you need to understand how standard sheet sizes translate into full-scale drawing sizes. Table 3.2 lists widths and heights of drawing areas in inches, according to scales and final printout sizes. The scales are listed in the far left column; the output sheet sizes are listed across the top.

Let's take an example: To find the area needed in AutoCAD for your bathroom drawing, look across from the scale 1"=1' to the column that reads 8½"×11" at the top. You'll find the value 102×132. This means the drawing area needs to fit within an area 102" x 132" (8.5 feet by 11 feet) in AutoCAD in order to fit a printout of a 1"=1'-0" scale drawing on an 8½×11" sheet of paper. You may want the drawing area to be oriented horizontally, so that the 11 feet will be in the x-axis and the 8.5 feet will be in the y-axis.

Now that you know the area you need, you can use the Limits command to set up the area.

1. Choose Format ➢ Drawing Limits.

2. At the ON/OFF/<Lower left corner> <0'-0",0'-0"> prompt, specify the lower-left corner of your work area. Press ↵ to accept the default.

TABLE 3.2: Work area in drawing units (inches) by scale and plotted sheet size

Scale	8½"×11"	11"×17"	17"×22"	18"×24"	22"×34"	24"×36"	30"×42"	36"×48"
3"=1'	34×44	44×68	68×88	72×96	88×136	96×144	120×168	144×192
1 1/2"=1'	68×88	88×136	136×176	144×192	176×272	192×288	240×336	288×384
1"=1'	102×132	132×204	204×264	216×288	264×408	288×432	360×504	432×576
3/4 "=1'	136×176	176×272	272×352	288×384	352×544	384×576	480×672	576×768
1/2"=1'	204×264	264×408	408×528	432×576	528×816	576×864	720×1008	864×1152
1/4"=1'	408×528	528×816	816×1056	864×1152	1056×1632	1152×1728	1440×2016	1728×2304
1/8"=1'	816×1056	1056×1632	1632×2112	1728×2304	2112×3264	2304×3456	2880×4032	3456×4608
1/16 "=1'	1632×2112	2112×3264	3264×4224	3456×4608	4224×6528	4608×6912	5760×8064	6912×9216
1/32 "=1'	3264×4224	4224×6528	6528×8448	6912×9216	8448×13056	9216×13824	11520×16128	13824×18432
1"=10'	1020×1320	1320×2040	2040×2640	2160×2880	2640×4080	2880×4320	3600×5040	4320×5760
1"=20'	2040×2640	2640×4080	4080×5280	4320×5760	5280×8160	5760×8640	7200×10080	8640×11520
1"=30'	3060×3960	3960×6120	6120×7920	6480×8640	7920×12240	8640×12960	10800×15120	12960×17280
1"=40'	4080×5280	5280×8160	8160×10560	8640×11520	10560×16320	11520×17280	14400×20160	17280×23040

3. At the `Upper right corner <1'0",0'9">` prompt, specify the upper-right corner of your work area. (The default is shown in brackets.) Enter **132,102**. Or if you prefer, you can enter **11',8'6**.

4. Next, choose View ➤ Zoom ➤ All. You can also select the Zoom All tool from the Zoom Window flyout on the Standard Toolbar, or type **Z** ↵ **A** ↵. Though it appears that nothing has changed, your drawing area is now set to a size that will allow you to draw your bathroom at full scale.

TIP   You can toggle through the different Coordinate Readout modes by pressing F6, or by double-clicking on the coordinate readout of the status bar. For more on the Coordinate Readout modes, see Chapter 1 and *Using the Coordinate Readout as Your Scale* section later in this chapter.

---

5. Move the cursor to the upper-right corner of the drawing area and watch the coordinate readout. You will see that now the upper-right corner has a Y coordinate of approximately 8' -6". The X coordinate will vary depending on the proportion of your AutoCAD window. The coordinate readout also displays distances in feet and inches.

In step 5 above, the coordinate readout shows you that your drawing area is larger than before, but there are no visual clues to tell you where you are or what distances you are dealing with. To help you get your bearings, you can use the Grid mode, which you will learn about shortly. But first, let's take a closer look at scale factors and how they work.

Understanding Scale Factors

When you draft manually, you work on the final drawing directly with pen and ink or pencil. With a CAD program, you are a few steps removed from the actual finished product. Because of this, you need to have a deeper understanding of your drawing scale and how it is derived. In particular, you will want to understand scale factors.

For example, one of the more common uses of scale factors is in translating text size in your CAD drawing to the final plotted text size. When you draw manually, you simply draw your notes at the size you want. In a CAD drawing, you need to translate the desired final text size to the drawing scale.

When you start adding text to your drawing (Chapter 8), you will have to specify a text height. The scale factor will help you determine the appropriate text height for a particular drawing scale. For example, you may want your text to appear 1/8" high in your final plot. But if you drew your text to 1/8" in your drawing, it would appear as a dot when plotted. The text has to be scaled up to a size that, when scaled back down at plot time, will appear 1/8" high. So for a 1/4" scale drawing you would multiply the 1/8" text height by a scale factor of 48 to get 6". Your text should be 6" high in the CAD drawing in order to appear 1/8" high in the final plot.

All the drawing sizes in Table 3.2 were derived by using scale factors. Table 3.3 shows scale factors as they relate to standard drawing scales. These scale factors are the values by which you multiply the desired final printout size to get the equivalent full-scale size. For example, if you have a sheet size of 11×17", and you want to know the equivalent full-scale size for a 1/4"-scale drawing, you multiply the sheet measurements by 48. In this way, 11" becomes 528" (48 × 11) and 17" becomes 816" (48 × 17). Your work area must be 528" by 816" if you intend to have a final output of 11" by 17" at 1/4"=1'. You can divide these inch measurements by 12" to get 44'×68'.

TIP   If you get the message **Outside limits, it means you have selected a point outside the area defined by the limits of your drawing *and* the Limits command's limits-checking feature is on. (Some third-party programs may use the limits-checking feature.) If you must select a point outside the limits, issue the Limits command and then enter **off** at the ON/OFF <Lower left corner>… prompt to turn off the limits-checking feature.

TIP   The scale factor for fractional inch scales is derived by multiplying the denominator of the scale by 12, and then dividing by the numerator. For example, the scale factor for 1/4"=1'-0" is (4×12)/1, or 48/1. For whole-foot scales like 1"=10', multiply the feet side of the equation by 12. Metric scales require simple decimal conversions.

If you are using the metric system, the drawing scale can be used directly as the scale factor. For example, a drawing scale of 1:10 would have a scale factor of 10; a drawing scale of 1:50 would have a scale factor of 50; and so on.

TABLE 3.3: Work area in metric units (millimeters) by scale and plotted sheet size

Scale	A0 or F 841mm× 1189mm (33.11"× 46.81")	A or D 594mm× 841mm (23.39"× 33.11")	A2 or C 420mm× 594mm (16.54"× 23.39")	A3 or B 297mm× 420mm (11.70"× 16.54")	A4 or A 210mm× 297mm (8.27"× 11.70")
1:2	1682mm× 2378mm	1188mm× 1682mm	840mm× 1188mm	594mm× 840mm	420mm× 594mm
1:5	4205mm× 5945mm	2970mm× 4205mm	2100mm× 2970mm	1485mm× 2100mm	1050mm× 1485mm
1:10	8410mm× 11890mm	5940mm× 8410mm	4200mm× 5940mm	2970mm× 4200mm	2100mm× 2970mm

You will be using scale factors to specify text height and dimension settings, so getting to understand them now will pay off later.

Using the AutoCAD Modes as Drafting Tools

After you have set up your work area, you can begin the plan of a typical bathroom in your studio. You will use this example to learn about some of AutoCAD's drawing aids. These tools might be compared to a background grid (the *Grid mode*), scale (the *Coordinate Readout mode*), and a T square and triangle (the *Ortho mode*). These drawing modes can be indispensable tools when used properly. The Drawing Aids dialog box helps you visualize the modes in an organized manner and simplifies their management.

Using the Grid Mode as a Background Grid

Using the *Grid mode* is like having a grid under your drawing to help you with layout. In AutoCAD, the Grid mode also lets you see the limits of your drawing and helps you visually determine the distances you are working with in any given view. In this section, you will learn how to control the grid's appearance. The F7 key toggles the Grid mode on and off; you can also double-click on the Grid button in the status bar. Start by setting the grid spacing.

1. Choose Tools ➤ Drawing Aids…, or type **Rm** ↵ to display the Drawing Aids dialog box, showing all the mode settings. You see four button groups: Modes, Snap, Grid, and Isometric Snap/Grid.

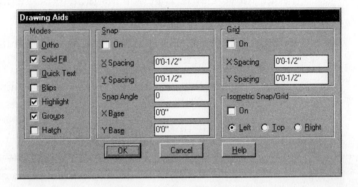

2. Let's start with the Grid group. Notice that the X Spacing input box contains a value of 0'0-1/2" .

3. Double-click on the X Spacing input box. The 0'0-1/2" highlights. You can now type in a new value for this setting.

TIP

You can use the Gridunit system variable to set the grid spacing. Enter **'Gridunit** ↵, and at the New value for GRIDUNIT <0'0",0'0">: prompt, enter **12,12**. Note that the Gridunit value must be entered as an x,y coordinate.

---

4. Enter **12** ↵ for 12". Notice that the Y Spacing input box automatically changes to 1'0" (the 12 you entered remains 12 until the next time you open this dialog box). AutoCAD assumes you want the X and Y grid spacing to be the same, unless you specifically ask for a different Y setting.

TIP

If you want to change an entry in an input box, you can double-click on it to highlight the whole entry, and then replace the entry by simply typing in a new one. If you just want to change a part of the entry, click on the input box and then use the cursor keys to move the vertical bar cursor to the exact character you want to change. You can use the Backspace key to delete characters.

---

5. Click on the On checkbox near the top of the Grid group. This setting makes the grid visible.

6. Click on OK. The grid now appears as an array of dots with a 12" spacing in your drawing area. They will not print or plot with your drawing.

With the grid at a 12-unit spacing, you can see your work area more clearly. Since the grid will appear only within the drawing limits, you are better able to see your work area. In the next section, you'll see how the Snap mode works.

7. Press F7, or double-click on the word "Grid" in the status bar (you can also hold down the Ctrl key and press **G**). The grid disappears.

8. Press F7 again to turn the grid back on again.

TIP   If your view is such that the grid spacing appears quite small, AutoCAD will not display the grid in order to preserve the readability of the drawing. If this situation occurs, you will see the message "Grid too dense to display" in the Command window.

TIP   In this exercise, you set the grid spacing to be equal to the scale factor of your drawing. This will make the grid spacing equivalent to 1" intervals of the final plotted drawing. For example, if your drawing is 1/4" = 1' -0" scale, you could set your grid spacing to 48. The grid spacing would then reflect the 1 inch spacing for a 1/4" scale drawing.

Using the Snap Mode

The *Snap mode* has no equivalent in hand drafting. This mode forces the cursor to step a specific distance. It is useful if you want to maintain accuracy while entering distances with the cursor. The F9 key toggles the Snap mode on and off. Or, just like the Grid mode, there is a Snap button in the status bar that you can double-click. Follow these steps to access the Snap mode.

1. Choose Tools ➤ Drawing Aids…, or type **Rm** ↵. The Drawing Aids dialog box appears again.

2. In the Snap group of the dialog box, double-click on the X Spacing input box and enter **4** ↵. As with the grid setting, AutoCAD assumes you want the X

and Y snap spacing to be the same, unless you specifically ask for a different Y setting.

3. Click on the On checkbox so a checkmark appears.

4. Click on OK, and start moving the cursor around. Notice how the cursor seems to move in "steps" rather than in a smooth motion. Also notice that the word "Snap" in the status bar is solid black, indicating that the Snap mode is on.

5. Press F9 or double-click on the word "Snap" in the status bar (you can also hold down the Ctrl key and press **B**); then move the cursor slowly around the drawing area. The Snap mode is now off.

6. Press F9 again to turn the Snap mode back on.

TIP   You can use the Snapunit system variable to set the snap spacing. Enter
'**Snapunit** ↵. Then at the New value for SNAPUNIT <0'0",0'0">
prompt, enter **4,4**. Note that the Snapunit value must be entered as an x,y
coordinate.

Take a moment to look at the Drawing Aids dialog box. The other options in the Snap group allow you to set the snap origin point (X Base and Y Base), rotate the cursor to an angle other than its current 0–90° (Snap angle), and set the horizontal snap spacing to a value different from the vertical spacing (X Spacing and Y Spacing). You can also adjust other settings, such as the grid/snap orientation that allow isometric-style drawings (Isometric Snap/Grid). We will look at these features in Chapters 6 and 15.

Using Grid and Snap Together

You can set the grid spacing to be the same as the snap setting, allowing you to see every snap point. Let's take a look at how grid and snap work together.

1. Open the Drawing Aids dialog box.

2. Double-click on the X Spacing input box in the Grid group, and enter 0 ↵.

3. Click on OK. Now the grid spacing has changed to reflect the 4" snap spacing. Move the cursor, and watch it snap to the grid points.

4. Open the Drawing Aids dialog box again.

5. Double-click on the X Spacing input box in the Snap group, and enter **1** ↵.

6. Click on OK. The grid automatically changes to conform to the new snap setting. When the grid spacing is set to 0, the grid then aligns with the snap points. At this density, the grid is overwhelming.

7. Open the Drawing Aids dialog box again.

8. Double-click on the X Spacing input box in the Grid group, and enter **12** ↵.

9. Click on OK. The grid spacing is now at 12 again, which is a more reasonable spacing for the current drawing scale.

   With the snap spacing set to 1, it is difficult to tell if Snap is turned on based on the behavior of the cursor, but the coordinate readout in the status bar gives you a clue. As you move your cursor, the coordinates appear as whole numbers with no fractional distances. Next, you'll look at other ways the coordinate readout helps you.

Using the Coordinate Readout as Your Scale

Now you will draw the first item in the bathroom: the toilet. It is composed of a rectangle representing the tank, and a truncated ellipse representing the seat.

As you move the cursor over the drawing area, the coordinate readout dynamically displays its position in absolute Cartesian coordinates. This allows you to find a position on your drawing by locating it in reference to the drawing origin—0,0—which is in the lower-left corner of the sheet. You can also set the coordinate readout to display relative coordinates. Throughout these exercises, coordinates will be provided to enable you to select points using the dynamic coordinate readout. (If you want to review the discussion of AutoCAD's coordinates display, see Chapter 1.)

1. Click on the Line tool on the Draw toolbar, or type **L** ↵. You could also select Draw ➤ Line from the pull-down menu.

2. Using your coordinate readout for guidance, start your line at the coordinate 5'-7", 6'-3".

3. Press F6 until you see the relative polar coordinates appear in the coordinate readout at the bottom of the AutoCAD window. You can also double-click on the coordinate readout. Polar coordinates allow you to see your current location in reference to the last point selected. This is helpful when you are using a command that requires distance and direction input.

4. Move the cursor until the coordinate readout lists 1'-10"< 0, 0' -0", and pick this point. As you move the cursor around, the rubber-banding line follows it at any angle.

5. You can also force the line to be orthogonal. Press F8, or double-click on the word "Ortho" in the status bar (you can also hold down the Ctrl key and press **O** to toggle on the Ortho mode), and move the cursor around. Now the rubber-banding line will only move vertically or horizontally.

NOTE   The Ortho mode (also available under Modes in the Drawing Aids dialog box) is analogous to the T square and triangle. Note that the word "Ortho" appears on the status bar to tell you that the Ortho mode is on.

6. Move the cursor down until the coordinate readout lists 0'- 9"< 270 and click on this point.

7. Continue drawing the other two sides of the rectangle by using the coordinate readout. You should have a drawing that looks like Figure 3.1.

FIGURE 3.1:

A Plan view of the toilet tank

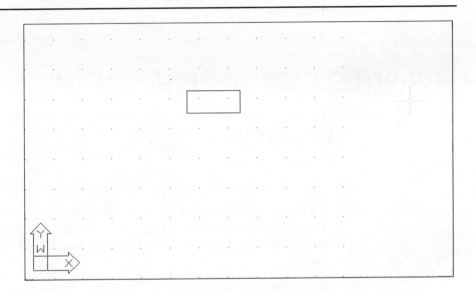

In steps 2 and 4, the coordinate readout showed some extra values. The 0' -0" that you see at the end of the coordinate readout listing indicates the Z value of the coordinate. This extra coordinate is significant only when you are doing 3D modeling; so for the time being, you can ignore it.

While this exercise tells you to use the line tool to draw the tank, you could also use the rectangle tool. The rectangle tool creates what is known as a *polyline*, which is a set of line or arc segments that acts like a single object. You'll learn more about polylines in Chapter 13.

NOTE   If you'd like to know more about the additional Z coordinate listing in the coordinate readout, see Chapter 16.

By using the Snap mode in conjunction with the coordinate readout, you can measure distances as you draw lines. This is similar to the way you would draw using a scale. Be aware that the smallest distance the coordinate readout will register depends on the area you have displayed in your drawing area. For example, if you are displaying an area the size of a football field, the smallest distance you can indicate with your cursor may be 6". On the other hand, if your view shows an area of only one square inch, you can indicate distances as small as 1/1000" using your cursor.

Exploring the Drawing Process

In this section, you will look at some of the more common commands and use them to complete a simple drawing. As you draw, watch the prompts and notice how your responses affect them. Also note how you use existing drawing elements as reference points.

While drawing with AutoCAD, you create gross geometric forms to determine the basic shapes of objects, and then modify the shapes to fill in detail. This is where the differences between drawing with AutoCAD and manual drafting become more apparent. In essence, you alternately create and edit objects to build your drawing.

AutoCAD offers 14 basic types of drawing. These are lines, arcs, circles, text, traces, polylines, points, 3D Faces, ellipses, elliptical arcs, spline curves, solids, regions, and multiline text. All drawings are built on these objects. In addition, there are five different 3D meshes, which are three-dimensional surfaces composed of 3D Faces. You are familiar with lines and arcs; these, along with circles, are the most commonly used objects. As you progress through the book, we will introduce you to the other objects and how they are used.

Locating an Object in Reference to Others

To define the toilet seat, you will use an ellipse.

1. Click on the Ellipse tool in the Draw toolbar, or type **El**⏎. You can also choose Draw ➤ Ellipse ➤ Axis, End.

2. At the `Arc/Center/<Axis endpoint 1>` prompt, pick the midpoint of the bottom horizontal line of the rectangle. Do this by bringing up the Osnap pop-up menu and selecting Midpoint; then move the cursor toward the bottom line. (Remember, to bring up the Osnap menu, Shift + click the right mouse button.) When you see the Midpoint Osnap marker appear on the line, press the left mouse button.

3. At the `Axis endpoint 2` prompt, move the cursor down until the coordinate readout lists 1'-10"< 270.

4. Pick this as the second axis endpoint.

5. At the `<Other axis distance>/Rotation` prompt, move the cursor horizontally from the center of the ellipse until the coordinate readout lists 0'-8"< 180.

6. Pick this as the axis distance defining the width of the ellipse. Your drawing should look like Figure 3.2.

FIGURE 3.2:

The ellipse added to
the tank

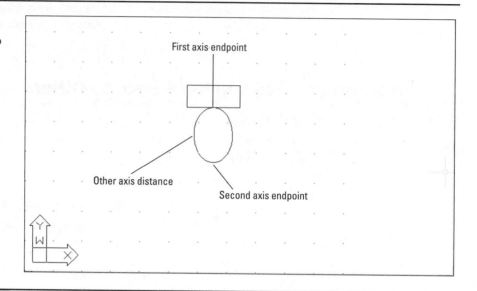

NOTE   As you work with AutoCAD, you will eventually run into NURBS. NURBS stands for Non-Uniform Rational B-Splines—a fancy term meaning that curved objects are based on accurate mathematical models. When you trim the ellipse in a later exercise, it becomes a NURBS curve, not a segmented polyline as in earlier versions of AutoCAD. You'll learn more about both polyline and NURBS curves in Chapter 13.

Getting a Closer Look

During the drawing process, you will want to enlarge areas of a drawing to more easily edit its objects. In Chapter 1, you already saw how the Zoom command is used for this purpose.

1.   Click on the Zoom Window tool from the Standard toolbar, or type **z** ↵ **w** ↵. You can also Choose View ➢ Zoom ➢ Window.

2. At the First corner prompt, pick a point below and to the left of your drawing at coordinate 5'-0", 3'-6".

3. At the Other corner prompt, pick a point above and to the right of the drawing at coordinate 8'-3", 6'-8", so that the toilet is completely enclosed by the view window. To obtain this view, use the Zoom Window tool. You can also use the Zoom Realtime tool in conjunction with the Pan Realtime tool. The toilet enlarges to fill more of the screen (see Figure 3.3).

TIP   To issue the Zoom Realtime tool from the keyboard, type **Z** ↵ ↵.

FIGURE 3.3:

A close-up of the toilet drawing

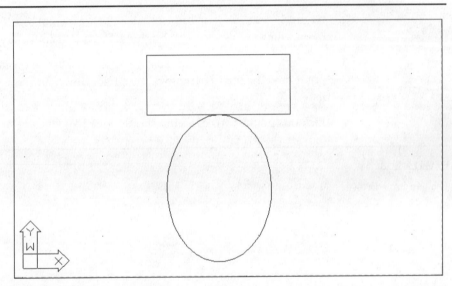

Modifying an Object

Now let's see how editing commands are used to construct an object. To define the back edge of the seat, let's put a copy of the line defining the front of the toilet tank 3" toward the center of the ellipse.

1. Click on the Copy Object tool in the Modify toolbar, or type **co** ↵. You can also select Modify ➤ Copy from the pull-down menu.

TIP

You can also use the Grip Edit tools to make the copy. See Chapter 2 for more on Grip editing.

---

2. At the `Select object` prompt, pick the horizontal line that touches the top of the ellipse. The line is highlighted. Press ↵ to confirm your selection.

3. At the `<Base point or displacement>/Multiple` prompt, pick a base point near the line. Then move the cursor down until the coordinate readout lists 0'-3"< 270.

4. Pick this point. Your drawing should look like Figure 3.4.

FIGURE 3.4:

The line copied down

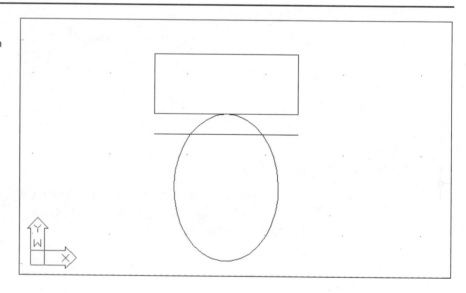

Architects and Their Symbols

You may be asking yourself if there is a set of architectural standard measurements for common items such as the aforementioned toilet tank. Some items, such as doors and kitchen appliances, do have "standard" sizes that architects would learn in the course of their professional training. In this particular example, the 3-inch offset is really arbitrary because the toilet symbol is just that, a *symbol* representing a toilet and not necessarily an exact representation of one. When you see a toilet symbol in an architectural drawing, it's saying "put the toilet here." The actual brand of toilet is specified in the *specs*, which are written documents that go with the drawings.

You will have noticed that the Copy command acts exactly like the Move command you used in Chapter 2, except that Copy does not alter the position of the objects you select.

Trimming an Object

Now you must delete the part of the ellipse that is not needed. You will use the Trim command to trim off parts of the ellipse.

1. First, turn the snap mode off by pressing F9 or double-clicking on the word "Snap" in the status bar. Snap may be a hindrance at this point in your editing session because it may keep you from picking the points you want. Snap mode forces the cursor to move to points at a given interval, so you will have difficulty selecting a point that doesn't fall exactly at one of those intervals.

2. Click on the Trim tool in the Modify toolbar.

You will see this prompt:

```
Select cutting edges: (Projmode=UCS, Edgemode=No extend)
Select objects:
```

3. Click on the line you just created—the one that crosses through the ellipse—and press ↵ to finish your selection.

4. At the `<Select object to trim>/Project/Edge/Undo` prompt, pick the topmost portion of the ellipse above the line. This trims the ellipse back to the line.

5. Press ↵ to exit the Trim command.

Selecting Close or Overlapping Objects

At times, you will want to select an object that is in close proximity to or lying underneath another object, and AutoCAD won't obey your mouse click. It's frustrating when you click on the object you want to select but AutoCAD selects the one next to it instead. To help you make your selections in these situations, AutoCAD provides Object Selection Cycling. To use it, you hold down the Ctrl key while simultaneously clicking on the object you want to select. If the wrong object is highlighted, press the left mouse button again (you do not need to hold down the Ctrl key for the second time), and the next object in close proximity will be highlighted. If several objects are overlapping or close together, just continue to press the left mouse button until the correct object is highlighted. When the object you want is finally highlighted, press ↵ and continue with further selections.

In step 2 of the foregoing exercise, the Trim command produces two messages in the prompt. The first message, `Select cutting edges…`, tells you that you must first select objects to define *the edge to which you wish to trim an object*. In step 4, you are again prompted to select objects, this time to select the *objects to trim*. Trim is one of a handful of AutoCAD commands that asks you to select two sets of objects: The first set defines a boundary, and the second is the set of objects you want to edit. The two sets of objects are not mutually exclusive. You can, for example, select the cutting edge objects as objects to trim. The next exercise shows how this works.

First you will undo the Trim you just did; then you will use the Trim command again in a slightly different way to finish off the toilet.

1. Click on the Undo button in the Standard toolbar, or enter **U** ↵ at the command prompt. The top of the ellipse reappears.

2. Start the Trim tool again by clicking on it in the Modify toolbar.

3. At the `Select cutting edges… Select objects` prompt, click on the ellipse and the line crossing the ellipse (see the top image of Figure 3.5).

4. Press ↵ to finish your selection and move to the next step.

These Trim options—Project, Edge, and Undo—are described in *The Trim Options* section later in this Chapter.

5. At the `<Select object to trim>/Project/Edge/Undo` prompt, click on the top portion of the ellipse, as you did in the previous exercise. The ellipse trims back.

6. Click on a point near the left end of the trim line, past the ellipse. The line trims back to the ellipse.

7. Click on the other end of the line. The right side of the line trims back to meet the ellipse. Your drawing should look like the bottom image of Figure 3.5.

8. Press ↵ to exit the Trim command.

Here you saw how the ellipse and the line are both used as trim objects, as well as the objects to be trimmed.

The Trim Options

AutoCAD offers three options for the Trim command: Edge, Project, and Undo. As described in the following paragraphs, these options give you a higher degree of control over how objects are trimmed.

Edge [E]   allows you to trim an object to an apparent intersection, even if the cutting-edge object does not intersect the object to be trimmed (see the top of Figure 3.6). Edge offers two options: Extend and No Extend. These can also be set using the Edgemode system variable.

Project [P]   is useful when working on 3D drawings. It controls how AutoCAD trims objects that are not coplanar. Project offers three options: None, UCS, and View. None causes Trim to ignore objects that are on different planes, so that only coplanar objects will be trimmed. If you choose UCS, the Trim command trims objects based on a Plan view of the current UCS and then disregards whether the objects are coplanar or not (see the middle of Figure 3.6). View is similar to UCS but uses the current view's "line of sight" to determine how non-coplanar objects are trimmed (see the bottom of Figure 3.6).

Undo [U]   causes the last trimmed object to revert to its original length.

FIGURE 3.5:

Trimming the ellipse and the line

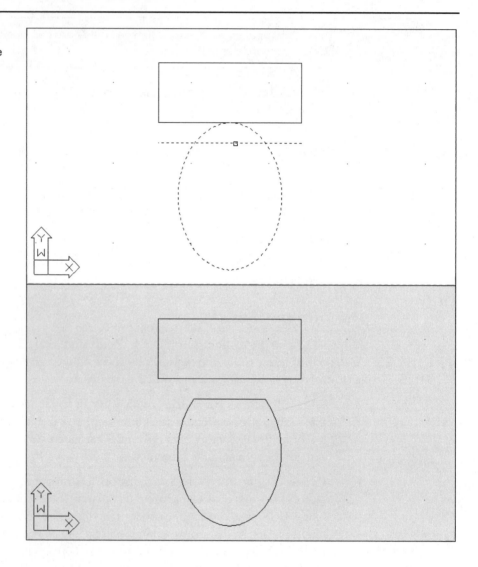

FIGURE 3.6:

The Trim tool's options

Imagined extension
of line

Actual
extent of
line

Result

With the Extend option, objects will trim even if the trim object
doesn't actually intersect with the object to be trimmed.

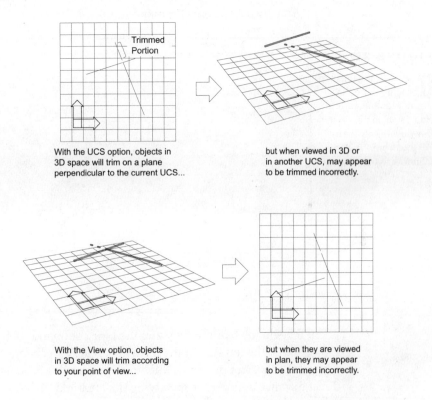

Trimmed
Portion

With the UCS option, objects in
3D space will trim on a plane
perpendicular to the current UCS...

but when viewed in 3D or
in another UCS, may appear
to be trimmed incorrectly.

With the View option, objects
in 3D space will trim according
to your point of view...

but when they are viewed
in plan, they may appear
to be trimmed incorrectly.

You've just seen one way to construct the toilet. However, there are many ways to construct objects. For example, you could have just trimmed the top of the ellipse, as you did in the first Trim exercise, and then used the Grips feature to move the endpoints of the line to meet the endpoints of the ellipse. As you become familiar with AutoCAD, you will start to develop your own ways of working, using the tools best suited to your style.

Planning and Laying Out a Drawing

For the next object, the bathtub, you will use some new commands to lay out parts of the drawing. This will help you get a feel for the kind of planning you must do to use AutoCAD effectively. You'll also get a chance to use some of the keyboard shortcuts built into AutoCAD. First, though, go back to the previous view of your drawing, and arrange some more room to work.

1. Return to your previous view; the one shown in Figure 3.7. A quick way to do this is to click on the Zoom Previous tool from the Standard toolbar, or Choose View ➤ Zoom ➤ Previous. Your view will return to the one you had before the last Zoom command (Figure 3.7).

FIGURE 3.7:

The view of the finished toilet after using the Zoom Previous tool. You can also obtain this view using the Zoom All tool from the Zoom Window flyout.

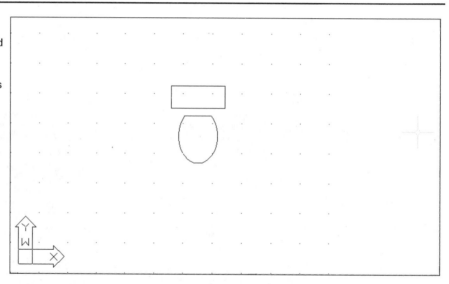

You'll begin the bathtub by using the Line command to draw a rectangle 2'-8"×5'-0" on the left side of the drawing area. For a change this time, you'll use a couple of shortcut methods: the Line command's keyboard shortcut and the direct distance method for specifying distance and direction.

2. Turn Snap mode on by pressing F9.

3. Type **L** ↵ and pick the coordinate location 0'-9", 0'-10" at the From point prompt. You can either use the cursor in conjunction with the coordinate readout or enter the coordinate through the keyboard.

4. Place your cursor so that the rubber-banding line is pointing directly to the left and type **2'8"**; then right-click the mouse for the first side of the tub. Notice that the rubber-banding line is now fixed at a length of 2' -8".

5. Now point the rubber-banding line upward toward the top of the screen and type **5'**; then right-click the mouse for the next side.

6. Point the rubber-banding line directly to the right of the last point and type **2'8"**; then right-click the mouse for the next side.

7. Type **C** ↵ to close the rectangle.

NOTE
Instead of right-clicking on the mouse during the direct distance entry method, you can press ↵ or the spacebar.

Now you have the outline of the tub. Notice that when you enter feet and inches through the keyboard, you must avoid hyphens or spaces. Thus, *2 feet 8 inches* is typed as 2'8". Also notice that you didn't have to enter the at sign (@) or angle specification. Instead, you used the *direct distance* method for specifying direction and distance. You can use this method for drawing lines or moving and copying objects at right angles. It is less effective if you want to specify exact angles other than right angles.

Besides the direct distance input method, you used a keyboard shortcut to start the Line command, instead of using the Line tool from the Draw toolbar.

TIP
Some of the keyboard shortcuts for tools or commands you've used in this chapter are C (Copy), E (Erase), EL (Ellipse), F (Fillet), M (Move), O (Offset), and TR (Trim). Remember that keyboard shortcuts, like keyboard commands, can only be entered when the command prompt is visible in the Command window.

Making a Preliminary Sketch

The following exercise will show you how planning ahead will make your use of AutoCAD more efficient. When drawing a complex object, you will often have to do some layout before you do the actual drawing. This is similar to drawing an accurate pencil sketch using construction lines that you later trace over to produce a finished drawing. The advantage of doing this in AutoCAD is that your drawing doesn't lose any accuracy between the sketch and the final product. Also, AutoCAD allows you to use the geometry of your sketch to aid you in drawing. While planning your drawing, think about what it is you want to draw, and then decide what drawing elements will help you create that object.

You will use the Offset command to establish reference lines to help you draw the inside of the tub. This is where the Osnap overrides are quite useful. See *The Osnap Options* sidebar, later in this chapter.

Setting Up a Layout

The Offset tool of the Modify toolbar allows you to make parallel copies of a set of objects, such as the lines forming the outside of your tub. Offset is different from the Copy command; Offset allows only one object to be copied at a time, but it can remember the distance you specify. The Offset option does not work with all types of objects. Only lines, arcs, circles, and 2D polylines can be offset.

In this exercise, you will use standard lines to layout your drawing. Standard lines are best suited for the layout of the bathtub in this situation. In Chapter 5 you will learn about two other objects, Construction Lines (Xlines) and Rays, which are specifically designed to help you layout a drawing.

1. Click on the Offset tool in the Modify toolbar, or type **o** ↵. You can also select Modify ➤ Offset from the pull-down menu.

2. At the Offset distance or Through <Through> prompt, enter **3** ↵. This enters the distance of 3" as the offset distance.

3. At the Select object to offset prompt, click on the bottom line of the rectangle you just drew.

4. At the Side to offset? prompt, pick a point inside the rectangle. A copy of the line appears. You don't have to be exact about where you pick the side to offset; AutoCAD only wants to know on which side of the line you want to make the offset copy.

5. The prompt Select an object to offset appears again. Click on another side to offset; then click again on a point inside the rectangle.

6. Continue to offset the other two sides; then offset these four new lines inside the rectangle toward the center. You will have a drawing that looks like Figure 3.8.

7. When you are done, exit the Offset command by pressing ↵.

FIGURE 3.8:

The completed layout

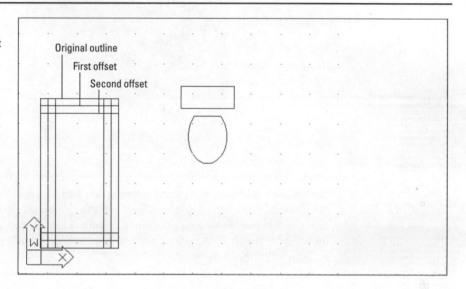

Using the Layout

Now you will begin to draw the inside of the tub, starting with the narrow end. You will use your offset lines as references to construct the arcs that make up the tub. Also in this exercise, you'll set up some of the Osnap tools to be available automatically whenever AutoCAD expects a point selection.

1. Choose Tools ➤ Object Snap Settings..., or type **os** ↵. This opens the Osnap Settings dialog box.

2. Make sure the Running Osnap tab is selected, and then click on the check-boxes labeled Endpoint, Midpoint, and Intersection so that an X appears in the boxes; then click OK.

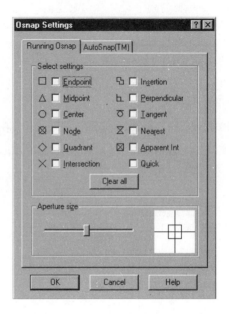

NOTE

Take a look at the graphic symbols next to each of the Osnap options in the Osnap Settings dialog box. These are the Osnap markers that appear in your drawing as you select Osnap points. Each Osnap option has its own marker symbol. As you work with the Osnaps, you'll become more familiar with how they work.

Understanding the AutoSnap Settings in the Osnap Settings Dialog Box

NEW!

When you select the AutoSnap tab of the Osnap Settings dialog box, you'll see a set of options pertaining to the new Release 14 AutoSnap feature. AutoSnap looks at the location of your cursor during Osnap selections and locates the Osnap point nearest your cursor. AutoSnap then displays a graphic called a *marker* showing you the Osnap point it has found. If it is the one you want, you simply left-click your mouse to select it.

The AutoSnap settings allow you to control its various features. The following is a listing of each of the settings and their purpose.

Marker   turns the graphic marker on or off.

Magnet   causes the Osnap cursor to "jump to" inferred Osnap points.

Snap Tip   turns the Osnap tool tip on or off.

Display aperture box   turns the old style Osnap cursor box on or off.

Marker size   controls the size of the graphic marker.

Marker color   controls the color of the graphic marker. ·

If you prefer the old method of using the Osnaps, you can turn off Marker, Magnet, and Snap tip, and then turn on Display aperture box. The Osnaps will then work as they did prior to Release 14. If you have problems seeing the graphic marker, you may want to change its color using the Marker color control.

You've just set up the Endpoint, Midpoint, and Intersection Osnaps to be on by default. This is called a Running Osnap where AutoCAD will automatically select the nearest Osnap point without your intervention. Now let's see how Running Osnaps works.

1. In the Draw toolbar, click on the Arc tool, or type **a** ↵. (See Figure 3.9 for other Arc options available from the pull-down menu. This figure shows each pull-down menu option name with a graphic above it depicting the arc and numbers indicating the sequence of points to select. For example, if you want to know how the Draw ➤ Arc ➤ Start, Center, End option works, you can look to the graphic at the bottom-right corner of the figure. It shows the point selection sequence for drawing an arc using that option; 1 for the start point, 2 for the center point, and then 3 for the end of the arc.)

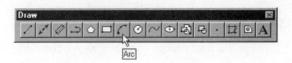

FIGURE 3.9:

If you look at the Draw ➤ Arc cascading menu, you'll see some additional options for drawing arcs. These options provide "canned" responses to the arc command so that you only have to select the appropriate points as indicated in the pull-down menu option name.

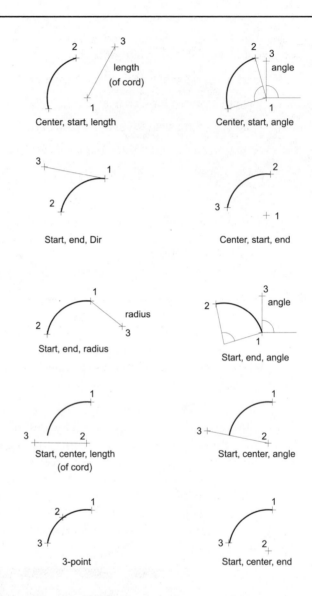

Center, start, length

Center, start, angle

Start, end, Dir

Center, start, end

Start, end, radius

Start, end, angle

Start, center, length (of cord)

Start, center, angle

3-point

Start, center, end

2. For the first point of the arc, move the cursor toward the intersection of the two lines located at coordinate 2'-11", 5'-4", as indicated in the first image of Figure 3.10. Notice that the Intersection Osnap marker appears on the intersection.

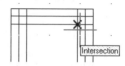

3. With the Intersection Osnap marker on the desired intersection, press the left mouse button.

4. Now move the cursor to the midpoint of the second horizontal line near the top. When the Midpoint Osnap marker appears at the midpoint of the line, press the left mouse button.

5. Finally, use the Intersection Osnap marker to locate and select the intersection of the two lines at coordinate 1'-3", 5'-4". An arc appears. The top image of Figure 3.10 shows the sequence we've just described.

TIP

When you see an Osnap marker on an object, you can have AutoCAD move to the next Osnap point on the object by pressing the Tab key. If you have several Running Osnap modes on (Endpoint, Midpoint, and Intersection, for example), pressing the Tab key will "cycle" through those Osnap points on the object. This feature can be especially useful in a crowded area of a drawing.

Next, you will draw an arc for the left side of the tub.

1. In the Draw toolbar, click on the Arc tool again.

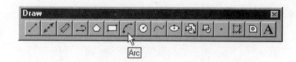

Then type @ ↵. This selects the last point you picked as the start of the next arc.

FIGURE 3.10:

The top, left side, and bottom of the tub

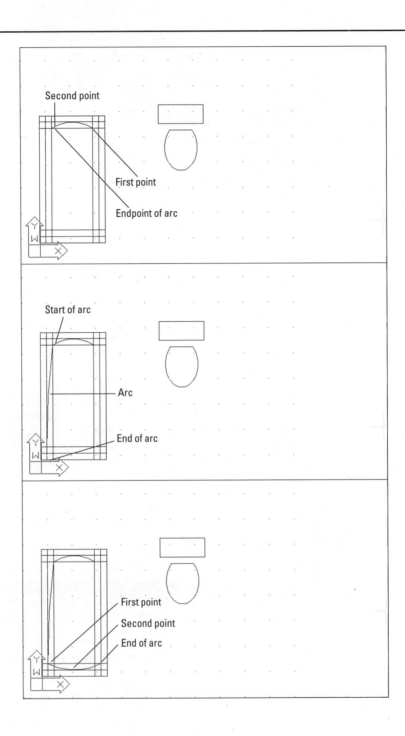

WARNING If you accidentally select additional points after the last exercise and prior to step 1, you may not get the results described here. If this happens, issue the Arc command again and then use the Endpoint Osnap and select the endpoint of the last arc.

2. Type **E** ↵ to tell AutoCAD that you want to specify the other arc, instead of the next point. Then at the End point prompt, use the Intersection Osnap to pick the intersection of the two lines at coordinate 1'-0", 1'-4" in the lower-left corner of the tub. See the middle image of Figure 3.10 for the location of this point.

3. Type **D** ↵ to select the Direction option. You will see the arc drag as you move the cursor, along with a rubber-banding line from the starting point of the arc. Then select "D" from the Angle/Direction/Radius/<Center Point>. This will make the command work as specified. Move the cursor to the left of the dragging arc until it touches the middle line on the left side of the tub. Then pick that as shown in the middle image of Figure 3.10.

TIP In step 3, the rubber-banding line indicates the direction of the arc. Be sure Ortho mode is off, because ortho will force the rubber-banding line and the arc in a direction you don't want. Check the status bar; if "Ortho" appears as solid black, not gray, press F8 to turn ortho off.

Now you will draw the bottom of the tub.

4. Click on the Arc tool in the Draw toolbar again. You can also press ↵ to replay the last command.

5. Using the Endpoint Osnap marker, pick the endpoint of the bottom of the arc just drawn.

6. Using the Midpoint Osnap marker, pick the middle horizontal line at the bottom of the tub.

7. Finally, pick the intersection of the two lines at coordinate 3'-2", 1'-4" (see the bottom image of Figure 3.10).

Now create the right side of the tub by mirroring the left side.

8. Click on the Mirror tool from the Modify toolbar.

9. At the `Select object` prompt, pick the long arc on the left side of the tub. The arc highlights. Press ↵ to indicate that you've finished your selection.

10. At the `First point of mirror line` prompt, pick the midpoint of the top horizontal line. By now, you should know how to use the automatic Osnap modes you set up earlier.

11. At the `Second point` prompt, turn on the Ortho mode and pick a point directly below the last point selected.

12. At the `Delete old objects?<N>` prompt, press ↵ to accept the default, No. A mirror image of the arc you picked appears on the right side of the tub. Your drawing should look like Figure 3.11.

FIGURE 3.11:

The inside of the tub completed with the lay-out lines still in place

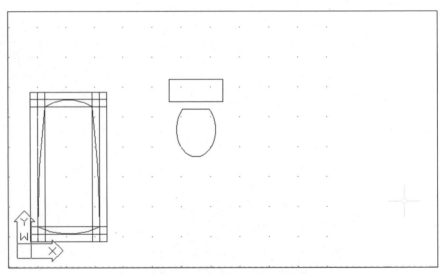

In this exercise, you were able to use the Osnaps in a Running Osnap mode. You'll find that you will use the Osnaps nearly all the time as you create your drawings. For this reason, you may choose to have Running Osnaps on all the

time. Even so, there will be times when Running Osnaps may get in the way. For example, they may be a nuisance in a crowded drawing when you want to use a Zoom window. The Osnaps can cause you to select an inappropriate window area by automatically selecting Osnap points.

Fortunately, you can turn Running Osnaps on and off quite easily by double-clicking on the Osnap label in the status bar. This toggles the Running Osnaps on or off. If you don't have any running Osnaps set, then double-clicking on the Osnap label will open the Osnap Settings dialog box.

Erasing the Layout Lines

For the next step, you will erase the layout lines you created using the Offset command. But this time, try selecting the lines *before* issuing the Erase command.

TIP
If the following exercise doesn't work as described, be sure you have the Noun/Verb selection setting turned on. See Appendix B for details.

1. Click on each internal layout lines individually.

If you have problems selecting just the lines, try using a window to select single lines. (Remember, a window selects only objects that are completely within the window.) You might also try the Object Selection Cycling option, as explained earlier in this chapter in the *Selecting Close or Overlapping Objects* sidebar.

2. Once all the layout lines are highlighted, enter **E** ↵. This is a keyboard short-cut to entering the Erase command. Your drawing will look like Figure 3.12.

TIP
If you find you need more control over the selection of objects, you will find the Add/Remove selection mode setting useful. This setting lets you de-select a set of objects within a set of objects you've already selected. While in Object Selection mode, enter **R** ↵; then proceed to use a window or other selection tool to remove objects from the selection set. Enter **A** ↵ to continue to add more options to the selection set. Or if you only need to de-select a single object, Shift + click on it.

FIGURE 3.12:

The drawing after eras-
ing the layout lines

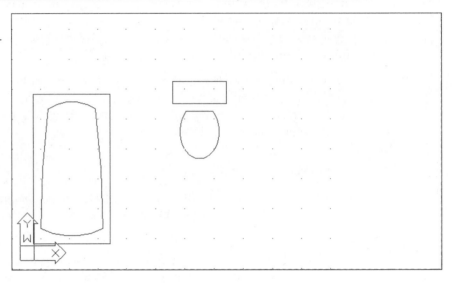

The Osnap Options

In the previous exercise, you made several of the Osnap settings automatic so that they were available without having to select them from the Osnap pop-up menu. Another way to invoke the Osnap options is by typing in their keyboard equivalents while selecting points.

Here is a summary of all the available Osnap options, including their keyboard shortcuts. You've already used many of these options in this and the previous chapter. Pay special attention to those options you haven't yet used in the exercises but may find useful to your style of work. The full name of each option is followed by its keyboard shortcut name in brackets. To use these options, you can enter either the full name or abbreviation at any point prompt. You can also pick these options from the pop-up menu obtained by Shift + clicking on the right mouse button.

Tip: Sometimes you'll want to have one or more of these Osnap options available as the default selection. You can set Osnaps to be on at all times (called a Running Osnap). Choose Tools ➢ Object Snap Settings from the pull-down menu.

Availabe Osnap options:

Apparent Intersection [apint]   selects the apparent intersection of two objects. This is useful when you want to select the intersection of two objects that do not actually intersect. You will be prompted to select the two objects.

Center [cen]   selects the center of an arc or circle. You must click on the arc or circle itself, not its apparent center.

Endpoint [endp]   selects all the endpoints of lines, polylines, arcs, curves, and 3D Face vertices.

From [fro]   selects a point relative to a picked point. For example, you can select a point that is 2 units to the left and 4 units to the right of a circle's center.

Insert [ins]   selects the insertion point of text, blocks, Xrefs, and overlays.

Intersection [int]   selects the intersection of objects.

Midpoint [mid]   selects the midpoint of a line or arc. In the case of a poly-line, it selects the midpoint of the polyline segment.

Nearest [nea]   selects a point on an object nearest the pick point.

Node [nod]   selects a point object.

None [non]   temporarily turns off Running Osnaps.

Perpendicular [per]   selects a position on an object that is perpendicular to the last point selected. Normally, this option is not valid for the first point selected in a string of points.

Quadpoint [qua]   selects the nearest cardinal (north, south, east, or west) point on an arc or circle.

Quick [qui]   by sacrificing accuracy, improves the speed at which AutoCAD selects geometry. You use Quick in conjunction with one of the other Osnap options. For example, to speed up the selection of an intersection, you would enter **QUICK,INT** ⏎ at a point prompt, and then select the intersection of two objects.

Tangent [tan]   selects a point on an arc or circle that represents the tangent from the last point selected. Like the Perpendicular option, Tangent is not valid for the first point in a string of points.

When preparing to erase an object that is close to other objects, you may want to select the object first, using the Noun/Verb method. This way you can carefully select objects you want to erase before you actually invoke the Erase command.

Putting On the Finishing Touches

The inside of the tub still has some sharp corners. To round out these corners, you can use the versatile Fillet command (on the Modify toolbar). Fillet allows you to join lines and arcs end to end, and it can add a radius where they join, so there is a smooth transition from arc to arc or line to line. Fillet can join two lines that do not intersect, and it can trim two crossing lines back to their point of intersection.

1. Click on the Fillet tool from the Modify toolbar, or type **f** ↵. You can also choose Modify ➣ Fillet from the pull-down menu.

2. At the Polyline/Radius/Trim/<Select first object> prompt, enter **R** ↵.

3. At the Enter fillet radius <0'1/2"> prompt, enter **4** ↵. This tells AutoCAD that you want a 4" radius for your fillet.

4. Press ↵ to invoke the Fillet command again; this time, pick two adjacent arcs. The fillet arc joins the two larger arcs.

5. Press ↵ again and fillet another corner. Repeat until all four corners are filleted. Your drawing should look like Figure 3.13.

6. Save the Bath file and exit AutoCAD.

FIGURE 3.13:

A view of the finished toilet and tub with the tub corners filleted

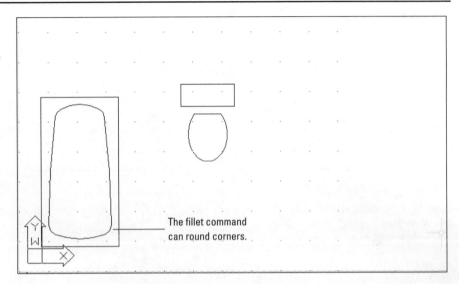

The fillet command can round corners.

Using AutoCAD's Automatic Save Feature

As you work with AutoCAD, you may notice that AutoCAD periodically saves your work for you. Your file is saved not as its current file name, but as a file called Auto.sv$. The default time interval between automatic saves is 120 minutes. You can change this interval by doing the following:

1. Enter **Savetime** ⏎ at the command prompt.

2. At the New value for SAVETIME < 120 >: prompt, enter the desired interval, in minutes. Or, to disable the automatic save feature entirely, enter 0 at the prompt.

If You Want to Experiment...

As you draw, you will notice that you are alternately creating objects, and then copying and editing them. This is where the difference between hand drafting and CAD really begins to show.

Try drawing the part shown in Figure 3.14. The figure shows you what to do, step by step. Notice how you are applying the concepts of layout and editing to this drawing.

FIGURE 3.14:

Drawing a Section view of a wide flange beam. Notice how objects are alternately created and edited instead of simply drawing each line segment of the wide flange.

1. Draw a box 7 units wide by 8 units high using the Line command.

2. Draw a vertical line through the center of the box.

3. Offset the top and bottom lines of the box a distance of 0.7 units. Offset the center at 0.35 units.

4. Break the sides of the box between the two offset lines.

5. Trim the top and bottom offset lines between the center three vertical lines.

6. Set the fillet radius to 0.4; then fillet the vertical offset lines with the horizontal offset lines.

7. Erase the center vertical line. You have finished the wide flange beam.

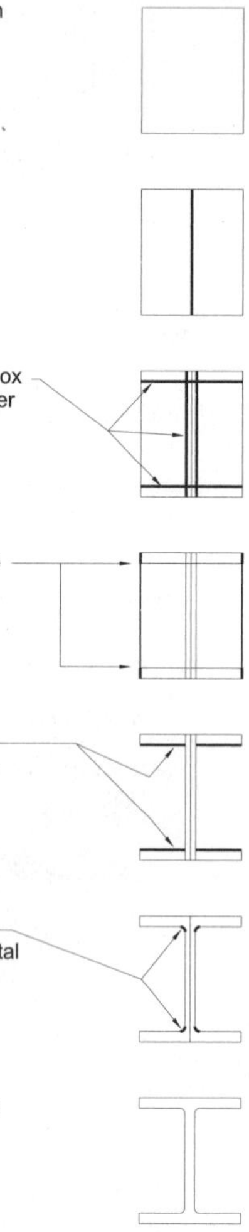

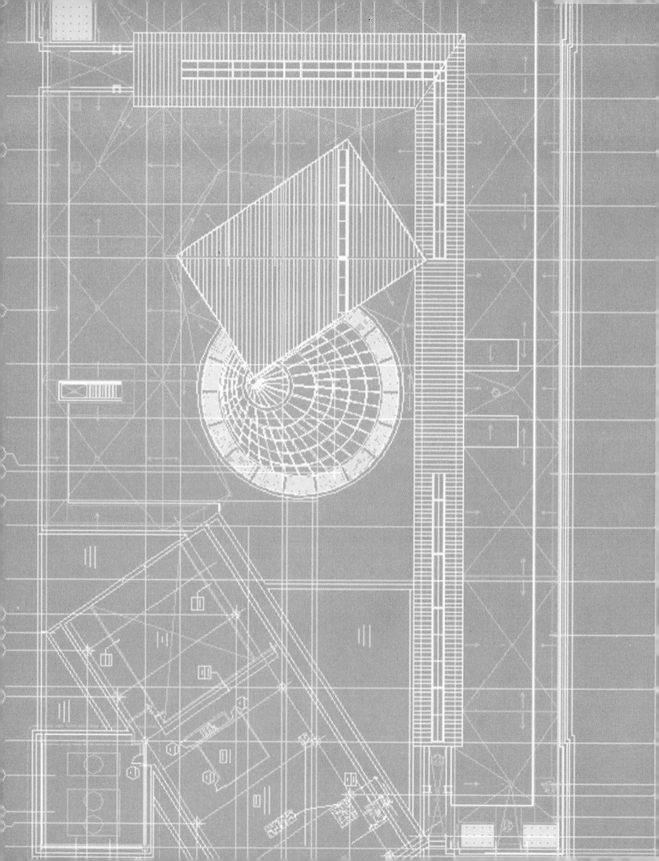

CHAPTER

FOUR

Organizing Your Work

- Creating a Symbol

- Inserting a Symbol

- Organizing Information with Layers

- Keeping Track of Blocks and Layers

- Finding Files on Your Hard Disk

- Inserting Symbols with Drag and Drop

Drawing the tub and toilet in Chapter 3 may have taken what seemed to you an inordinate amount of time. As you continue to use AutoCAD, however, you will learn to draw objects more quickly. You will also need to draw fewer of them because you can save drawings as symbols to be used like rubber stamps, duplicating drawings instantaneously wherever they are needed. This will save you a lot of time when you're composing drawings.

To make effective use of AutoCAD, you should begin a *symbols library* of drawings you use frequently. A mechanical designer might have a library of symbols for fasteners, cams, valves, or any type of parts for his or her application. An electrical engineer might have a symbols library of capacitors, resistors, switches, and the like. And a circuit designer will have yet another unique set of frequently used symbols. On this book's companion CD-ROM, you'll find a variety of ready-to-use symbols libraries. Check them out—you're likely to find some you can use.

In Chapter 3, you drew two objects—a bathtub and a toilet—that architects often use. In this chapter, you will see how to create symbols from those drawings. You will also learn about layers and how you can use them to organize information.

Symbols for Projects Large and Small

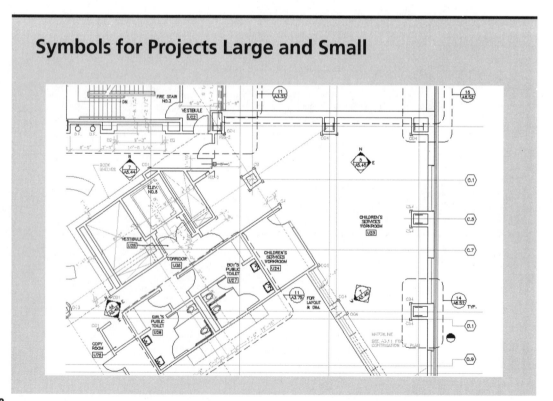

A symbols library was a crucial part of the production of the San Francisco Main Library construction documents. Shown here is a portion of an AutoCAD floor plan of the library where some typical symbols were used.

Notice the familiar door symbols, like the door you created in Chapter 2. And yes, there are even toilets in the lower half of the plan in the public restrooms. The method for drawing the wide flange demonstrated at the end of Chapter 3 is similar to the one that was used to create the I-beam column symbols shown here.

Symbol use isn't restricted to the building components. Room number labels, diamond-shaped interior elevation reference symbols, and the hexagonal column grid symbols are all common to an architectural drawing, regardless of the project's size. As you work through this chapter, keep in mind that all of the symbols used in the library drawings were created using the tools presented here.

Creating a Symbol

To save a drawing as a symbol, you use the Block tool. In word processors, the term block refers to a group of words or sentences selected for moving, saving, or deletion. A block of text can be copied elsewhere within the same file, to other files, or to a separate file on disk for future use. AutoCAD uses blocks in a similar fashion. Within a file, you can turn parts of your drawing into blocks that can be saved and recalled at any time. You can also use entire existing files as blocks.

1. Start AutoCAD and open the existing Bath file. Use the one you created in Chapter 3 or open 04-BATH.dwg on the companion CD-ROM. The drawing appears just as you left it in the last session.

2. In the Draw toolbar, click on the Make Block tool or type **B** ↵, the keyboard shortcut for the Make Block tool.

The Block definition dialog box appears.

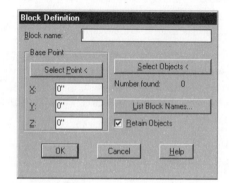

3. Type **Toilet** ↵ into the Block name input box.

4. In the Base Point button group of the dialog box, click on Select Point <. This option enables you to select a base point for the block using your cursor. (The insertion base point of a block is similar to the base point you used as a handle on an object in Chapter 2.) When you've selected this option, the dialog box will temporarily disappear.

NOTE Notice that the Block Definition dialog box gives you the option to specify the x, y and z coordinates for the base point, instead of selecting a point.

5. Using the Midpoint Osnap, pick the midpoint of the back of the toilet as the base point. Remember that you learned how to set up some Running Osnaps in Chapter 3; all you need to do is point to the midpoint of a line to display the Midpoint Osnap marker, and then left-click on your mouse. Once you've selected a point, the Block Definition dialog box will reappear.

6. Next, you need to select the actual objects that you want as part of the block. Click on the Select Objects < button. Once again, the dialog box will momentarily disappear. You now see the familiar object selection prompt in the Command window. Click on a point below and to the left of the toilet. Then window the entire toilet. It will now be highlighted.

WARNING Make sure you use the Select Objects < option in the Block Definition dialog box to select the objects you want to turn into a block. AutoCAD will let you create a block that contains no objects. This can cause some confusion and frustration, even for an experienced user.

7. Press ↵ to confirm your selection. The dialog box appears again. Make sure the Retain Objects option is checked, and then click OK. The toilet drawing is now a block with the name Toilet.

8. Repeat the blocking process for the tub, but this time use the upper-left corner of the tub as the insertion base point and give the block the name Tub.

NOTE   You can press ↵ or right-click on the mouse to start the Make Block tool again.

When you turn an object into a block, it is stored within the drawing file, ready to be recalled at any time. The block remains part of the drawing file even when you end the editing session. When you open the file again, the block will be available for your use. A block acts like a single object, even though it is really made up of several objects. It can only be modified by unblocking it using the *Explode* tool in the Modify toolbar. You can then edit it and turn it back into a block. We will look at the block-editing process later in this chapter.

Restoring Objects That Have Been Removed By the Make Block Tool or Block Command

In prior versions of AutoCAD, the Block command was the only command available to create blocks. This is a command-line version of the Make Block tool and is still available to those users who are more comfortable entering commands via the keyboard. When you use the Block command, the objects you turn into a block will automatically disappear. Release 14's new Make Block tool (Bmake) gives you the option of removing or maintaining the block's source objects by way of the Retain Objects option shown above in step 7.

If you use the Block command, or if for some reason you leave the Retain Objects option unchecked in the Block Definition dialog box, the source objects you select for the block will disappear. You can restore the source using the Oops command. Oops can also be used in any situation where you want to restore an object you accidentally erased. To use it, simply type **OOPS** ↵ at the command prompt. The source objects reappears in their former condition and location, not as a block.

Inserting a Symbol

The tub and toilet blocks can be recalled at any time, as many times as you want. In the following exercise you'll first draw the interior walls of the bathroom and then insert the tub and toilet.

1. First, delete the original tub and toilet drawings. Click on the Erase tool in the Modify toolbar; then enter **All** ↵↵. This erases the entire visible contents of the drawing. (It has no effect on the blocks you created previously.)

2. Draw a rectangle 5 '×7' -6 ". Orient the rectangle so the long sides go from left to right and the lower-left corner is at coordinate 1 ' -10 ", 1' -10 ". If you draw the rectangle using the Rectangle tool, make sure you explode it using the Explode tool. This is important for later exercises. Your drawing should now look like Figure 4.1.

TIP

If you're in a hurry, enter **Insert** ↵ at the command prompt, then enter **Tub** ↵, and then go to step 6 in this exercise.

FIGURE 4.1:

The interior walls of the bathroom

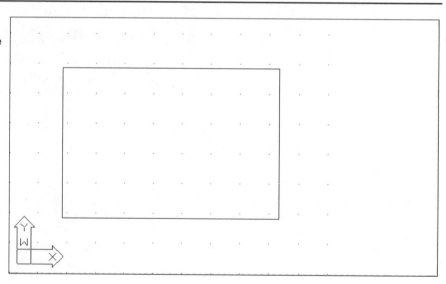

The Insert Block tool can also be found in the Insert toolbar. The Insert toolbar can be opened using the Toolbars dialog box. To open the Toolbars dialog box, right-click on any open toolbar, or choose View ➤ Toolbar....

3. In the Draw toolbar, click on the Insert Block tool or type **I** ↵.

The Insert dialog box appears.

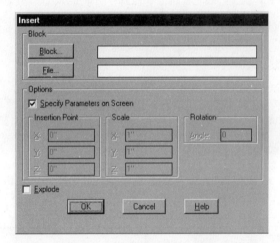

4. Click on the Block button at the top of the dialog box. The Defined Blocks dialog box appears, with a list of the available blocks in the current drawing.

5. Double-click on the block name TUB. The Insert dialog box returns with TUB in the input box next to the Block button.

6. Click on OK and you see a preview image of the tub attached to the cursor. The upper-left corner you picked for the tub's base point is now on the cursor intersection.

7. At the Insertion point prompt, pick the upper-left intersection of the room as your insertion point. Once you've picked the insertion point, notice that as you move your cursor, the preview image of the tub appears distorted.

8. At the X scale factor <1> / Corner / XYZ prompt, press ↵ to accept the default, 1.

9. At the Y scale factor (default=X) prompt, press ↵ to accept (default=X). This means you are accepting that the X scale equals the Y scale, which in turn equals 1.

NOTE   The X scale factor and Y scale factor prompts let you stretch the block in one direction or another. You can even specify a negative value to mirror the block. The defaults on these prompts are always 1, which inserts the block or file at the same size as it was created.

---

10. At the Rotation angle <0> prompt, press ↵ to accept the default of 0. You should have a drawing that looks like the top image of Figure 4.2.

11. Repeat steps 2 through 10, but this time, in steps 3 and 4 click on the Block input box and select TOILET. Place the toilet along the top of the rectangle representing the room, just to the right of the tub at coordinate 5'-8", 6'-10",

as shown in the bottom image of Figure 4.2. You may enter the coordinates through the keyboard.

WARNING If you decide to use your cursor to select the toilet insertion point, toggle the Running Osnaps off by double-clicking on the word "Osnap" in the status bar, or by pressing the F3 function key. This will prevent you from accidentally selecting the midpoint of the wall where you are placing the toilet.

FIGURE 4.2:

The bathroom, first with the tub and then with the toilet inserted

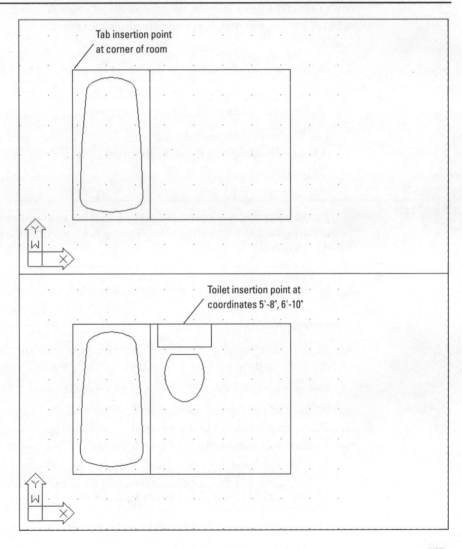

You might have noticed that as you moved the cursor in step 7, the tub became distorted. This demonstrates how the x and y scale factors can affect the item being inserted. Also, in step 10, you can see the tub rotate as you move the cursor. You can pick a point to fix the block in place, or you can enter a rotation value. The default 0° angle inserts the block or file with the orientation at which it was created.

Using an Existing Drawing as a Symbol

Now you need a door into the bathroom. Since you have already drawn a door and saved it as a file, you can bring the door into this drawing file and use it as a block.

1. In the Draw toolbar, click on the Insert Block tool or type **I** ↵.

2. In the Insert dialog box, click on the File button just below the Block button. The Select Drawing File dialog box appears.

3. Locate the door file and double-click on it. You may need to go to a different drive and folder from the default folder shown in the Select Drawing File dialog box.

TIP

You can also browse your hard disk by looking at thumbnail views of the drawing files in a directory. See *Finding Files on Your Hard Disk* later in this chapter.

---

4. When you return to the Insert dialog box, click OK. As you move the cursor around, you will notice the door appear above and to the right of the cursor intersection, as in Figure 4.3.

5. At this point, the door looks too small for this bathroom. This is because you drew it 3 units long, which translates to 3". Pick a point near coordinate 7'-2",2'-4", so that the door is placed in the lower-right corner of the room.

6. If you take the default setting for the X scale of the inserted block, the door will remain 3" long. However, as mentioned earlier, you can specify a smaller or larger size for an inserted object. In this case, you want a 3' door. To get that from a 3" door, you need an X scale factor of 12. (You may want to look again at Table 3.3 in Chapter 3 to see how this is determined.) Enter **12** ↵ now, at the X scale factor prompt.

7. Press ↵ twice to accept the default y = x and the rotation angle of 0°.

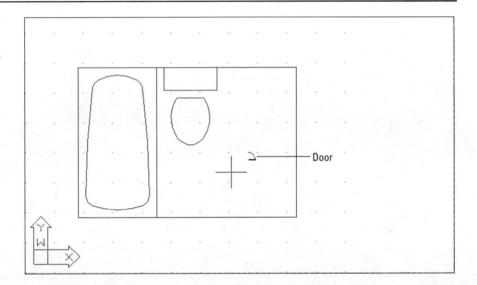

Now the command prompt appears, but nothing seems to happen to the drawing. This is because when you enlarged the door, you also enlarged the distance between the base point and the object. This brings up another issue to be aware of when you're considering drawings as symbols: All drawings have base points. The default base point is the absolute coordinate 0,0, otherwise known as the *origin*, which is located in the lower-left corner of any new drawing. When you drew the door in Chapter 2, you didn't specify the base point. So when you try to bring the door into this drawing, AutoCAD uses the origin of the door drawing as its base point (see Figure 4.4).

Because the door appears outside the bathroom, you must first use the Zoom ➤ All option to show more of the drawing, and then the Move command on the Modify toolbar to move the door to the right-side wall of the bathroom. Let's do this now.

1. Click on View ➤ Zoom ➤ All from the menu bar pull-down menu. Zoom All displays the area set by the Limits of your drawing (Format ➤ Drawing Limits) plus any other objects that may be outside those limits. The view of the room shrinks away and the door is revealed. Notice that it is now the proper size for your drawing (see Figure 4.5).

FIGURE 4.4:

By default, a drawing's origin is also its insertion point. You can change a drawing's insertion point using the Base command.

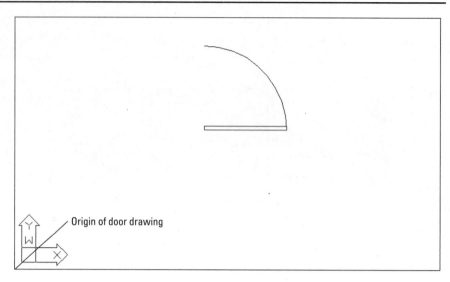

Origin of door drawing

FIGURE 4.5:

The enlarged door

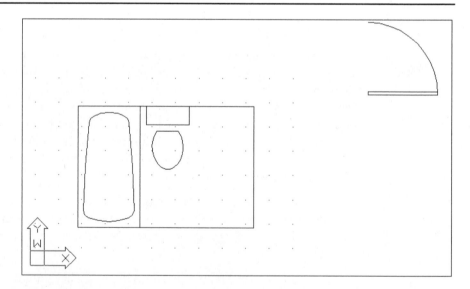

2. Choose Move from the Modify toolbar, or type **M** ↵.

3. To pick the door you just inserted, at the Select objects prompt, click on a point anywhere on the door and press ↵. Notice that now the entire door

highlights. This is because a block is treated like a single object, even though it may be made up of several lines, arcs, and so on.

4. At the Base point prompt, turn the Running Osnaps back on and pick the lower-left corner of the door. Remember that pressing the F3 function key or double-clicking on the word "Osnap" in the status bar will toggle the Running Osnaps on or off.

5. At the Second point prompt, use the Nearest Osnap override, and position the door so your drawing looks like Figure 4.6.

FIGURE 4.6:

The door on the right-side wall of the bathroom

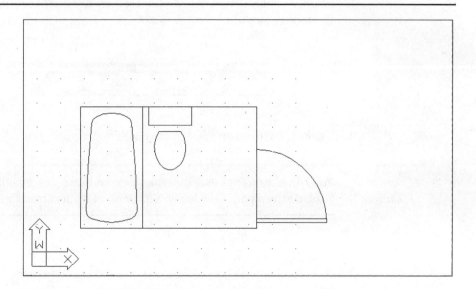

Because the door is an object you will use often, it should be a common size, so you don't have to specify an odd value every time you insert it. It would also be helpful if the door's insertion base point were in a more convenient location; that is, a location that would allow you to place the door accurately within a wall opening. Next, you will modify the Door block to better suit your needs.

Unblocking and Modifying a Block

To modify a block, you break it down into its components, edit them, and then turn them back into a block. This is called *redefining* a block. If you redefine a block that has been inserted in a drawing, each occurrence of that block within the current file will change to reflect the new block definition. You can use this block redefinition feature to make rapid changes to a design.

TIP

> If the Regenauto setting is turned off, you will have to issue a Regen command to see changes made to redefined blocks. See Chapter 6 for more on Regenauto.

To separate a block into its components, you use the Explode command.

1. Choose Explode from the Modify toolbar. You can also type **X** ↵ to start the Explode command.

2. Click on the door and press ↵ to confirm your selection.

TIP

> You can simultaneously insert and explode a block by clicking on the Explode checkbox in the lower-left corner of the Insert dialog box.

Now you can edit the individual objects that make up the door, if you so desire. In this case, you only want to change the door's insertion point because you have already made it a more convenient size. So now you'll turn the door back into a block, this time using the door's lower-left corner for its insertion base point.

3. In the Draw toolbar, select Make Block or type **B** ↵.

4. In the Block Definition dialog box, enter **Door** for the block name.

5. Click on the Select Point < button and pick the lower-left corner of the door.

6. Click on the Select Objects < button and select the components of the door. Press ↵ when you've finished making your selection.

7. Now click OK. You see a warning message that reads: "A Block with this name already exists in the drawing. Do you want to redefine it?" You don't want to accidentally redefine an existing block. In this case, you know you want to redefine the door, so click the Redefine button to proceed.

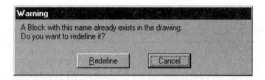

8. Erase the old door still remaining in the drawing.

9. Now insert the door block again, using the Block button in the Insert dialog box. This time, however, use the Nearest Osnap override and pick a point on the right-side wall of the bathroom, near coordinate 9'-4", 2'-1".

10. After you complete this, use the Grips feature to mirror the door, using the wall as the mirror axis so that the door is inside the room. Your drawing will look like Figure 4.7.

TIP To mirror an object using grips, first be sure the Grips feature is on. Select the objects to mirror, click on a grip, and then press the right mouse button. You can then select Mirror from the pop-up list that appears; then indicate a mirror axis with the cursor.

FIGURE 4.7:

The bathroom floor plan thus far

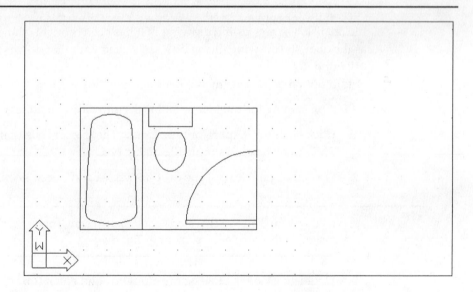

In step 7, you received a warning message telling you that you were about to redefine the existing door block. But you had inserted the door as a file, not as a block. Whenever you insert a drawing file using the Insert Block tool, the drawing automatically becomes a block in the current drawing. When you redefine a block, however, you do not affect the drawing file you imported. AutoCAD only changes the block within the current file. Next, you'll see how you can update an external file with a redefined block.

> **TIP**
> You may have noticed that both the Select Object button and the Select Point button are both followed by the less-than symbol (<). Whenever you see this symbol, you know that by selecting that option, AutoCAD will temporarily close the dialog box and allow you to select objects, pick points, or perform other operations that require a clear view of the drawing area.

Saving a Block as a Drawing File

You've seen that, with very little effort, you can create a symbol that can be placed anywhere in a file. Suppose you want to use this symbol in other files. When you create a block using the Block command, the block exists within the current file only until you specifically instruct AutoCAD to save it as a drawing file on disk. For an existing drawing that has been brought in and modified, such as the door, the drawing file on disk associated with that door is not automatically updated. To update the door file, you must take an extra step and use the Export option on the File menu. Let's see how this works.

Start by turning the tub and toilet blocks into individual files on disk.

1. Click on File ➤ Export, or type **Exp** ↵. The Export Data dialog box opens. This dialog box is a simple file dialog box.

2. Open the List Files of Type drop-down list and select Block (*.dwg).

> **TIP**
> If you prefer, you can skip step 2, and then in step 3 enter the full file name including the .dwg extension, as in **Tub.dwg.**

3. Double-click on the File Name input box and enter **Tub**.

4. Click the Save button. The dialog box closes.

5. At the Block name prompt, enter the name of the block you wish to save on disk as the tub file—in this case, also Tub. The Tub block is now saved as a file.

6. Repeat steps 1 through 3 for the toilet block. Give the file the same name as the block.

NOTE AutoCAD gives you the option to save a block's file under the same name as the original block or with a different name. Usually you will want to use the same name, which you can do by entering an equals sign (=) after the prompt.

NOTE Normally, AutoCAD will save a preview image with a file. This allows you to preview a drawing file prior to opening it. Preview images are not included with files that are exported with the File ➤ Export option or the Wblock command, which is discussed in the next section.

Replacing Existing Files with Blocks

The Wblock command does the same thing as File ➤ Export, but output is limited to AutoCAD .dwg files. (Veteran AutoCAD users will want to note that Wblock is now incorporated into the File ➤ Export option.) Let's try using the Wblock command this time to save the door block you modified.

1. Issue the Wblock command by typing **Wblock** ↵, or use the keyboard shortcut by typing **w** ↵.

2. At the Create Drawing File dialog box, enter the file name **Door**. A warning message appears:

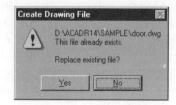

3. In this case, you want to update the door you drew in Chapter 2, so click on Yes.

4. You'll see a prompt asking for a block name. Enter **Door** ↵. The new door will replace the old one.

5. Save the current drawing.

In this exercise, you typed the Wblock command at the command prompt instead of using File ➢ Export. The results are the same, regardless of which method you use. If you are in a hurry, the Wblock command is a quick way to save part of your drawing as a file. The File ➢ Export option may be easier for new users to remember.

Other Uses for Blocks

So far, you have used the Make Block tool to create symbols, and the Export and Wblock commands to save those symbols to disk. As you can see, symbols can be created and saved at any time while you are drawing. You have made the tub and toilet symbols into drawing files that you can see when you check the contents of your current directory.

However, creating symbols is not the only use for Insert Block, Block, Export, and Wblock. You can use them in any situation that requires grouping objects (though you may prefer to use the more flexible Object Group command discussed in the next section). You can also use blocks to stretch a set of objects along one axis. Export and Wblock also allow you to save a part of a drawing to disk. You will see instances of these other uses of Block, Export, and Wblock through-out Chapters 5–8 and in Chapter 12.

Make Block, Export, and Wblock are extremely versatile and, if used judi-ciously, can boost your productivity and simplify your work. If you are not care-ful, however, you can also get carried away and create more blocks than you can keep track of. Planning your drawings helps you determine which elements will work best as blocks, and to recognize situations where other methods of organi-zation will be more suitable.

An Alternative to Blocks

Another way to create symbols is by creating shapes. Shapes are special objects made up of lines, arcs, and circles. They can regenerate faster than blocks, and they take up less file space. Unfortunately, shapes are considerably more difficult to create and less flexible to use than blocks.

You create shapes by using a coding system developed by Autodesk. The codes define the sizes and orientations of lines, arcs, and circles. You first sketch your shape, convert it into the code, and then copy that code into a DOS text file. We won't get into detail on this subject, so if you want to know more about shapes, see your *AutoCAD Customization Manual*.

Another way of using symbols is to use AutoCAD's external reference capabilities. External referenced files, otherwise know as *Xrefs*, are files inserted into a drawing in a way similar to blocks—the difference is that Xrefs do not actually become part of the drawing's database. Instead, they are loaded along with the current file at start-up time. It is as if AutoCAD opens several drawings at once: the main file you specify when you start AutoCAD, and Xrefs associated with the main file.

By keeping Xrefs independent from the current file, you make sure that any changes made to the Xrefs will automatically appear in the current file. You don't have to update the Xrefs as you must for blocks. For example, if you used the External Reference option on the Reference toolbar (to be discussed in Chapter 12) to insert the Tub drawing, and you later made changes to the tub, the next time you opened the Bath file, you would see the new version of the tub.

Xrefs are especially useful in workgroup environments, where several people are working on the same project. One person might be updating several files that have been inserted into a variety of other files. Before Xrefs were available, everyone in the workgroup would have had to be notified of the changes and update all the affected blocks in all the drawings that contained them. With Xrefs, the updating is automatic. There are many other features unique to these files, discussed in more detail in Chapters 6 and 12.

Grouping Objects

Blocks are an extremely useful tool, but for some situations, they are too restricting. At times, you will want to group objects together so they are connected, yet can still be edited individually. For example, consider a space planner who has to place workstations in a floor plan. Though each workstation is basically the same, there may be some slight variations in each station that would make the use of blocks unwieldy. For instance, one workstation may need a different configuration to accommodate special equipment while another may need to be slightly larger than the standard size. A better way is to draw a prototype workstation, and then turn it into a group. The group can be copied into position, then edited for each individual situation, without the group losing its identity as a group. The following exercises demonstrate how this works.

1. Open the drawing named office1.dwg from the companion CD-ROM.

2. Use the Zoom command to enlarge just the view of the workstation, as shown in the top image of Figure 4.8.

3. Choose Tools ➤ Object Group…, or use the keyboard shortcut **G** ↵. The Object Grouping dialog box appears.

4. Type **Station1**. As you type, your entry appears in the Group Name input box.

5. Click on New in the Create Group button group, about midway in the dialog box. The dialog box temporarily disappears to allow you to select objects for your new group.

6. At the Select objects prompt, window the entire workstation and press ↵. The Object Grouping dialog box returns. Notice that the name "Station1" appears in the Group Name list box at the top of the dialog box.

7. Click OK. You have just created a group.

FIGURE 4.8:

A workstation in an office plan

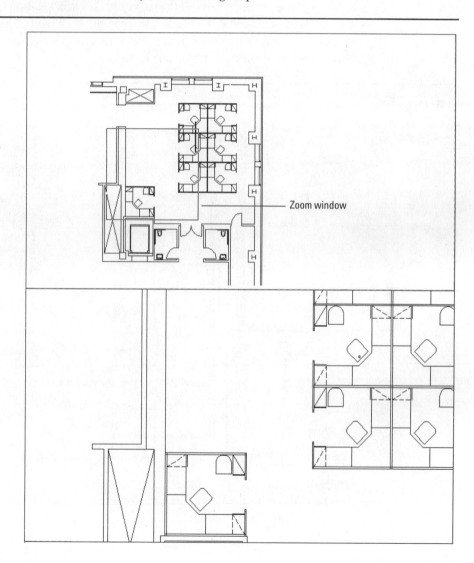

Zoom window

Now, whenever you want to select the workstation, you can click on any part of it and the entire group will be selected. At the same time, you will still be able to modify individual parts of the group—the desk, partition, and so on—without losing the grouping of objects.

Modifying Members of a Group

Next, you will make copies of the original group and modify the copies. Figure 4.9 is a sketch of the proposed layout that uses the new workstations. Look carefully and you'll see that some of the workstations in the sketch are missing a few of the standard components that exist in the Station1 group. One pair of stations has a partition removed; another station has no desk.

FIGURE 4.9:

A sketch of the new office layout

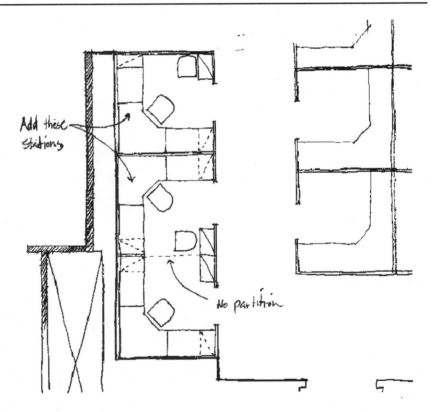

This next exercise shows you how to complete your drawing to reflect the design requirements of the sketch.

1. Click on Copy in the Modify toolbar or type **Co** ⏎, and click on the
   `Station1` group you just created. Notice that you can click on any part
   of the station to select the entire station.

2. Press ⏎ to finish your selection.

3. At the `Base point` prompt, enter @ ⏎. Then enter **@8'2"<90** to copy the
   workstation 8 feet, 2 inches vertically.

In step 2, you can also use the direct distance method by typing @ ⏎; then
pointing the rubber-banding line 90 degrees and typing 8'2" ⏎.

4. Issue the Copy command again, but this time click on the copy of the workstation you just created. Notice that it, too, is a group.

5. Copy this workstation 8'2" vertically, just as you did the original workstation.

6. Next, you'll use grips to mirror the first workstation copy. Click on the middle workstation to highlight it, and notice that grips appear for all the entities in the group.

7. Click on the grip in the middle-left side, as shown in Figure 4.10.

FIGURE 4.10:

Mirroring the new
group using grips

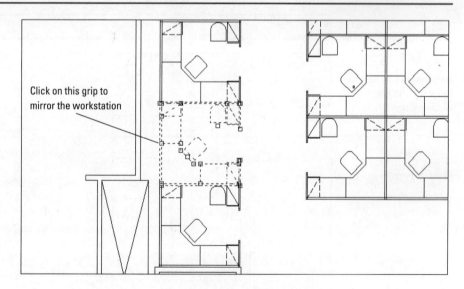

Click on this grip to
mirror the workstation

8. Right-click the mouse and select Mirror from the pop-up list. Notice that a temporary mirror image of the workstation follows the movement of your cursor.

9. Turn on the Ortho mode and pick a point directly to the right of the hot grip you picked in step 6. The workstation is mirrored to a new orientation.

10. Press the Esc key twice to clear the grip selection.

Now that you've got the workstations laid out, you need to remove some of the partitions between the new workstations. If you had used blocks for the workstations, you would have to first explode the workstations whose partitions you wish to edit. Groups, however, let you make changes without undoing their grouping.

1. Press Ctrl + A. This temporarily turns off groupings. You'll see the message <Group off> in the Command window.

2. Using a window, erase the short partition that divides the two copies of the workstations, as shown in Figure 4.11.

3. Press Ctrl + A again to turn groupings back on. You'll see the message <Group on> in the Command window.

4. To check your workstations, click on one of them to see if all of its components are highlighted together.

TIP   You can also use the Pickstyle system variable to control groupings. See Appendix D for more on Pickstyle.

FIGURE 4.11:

Remove the partitions between the two workstations

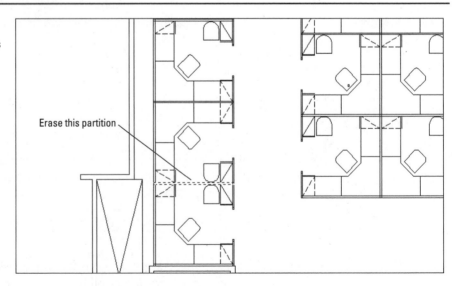

Erase this partition

Working with the Object Grouping Dialog Box

Each group has a unique name, and you can also attach a brief description of the group in the Object Grouping dialog box. When you copy a group, AutoCAD assigns an arbitrary name to the newly created group. Copies of groups are considered unnamed, but still can be listed in the Object Grouping dialog box by clicking the Unnamed checkbox. You can use the Rename button in the Object Grouping dialog box to rename unnamed groups appropriately.

Objects within a group are not bound solely to that group. One object can be a member of several groups, and you can have nested groups.

Here are descriptions of the options available in the Object Grouping dialog box:

Group Identification   Use this button group to identify your groups, using unique elements that let you remember what each group is for.

> **Group Name**   input box lets you create a new group by naming it first.
>
> **Description**   input box lets you include a brief description of the group.
>
> **Find Name**   button lets you find the name of a group by temporarily closing the dialog box so you can click on a group.
>
> **Highlight**   button highlights a group that has been selected from the group list. This helps you locate a group in a crowded drawing.
>
> **Include Unnamed**   checkbox determines whether unnamed groups are included in the Group Name list. Check this box to display the names of copies of groups for processing by this dialog box.

Create Group   Here's where you control how a group is created.

> **New**   lets you create a new group. It temporarily closes the dialog box so you can select objects for grouping. To use this button, you must have either entered a group name or checked the Unnamed checkbox.
>
> **Selectable**   checkbox lets you control whether the group you will create is selectable or not. See the description of the Selectable button in the Change Group just below.
>
> **Unnamed**   checkbox lets you create a new group without naming it.

Change Group   These buttons are available only when a group name is highlighted in the Group Name list at the top of the dialog box.

> **Remove**   lets you remove objects from a group.

161

Add   lets you add objects to a group. While using this option, grouping is temporarily turned off to allow you to select objects from other groups.

Rename   lets you rename a group.

Reorder   lets you change the order of objects in a group.

Description   lets you modify the description of a group.

Explode   separates a group into its individual components.

Selectable   turns individual groupings on and off. When a group is selectable, it is selectable as a group. When a group is not selectable, the individual objects in a group can be selected, but not the group.

Organizing Information with Layers

Another tool for organization is the *layer.* Layers are like overlays on which you keep various types of information (see Figure 4.12). In a floor plan of a building, for example, you want to keep the walls, ceiling, plumbing fixtures, wiring, and furniture separate, so you can display or plot them individually or combine them in different ways. It's also a good idea to keep notes and reference symbols about each element of the drawing, as well as the drawing's dimensions, on their own layers. As your drawing becomes more complex, the various layers can be turned on and off to allow easier display and modification.

For example, one of your consultants may need a plot of just the dimensions and walls, without all the other information; another consultant may need only a furniture layout. Using manual drafting, you would have to redraw your plan for each consultant. With AutoCAD, you can turn off the layers you don't need and plot a drawing containing only the required information. A carefully planned layering scheme helps you produce a document that combines the different types of information needed in each case.

Using layers also enables you to modify your drawings more easily. For example, suppose you have an architectural drawing with separate layers for the walls, the ceiling plan, and the floor plan. If any change occurs in the wall locations, you can turn on the ceiling plan layer to see where the new wall locations will affect the ceiling, and then make the proper adjustments.

AutoCAD allows an unlimited number of layers, and you can name each layer anything you want.

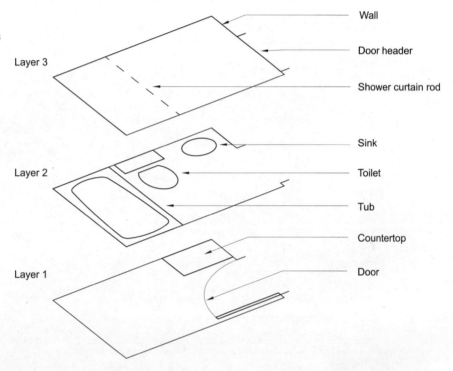

FIGURE 4.12:

A comparison of layers and overlays

Layer 3

Layer 2

Layer 1

Wall

Door header

Shower curtain rod

Sink

Toilet

Tub

Countertop

Door

Creating and Assigning Layers

To continue with your bathroom, you will create some new layers.

1. Open the Bath file you created earlier in this chapter. If you didn't create one, use the file 04b-bath.dwg from the companion CD-ROM.

2. To display the Layer & Linetype Properties dialog box, click on the Layers tool in the Properties toolbar, or choose Format ➤ Layers... from the pull-down menu. You can also type **LA** ↵ to use the keyboard shortcut.

Getting Multiple Use from a Drawing Using Layers

Layering can allow you to use a single AutoCAD drawing for multiple purposes. A single drawing may serve to show both the general layout of the plan and more detailed information such as equipment layout or floor paving layout.

These two reproductions of the San Francisco Main Library's lower level show how one floor plan file was used for two different purposes. The top view shows the layout of furnishings and the bottom shows a paving layout. In each case, the same floor plan file was used, but in the upper panel, the paving information is on a layer that is turned off. Layers also facilitate the use of differing scales in the same drawing. Frequently, a small-scale drawing of an overall plan will contain the same data for an enlarged view of other portions of the plan, such as a stairwell or elevator core. The detailed information, such as notes and dimensions, may be on a layer that is turned off for the overall plan.

NOTE   The Layer & Linetype Properties dialog box shows you at a glance the status of your layers. Right now, you only have one layer, but as your work expands, so will the number of layers. You will then find this dialog box indispensable.

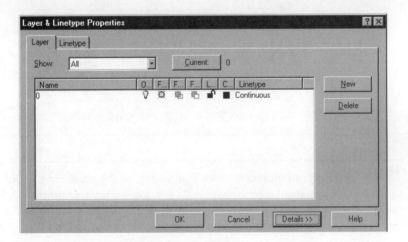

3.   Click on the New button in the upper-right corner of the dialog box. A new layer named Layer 1 appears in the list box. Notice that the name is highlighted. This tells you that by typing, you can change the default name to something better suited to your needs.

4. Type **Wall**; as you type, your entry replaced the Layer 1 name in the list box.

5. Click on the Details >> button near the bottom of the dialog box. Additional layer options appear.

6. With the Wall layer name highlighted, click on the downward pointing arrow to the right of the Color drop-down list. You see a listing of colors that you can assign to the Wall layer.

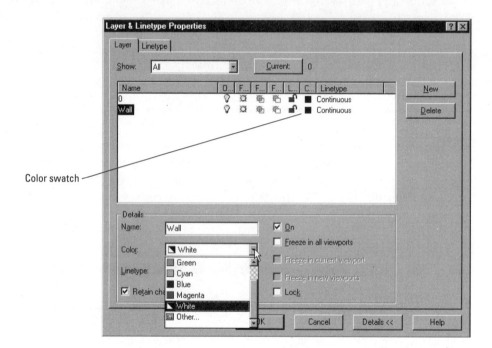

At first glance, this list may seem a bit limited, but you actually have a choice from 256 colors.

NOTE

Though it isn't readily apparent, all the colors in the Color drop-down list except for the first seven are designated by numbers. So when you select a color after the seventh color, the color's number rather than its name appears in the Color input box at the bottom of the dialog box.

---

7. Click on Other from the list, or click on the black color swatch in the Wall layer listing, next to the word "Continuous."

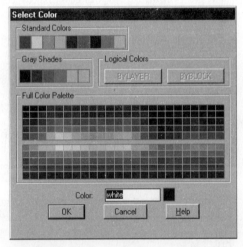

8. In the top row of Standard Colors, click on the green square and then on OK. Notice that the color swatch in the Wall layer listing is now green. You could have just chosen green from the Colors drop-down list, but I wanted you to select green from the Select Color dialog box so you would be aware that many other colors are available.

9. When the Layer & Linetype Properties dialog box returns, click on OK to close it.

The New Release 14 Layer Dialog Box

The Release 14 Layer dialog box conforms to the Windows interface standard. You'll notice that the bar at the top of the Layer Name list box offers several buttons for the various layer properties. Just as you can adjust the Windows Explorer, you can adjust the width of each column in list of layers by clicking and dragging either side of the column head buttons. You can also sort the layer list based on a property simply by clicking on the property name at the top of the list. And, just as with other Windows list boxes, you can Shift + click on names to select a block of layer names, or Ctrl + click on individual names to select multiples that do not appear together. These features will become helpful as your list of layers enlarges.

Controlling Layers through the Layer Command

You have seen how the Layer & Linetype Properties dialog box makes it easy to view and edit layer information, and how layer colors can be easily selected from an on-screen toolbar. But layers can also be controlled through the command prompt.

1. First press Esc to make sure any current command is canceled.

2. At the command prompt, enter **-Layer** ↵. Make sure you include the minus sign in front of the word Layer. The following prompt appears:

   ?/Make/Set/New/ON/OFF/Color/Ltype/Freeze/Thaw/Lock/Unlock:

   You'll learn about many of the options in this prompt as you work through this chapter.

3. Enter **N** ↵ to select the New option.

4. At the New layer name(s) prompt, enter **Wall2** ↵. The ?/Make/Set/New... prompt appears again.

5. Enter **C** ↵.

6. At the Color prompt, enter **Yellow** ↵. Or you can enter **2** ↵, the numeric equivalent to the color yellow in AutoCAD.

7. At the Layer Names for color 2 (yellow) <0>: prompt, enter **Wall2** ↵. The ?/Make/Set/New... prompt appears again.

8. Press ↵ to exit the Layer command.

Each method of controlling layers has its own advantages: The Layer & Linetype Properties dialog box offers more information about your layers at a glance. On the other hand, the Layer command offers a quick way to control and create layers if you're in a hurry. Also, if you intend to write custom macros, you will want to know how to use the Layer command as opposed to the dialog box, because dialog boxes cannot be controlled through custom toolbar buttons or scripts.

TIP
Another advantage to using the keyboard commands is that you can recall previously entered keystrokes by using the up and down arrow cursor keys. For example, to recall the layer named Wall2 you entered in step 4 above, press the up arrow key until Wall2 appears in the prompt. This can save time when you are performing repetitive operations such as creating multiple layers. This feature does not work with tools selected from the toolbars.

Assigning Layers to Objects

When you create an object, that object is assigned to the current layer. Until now, only one layer has existed, Layer 0—which contains all the objects you've drawn so far. Now that you've created some new layers, you can reassign objects to them using the Properties tool on the Object Properties toolbar.

1. Choose Properties from the Properties toolbar.

2. At the `Select objects` prompt, click on the four lines representing the bathroom walls. If you have problems singling out the wall to the left, use a window to select the wall line.

3. Press ↵ to confirm your selection. The Change Properties dialog box appears.

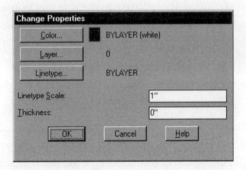

This dialog box allows you to change the layer assignment, color, line type, and thickness of an object. You'll learn about line types later in this chapter and object thickness in Chapter 15.

4. Click on the Layer button. Next you see the Select Layer dialog box, listing all the existing layers, including the ones you just created.

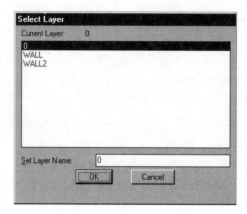

5. Double-click on the Wall layer. You return to the Change Properties dialog box.

6. Click on OK to close the dialog box.

The bathroom walls are now on the new layer, Wall, and the walls are changed to green. Layers are more easily distinguished from one another when colors are used to set them apart.

Next, you will practice the commands you learned in this section by creating some new layers and changing the layer assignments of the rest of the objects in your bathroom.

1. Bring up the Layer & Linetype Properties dialog box (use Format ≻ Layers or click on the Layers button in the Properties toolbar). Create a new layer called **Fixture** and give it the color blue.

TIP   You can change the name of a layer by clicking on it in the Layer & Linetype Properties dialog box; then once it is highlighted, click on it again so a box surrounds the name. You can then rename the layer. This works in the same way as renaming a file or folder in Windows 95.

---

2. Use the Change Properties dialog box (click the Properties button on the Object Properties toolbar) to change the tub and toilet to the Fixture layer.

3. Now create a new layer for the door, name the layer **Door,** and make it red.

NOTE   Within a block, you can change the color assignment and line type of only the objects that are on layer 0. See the sidebar, *Controlling Colors and Line Types of Blocked Objects* in this chapter.

4. Use the Properties tool on the Properties toolbar to open the Modify Block Insertion dialog box and change the door to the Door layer. Click on the Layer button in the Modify Block Insertion dialog box to open the Select Layer dialog box; then select the Door layer.

5. Use the Layer & Linetype Properties dialog box to create three more layers for the ceiling, door jambs, and floor, as shown in Table 4.1. Remember that you can open the Select Color dialog box by clicking on the color swatch of the layer listing.

TABLE 4.1: Create these layers and set their colors as indicated

Layer Name	Layer Color (Number)
Ceiling	Magenta (6)
Jamb	Green (3)
Floor	Cyan (4)

In step 4 above, you used a dialog box that offered several options for modifying the block. When you click the Properties tool on the Object Properties toolbar, the dialog box displayed will depend on whether you have selected one object or several. With only one object selected, AutoCAD presents options that apply specifically to that object. With several objects selected, you'll see a more limited set of options because AutoCAD can change only the properties that are common to all the objects selected.

NOTE   The Properties button on the Object Properties toolbar issues one of two commands, based on how many objects you selected. Dchprop is the command that opens the Change Properties dialog box; Dmodify opens the Modify Properties dialog box.

Controlling Colors and Line Types of Blocked Objects

Layer 0 has special importance to blocks. When objects assigned to Layer 0 are used as parts of a block, those objects take on the characteristics of the layer on which the block is inserted. On the other hand, if those objects are on a layer other than 0, they will maintain their original layer characteristics even if you insert or change that block to another layer. For example, suppose the tub is drawn on the Door layer, instead of on layer 0. If you turn the tub into a block and insert it on the Fixture layer, the objects the tub is composed of will maintain their assignment to the Door layer, although the Tub block is assigned to the Fixture layer.

It might help to think of the block function as a clear plastic bag that holds together the objects that make up the tub. The objects inside the bag maintain their assignment to the Door layer even while the bag itself is assigned to the Fixture layer.

AutoCAD also allows you to have more than one color or line type on a layer. For example, you can use the Color and Linetype buttons in the Change Properties dialog box (the Object Properties button on the Standard toolbar) to alter the color or line type of an object on layer 0. That object then maintains its assigned color and line type—no matter what its layer assignment. Likewise, objects specifically assigned a color or line type will not be affected by their inclusion into blocks.

Working on Layers

So far you have created layers and then assigned objects to those layers. However, the current layer is still 0, and every new object you draw will be on layer 0. Here's how to change the current layer.

1. Click on the arrow button next to the layer name on the Object Properties toolbar. A drop-down list opens, showing you all the layers available in the drawing.

   Notice the icons that appear next to the layer names; these control the status of the layer. You'll learn how to work with these icons later in this chapter. Also notice the box directly to the left of each layer name. This shows you the color of the layer.

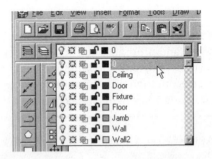

2. Click on the Jamb layer name. The drop-down list closes, and the name Jamb appears in the toolbar's layer name box. Jamb is now the current layer.

NOTE
You can also use the Layer command to reset the current layer. To do this here, enter **-Layer** (be sure to include the minus sign) at the command prompt, and at the ?/Make... prompt, enter **S** for set. At the New current layer prompt, enter **Jamb** and then press ↵ twice to exit the Layer command.

3. Zoom in to the door and draw a 5" line; start at the lower-right corner of the door and draw toward the right.

4. Draw a similar line from the top-right end of the arc. Your drawing should look like Figure 4.13.

Because you assigned the color green to the Jamb layer, the two lines you just drew to represent the door jambs are green. This gives you immediate feedback about what layer you are on as you draw.

Now you will use the part of the wall between the jambs as a line representing the door header (the part of the wall above the door). To do this, you will have to cut the line into three line segments, and then change the layer assignment of the segment between the jambs.

1. In the Modify toolbar, click on the Break tool.

NOTE

You can also start the Break command by typing **Break** ↵ or **BR** ↵ at the command prompt. Once you select an object, you enter **F** ↵ for the First point option, allowing you to select two points defining the location of the break. You then pick the break point and type **@** ↵ to break an object into two parts without making a gap.

2. At the Select objects prompt, click on the wall between the two jambs.

3. At the Enter second point (or F for first point) type **F** ↵. This issues the first point option.

4. At the first point prompt, use the Endpoint Osnap override to pick the endpoint of the door's arc that is touching the wall, as shown in Figure 4.13.

5. At the Enter second point prompt, type **@** ↵ to signify that you want the second point of the break to be at the same location as the first point.

6. Click on Break from the Modify toolbar, and then repeat steps 2 through 5, this time using the jamb near the door hinge location to locate the break point (see Figure 4.13).

FIGURE 4.13:

Door at wall with door jamb added

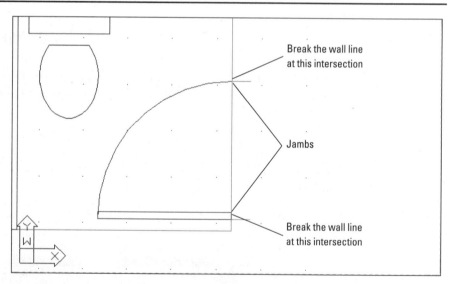

Though it may not be obvious, you've just broken the right-side wall line into 3 line segments; one at the door opening and two more on either side of the jambs. You can also use break to produce a gap in a line segment.

Next, you'll change the layer property of the line between the two jambs to the Ceiling layer. But instead of using the Properties tool, as you've done in earlier exercises, you'll use a shortcut method.

1. Click on the line between the door jambs to highlight it. Notice that the layer listing in the Properties toolbar changes to Wall. Whenever you select an object to expose its grips, both the Layer, Color, and Linetype listing in the Properties toolbar will change to reflect those properties of the selected object.

2. Click on the layer name in the Properties toolbar. The Layer drop-down list will open.

3. Click on the Ceiling layer name. The list closes and the line you selected changes to the magenta color showing you that it is now on the Ceiling layer. Also notice that the color list in the Properties toolbar also changes to reflect the new color for the line.

4. Press Esc twice to clear the grip selection. Notice that the layer returns to Jamb, the current layer.

5. Click on the Zoom Previous tool in the Standard toolbar, or choose View ➤ Zoom ➤ Previous to return to the previous view.

In this exercise, you were shown that by selecting an object with no command active, the object's properties are immediately displayed in the Properties toolbar under the Layer, Color, and Linetype boxes. Using this method, you can also change an object's color and line type independent of its layer. Just as with the Properties tool, you can select multiple objects and change their layers through the Layer drop-down list.

Now you'll finish the bathroom by adding a sink to a layer named Casework.

1. Open the Layer & Linetype Properties dialog box and create a new layer called **Casework**.

2. When the Casework layer name appears in the Layer drop-down list, click on the button labeled Current at the top of the dialog box.

3. Click on the color swatch for the Casework layer, and then select Blue from the Select Color dialog box. Click OK to exit the dialog box.

4. Click OK at the Layer & Linetype Properties dialog box. Notice that the layer listing in the Properties toolbar indicates that the current layer is Casework.

Now you'll add the sink. As you draw, the objects will appear in blue, the color of the Casework layer.

5. Click on View ➤ Zoom ➤ All.

6. Click on Rectangle in the Draw toolbar and draw a rectangle 28"×18" representing a sink countertop. Orient the countertop so that it fits into the upper-right corner of the room, as shown in Figure 4.14. Use coordinate 7'-0", 5'-4" for the lower-left corner of the countertop.

7. Use the Ellipse tool from the Draw toolbar and draw an ellipse 17"×14" in the center of the countertop.

8. Use the Change Properties dialog box to change the ellipse to the Fixture layer. Your drawing will look like Figure 4.14.

FIGURE 4.14:

Bathroom with sink and countertop added

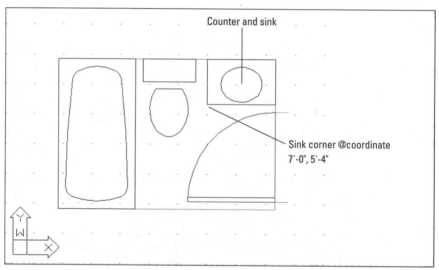

Controlling Layer Visibility

I mentioned earlier that at times you'll want to be selective about what layers you are working with on a drawing. In this bathroom, there is a door header that would normally appear only in a reflected ceiling plan. To turn off a layer so that it becomes invisible, use the Off button in the Layer & Linetype Properties dialog box.

1. Open the Layer & Linetype Properties dialog box by clicking on the Layers tool in the Properties toolbar.

2. Click on the Ceiling layer in the Layer drop-down list.

3. Click on the lightbulb icon in the Layer drop-dwon list next to the Ceiling layer name. You can also click on the checkbox labeled On in the Details section of the dialog box so that no check appears there. In either case, the lightbulb icon changes from yellow to gray to indicate that the layer is off.

TIP   By momentarily placing the cursor on an icon in the layer, you will get a tool tip giving you a brief description of the icon's purpose.

4. Click on the OK button to exit the dialog box. When you return to the drawing, the header disappears because you have made it invisible by turning off its layer (see Figure 4.15).

FIGURE 4.15:

Bathroom with Ceiling layer turned off

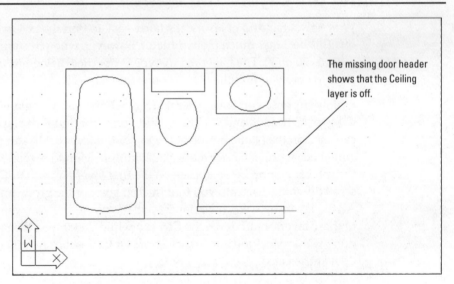

The missing door header shows that the Ceiling layer is off.

You can also control layer visibility using the Layer drop-down list on the Object Properties toolbar.

1. On the Object Properties toolbar, click the Layer drop-down list.

2. Find the Ceiling layer and notice that its lightbulb icon is gray. This tells you that the layer is off and not visible.

3. Click on the lightbulb icon to make it yellow.

4. Now click on the drawing area to close the Layer drop-down list, and the door header reappears.

Figure 4.16 explains the role of the other icons in the Layer drop-down list.

FIGURE 4.16:

The drop-down Layer list icons

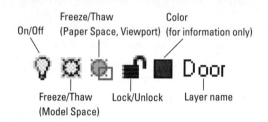

Finding the Layers You Want

With only a handful of layers, it's fairly easy to find the layer you want to turn off. This becomes much more difficult, however, when the number of layers exceeds 20 or 30. The Layer & Linetype Properties dialog box offers some useful tools to help you find the layers you want fast.

Now suppose you have several layers whose names begin with C, such as C-lights, C-header, and C-pattern, and you want find those layers quickly. You can click on the Name button at the top of the layer list to sort the layer names in alphabetical order. Click on the Name button again to reverse the order. To select those layers for processing, click on the first layer name that starts with C; then scroll down the list until you find the last layer of the group and Shift click on it. All the layers between those layers will be selected. If you want to deselect some of those layers, hold down the Ctrl key while clicking on the layer names you don't want to include in your selection. Or Ctrl + click on other layer names you do want selected.

The Color and Linetype buttons at the top of the list let you control what layers appear in the list by virtue of their color or line-type assignments. Other buttons will sort the list by virtue of the status: On/Off, Freeze/Thawed, Locked/Unlocked, and so forth. See the *Other Layer Options* sidebar later in this chapter.

NOTE　To delete all the objects on a layer, you can set the current layer to the one you want to edit, and then freeze or lock all the others. Click on Erase in the Modify toolbar and then type **A** ⏎⏎. The A issues the All selection option.

Now try changing the layer settings again, turning off all the layers except Wall and Ceiling and leaving just a simple rectangle. In the exercise, you'll get a chance to experiment with the On/Off options of the Layer & Linetype Properties dialog box.

1. Click on the Layers button in the Object Properties toolbar, or on Format ➤ Layers in the pull-down menus.

2. Click on the topmost layer name in the List box; then Shift + click on the bottom-most layer name. All the layer names will highlight.

TIP　Another way to select all the layers at once in the Layers & Linetype Properties dialog box is to right-click on the layer list box; then click on the Select All option from the pop-up menu that appears. And if you want to clear your selections, you can right-click on the layer list and select Clear all.

---

3. Control + click on the Wall and Ceiling layers to deselect them and thus exempt them from your next action.

4. Click on a lightbulb icon of any of the highlighted layer names or click on the On checkbox in the Details section of the dialog box to clear the checkmark.

5. A message appears warning you that the current layer will be turned off. Click OK in the message box. The lightbulb icons turn gray to show that the selected layers have been turned off.

6. Click on the OK button. The drawing now appears with only the Wall and Ceiling layers displayed (see Figure 4.17).

7. Open the Layer & Linetype Properties dialog box again and select all the layers as you did in step 2 and 3, and then click on the On button, or on any of the gray light bulbs, to turn on all the layers at once.

8. Click on OK to return to the drawing.

FIGURE 4.17:

Bathroom with all layers except Wall and Ceiling turned off

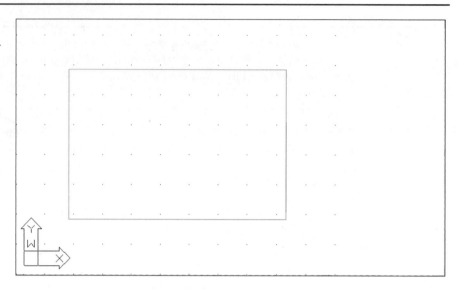

In this exercise, you turned off a set of layers with a single click on a lightbulb icon. You can freeze/thaw, lock/unlock, or change the color of a group of layers in a similar manner by clicking on the appropriate layer property. For example, if you had clicked on a color swatch of one of the selected layers, the Select Color dialog box would appear, allowing you to set the color for all the selected layers.

Other Layer Options

You may have noticed the *Freeze* and *Thaw* buttons in the Layer & Linetype Properties dialog box. These options are similar to the On and Off buttons—however, Freeze not only makes layers invisible, it also tells AutoCAD to ignore the contents of those layers when you use the All response to the Select object prompt. Freezing layers can also save time when you issue a command that regenerates a complex drawing. This is because AutoCAD ignores objects on frozen layers during Regen. You will get firsthand experience with Freeze and Thaw in Chapter 6.

Another pair of Layer & Linetype Properties options, *Lock* and *Unlock*, offer a function similar to Freeze and Thaw. If you lock a layer, you will be able to view and snap to objects on that layer, but you won't be able to edit those objects. This feature is useful when you are working on a crowded drawing and you don't want to accidentally edit portions of it. You can lock all the layers except those you intend to edit, and then proceed to work without fear of making accidental changes.

Taming an Unwieldy List of Layers

Chances are, you will eventually end up with a fairly long list of layers. Managing such a list can become a nightmare, but AutoCAD provides the Layer Filter dialog box to help you locate and isolate only those layers you need to work with.

To use layer filters, you click on the Show drop-down list near the top of the Layer & Linetype Properties dialog box. This drop-down list contains a list of options described here in Table 4.2. See *Using External References* in Chapter 6 for information on Xref-dependent layers.

TABLE 4.2: The Filter options

Filter Options	What It Filters
All	All layers regardless of their status
All in use	All layers that have objects assigned to them
All unused	All layers that do not have objects assigned to them
All Xref dependent	All layers that contain Xref objects
All not Xref dependent	All layers that do not contain Xref objects
All that pass filter	All layers that conform to filter criteria set in the Set Filter dialog box
Set Filter Dialog...	Opens the Set Filter dialog box

If you click on the Set Filter Dialog… option at the bottom of the list, you open the Set Filter dialog box. Here you can filter out the layers you want to show in the layer list by indicating the layers' characteristics.

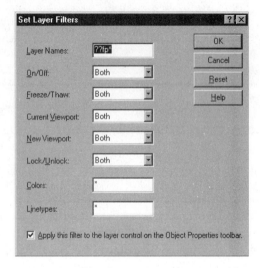

Now suppose you have a drawing whose layer names are set up to help you easily identify floor plan data versus ceiling plan data as in the following list.

A-FP-WALL-JAMB

A-RP-WIND-JAMB

A-FP-WIND-SILL

A-CP-WIND-HEAD

A-CP-DOOR-HEAD

L-FP-CURB

C-FP-ELEV

NOTE These layer examples are loosely based on a layer naming convention devised by the American Institute of Architects. As you can see from this example, careful naming of layers can help you manage them.

The first character in the layer name designates the discipline related to that layer: *A* for architectural, *L* for landscape, *C* for civil, and so on. In this example, layers whose names contain the two characters FP signify floor plan layers. CP designates ceiling information.

If you want to isolate only those layers that have to do with floor plans, regardless of their discipline, you enter **??FP*** in the Layer Names input box, and then click on OK. Now only the layers whose names contain the letters FP as their third and fourth character will appear in the list of layers. You can then easily turn all these layers off, change their color assignment, or change other settings quickly, without having to wade through other layers you don't want to touch.

NOTE In the ??FP* example, the question marks tell AutoCAD that the first two characters in the layer name can be anything. The "FP" tells AutoCAD that the layer name must contain F and P in these two places of the name. The asterisk (*) at the end tells AutoCAD that the remaining characters can be anything. The question marks (??) and asterisk are known as wildcard characters. They are commonly used filtering tools for DOS and UNIX operating systems.

The other two input boxes near the bottom, Colors and Linetypes, let you control what layers appear in the list by virtue of their color or line-type assignments. The five pop-up lists let you filter layers by virtue of the status: On/Off, Freeze/Thawed, Locked/Unlocked, and so forth. See the *Other Layer Options* sidebar earlier in this chapter.

As the number of layers in a drawing grows, you will find layer filters to be an indispensable tool. But bear in mind that the successful use of the layer filters depends on a careful layer-naming convention. If you are producing architectural plans, you may want to consider the American Institute of Architects (AIA) layering guidelines.

Assigning Line Types to Layers

You will often want to use different line types to show hidden lines, center lines, fence lines, or other non-continuous lines. You can set a layer to have not only a color assignment but also a line-type assignment. AutoCAD comes with several line types, as shown in Figure 4.18. From the top of one image to the bottom of the continued image of Figure 4.18, we can see Standard line types, then ISO and

Complex line types, and then a series of lines that can be used to illustrate gas and water lines in civil work, or batt insulation in a wall cavity. ISO line types are designed to be used with specific plotted line widths and line-type scales. For example, if you are using a pen width of .5mm, the line type scale of the drawing should be set to .5 as well (see Chapter 12 for more information on plotting and line-type scale). The complex line types at the bottom of the figure offer industry specific lines such as gas and water lines for civil work, and a line type that can be used to symbolize batt insulation in a wall cavity. You can also create your own line types (see Chapter 19).

WARNING Be aware that line types that contain text, such as the gas sample, will use the current text height and font to determine the size and appearance of the text displayed in the line. A text height of 0 (zero) will display the text properly in most cases. See Chapter 8 for more on text styles.

AutoCAD stores line-type descriptions in an external file named Acad.lin. You can edit this file in a word processor to create new line types or to modify existing ones. You will see how this is done in Chapter 19.

Adding a Line Type to a Drawing

To see how line types work, add a dash-dot line in the bathroom plan to indicate a shower curtain rod.

1. Open the Layers & Linetype Properties dialog box.

2. Click New and then type **Pole** to create a new layer called Pole.

TIP If you are in a hurry, you can simultaneously load a line type and assign it to a layer by using the Layer command. In this exercise, you would enter **-Layer** ↵ at the command prompt. Then enter **L** ↵, **dashdot** ↵, **pole** ↵, and then ↵ to exit the Layer command.

3. Click on the word "Continuous" at the far right of the Pole layer listing (under the Linetype column).

The Select Linetype dialog box appears.

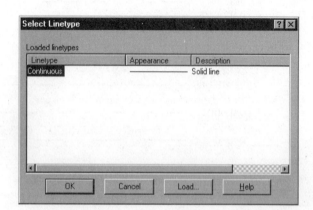

This dialog box offers a list of line types to choose from. In a new file such as the Bath file, only one line type is available by default. You must load any additional line type you may want to use.

4. Click on the Load at the bottom of the dialog box. The Load or Reload Linetype dialog box appears.

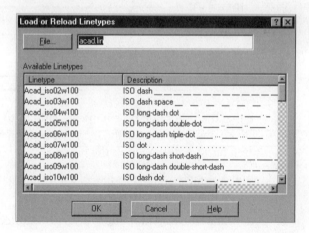

FIGURE 4.18:

Standard AutoCAD line types

BORDER	—— — —— —— —— —— —— —— • —— —— ——
BORDER2	– – –– – –– – –– –– – –– –– – –– –– –
BORDERX2	——— ——— • ——— ——— • ——— ——— • ———
CENTER	—— – —— – —— – —— – —— – —
CENTER2	— – —— – —— – —— – —— – —— – —— – ——
CENTERX2	——— —— ——— —— ——— —— ———
DASHDOT	— • — • — • — • — • — • — • — • — • —
DASHDOT2	– • – • – • – • – • – • – • – • – • – • – • – • – •
DASHDOTX2	——— • ——— • ——— • ——— • ———
DASHED	— — — — — — — — — — — — —
DASHED2	– –
DASHEDX2	——— ——— ——— ——— ——— ——— ———
DIVIDE	— • • — • • — • • — • • — • • — • • —
DIVIDE2	– • • – • • – • • – • • – • • – • • – • • – •
DIVIDEX2	——— • • ——— • • ——— • • ——— • • ———
DOT	• •
DOT2	••
DOTX2	• • • • • • • • • • • • • • • • • • •
HIDDEN	– –
HIDDEN2	--
HIDDENX2	— — — — — — — — — — — — — — — —
PHANTOM	—— – – —— – – —— – – —— – – ——
PHANTOM2	— – – — – – — – – — – – — – – — – – —
	—— — — —— — — —— — — ——

Notice that the list of line type names is similar to theLayer drop-down list. You can sort the names alphabetically or by description by clicking on the Linetype or Description buttons at the top of the list.

5. In the Available Linetypes list, scroll down to locate the Dashdot line type, click on it, and then click OK.

6. Notice that the Dashdot line type is now added to the line types available in the Select Linetype dialog box.

7. Click on Dashdot to highlight it; then click OK. Now Dashdot appears in the Pole layer listing under Linetype.

8. With the Pole layer still highlighted, click the Current button to make the Pole layer current.

FIGURE 4.18:
CONTINUED

Standard AutoCAD
line types

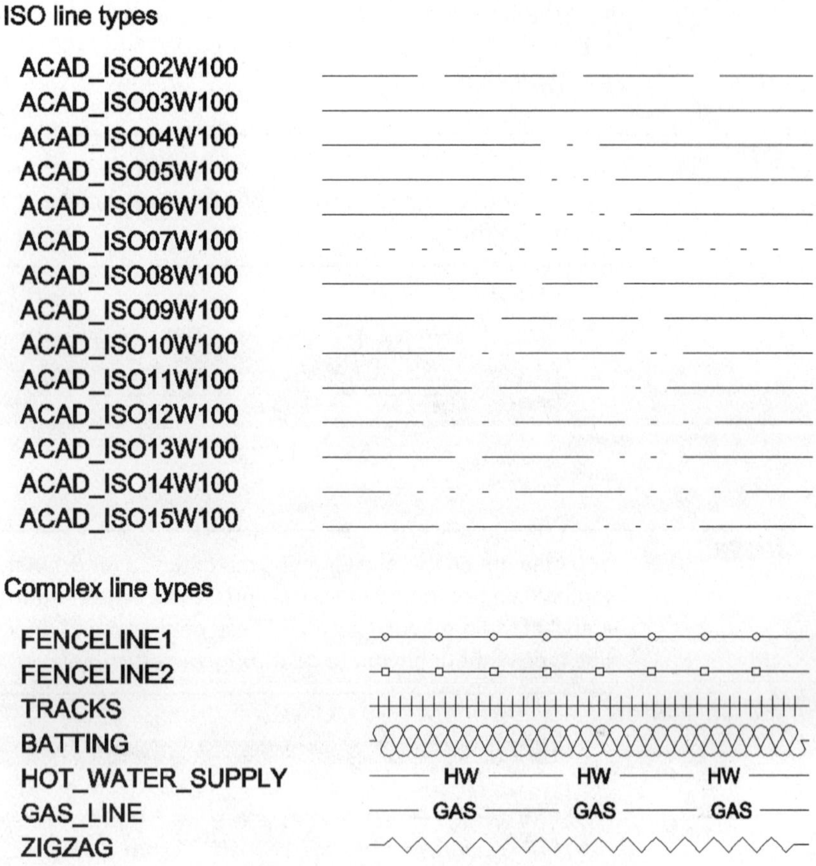

ISO line types

ACAD_ISO02W100	_____
ACAD_ISO03W100	_____
ACAD_ISO04W100	_____
ACAD_ISO05W100	_____
ACAD_ISO06W100	_____
ACAD_ISO07W100	_____
ACAD_ISO08W100	_____
ACAD_ISO09W100	_____
ACAD_ISO10W100	_____
ACAD_ISO11W100	_____
ACAD_ISO12W100	_____
ACAD_ISO13W100	_____
ACAD_ISO14W100	_____
ACAD_ISO15W100	_____

Complex line types

FENCELINE1
FENCELINE2
TRACKS
BATTING
HOT_WATER_SUPPLY
GAS_LINE
ZIGZAG

9. Click on OK to exit the dialog box.

10. Turn off the Running Osnap mode; then draw a line across the opening of the tub area, from coordinate 4'-4", 1'-10" to coordinate 4'-4", 6'-10".

Controlling Line Type Scale

Although you have designated this line to be a Dashdot line, it appears to be solid. Zoom in to a small part of the line, and you'll see that the line is indeed as you specified.

Since you are working at a scale of 1"=1', you must adjust the scale of your line types accordingly. This, too, is accomplished in the Layer & Linetype Properties dialog box.

1. Click on the Linetype button in the Properties toolbar, or on Format ➤ Linetype in the pull-down menus. The Layer &Linetype Properties dialog box appears. This is the same dialog box you see when you click on the Layers tool, but in this case the Linetypes tab is visible.

TIP

You can also use the Ltscale system variable to set the line-type scale. Type **Ltscale** ↵, and at the LTSCALE New scale factor <1.0000> prompt, enter **12** ↵.

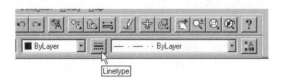

NOTE

You may notice that the Linetype tab of the Layer & Linetype Properties dialog box also contains the Load and Delete button options that you saw in step 4 of the previous exercise. These offer a way to directly load or delete a line type without having to go through a particular layer's line type setting.

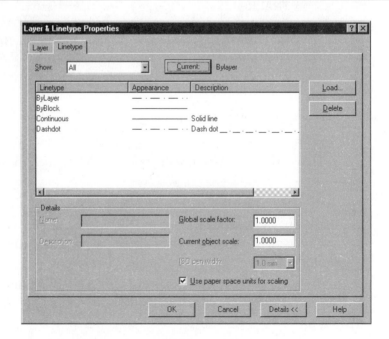

2. Double-click on the Global Scale Factor input box, and then type **12**. This is the scale conversion factor for a 1"=1' scale (see Table 3.3).

3. Click on OK. The drawing regenerates, and the shower curtain rod is displayed in the line type and at the scale you designated.

4. Click on the Zoom Previous tool so your drawing looks like Figure 4.19.

FIGURE 4.19:

The completed
bathroom

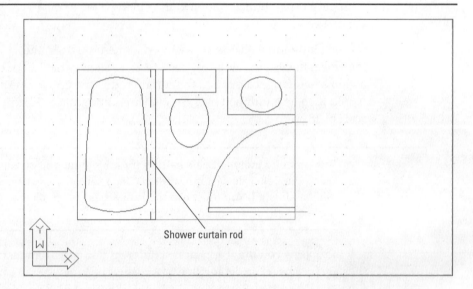

Shower curtain rod

TIP

If you change the line type of a layer or object but the object remains a continuous line, check the Ltscale system variable. It should be set to your drawing scale factor. If this doesn't work, set the Viewres system variable to a higher value (see Chapter 6). Also, line-type scales act differently depending on whether you are in Model Space or Paper Space. See Chapter 12 for more on Model and Paper Space.

Remember that if you assign a line type to a layer, everything you draw on that layer will be of that line type. This includes arcs, polylines, circles, and traces. As explained in the *Setting Individual Colors, Line Types, and Line-Type Scales* sidebar late in this chapter, you can also assign different colors and line types to individual objects, rather than relying on their layer assignment to define color and line type. However, you may want to avoid assigning colors and line types directly to objects until you have some experience with AutoCAD and a good grasp of your drawing's organization.

In the last exercise, you changed the global line-type scale setting. This affects all non-continuous line-types within the current drawing. You can also change the line-type scale of individual objects, using the Properties button on the Object Properties toolbar. Or you can set a default line-type scale for all new objects, with the Current button option in the Linetype tab of the Layer & Linetype Properties dialog box.

When individual objects are assigned a line-type scale, they are still affected by the global line-type scale set by the Ltscale system variable. For example, say you assign a line-type scale of 2 to the curtain rod in the previous example. This scale would then be multiplied by the global line-type scale of 12, for a final line-type scale of 48.

TIP

The default Linetype Scale setting for individual objects can also be set using the Celtscale system variable. Once set, only newly created objects will be affected. You must use the Properties tool to change the line-type scale of individual existing objects.

If the objects you draw appear in a different line type from that of the layer they are on, check the default line type, using the Linetype tab of the Layer and Linetype Properties dialog box. Click on Format ➤ Linetype. Highlight Bylayer in the Linetype list, and then click the Current button. Also, check the line-type scale of the object itself, using the Properties button. A different line-type scale can make a line appear to have an assigned line type that may not be what you expect. See the *Setting Individual Colors, Line Types, and Line-Type Scales* sidebar below.

WARNING

The display of line types also depends on whether you are in Paper Space or Model Space. If your efforts to control line-type scale have no effect on your line type's visibility, you may be in Paper Space. See Chapter 12 for more information on how to control line-type scale while in Paper Space.

If you are working through the tutorial, your last task here is to set up an insertion point for the current drawing, to facilitate its insertion into other drawings in the future.

1. Type **Base** ↵.

2. At the Base point <0'-0",0'-0">: prompt, pick the upper-left corner of the bathroom. The bathroom drawing is now complete.

3. Choose File ➤ Save to record your work up to now.

Setting Individual Colors, Line Types, and Line-Type Scales

If you prefer, you can set up AutoCAD to assign specific colors and line types to objects, instead of having objects take on the color and line-type settings of the layer on which they reside. Normally, objects are given a default color and line type called Bylayer, which means each object takes on the color or line type of its assigned layer. (You've probably noticed the word Bylayer in the Object Properties toolbar and in various dialog boxes.)

Use the Properties tool on the Object Properties toolbar to change the color or line type of existing objects. This tool opens a dialog box that lets you set the properties of individual objects. For new objects, use the Color tool on the Object Properties toolbar to set the current default color to red (for example), instead of Bylayer. The Color tool opens the Select Color dialog box, where you select your color from a toolbar. Then everything you draw will be red, regardless of the current layer color.

For line types, you can use the Line Type drop-down list in the Object Properties toolbar to select a default line type for all new objects. The list only shows line types that have already been loaded into the drawing, so you must have first loaded a line type before you can select it.

Another possible color and line-type assignment is Byblock, which is also set with the Properties button. Byblock makes everything you draw white, until you turn your drawing into a block and then insert the block on a layer with an assigned color. The objects then take on the color of that layer. This behavior is similar to that of objects drawn on layer 0. The Byblock line type works similarly to the Byblock color.

Finally, if you want to set the line-type scale for each individual object, instead of relying on the global line-type scale (the Ltscale system variable), you can use the Properties button to modify the line-type scale of individual objects. Or you can use the Object Creation Modes dialog box (via the Object Creation button in

Continued on next page

the Object Properties toolbar) to set the line-type scale to be applied to new objects. In place of using the Properties button, you can set the Celtscale system variable to the line-type scale you want for new objects.

As we mentioned earlier, you should stay away from assigning colors and line-types to individual objects until you are comfortable with AutoCAD; and even then, use color and line type assignments carefully. Other users who work on your drawing may have difficulty understanding your drawing's organization if you assign color and line type properties indiscriminately.

Keeping Track of Blocks and Layers

The Insert and the Layer & Linetype Properties dialog boxes let you view the blocks and layers available in your drawing, by listing them in a window. The Layer & Linetype Properties dialog box also includes information on the status of layers. However, you may forget the layer on which an object resides. The List button on the Object Properties toolbar enables you to get information about individual objects, as well as blocks.

1. Click and hold the Distance tool so that a flyout appears.

2. Drag the pointer down to the List tool and select it.

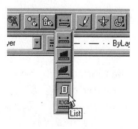

TIP

If you just want to quickly check what layer an object is on, click on it. Its layer will appear in the Layer list of the Properties toolbar. You can also click on the Properties tool in the Standard toolbar, and then click on the object in question. You will get a dialog box showing you the basic properties of the object, including its layer setting.

3. At the `Select object` prompt, click on the Tub and then press ↵. The AutoCAD Text Window appears.

4. In the Text Window, you will see a listing that shows not only the layer that the tub is on, but its space, insertion point, name, color, line type, rotation angle, and scale.

NOTE
The Space property you see listed for the Tub block designates whether the object resides in Model Space or Paper Space. You'll learn more about these spaces in Chapters 6 and 12.

Using the Log File Feature

NEW!

Eventually, you will want a permanent record of block and layer listings. This is especially true if you work on drawing files that are being used by others. Here's a way to get a permanent record of the layers and blocks within a drawing, using the Log File option under the Environment Preferences.

1. Minimize the Text Window (click on the Minimize button in the upper-right corner of the text window).

2. Click on Tools ➤ Preferences, or type **pr** ↵. The Preferences dialog box appears.

3. Click on the General tab at the top of the dialog box.

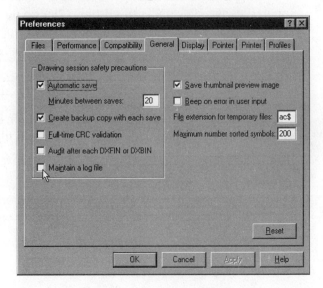

4. Click on the Maintain a Log File checkbox in the bottom-left side of the dialog box. An X appears in the checkbox.

5. Click on OK; then type -**LAYER** ↵ (don't forget the minus sign) at the command prompt, and then **?** ↵ ↵. The AutoCAD Text Window appears and a listing of all the layers scrolls into view.

6. Press F2 to return to the AutoCAD drawing screen. Then click on Tools ➤ Preferences to reopen the Preferences dialog box.

7. Deselect the Maintain a log file checkbox, and then click on OK.

8. Use the Windows Notepad to open the AutoCAD log file, Acad.log, located in the \AutoCAD 14\ directory. You will see that the layer listing is recorded there.

With the Log File feature, you can record virtually anything that appears in the command prompt. You can even record an entire AutoCAD session. The log file can also be helpful in constructing Script files to automate tasks (see *Automating a Slide Presentation* in Chapter 15 for more on Scripts). To have hard copy of the log file, just print it from an application such as Windows Notepad or your favorite word processor.

If you wish, you can arrange to keep the Acad.log file in a directory other than the default AutoCAD subdirectory. This setting is also in the Preferences dialog box under the Files tab. Locate the Menu, Help, Log, and Miscellaneous File Names listing in the Search Path, File Names, and File Locations list box. Click on the plus sign next to this listing. The listing expands to show the different types of support files available under this listing. Click on the plus sign next to the Log File listing. You will see the location for the Acad.log file.

NOTE   See Appendix B for more on the AutoCAD Preferences dialog box settings.

You can double-click on the acad.log file location listing to open a Select a File dialog box and specify a different location and file name for your log file. This dialog box is a typical Windows file dialog box.

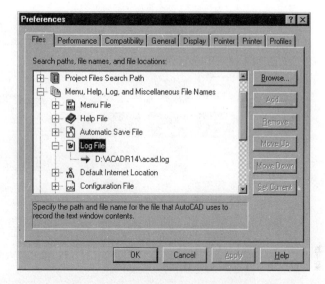

TIP

Once you've settled on a location on disk for the log file, use the File Manager to associate the log file with the Windows Notepad or Write application. Then click and drag the file to the AutoCAD program group. This gives you quick access to your log file by simply double-clicking on its icon in the AutoCAD program group.

Finding Files on Your Hard Disk

As your library of symbols and files grows, you may begin to have difficulty keeping track of them. Fortunately, AutoCAD offers a utility that lets you quickly locate a file anywhere in your computer. The Find File utility searches your hard disk for specific files. You can have it search one drive or several, or you can limit the search to one directory. You can limit the search to specific file names or use DOS wildcards to search for files with similar names.

The following exercise steps you through a sample Find File task.

1. Click on File ➤ Open. In the Select File dialog box, click on Find File to display the Browse/Search dialog box.

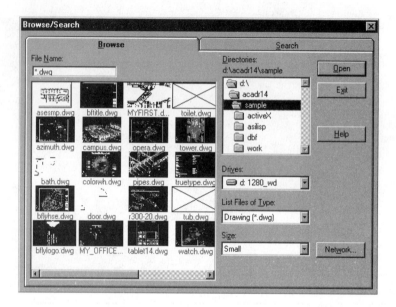

Find File can also be accessed using the Find File button in any AutoCAD file dialog box, including the File option of the Insert Block tool. Find File can help you access and maintain your symbols library.

The Browse/Search dialog box has two tabs: Browse and Search. In the Browse page are all the drawings in the current directory, displayed as thumbnail views so you can easily identify them. You can open a file by double-clicking on its thumbnail view, or by entering its name in the File Name input box at the top.

The Size drop-down list in the Browse page of the Browse/Search dialog box lets you choose the size of the thumbnail views shown in the list box—small, medium, and large. You can scroll through the views using the scroll bars at the bottom of the list box.

2. Click on the Search tab to open the page of Search functions. Use the Search Pattern input box to enter the name of the file for which you wish to search. The default is *.dwg, which will cause Find File to search for all AutoCAD drawing files. Several other input boxes help you set a variety of other search criteria, such as the date stamp of the drawing, the type of drawing, and the drive and path to be searched. For now, leave these settings as is.

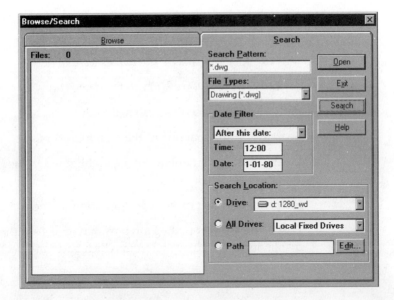

3. Click on the Search button. In a few seconds, a listing of files that meet the criteria specified in the input boxes appears in the Files list on the left, along with thumbnail views of each file. You can click on a file name in the list, and then click on the Open button to open the file in the drawing editor.

4. When you're ready, click on Exit to exit the Browse/Search dialog box, and then click on Cancel to exit the Open File dialog box.

NOTE   In the Browse/Search dialog box, a drawing from a pre-Release 13 version of AutoCAD will be represented as a box with an X through it.

In this exercise you performed a search using the default settings. These settings caused AutoCAD to search for files with the .dwg file name extension, created after 12:00 midnight on January 1, 1980, in the \ACADWIN directory.

Here are descriptions of the items in the Browse/Search dialog box:

Search Pattern   lets you give specific file-name search criteria using DOS wildcard characters.

File Types   lets you select from a set of standard file types.

Time and Date let you specify a cutoff time and date. Files created before the specified time and date are ignored.

Drives lets you specify the drives to search.

All Drives lets you search all the drives on your computer.

Path lets you specify a path to search.

Search button that begins the search process.

Open button that opens the file highlighted in the file list, after a search is performed.

Help button that provides information on the use of Browse/Search.

Edit button, next to the Path box, that opens another dialog box, displaying a directory tree from which you can select a search path.

Inserting Symbols with Drag and Drop

If you prefer to manage your symbols library using the Windows Explorer, or to use another third-party file manager for locating and managing your symbols, you'll appreciate AutoCAD's support for Drag and Drop. With this feature, you can click and drag a file from the Windows Explorer into the AutoCAD window. You can also drag and drop from the Windows Find File or Folder utility. Auto-CAD will automatically start the Insert command to insert the file. Drag and Drop also works with a variety of other AutoCAD support files. AutoCAD also supports Drag and Drop for other types of data from applications that support Microsoft's ActiveX technology. Table 4.3 shows a list of files with which you can use Drag and Drop, and the functions associated with them.

TABLE 4.3: AutoCAD support for Drag and Drop

File Type	Command Issued	Function Performed When File Is Dropped
.dxf	Dxfin,	Imports .dxf files
.dwg	Insert	Imports or plots drawing files
.txt	Dtext	Imports texts via Dtext
.lin	Linetype	Loads line types

TABLE 4.3 CONTINUED: AutoCAD support for Drag and Drop

File Type	Command Issued	Function Performed When File Is Dropped
.mnu, .mnx	Menu	Loads menus
.ps	Psin	Imports PostScript files
.psb, .shp, .shx	Style	Loads fonts or shapes
.scr	Script	Runs Script
.lsp	(Load..)	Loads AutoLISP routine
.exe, .exp	(Xload..)	Loads ADS application

TIP You can also drag and drop from folder shortcuts placed on your desktop or even from a Web site.

If You Want to Experiment...

If your application is not architecture, you may want to experiment with creating some other types of symbols. You might also start thinking about a layering system that suits your particular needs.

Open a new file called Mytemp. In it, create layers named 1 through 8 and assign each layer the color that corresponds to its number. For example, give layer 1 the color 1 (red), layer 2 the color 2 (yellow), and so on. Draw each part shown in Figure 4.20, and turn each part into a file on disk using the Export (File ➤ Export) or the Wblock command. When specifying a file name, use the name indicated for each part in the figure. For the insertion point, also use the points indicated in the figure. Use the Osnap modes (Chapter 2) to select the insertion points.

When you are done creating the parts, exit the file using File ➤ Exit, and then open a new file. Set up the drawing as an engineering drawing with a scale of 1/4"=1" on an 11"×17" sheet. Create the drawing in Figure 4.21 using the Insert Block command to place your newly created parts.

FIGURE 4.20:

A typical set of symbols

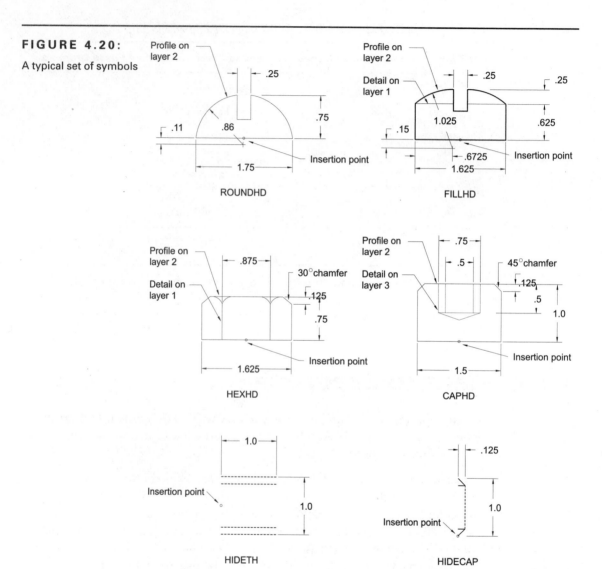

Note:
Give layer 3 the HIDDEN line type.
Put all of HIDETH and HIDECAP on layer 3.
Don't draw dimensions, just use them for reference.

FIGURE 4.21:

Draw this part using
the symbols you create

1. Set the snap mode to .125 and be sure it is on.
   Set Ltscale to .25. Draw the figure at right
   using the dimensions shown as a guide.

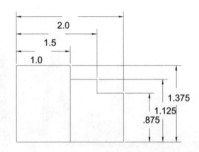

2. Insert the HEXHD drawing at the location shown
   in the figure at right. Enter .25 for a scale
   value and when you are asked for a rotation
   angle, visually orient it as shown.

3. Insert the HIDETH file at the same point and scale
   as the HEXHD file, and then explode it.

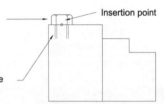

4. Insert the HIDECAP file as shown at right.
   Enter .25 for the scale and rotate it so it looks
   like this figure.

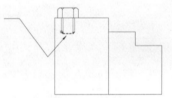

5. Do the same sequence of steps to add the screw
   shown at right. This time, use a scale factor
   of .125 when you insert the ROUNDHD file. When
   you insert the HIDETH file, enter a value of 1
   for the X scale factor and .125 for the Y scale
   factor.

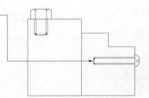

PART II

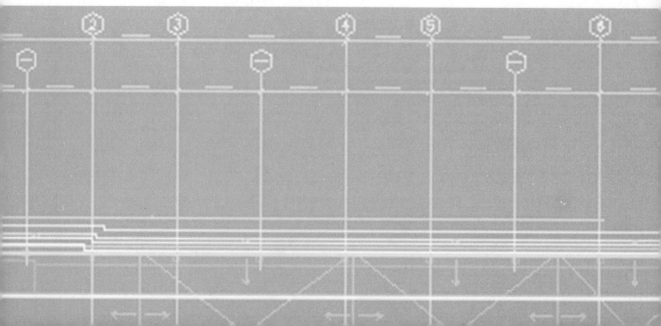

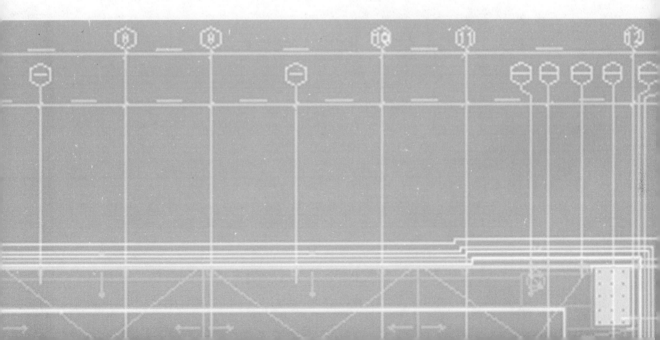

Building on the Basics

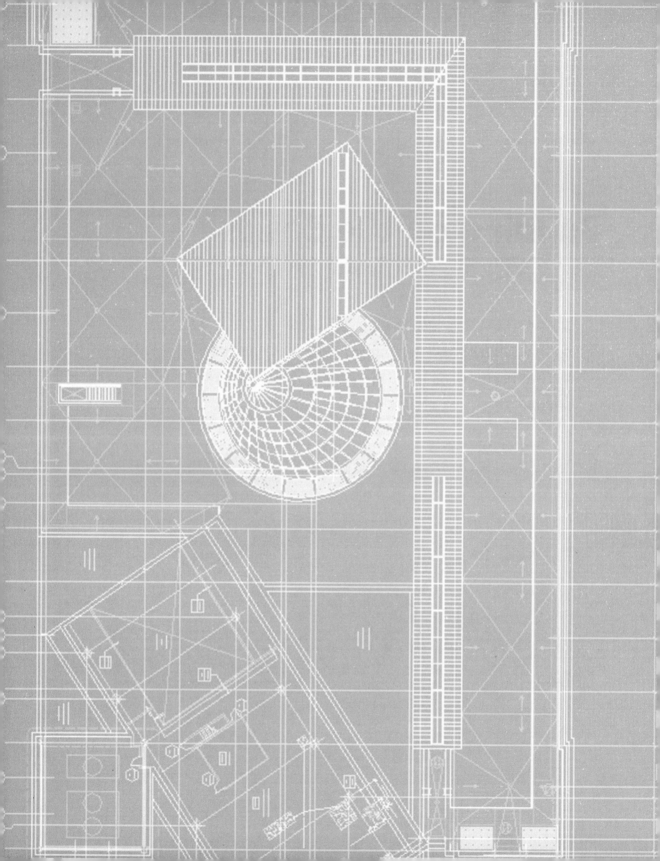

Editing
for Productivity

- Creating and Using Templates

- Copying an Object Multiple Times

- Developing Your Drawing

- Drawing Parallel Lines

- Eliminating Layers, Line Types, Shapes, and Styles

There are at least five commands devoted to duplicating objects, ten if you include the Grips options. Why so many? If you're an experienced drafter, you know that technical drawing is often tedious. So AutoCAD offers a variety of ways to reuse existing geometry, thereby automating much of the repetitious work usually associated with manual drafting.

In this chapter, as you finish drawing the studio apartment unit, you will explore some of the ways to exploit existing files and objects while constructing your drawing. For example, you will use existing files as prototypes for new files, eliminating the need to set up layers, scales, and sheet sizes for similar drawings. With AutoCAD you can also duplicate objects in multiple arrays. You have already seen how to use the Osnap overrides on objects to locate points for drawing complex forms. We will look at other ways of using lines to aid your drawing.

And, because you will begin to use Zoom more in the exercises of this chapter, we will review this command as we go along. You'll also discover the Pan command—another tool to help you get around in your drawing.

You're already familiar with many of the commands you will use to draw the apartment unit. So, rather than going through every step of the drawing process, the exercises will sometimes ask you to copy the drawing from a figure, using notes and dimensions as guides and putting objects on the indicated layers. If you have trouble remembering a command you've already learned, just go back and review the appropriate section of the book.

Creating and Using Templates

If you are familiar with the Microsoft Office suite, you are probably familiar with templates. A template is a blank file that is already set up for a specific application. For example, you might want to have letters set up in a way that is different from a report or invoice. You can have a template for each type of document, each set up for the needs of that document. That way, you don't have to spend time reformatting each new document you create.

Similarly, AutoCAD offers templates, which are drawing files that contain custom settings designed for a particular function. Out of the box, AutoCAD offers templates for ISO, ANSI, DIN, and JIS standard drawing formats. But you aren't limited to these "canned" templates. You can create your own templates set up for your particular style and method of drawing.

If you find that you use a particular drawing setup frequently, you can turn one or more of your typical drawings into a template. For example, you may want to create a set of drawings with the same scale and sheet size as an existing drawing. By turning a typical drawing into a template, you can save a lot of setup time for subsequent drawings.

Creating a Template

The following exercise guides you through creating and using a template drawing for your studio's kitchenette. Because the kitchenette will use the same layers, settings, scale, and sheet size as the bathroom drawing, you can use the Bath file as a prototype.

1. Start AutoCAD in the usual way.

2. Click on File ➤ Open.

3. At the Select File dialog box, locate the Bath file you created in the last chapter. You can also use the file 04c-bath.dwg from the companion CD-ROM.

4. Click on the Erase button in the Modify toolbar; then type **A** ↵↵. This will erase all the objects that make up the bathroom.

5. Choose File ➤ Save As; then at the Save Drawing As dialog box, open the Save as Type drop-down list and select Drawing Template File (*.dwt). The file list window will change to display the current template files in the \Template folder.

NOTE   When you choose the Drawing Template File option in the Save Drawing As dialog box, AutoCAD automatically opens the folder containing the template files. The standard installation creates the folder named Template to contain the template files. If you wish to place your templates in a different folder, you can change the default template location using the Preferences dialog box. (Tools ➤ Preferences). Use the Files tab and then double-click on Template Drawing File Location in the list. Double-click on the folder name that appears just below Template Drawing File Location; then select a new location from the Browse for Folder dialog box that appears.

---

6. Double click on the File Name input box and enter the name **8x11h.**

7. Click OK. The Template Description dialog box appears.

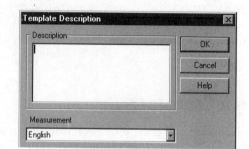

8. Enter the following description:

"Architectural half inch scale drawing on 8 1/2 by 11 inch media."

9. Click Save. You have just created a template.

TIP

While AutoCAD allows long names, only 8 character names appear correctly in the Use a Template list box that you will see in the next exercise. The Template Description dialog box lets you supply more descriptive information regarding your template.

Notice that the current drawing is now the template file you just saved. As with other Windows programs, the File ➤ Save As option makes the saved file current. This also shows that you can edit template files just as you would regular drawing files.

Using a Template

Now let's see how a template is used. You'll use the template you just created as the basis for a new drawing you will work on in this chapter.

1. Choose File New.

2. At the Create New Drawing dialog box, click on the Use a Template button. A list box entitled Select a Template appears, along with a Preview window.

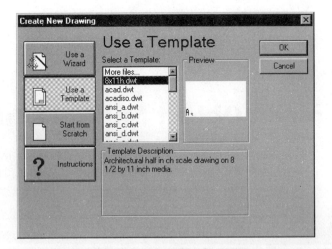

3. Click on 8x11h.dwt from the Use a Template list box. The file is displayed in the Preview window. Since it is a blank file, nothing is displayed in the preview box. Also notice that the description you entered earlier in the Template Description dialog box appears in the Template Description area below the list.

TIP The More Files... option at the top of the Use a Template list box lets you browse your hard drive to locate other files for use as a template.

4. Click OK. It may not be obvious, but your new file is set up with the same architectural units and drawing limits as the bathroom drawing. It also contains the door, toilet, and tub blocks.

5. Now you need to give your new file a name. Choose File ➢ Save As. Then at the Save Drawing As dialog box, enter **Kitchen** for the file name and select the appropriate folder in which to save your new kitchen file.

6. Click Save to create the Kitchen file and close the dialog box.

You've created and used your own template file. Later, when you have established a comfortable working relationship with AutoCAD, you can create a set of templates that are custom made to your particular needs.

However, you don't need to create a template every time you want to re-use settings from another file. You can use an existing file as the basis or prototype for a new file without creating a template. Open the prototype file and then use File ➤ Save As to create a new version of the file under a new name. You can then edit the new version without affecting the original prototype file.

Copying an Object Multiple Times

Now let's explore the tools that let you quickly duplicate objects. In the next exercise, you will begin to draw parts to a small kitchen. The first exercise introduces the Array command, which enables you to draw the gas burners of a range top.

NOTE An array can be in either a circular pattern called a *polar array,* or a matrix of columns and rows called a *rectangular array.*

Making Circular Copies

To start the range top, you have to first set the layer on which you want to draw, and then draw a circle representing the edge of one burner.

1. Set the current layer to Fixture, and toggle the Snap mode on.

NOTE Since you used the Bath file as a template, the Running Osnaps for Endpoint, Midpoint, and Intersection are already turned on and available in this new file.

2. Click on Circle from the Draw toolbar, or type **C** ↵.

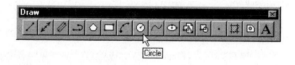

3. At the 3P/2P/TTR/<Center point> prompt, pick a point at coordinate 4',4'.

4. At the Diameter/<Radius> Drag prompt, enter **3** ↵. The circle appears.

Now you're ready to use the Array command to draw the burner grill. You will first draw one line representing part of the grill, and then use Array to create the copies.

1. Draw a 4"-long line starting from the coordinate 4'-1", 4'-0" and ending to the right of that point.

2. Zoom into the circle and line to get a better view. Your drawing should look like Figure 5.1.

FIGURE 5.1:

A close-up of the circle and line

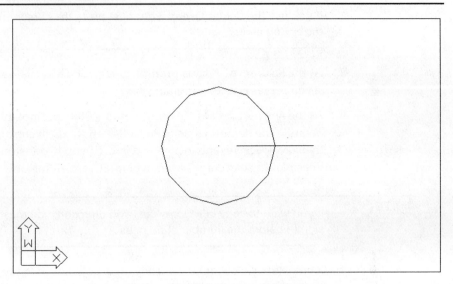

3. Click Array from the Modify toolbar, or type **AR** ↵.

4. At the Select object prompt, enter **L** ↵. This highlights the line you just drew.

5. Press ↵ to confirm your selection.

6. At the Rectangular or Polar array (<R>/P), type **P** ↵ to use the polar array option.

7. At the `Specify Center point of array` prompt, pick the center of the circle. You can either use the snap point at the center of the circle at coordinate 4',4', or use the Center Osnap.

TIP

Remember, to access Osnaps other than those set up as Running Osnaps, Shift + right-click the mouse; then select the Osnap from the pop-up menu.

WARNING

If you use the Center Osnap, you must place the cursor on the circle, not the circle's center point.

---

8. At the `Number of items` prompt, enter **8** ↵. This tells AutoCAD you want seven copies plus the original.

9. At the `Angle to fill (+=ccw,-=cw) <360>` prompt, press ↵ to accept the default. The default value of 360 tells AutoCAD to copy the objects so that they are spaced evenly over a 360° arc. (If you had instead entered 180°, the lines would be evenly spaced over a 180° arc, filling only half the circle.)

NOTE

If you want to copy in a clockwise (CW) direction, you must enter a minus sign (-) before the number of degrees.

---

10. At the `Rotate objects as they are copied?` `<Y>` prompt, press ↵ again to accept the default. The line copies around the center of the circle, rotating as it copies. Your drawing will look like Figure 5.2.

NOTE

In step 10, you could have the line maintain its horizontal orientation as it is copied around by entering **N** ↵. But since you want it to rotate about the array center, accept the default, **Y**.

FIGURE 5.2:

The completed gas burner

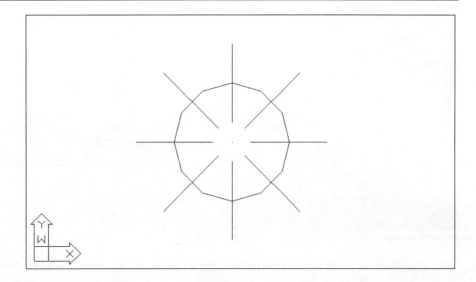

Making Row and Column Copies

Now you will draw the other three burners of the gas range by creating a rectangular array from the burner you just drew. You will first zoom back a bit to get a view of a larger area. Then you will proceed with the Array command.

1. Choose View ➢ Zoom ➢ Scale, or type **Z** ↵ **S** ↵.

2. Enter **.5x** ↵. Your drawing will look like Figure 5.3.

> **TIP** If you're not too fussy about the amount you want to zoom out, you can choose View ➢ Zoom ➢ Out to quickly reduce your view.

Entering **.5x** for the Zoom Scale value tells AutoCAD you want a view that reduces the width of the current view to fill half the display area, allowing you to see more of the work area. If you specify a Scale value greater than 1 (5, for example), you will magnify your current view. If you leave off the x, your new view will be in relation to the drawing limits rather than the current view.

Now you will finish the range top. Here you will get a chance to use the Rectangular Array option to create three additional burners.

213

FIGURE 5.3:

The preceding view
reduced by a factor of
0.5 times (0.5x)

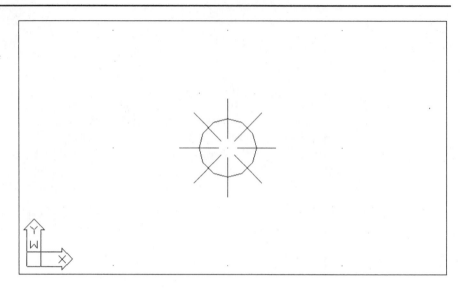

3. Click Array in the Modify toolbar again, or type **AR** ↵.

4. At the Select objects prompt, use a window to select the entire burner. Then press ↵ to confirm you selection.

5. Enter **R** ↵ at the Rectangular or Polar array (R/<P>) prompt to select the Rectangular option.

TIP   You can also type **Array** ↵ to start the Array command. Then, after confirming your selection of objects in step 4, type **R** ↵.

---

6. As mentioned earlier, a rectangular array is a matrix of columns and rows. At the Number of rows (--) <1> prompt, enter **2** ↵. This tells AutoCAD the number of copies you want vertically.

7. At the Number of columns (BV BV BV BV) <1> prompt, enter **2** ↵ again. This tells AutoCAD the number of copies you want horizontally.

8. At the Unit cell or distance between rows (—) prompt, enter **14** ↵. This tells AutoCAD that the vertical distance between the rows of burners is 14".

9. At the Distance between columns (BV BV BV BV) prompt, enter **16** ↵ to tell AutoCAD you want the horizontal distance between the columns of burners to be 16". Your screen will look like Figure 5.4.

NOTE Unlike prior versions of AutoCAD, the Array command now "remembers" whether you last used the polar or rectangular array option and offers that option as the default.

FIGURE 5.4:

The burners arrayed

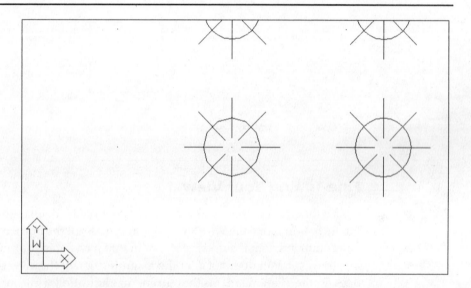

AutoCAD usually draws a rectangular array from bottom to top, and from left to right. You can reverse the direction of the array by giving negative values for the distance between columns and rows.

TIP At times you may want to do a rectangular array at an angle. To accomplish this you must first set the Snap Angle setting in the Drawing Aids dialog box (Tools ➤ Drawing Aids) to the desired angle. Then proceed with the Array command. Another method is to set the UCS to the desired angle. See *Defining a UCS* in Chapter 11.

You can also use the cursor to graphically indicate an *array cell* (see Figure 5.5). An array cell is a rectangle defining the distance between rows and columns. You may want to use this option when an object is available to use as a reference from which to determine column and row distances. For example, you may have drawn a crosshatch pattern, as on a calendar, within which you want to array an object. You would use the intersections of the hatch lines as references to define the array cell, which would be one square in the hatch pattern.

FIGURE 5.5:

An array cell

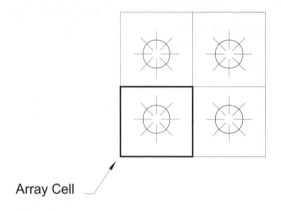

Array Cell

Fine-Tuning Your View

Notice that most of the burners do not appear on the display shown in back in Figure 5.4. To move the view over so you can see all the burners, you can use the Pan command. Pan is similar to Zoom in that it changes your view of the drawing; however, Pan does not alter the magnification of the view the way Zoom does. Rather, Pan maintains the current magnification while moving your view across the drawing, just as you would pan a camera across a landscape.

NOTE Pan is especially helpful when you have magnified an area to do some editing, and you need to get to a part of the drawing that is near your current view.

To activate the Pan command, follow these steps.

1. Click on the Pan Realtime tool in the Standard toolbar, or type **P** ↵.

A small hand-shaped cursor appears in place of the AutoCAD cursor.

2. Place the hand cursor in the center of the drawing area and then click and drag it downward and to the left. The view follows the motion of your mouse.

3. Continue to drag the view until it looks similar to Figure 5.6; then let go of the mouse.

To finish the kitchen, you will want a view that shows more of the drawing area. Continue with the following steps.

4. Now right-click the mouse. A pop-up list appears.

NOTE   The Pan/Zoom pop-up menu also appears when you right-click on your mouse during the Zoom Realtime command.

---

5. Select Zoom from the list. The cursor changes to the Zoom Realtime cursor.

6. Now place the cursor close to the top of the screen and click and drag the cursor downward to zoom out until your view looks like the top panel of

Figure 5.7. You may need to click and drag the zoom cursor a second time to achieve this view.

7. Right-click the mouse again, and then choose Exit from the pop-up menu. You're now ready to add more information to the kitchen drawing.

NOTE To exit the Pan Realtime or Zoom Realtime command without opening the pop-up menu, press the Esc key.

8. Now complete the kitchenette as indicated in the bottom panel of Figure 5.7.

FIGURE 5.6:

The Panned view of the top range

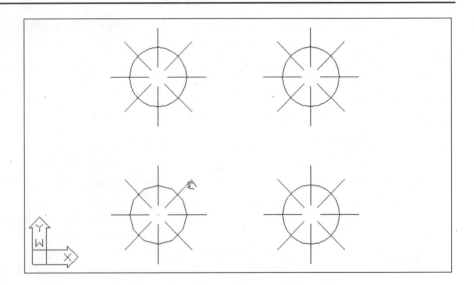

This exercise showed you how you can fine-tune your view by easily switching between Pan Realtime and Zoom Realtime. Once you get the hang of these two tools working together, you'll be able to quickly access the best view for your needs. The other options in the pop-up list—Zoom Window, Zoom Previous, and Zoom Extents—perform the same functions as the tools of the same name on the Standard toolbar and View pull-down menu.

NOTE The Zoom Window option in the Zoom pop-up menu functions in a slightly different way from the standard Zoom Window. Instead of picking two points, you click and drag a window across your view.

FIGURE 5.7:

The final view of the range top burners (top image) and the finished kitchen (bottom image)

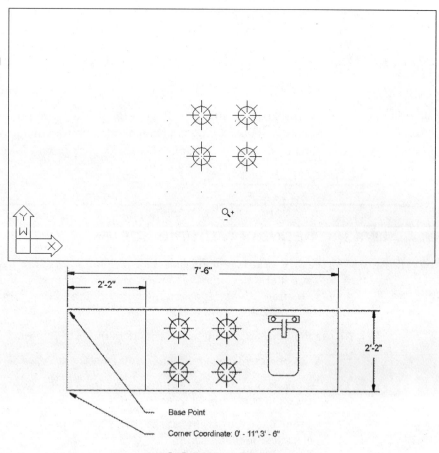

Base Point

Corner Coordinate: 0' - 11",3' - 6"

Put Entire Kitchen on Fixture Layer

While we're on the subject of display tools, don't forget the scroll bars to the right and bottom of the AutoCAD drawing area. They work like any other Windows scroll bar, offering a simple way to move up, down, left, or right of your current view.

TIP

If for some reason the scroll bars do not appear in AutoCAD, or if you prefer to turn them off, do the following. Go to the Display tab of the Preferences dialog box (Tools ➤ Preferences...) and make sure the Display scroll bars in Drawing Window option is either checked to turn them on or unchecked to turn them off.

Before you save and close the kitchen file, there is one more thing you need to do. You will be using this drawing as a symbol and inserting it into the overall plan of the apartment studio unit. To facilitate accurate placement of the kitchen, you will want to change the location of the base point of this drawing to the upper-left corner of the kitchen. This will then be the "handle" of the drawing.

1. Choose Draw ➢ Block ➢ Base from the pull-down menu.

2. At the Base point <1'-10",6'-10",0'-0"> prompt, pick the upper-left corner of the kitchen, as indicated in the bottom image of Figure 5.7. The kitchen drawing is complete.

3. Click on File ➢ Save.

Making Random Multiple Copies

The Draw ➢ Array command is useful when you want to make multiple copies in a regular pattern. But what if you need to make copies in a random pattern? You have two alternatives for accomplishing this: the Copy command's Multiple option and the Grips Move option.

To use the Copy command to make random multiple copies:

1. Click on Copy Object from the Modify toolbar, or type **CO** ⏎.

2. At the Select object prompt, select the objects you want to copy and press ⏎ to confirm your selections.

3. At the <Base point or displacement>/Multiple prompt, enter **M** ⏎ to select the Multiple option.

4. At the Base point prompt, select a base point as usual.

5. At the Second point prompt, select a point for the copy. You will be prompted again for a second point, allowing you to make yet another copy of your object.

6. Continue to select points for more copies as desired.

7. Press ⏎ to exit the Copy command when you are done.

When you use the Grips feature to make multiple random copies, you get an added level of functionality because you can also rotate, mirror, and stretch copies by using the pop-up menu (right-click while a grip is selected). Of course,

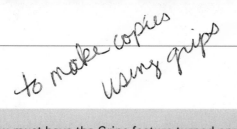
to make copies using grips

you must have the Grips feature turned on; it is usually on by default but you may find yourself on a system that has it turned off for some reason.

1. Press the Esc key twice to make sure you are not in the middle of a command; then select the objects you want to copy.

2. Click on a grip point as your base point.

3. Right-click your mouse and select Move.

4. Right-click again and select Copy.

5. Click on the location for the copy. Notice that the rubber-banding line persists and you still see the selected objects follow the cursor.

6. If desired, click on other locations for more copies.

Finally, you can make square arrayed copies using grips by doing steps 1 through 3 above, but instead of step 4, Shift + click on a copy location. Continue to hold down the Shift key and select points. The copies will snap to the angle and distance you indicate with the first Shift-select point. Release the Shift key and you can make multiple random copies.

Developing Your Drawing

As mentioned briefly in Chapter 3, when using AutoCAD, you first create the most basic forms of your drawing; then you refine them. In this section you will create two drawings—the studio apartment unit and the lobby—that demonstrate this process in more detail.

First you will construct a typical studio apartment unit using the drawings you have created thus far. In the process, you will explore the use of lines as reference objects.

You will also further examine how to use existing files as blocks. In Chapter 4, you inserted a file into another file. There is no limit to the size or number of files you can insert. As you may already have guessed, you can also *nest* files and blocks; that is, insert blocks or files within other blocks or files. Nesting can help reduce your drawing time by allowing you to build one block out of smaller blocks. For example, you can insert your door drawing into the bathroom plan. The bathroom plan can in turn be inserted into the studio unit plan, which also contains doors. Finally, the unit plan can be inserted into the overall floor plan for the studio apartment building.

Importing Settings

In this exercise, you will use the Bath file as a prototype for the studio unit plan. However, you must make a few changes to it first. Once the changes are made, you will import the bathroom and thereby import the layers and blocks contained in the bathroom file.

As you go through this exercise, observe how the drawings begin to evolve from simple forms to complex, assembled forms.

1. First, open the Bath file. If you skipped drawing the Bath file in the last chapter, use the file named `04c-bath.dwg` from the companion CD-ROM.

2. Use the Base command and select the upper-left corner of the bathroom as the new base point for this drawing, so you can position the Bath file more accurately.

3. Save the Bath file. If you use the file from the CD-ROM, use File ➣ Save As and save it as **Bath**.

Next, you will create a new file. But this time, instead of using the Start from Scratch or Use a Template option in the Create New Drawing dialog box, you'll try out the Use a Wizard option.

4. Choose File ➣ New.

5. At the Create New Drawing dialog box, choose Use a Wizard. You'll see two options in the Select a Wizard list box. Choose Quick Setup and then click OK. The Quick Setup dialog box appears. Note the two tabs labeled Step1: Units and Step 2: Area.

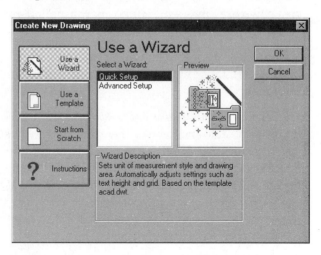

6. Click on the Architectural radio button in the Step 1: Units tab.

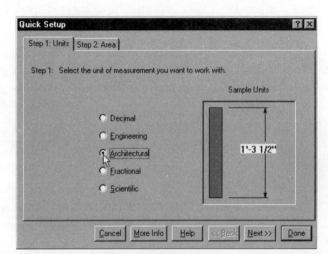

7. Click on the Architectural radio button.

8. Click on the Step 2: Area tab.

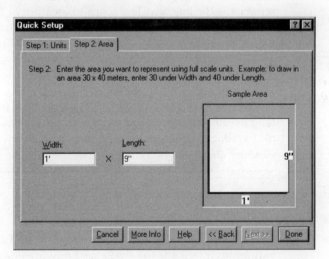

9. Enter **528** in the Width input box and **408** in the length input box. These are the appropriate dimensions for an 8½x11" drawing at 1/4"=1'-0" scale.

10. Click Done.

11. Use Tools ➤ Drawing Aids… to set the snap spacing to 1" and the grid spacing to 48". This sets the grid spacing to display the equivalent of 1 inch intervals for a 1/4"=1' -0" scale drawing.

> **NOTE**
>
> If you need to find out the equivalent drawing area for a given sheet size and scale, see *Setting Up a Work Area* in Chapter 3.

You're drawing is now set up. However, this time, you used the Quick Setup Wizard option to set it up. In fact, the Quick Setup Wizard does nothing more than combine the Format ➤ Units and Format ➤ Drawing Limits options into one dialog box.

Now let's continue by laying out a typical studio unit. You'll also discover how importing a file also imports a variety of drawing items such as layers and line types.

1. Begin the unit by drawing two rectangles, one 14' wide by 24' long, and the other 14' wide by 4' long. Place them as shown in Figure 5.8. The large rectangle represents the interior of the apartment unit, and the small rectangle represents the balcony. The size and location of the rectangles are indicated in the figure.

> **NOTE**
>
> If you used the Rectangle tool to draw the interior and balcony of the apartment unit, then make sure you use the Explode tool on the Modify toolbar to explode the rectangles. The Rectangle tool draws a polyline rectangle instead of simple line segments, so you need to explode the rectangle to reduce it to its component lines. You'll learn more about Polylines in Chapter 13.

2. Click the Insert Block tool on the Draw toolbar, and then click the File button to insert the bathroom drawing.

3. At the Insert Dialog box, click on the File button and locate and select the bathroom drawing using the Select Drawing File dialog box. Then click Open.

FIGURE 5.8:

The apartment unit interior and balcony

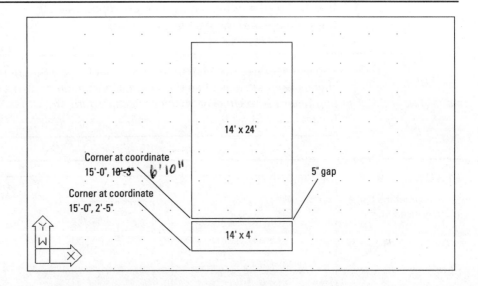

If you are using the 04c-bath.dwg file from the CD-ROM, do the following: After performing step 3, change the name that appears in the Block input box to Bath instead of 04c-bath before you click OK. This will give the inserted file a block name of Bath, even though its originating file's name is 04c-bath.

4. Click OK in the Insert dialog box, and then click on the upper-left corner of the unit's interior as the insertion point (see Figure 5.9). You can use the Endpoint Osnap to accurately place the bathroom. Use a scale factor of 1.0 and a rotation angle of 0°.

Because the Running Osnaps have not been set up in this file, you will need to use the Osnap pop-up menu (Shift + right-click) to access the Endpoint Osnap. You can set up the Running Osnaps to take advantage of Release 14's Auto Snap functions by double-clicking on the OSNAP box in the status bar. Set the Running Osnaps as described in *Using the Layout* section of Chapter 3.

5. Use the Properties tool on the Object Properties toolbar to change all the lines you drew to the Wall layer.

TIP
You can also use the Match Properties tool in the Standard toolbar to change layer settings of an object to those of another object in the drawing. See *How to Quickly Match a Hatch Pattern and Other Properties* in Chapter 6.

FIGURE 5.9:

The unit after the bathroom is inserted

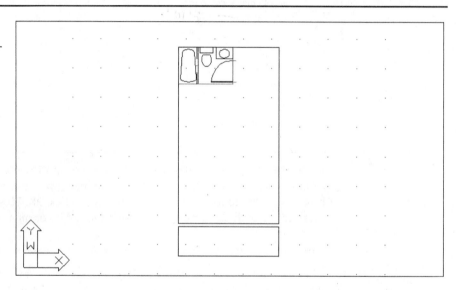

By inserting the bathroom, you imported the layers and blocks contained in the Bath file. You were then able to move previously drawn objects to the imported layers. If you are in a hurry, this can be a quick way to duplicate layers that you know exist in another drawing. This method is similar to using an existing drawing as a template, but it allows you to start work on a drawing before deciding which template to use.

WARNING
If two drawings contain the same layers and blocks, and one of these drawings is imported into the other, the layer settings and block definitions of the *current* file will take priority over those of the *imported* file. This is a point to remember in cases where the layer settings and block definitions are different in the two files.

Importing Settings from External Reference Files

As explained in the Chapter 4 sidebar, *An Alternative to Blocks*, you can use the External Reference (Xref) Attach option to use another file as a background or Xref file. Xref files are similar to blocks except that they do not actually become part of the current drawing's database; nor do the settings from the cross-referenced file automatically become part of the current drawing.

If you want to import layers, line types, text styles, and so forth from a Xref file, you must use the Xbind command, which you will learn more about as you work through this book. Xbind allows you to attach dimension style settings (discussed in Chapter 9 and in Appendix D), layers, line types, or text styles (discussed in Chapter 8) from a cross-referenced file to the current file.

You can also use Xbind to turn a cross-referenced file into an ordinary block, thereby importing all the new settings contained in that file.

See Chapter 12 for a more detailed description of how to use the External References (Xref) and Xbind commands.

Using and Editing Lines

You will draw lines in the majority of your work, so it is important to know how to manipulate lines to your best advantage. In this section, you will look at some of the more common ways to use and edit these fundamental drawing objects. The following exercises show you the process of drawing lines, rather than just how individual commands work.

Roughing In the Line Work

The bathroom you inserted in the last section has only one side of its interior walls drawn (walls are usually shown by double lines). In this next exercise, you will draw the other side. Rather than trying to draw the wall in perfectly the first time, you will "sketch" in the line work and then work through a clean-up process, in a way similar to manual drafting.

1. Zoom into the bathroom so that the entire bathroom and part of the area around it are displayed on the screen, as in Figure 5.10.

NOTE

You may notice that some of the arcs in your bathroom drawing are not smooth. Don't be alarmed; this is how AutoCAD displays arcs and circles in enlarged views. The arcs will be smooth when they are plotted. If you want to see them now as they actually are stored in the file, you can regenerate the drawing by typing **Regen** ↵ at the command prompt. We will look more closely at regeneration in *Chapter 6*.

FIGURE 5.10:

The enlarged view of the bathroom

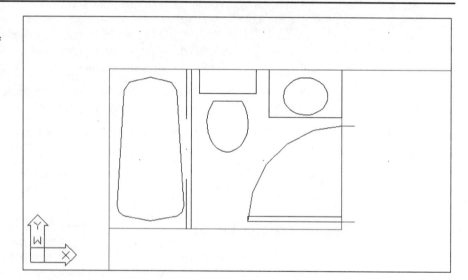

2. Select Wall from the Layer drop-down list in the Properties toolbar to make Wall the current layer.

3. Choose Line from the Draw menu, or type **L** ↵.

4. Shift + right-click the mouse to open the Osnap menu; then select From. This option lets you select a point relative to another point.

5. At the From prompt, open the Osnap menu again and using the Endpoint Osnap, click on the lower-right corner of the bathroom (see the top image of Figure 5.11). Nothing appears in the drawing area yet.

6. Type **@5<-90** ↵. Now a line starts 5" below the lower-right corner of the bathroom.

7. Continue the line horizontally to the left to slightly across the left wall of the apartment unit, as illustrated in the top image of Figure 5.11. You can turn on the Ortho mode to ensure that the line is exactly horizontal.

FIGURE 5.11:

The first wall line and the wall line by the door

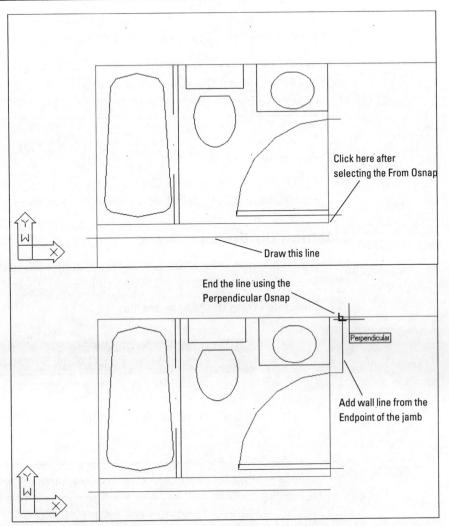

Click here after selecting the From Osnap

Draw this line

End the line using the Perpendicular Osnap

Perpendicular

Add wall line from the Endpoint of the jamb

In the foregoing exercise, the From Osnap allows you to specify a point in space relative to the corner of the bathroom. In step 5, you used a polar coordinate to indicate the distance from the corner at which you wanted the line to start. You can also use relative or absolute Cartesian coordinates. Now let's continue with the line work.

1. Draw another line upward from the endpoint of the top door jamb at coordinate 22'-11", 29'-2" to meet the top wall of the unit (see the bottom image

of Figure 5.11). Use the Ortho mode and the Perpendicular Osnap to pick the top wall of the unit. This causes the line to end precisely on the wall line in perpendicular position, as in the bottom image of Figure 5.11.

TIP

The Perpendicular Osnap override can also be used to draw a line perpendicular to a nonorthogonal line—one at a 45° angle, for instance.

2. Draw a line connecting the two door jambs. Then change that line to the Ceiling layer (see first panel of Figure 5.12).

3. Draw a line 6" downward from the endpoint of the jamb nearest the corner at coordinate 22'-11", 26'-0", as shown in the bottom image of Figure 5.12.

Cleaning Up the Line Work

You've drawn some of the wall lines, approximating their endpoint locations. Next you will use the Fillet command to join lines exactly end to end.

1. Click Fillet from the Modify toolbar.

2. Type **R** ↵ **0** ↵ to set the fillet radius to 0; then press ↵ to repeat the Fillet command.

NOTE

There is another command, the *Chamfer* command, that performs a similar function to Fillet. Unlike Fillet, the Chamfer command allows you to join two lines with an intermediate beveled line rather than an arc. Chamfer can be set to join two lines at a corner in exactly the same manner as Fillet.

3. Fillet the two lines by picking the vertical and horizontal lines, as indicated in Figure 5.12. Notice that these points lie on the portion of the line you want to keep. Your drawing will look like the bottom image of Figure 5.12.

WARNING

If you are a veteran AutoCAD user, you should note that the default value for the Fillet command is now .5 instead of 0.

4. Fillet the bottom wall of the bathroom with the left wall of the unit, as shown in Figure 5.13. Make sure the points you pick on the wall lines are on the side of the line you want to keep, not the side you want trimmed.

5. Fillet the top wall of the unit with the right side wall of the bathroom as shown in Figure 5.13.

FIGURE 5.12:

The corner of the bathroom wall and the filleted wall around the bathroom

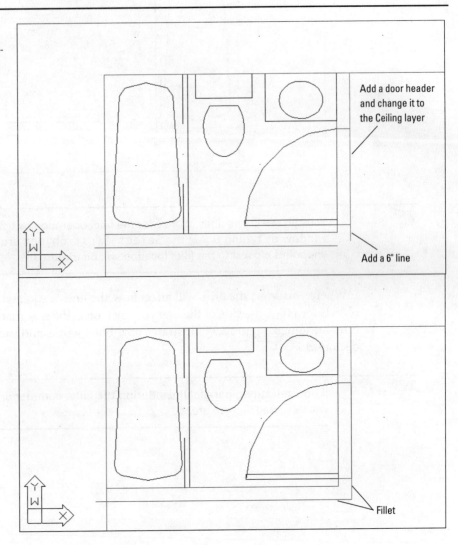

Add a door header and change it to the Ceiling layer

Add a 6" line

Fillet

The cleaned up wall
intersections

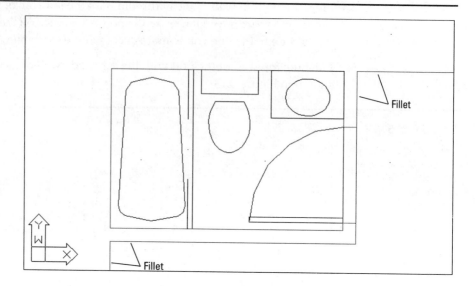

You can select two lines at once for the fillet operation by using a Crossing window by typing **C** ↵ at the Select first object prompt. The two endpoints closest to the fillet location will be trimmed.

Where you select the lines will affect how the lines are joined. As you select objects for Fillet, the side of the line you click on is the side that remains when the lines are joined. Figure 5.14 illustrates how Fillet works and shows what the fillet options do.

If you select two parallel lines during the Fillet command, the two lines will be joined with an arc.

FIGURE 5.14:

The place where you click on the object to select it determines what part of an object gets filleted.

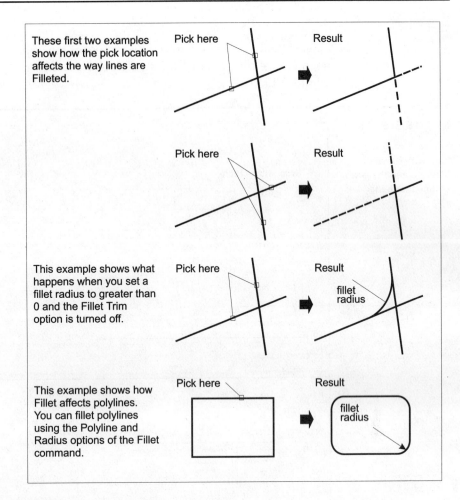

Now let's finish this end of the Unit plan.

1. Insert Block from the Draw toolbar to place the kitchen drawing at the wall intersection below the bathroom at coordinate 15'-0", 25'-5" (see the top image of Figure 5.15). You can also insert the kitchen at approximately the place where you want it, and then move it into a more exact position.

TIP

If you didn't complete the kitchen earlier in this chapter, you can insert the 05a-kitchen.dwg file from the companion CD-ROM.

2. Press ↵ three times to accept the default X and Y Scale factors of 1.0, and a Rotation Angle of 0°.

3. Adjust your view with Pan and Zoom so that the upper portion of the apartment unit is centered in drawing area, as illustrated in the top image of Figure 5.15.

FIGURE 5.15:

The view after using Pan, with the door inserted and the jamb and header added

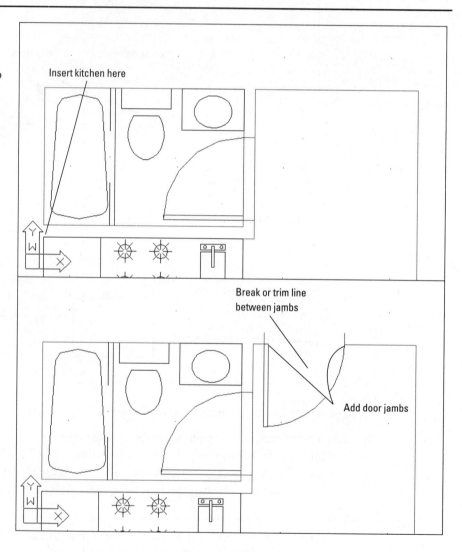

4. Insert a door on the unit wall at coordinate 23'-4", 30'- 10". Then press ↵ twice to accept the default Scale factors.

5. At the Rotation angle prompt, enter **270** ↵. You can also use the cursor (make sure the Ortho mode is on) to orient the door so that it is swinging *into* the studio. This is the entry door to the studio apartment.

6. Make sure the door is on the Door layer.

TIP   As a shortcut to setting an object's layer, you can select the object or objects, and then select a layer from the Layer drop-down list in the Properties toolbar.

---

7. Add 5" door jambs and change their layer property to the Jamb layer, as shown in Figure 5.15.

8. Choose the Break tool in the Modify toolbar, and then select the header over the entry door (see the bottom image of Figure 5.15).

NOTE   If you need some help with the Break command, see *Modifying an Object* in Chapter 3, and the *Different Methods for Using the Break Command* sidebar, here in Chapter 5.

---

9. Type **F** ↵ to use the first point option; then select the endpoint of one of the jambs.

10. At the second point prompt, select the endpoint of the other jamb as shown in Figure 5.15.

11. Draw the door header on the Ceiling layer as shown in Figure 5.16.

12. Click Offset from the Modify toolbar and offset the top wall lines of the unit and the door header up 5", so they connect with the top end of the door jamb, as shown in Figure 5.16. Don't forget to include the short wall line from the door to the bathroom wall.

13. Use File ➤ Save As to save your file under the name Unit.

FIGURE 5.16:

The other side of the wall

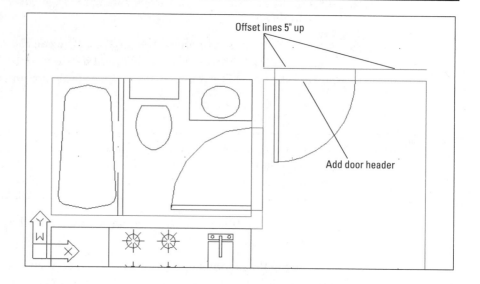

Different Methods for Using the Break Command

In the exercise for finishing the Unit plan, you used the Break command to accurately place a gap in a line over the entry door. In Chapter 3, you broke a line at a single point to create multiple, contiguous line segments. In both cases you used the F option. You can also break a line without the F option with a little less accuracy. By not using the F option, the point at which you select the object is used as the first break point. If you're in a hurry, you can dispense with the F option and simply place a gap in an approximate location. You can then later use other tools to adjust the gap.

In addition, you can use locations on other objects to select the first and second points of a break. For example, you may want to align an opening with another opening some distance away. Once you've selected the line to break, you can then use the F option and select two points on the existing opening to define the first and second break points. The break points will align in an orthogonal direction to the selected points.

Using Construction Lines as Tools

Now you need to extend the upper wall line 5" beyond the right-side interior wall of the unit. To accomplish this, you will draw some line objects specifically designed to help with layout. Start by drawing a Ray line.

1. Choose Draw ➤ Ray from the pull-down menu.

2. At the Start point prompt, start the Ray line from the upper-right corner of the unit at coordinate 29'-0", 30'-10". If the Ortho mode is on, turn it off. As you move your mouse, you'll see the Ray follow its direction. (See the top image of Figure 5.17.)

3. Type @1<45. The Ray line is fixed in a 45° angle. The Ray command persists allowing you to add more lines.

4. Press ↵ to exit the Ray command.

NOTE   A Ray is a line that starts from a point you select and continues off to some infinite distance. For this reason, you weren't required to enter a distance value in step 3.

---

5. Fillet this Ray with the wall line you wish to extend, and then erase the Ray when you are done. Your drawing should look like the bottom image of Figure 5.17.

6. Pan your view to see more of the left side of the unit.

7. Draw another Ray from the upper-left corner of the bathroom at an angle of 135°. Then use Fillet to join this line with the wall line (see Figure 5.18).

8. Erase the last Ray you drew.

9. Click on View ➤ Zoom ➤ All to view the entire drawing. It will look like Figure 5.19.

FIGURE 5.17:

A Ray used to extend the wall line; and the extended line

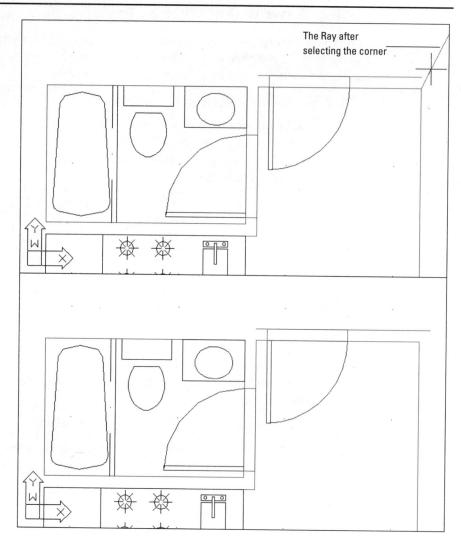

The Ray after selecting the corner

FIGURE 5.18:

The left-side wall line, extended

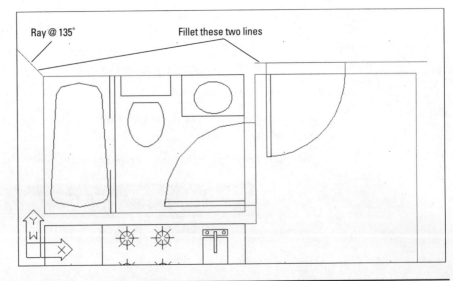

FIGURE 5.19:

The Studio unit thus far

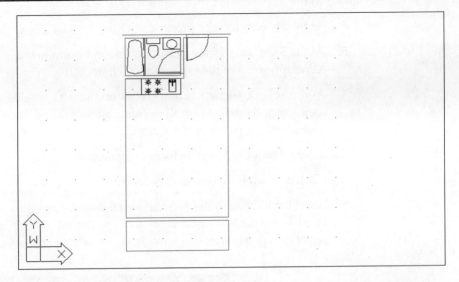

In this exercise, you used Rays to help accurately position two other lines used for the exterior walls of the studio unit. This shows that you can freely use objects to help construct your drawing.

Now you will finish the balcony by adding a sliding glass door and a rail. Again, you will use lines for construction as well as for parts of the drawing. First, you'll add the door jamb by drawing an Xline. An Xline is a line that has an infinite length, but unlike the Ray, it extends in both directions. After drawing the Xline, you'll use it to quickly position the door jambs.

1. Zoom into the balcony area.

2. Click on the Construction Line tool from the Draw toolbar, or type **XL** ↵. You'll see this prompt:

    ```
    Hor/Ver/Ang/Bisect/Offset/<From point>:
    ```

3. Type **O** ↵ to select the Offset.

4. At the Offset distance prompt, type **4'** ↵.

5. At the Select object prompt, click on the wall line at the right of the unit.

6. At the Side to offset prompt, click on a point to the left of the wall. The Xline appears (see the top image of Figure 5.20).

7. At the Select object prompt, click on the left wall line, and then click to the right of the selected wall to create another Xline. Your drawing should look like the top image of Figure 5.20.

    Next, you'll edit the Xlines to form the jambs.

8. Click on Trim from the Modify toolbar.

9. Select the Xlines and the two horizontal lines representing the wall between the unit and the balcony, and press ↵. You can use either a crossing window or select each line individually. You have just selected the objects to which to trim.

FIGURE 5.20:

The door opening

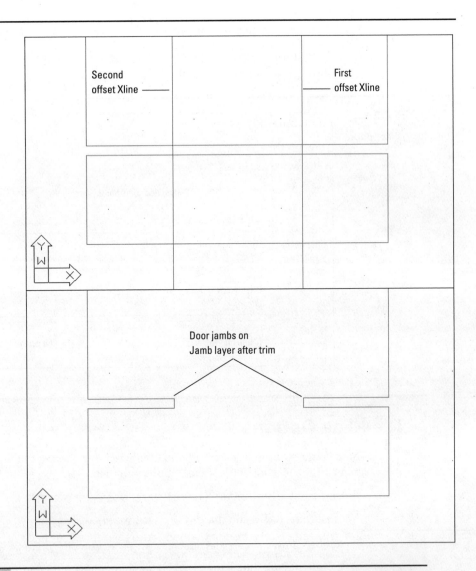

Second offset Xline ——

First —— offset Xline

Door jambs on Jamb layer after trim

TIP   You can also use the Fence selection option to select the lines to be trimmed. See *Other Selection Options* in Chapter 2 or *Building on Previously Drawn Objects* in Chapter 12.

10. Click on the horizontal lines at any point between the two Xlines. Then click on the Xlines above and below the horizontal lines to trim them. Your drawing will look like the bottom image of Figure 5.20.

11. Add lines on the Ceiling layer to represent the door header.

12. Now draw lines between the two jambs (on the Door layer) to indicate a sliding glass door (see Figure 5.21).

FIGURE 5.21:

The sliding glass door

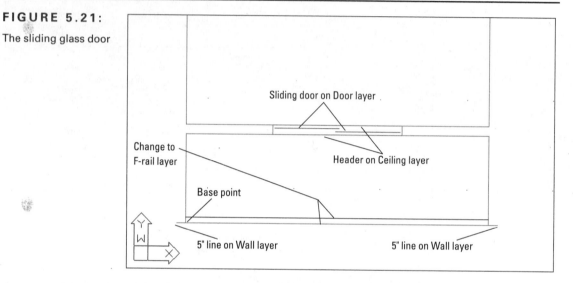

The Xline Options

There is more to the Xline command than you have seen in the exercises of this chapter. Here is a list of the Xline options and their use:

Hor draws horizontal Xlines as you click on points.

Ver draws vertical Xlines as you click on points.

Angle draws Xlines at a specified angle as you pick points.

Bisect draws Xlines bisecting an angle or a location between two points.

The wall facing the balcony is now complete. To finish off the unit, you need to show a handrail and the corners of the balcony wall.

1. Offset the bottom line of the balcony 3" toward the top of the drawing.

2. Create a new layer called **F-rail**, and assign this offset line to it.

3. Add a 5" horizontal line to the lower corners of the balcony, as shown in Figure 5.21.

4. Now choose Draw ➤ Block ➤ Base from the pull-down menu to set the base point at the lower-left corner of the balcony, at the coordinates 15', 2'-5".

5. Change the lines indicating walls to the Wall layer, and put the sliding glass door on the Door layer (see Figure 5.21).

6. Zoom back to the previous view. Your drawing should now look like Figure 5.22.

7. Click on File ➤ Save to save the drawing.

FIGURE 5.22:

The completed studio apartment unit

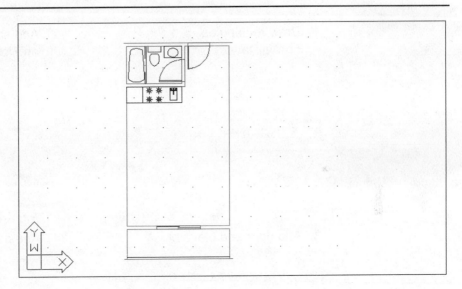

Your studio apartment unit plan is now complete. The exercises you've just completed show you a typical set of operations you'll perform while building your drawings. In fact, nearly 80 percent of what you will do in AutoCAD is represented here.

Now, to review the drawing process, and to create a drawing you'll use later, we're going to draw the apartment building's lobby. As you follow the steps, refer to Figure 5.23. As is usual in floor plans, the elevator is indicated by the box with the large X through it, and the stair shaft is indicated by the box with the row of vertical lines through it.If you are in a hurry, there is a finished version of this file on the companion CD-ROM.

FIGURE 5.23:

Drawing the lobby plan

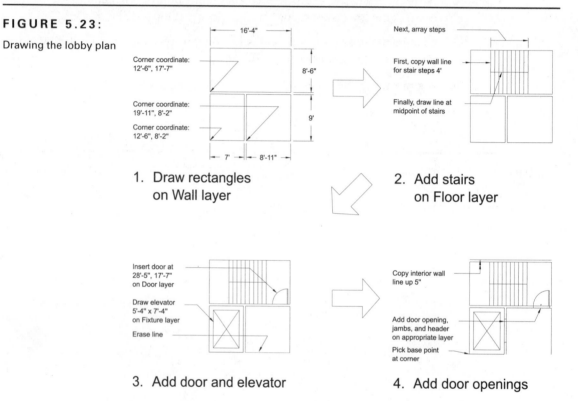

1. Draw rectangles on Wall layer

2. Add stairs on Floor layer

3. Add door and elevator

4. Add door openings

Here are the steps.

1. Create a new file called Lobby, using the Unit file as a prototype (open the Unit file, choose File ➤ Save As, and enter **Lobby** for the new file name).

2. Erase the entire unit (Erase ➤ All).

3. Begin by drawing the three main rectangles representing the outlines of the stair shaft, the elevator shaft, and the lobby.

4. To draw the stairs, offset the stair shaft's left wall to the right a distance of 4'. This creates the first line representing the steps.

5. Array this line in one row of ten columns, using an 11" column spacing.

6. Draw the center line dividing the two flights of stairs.

7. Draw the elevator and insert the door. Practice using Xlines here.

8. Draw in the door jambs; then edit the door openings to add the door headers. Your plan should resemble the one in Figure 5.23, step 4.

9. Once you are finished, save the Lobby file.

How to Quickly Set the Current Layer to That of an Existing Object

 As your list of layers grows, you may find it difficult to quickly locate the exact layer you want. You may know that you want to draw objects on the same layer as an existing object in a drawing, but you are not sure what that layer is.

In previous versions of AutoCAD, you would have to take the following steps: First determine the layer of the object whose layer you want to match. Next, open the layer list, scroll down the list until you find the layer name, and then select it. If the list of layers is quite long, you may forget the name of the layer before you find it in the list!

AutoCAD offers the *Make Object's Layer Current* tool to help you easily set the current layer. This tool can be found on the Object Properties toolbar next to the Layers tool.

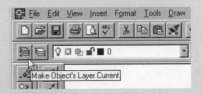

The Make Object's Layer Current tool is a simple yet powerful tool that lets you set the current layer by selecting an object in the drawing instead of selecting its name from a list. To use it, click on the Make Object's Layer Current tool and then click on the object whose layer you want to make current. This reduces the three or four step process of earlier AutoCAD versions to one click.

Remember this tool the next time you are faced with a drawing that has a very large list of layers.

Finding Distances Along Arcs

You've seen how you can use lines to help locate objects and geometry in your drawing. But if you need to find distances along a curved object such as an arc, lines don't always help. Following are two ways of finding exact distances on arcs. Try these exercises when you're not working through the main tutorial.

Finding a Point a Particular Distance from Another Point   At times you'll need to find the location of a point on an arc that lies at a known distance from another point on the arc. The distance could be described as a cord of the arc, but how do you find the exact cord location? To find a cord along an arc, follow these steps.

1. Click on Circle from the Draw toolbar.

2. Use the Endpoint Osnap to click on the endpoint of the arc.

3. At the End of diameter/<radius> prompt, enter the length of the cord distance you wish to locate along the arc.

The point where the circle intersects the arc is the endpoint of the cord distance from the endpoint of the arc (see Figure 5.24). You can then use the Intersect Osnap override to select the circle and arc intersection.

FIGURE 5.24:

Finding a cord distance along an arc using a circle

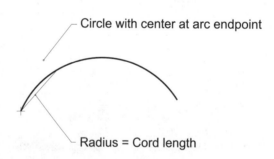

Circle with center at arc endpoint

Radius = Cord length

Finding an Exact Distance Along an Arc   To find an exact distance along an arc or curve (nonlinear), or to mark off specific distance increments along an arc or curve, do the following:

1. Choose Format ➤ Point Style from the pull-down menu to open the Point Style dialog box.

TIP

You can also set the point style by setting the Pdmode system variable to 3. See Appendix D for more on Pdmode.

2. At the Point Style dialog box, click on the icon that looks like an *X*, in the top row. Also be sure the Set Size Relative to Screen radio button is selected. Then click on OK.

3. Choose Draw ➣ Point ➣ Measure from the pull-down menu.

TIP

Another command called Divide (Draw ➣ Point ➣ Divide) marks off a line, arc, or curve into equal divisions, as opposed to divisions of a length you specify. You would use Divide to divide an object into twelve equal segments, for example. Aside from this difference in function, divide works in exactly the same way as Measure.

4. At the `Select object to measure` prompt, click on the arc near the end from which you wish to find the distance.

5. At the `<Segment length>/Block` prompt, enter the distance you are interested in. A series of *X*s appears on the arc, marking off the specified distance along the arc. You can select the exact location of the *X*s using the Node Osnap override (Figure 5.25).

TIP The Block option of the Measure command allows you to specify a block to be inserted at the specified segment length, in place of the Xs on the arc. You have the option of aligning the block with the arc as it is inserted. (This is similar to the polar array's Rotate Objects As They Are Copied option.)

FIGURE 5.25:

Finding an exact distance along an arc using points and the Measure command

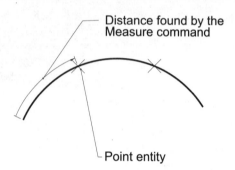

The Measure command also works on Bezier curves. You'll get a more detailed look at the Measure command in Chapter 13.

As you work with AutoCAD, you'll find that constructing temporary geometry such as the circle and points in the two foregoing examples will help you solve problems in new ways. Don't hesitate to experiment! Remember, you've always got the Save and U commands to help you recover from mistakes.

Changing the Length of Objects

Suppose, after finding the length of an arc, you realize you need to lengthen the arc by a specific amount. The Modify ➤ Lengthen command lets you lengthen or shorten arcs, lines, splines, and elliptical arcs. Here's how to lengthen an arc.

1. Click Lengthen from the Modify toolbar.

2. At the `DElta/Percent/Total/DYnamic/,Select object>` prompt, type **T** ⏎.

3. At the `Angle/<Enter total length (1.0000)>` prompt, enter the length you want for the arc.

4. At the `<Select object to change>/Undo` prompt, click on the arc you wish to change. Be sure to click at a point nearest the end you want to lengthen. The arc increases in length to the size you specified.

Lengthen will also shorten an object if it is currently longer than the value you enter.

In this short example, we have demonstrated how to change an object to a specific length. You can use other criteria to change an object's length, using these options available in the Lengthen command:

DElta lets you lengthen or shorten an object by a specific length. To specify an angle rather than a length, use the Angle suboption.

Percent is for increasing or decreasing the length of an object by a percentage of its current length.

Total lets you specify the total length or angle of an object.

DYnamic lets you graphically change the length of an object using your cursor.

Creating a New Drawing Using Parts from Another Drawing

In this section you will use the Wblock command (which you learned about in Chapter 4), to create a separate stair drawing using the stair you've already drawn for the lobby. Although you haven't turned the existing stair into a block, you can still use Wblock to turn parts of a drawing into a file.

1. If you have closed the Lobby file, open it now.

NOTE If you have closed the Lobby drawing, open it now for the following exercise. If you didn't create the lobby drawing, open the Lobby.dwg file from the companion CD-ROM for this exercise.

2. Click on File ➤ Export....

3. When the Export Data File dialog box appears, enter **stair.dwg** in the file name input box and click Save. By including the .dwg file name extension, AutoCAD knows that you want to export to a drawing file and not some other format, such as a .dxf or .wmf format file.

4. At the Block name prompt, press ↵. When you export to a .dwg format, AutoCAD assumes you want to export a block. Bypassing this prompt by pressing ↵ tells AutoCAD that you want to create a file from part of the drawing, rather than from a block.

5. At the Insertion base point prompt, pick the lower-right corner of the stair shaft, at coordinate 28'-10", 17'-7". This tells AutoCAD the base point for the new drawing.

6. At the Select objects prompt, use a window to select the stair shaft, as shown in Figure 5.26.

7. When the stair shaft, including the door, is highlighted, press ↵ to confirm your selection. The stair disappears.

8. Since you want the stair to remain in the lobby drawing, click on the Undo button to bring it back. Undo will not affect any files you may export with File ➤ Export, Wblock, or the Make Block tool.

FIGURE 5.26:

A selection window enclosing the stair shaft

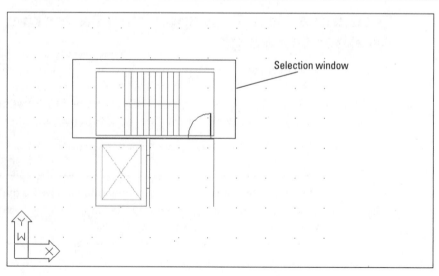

Drawing Parallel Lines

Frequently, when working on an architectural project, you will first do your schematic layout using simple lines for walls. Then, as the design requirements begin to take shape, you can start to add more detailed information about the walls; for example, indicating wall materials or locations for insulation. Auto-CAD provides *multilines* (the Mline command), which are double lines that can be used to represent walls. Mline can also be customized to display solid fills, center lines, and additional line types shown in Figure 5.27. You can save your custom multilines as Mline styles, which are in turn saved in special files for easy access from other drawings.

TIP   Multilines are especially useful for Metric users who need to represent cavity walls.

FIGURE 5.27:

Samples of Multiline styles

Dots indicate pick points.

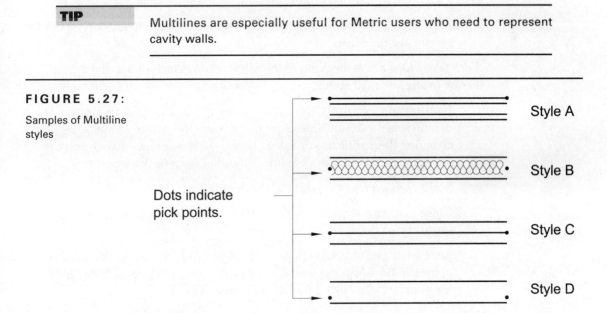

Style A

Style B

Style C

Style D

The following exercise shows you how you might continue to build information into your drawings by using Multilines to indicate wall types.

1. Click Multiline from the Draw menu, or type **ML** ↵. You'll see two lines in the prompt area:

   ```
   Justification = Top, Scale = 1.00, Style = Standard
   Justification/Scale/STyle/<From point>:
   ```

The first line in the prompt area gives you the current settings for Mline.

2. At the `Justification/Scale/Style/<From Point>` prompt, type **S** ↵ (for Scale).

3. At the `Set Mline Scale <0.00>` prompt, type **5** ↵.

4. Pick a point to start the double line.

5. Continue to select points to draw more double line segments, or type **C** ↵ to close the series of lines.

Let's take a look at the meaning of the Mline settings included in the prompt you saw in steps 1 and 2 above.

Justification   controls how far off center the double lines are drawn. The default sets the double lines equidistant from the points you pick. By changing the justification value to be greater than or less than 0, you can have AutoCAD draw double lines off center from the pick points.

Scale   lets you set the width of the double line.

Close   closes a sequence of double lines, much as the Line command's Close option does.

Style   lets you select a style for Multilines. You can control the number of lines in the Multiline, as well as the line types used for each line in the Multiline style, by using the Mledit command.

Customizing Multilines

In Chapter 4 you learned how to make a line appear dashed or dotted, using line types. In a similar way, you can control the appearance of Multilines using the Multiline Style dialog box. This dialog box allows you to

- Set the number of lines that appear in the multiline

- Control the color of each line

- Control the line type of each line

- Apply a fill between the outermost lines of a multiline

- Control if and how ends of multilines are closed

To access the Multiline Style dialog box, choose Format ➤ Multiline Style… from the pull-down menu, or type **Mlstyle** ↵ at the command prompt. Here is the Multiline Styles dialog box:

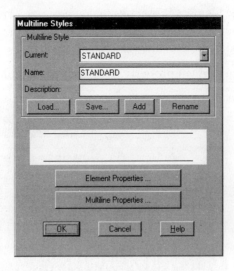

Once you have drawn a multiline in a particular style, you cannot modify the style settings for that style in the Element Properties and Multiline Properties dialog box described later in this section. The Multiline Styles dialog box only allows you to set up style before they are used in a drawing.

At the top of the dialog, a group of buttons and input boxes allow you to select the Multiline Style you want to work with. The Current pop-up list offers you a selection of existing styles. In the Name input box you can name a new style you are creating, or rename an existing style. The Description input box lets you attach a description to an Mline style for easy identification. You use the Add and Save buttons to create and save Multiline styles as files so they can be accessed by any AutoCAD drawing, and with the Load button you retrieve a saved style for use in the current drawing. Rename lets you change the name of an Mline style (the default style in a new drawing is called Standard).

In the lower half of the Multiline Styles dialog box are two buttons—Element Properties and Multiline Properties—that allow you to make adjustments to the Mline style currently indicated at the top of the dialog box. This Mline is also previewed in the middle of the dialog box.

Element Properties

In the Element Properties dialog box, you control the properties of the individual elements of a newly created style, including the number of lines that appear in the Mline, their color, and the distance they appear from your pick points.

The element property settings are not available for existing Mline styles.

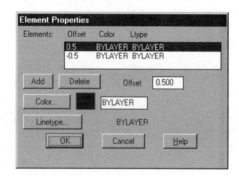

For example, click on the Add button, and another line is added to your multiline. The offset distance of the new line appears in the list box. The default value for new lines is 0.0, which places the line at the center of the standard multiline. To delete a line, highlight its offset value in the list box and click the Delete button. To change the amount of offset, highlight it and enter a new value in the Offset input box.

To change the color and line type of individual lines, use the Color... and Linetype... buttons, which open the Color and Select Linetype dialog boxes, both of which you have already worked with. In Figure 5.28 you see some examples of multilines and their corresponding Element Properties settings.

FIGURE 5.28:

Samples of Mline styles you can create

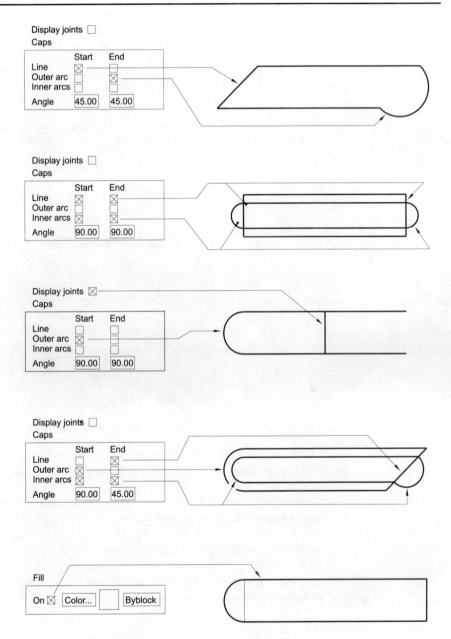

TIP

You can easily indicate an insulated wall in an architectural drawing by adding a third center line (offset of 0.0), and giving that center line a Batting line. This line type draws an S-shaped pattern typically used to represent fiberglass batt insulation in a floor plan. To see how other wall patterns can be created, see the sections on line-type customization in Chapter 21.

Multiline Properties

The Multiline Properties... button lets you control how the Mline is capped at its ends, as well as whether joints are displayed.

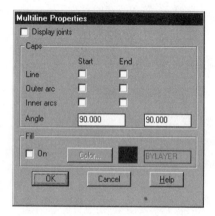

To turn a cap on, you click on the checkbox next to the type of cap you want. If you prefer, you can give your Multiline Style a solid fill, using the Fill checkbox.

TIP

A solid-filled Multiline can be used where you need to fill in a wall with a solid shade (or *poche,* to use the drafting term). You can quickly add a poche by setting one multiline offset to be 0.0 and the other to be the width of the wall. Then trace either the inside or outside of the wall to be poched, using the Multiline style with the Fill option turned on.

Joining and Editing Multilines

Multilines are unique in their ability to combine several line types and colors into one entity. For this reason, you need special tools to edit them. On the Modify menu, the Edit multiline option (and the Mledit command) have the sole purpose of allowing you to join multilines in a variety of ways, as demonstrated in Figure 5.29.

FIGURE 5.29:

The Mledit options and their meanings

CLOSED CROSS Trims one of two intersecting multilines so that they appear overlapping.		
OPEN CROSS Trims the outer lines of two intersecting multilines.		
MERGED CROSS Joins two Multilines into one multiline.		
CLOSED TEE Trims the leg of a tee intersection to the first line.		
OPEN TEE Joins the outer lines of a multiline tee intersection.		
MERGED TEE Joins all the lines in a multiline tee intersection		
CORNER JOINT Joins two multilines into a corner joint.		
ADD VERTEX Adds a vertex to a multiline. The vertex can later be moved.		
DELETE VERTEX Deletes a vertex to straighten a multiline.		
CUT SINGLE Creates an opening in a single line of a multiline.		
CUT ALL Creates a break across all lines in a multiline.		
WELD Closes a break in a multiline.		

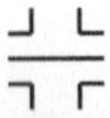

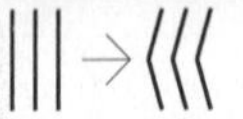

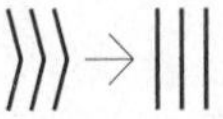

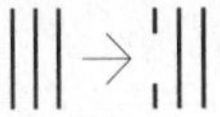

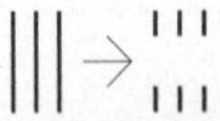

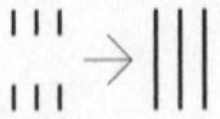

Here's how the Mledit command is used.

1. Type **Mledit** ↵ at the command prompt. The Multiline Edit Tools dialog box appears (see Figure 5.30), offering a variety of ways to edit your Multilines.

FIGURE 5.30:

Multiline Edit Tools

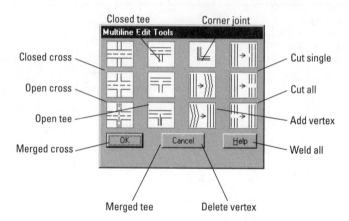

2. Click on the graphic that best matches the edit you want to perform.

3. Select the Multilines you want to join or edit.

Another option is to explode multilines and edit them using the editing tools you've used in this and previous chapters. When a multiline is exploded, it is reduced to its component lines. Line-type assignments and layers are maintained for each component.

If you are doing a lot of work with Multilines, you can open the Modify II toolbar. It contains a multiline edit tool button that opens the Multiline Edit Tools dialog box. To open the Modify II toolbar, right-click on any toolbar and then click on the Modify II checkbox in the Toolbar dialog box.

Eliminating Blocks, Layers, Line Types, Shapes, and Styles

A prototype may contain blocks and layers you don't need in your new file. For example, the lobby you just completed contains the bathroom block because you used the unit file as a prototype. Even though you erased this block, it remains in the drawing file's database. It is considered "unused" because it doesn't appear as part of the drawing. Such extra blocks can slow you down by increasing the amount of time needed to open the file. They will also increase the size of your file unnecessarily. There are two commands for eliminating unused elements from a drawing: Purge and Wblock.

Selectively Removing Unused Elements

The Purge command is used to remove unused individual blocks, layers, line types, shapes, and text styles from a drawing file. To help keep the file size down and to make layer maintenance easier, you will want to purge your drawing of unused elements.

As you will see in the File ➤ Drawing Utilities ➤ Purge cascading menu and the Purge command prompt, you can purge other unused drawing elements, such as line types and layers, as well. Bear in mind, however, that Purge will not delete certain primary drawing elements—namely, layer 0, the Continuous line type, and the standard text style.

1. Click on File ➤ Open and open the Lobby file.

2. Click on File ➤ Drawing Utilities ➤ Purge ➤ Blocks.

3. At the `Names to purge <*>` prompt, you can enter the name of a specific block, or press ↵ to purge all the blocks.

4. Go ahead and press ↵. You should now see the `Verify each name to be purged? <Y>` prompt. This lets you selectively purge blocks by displaying each block name in succession.

5. Press ↵ again.

6. At the Purge block BATH? <N> prompt, enter **Y** ↵. The Purge block prompt will repeat for each unused block in the file. Continue to enter **Y** ↵ to all the prompts until the Purge command is completed.

The Lobby file is now purged of most, but not all, of the unused blocks. Now let's take a look at how to delete all the unused elements at once.

Opening a File as Read-Only

When you open an existing file, you might have noticed the Read Only Mode checkbox in the Open Drawing dialog box. If you open a file with this option checked, AutoCAD will not let you save the file under its original name. You can still edit the drawing any way you please, but if you attempt to use File ➤ Save, you will get the message "Drawing file is write-protected." You can, however, save your changed file under another name.

The read-only mode provides a way to protect important files from accidental corruption. It also offers another method for reusing settings and objects from existing files by letting you open a file as a prototype, and then saving the file under another name.

Removing All Unused Elements

Purge does not remove nested blocks on its first pass. For example, although you purged the Bath block from the Lobby file, it still contains the Tub and Toilet blocks that were nested in the Bath block. To remove them using Purge, you must start the command again and remove the nested blocks. For this reason, Purge can be a time-consuming way to delete large numbers of elements.

NOTE Cross-referenced files do not have to be purged because they never actually become part of the drawing's database.

In contrast, the File ➤ Export… option (Wblock) enables you to remove *all* unused elements—including blocks, nested blocks, layers, line types, shapes, and styles—all at once. You cannot select specific elements or types of elements to remove.

Be careful: In a given file, there may be a block that is unused but that you want to keep, so you may want to keep a copy of the unpurged file.

1. Choose File ➤ Open and at the Save Changes to Drawing warning, and then click on No.

2. At the Select File dialog box, select the Lobby file again. Because you didn't save changes to it from the last exercise, this has the effect of reverting back to the condition before you used the Purge command.

3. Click on File ➤ Export....

4. At the Export Data File dialog box, enter **Lobby1.dwg**. This tells AutoCAD to create a new file called Lobby1, which will be the Lobby file with the unused elements removed.

NOTE   If you specify an existing file, you will get a warning message telling you that a file with that name already exists, and a request to confirm if you want to replace it. Click on Yes to replace the file or No to enter a new name.

---

5. At the Block name prompt, enter * ↵. This tells AutoCAD that you want to create a new file containing all the drawing elements of the current file, including settings. AutoCAD saves the current file to disk, omitting all the unused blocks, layers, and so forth.

6. Now open the Lobby1 file and click on Insert Block from the Draw toolbar.

7. Click on the Block button to get a view of blocks contained in this file. Note that the list shows only the Door block. All the unused blocks have been purged.

Remember: Though Wblock offers a quick way of clearing out the deadwood in a file, the command indiscriminately strips a file of all unused elements. So exercise care when you use this method of purging files.

If You Want to Experiment...

Try using the techniques you learned in this chapter to create new files. Use the files you created in Chapter 4 as prototypes to create the symbols shown in Figure 5.31.

FIGURE 5.31:

Mechanical symbols

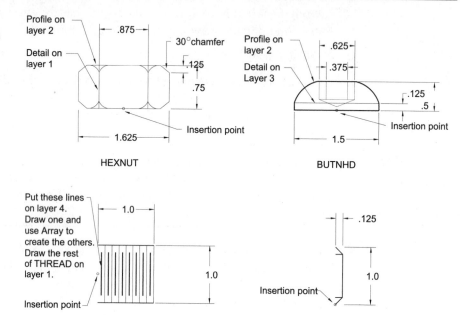

Note:
Create four layers named 1, 2, 3, and 4, if they do not already exist.
Give each layer the same color as their number.
Give layer 3 the HIDDEN line type.
Don't draw dimensions, just use them for reference.

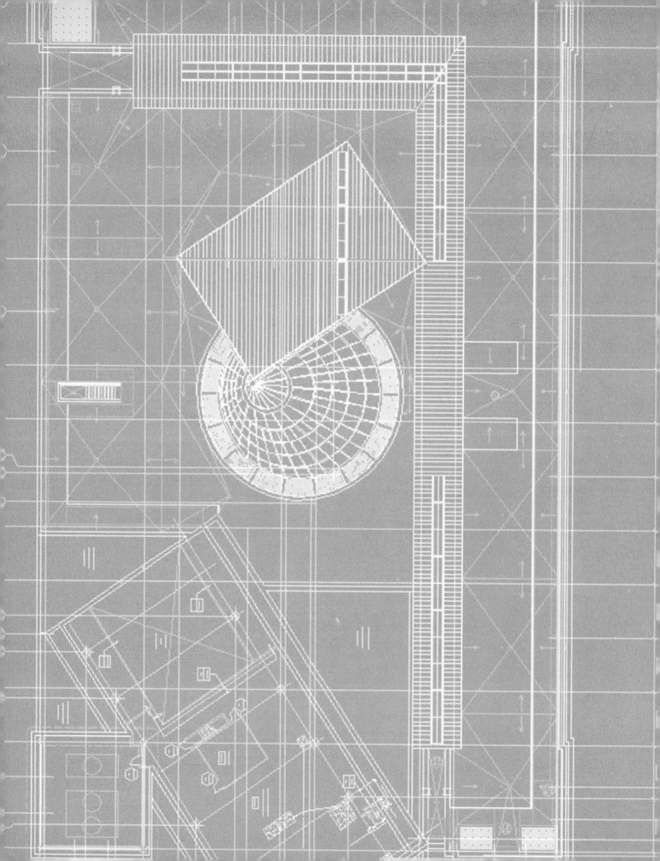

CHAPTER

SIX

6

Enhancing Your Drawing Skills

- Assembling the Parts

- Taking Control of the AutoCAD Display

- Using Hatch Patterns in Your Drawings

- Updating Blocks

- Using External References

Now that you have created drawings of a typical apartment unit, and the apartment building's lobby and stairs, you can assemble them to complete the first floor of the apartment building. In this chapter, you will take full advantage of AutoCAD's features to enhance your drawing skills, as well as to reduce the time it takes for you to create accurate drawings.

As your drawing becomes larger, you will find that you need to use the Zoom and Pan commands more often. Larger drawings also require some special editing techniques. You will learn how to assemble and view drawings in ways that will save you time and effort as your design progresses. Along the way, you'll see how you can enhance the appearance of your drawings by adding hatch patterns.

Assembling the Parts

Start by creating a new file for the first floor, and inserting and copying the unit file.

1. Create a new file named Plan, to contain the drawing of the apartment building's first floor. This is the file that you will use to assemble the unit plans into an apartment building.

TIP

If you're just opening AutoCAD, you can click on the Open a Drawing button in the Start Up dialog box, and then double click on More files... from the Select a File list.

---

2. Set the Units style to Architectural (Format ➤ Units...).

3. Set up the drawing for a 1/8"=1'-0" scale on an 24"×18" drawing area (Format ➤ Drawing Limits). If you look at Table 3.2 in Chapter 3 you'll see that such a drawing requires an area 2304 wide units by 1728 units deep.

4. Create a layer called **Plan1** and make it the current layer.

5. Use the Drawing Aids dialog box to set the Snap mode to 1, and set the grid to 8' which is the distance required to display 1 inch divisions in an 1/8"=1'-0" scale drawing.

6. Turn on the grid.

7. Choose View ➤ Zoom ➤ All, or type **Z** ↵ **A** ↵, to get an overall view of the drawing area.

If you prefer, you can specify the insertion point in the dialog box by removing the checkmark from the Specify Parameters on Screen checkbox. The Input options will then become available to receive your input.

---

8. Insert the Unit.dwg drawing at coordinate 31'–5", 43'–8". Accept the default values at all the prompts, since you want to insert this drawing just as you drew it.

9. Zoom in to the apartment unit plan.

10. Click on Mirror from the Modify toolbar. Then select the unit plan and press ↵.

11. At the First point of the mirror line prompt, Shift + right-click the mouse and select From.

12. Shift + right-click again and select Endpoint.

13. Select the endpoint of the upper-right corner of the apartment unit, as shown in Figure 6.1.

14. Enter @2.5<0 ↵. A rubber-banding line appears indicating the mirror axis.

15. Turn on the Ortho mode and select any point to make the mirror axis point in a vertical orientation.

16. At the Delete Old Objects prompt, press ↵. You will thus get a 5" wall thickness between two studio units. Your drawing should be similar to Figure 6.1.

17. Press ↵ to reissue the Mirror command again and select both units.

18. Use the From Osnap again and, using the Endpoint Osnap, select the same corner you selected in step 10.

19. Enter @24<90 to start a mirror axis 24 inches directly above the selected point.

20. With the Ortho mode on, select a point so that the mirror axis is exactly horizontal.

21. Press ↵ to keep the original units and complete the mirror operation.

FIGURE 6.1:

The unit plan mirrored

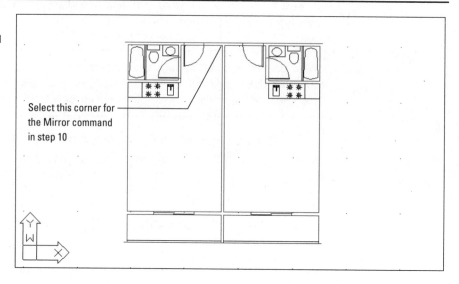

Select this corner for the Mirror command in step 10

NOTE   The Extents option forces the entire drawing to fill the screen at the left-most side of the display area.

With the tools you've learned about so far, you've quickly and accurately set up a fairly good portion of the floor plan. Continue with the next few steps to "rough-in" the main components of the floor.

1. Click on View ➤ Zoom ➤ Extents, or type **Z** ↵ **E** ↵, to get a view of the four plans. You can also use the Extents tool on the Zoom Window tool flyout. Your drawing will look like Figure 6.2.

TIP   If you happen to insert a block in the wrong coordinate location, you can use the Properties tool in the Object Properties toolbar to change the insertion point for the block.

2. Copy the 4 units to the right at a distance of 28'-10", which is the width of two units from centerline to centerline of walls.

3. Insert the lobby at coordinate 89'-1", 76'-1".

FIGURE 6.2:

The unit plan, dupli-
cated four times

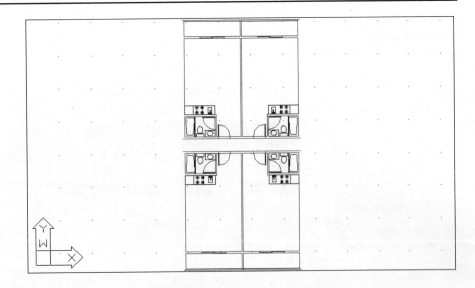

4. Copy all the unit plans to the right 74'–5", the width of four units plus the width of the lobby.

NOTE From this point on, we will use the nickname "Zoom All" to refer to the View ➢ Zoom ➢ All command.

---

5. Click on View ➢ Zoom ➢ All, or type **Z** ↵ **A** ↵, to view the entire drawing, which will look like Figure 6.3. You can also use the Zoom All tool on the Zoom Window flyout.

6. Now use the File ➢ Save option to save this file to disk.

Taking Control of the AutoCAD Display

By now you should be familiar with the Pan and Zoom functions in AutoCAD. There are many other tools at your disposal that can help you get around in your drawing. In this section, you'll get a closer look at the different ways you can view your drawing.

FIGURE 6.3:

The Plan drawing

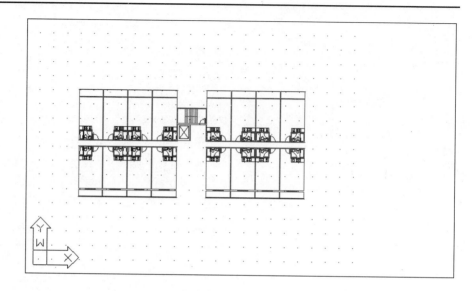

Understanding Regeneration and Redraw

AutoCAD uses two methods for refreshing your drawing display: the drawing regeneration or *regen* and the *redraw*. Each serves a particular purpose, though they may not be clear to a new user.

AutoCAD stores drawing data in two ways; one is like a database of highly accurate coordinate information and object properties. This is the core information you supply as you draw and edit your drawing. The other way is a less accurate, simplified database of just the display information. AutoCAD uses this second database to allow quick manipulation of the display of your drawing. For the purposes of this discussion, I'll call this simplified database the "virtual display" because it is like a computer model of the overall display of your drawing. This virtual display is in turn used as the basis for what is shown in the drawing area. When you issue a redraw, you are telling AutoCAD to re-read this virtual display data and display that information in the drawing area. A regen, on the other hand, causes AutoCAD to re-build the virtual display based on information from the core drawing database.

As you edit drawings, you may find that some of the lines in the display disappear or otherwise appear corrupted. Redraw will usually restore such distortions in the display. In earlier versions of AutoCAD, the Blipmode system variable was turned on by default, causing markers called blips to appear wherever points were selected. Redraw was, and still is, useful in clearing the screen of these blips.

Regens are used less frequently, and are brought to bear when changes occur to settings and options that have a global effect on a drawing, such as a line-type scale change, layer color change, or text style changes (you'll learn more about text styles in Chapter 8). In fact, regens are normally issued automatically when such changes occur. You usually don't have to issue the Regen command on your own, except under certain situations.

Regens can also occur when you select a view of a drawing that is not currently included as part of the virtual display. The virtual display contains display data for a limited area of a drawing. If you zoom or pan to a view that is outside that virtual display area, a regen occurs.

NOTE You may notice that Pan Realtime and Zoom Realtime will not work beyond a certain area in the display. When you've reached a point when these commands seem to stop working, you've come to the limits of the virtual display data. In order to go beyond these limits, AutoCAD must rebuild the virtual display data from the core data; in other words, do a drawing regeneration.

In past versions of AutoCAD, regens were to be avoided at all cost, especially in large files. A regen on a very large file could take several minutes to complete. Today, with faster processors, large amounts of RAM, and a retooled AutoCAD, regens are not the problem they once were. Still, they can be annoying in multi-megabyte files, and if you are using an older Pentium-based computer, regens can still be a major headache. For these reasons, it pays to understand the finer points of controlling regens.

In this section, you will discover how to manage regens, thus reducing their impact on complex drawing. You can control how regens impact your work in three ways:

- By taking advantage of AutoCAD's many display-related tools

- By setting up AutoCAD so that regens do not occur automatically

- By freezing layers that do not need to be viewed or edited

We will explore these methods in the upcoming sections.

Exploring Other Ways of Controlling AutoCAD's Display

Perhaps one of the easiest ways of avoiding regens is by making sure you don't cross into an area of your drawing that falls outside of the virtual display's area. If you use Pan Realtime and Zoom Realtime, you are automatically kept safely within the bounds of the display list. In this section, you'll be introduced to other tools that will help keep you within those boundaries.

Controlling Display Smoothness

The virtual display can be turned on or off using the Viewres command. The Viewres setting is on by default, and for the most part, should remain on. You can turn it off by typing **Viewres** ⤶ **No** ⤶ at the command prompt. However, I wouldn't recommend this. With Viewres off, a regen occurs every time you change your view using pan or zoom.

The Viewres command also controls the smoothness of line types, arcs, and circles when they appear in an enlarged view. With the display list active, line types sometimes appear as continuous even when they are supposed to be dotted or dashed. You may have noticed in previous chapters that on-screen arcs appear to be segmented lines, though they are always plotted as smooth curves. You can adjust the Viewres value to control the number of segments an arc appears to have: the lower the value, the fewer the segments and the faster the redraw and regeneration. However, a low Viewres value will cause noncontinuous line types, such as dashes or center lines, to appear as continuous.

TIP

You can set the Viewres value in the Performance tab of the Preferences dialog box under the setting labeled *Arc and Circle Smoothness*.

Another way to accelerate screen redraw is to keep your drawing limits to a minimum area. If the limits are set unnecessarily high, AutoCAD may slow down noticeably. Also, make sure the drawing origin falls within the drawing limits.

TIP

A good value for the Viewres setting is 500. At this setting, line types display properly, and arcs and circles have a reasonably smooth appearance. At the same time, redraw speed is not noticeably degraded. However, you may want to keep Viewres lower still if you have a limited amount of RAM. High Viewres settings can adversely affect AutoCAD's overall use of memory.

Using the Aerial View

Let's take a tour of a tool that lets you navigate drawings that represent very large areas. It's called the Aerial View.

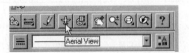

1. Click on Aerial View from the Standard Toolbar. The Aerial View window appears, as shown in Figure 6.4.

2. Move your cursor over the Aerial View window. Notice that you have a dotted crosshair cursor in the window. This is the Aerial View zoom cursor.

FIGURE 6.4:

The Aerial View window and its components

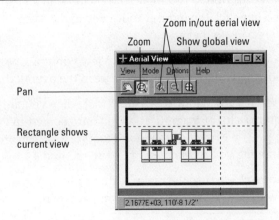

3. Click on a point in the lower-left corner of the aerial view. A view window appears.

4. Click on a point above and to the right of the first point you selected. Your view in the main AutoCAD drawing area enlarges to display the area you just selected. You also see a bold rectangle in the Aerial View window showing the location of your drawing area view.

The Aerial View doesn't zoom in. It continues to display the overall view of your drawing. The bold rectangle shows you exactly where you are in the overall drawing at any given time. This feature is especially useful in drawings of large areas that may take several pans to cross.

TIP   The View ➤ Zoom ➤ Dynamic option performs a similar function to the Aerial View window, but instead of opening a separate window, Dynamic temporarily displays the overall view in the drawing area.

Now let's look at the pan feature on the Aerial View toolbar. The pan feature can be helpful if you are moving or copying objects from one part of a drawing to another.

1. Choose Mode ➤ Pan from the Aerial View menu bar, or click on the Pan tool on the Aerial View toolbar. Now as you move your cursor over the Aerial View window, you see a dotted rectangle. This lets you pan to any location in the view.

2. Move the dotted rectangle so it encloses an area in the upper-right corner and left-click the mouse. Your view in the AutoCAD Drawing area immediately pans to that area.

Once again, the view in the Aerial View window doesn't change during the pan, allowing you to see where you are in the overall drawing.

The Aerial View window is a great tool when you are working on a drawing that requires a lot of magnification in your zoomed-in views. You may not find it very helpful on drawings that don't require lots of magnification, like the bathroom drawing you worked on in Chapters 3 and 4.

You were able to use the major features of the Aerial view in this exercise. Here are a few more features you can try on your own:

View ➤ Zoom In   zooms in on the view in the Aerial View.

View ➤ Zoom Out   zooms out on the view in the Aerial View.

View ➤ Global   displays an overall view of your drawing in the Aerial View window. Global is like a View ➤ Zoom ➤ Extents option for the Aerial View.

Options ➤ Auto Viewport   controls whether a selected viewport is automatically displayed in the Aerial View window. When checked, this option will cause the Aerial View window to automatically display the contents of a viewport when it becomes active. (See Chapters 12 and 16 for more on viewports.)

Options ➤ Dynamic Update   controls how often changes in your drawing are updated in the Aerial View. When this option is checked, the Aerial

View window is updated as you work. You may want to turn this feature off in very complex drawing as it can slow down redraw times.

Saving Views

Another way of controlling your views is by saving them. You might think of saving views as a way of creating a bookmark or placeholder in your drawing. You'll see how to save views in the following set of exercises.

A few walls in the Plan drawing are not complete. You'll need to zoom in to the areas that need work to add the lines, but these areas are spread out over the drawing. You could use the Aerial View window to view each area. There is, however, another way to edit widely separated areas: First, save views of the areas you want to work on, and then jump from saved view to saved view. This technique is especially helpful when you know you will often want to return to a specific area of your drawing.

1. First, close the Aerial View window by clicking on the Close button in the upper-left corner of the window.

2. Click on View ➢ Zoom ➢ All, or type **Z** ⏎ **a** ⏎, to get an overall view of the plan.

3. Click on View ➢ Named Views.... The View Control dialog box appears.

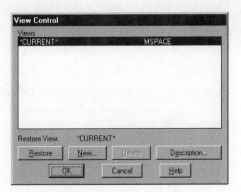

NOTE From this dialog box, you can call up an existing view (Restore), create a new view (New...), or get detailed information about a view (Description...).

4. Click on the New... button. The Define New View dialog box appears.

5. Click on the Define Window radio button. Notice that the grayed options become available.

6. Click on Window <. The dialog boxes momentarily disappear.

7. At the First corner prompt, click near the coordinate 26', 40'. You don't have to be exact because you are selecting view windows.

8. At the Other corner prompt, click on a location near the coordinate 91', 82'. The dialog boxes reappear.

9. Type **first** for the name of the view you just defined. As you type, the name appears in the New Name input box.

10. Click on the Save View button. The Define New View dialog box closes, and you see FIRST listed in the View Control list.

11. Repeat steps 3 through 9 to define five more views, named SECOND, THIRD, etc. Use Figure 6.5 as a guide for where to define the windows. Click on OK when you are done.

Now let's see how you recall these views that you've saved.

1. With the View Control dialog box open, click on FIRST in the list of views.

(Named Views)

TIP

A quick way to restore saved views is to type **View** ↵ **R** ↵ then enter the name of the view you wish to restore.

FIGURE 6.5:

Save view windows in these locations for the Plan drawing

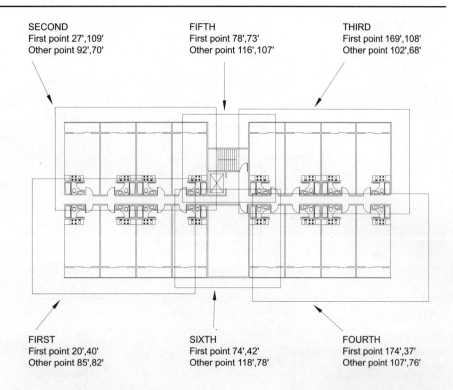

SECOND
First point 27',109'
Other point 92',70'

FIFTH
First point 78',73'
Other point 116',107'

THIRD
First point 169',108'
Other point 102',68'

FIRST
First point 20',40'
Other point 85',82'

SIXTH
First point 74',42'
Other point 118',78'

FOURTH
First point 174',37'
Other point 107',76'

2. Click on the Restore button and then click on OK. Your screen displays the first view you selected.

3. Set the current layer to Wall, and proceed to add the stairs and exterior walls of the building, as shown in Figure 6.6. (Remember that you exported the stairs from the lobby drawing in the last chapter. You can also use the Stair.dwg file from the companion CD-ROM.)

4. Use the View Control dialog box again to restore the view named SECOND. Then add the walls shown in Figure 6.7.

5. Continue to the other views and add the rest of the exterior walls, as you have done with FIRST and SECOND. Use the four panels of Figure 6.8 as a guide to completing the views.

FIGURE 6.6:

The stairs added to the restored FIRST view

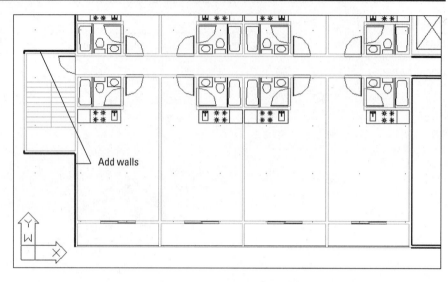

FIGURE 6.7:

Walls added to the restored SECOND view

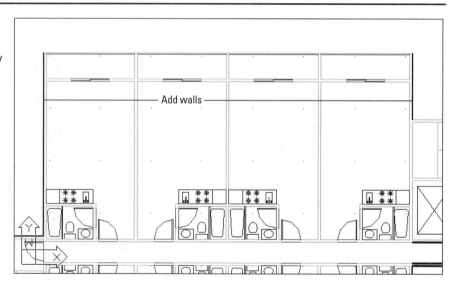

FIGURE 6.8:

Walls, stairs, and
doors added to the
other views

THIRD view

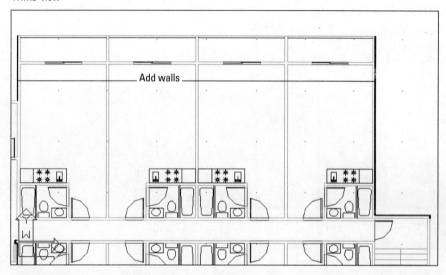

FOURTH view

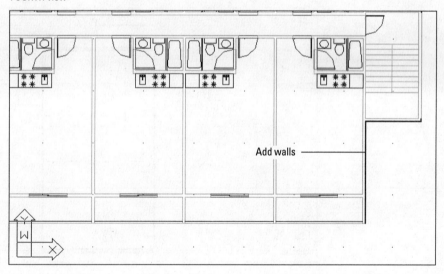

FIGURE 6.8: CONTINUED

Walls, stairs, and doors added to the other views

FIFTH view

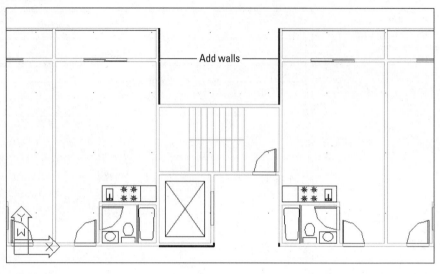

SIXTH view

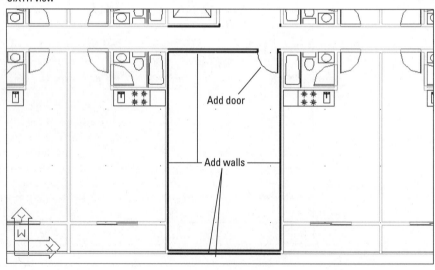

If you prefer, you can use the keyboard to invoke the View command and thus avoid all the dialog boxes.

1. Click on View ➢ Zoom ➢ Extents, or type **Z ↵ E ↵**.

2. Enter **View** ↵ **s** ↵ at the command prompt.

3. At the View name to save prompt, enter **Overall** ↵.

4. Now save the Plan file to disk.

NOTE In prior versions of AutoCAD, Zoom ➤ Extents caused a regen to occur. Regens no longer occur with this command in Release 14.

As you can see, this is a quick way to save a view. With the name OVERALL assigned to this view, you can easily recall the overall view at any time. (The View ➤ Zoom ➤ All option gives you an overall view, too, but it may zoom out too far for some purposes, or it may not show what you might consider to be an overall view.)

TIP Another useful tool for getting around in your drawing is the Zoom toolbar. It contains tools for Zoom Window, Dynamic, Scale, Center, In, Out, All, and Extent. To open the Zoom toolbar, right-click on any toolbar, then click on the Zoom checkbox in the Toolbar dialog box that appears.

Opening a File to a Particular View

The Open Drawing dialog box contains a Select Initial View checkbox. If you open an existing drawing with this option checked, you are greeted with a Select Initial View dialog box just before the opened file appears on the screen. This dialog box lists any views saved in the file. You can then go directly to a view by double-clicking on the view name. If you have saved views and you know the name of the view you want, using Select Initial View saves time when you're opening very large files.

Freezing Layers to Control Regeneration Time

As mentioned earlier, you may wish to turn certain layers off altogether to plot a drawing containing only selected layers. But even when layers are turned off, AutoCAD still takes the time to redraw and regenerate them. The Layer &

Linetype Properties dialog box offers the Freeze option that acts like the Off option, except that Freeze causes AutoCAD to ignore frozen layers when redrawing and regenerating a drawing. By freezing layers that are not needed for reference or editing, you can reduce the time AutoCAD takes to perform regens.

You should be aware, however, that the Freeze options affect blocks in an unusual way. Try the following exercise to see firsthand how the Freeze option makes entire blocks invisible.

1. Use the Layers & Linetype Properties dialog box to set the current layer to 0.

TIP   You can freeze and thaw individual layers by clicking on the Sun icon in the layer pop-up list in the Properties toolbar.

---

2. Click on the yellow lightbulb icon in the Plan1 layer listing to turn off that layer, and then click OK. Nothing happens to your drawing. Turning off the Plan1 layer, the layer on which the unit blocks were inserted, has no affect.

3. Now use the Layer & Linetype Properties dialog box to turn off all of the layers.

4. Choose View ➣ Regen, or type **re** ↵. Note the time it takes to perform a regen.

5. Open the Layers & Linetype Properties dialog box again and turn all of the layers back on.

6. Now click on the Plan1 layer's Freeze/Thaw icon, which is the one that looks like a sun. (Note that you cannot freeze the current layer.) The yellow sun icon changes to a gray snowflake indicating that the layer is now frozen.

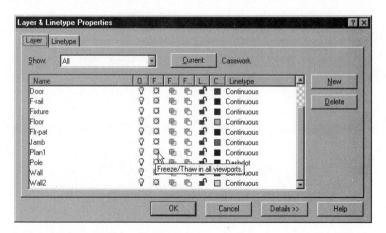

7. Click on OK. Now the unit blocks disappear. Even though none of the objects within the unit blocks were drawn on layer Plan1, when Plan1 is frozen, so are the entire contents of the blocks assigned to the Plan1 layer.

TIP   Remember that you can right-click on a blank area of the Layers & Linetype properties dialog box, then choose Select All from the pop-up menu to select all the layers at once.

---

8. Issue the Regen command again and pay attention to the time it takes. The regen is faster this time.

9. Now, "thaw" layer Plan1 by opening the Layer & Linetype Properties dialog box and clicking on the Snowflake icon in the Plan1 layer listing.

10. Turn off the Ceiling layer, exit the dialog box, and use File ➤ Exit to exit the Plan file. You needn't save the change. In this relatively small file, the differences between the regen times of the off state versus the freeze state is small. But in larger files, the difference can be significant. As your drawings become larger, try this exercise again to see how Off versus Freeze affects your regen speed.

Block Visibility with Freeze and Off

 The previous exercise showed the effect that freezing a layer has on blocks. When the layer of a block is frozen, the entire block is made invisible, regardless of the layers assignments of the objects contained in the block.

Keep in mind that when blocks are on layers that are not frozen, the individual objects that are a part of a block are still affected by the status of the layer to which they are assigned.

You can take advantage of this feature by using layers to store parts of a drawing that you may want to plot separately. For example, three floors in your apartment building plan may contain the same information, with some specific variation on each floor. In this case, you can have one layer contain blocks of the objects common to all the floors. Another layer contains the blocks and objects specific to the first floor, and additional layers contain information specific to the second and third floors. When you want to view or plot one floor, you can freeze the layers associated with the others. With respect to Freeze/Thaw visibility, external referenced files inserted using the external reference (Xref) command also act like blocks. For example, you can Xref several drawings on different layers. Then, when you want to view a particular Xref drawing, you can freeze all the layers except the one containing that drawing.

Using layers and blocks in these ways requires careful planning and record keeping. If used successfully, however, this technique can save substantial time when you're working with drawings that use repetitive objects or that require similar information that can be overlaid.

Taking Control of Regens

Another way to control regeneration time is by setting the Regenmode system variable to 0 (zero). You can also use the Regenauto command to accomplish the same thing, by typing **Regenauto ⏎ Off ⏎**.

If you then issue a command that normally triggers a regen, AutoCAD will give the message "Regen queued." For example, when you globally edit attributes, redefine blocks, thaw frozen layers, change the LTSCALE setting, or, in some cases, change a text's style, you will get the "Regen queued" message. You can "Que-up" regens then at a time you choose. You can issue a regen to update all the changes at once by choosing View ➤ Regen, or by typing **RE ⏎**. This way, only one regen occurs instead of several.

By taking control of when regens occur, you can reduce the overall time you spend editing large files.

Using Hatch Patterns in Your Drawings

To help communicate your ideas to others, you will want to add graphic elements that represent types of materials, special regions, or textures. AutoCAD provides *hatch patterns* for quickly placing a texture over an area of your drawing. In this section, you will add a hatch pattern to the floor of the studio apartment unit, thereby instantly enhancing the appearance of one drawing. Later in the chapter you'll learn how you can quickly update all the units in the overall floor plan to reflect the changes in the unit.

Creating Multiple Views

So far, you've looked at ways to help you get around in your drawing while using a single view window. You also have the capability to set up multiple views of your drawing, called viewports. With viewports, you can display more than one view of your drawing at one time in the AutoCAD drawing area. For example, you can have one viewport to show a close-up of the bathroom, another viewport to display the overall plan view, and yet another to display the unit plan.

When viewports are combined with AutoCAD's Paper Space feature, you can plot multiple views of your drawing. Paper Space is a display mode that lets you "paste-up" multiple views of a drawing, much like a page layout program. To find out more about Viewports and Paper Space, see Chapter 12.

Placing a Hatch Pattern in a Specific Area

It's always a good idea to provide a separate layer for hatch patterns. By doing so, you can turn them off if you need to. For example, in Chapter 3, you saw how the San Francisco Main Library floor plan displayed the floor paving pattern in one drawing while in another drawing, it was turned off so it wouldn't distract from other information.

In the following exercise, you will add a hatch pattern representing floor tile. This will give you the opportunity to learn the different methods of creating and controlling hatch patterns.

1. Open the Unit file.

2. Zoom into the bathroom and kitchen area.

3. Create a new layer called Flr-pat.

4. Make Flr-pat the current layer.

Once you've set up the layer for the hatch pattern, you can place the pattern in the drawing.

1. Click on the Hatch tool on the Draw Toolbar or type **H** ↵. Hatch is also located in the Draw pull-down menu.

The Boundary Hatch dialog box appears.

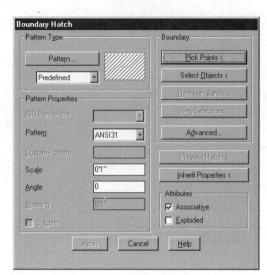

TIP

Say you want to add a hatch pattern you have previously inserted in another part of the drawing. You may think that you have to guess at its scale and rotation angle. But with the Inherit Properties option in the Boundary Hatch dialog box, you can select a previously inserted hatch pattern as a prototype for the current hatch pattern. However, this feature does not work with exploded hatch patterns.

---

2. Under Pattern Type, open the pop-up list and select User-Defined. The User-Defined option lets you define a simple crosshatch pattern by specifying the line spacing of the hatch and whether it is a single- or double-hatch pattern. The Angle and Spacing input boxes become available in the Pattern Properties group, so you can enter values.

3. Double-click on the Spacing input box near the bottom and enter **6**. This tells AutoCAD you want the hatch's line spacing to be 6". Leave the Angle value at 0. Because we want the pattern to be aligned with the bathroom.

4. Click on the checkbox labeled Double (at the lower-left of the Pattern Properties group). This tells AutoCAD you want the hatch pattern to run both vertically and horizontally.

5. Click on the Pick Points button. The dialog box momentarily disappears, allowing you to pick a point inside the area you want hatched.

6. Click on a point anywhere inside the bathroom floor area, below the toilet. Notice that a highlighted outline appears in the bathroom. This is the boundary AutoCAD has selected to enclose the hatch pattern. It outlines everything including the door swing arc.

TIP If you have text in the hatch boundary, AutoCAD will avoid hatching over it, unless the Ignore is selected in the Boundary Style options of the Advanced Hatch settings. See Using Advanced Hatch Settings in this chapter for more on the Ignore setting.

7. Press ↵ to return to the Boundary Hatch dialog box.

8. Click on the Preview Hatch button. The hatch pattern appears everywhere on the floor except where the door swing occurs.

9. Click on Continue to return to the dialog box.

10. Click on Pick Points again, pick a point inside the door swing, and press ↵.

11. Click on Preview Hatch again. The hatch pattern now covers the entire floor area.

12. Click on Continue to return to the dialog box.

13. Click on the Apply button to place the hatch pattern in the drawing.

The Hatch dialog box lets you first define the boundary within which you want to place a hatch pattern. You do this by simply clicking on a location inside the boundary area, as in step 6. AutoCAD finds the actual boundary for you.

The Boundary Hatch dialog box also lets you set the hatch pattern (Pattern Type and Pattern Properties), pick a point that is bounded by the area to be hatched (Pick Points), select objects to define the hatch area (Select Objects), and use advanced boundary selection options for complex hatch patterns (Advanced…). Other options let you preview the hatch pattern in place (Preview Hatch), or view the hatch boundaries (View Selections).

Using the Advanced Hatch Options

AutoCAD's Boundary Hatch command has a fair amount of intelligence. As you saw in the last exercise, it was able to detect not only the outline of the floor area, but also the toilet seat that represents an island within the pattern area. If you prefer, you can control how AutoCAD treats these island conditions and other situations by selecting options available when you click on the Advanced button in the Boundary Hatch dialog box. This button displays the Advanced Options dialog box.

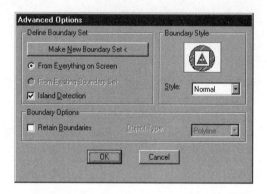

In addition to controlling the Island Detection feature of hatch patterns, the Advanced Options let you fine-tune other aspects of hatch pattern creation.

Style

The Style pop-up list in the middle of the dialog box controls how nested boundaries affect the hatch pattern. When you select a Style option, the graphic to the right of the pop-up list shows an example of the effect of the selected option. The Style options include the following:

Normal   causes the hatch pattern to alternate between nested boundaries. The outer boundary is hatched; if there is a closed object within the boundary, it is not hatched. If another closed object *is* inside the first closed object, *that* object is hatched. This is the default setting.

Outer   applies the hatch pattern to an area defined by the outermost boundary and any boundaries nested within the outermost boundary. Any boundaries nested within the nested boundaries are ignored.

Ignore   applies the hatch pattern to the entire area within the outermost boundary, ignoring any nested boundaries.

NOTE Hatch patterns are like blocks, in that they act like single objects. You can explode a hatch pattern to edit its individual lines. You can also automatically explode the hatch after it is placed in the drawing by selecting the Exploded checkbox in the Pattern Properties group of the Boundary Hatch dialog box.

Object Type

The Object Type pull-down list lets you select the type of object used to define the boundary. The default is Polyline, which creates a simple outline using a polyline. The other option is Region, which creates an object that is like a flat plane in the shape of the hatch area.

Define Boundary Set

A Boundary Set is the set of objects that you want AutoCAD to use to define the outline of the hatch pattern. Within this group, you'll find the following:

From Everything on Screen   is on by default, unless you have already used Boundary Hatch to generate a hatch boundary. If it isn't already on, clicking on this button creates a new boundary set based on everything visible on the screen. This operation can take some time if the current view is dense with objects.

From Existing Working Set   is on by default if you have used the Select Object option to generate a hatch boundary. This setting simply indicates that you have selected objects to be used in defining the boundary. These selected objects will be used unless the From Everything on Screen option button is selected or you click on the Make New Boundary Set button.

Make New Boundary Set   lets you select the objects from which you want AutoCAD to determine the hatch boundary. The screen clears and lets you select objects. This option discards previous boundary sets. It is useful for hatching areas in a drawing that may contain many objects that you do not want to include in the hatch boundary.

Island Detection   This checkbox controls the Island Detection feature, a method of finding boundaries within the selected area. It is capable of finding nested areas.

Retain Boundaries   The Boundary Hatch command can also create an outline of the hatch area using one of two objects: 2D regions, which are like 2D planes, or polyline outlines. Boundary Hatch actually creates such a polyline boundary temporarily, to establish the hatch area. These boundaries are automatically removed after the hatch pattern is inserted. If you want to retain the polyline boundaries in the drawing, make sure the Retain Boundaries checkbox is turned on. Retaining the boundary can be useful in situations where you know you will be hatching the area more than once, or if you are hatching a fairly complex area.

TIP   Retaining a hatch boundary is useful if you want to know the hatched area's dimensions in square inches or feet, because you can find the area of a closed polyline using the List command. Another command called *Boundary* will create a polyline outline or region within a selected area. It works much like the Bondary Hatch command but does not add a hatch pattern. The keyboard shortcut for Boundary is **B** ↵.

Tips for Using the Boundary Hatch

Here are a few tips on using the Boundary Hatch feature:

- Watch out for boundary areas that are part of a very large block. AutoCAD will examine the entire block when defining boundaries. This can take time if the block is quite large.

- The Boundary Hatch feature is view dependent; that is, it locates boundaries based on what is visible in the current view. To ensure that AutoCAD finds every detail, zoom in to the area to be hatched.

- If the area to be hatched will cover a very large area yet will require fine detail, first outline the hatch area using a polyline (see Chapter 13 for more on Polylines). Then use the Select Object option in the Boundary Hatch dialog box to select the polyline boundary manually, instead of depending on Boundary Hatch to find the boundary for you.

- Consider turning off layers that might interfere with AutoCAD's ability to find a boundary. For example, in the previous exercise, you could have turned off the Door layer, and then used Pick Points to locate the boundary of the hatch pattern.

- Boundary Hatch works on nested blocks as long as the nested block entities are parallel to the current UCS and are uniformly scaled in the *x*- and *y*-axes.

Positioning Hatch Patterns Accurately

In the last exercise, the hatch pattern was placed in the bathroom without regard for the location of the lines that make up the pattern. In most cases, however, you will want to control where the lines of the pattern are placed.

TIP You can also click on Graphic in the Pattern Type list to "page" through each of the predefined hatch patterns.

Hatch patterns use the same origin as the snap origin (see Chapter 3 for more information about the snap origin). By default, this origin is the same as the drawing origin, 0,0. You can change the snap origin (and thus the hatch pattern origin) by using the Snapbase system variable. The following exercise guides you through the process of placing a hatch pattern accurately, using the example of adding floor tile to the kitchenette.

1. Pan your view so that you can see the area below the kitchenette, and using the Rectangle tool in the Draw toolbar, draw the 3'–0"×8'–0" outline of the floor tile area, as shown in Figure 6.9. You may also use a closed polyline.

TIP If you know the coordinates of the new snap origin, you can enter them in the Drawing Aids dialog box under the X Base and Y Base input box instead of using the Snapbase system variable.

2. At the command prompt, type **Snapbase** ↵.

3. At the New value for Snapbase <0'-0",0'-0"> prompt, use the Endpoint Osnap and click on the lower-left corner of the area you just defined (see Figure 6.11).

FIGURE 6.9:

The area below the kitchen showing the outline of the floor tile area

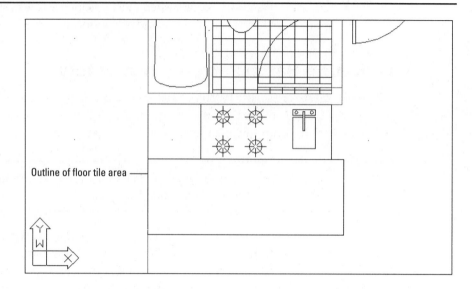

Outline of floor tile area

4. Click on Hatch in the Draw toolbar.

5. At the Boundary Hatch dialog box, make sure Predefined is selected in the Pattern Type pull-down list.

6. In the Pattern Type group, click on the button labeled Pattern.... The Hatch Pattern Palette dialog box appears.

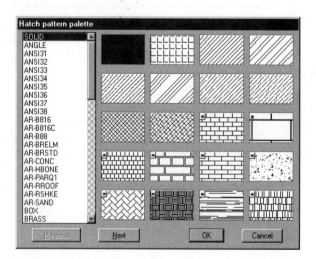

NOTE   If you know the name of the pattern you want, you can also select it from the Pattern drop-down list in the Pattern Properties group.

7. This dialog box lets you select a pre-defined pattern either from a list to the left, or from a graphic that shows what the pattern looks like.

8. Locate and click on AR-PARQ1 from the list to the left. The sample pattern is highlighted in the right portion of the dialog box.

9. Click on OK to exit the dialog box.

10. Click on the Pick Points button.

11. Click on the interior of the area to be tiled, and press ↵.

12. Click on Apply. A parquet-style tile pattern appears in the defined area.

TIP   You can use the Solid predefined hatch pattern at the top of the list to create solid fills. This is a vast improvement over the Solid command that was used for solid fills in earlier versions of AutoCAD.

Notice that each tile is shown whole; none of the tiles is cut off as in the bathroom example. This is because you first used the Snapbase system variable to set the origin for the hatch pattern. You can now move the Snapbase setting back to the 0,0 setting and not affect the hatch pattern.

In the foregoing exercise, you got a chance to use a predefined hatch pattern. Figure 6.10 shows you all the patterns available. You can also create your own custom patterns, as described in Chapter 21.

NOTE   The predefined patterns with the AR prefix are architectural patterns that are drawn to full scale. In general, you will want to leave their scale settings at 1. You can adjust the scale after you have placed the hatch pattern using the Properties tool, as described later in this chapter.

NOTE   If you are a veteran AutoCAD user, you may hesitate to use many hatch patterns in an already crowded drawing. In the past, hatch patterns were memory hogs. You'll be happy to know that Release 14 has made hatch patterns much more memory efficient. Also, Release 14 now has a solid hatch for solid fills.

FIGURE 6.10:

Predefined hatch patterns available in AutoCAD

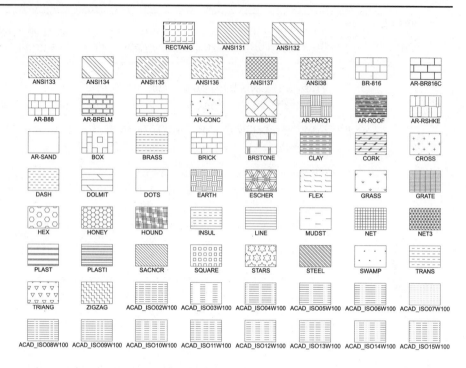

Changing the Hatch Area

You may have noticed the Associative option in the Boundary Hatch dialog box. When this option is checked, AutoCAD creates an Associative hatch pattern. Associative hatches will adjust their shapes to any changes in their associated boundary, hence the name. The following exercise demonstrates how this works.

Suppose you want to enlarge the tiled area of the kitchen by one tile. Here's how it's done.

1. Click on the outline border of the hatch pattern you just created. Notice the grips that appear around the hatch pattern area.

NOTE   You may need to zoom in closer to the pattern area or use the object selection cycling feature to select the hatch boundary. For more on selection cycling, see *Singling Out Proximate Objects* in Chapter 12.

2. Shift + click on the grip in the lower-left corner of the hatch area.

TIP　If the boundary of the hatch pattern consists of line segments, you can use a crossing window or polygon crossing window to select the corner grips of the hatch pattern.

3. With the lower-left grip highlighted, Shift + click on the lower-right grip.

4. Now click on the lower-right grip again, but don't Shift + click this time.

5. Enter @12<−90 to widen the hatch pattern by 1 foot. The hatch pattern adjusts to the new size of the hatch boundary.

The Associative feature of hatch patterns can save time when you need to make modifications to your drawing. But you should be aware of its limitations. There are several ways a hatch pattern can lose its associativity. They are:

- Erasing or exploding a hatch boundary
- Erasing or exploding a block that forms part of the boundary
- Moving a hatch pattern away from its boundary
- Moving a hatch boundary away from the hatch pattern

These situations frequently arise when you edit an unfamiliar drawing. Often, boundary objects are placed on a layer that is off or frozen, so the boundary objects are not visible. Or the hatch pattern may be on a layer that is turned off and you proceed to edit the file not knowing that a hatch pattern exists. When you encounter such a file, take a moment to check for hatch boundaries so you can deal with them properly.

Modifying a Hatch Pattern

Like everything else, you or someone involved in your project will eventually want to change a hatch pattern in some way. The Properties tool in the Object Properties toolbar offers most of the settings you'll need to make changes to your hatch patterns.

1. Press the Esc key twice to clear any grip selections.

2. Click on the Properties tool in the Object Properties toolbar, and then click on the hatch pattern and press ⌐. You'll see the Modify Hatch dialog box,

which is similar to the typical Change Properties dialog box. But this one has an additional Hatch Edit... Button.

3. Click on the Hatch Edit... Button. The Boundary Hatch dialog box appears again. You can now select any option that is available (not grayed out) to modify the hatch pattern.

TIP You can also go directly to the Boundary Hatch dialog box by using the Hatchedit command (Modify ➤ Object ➤ Hatch). The keyboard shortcut for Hatchedit is **HE** ⏎. Hatchedit also allows you to acquire a hatch pattern from an existing one in your drawing. This option is not available when you select Hatch Edit from the Modify Hatch dialog box.

4. Make sure Predefined is selected in the Pattern Type list box; then click on the graphic beside the Pattern Type list box. Notice how it changes and how, as it changes, the name of the pattern in the Pattern Properties group changes with it, to identify the pattern.

5. Open the Pattern drop-down list in the Pattern Properties group and choose AR-BRSTD. You will have to scroll up the list to find it.

6. Click on the Apply button to change the hatch pattern area to the new pattern.

7. Click on OK at the Modify Hatch dialog box.

8. We want to keep the old pattern in our drawing, so click on the Undo button on the Standard toolbar, or type **U** ⏎ to return to the previous hatch pattern.

9. Now save this version of the Unit file.

As you saw in the last exercise, not all the Boundary Hatch options are available to you. Still, you can change the pattern to a predefined or custom pattern, or to one that already exists in the drawing. You can also change the angle and scale of a pattern, as well as the origin. To adjust the position of an existing hatch pattern, set the snap origin, then use the Properties tool to redefine the hatch pattern.

If you find that you are creating and editing hatch patterns frequently, you will find the Modify II toolbar useful. It contains an Edit Hatch tool that gives you ready access to the Hatchedit dialog box. To open the Modify II toolbar, right-click on any toolbar, and then click on the Modify II checkbox in the Toolbars dialog box that appears.

A Review of Other Boundary Hatch Options

Before exiting this section, you might want to look over the descriptions of options in the Boundary Hatch dialog box that weren't discussed in the exercises.

ISO Pen Width   lets you select a pen width to associate with the hatch patterns. These pen widths are meaningful only when used with the ISO standard hatch patterns. When you set the ISO pen width, the scale of the pattern is adjusted accordingly. However, you must manually set the width of the actual plotter pen at plot time. (See Chapter 7 for more on pen-width adjustments.)

Exploded   draws the hatch pattern as individual objects, instead of an associative hatch pattern. This option can greatly increase the size of a file because hatch lines are converted to individual objects. Use it with caution.

Associative   draws a hatch pattern that will automatically update whenever the boundary of the hatch pattern changes.

Remove Islands   allows you to remove nested or island boundaries that have been included when you pick a point to define a boundary. This is useful when you want to force a hatch pattern to fall inside an island that occurs in a boundary.

View Selections   lets you review the boundaries that have been selected at any given time during the Boundary Hatch process.

Inherit Properties   lets you designate a hatch pattern, scale, and angle by selecting an existing hatch pattern in your drawing. When you choose this option, the dialog box momentarily disappears so you can select a pattern from your drawing. The properties of the selected pattern become the settings for the current boundary hatch session.

Default Properties   sets the Boundary Hatch options to their current default settings.

How to Quickly Match a Hatch Pattern and Other Properties

Another tool to help you edit hatch patterns is the Match Property tool, which is similar to the Format Painter in the Microsoft Office Suite. This tool lets you change an existing hatch pattern to match another existing hatch pattern. Here's how to use it.

1. Click on the Match Properties tool in the Standard toolbar.

2. Click on the hatch pattern you want to copy.

3. Click on the hatch pattern you want to change.

The pattern selected will change to match the pattern selected in step 2.

The Property Painter transfers other properties as well, such as layer, color, and line type settings. You can select the properties that are transferred by opening the Property Settings dialog box.

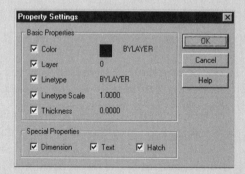

To open this dialog box, type **S** ↵ after selecting the object in step 2. You can then select the properties you wish to transfer from the options shown. All the properties are selected by default. Note that text and dimension style settings can also be transferred. You'll learn more about text and dimension styles in Chapters 8 and 9.

Space Planning and Hatch Patterns

Suppose you are working on a plan within which you are constantly repositioning equipment and furniture, or you are in the process of designing the floor covering. You may be a little hesitant to place a hatch pattern on the floor because you don't want to have to rehatch the area every time you move a piece of equipment or change the flooring. You have two options in this situation: You can use the Boundary Hatch's associative capabilities to include the furnishings in the boundary set, or you can put AutoCAD's 3D features to work.

Using Associative Hatch

Associative Hatch is the most straightforward method. Make sure the Associative option is checked in the Boundary Hatch dialog box and include your equipment or furniture in the boundary set. You can do this by using the Select Objects option in the dialog box.

Once the pattern is in place, you can move the furnishings in your drawing and the hatch pattern will automatically adjust to their new location. One drawback, however, is that AutoCAD will attempt to hatch the interior of your furnishings if it crosses over the outer boundary of the hatch pattern. Also, if any boundary objects are erased or exploded, the hatch pattern will no longer follow the location of your furnishings. To avoid these problems, you can use the following method.

Using 3D Features to Trick AutoCAD

The second method for masking hatch patterns requires the use of some 3D features of AutoCAD. First, draw the equipment at an elevation above the floor level by setting up AutoCAD to draw objects with a Z coordinate other than 0. Use the 3DFace command to generate a 3D surface that matches the outline of the equipment. Or, if your equipment outline is a fairly complex shape, use a region (regions are discussed in Chapter 18). Make sure the 3D Faces are drawn at an elevation that places them between the floor and the equipment. Turn each individual piece of equipment, complete with 3D Face, into blocks or groups so that you can easily move around. Once this is done, hatch the entire floor, making sure the hatch pattern is at an elevation below the 3D Face elevation (see Figure 6.11).

NOTE   See Chapter 15 for more on drawing objects in 3D.

TIP

You can change the Z coordinate of virtually any object by using the Properties tool in the Object Properties toolbar.

FIGURE 6.11:

Using 3D functions for space planning

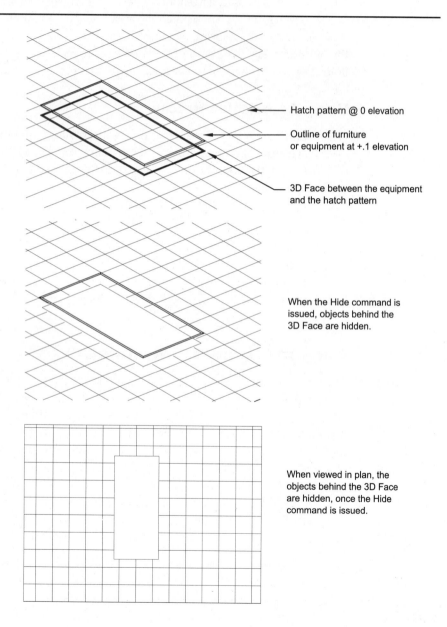

Hatch pattern @ 0 elevation

Outline of furniture or equipment at +.1 elevation

3D Face between the equipment and the hatch pattern

When the Hide command is issued, objects behind the 3D Face are hidden.

When viewed in plan, the objects behind the 3D Face are hidden, once the Hide command is issued.

WARNING   One drawback to the 3D method is that the Hide command turns solids and wide polylines into outlines.

As you work with the drawing, the floor pattern will show through the equipment. (Don't worry—when it's time to plot your drawing, you can use the Plot command's Hide option, discussed in Chapter 15, or the Mview command's Hideplot option, discussed in Chapter 18.) This causes anything behind the 3D Face to be hidden in the plotter output, which means any hatch pattern underneath your equipment will not appear. You can also use the Hide command from time to time to see what your design will look like without having to wait for hard copy—like using paper cutouts over a plan.

Using AutoCAD 3D features this way can save you time and give you more flexibility in your work. And although the Hide command takes a minute or two to do its work, it is still faster than rehatching an area each time you make a change to its configuration. For more on the 3D functions mentioned here, see Part IV of this book.

NOTE   A third method for masking hatch patterns is to use two bonus tools called Wipeout and Text Mask. Text Mask will mask the area behind text to make text more readable when situated over a hatch pattern. Wipeout is a more generalized masking tool. See Chapter 19 for details on both these tools.

Updating Blocks

As you progress through a design project, you make countless revisions. With traditional drafting methods, revising a drawing like our studio apartment floor plan takes a good deal of time. If the bathroom layout is changed, for example, you have to erase every occurrence of the bathroom and redraw it 16 times. With AutoCAD, on the other hand, revising this drawing can be a very quick operation. The studio unit you just modified can be updated throughout the overall plan drawing by replacing the current Unit block with the updated Unit file. AutoCAD automatically updates all occurrences of the Unit block. In the following exercise, we show you how this is accomplished.

1. Start by opening the Plan file.

This method does not update exploded blocks. If you plan to use this method to update parts of a drawing, do not explode the blocks you plan to update. See Chapter 4.

2. Click on Insert Block from the Draw toolbar.

3. Click on the File button, and from the Select Drawing File dialog box, double-click on the Unit file name.

4. Click on OK. A warning message tells you that a block already exists with the same name as the file. You have the option to cancel the operation or redefine the block in the current drawing.

5. Click on OK. The drawing will regenerate (unless you have Regenauto turned off.

6. At the Insertion point prompt, press Esc. You do this because you really don't want to insert a Unit plan into your drawing, but rather are just using the Insert feature to update an existing block.

7. If Regenauto is turned off, type **Regen** ↵ to turn it on.

If Regenauto is turned off, you must use the Regen command to force a regeneration of the drawing before the updated Unit block will appear on the display, even though the drawing database has been updated.

8. Now zoom in to one of the units. You will see that the floor tile appears in the unit as you drew it in the Unit file (see Figure 6.12).

Nested blocks must be updated independently of the parent block. For example, if you had modified the Toilet block while editing the Unit file, and then updated the Unit drawing in the Plan file, the old Toilet block would not have been updated. Even though the toilet is part of the Unit file, it is still a unique, independent block in the Plan file, and AutoCAD will not modify it unless specifically instructed to do so. In this situation, you must edit the original Toilet file, and then update it in both the Plan and Unit files.

FIGURE 6.12:

The Plan drawing thus far

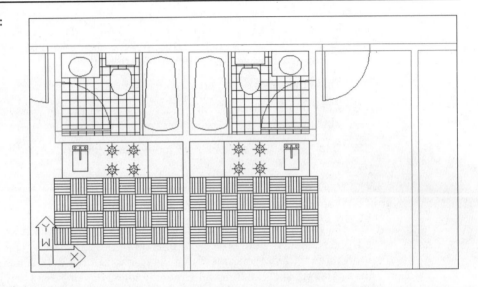

TIP   If you want to substitute one block with another within the current file, type **Insert** ↵. At the Block name prompt, enter the block name followed by an equals sign, then the name of the new block or file name. Do not include spaces between the names and the equals sign.

Also, block references and layer settings of the current file take priority over those of the imported file. For example, if a file to be imported has layers of the same name as the current file, but those layers have color and line-type assignments that are different from the current file's, the current file's layer color and line type assignments will determine those of the imported file. This does not mean, however, that the actual imported file on disk is changed; only the inserted drawing is effected.

Substituting Blocks

In the example under the section *Updating Blocks,* you updated a block in your Plan file using the File option in the Insert dialog box. In that exercise, the block name and the file name were the same. You can also replace a block with another block or file of a different name. Here's how to do this.

1. Open the Insert dialog box.

2. Click on the File button and locate and select the file you want to use as a substitute, and then click on OK. You will return to the Insert dialog box.

3. Change the name in the Block input box to the name of the block you want replaced.

4. Click on OK. You will see a warning message telling you that a block with this name already exists. Click on OK again to proceed with the block substitution.

You can use this method of replacing blocks if you would like to see how changing one element of your project can change your design. You might, for example, draw three different apartment unit plans, each with a unique name. You could then generate and plot three apartment building designs in a fraction of the time it would take you to do it by hand.

Block substitution can also reduce a drawing's complexity and accelerate regenerations. To do this, you temporarily replace large, complex blocks with schematic versions of those blocks. For example, you might replace the Unit block in the Plan drawing with another drawing that contains just a single-line representation of the walls and bathroom fixtures. You would still have the wall lines for reference when inserting other symbols or adding mechanical or electrical information, but the drawing would regenerate much faster. When doing the final plot, you would reinsert the original Unit block showing every detail.

Using External References

In this chapter's discussion about freezing layers, I mentioned that you can insert drawing files as external references, in a way similar to inserting blocks. To accomplish this, you use the Insert ➤ External Reference… (Xref) command. The difference between Xref files and blocks is that Xref files do not actually become part of the drawing's database. Instead, they are "loaded" along with the current file at start-up time. It is as if AutoCAD were opening several drawings at once: the currently active file you specify when you start AutoCAD, and any file inserted as an Xref.

If you keep Xref files independent from the current file, any changes you make to the Xref will automatically appear in the current file. You don't have to manually update the Xref file as you do blocks. For example, if you used Xref to insert the Unit file into the Plan file, and you later made changes to the Unit file, the next time you opened the Plan file you would see the new version of the Unit file in place of the old.

TIP   You cannot Xref a file if the file has the same name as a block in the current drawing. If this situation occurs, but you still need to use the file as an External reference, you can rename the block of the same name using the Rename command. See Chapter 8.

Another advantage to Xref files is that since they do not actually become part of a drawing's database, drawing size is kept to a minimum. This translates to more efficient use of your hard disk space.

NOTE   Xref files, like blocks, cannot be edited. You can, however, use Osnaps to snap to location in an Xref file, or freeze or turn off the Xref file's insertion layer to make it invisible.

Attaching a Drawing as an External Reference

The next exercise shows how you can use an External Reference in place of an inserted block to construct the studio apartment building. You'll start with creating a new unit file by copying the old one. Then you bring a new toolbar, the External Reference Toolbar, to the screen.

1. Use the Windows Explorer to make a copy of the Unit file and name the copy Unitxref.dwg. You can also use the Unitxref.dwg file from the companion CD-ROM.

2. Open the Plan file, and then choose Save As and save the file under the name Planxref. The current file is now Planxref.

3. Erase all of the objects (**E** ↵ **All** ↵) and purge the Unit, Stair, and Lobby block. (By doing steps 2 and 3, you save yourself from having to set up a new file.)

4. Click on Insert ➤ External Reference, or type **XR** ↵, to open the External Reference dialog box.

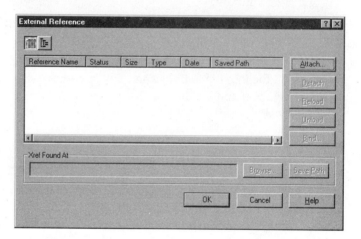

5. Click on the Attach button in the dialog box. The Select File to Attach dialog box appears. This is a typical AutoCAD File dialog box complete with a preview window.

6. Locate and select the Unitxref.dwg file, and then click on Open. The Attach Xref dialog box appears.

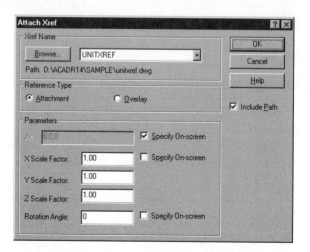

7. You'll get a description of the options presented in this dialog box. For now, click on OK.

8. Enter **31'–5",43'–8"** for the insertion point.

9. After the Unitxref.dwg file is inserted, recreate the same layout of the floor plan you created in the first section of this chapter by copying and mirroring the the Unitxref.dwg external reference.

10. Save the Planxref.dwg file. Then open Unitxref.dwg.

11. Erase the hatch pattern and kitchen outline for the floors, and save the file.

12. Open Planxref.dwg again, and notice what happens to the Unitxref.dwg file you inserted using the External Reference command.

Importing Blocks, Layers, and Other Named Elements from External Files

You can use the tool labeled External Reference Bind in the Reference toolbar to import blocks and other drawing components from another file. First use Extranal Reference Attach to cross-reference a file; then click on External Reference Bind. At the Xbind dialog box, click on the plus sign next to the external reference file name, and then select Block. Locate the name of the block you want to import, click on the Add button, and click OK. Finally, use Detach from the Reference dialog box to remove the Xref file. The imported block will remain as part of the current file. (See Chapter 12 for details on importing drawing components.)

Here you saw how an Xref file doesn't have to be updated the way blocks do. Also, you avoid the task of having to update nested blocks, because AutoCAD updates nested Xrefs, as well as non-nested Xrefs.

TIP If you find that you use the Xrefs frequently, you may want to place the Insert toolbar permanently in your AutoCAD window. It contains tools for inserting both blocks and Xrefs. To open the Insert toolbar, right-click on any toolbar, and then click on the Insert check box in the toolbar's dialog box.

Other Differences between External References and Blocks

Here are a few other differences between external references (Xref) and inserted blocks that you will want to keep in mind:

- Any new layers, text styles, or line types brought in with cross-referenced files do not become part of the current file. You must use the Xbind command (described in Chapter 12).

- If you make changes to the layers of a cross-referenced file, those changes will not be retained when the file is saved, unless the Retain Changes to Xref-dependant Layers option is checked. This option will then instruct AutoCAD to remember any layer color or visibility settings from one editing session to the next. In the standard AutoCAD settings, this option is on by default.

> **TIP**
>
> Another way to ensure that layer settings for Xrefs are retained is to enter **Visretain** ↵ at the command prompt. At the New value for VISRETAIN <0> prompt, enter **1**.

- To segregate layers on a cross-referenced file from the ones in the current drawing, the cross referenced file's layers are prefixed with their file's name. A vertical bar separates the file-name prefix and the layer name, as in Unitxref | wall.

- Xrefs cannot be exploded. You can, however, convert an Xref into a block, and then explode it. To do this, you must use the Bind button in the External Reference dialog box. This opens another dialog box that offers two ways of converting an Xref into a block. See the *Options in the External Reference Dialog Box* section for more information on this dialog box.

> **TIP**
>
> You can convert an Xref into a block by using the Bind option of the External Reference dialog box.

- If an Xref is renamed or moved to another location on your hard disk, AutoCAD won't be able to find that file when it opens other files to which the Xref is attached. If this happens, you must use the Browse option on the

External Reference dialog box to tell AutoCAD where to find the cross-reference file.

WARNING   Take care when relocating an Xref file with the Browse button. The Browse button can assign a file of a different name to an existing Xref as a substitution.

Xref files are especially useful in workgroup environments where several people are working on the same project. For example, one person might be updating several files that are inserted into a variety of other files. Using blocks, everyone in the workgroup would have to be notified of the changes and would have to update all the affected blocks in all the drawings that contained them. With cross-referenced files, however, the updating is automatic, so you avoid confusion about which files need to have their blocks updated.

External References in the San Francisco Main Library Project

While these exercises demonstrate how Xrefs work, you aren't limited to using them in the way shown here. Perhaps one of the more common ways of using Xrefs is to combine a single floor plan with different title block drawings, each with its own layer settings and title block information. In this way, single drawing files can be reused in several drawing sheets of a final construction document set. This helps keep data consistent across drawings and reduces the number of overall drawings needed.

This is exactly how Xrefs were used in the San Francisco Main Library drawings. One floor plan file contained most of the main information for that floor. The floor plan was then used as an Xref in another file that contained the title block, as well as additional information, such as furnishings or floor finish reference symbols. Layer visibility was controlled in each title block drawing so only the data related to that drawing appeared.

Multiple Xref files were also used by segregating the structural column grid layout drawings from the floor plan files. In other cases, portions of plans from different floors were combined into a single drawing using Xrefs, as shown in Figure 6.13.

FIGURE 6.13:

A sample sheet from the San Francisco Main Library construction documents showing enlarged paving plans from various floors. Each floor is an Xref from a complete floor plan drawing file.

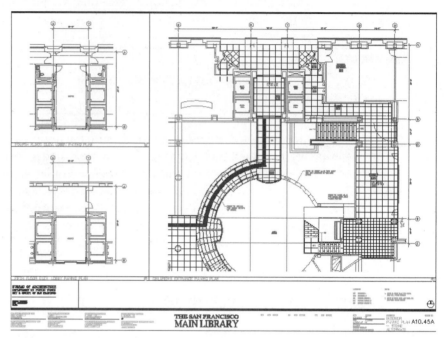

Other External Reference Options

There are many other features unique to cross-referenced files. Let's briefly look at some of the options in the External Reference dialog box we haven't yet discussed.

Options in the External Reference Dialog Box

The following options are found in the main External Reference dialog box. All but the Attach option are available only when an Xref is present in the current drawing and its name is selected from the list of Xrefs shown in the main part of the dialog box.

Attach opens the Attach Xref dialog box allowing you to select a file to attach and set the parameters for the attachment.

Detach detaches an Xref from the current file. The file will then be completely disassociated from the current file.

Unload is similar to detach but maintains a link to the Xref file so that it can be quickly reattached. This has an effect similar to freezing a layer and can reduce redraw, regen, and file-loading times.

Reload restores an unloaded Xref.

Bind converts an Xref into a block. Bind offers two options: Bind (again) and Insert. The Bind's Bind option will maintain the Xref's named elements (Layers, Linetypes, and text and dimension styles) by creating new layers in the current file with the Xref's file name prefix (see Chapter 12). The Insert option will not attempt to maintain the Xref's named elements but will merge them with named elements of the same name in the current file. For example, if both the Xref and the current file have layers of the same name, the objects in the Xref will be placed in the layers of the same name in the current file.

Browse opens the Select New Path dialog box from which you can select a new file or location for a selected Xref.

Save Path saves the file path displayed in the Xref Found At input box. See the Include Path option in the following section.

List View/Tree View are two buttons in the upper-right corner of the dialog box. They let you switch between a List view of your Xrefs, or a hierarchical Tree view. The Tree view can be helpful in determining how Xrefs are nested.

NOTE The Xref list works like other Windows lists, offering the ability to sort by name, status, size, type, date, or path. To sort by name, for example, click on the Reference Name button at the top of the list.

The Attach Xref Dialog Box

The Attach Xref dialog box shown in the previous exercise offers these options:

Attachment causes AutoCAD to include other Xref attachments that are nested in the selected file.

Overlay causes AutoCAD to ignore other Xref attachments that are nested in the selected file. This avoids multiple attachments of other files and eliminates the possibility of circular references (referencing the current file into itself through another file).

Include Path lets you determine whether AutoCAD stores the path information to the Xref in the current drawings database, or discards it. If you choose not to use this option, AutoCAD will use the default file search path to locate the Xref the next time the current file is open. If you plan to send your files to someone else, you may want to turn this option off, otherwise the person you send the file to will have to duplicate the exact file path structure of your computer before the Xrefs will load properly.

Specify On-screen gives you the option to enter insertion point, scale factors, and rotation angles within the dialog box or in the command window, in a way similar to inserting blocks. If you check this option for any of the corresponding parameters, the parameters change to allow input. If they are not checked, you are prompted for those parameters after you click OK to close the dialog box. With all three Specify On-screen checkboxes unchecked, you receive the same set of prompts as those for the Insert dialog box.

Clipping Xref Views and Improving Performance

Xrefs are frequently used to import large drawings for reference or backgrounds. Multiple Xrefs, such as a floor plan, column grid layout, and site plan drawing, might be combined into one file. One drawback to multiple Xrefs in earlier versions of AutoCAD, is that the entire Xref is loaded into memory, even if only a small portion of the Xref is used for the final plotted output. For computers with limited resources, multiple Xrefs could slow the system to a crawl.

Release 14 offers two tools that will help make display and memory use more efficient when using Xref: The Xclip command and the Demand load option in the Preferences dialog box.

Clipping Views

Xclip is the name of a command accessed by choosing Modify ➤ Object ➤ Clip. This command allows you to clip the display of an Xref or block to any shape you desire as shown in Figure 6.14. For example, you may want to display only an L-shaped portion of a floor plan to be part of your current drawing. Xclip lets you define such a view.

FIGURE 6.14:

The top panel shows a polyline outline of the area to be isolated with Xclip. The middle panel shows how the Xref appears after Xclip is applied. The bottom panel shows a view of the plan with the polyline's layer turned off.

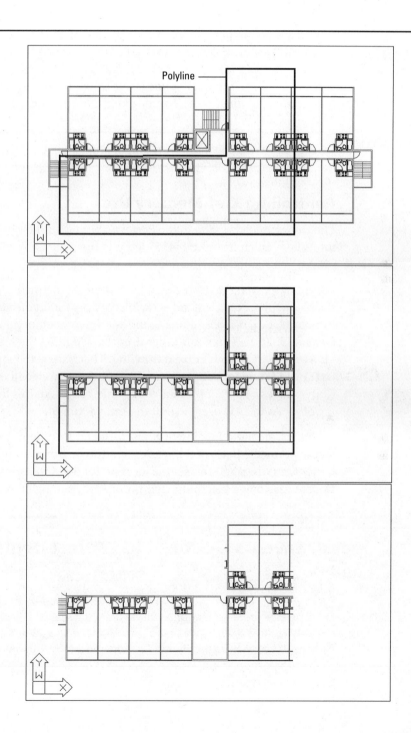

Blocks and Multiple Xrefs can be clipped as well. And you can specify a front and back clipping distance so that visibility of objects in 3D space can be controlled (see *Using 3D Features to Trick AutoCAD* in this chapter). You can define a clip area using polylines or spline curves, though curve-fitted polylines will revert to decurved polylines (see Chapter 13 for more on polylines and spline curves).

NOTE   To see a detailed tutorial on clipping Xrefs, see Chapter 12.

Controlling Xref Memory Use

The Demand load option in the Performance tab of the Preferences dialog box limits how much of an Xref is loaded into memory. Only the portion that is displayed gets loaded into memory.

Demand load has a drop-down list with three settings: Disabled, Enabled, and Enabled with Copy. Demand is enabled by default in the standard AutoCAD drawing setup. Besides reducing the amount of memory an Xref consumes, Demand load also prevents other users from editing the Xref while it is being viewed as part of your current drawing. This is done to help aid drawing version control and drawing managment. The third demand load option, Enabled with Copy, creates a copy of the source Xref file, and then uses the copy, thereby allowing other AutoCAD users to edit the source Xref file.

Controls demand loading of Xrefs. Demand loading improves performance by loading only the parts of the referenced drawing that are needed to regenerate the current drawing. You can set the location for the Xref copy in the Files tab of the Preferences dialog box under Temporary External Reference Location.

Special Save As Options That Affect Demand Loading

AutoCAD offers a few additional settings that will boost the performance of the Demand load feature mentioned in the previous section. When you choose File ➢ Save As to save a file in the standard .dwg format, you will see a button labeled Options. If you click on the Options button, the Export Options dialog box appears.

This dialog box offers the Index Type drop-down list. The index referred to can help improve the speed of demand loading. The index options are:

None   No index is created.

Layer   AutoCAD will load only layers that are both turned on and thawed.

Spacial   AutoCAD will load only portions of an Xref or raster image within a clipped boundary.

Layer & Spacial   This option turns on both the Layer and Spacial options.

If You Want to Experiment...

If you'd like to see firsthand how block substitution works, try doing the exercise in Figure 6.15. It shows how quickly you can change the configuration of a drawing by careful use of block substitution. As you work through the exercise, keep in mind that some planning is required to use blocks in this way. If you know that you will have to try various configurations in a drawing, you can plan to set up files to accommodate them.

You might also want to try the exercise using Xrefs instead of inserting files as blocks. Once you've attached the Xref, try substituting the Tab1 Xref with the Tab2 Xref by using the Browse button in the External Reference dialog box. Highlight Tab1 from the list of Xrefs, and then click on Browse and select Tab2. The current file will still call the Xref Tab1 by its original name, but will instead load Tab2 in its place.

TIP   You can substitute Xrefs in a way similar to blocks as shown in this example.

By now, you may be anxious to see how your drawings look on paper. In the next chapter you will explore the use of AutoCAD's printing and plotting commands.

FIGURE 6.15:

An exercise in block substitution

1. Open a file called PART1 and draw the object shown at right.

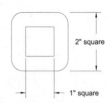

2. Next to that object, draw the object shown at right. Use the Wblock command and turn it into a file called TAB1. (Note the insertion point location.)

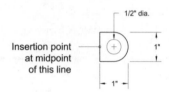

3. Draw the object shown at right and turn it into a file called TAB2.

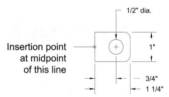

4. Insert TAB1 into the drawing in four places as shown in here. You can insert one then use the Polar option under the Array command for the other three tabs.

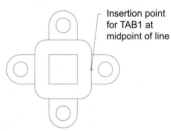

5. Start the Insert command again, but at the prompt

   Block name (or ?):

   enter **TAB1=TAB2**. The drawing regenerates and an alternate version of the part appears with TAB2 replacing TAB1. Cancel the Insert command.

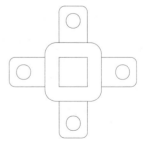

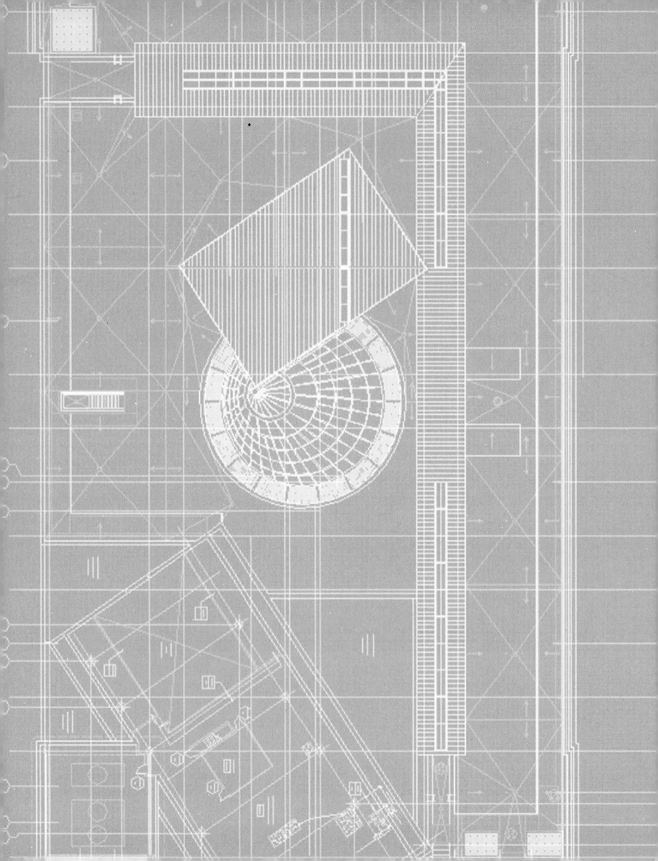

CHAPTER

SEVEN

7

Printing and Plotting

- Plotting the Plan

- Selecting the Output Device

- Selecting a Paper Size and Orientation

- Controlling the Appearance of Output

- Controlling Scale and Location

- Adjusting Pen Parameters and Plotter Optimization

- Other Plot Controls

- Batch Plotting

- Sending Your Drawings to a Service Bureau

Getting hard copy output from AutoCAD is something of an art. You'll need to be intimately familiar with both your output device and the settings available in AutoCAD. You will probably spend a good deal of time experimenting with AutoCAD's plotter settings and your printer or plotter to get your equipment set up just the way you want.

With the huge array of output options available, this chapter can only provide a general discussion of plotting. It's up to you to work out the details and fine-tune the way you and AutoCAD together work with your plotter. Here we'll take a look at the features available in AutoCAD and discuss some general rules and guidelines to follow when setting up your plots. We'll also discuss alternatives to using a plotter, such as plotter service bureaus and common desktop printers. There won't be much in the way of a tutorial, so consider this chapter more of a reference.

NOTE For more information on choosing between printers and plotters, see Appendix A.

Plotting the Plan

To see firsthand how the Plot command works, you'll plot the Plan file using the default settings on your system. But first, take a preview of your plot using the new Release 14 Plot Preview option.

1. First, be sure your printer or plotter is connected to your computer and is turned on.

2. Start AutoCAD and open the Plan file.

3. Click on View ➤ Zoom ➤ All to display the entire drawing.

4. Choose File ➤ Print Preview. The display changes to show you how the Plan file will look as output from your printer or plotter.

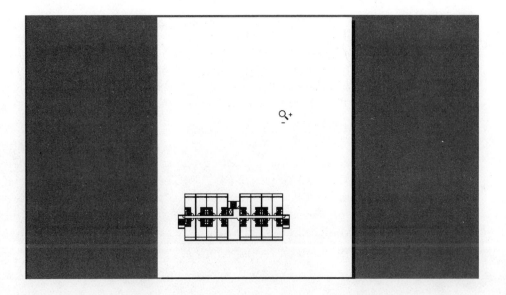

Your print preview will depend on the type of output device you chose when you installed AutoCAD or when you last selected a Plotter Device option (described in *Selecting an Output Device* in this chapter). It will also be affected by other settings in the Plot Configuration dialog box; such as those in the Additional Parameters group and Scale, Rotation and Origin group. This example shows a typical preview view using the Windows default system printer in portrait mode.

Notice that the view also shows the Zoom Realtime cursor. You can use the Zoom/Pan Realtime tool to get a close-up look at your print preview. Now go ahead and plot the file.

5. Click on File ➤ Print, or type **Plot** ↵, at the command prompt. The Print/Plot Configuration dialog box appears.

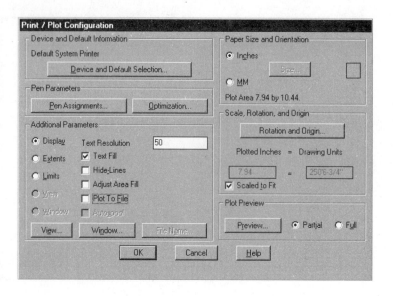

If you see prompts in the Command window instead of the Plot Configuration dialog box, and then change the Cmddia system variable to 1. To do this, type **Cmddia** ⏎ **1** ⏎.

6. Click on OK. The dialog box closes and you see the following message:

   ```
   Command: PLOT Effective plotting area:   10.50 wide by 7.59 high
   ```

   The width and height values shown in this message will depend on your system setup:

7. Your plotter or printer will print out the plan to no particular scale. You may see various messages while AutoCAD is plotting. When the plot is done, you see the message:

   ```
   Regeneration done 100% Plot complete.
   ```

   You've just done your first printout. Now let's take a look at the wealth of settings available when you plot, starting with the selection of an output device.

Selecting an Output Device

Many of you have more than one device for output. You may have a laser printer for your word-processed documents, in addition to a plotter. You may also require PostScript file output for presentations. AutoCAD offers you the flexibility of using several types of devices, quickly and easily.

When you configure AutoCAD, you have the option to specify more than one output device. Once you've configured several printers and plotters, you can select the desired device using the Device and Default Selection button. The current default device is shown just above this button. When you click this button, you will see the Device and Default Selection dialog box.

NOTE   This graphic shows some sample plotter configurations in the Device Configuration list. Your system will show a different list, or only one plotter or printer.

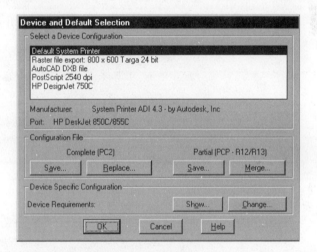

Using the Windows System Printer

Under Windows, you have even more output options than those provided by AutoCAD because Windows itself offers you the option to output to a wide range of plotters and printers. If you configure AutoCAD to use the System Printer, AutoCAD will then use the Windows output device. You set the Windows output device through the Printers option of the Windows Control Panel. Consult your Windows manual for more on the use of output devices and Windows.

To select a device, highlight the device name from the list and click on OK. The rest of the Plot Configuration options will then reflect the requirements of the chosen device. For this reason, be sure you select the output device you want *before* you adjust the other plotter settings.

Adding an Output Device

Before you can select more than one device from the list in the Device and Default Selection dialog box, you'll need to configure AutoCAD for multiple output devices. You have the opportunity to configure AutoCAD plotters or printers when you install AutoCAD. You can also configure additional printers through the Preferences dialog box. Here's how it's done.

1. Choose Tools ➤ Preferences....

2. Click on the Printer tab. The Printer options appear.

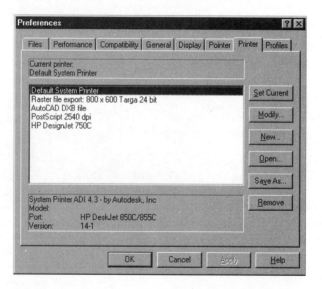

3. You'll see a listing of the current printer drivers that have already been installed. To the right of the list, you see several buttons.

4. Click on the button labeled New.... The Add a Printer dialog box appears.

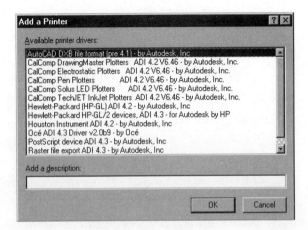

5. Select a printer from the list in the dialog box.

6. Add a description of your selection.

7. Click on OK, you'll then be presented with a series of prompts asking you for more detailed information on how you would like your device configured. You can generally accept the default answers to each prompt, since they are presented to you in the Plot Configuration dialog box when you plot. The exception to this is the Raster File and DXB output options, which will ask for a specific image size and resolution.

8. When you are done replying to the prompts, you are returned to the Preferences dialog box.

If you find that the settings you selected in step 7 are inappropriate, you can use the Modify button to change the printer configuration settings. Highlight the printer you want to reconfigure from the list, and then click on Modify. The Reconfigure a Printer dialog box appears.

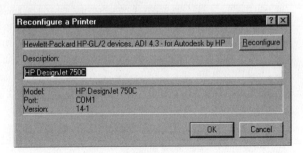

You can enter a new description for the printer in the Description input box. Click on Reconfigure to change the configuration settings. You will then see the prompts you saw in step 7.

Other options in the Printer tab of the Preferences dialog box let you store or load PC2 plot configuration files (see *Storing Plotter Settings*) or remove a configuration from the list. Here is a summary of the printer options:

Set Current   makes the highlighted printer or plotter the current output device.

Modify   lets you change the printer description shown in the list and also allows you to change configuration settings for the selected printer.

New   lets you add a printer to the list of printers available at plot time.

Open   lets you load a PC2 plot configuration file.

Save As   lets you save the current configuration of a plotter as a PC2 file.

Remove   removes a plotter from the list.

Plotting Image Files

If your work involves the production of manuals, reports, or similar documents, you may want to add the Raster File Export option to your list of plotter configurations. The Raster File Export option lets you plot your drawings as PCX, Targa, Tiff, or BMP files that you can later import into documents that accept bitmap images. Images can be up to 8000 x 8000 pixels and can contain 256 colors. If you need several different raster formats, you can use multiple instances of this or any plotter configuration.

If you would like to convert your 3D wireframe models into 2D line drawings, add the AutoCAD DXB file format to your list of plotters. Then you can plot your hidden-line 3D models to a DXB file format. Once you have a DXB file, choose File ➤ Import to import the DXB plot file. AutoCAD will create a 2D line drawing from the plot file data. For best results, use a value of 2900 for the Plotter Steps per Drawing unit setting.

Another tool for 3D is the PostScript file output format. Like the DXB option, you can plot a 3D image to a file, and then import the resultant EPS file using File ➤ Import. For best results, make sure that when you configure the PostScript printer you use the highest resolution available, and that you use the largest media size possible when you're plotting.

Storing Plotter Settings

In addition to the ability to set up multiple output devices, AutoCAD also lets you store setup information for each device, such as default paper sizes, sheet orientation, what to plot, and so on. This information is stored as a file in one of two formats: the older PCP format used in Release 12 and 13, or the new PC2 format, which stores device-specific information as well as the general information stored in the PCP file.

If you find that you frequently plot your drawings using a particular plotter setup, the PCP and PC2 setup files will be especially helpful for saving time. They are also a crucial component for batch plotting as you'll see later in this chapter.

Understanding Your Plotter's Limits

If you're familiar with a word-processing or desktop-publishing program, you know that you can set the margins of a page, thereby telling the program exactly how far from each edge of the paper you want the text to appear. With AutoCAD, you don't have that luxury. To accurately place a plot on your paper, you must know the plotter's *hard clip limits*. The hard clip limits are like built-in margins, beyond which the plotter will not plot. These limits vary from plotter to plotter (see Figure 7.1).

It's crucial that you know your printer/plotter's hard clip limits, in order to accurately place your drawings on the sheet. Take some time to study your plotter manual and find out exactly what these limits are. Then make a record of them and store it somewhere, in case you or someone else needs to format a sheet in a special way.

Hard clip limits for printers are often dependent on the software that drives them. You may need to consult your printer manual, or use the trial-and-error method of plotting several samples to see how they come out.

Once you've established the limits of your plotter or printer, you can begin to lay out your drawings to fit within those limits (see *Setting the Output's Origin and Rotation* later in this chapter). You can then establish some standard drawing limits based on your plotter's limits. You'll also need to know the dimension of those hard clip limits to define your plotter sheet sizes. While AutoCAD offers standard sheet sizes in the Paper Size and Orientation button group of the Plot Configuration dialog box, these sizes do not take into account the hard clip limits.

FIGURE 7.1:

The hard clip limits of a plotter

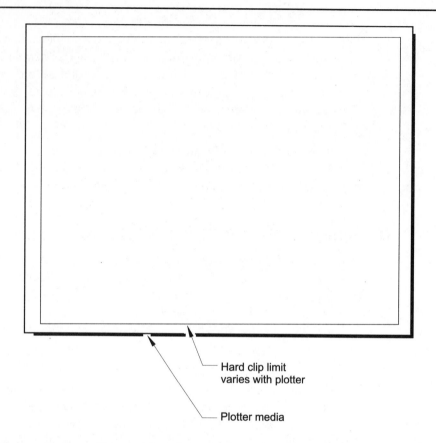

Hard clip limit
varies with plotter

Plotter media

Knowing Your Plotter's Origins

Another important consideration is the location of your plotter's origin. For example, on some plotters the lower-left corner of the plot area is used as the origin. Other plotters will use the center of the plot area as the origin. When you plot a drawing that is too large to fit the sheet on a plotter that uses a corner for the origin, the image is pushed toward the top and to the right of the sheet (see Figure 7.2). When you plot a drawing that is too large to fit on a plotter that uses the center of the paper as the origin, the image is pushed outward in all directions from the center of the sheet.

FIGURE 7.2:

Plotting an oversized image on a plotter that uses the lower-left corner for its origin

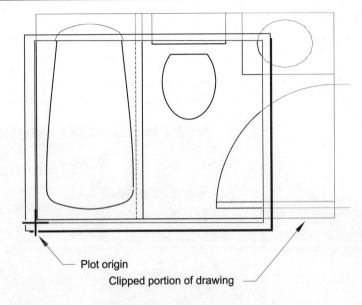

Plot origin

Clipped portion of drawing

In each situation, the origin determines a point of reference from which you can relate your drawing in the computer to the physical output. Once you understand this, you're better equipped to accurately place your electronic drawing on the physical media.

Selecting a Paper Size and Orientation

Next let's look at the Paper Size and Orientation button group in the Plot Configuration dialog box. This is where you determine the size of your media and the standard unit of measure you will use. The Inches and MM radio buttons let you determine the unit of measure you want to work with in this dialog box. This is the unit of measure you will use when specifying sheet sizes and view locations on the sheet. If you choose MM, sheet sizes are shown in millimeters, and you must specify distances and scales in millimeters for other options.

TIP

If you need to convert from inches to millimeters, the scale factor is 1" = 25.4 mm.

Once you've chosen a unit of measure, you can click on the Size... button to select a sheet size. This brings up the Paper Size dialog box.

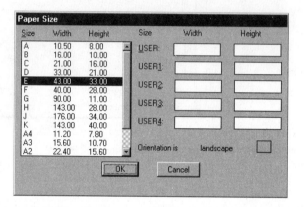

NOTE

If you are using the System Printer, the Size option is not available. To set the size, you must use the Printers option in the Windows Control Panel, or click on the Device and Default Selection button, and with the Default System Printer selected in the list, click on Change in the Device Specific Configuration button group. This opens the Print Setup dialog box from which you can change your printer settings.

The range of sheet sizes will vary, depending on which plotter you have selected in the Device and Default selection option (described later in this chapter). To select a sheet size, you simply highlight it in the list box on the left and click on OK. If you choose, you can enter a nonstandard sheet size in the input boxes to the right. As you can see, you can store up to five custom sheet sizes.

Controlling the Appearance of Output

On the left side of the Plot Configuration dialog box is the Additional Parameters button group. These options give you the most control over the appearance of your plot. From here, you can control what gets plotted and how.

Designating Hidden Lines, Fills, and Text Quality

Let's start by looking at the six options down the right side of this group. Using these checkboxes, you can tell AutoCAD to store the plot in a file on disk, instead of sending the plot data to a plotter or printer for immediate output. You can specify whether to plot a 3D drawing with hidden lines removed, or whether your plotter is to compensate for pen widths when drawing solid fills.

Text Resolution

The Text Resolution input box controls the appearance of filled fonts such as New Times Roman True Type or Helvetica PostScript. A higher number generates smoother edges around the font characters. A lower number causes the characters to appear rough. The default is 50 with a range from 0 to 100.

Text Fill

If you want your filled fonts to appear as outline fonts, make sure this option is *not* checked. Leave it checked for filled fonts.

Hide Lines

The Hide Lines checkbox is generally only used for 3D images. When this option is on, AutoCAD will remove hidden lines from a 3D drawing as it is plotted. This operation will add a minute or two to your plotting time.

WARNING   Hide Lines is not required for Paper Space viewports that have been set to hide lines using the Hideplot option of the Mview command (View ➤ Floating Viewports ➤ Hideplot). For more on Hideplot, see Chapter 18.

Adjust Area Fill

Turning on Adjust Area Fill tells AutoCAD to compensate for pen width around the edges of a solid filled area in order to maintain dimensional accuracy of the plot. To understand this feature, you need to understand how most plotters draw solid areas.

Plotters draw solid fills by first outlining the fill area and then cross-hatching the area with a series of lines, much as you would do by hand. For example, if a solid filled area is drawn at a width of 0.090", the plotter will outline the area using the edge of the outline as the centerline for the pen, and then proceed to fill the area with a cross-hatch motion. Unfortunately, by using the outline as the centerline for the pen, the solid fill's actual width is 0.090" *plus* the width of the pen.

NOTE   Generally, compensation for pen width is critical only when you are producing drawings as a basis for photo etchings or similar artwork, where close tolerances must be adhered to.

When you check the Adjust Area Fill box, AutoCAD pulls in the outline of the solid area by half the pen width. To determine the amount of offset to use, AutoCAD uses the pen width setting you enter under the Pen Assignments dialog box (described later in this chapter). Figure 7.3 illustrates the operation of Adjust Area Fill.

Plot To File

Turn this option on when you want to divert your printout to a file on disk and print it later. This can be useful if you are in an office in which a plotter is shared among several CAD stations. When the plotter is busy, or if a plotter buffer or spooler is full, plot to a file. Later you can download the plot file when your plotter is available. The following steps show you how to use this option.

1. Click on the Plot To File checkbox.

2. Click on the File Name button (just below the checkbox). You'll see the Create Plot File dialog box, which is the same as the one used for most other file creation operations.

3. Enter the name for your plot file, or just accept the default file name, which is usually the same as the current file. The .plt file name extension is the default.

4. Click on OK to accept the file name.

FIGURE 7.3:

A solid area shown without pen-width compensation and with pen-width compensation

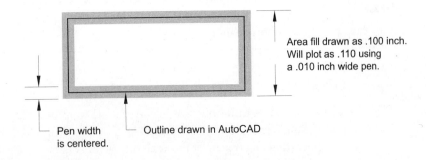

Area fill drawn as .100 inch. Will plot as .110 using a .010 inch wide pen.

Pen width is centered.

Outline drawn in AutoCAD

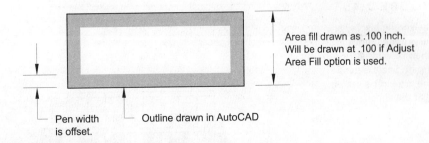

Area fill drawn as .100 inch. Will be drawn at .100 if Adjust Area Fill option is used.

Pen width is offset.

Outline drawn in AutoCAD

AutoSpool

This option is only available for certain AutoCAD ADI plotter configurations and only when the Plot to File option is selected. With AutoSpool selected, AutoCAD will create a Plot spool file in the directory specified in the Files tab of the Preferences dialog box (you can access the dialog box by choosing Tools ➢ Preferences…) under Print Spooler File Location. This option is usually associated with a Print Spooler application that reads the Print spool file and sends it to the appropriate device. AutoCAD can be directed to the print spooler application by way of the Print file, Spooler, and Prolog Section Names listing in the Files tab of the Preferences dialog box.

Determining What to Print

The radio buttons on the left side of the Additional Parameters button group let you specify which part of your drawing you wish to plot. You might notice some similarities between these settings and the Zoom command options.

NOTE   The File ➤ Print Preview option will display a preview based on the settings in this section.

Display

Display is the default option; it tells AutoCAD to plot what is currently displayed on the screen (see panel 1 of Figure 7.4). If you let AutoCAD fit the drawing onto the sheet (that is, you check the Scaled to Fit checkbox), the plot will be exactly the same as what you see on your screen (panel 2 of Figure 7.4).

FIGURE 7.4:

The screen display and the printed output when Display is chosen and no Scale is used (the drawing is scaled to fit the sheet)

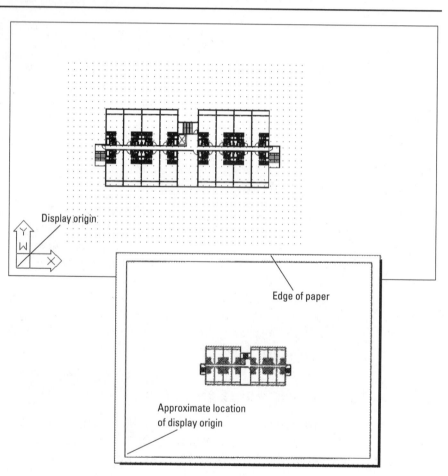

Display origin

Edge of paper

Approximate location
of display origin

Extents

The Extents option draws the entire drawing, eliminating any space that may border the drawing (see Figure 7.5). If you let AutoCAD fit the drawing onto the sheet (that is, you check the Scaled to Fit checkbox), the plot will display exactly the same thing that you would see on the screen had you clicked on View ➢ Zoom ➢ Extents.

FIGURE 7.5:

The printed output when Extents is chosen

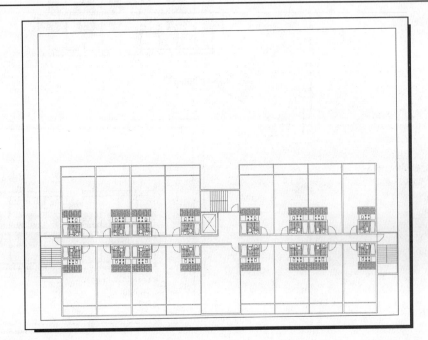

Limits

The Limits printing option uses the limits of the drawing to determine what to print (see Figure 7.6). If you let AutoCAD fit the drawing onto the sheet (by selecting Scaled to Fit), the plot will display exactly the same thing that you would see on the screen had you clicked on View ➢ Zoom ➢ All.

FIGURE 7.6:

The screen display and
the printed output
when Limits is chosen

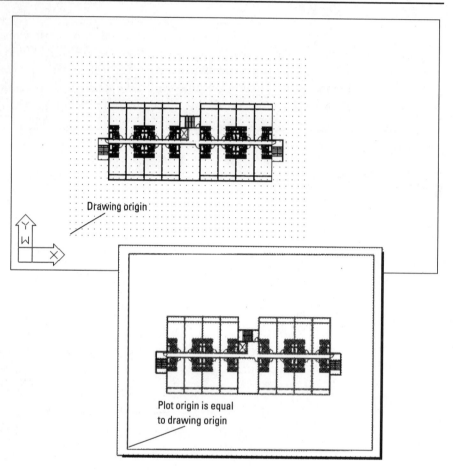

View

The View printing option uses a previously saved view to determine what to print (see Figure 7.7). To use this option, you must first create a view. Then click on the View… button in the Plot Configuration dialog box, and double-click on the desired view name in the dialog box list that appears.

FIGURE 7.7:

A comparison of the saved view and the printed output

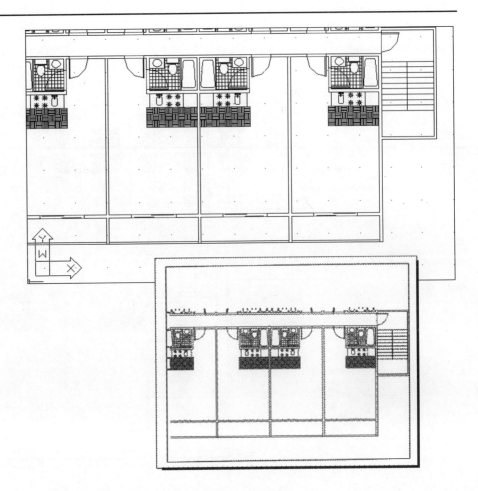

If you let AutoCAD fit the drawing onto the sheet (by selecting Scaled to Fit), the plot will display exactly the same thing that you would see on the screen if you recalled the view you are plotting.

Window

Finally, the Window option allows you to use a window to indicate the area you wish to plot (see Figure 7.8). Nothing outside the window will print.

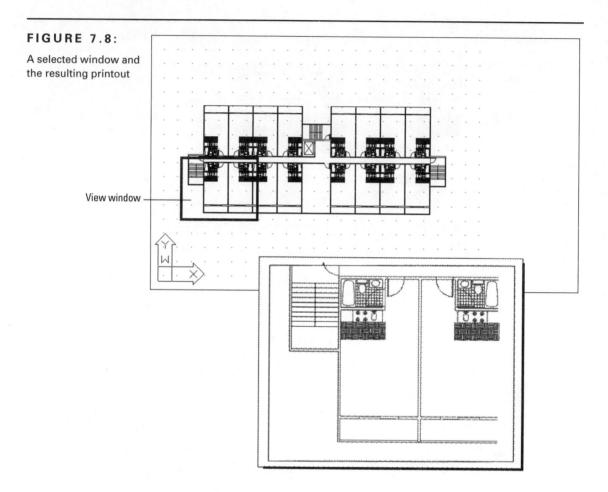

FIGURE 7.8:

A selected window and the resulting printout

View window

To use this option, click on the Window... button. Then enter the coordinates of the window in the appropriate input boxes. Or you can click on the Pick button to indicate a window in the drawing editor. The dialog box will temporarily close to allow you to select points. When you're done, click on OK.

If you let AutoCAD fit the drawing onto the sheet using the Scale to Fit checkbox, the plot will display exactly the same thing that you enclose within the window.

Do you get a blank print, even though you selected Extents or Display? Chances are the Scale to Fit option is unchecked, or the Plotted Inches = Drawing Units setting is inappropriate for the sheet size and scale of your drawing. If you don't care about the scale of the drawing, then make sure the Scale to Fit checkbox is checked. Otherwise, make sure the Plotted Inches = Drawing Units setting is set correctly. The next section describes how to set the scale for your plots.

Controlling Scale and Location

The Scale, Rotation, and Origin button group is where you tell AutoCAD the scale of your drawing, as well as how the image is to be rotated on the sheet, and the location of the drawing origin on the paper.

In the previous section, the descriptions of several options indicate that the Scale to Fit checkbox must be checked. Bear in mind that when you apply a scale factor to your plot, it changes the results of the Additional Parameters settings, and some subtle problems can arise. This is usually where most new users have difficulty.

For example, the apartment plan drawing fits nicely on the paper when you use Scale to Fit. But if you tried to plot the drawing at a scale of 1"=1', you would probably get a blank piece of paper because, at that scale, hardly any of the drawing would fit on your paper. AutoCAD would tell you that it was plotting and then that the plot was finished. You wouldn't have a clue as to why your sheet was blank.

If an image is too large to fit on a sheet of paper because of improper scaling, the plot image will be clipped differently depending on whether the plotter uses the center of the image or the lower-left corner for its origin (see Figure 7.1). Keep this in mind as you specify Scale factors in this area of the dialog box.

Specifying Drawing Scale

To indicate scale, two input boxes are provided in the Scale, Rotation, and Origin button group: Plotted Inches (or Plotted MM if you use metric units) and Drawing Units. For example, if your drawing is of a scale factor of 96, follow these steps.

1. Double-click on the Plotted Inches (or Plotted MM) input box, and enter **1** ↵.

2. Double-click on the Drawing Units input box, and enter **96**.

For a drawing set up using the Architectural unit style, you can enter a scale as a fraction of 1" = 1'. For example, for a 1/8" scale drawing:

1. Double-click on the Plotted Inches (or Plotted MM) input box, and enter **1/8"**.

2. Double-click on the Drawing Units input box, and enter **1'**.

You can specify a different scale from the one you chose while setting up your drawing, and AutoCAD will plot your drawing to that scale. You are not restricted in any way as to scale, but entering the correct scale is important: If it is too large, AutoCAD will think your drawing is too large to fit on the sheet, though it will attempt to plot your drawing anyway.

NOTE See Chapter 3 for a discussion on unit styles and scale factors.

TIP If you plot to a scale that is different from the scale you originally intended, objects and text will appear smaller or larger than would be appropriate for your plot. You'll need to edit your text size to match the new scale. This can be done using a utility found on the companion CD-ROM. See Appendix C for details.

The Scale to Fit checkbox, as already described, allows you to avoid giving a scale altogether and forces the drawing to fit on the sheet. This works fine if you are doing illustrations that are not to scale.

Setting the Output's Origin and Rotation

To adjust the position of your drawing on the media, you enter the location of the view origin in relation to the plotter origin in x and y coordinates (see Figure 7.9).

FIGURE 7.9:

Adjusting the image
location on a sheet

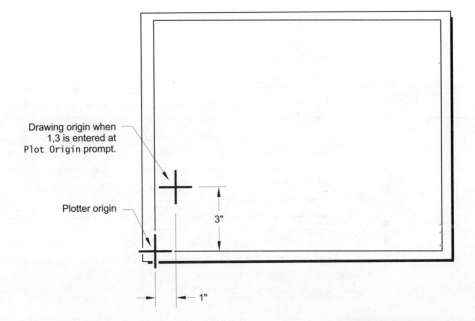

Drawing origin when
1,3 is entered at
`Plot Origin` prompt.

Plotter origin

3"

1"

For example, suppose you plot a drawing, then realize that it needs to be moved 1" to the right and 3" up on the sheet. You would replot the drawing by making the following changes.

1. In the Plot Configuration dialog box, click on the Rotation and Origin... button in the Scale, Rotation, and Origin button group. The Plot Rotation and Origin dialog box appears.

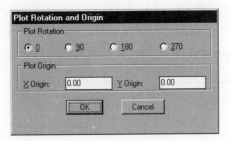

2. Double-click on the X Origin input box and type **1**.

3. Double-click on the Y Origin input box and type **3**.

4. Click on OK.

Now proceed with the rest of the plot configuration. With the above settings, when the plot is done, the image will be shifted on the paper exactly 1" to the right and 3" up.

TIP If you encounter problems with rotating plots, try setting up a UCS that is rotated 90° from the World Coordinate System. Then use the Plan command (View ≻ 3D Viewport Presets ≻ Plan View) to view your drawing in the new rotated orientation. Next, save the view using the View command (View ≻ Named Views…). Once you do this, you can use the View button in the Additional Parameters group to plot the rotated view. See Chapter 16 for more on UCS.

The four radio buttons labeled 0, 90, 180, and 270 allow you to rotate the plot on the sheet. Each value indicates the number of degrees of rotation for the plot. The default is 0, but if you need to rotate the image to a different angle, click on the appropriate radio button.

Adjusting Pen Parameters and Plotter Optimization

The Pen Parameters group of the Plot Configuration dialog box contains two buttons: Pen Assignments…, which helps you control line weight and color, and Optimization…, which lets you control pen motion in pen plotters.

Working with Pen Assignments and Line Weights

In most graphics programs, you control line weights by adjusting the actual width of lines in the drawing. In AutoCAD, you generally take a different approach to line weights. Instead of specifying a line weight in the drawing editor, you match plotter pen widths to colors in your drawing. For example, you might designate the color red to correspond to a fine line weight or the color blue to a very heavy line weight. To make these correlations between colors and line weights, you tell AutoCAD to plot with a particular pen for each color in the drawing.

You can also control line weights through the use of polylines. See Chapter 13 for details.

The Pen Assignments... button in the Plot Configuration dialog box is the entry point to setting the drawing colors for the pens on your plotter. When you click on this button, the Pen Assignment dialog box appears.

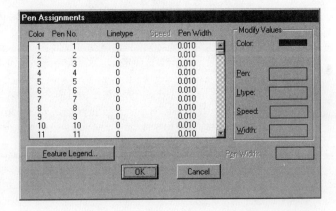

This dialog box shows a listing for a Hewlett-Packard 750c plotter.

The predominant feature of this dialog box is the list of pen assignments. The color numbers in the first column of the list correspond to the colors in your drawing. The other columns show you what pen number, line type, pen speed, and pen width are assigned to those colors.

To change these settings, you click on the item in the list you want to change. The values for that selected item appear in the appropriate input boxes under Modify Values at the right. You can then change the values in the input boxes. You can highlight more than one color at a time to change the pen assignments of several colors at once.

WARNING   Not all printers and plotters will offer all of the options presented here. System printers may have separate options in the Windows control panel for many of these options. Some plotters offer a "software mode" that will allow AutoCAD to have more control over the plots. Check the documentation for your particular output device for more detailed information.

ISO Pen Widths

You may have noticed a setting called ISO Pen Widths in the Linetype tab of the Layer & Linetype Properties dialog box discussed in Chapter 4 (Format ➤ Linetype...). This setting is in the form of a pull-down list. When you select a pen width from that list, the line-type scale is updated to conform to the ISO standard for that width. However, this setting has no effect on the actual plotter output. If you are using ISO standard widths, it is up to you to match the color of the lines to their corresponding widths in the Plot Configuration dialog box. Use the Pen Assignments dialog box to set the line colors to pen widths.

Pen No.

For pen plotters, you assign line weights to colors by entering a pen number in the Pen input box. The default for the color red, for example, is pen 1. If you have a pen plotter, you can then place a pen with a fine tip in the slot designated for pen 1 in your plotter. Then everything that is red in your AutoCAD drawing will be plotted with the fine pen.

Most ink jet and laser printers allow you to set line widths through the Width option discussed later in this section, or in the Printers folder of the Windows Control Panel.

NOTE   If you have a Hewlett-Packard ink jet plotter, you can also control pen settings through the Hpconfig command by typing **Hpconfig** ↵ at the command prompt. This option allows you to store and retrieve advanced plotter configurations in addition to those found in the Plot Configuration dialog box. These options include solid fill shading and area fill control. Other plotter manufacturers may offer similar configuration options. Consult your plotter manual for details.

Ltype

Some plotters offer line types independent of AutoCAD's line types. Using the Ltype input box, you can force a pen assignment to one of these hardware line types. If your plotter supports hardware line types, you can click on the Feature Legend button to see what line types are available and their designations. Usually line types are given numeric designations, so a row of dots might be designated as line type 1, or a dash-dot might be line type 5.

If your plotter can generate its own line types, you can also assign line types to colors. But this method is very seldom used, because it is simpler to assign line types to layers directly in the drawing.

Speed

The Speed setting lets you adjust the pen speed in inches per second for pen plotters. This is important because various pens have their own speed requirements. Refillable technical pens that use India ink generally require the slowest settings; roller pens are capable of very high speeds. Pen speeds will also be affected by the media you are using.

Selecting pens and media for your plotter can be a trial-and-error proposition. If you are in a high production environment, you may want to consider purchasing or leasing a modern ink jet plotter, as they are easier to maintain and considerably faster than pen plotters.

Width

If you have an ink jet or laser plotter, this option usually allows you to control the line weights of your plots. Here you can set the line width for each AutoCAD color. The default line width is 0.010, though you can usually specify a finer width than this, depending on your plotter or printer's resolution (usually rated in dots per inch). Of course, you can specify a thicker line weight as well.

AutoCAD also uses this setting in conjunction with the Adjust Area Fill option under the Additional Parameters button group (discussed earlier). When AutoCAD draws solid fills, it draws a series of lines close together—much as you would do by hand (see Figure 7.10). To do this efficiently, AutoCAD must know the pen width. If the Width setting is too low, AutoCAD will take longer than necessary to draw a solid fill; if it is too high, solid fills will appear as crosshatches instead of solids.

FIGURE 7.10:

How solid fill areas are
drawn by a plotter

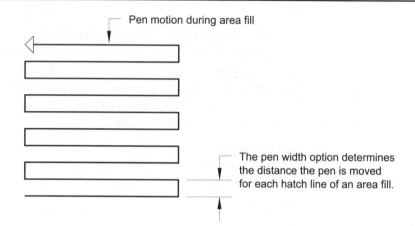

Pen motion during area fill

The pen width option determines
the distance the pen is moved
for each hatch line of an area fill.

Colors and Line Weights in the San Francisco Main Library

Technical drawings can have a beauty of their own, but they can also be deadly boring. What really sets a good technical drawing apart from a poor one is the control of line weights. Knowing how to vary and control line weights in both manual and CAD drawings can make a huge difference in the readability of the drawing.

In the San Francisco Main Library project, the designers at SMWM Associates were especially concerned with line weights in the reflected ceiling plan. Figure 7.11 shows a portion of the reflected ceiling plan from the library drawings. As you can see, it contained a good deal of graphical information which, without careful line weight control, could become confusing. (While you can't see it in the black and white print, a multitude of colors were used to vary line weight.) When the electronic drawings were plotted, colors were converted into lines of varying thickness. Bolder lines were used to create emphasis in components such as walls and ceiling openings, while fine lines were used to indicate ceiling tile patterns.

By emphasizing certain lines over others, visual monotony is avoided and the various components of the drawing can be seen more easily.

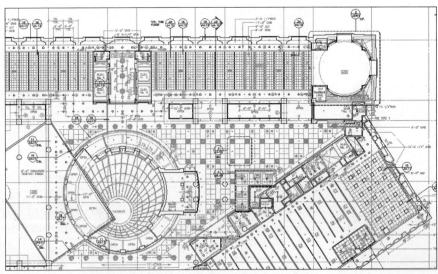

FIGURE 7.11:

A sample portion of the reflected ceiling plan of the San Francisco Main Library. These plans were carefully color coded to control the line weights of the plotter drawing.

Optimizing Plotter Speed

AutoCAD does a lot of preparation before sending your drawing to the plotter. If you are using a pen plotter, one of the things it does is optimize the way it sends vectors to your plotter, so your plotter doesn't waste time making frequent pen changes and moving from one end of the plot to another just to draw a single line.

The Optimization… button in the Pen Parameters group opens a dialog box that lets you control the level of pen optimization AutoCAD performs on your plots.

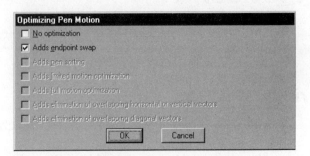

Here are brief descriptions of each setting:

No optimization causes AutoCAD to plot the drawing just as it is regenerated on the screen.

Adds endpoint swap   forces the plotter to draw (as best it can) parallel lines in a back-and-forth motion, so that the pen moves the minimum distance between the end of one line and the beginning of another.

Adds pen sorting   sorts pens so that all of one color is plotted at once. This is fine if your plotter has a self-capping penholder, or if it is a single-pen plotter. You may not want to enable this option if you have a multipen plotter that does not cap the pens.

Adds limited motion optimization and **Adds full motion optimization** further minimize pen travel over a plot.

Adds elimination of overlapping horizontal or vertical vectors   does just what it says: It eliminates overlapping lines. With pen plotters, overlapping lines can cause the weight of the line to increase noticeably. This setting helps reduce line weight build-up when a drawing contains numerous line overlaps. This setting does not affect raster plotters or printers.

Adds elimination of overlapping diagonal vectors   performs a similar function as the previous option, but on diagonal lines.

NOTE   None of these options, except the No Optimization and the Adds Endpoint Swap options, have any effect on dot-matrix and laser printers, or on ink jet plotters.

Other Plot Controls

Here are a couple of other handy, timesaving features available to you in the Plot Configuration dialog box.

Previewing a Plot

If you're a seasoned AutoCAD user, you're probably all too familiar with the following scenario:

You're rushing to meet a deadline. You've got one hour to plot a drawing that you know takes 45 minutes to plot. You set up AutoCAD and start the plot, and then run off to finish some paperwork. When you come back 45 minutes later, the plot image is half the size it is supposed to be.

You can avoid facing predicaments like this one with the Plot Preview feature. Once you've chosen all the settings you think you need for plotting your drawing, turn on the Full radio button in the Plot Preview group, and then click on Preview.... AutoCAD will show you what your drawing will look like based on the settings you've chosen. Preview also lists any warning messages that would appear during the actual plotting process.

TIP   You can press the Esc key to speed up the preview. Once the preview plot is done, you are immediately returned to the Plot Configuration dialog box. You can also press Ctrl + C to terminate the preview generation when you've seen enough.

While in the Full Preview, you can zoom in on an area and pan around, just as you could with the File ➤ Print Preview option.

The Full Preview is worth using on a regular basis since it is considerably faster than an actual plot. If you're just interested in seeing how the drawing fits on the sheet, you can choose Partial instead of Full before clicking on Preview. The Partial option shows the sheet edge, image orientation triangle, and image boundary. The image itself is not shown. Using a small triangle in the corner of the drawing to indicate the lower-left corner of the drawing, AutoCAD shows you how the image is oriented on the sheet.

Reinitializing Your Input/Output Ports

If you are using two output devices (such as a printer and a plotter) on the same port, you may want to know about the Reinit command. This command lets you reinitialize a port for use by AutoCAD after another program has used the port.

To use Reinit, enter Reinit at the command prompt or select Reinitialize... on the Tools menu. You will see a dialog box containing checkboxes labeled Digitizer, Plotter, Display, and PGP File. You can check them all, if you like, or just check the items you are most concerned with.

Reinit can also be accessed using the Reinit system variable.

Saving Your Settings

At times, drawings will require special plotter settings, or you may find that you frequently use one particular setting configuration. Instead of trying to remember the settings every time you plot, you can store settings as files that you can recall at any time.

In Release 14, you can now store plotter settings in two different formats. For compatibility with earlier versions of AutoCAD, you can store and load configuration files in the PCP format. This format stores the general plot configuration information you set up in the Plot configuration dialog box, such as sheet size, plot scale, and orientation. A new format called PC2 will store the same information as the PCP file, with additional configuration information regarding the specific plotter you are using. Here's a step-by-step description of how to store and recall plotter settings.

1. Set up the plotter settings exactly as you want them.

2. Click the Device and Default Selection... button.

3. In the Device and Default Selection dialog box, click under the Save... button in either the Complete PC2 or Partial (PCP - R12/R13) heading. The Save to File dialog box appears.

4. Enter a name for the group of settings. The default name is the same as the current drawing name, with the PCP or PC2 file name extension.

5. Click on OK to create your plot file of settings.

To recall a settings file:

1. Click on File ➤ Print (or type **Plot** ↵ at the command line).

2. Click on the Device and Default Selection... button.

3. In the Device and Default Selection dialog box, click on either the Replace button to recall a PC2 setup or on the Merge button to recall settings from a PCP file.

4. Click on the name of the desired plotter settings file.

5. Click on OK, and the settings will be loaded. You can then proceed with your plot.

The ability to store plotter settings in PC2 and PCP files gives you greater control over your output quality. It helps you to reproduce similar plots more easily when you need them later. You can store several different plotter configurations for one file, each for a different output device. In addition, PC2 files are required for performing batch plots to multiple devices (see the next section, *Batch Plotting*).

You can also open a plot configuration file with a text editor. You can even create your own PCP file by copying an existing one and editing it.

Batch Plotting

Release 14 includes a tool that enables you to plot several unattended drawings at once. This can be helpful when you've finished a set of drawings and would like to plot them during a break or overnight. Here's how to use the Batch Plot utility.

1. From the Windows Desktop, choose Start ➤ Programs ➤ AutoCAD R14 ➤ Batch Plot Utility. The Batch Plot Utility program opens, along with an AutoCAD session.

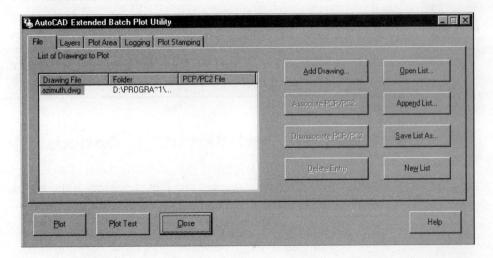

2. Click on the Add Drawing button. The Add Drawing dialog box opens. This is a typical Windows file dialog box.

3. Locate and select a file you wish to plot. The name of the file you select appears in the list box of the Batch Plot Utility Window.

4. Click on the file name in the list. The three buttons labeled Associate PCP/PC2..., Disassociate PCP/PC2, and Delete Entry become available. The Delete Entry option deletes the highlighted option.

5. Click on the Associate PCP/PC2... button. The Associate PCP/PC2 File dialog box appears. This is also a typical Windows file dialog box.

6. Locate and select a PCP or PC2 plot configuration file that contains the settings you want to use in conjunction with this file. If you want to plot to different devices for each drawing, you must use the PC2 plot configuration format.

7. Repeat steps 2 through 6 for additional files.

8. When you have selected all the files and associated a plot configuration file with each one, click on Plot to proceed with the plots.

If you need to, you can store the list of files to plot so you can quickly recall them later. Click on the Save List As... button and a file dialog box appears. You can then save the list under any name you choose. The file will have the BP2 file extension. To restore a saved list, choose Open List; if you want to add a saved list to the current list, choose Append list.

TIP   If you have already set up a system using Scripts for accessing the Plot command, you can restore the command line version of Plot by changing the Cmddia system variable to 0. Bear in mind that, due to minor changes in the way the command line plotting works, you may need to make changes to your plot script. See Chapter 15 for more on scripts.

Other Extended Batch Plot Utility Options

In addition to the main File tab of the Extended Batch Plot Utility, four other tabs—Layers, Plot Area, Logging, and Plot Stamping—offer additional settings that allow greater control over your plots.

The Layers Tab lets you set the layer on/off status for each file in the list of drawings to plot. The settings you make here don't affect the drawing, but they're stored with the BP2 batch plot file so they can be recalled during your batch plots. A Plot Test button is provided to test your batch plot settings. No plot is produced, but if errors are encountered, you will see messages describing them.

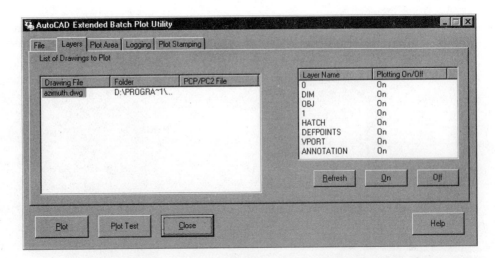

The Plot Area Tab allows you to determine the portion of the drawing that is to be plotted. The options presented here are the same as those in the Plot Configuration dialog box.

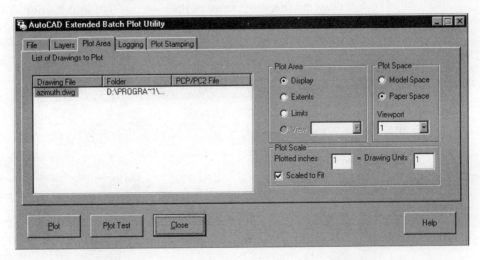

The Logging Tab controls if and where a plot log file is generated at plot time. Log files are helpful in determining where problems are occurring when a batch plot fails. From here, you can set the location and name for the log file, or you can add user comments or header information.

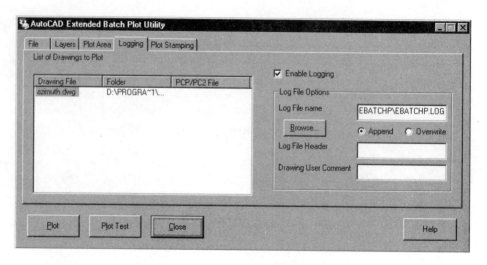

The Plot Stamping Tab controls the plot stamping feature that places a brief message on the plotter output to help identify the plot or otherwise add a stamp to the plot. This can be helpful in associating a plot with a drawing file, the creator of the plot, or other information. To add or change the text of a stamp, use the Change button. This opens another dialog box that allows you to edit the stamp's contents. The Change button also allows you to select an external text file for the contents of the stamp.

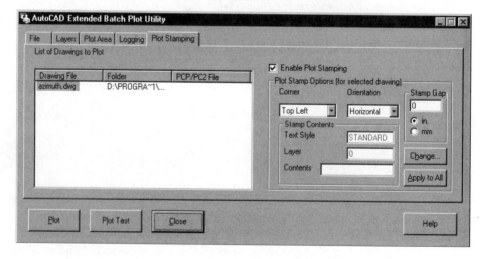

Sending Your Drawings to a Service Bureau

Using a plotting service can be a good alternative to purchasing your own plotter. Or you might consider using a low-cost plotter for check plots and then sending the files to a service for your final product. Many reprographic services, such as blueprinters, offer plotting in conjunction with their other services. Quite often these services include a high-speed modem that allows you to send files over phone lines, eliminating the need for using courier services or regular mail.

Service bureaus will often use an *electrostatic plotter*—it's like a very large laser printer, and is often capable of producing color plots. These plotters are costly, and you probably won't want to purchase one yourself. However, they are excellent for situations requiring high volume and fast turnaround. The electrostatic plotter produces high-quality plots, and it's fast: A 30"×42" plot can take as little as two minutes. One limitation, however, is that these plotters require special media, so you can't use your preprinted title blocks. Ask your prospective plotter service organization about the media limitations.

Another device used by service bureaus is the *laser photo plotter*. This device uses a laser to plot a drawing on a piece of film. The film negative is later enlarged to the finished drawing size by means of standard reprographic techniques. Laser photo plotters yield the highest-quality output of any device, and they offer the flexibility of reproducing drawings at any size.

Finally, many service bureaus can produce full E-size plots of PostScript files. With AutoCAD's full PostScript support, you can get presentation-quality plots from any AutoCAD drawing. See Chapter 14 for more on PostScript and AutoCAD.

If You Want to Experiment...

At this point, since you aren't rushing to meet a deadline, you may want to experiment with some of the plotter and printer variables and see firsthand what each one does. Figure 7.12 shows an exercise you can do to try printing a view and scale different from those used in the exercises.

FIGURE 7.12:

Printing the tub at
1/2"=1'-0" scale

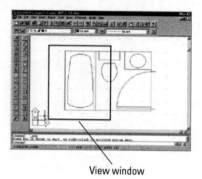

1. Open the Bath file and then use the Window option under the View command to create a view of the bathtub. Name the view **Bath**.

2. Start the Prplot command. At the What to Plot prompt, enter **V** for View. At the View Name prompt, enter **Bath**.

3. Enter **Y** at the Do You Want to Change Anything prompt.

4. Press return at all the defaults until you get to the scale prompt. Enter ½" = **1'** for a plot scale of ½" =1'-0".

5. Proceed with the plot by pressing ↵ at the rest of the prompts. You will get a printout of the tub and part of the toilet.

View window

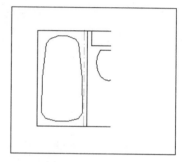

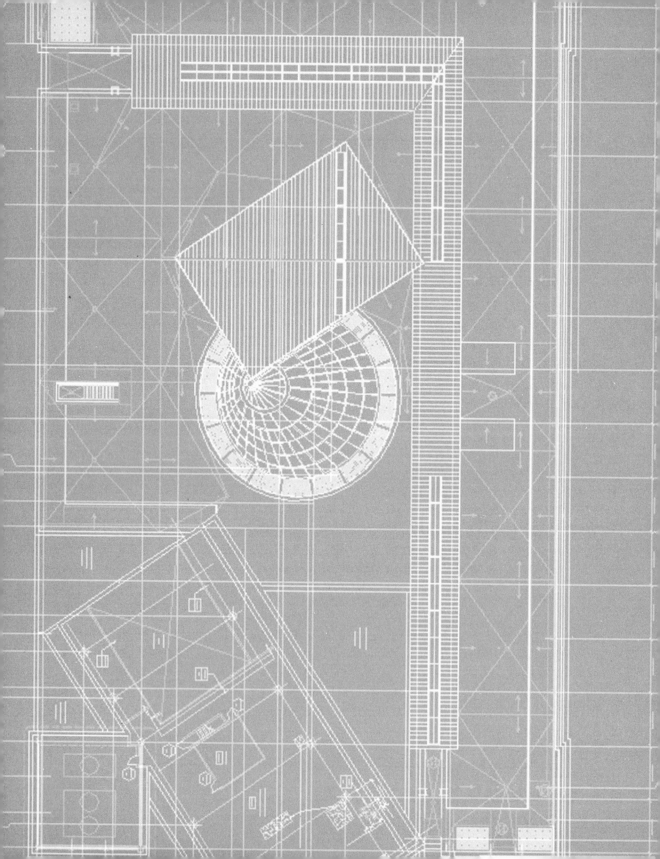

CHAPTER

EIGHT

8

Adding Text to Drawings

- Adding Text to a Drawing

- Understanding Text Formatting in AutoCAD

- Organizing Text by Styles

- What Do the Fonts Look Like?

- Adding Special Characters

- Adding Simple Text Objects

- Checking Spelling

- Substituting Fonts

- Accelerating Zooms and Regens with Qtext

One of the more tedious drafting tasks is applying notes to your drawing. Anyone who has had to draft a large drawing containing a lot of notes knows the true meaning of writer's cramp. AutoCAD not only makes this job go faster by allowing you to type your notes right into the same document as the corresponding drawing, it also helps you to create more professional-looking notes by using a variety of fonts, type sizes, and type styles. And with Release 14, you have an improved text tool that simplifies access to all the text features.

In this chapter, you will add notes to your apartment building plan. In the process, you will explore some of AutoCAD's text creation and editing features. You will learn how to control the size, slant, type style, and orientation of text, and how to import text files.

Adding Text to a Drawing

In this first section, you will add some simple labels to your Unit drawing to identify the general design elements: the bathroom, kitchen, and living room.

1. Start AutoCAD and open the Unit file. If you haven't created the Unit file, you can use the file called `08a-unit.dwg` from the companion CD-ROM. Once open, use File ➢ Save As to save as a file called `Unit.dwg`.

2. Create a layer called Notes and make it the current layer. Notes is the layer on which you will keep all your text information.

3. Turn off the Flr-pat layer. Otherwise, the floor pattern you added previously will obscure the text you will enter in this chapter.

TIP   It's a good idea to keep your notes on a separate layer, so you can plot drawings containing only the graphics information, or freeze the notes layer to save redraw/regeneration time.

---

4. Set up your view so it looks similar to Figure 8.1

5. Choose Multiline Text from the Draw toolbar, or type **MT** ↵.

6. Click in on the first point indicated in the top image of Figure 8.1 to start the text boundary window. This boundary window indicates the area in which to place the text. Notice the arrow near the bottom of the window. It indicates the direction of the text flow.

NOTE You don't have to be too precise about where you select the points for the boundary because you can make adjustments to the location and size later.

7. Click the second point indicated in the top image of Figure 8.1. The Multiline Text Editor appears.

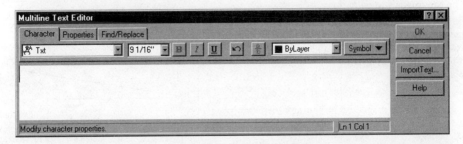

8. You could start typing the text for the room label, but first you need to select a size. Point to the Font Height drop-down list and click on it. The default size highlights.

9. Enter **6** to make the default height 6 inches.

NOTE Why make the text so high? Remember that you are drawing at full scale, and anything you draw will be reduced in the plotted drawing. We will discuss text height in more detail later in this chapter.

10. Click in the main text window and type the word **Entry**. As you type, the word appears in the text window, just as it will appear in your drawing. As you will see later, the text also appears in the same font as the final text.

NOTE   The default font is a native AutoCAD font called Txt. It. As you will see, you can also use TrueType fonts and PostScript fonts.

11.   Press ↵ to advance one line; then enter **6' by 7'**.

12.   Press ↵ again to advance another line and enter **carpet floor**.

13.   Click OK. The text appears in the drawing (see the second image of Figure 8.1).

FIGURE 8.1:

The top image shows the points to pick to place the text boundary window. The bottom image shows the completed text.

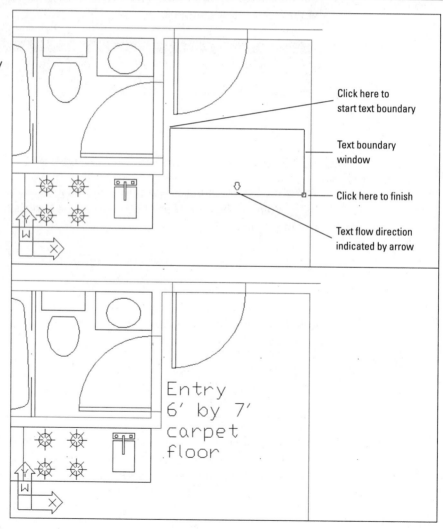

Click here to start text boundary

Text boundary window

Click here to finish

Text flow direction indicated by arrow

The Text window works like any text editor, so if you make a typing error, you can highlight the error and then retype the letter or word. You can also perform many other functions such as search and replace, import text, or make font changes.

The following sections discuss some of the many options you have available for formatting text.

TIP   If text is included in an area where a hatch pattern is to be placed, AutoCAD will automatically avoid hatching over the text. If you add text over a hatched area, you must re-hatch the area to include the text in the hatch boundary.

Understanding Text Formatting in AutoCAD

AutoCAD offers a wide range of text formatting options. You can control fonts, text height, justification, and width. You can even include special characters such as degree symbols or stacked fractions. In a departure from the somewhat clumsy text implementation of earlier AutoCAD versions, you now have a much wider range of controls over your text.

Adjusting the Text Height and Font

Let's continue our look at AutoCAD text by adding a label for the living room of the studio apartment. You'll use the Multiline Text tool again, but this time you'll get to try out some of its other features. In this first exercise, you'll see how you can adjust the size of text in the editor.

1. Pan your view so that the kitchen is just at the top of the drawing, as shown in the top image of Figure 8.2.

2. Click the Multiline Text tool again; then select a text boundary window, as shown in the top image of Figure 8.2.

3. At the Multiline Text dialog box, start typing the following text:

```
Living Room ↵
14'-0" by 16'-5"
```

As you type, you will notice that the words "Living" and "Room" become two separate lines even though you did not press ↵ between them. Auto-CAD uses word wrap to fit the text inside the text boundary area.

4. Highlight the text 14'-0" by 16'-5" as you would in any word processor. For example, you can click on the end of the line to place the cursor there; then Shift + click on the beginning of the line to highlight the whole line.

5. Click on the Font Height drop-down list and enter **6** ↵. The highlighted text changes to a smaller size.

6. Highlight the words "Living Room."

7. Click on the Font drop-down list. A list of font options appears.

8. Scroll up the list until you find Arial. This is a standard TrueType font available in all installations of Windows NT or 95. Notice that the text changes to reflect the new font.

9. With the Living Room text still highlighted, click the Underline tool.

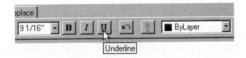

10. Click OK. The label appears in the area you indicated in step 2 (see the bottom image of Figure 8.2).

FIGURE 8.2:

Placing the text boundary window for the living room label and the final label

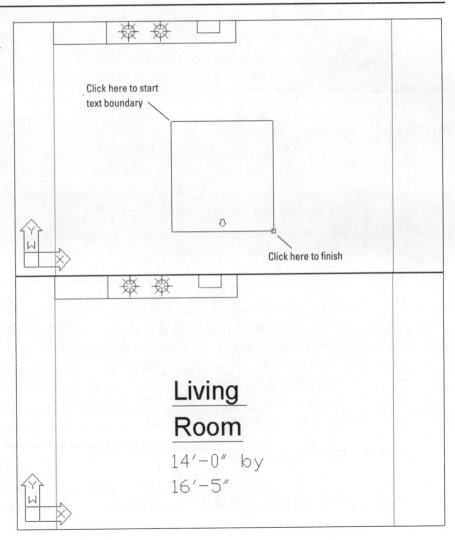

Using PostScript Fonts

If you have PostScript fonts that you would like to use in AutoCAD, you will need to compile them into AutoCAD's native font format. The following steps show you how it's done.

1. Type **Compile** ↵. The Compile Shape or Font File dialog box appears.

2. Select PostScript Font (*.pfb) from the File of Type drop-down list.

3. Double-click on the PostScript font you want to convert into the AutoCAD format. AutoCAD will work for a moment; then you'll see this message:

   ```
   "Compiling shape/font description file"
   Compilation successful. Output file Program Files\AutoCAD 14\
   FONTS\fontname.shx contains 59578 bytes.
   ```

When AutoCAD is done, you have a file with the same name as the PostScript font file, but with the .shx file name extension. If you place your newly compiled font in AutoCAD's Fonts folder, it will be available in the Style dialog box.

When you work with AutoCAD's .shx font files, it is important to remember that

- license restrictions still apply to the AutoCAD-compiled version of the PostScript font.

- like other fonts, compiled PostScript fonts can use up substantial disk space, so compile only the fonts you need.

While using the Multiline Text tool, you may have noticed the [Height/Justify/Rotation/Style/Width] prompt immediately after you picked the first point of the text boundary. You can use any of these options to make on-the-fly modifications to the height, justification, rotation style, or width of the Multiline text.

For example, right after clicking on the first point for the text boundary, you can type **R** ↵ and then specify a rotation angle for the text windows, either graphically with a rubber-banding line or by entering an angle value. Once you've entered a rotation angle, you can resume selecting the text boundary.

Adding Color, Stacked Fractions, and Special Symbols

In the previous exercise, you were able to adjust the text height and font, just as you would in any word processor. You saw how you can easily underline portions of your text using the tool buttons in the editor. Other tools allow you to set the color for individual characters or words in the text, create stacked fractions, or insert special characters. Here's a brief description of how these tools work:

- To change the color of text, highlight it and then select the color from the Text Color drop-down list.

- To turn a fraction into a stacked fraction, highlight the fraction and then click the Stack/Unstack tool.

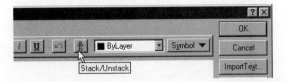

- To add a special character, place the cursor at the location of the character and then click on the Symbol tool. A drop-down list appears offering options for special characters.

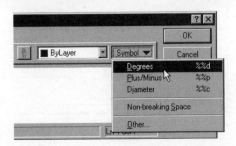

The Symbol tool offers three standard options that are typical for most technical drawings: the Degree, Plus/Minus, and Diameter signs. When you select these options, AutoCAD will insert the proper AutoCAD text code in the text that corresponds to these symbols. They won't appear in the editor as symbols. Instead, they will appear as a special code. However, once you return to the drawing, you will see the text with the proper symbol. You'll get a more detailed look at special symbols later in this chapter.

Adjusting the Width of the Text Boundary Window

While your text font and height is formatted correctly, it appears stacked in a way that is too tall and narrow. The following steps will show you how to change the boundary to fit the text.

1. Click on any part of the text you just entered to highlight it.

2. Click on the upper-right grip.

3. Drag the grip to the right to the location shown in Figure 8.3; then click that point.

4. Click on any grip and then right-click on the mouse and select Move.

5. Move the text to a location that is more centered in the room.

FIGURE 8.3:

Adjusting the text boundary window

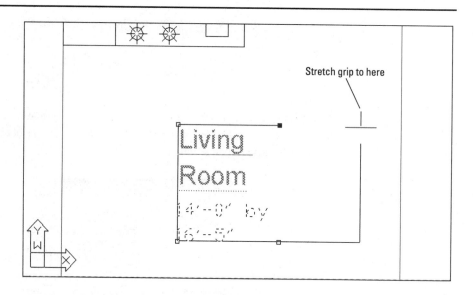

AutoCAD's word wrap feature automatically adjusts the text formatting to fit the text boundary window. This feature is especially useful to AutoCAD users because other drawing objects often impact the placement of text. As your drawing changes you will need to make adjustments to the location and boundary of your notes and labels.

Adjusting the Text Alignment

The text is currently aligned on the left side of the text boundary. For a label such as the one in the living room, it would be more appropriate to center the text. Here's how you can make changes to the text alignment.

1. If the text is not yet selected, click on it.

2. Click on the Properties tool on the Object Properties toolbar. The Modify Mtext dialog box appears.

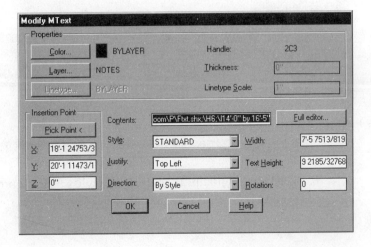

If you click on multiple text objects while using the Properties tool, you will only get the abbreviated Change Properties dialog box.

3. Notice that the text appears in the Contents input box. Also included is some special code that helps format the text. If you only wanted to make changes to the text, this is one place you could do it.

The code you see mixed in with the text in the Contents input box is normally hidden from you in the Multiline text editor, and you don't really need to concern yourself with it. If you edit the text in the Contents input box, make sure you don't change the coding unless you know what you are doing.

4. Click the button labeled Full Editor.... The Multiline Text Editor appears with the text.

TIP

You can go directly to the Multiline Text Editor by using the Ddedit command. Type **Ddedit** ↵ or **ED** ↵ for the keyboard shortcut; then select the text you wish to edit.

5. Click the Properties tab. The editor changes to display a different set of options.

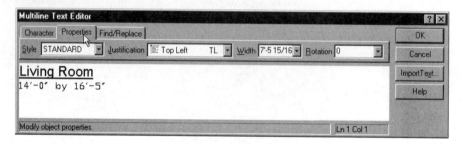

6. Click on the Justification drop-down list. The alignment options appear.

7. Click on Top Center. The living room label moves to a centered position above the second line.

8. Click OK and then at the Modify Mtext dialog box, click OK again. The text changes to align through the center of the text, as shown in Figure 8.4.

FIGURE 8.4:

The text aligned using the Top Center alignment option

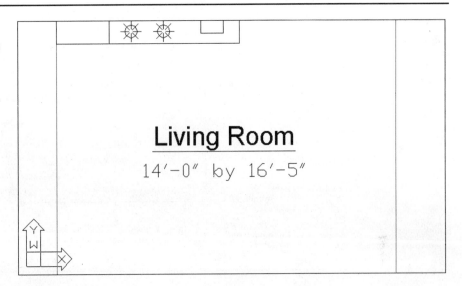

Text Alignment and Osnaps

While it's clear that the text is now aligned through the center of the text, one important change occurred that is not so obvious. You may have noticed that the object alignment list offered three centered options: Top Center, Middle Center, and Bottom Center. All three of these options will have the same effect on the text's appearance, but they each have a different effect on how Osnaps act upon the text. Figure 8.5 shows where the Osnap point occurs on a text boundary depending on which alignment option is selected. A multiline text object will only have one insertion point on its boundary that you can access with the Insert Osnap.

The Osnap point will also appear as an extra grip point on the text boundary when you click on the text. If you click on the text you just entered, you will see that a grip point now appears at the top center of the text boundary.

FIGURE 8.5:

The location of the Insert Osnap points on a text boundary based on its alignment setting

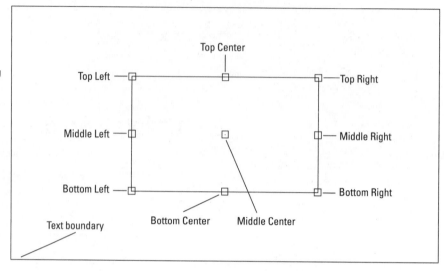

Knowing where the Osnap points occur can be helpful when you want to align the text with other objects in your drawing. In most cases, you can use the grips to align your text boundary, but the center and middle alignment options allow you to use the center and middle portions of your text to align the text with other objects.

Editing Existing Text

It is helpful to think of text in AutoCAD as a collection of text documents. Each text boundary window you place is like a separate document. To create and edit these documents, you use the Multiline Text editor.

You've already seen how you can access existing text using the Properties tool on the Object Properties toolbar when you modified the formatting of the living room label. Of course, you can use the same tool to change the content of the text. In the following example, you'll use a shortcut to the Multiline Text dialog box to add more text to the living room label.

1. Type **Ed** ↵ or choose Modify ➤ Object ➤ Text…. This issues the Ddedit command.

NOTE   The Ddedit command does not allow Noun/Verb selection.

2. Click on the words "Living Room." The Multiline Text dialog box appears.

3. Place and click the text cursor on the end of the line that reads "Living Room"; then type ↵ **230 square feet**.

4. Click OK. The text appears in the drawing with the addition line.

5. The Ddedit command is still active, so press ↵ to exit Ddedit.

TIP You can also add or delete text using the Properties tool in the Object Properties toolbar. When you select a single text object, the Modify Mtext dialog box appears displaying the text in the Contents input box; you can change the text here.

In step 5, the Ddedit command remains active so you can continue to edit other text objects. In addition to pressing ↵ to exit the command, you can select another text object.

As with the prior exercise, you can change the formatting of the existing or new text while in the Multiline Text dialog box. Notice that the formatting of the new text is the same as the text that preceded it. Just as in Microsoft Word, the formatting of text is dependent on the paragraph or word to which it is added. If you had added the text after the last line, it would appear in the AutoCAD Txt font and in the same 6-inch height.

Understanding Text and Scale

In the first few exercises of this chapter, you were asked to make the text height 6 inches. This is necessary to give the text the proper scale for the drawing. But where did we come up with the number 6? Why not 4 or 10? The 6-inch height was derived by carefully considering the desired final height of the text in relation to the designated scale of the drawing. Just as in Chapter 3 where we applied a scale factor to a drawing's final sheet size to accommodate a full scale drawing, we need to make a scale conversion for our text size to make the text conform to the drawings intended scale.

Text scale conversion is a concept many people have difficulty grasping. As you discovered in previous chapters, AutoCAD allows you to draw at full scale; that is, to represent distances as values equivalent to the actual size of the object. When you later plot the drawing, you tell AutoCAD at what scale you wish to plot and the program reduces the drawing accordingly. This allows you the freedom to input measurements at full scale and not worry about converting them to various scales every time you enter a distance. Unfortunately, this feature can also create problems when you enter text and dimensions. Just as you had to convert the plotted sheet size to an enlarged size equivalent at full scale in the drawing editor, you must convert your text size to its equivalent at full scale.

To illustrate this point, imagine you are drawing the unit plan at full size on a very large sheet of paper. When you are done with this drawing, it will be reduced to a scale that will allow it to fit on an $8\frac{1}{2}\times11$" sheet of paper. So you have to make your text quite large to keep it legible once it is reduced. This means that if you want text to appear 1/8" high when the drawing is plotted, you must convert it to a considerably larger size when you draw it. To do this, you multiply the desired height of the final plotted text by a scale conversion factor.

If your drawing is at 1/8"=1' scale, you multiply the desired text height, 1/8", by the scale conversion factor of 96 (Table 3.3 shows scale factors as they relate to standard drawing scales) to get a height of 12". This is the height you must make your text to get 1/8"-high text in the final plot. Table 8.1 shows you some other examples of text height to scale.

TABLE 8.1: 1/8"-high text converted to size for various drawing scales

Drawing Scale	Scale Factor	AutoCAD Drawing Height for 1/8"-High Text
1/16" = 1'-0"	192	24.0"
1/8" = 1'-0"	96	12.0"
1/4" = 1'-0"	48	6.0"
1/2" = 1'-0"	24	3.0"
3/4" = 1'-0"	16	2.0"
1" = 1'-0"	12	1.5"
1 1/2" = 1'-0"	8	1.0"
3" = 1'-0"	4	0.5"

Organizing Text by Styles

If you understand the Multiline Text Editor and text scale, you know all you need to know to start labeling your drawings. As you expand your drawing skills and your drawings become larger, you will want to start organizing your text into *styles*. You can think of text styles as a way to store your most common text formatting. Styles will store text height and font information, so you don't have to reset these options every time you enter text. But styles also include some settings not available in the Multiline Text Editor.

Creating a Style

In the prior examples, you entered text using the AutoCAD default settings for text. Whether you knew it or not, you were also using a text style: AutoCAD's default style called Standard. The Standard style uses the AutoCAD Txt font and numerous other settings that you will learn about in this section. These other settings include width factor, obliquing, and default height.

TIP If you don't like the way the AutoCAD Default style is set up, open the Acad.dwt file and change the Standard text style settings to your liking. You can also add other styles that you use frequently.

The previous exercises in this chapter demonstrate that you can modify the formatting of a style as you enter the text. But for the most part, once you've set up a few styles, you won't need to adjust settings like fonts and text height each time you enter text. You will be able to select from a list of styles you've previously created, and just start typing.

To create a style, you use Format ➤ Text Style ➤ and then select from the fonts available. This next exercise will show you how to create a style.

1. Click on Format ➤ Text Style, or type **St** ⏎. The Text Style dialog box appears.

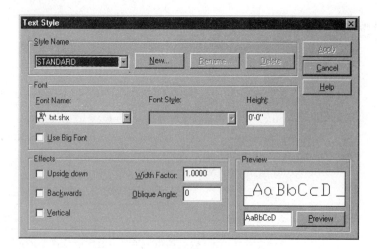

2. Click the New button in the Style Name group. The New Text Style dialog box appears.

3. Enter **Note1** for the name of your new style; then click OK.

4. Now select a font for your style. Click on the Font Name in the Font group.

5. Locate the Courier New TrueType font and select it.

6. In the Height input box, enter **6**.

7. Click Apply and then click Close.

Dressing Up Your Drawings with Display Fonts

Display fonts are fonts used in situations where appearances are important. In a typical architectural project, for example, display fonts are frequently used for presentation drawings of floor plans and building elevations. Traditionally, architects have used a device called a Kroy label machine to generate text for presentations. The Kroy machine is slow and somewhat time-consuming to use because you have to apply the lettering by hand to your artwork. With TrueType support, you can add display fonts directly to your CAD drawings, thereby saving time and gaining a higher degree of control over your presentation artwork.

Using a Type Style

Now let's see how your new text style looks by adding more text to the `Unit.dwg` drawing.

1. Pan your view so the balcony is centered in the AutoCAD drawing area, as shown in Figure 8.6.

2. Click on the Multiline Text tool on the Draw toolbar.

3. Place the text boundary as shown in the top image of Figure 8.6. Notice that the font and height settings reflect the Note1 style you created earlier.

4. Enter the following text:

   ```
   Balcony ↵
   56 SF↵
   14'-0" by 4'-0"
   ```

5. Highlight the word "Balcony," and then click the Underline button.

6. With Balcony still highlighted, click on the Height input box and enter **9** ↵.

7. Click the Properties tab.

8. Highlight all of the text and then select the Top Center from the Object Alignment drop-down list.

9. Click OK. The text appears over the balcony in the style you selected.

A newly created style becomes the default style, and you didn't have to explicitly select your new Note1 style in order to use it.

You can also change an existing piece of text to a different style. The following steps show you how.

1. Return to your previous view of the "Living Room" text.

2. Type **Ed** ↵ and select the text.

3. Click on the Properties tab in the Multiline Text Editor.

4. Highlight one line of the text.

5. Click on the Style drop-down list and select Note1. Notice that all the text is converted to the new style.

WARNING   When you change the style of a text object, it loses any custom formatting it may have, such as font or height changes that are different from those of the text's default style settings.

6. Click OK. The living room label is now in your Note1 style (see Figure 8.7).

FIGURE 8.6:

Adding the balcony label using the Note1 text style

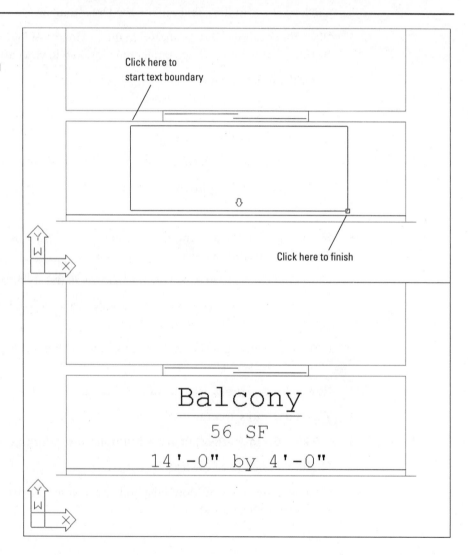

Click here to start text boundary

Click here to finish

Balcony

56 SF

14'-0" by 4'-0"

FIGURE 8.7:

The living room label converted to the Note1 Style

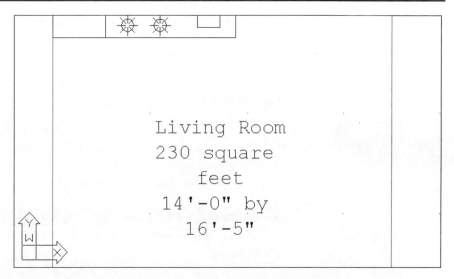

```
Living Room
230 square
   feet
14'-0" by
 16'-5"
```

> **WARNING** The Style input box in the Modify Mtext dialog box (found via the Properties tool) will allow you to select a new style for a text object. This option does not affect the style of text if the text has other custom format changes, such as a font and size change from its default settings.

Setting the Current Default Style

The last exercise showed you how you can change the style of existing text. But suppose you want all the new text you create to be of a different style than the current default style. You can change the current style by using the Style dialog box. Here's how it's done.

1. Click on Format ➤ Text Style, or type **St** ↵. The Text Style dialog box appears.

2. Select a style name from the Style Name drop-down list. For this exercise, choose Standard to return to the Standard style.

3. Click Close....

Once you've done this, the selected style will be the default until you select a different style. AutoCAD will record the current default style with the drawing data when you issue a File ➤ Save command, so the next time you work on the file you will still have the same default style.

Understanding the Text Style Dialog Box Options

Now you know how to create a new style. As I mentioned before, there are other settings in the Text Style dialog box that you didn't apply in an exercise. Here is a listing of those settings and their purposes. Some of them, like the Width factor, can be quite useful. Others like the Backward and Vertical options are rarely used.

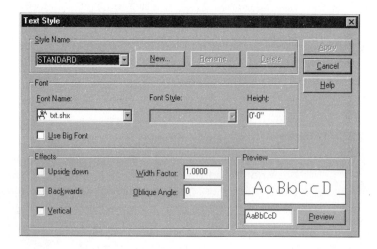

Style Name

New   lets you create a new text style.

Rename   lets you rename an existing style. This option is not available for the Standard style.

Delete   deletes a style. This option is not available for the Standard style.

Font

Font Name   lets you select a font from a list of available fonts. The list is derived from the font resources available to Windows NT or 95, plus the standard AutoCAD fonts.

Font Style   offers variations of a font such as italic or bold, when they are available.

Height   lets you enter a font size. A 0 height has special meaning when entering text using the Dtext command described later in this chapter.

Effects

Upside down   prints the text upside down.

Backwards   prints the text backwards.

Width Factor   adjusts the width and spacing of the characters in the text. A value of 1 keeps the text at the its normal width. Values greater than 1 will expand the text while values less than 1 will compress the text.

This is the Simplex font expanded by 1.4

This is the simplex font using a width factor of 1

This is the simplex font compressed by .6

Oblique Angle   skews the text at an angle. When this option is set to a value greater than 0, the text appears to be italicized. A value of less than 0 (-12, for example) will cause the text to "lean" to the left.

*This is the simplex font
using a 12—degree oblique angle*

Renaming a Text Style

You can use the Rename option in the Text Style dialog box to rename a style. An alternate method is to use the Ddrename command. This is a command that allows you to rename a variety of AutoCAD settings. Here's how to use it.

NOTE This exercise is not part of the main tutorial. If you are working through the tutorial, make note of it and then try it out later.

1. Click on Format ➤ Rename…, or enter **Ren** ↵ at the command prompt. The Rename dialog box appears.

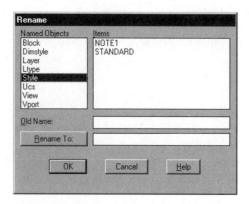

NOTE The Ddrename command allows you to rename blocks, dimension styles, layers, line types, user coordinate systems, viewports, and views, as well as text styles.

2. In the Named Objects list box, click on Style.

3. Click on the name of the style you wish to change from the list to the right; the name appears in the Old Name input box below the list.

4. In the input box next to the Rename To button, enter the new name, click the Rename To button, and then click OK.

NOTE If you are an experienced AutoCAD user and accustomed to entering the Rename command at the command prompt, you still can. Then answer the prompts that appear.

TIP If you need to change the style of one text object to match that of another, you can use the Match Properties tool. See the *How to Quickly Match a Hatch Pattern and Other Properties* sidebar in Chapter 6 for details on how to use this tool.

What Do the Fonts Look Like?

You've already seen a few of the fonts available in AutoCAD. Chances are, you are familiar with the TrueType fonts available in Windows. You have some additional AutoCAD fonts from which to choose. In fact, you may want to stick with the AutoCAD fonts for all but your presentation drawings, as other font's can consume more memory.

Figure 8.8 shows the basic AutoCAD text fonts. The Roman font is perhaps the most widely used because it offers a reasonable appearance while not consuming much memory. Figure 8.9 shows the Symbols, Greek, and Cyrillic fonts.

FIGURE 8.8:

The Standard AutoCAD text fonts

This is Txt
This is Monotxt
This is Simplex   (Old version of Roman Simplex)
This is Complex   (Old version of Roman Complex)
This is Italic   (Old version of Italic Complex)
This is Romans   (Roman Simplex)
This is Romand   (Roman double stroke)
This is Romanc   (Roman Complex)
This is Romant   (Roman triple stroke)
This is Scripts   (Script Simplex)
This is Scriptc   (Script Complex)
This is Italicc   (Italic Complex)
This is Italict   (Italic triple stroke)
Τηισ ισ Γρεεκσ   (This is Greeks - Greek Simplex)
Τηισ ισ Γρεεκχ   (This is Greekc - Greek Complex)
Узит ит Вшсиллив   (This is Cyrillic - Alphabetical)
Тхис ис Чйрилтлч   (This is Cyriltlc - Transliteration)
This is Gothice   (Gothic English)
Thif if Gothicg   (Gothic German)
This is Gothici   (Gothic Italian)

FIGURE 8.9:

The AutoCAD Symbols, Greek, and Cyrillic fonts

font\key	A	B	C	D	E	F	G	H	I	J	K	L	M	N	O	P	Q	R	S	T	U	V	W	X	Y	Z	[	\	]	^	_
Symap																											[	\	]	~	_
Syastro																											[	\	]	~	_
Symath																											[	\	]	~	_
Symeteo																											[	\	]	~	_
Symusic																											[	\	]	~	_
Greeks	Α	Β	Χ	Δ	Ε	Φ	Γ	Η	Ι	ϑ	Κ	Λ	Μ	Ν	Ο	Π	Θ	Ρ	Σ	Τ	Τ	∇	Ω	Ξ	Ψ	Ζ	[	\	]	~	_
Greekc	Α	Β	Χ	Δ	Ε	Φ	Γ	Η	Ι	ϑ	Κ	Λ	Μ	Ν	Ο	Π	Θ	Ρ	Σ	Τ	Τ	∇	Ω	Ξ	Ψ	Ζ	[	\	]	~	_
Cyrillic	А	Б	В	Г	Д	Е	Ж	З	И	Й	К	Л	М	Н	О	П	Р	С	Т	У	Ф	Х	Ц	Ч	Ш	Щ	Ъ	Ы	Ь	Э	Ю	Я
Cyriltlc	А	Б	Ч	Д	Е	Ф	Г	Х	И	Щ	К	Л	М	Н	О	П	Ц	Р	С	Т	У	В	Ш	Ж	Й	З	Ь	Ы	Ъ	Э	Ю	Я

font\key	a	b	c	d	e	f	g	h	i	j	k	l	m	n	o	p	q	r	s	t	u	v	w	x	y	z	{	|	}	~	❖	⚘
Symap																											{	|	}	~	<	>
Syastro																											{	|	}	~	<	>
Symath																											{	|	}	~	<	>
Symeteo																											{	|	}	~	<	>
Symusic																											{	|	}	~	<	>
Greeks	α	β	χ	δ	ε	φ	γ	η	ι	∂	κ	λ	μ	ν	ο	π	ϑ	ρ	σ	τ	υ	ϖ	ω	ξ	ψ	ζ	{	|	}	~	<	>
Greekc	α	β	χ	δ	ε	φ	γ	η	ι	∂	κ	λ	μ	ν	ο	π	ϑ	ρ	σ	τ	υ	ϖ	ω	ξ	ψ	ζ	{	|	}	~	<	>
Cyrillic	а	б	в	г	д	е	ж	з	и	й	к	л	м	н	о	п	р	с	т	у	ф	х	ц	ч	ш	щ	ъ	ы	ь	э	ю	я
Cyriltlc	а	б	ч	д	е	ф	г	х	и	щ	к	л	м	н	о	п	ц	р	с	т	у	в	ш	ж	й	з	ь	ы	ъ	э	ю	я

The Textfill System Variable

Unlike the standard sticklike AutoCAD fonts, TrueType and PostScript fonts have filled areas. These filled areas take more time to generate, so if you have a lot of text in these fonts, your redraw and regen times will increase. To help reduce redraw and regen times, you can set AutoCAD to display and plot these fonts as outline fonts, even though they are filled in their true appearance.

To change its setting, type **Textfill** ↵ and then type **0** ↵. This turns off text fill for PostScript and TrueType fonts. For plots, you can remove the checkmark on the option labeled Text Fill (this is the same as setting the Textfill system variable to 0).

We've shown you samples of the AutoCAD fonts in this section. You can see samples of all the fonts, including TrueType fonts, in the Preview window of the Text Style dialog box. If you use a word processor, you're probably familiar with at least some of the TrueType fonts available in Windows and AutoCAD.

Adding Special Characters

I mentioned earlier that you can add special characters using the Symbol button in the Multiline Text Editor. For example, the Degree symbol to designate angles, the Plus/Minus symbol for showing tolerance information, and the Diameter characters are already available as special characters. AutoCAD also offers a nonbreaking space. You can use the nonbreaking space when you have a space between two words but you do not want the two words to be separated by a line break.

By clicking the Other... option in the Symbols drop-down list, you can also add other special characters from the Windows Character Map dialog box.

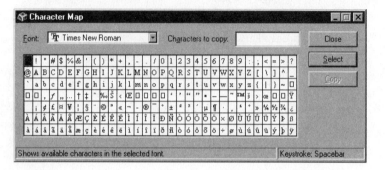

Characters such as the Trademark (™) and copyright (©) symbols are often available. The contents of the list will vary depending on the font you have currently selected. You can click and drag or just click your mouse over the Character Map to see an enlarged view of the character you are pointing to.

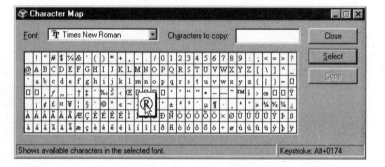

To use the characters from this dialog box, proceed with the following steps.

1. Chose Other from the Symbols button of the Multiline Text Editor.

NOTE   This is not part of the regular tutorial in this chapter, though you can experiment with these steps on your own.

---

2. Highlight the character you want.

3. Either double-click on the character or click on the Select button. The character appears in the box at the upper-right corner of the dialog box.

4. Click Copy to copy the character to the clipboard.

5. Close the dialog box.

6. In the Editor, place the cursor where you want the special character to appear.

7. Press Ctrl+V to paste the character into your text. You can also right-click on the mouse and choose Paste from the pop-up list.

Importing Text Files

With Multiline text objects, AutoCAD allows you to import ASCII text or Rich Text Format files. Here's how you go about importing text files.

1. From the Multiline Text Edit dialog box, click on Import Text.

2. At the Open dialog box, locate a valid text file. It must be either a file in a raw text (ASCII) format, such as a Notepad (.txt), or a Rich Text Format (.rtf) file. RFT files are capable of storing formatting information, such as bold-face and varying point sizes.

3. Once you've highlighted the file you want, double-click on it or click on OK. The text appears in the Edit Mtext window.

4. You can then click on OK and the text will appear in your drawing.

In addition, you can use the Windows clipboard and Cut and Paste feature to add text to a drawing. To do this, take the following steps:

1. Use the Cut or Copy option in any other Windows program to place text into the Windows clipboard.

2. Go to AutoCAD and then choose Edit ➤ Paste. The text appears in the upper-left corner of the AutoCAD drawing window. It is not, however, editable within AutoCAD.

Because AutoCAD is an OLE client, you can also attach other types of documents to an AutoCAD drawing file. See Chapter 14 for more on AutoCAD's OLE support.

Adding Simple Text Objects

You may find that you are entering a lot of single words or simple labels that don't require all the bells and whistles of the Multiline Text Editor. AutoCAD offers the *single-line text object* that is simpler to use and can speed text entry if you are only adding small pieces of text.

Continue the tutorial on the Unit.dwg file by trying the following exercise.

1. Adjust your view so it looks like Figure 8.10.

2. Enter **Dt** ↵, or choose Draw ➤ Text ➤ Single Line Text. This issues the Dtext command.

3. At the DTEXT Justify/Style/<Start point> prompt, pick the starting point for the text you are about to enter, just below the kitchen at coordinate 16'-2", 21'-8". By picking a point, you are accepting <start point>, which is the default.

4. At the Height prompt, enter **6"** to indicate the text height.

5. At the Insertion angle <0> prompt, press ↵ to accept the default, 0°. You can specify any angle other than horizontal (for example, if you want your text to be aligned with a rotated object). You'll see a text I-beam cursor at the point you picked in step 3.

6. At the Text prompt, enter the word **Kitchenette**. As you type, the word appears in the drawing as well as in the Command window.

NOTE   If you make a typing error, use the right and left arrow key to move the text cursor in the Command window to the error; then use the backspace key to correct the error. You can also paste text from the clipboard into the cursor location using the Ctrl+V keyboard shortcut or by right-clicking in the Command window to access the pop-up menu.

---

7. Press ↵ to move the cursor down to start a new line.

8. This time you want to label the bathroom. Pick a point to the right of the door swing at coordinate 19'-11", 26'-5". The text cursor moves to that point.

9. Type **Bathroom** ↵. Figure 8.10 shows how your drawing should look now.

10. Press ↵ again to exit the Dtext command.

FIGURE 8.10:

Adding simple labels
to the kitchen and bath
using the Dtext
command

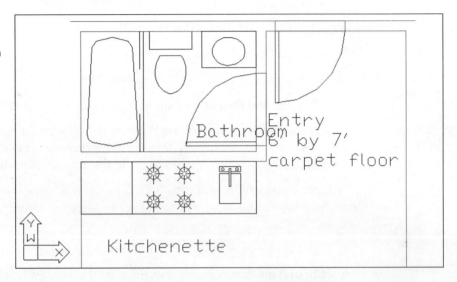

If for some reason you need to stop entering single-line text objects to do
something else in AutoCAD, you can continue text where you left off by
pressing ↵ at the Start point prompt of the Dtext command. The text will
continue immediately below the last line of text entered.

Here you were able to add two single lines of text in different parts of your
drawing fairly quickly. Dtext will use the current default text style settings
(remember that earlier you set the style to Standard), so the kitchen and bath
labels used the Standard style.

Editing Single-Line Text Objects

Editing single-line text uses the same tools as those for multiline text, though the
dialog boxes that result are different. In this exercise, you'll change the labels in
both the kitchen and bath using the Dedit command.

1. Type **ED** ↵ or choose Modify ➢ Object ➢ Text.

2. Click on the Kitchenette label. A small Edit Text dialog box appears.

3. Using the cursor, highlight the "ette" in kitchenette and delete it.

4. Click OK. (Notice that Ddedit is still active.)

5. Click on the Bath label.

6. In the dialog box, change Bathroom to **Bath**.

7. Click OK and then press ↵ to exit the Ddedit command.

As you can see, even the editing is simplified. You are limited to editing the text only. This can be an advantage, however, when you need to edit several pieces of text. You don't have other options to get in the way of your editing.

You can change other properties of single-line text using the Properties dialog box. For example, suppose you want to change the bathroom label to a height of 9 inches.

1. Click on the Properties tool in the Object Properties toolbar.

2. Click on the Bath text and then press ↵. The Modify Text dialog appears.

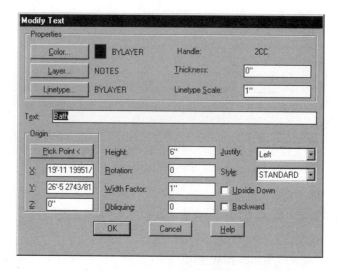

Notice that in this case, you do not see the Full Editor... option.

3. Double-click on the Height input box and enter **9** ↵.

4. Click OK. The text increases in size to 9-inches high.

5. Click the Undo Tool on the menu bar to undo the change in text height.

6. Click File ➢ Save to save the changes you've made thus far.

The Modify Text dialog box lets you change the Height, Rotation, Width Factor, Obliquing, Justification, and style of a single-line text object. You can also modify the text content.

TIP

Unlike prior version of AutoCAD, the `Height` prompt appears in the Dtext command even if the current style has a non-zero height.

Justifying Single-Line Text Objects

Justifying single-line text objects works in a slightly different way from multiline text. For example, if you change the justification setting to Center, the text will move so the center of the text will be placed at the text insertion point. In other words, the insertion point stays in place while the text location adjusts to the new justification setting. Figure 8.11 shows the relationship between single-line text and the insertion point based on different justification settings.

FIGURE 8.11:

Text inserted using the various Justify options

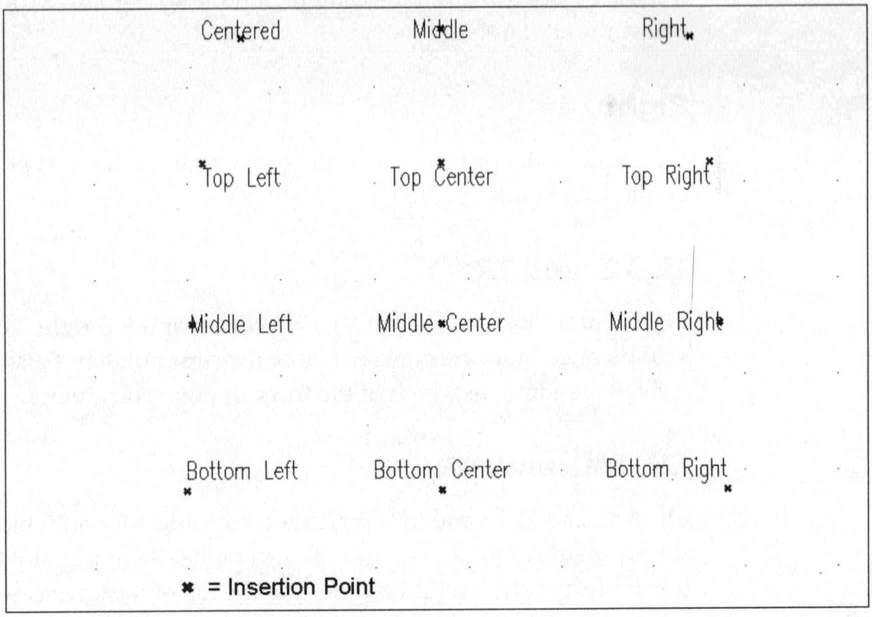
Centered
Middle
Right
Top Left
Top Center
Top Right
Middle Left
Middle Center
Middle Right
Bottom Left
Bottom Center
Bottom Right
* = Insertion Point

To set the justification of text as you enter it, you must enter **J** ↵ at the Justify/Style/<Start point> prompt after issuing the Dtext command.

NOTE   You can also change the current default style by entering **S** ↵ and then the name of the style at the Justify/Style/<Start point> prompt.

Once you've issued the Dtext's Justify option, you will then get the prompt:

Align/Fit/Center/Middle/Right/TL/TC/TR/ML/MC/MR/BL/BC/BR:

Here are descriptions of each of these options (I've left Fit and Align until last, as these options require a bit more explanation):

Center

Center causes the text to be centered on the start point, with the baseline on the start point.

Middle

Middle causes the text to be centered on the start point, with the baseline slightly below the start point.

Right

Right causes the text to be justified to the right of the start point, with the baseline on the start point.

TL, TC, and TR

TL, TC, and TR stand for top left, top center, and top right. Text using these justification styles appears entirely below the start point and justified left, center, or right, depending on which of the three options you choose.

ML, MC, and MR

ML, MC, and MR stand for middle left, middle center, and middle right. These styles are similar to TL, TC, and TR, except that the start point will determine a location midway between the baseline and the top of the lowercase letters of the text.

BL, BC, and BR

BL, BC, and BR stand for bottom left, bottom center, and bottom right. These styles, too, are similar to TL, TC, and TR, but here the start point determines the bottom-most location of the letters of the text (the bottom of letters that have descenders, such as *p*, *q*, and *g*).

Align and Fit Options

With the Fit and Align justification options, you must specify a dimension within which the text is to fit. For example, suppose you want the word "Refrigerator" to fit within the 26"-wide box representing the refrigerator. You can use either the Fit or the Align option to accomplish this. With Fit, AutoCAD prompts you to select start and end points, and then stretches or compresses the letters to fit within the two points you specify. You use this option when the text must be a consistent height throughout the drawing and you don't care about distorting the font. Align works like Fit, but instead of maintaining the current text style height, Align adjusts the text height to keep it proportional to the text width, without distorting the font. Use this option when it is important to maintain the font's shape and proportion. Figure 8.12 demonstrates how Fit and Align work.

FIGURE 8.12:

The word "Refrigerator" as it appears normally and with the Fit and Align options selected

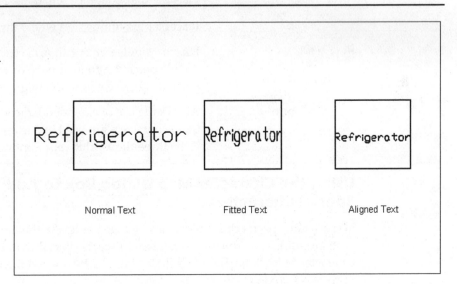

Normal Text   Fitted Text   Aligned Text

Using Special Characters with Single-Line Text Objects

Just as with multiline text, you can add a limited set of special characters to single-line text objects. For example, you can place the degree symbol (o) after a number, or you can *underscore* (underline) text. To accomplish this, you use double percent (%%) signs in conjunction with a special code. For example, to underscore text, you enclose that text with the %% signs and follow it with the underscore code. So, to get this text: "This is underscored text." you would enter this at the prompt:

This is %%uunderscored%%u text.

Overscoring (putting a line above the text) operates in the same manner. To insert codes for symbols, you just place the codes in the correct positions for the symbols they represent. For example, to enter 100.5°, you type **100.5%%d**.

Here is a list of the codes you can use:

Code Special	Characters
%%o	Toggles overscore on and off.
%%u	Toggles underscore on and off.
%%d	Places a degree sign (°) where the code occurs.
%%p	Places a plus-minus sign where the code occurs.
%%%	Forces a single percent sign; useful when you want a double percent sign to appear, or when you want a percent sign in conjunction with another code.
%%nnn	Allows the use of extended Unicode characters when these characters are used in a text-definition file; *nnn* is the three-digit value representing the character.

Using the Character Map Dialog Box to Add Special Characters

You can add special characters to a single line of text in the same way you would with multiline text. You may recall that to access special characters, you use the Character Map dialog box. This dialog box can be opened directly from the Windows Explorer.

Using the Explorer, locate the file Charmap.exe in the Windows folder. Double-click on it and the Character Map dialog box appears. You can then use the procedure discussed in the *Adding Special Characters* section earlier in this chapter to cut and paste a character from the Character Map dialog box. If you find you use the Character Map dialog box often, create a shortcut for it and place the shortcut in your AutoCAD Program group.

Keeping Text from Mirroring

At times you will want to mirror a group of objects that contain some text. This operation will cause the mirrored text to appear backward. You can change a setting in AutoCAD to make the text read normally, even when it is mirrored.

1. Enter **Mirrtext** ↵.

2. At the New value for MIRRTEXT <1> prompt, enter **0** ↵.

Now any mirrored text that is not in a block will read normally. The text's *position*, however, will still be mirrored, as shown in the graphic below. Mirrtext is set to 0 by default.

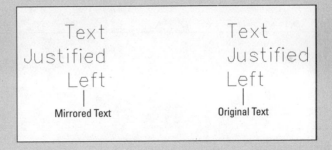

Mirrored Text   Original Text

Checking Spelling

Although AutoCAD is primarily a drawing program, you will find that some of your drawings contain more text than graphics. Autodesk has recognized this and has included a spelling checker in AutoCAD Release 14. If you've ever used the spelling checker in a typical word processor, such as Microsoft Word, the AutoCAD spelling checker's operation will be familiar to you. These steps show you how it works.

1. Click the Spelling tool on the Standard toolbar, or type **Sp** ⏎.

2. At the `Select object` prompt, select any text object you want to check. You can select a mixture of multiline and single-line text. When the spelling checker finds a word it does not recognize, the Check Spelling dialog box appears.

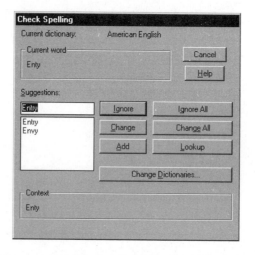

In the Check Spelling dialog box, you'll see the word in question, along with the spelling checker's suggested alternate word in the Suggestions input box. If the spelling checker finds more than one suggestion, a list of suggested replacement words appears below the input box. You can then highlight the desired replacement and click the Change button to change the misspelled word, or click Change All to change all occurrences of the word in the selected text. If the suggested word is inappropriate, choose another word from the replacement list (if any), or enter your own spelling in the Suggestions input box. Then choose Change or Change All.

Here is a list of the options available in the Check Spelling dialog box:

Ignore skips the word.

Ignore All skips all the occurrences of the word in the selected text.

Change changes the word in question to the word you have selected (or entered) from the Suggestions input box.

Change All changes all occurrences of the current word, when there are multiple instances of the misspelling.

Add adds the word in question to the current dictionary.

Lookup checks the spelling of the word in question. This option is for the times when you want to find another word that doesn't appear in the Suggestions input box.

Change Dictionaries lets you use a different dictionary to check spelling. This option opens the Change Dictionaries dialog box, described in the upcoming section.

Choosing a Dictionary

The Change Dictionaries option opens the Change Dictionaries dialog box, where you can select a particular main dictionary for foreign languages, or create or choose a custom dictionary. Main dictionary files have the .dct extension. The Main dictionary for the U.S. version of AutoCAD is Enu.dct.

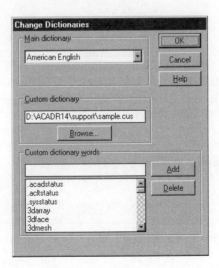

In this dialog box, you can also add or delete words from a custom dictionary. Custom dictionary files are ASCII files with the .cus extension. Because they are ASCII files, they can be edited outside of AutoCAD. The Browse button lets you view a list of existing custom dictionaries.

If you prefer, you can also select a main or custom dictionary using the Dctust and Dctmain system variables. See Appendix D for more on these system variables.

A third place where you can select a dictionary is in the Files tab of the Preferences dialog box (Tools ➤ Preferences). You can find the Dictionary listing under Text Editor, Dictionary, and Font File Names. Click the plus sign next to this listing and then click the plus sign next to the Main Dictionary listing to expose the dictionary options.

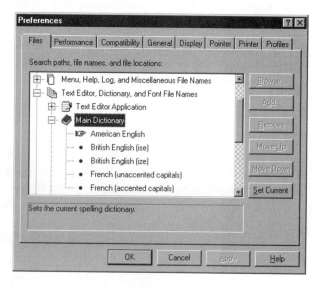

From here, you can double-click on the dictionary you prefer. The pointing hand icon will move to the selected dictionary.

Substituting Fonts

There will be times when you will want to change all the fonts in a drawing quickly. For instance, you may want to convert PostScript fonts into a simple Txt.shx font to help shorten redraw times while you are editing. Or you may need to convert the font of a drawing received from another office to a font that conforms to your own office standards. In AutoCAD Release 14, the Fontmap system variable works in conjunction with a font-mapping table, allowing you to easily substitute fonts in a drawing.

The font-mapping table is an ASCII file called `Acad.fmp`. You can also use a file you create yourself. You can give this file any name you choose, as long as it has the .fmp extension.

This font-mapping table contains one line for each font substitution you want AutoCAD to make. A typical line in this file would read as follows:

```
romant; C:\acadr14\common\font\Txt.shx
```

In this example, AutoCAD is directed to use the `Txt.shx` font in place of the Romant font. To execute this substitution, you would type:

```
Fontmap ↵ Fontmap_filename
```

where *Fontmap_filename* is the font-mapping table you've created. This tells AutoCAD where to look for the font-mapping information. Then you would issue the Regen command to view the font changes. To disable the font-mapping table, you type:

```
Fontmap ↵ .↵
```

You can also specify a font-mapping file in the Files tab of the Preferences dialog box. Look for the Text Editor, Dictionary, and Font File listing. Click the plus sign next to this listing and then click the plus sign next to the Font Mapping File listing to expose the current default font-mapping file name.

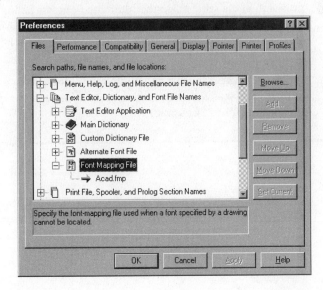

You can double-click on this file name to open a Select a File dialog box. From there you can select a different font-mapping file.

See Appendix D for more on Fontmap and other system variables.

Making Substitutions for Missing Fonts

When text styles are created, the associated fonts do not become part of the drawing file. Instead, AutoCAD loads the needed font file at the same time that the drawing is loaded. So if a text style in a drawing requires a particular font, AutoCAD looks for the font in the AutoCAD search path; if the font is there, it is loaded. Usually this isn't a problem if the drawing file uses the standard fonts that come with AutoCAD or Windows. But occasionally you will encounter a file hat uses a custom font.

In earlier versions of AutoCAD, when you attempted to open such a file, you saw an error message. This missing-font message would often send the new AutoCAD user into a panic.

Fortunately, Release 14 offers a solution: AutoCAD automatically substitutes an existing font for the missing font in a drawing. By default, AutoCAD substitutes the Txt.shx font, but you can specify another one using the Fontalt system variable. Type **Fontalt** ↵ at the command prompt and then enter the name of the font you want to use as the substitute.

You can also select an alternate font through the Files tab of the Preferences dialog box. Locate the Text Editor, Dictionary, and Font File Names listing and then click the plus sign at the left. Locate the Alternate Font File listing that appears and click on the plus sign at the left. The current alternate is listed. You can double-click on the font name to select a different font through a Standard File dialog box.

Be aware that the text in your drawing will change in appearance, sometimes radically, when you use a substitute font. If the text in the drawing must retain its appearance, you will want to substitute a font that is as similar in appearance to the original font as possible.

Accelerating Zooms and Regens with Qtext

If you need to edit a drawing that contains a lot of text, but you don't need to edit the text, you can use the Qtext command to help accelerate redraws and regenerations when you are working on the drawing. Qtext turns lines of text into rectangular boxes, saving AutoCAD from having to form every letter. This allows you to see the note locations so you don't accidentally draw over them.

TIP Selecting a large set of text objects for editing can be annoyingly slow. To improve the speed of text selection (and object selection in general), turn off the Highlight and Drag mode system variables. This will disable certain convenience features but may improve overall performance, especially on large drawings. See Appendix D for more information.

These steps tell you how to turn on Qtext.

1. Select Tools ➤ Drawing Aids… and turn on the Quick Text checkbox, or enter **Qtext** ↵ at the command prompt.

2. At the ON/OFF <OFF> prompt, enter **ON** ↵.

3. To display the results of Qtext, issue the Regen command from the prompt.

When Qtext is off, text is generated normally. When Qtext is on, rectangles show the approximate size and length of text, as shown in Figure 8.13.

FIGURE 8.13:

View of the Unit file labels with the Qtext system variable turned on

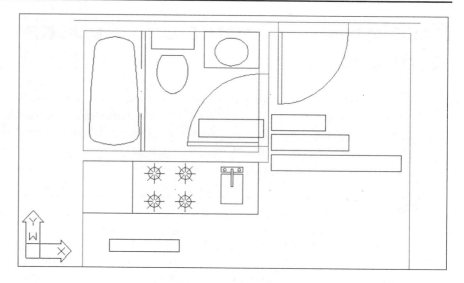

Manipulating Text beyond Labels

This chapter concentrates on methods for adding labels to your drawing, but you also use text in other ways with AutoCAD. Many of the inquiry tools in AutoCAD, such as Dist and List, produce text data. You can use the Windows clipboard to manipulate such data to your benefit.

For example, you can duplicate the exact length of a line by first using the List command to get a listing of its properties. Once you have the property list in the AutoCAD Text window, you can highlight its length listing and then press Ctrl+C to copy it to the Windows Clipboard. Next, you can start the line command and then pick the start point for the new line. Press Ctrl+V to paste the line length data into the Command window; then add the angle data or use the direct distance method to draw the line.

Any text data from dialog box input boxes or the AutoCAD Text window can be copied to the clipboard using the Ctrl+C keyboard shortcut. That data can likewise be imported into any part of AutoCAD that accepts text.

Consider using the clipboard the next time you need to transfer data within AutoCAD, or even when you need to import text from some other application.

Bonus Text Editing Utilities

Finally, before ending this chapter, you will want to know about a set of Bonus Utilities that give you the following capabilities:

- Draw text along an arc. If the arc changes, the text follows.

- Globally change the Height, Justification, Location, Rotation, Style, Text, and Width factor of a set of text objects you select.

- Adjust the width of a single-line text object to fit within a specified area.

- Explode text into lines.

- Mask areas behind text so the text is readable when placed over hatch or solid filled patterns.

- Search and replace text for a set of single-line text objects.

These functions can save hours of your time when editing a complex drawing that is full of text. You can find out how access these tools in Chapter 19.

We also include some additional text editing tools on the companion CD-ROM. These tools let you edit single-line text objects in a word-processor environment (Edsp.lsp), change the oblique angle of a set of text (Oblique.lsp), and change a set of single-line text objects into sequential numbers (Ets.lsp). See Appendix C for details.

If You Want to Experiment...

At this point, you may want to try adding some notes to drawings you have created in other *If You Want to Experiment...* sections of this book. Also, try the exercise shown in Figure 8.14. In addition, you might try importing a finish or door schedule from a word processor in the Monotxt font, to see how that works. If your application is mechanical, you might try importing a parts list.

FIGURE 8.14:

The sample mechanical drawing with notes added

1. Open the file called PART1. Using the Style command, create a style called Notes. Use the Romans font and give the style a height of .12 units and a width factor of .8.

2. Add the notes shown in this figure using the Dtext command. Place the notes approximately as shown.

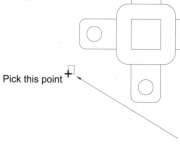

Note:
PARTS MUST BE
CLEAN AND FREE
OF LOOSE BURRS
AND DUST PRIOR
TO PACKAGING.

3. When you've finished typing the note, but before you exit Dtext, pick the point shown in this figure. Notice that the Dtext cursor moves to the point you pick.

Pick this point ✛

Note:
PARTS MUST BE
CLEAN AND FREE
OF LOOSE BURRS
AND DUST PRIOR
TO PACKAGING.

4. Continue to add this second note to your drawing. Press return twice at the end of the last line to exit the Dtext command.

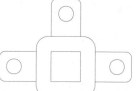

BREAK ALL
CORNERS
UNLESS
OTHERWISE
NOTED

Note:
PARTS MUST BE
CLEAN AND FREE
OF LOOSE BURRS
AND DUST PRIOR
TO PACKAGING.

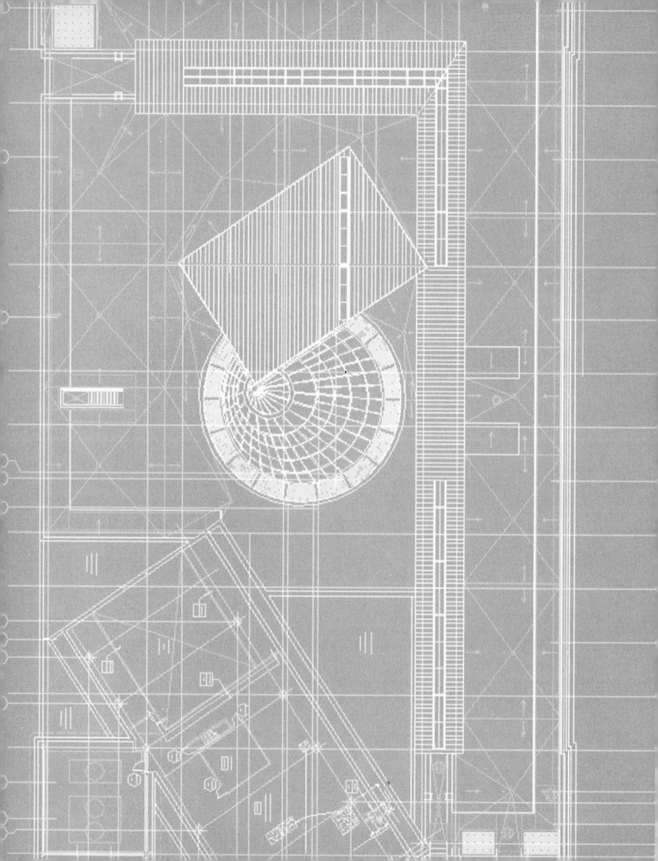

CHAPTER

NINE

Using Dimensions

- Creating a Dimension Style

- Drawing Linear Dimensions

- Editing Dimensions

- Dimensioning Nonorthogonal Objects

- Adding a Note with an Arrow

- Skewing Dimension Lines

- Applying Ordinate Dimensions

- Adding Tolerance Notation

Before you determine the dimensions of a project, your design is in flux and many questions may be unanswered. Once you begin dimensioning, you begin to see if things fit or work together. Dimensioning can be crucial to how well a design works and how quickly it develops. The dimensions answer questions about code conformance if you are an architect; they answer questions about tolerances, fit, and interference if you are involved in mechanical applications. Once you and your design team have reached a design on a schematic level, communicating even tentative dimensions to others on the team can accelerate design development. Dimensions represent a point from which you can further develop your ideas.

With AutoCAD, you can easily add tentative or final dimensions to any drawing. AutoCAD gives you an accurate dimension without your having to take measurements. You simply pick the two points to be dimensioned and the dimension line location, and AutoCAD does the rest. AutoCAD's *associative dimensioning* capability automatically updates dimensions whenever the size or shape of the dimensioned object is changed. These dimensioning features can save you valuable time and reduce the number of dimensional errors in your drawings.

AutoCAD's dimensioning feature has a substantial number of settings. Though they give you an enormous amount of flexibility in formatting your dimensions, all these settings can be somewhat intimidating to the new user. This chapter will ease you into dimensioning by first showing you how to create a *dimension style*.

Creating a Dimension Style

Dimension styles are similar to text styles. They determine the look of your dimensions as well as the size of dimensioning features, such as the dimension text and arrows. You might set up a dimension style to have special types of arrows, for instance, or to position the dimension text above or in line with the dimension line. Dimension styles also make your work easier by allowing you to store and duplicate your most common dimension settings.

AutoCAD gives you a default dimension style called *Standard*, which is set up for mechanical drafting. You will probably add many other styles to suit the style of drawings you are creating. You can also create variations of a general style for those situations that call for only minor changes in the dimension's appearance.

In this first section you'll see how to set up a dimension style that is more appropriate for architectural drawings (see Figure 9.1).

FIGURE 9.1:

AutoCAD's Standard dimension style compared with an architectural-style dimension

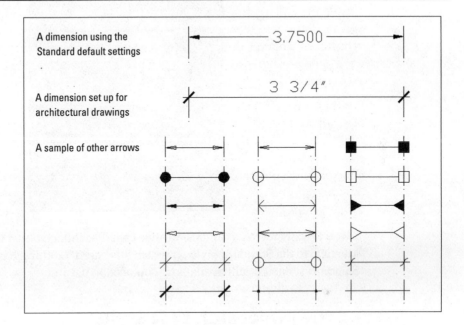

1. Open the Unit file you edited in the last chapter. If you didn't create one, use the 09a-unit.dwg file on the companion CD-ROM and rename it Unit.dwg.

2. Issue a Zoom All to display the entire floor plan.

3. Click on Format ➤ Dimension Style…, or type **D** ↵ at the command prompt. The Dimension Styles dialog box appears.

4. Click on the Current drop-down list at the top of the dialog box, and then click Standard.

5. Double-click on the Name input box to highlight STANDARD, and then type in **architect**.

6. Click on Save. Notice the message at the bottom of the dialog box telling you that the architect style was created based on the Standard style.

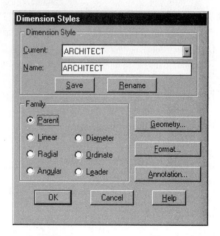

You've just created a dimension style called Architect; but at this point, it is identical to the Standard style on which it is based. Nothing has happened to the Standard style; it is still available if you need to use it.

Setting the Dimension Unit Style

Now you need to modify the new Architect dimension style so that it conforms to the architectural style of dimensioning. Let's start by changing the unit style for the dimension text. Just as you changed the overall unit style of AutoCAD to a foot-and-inches style for your toilet and tub drawing in Chapter 3, you must do the same for your dimension styles. Setting the overall unit style does not automatically set the dimension unit style.

1. In the Dimension Styles dialog box, click on the Annotation... button. The Annotation dialog box appears.

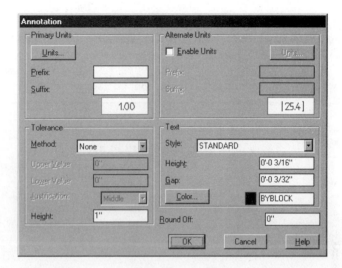

2. In the Primary Units group, click on the Units... button. The Primary Units dialog box appears.

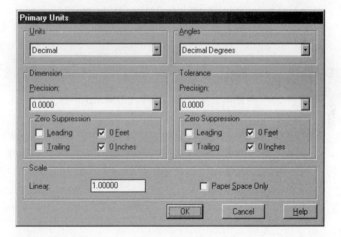

3. Open the Units drop-down list and choose Architectural. Notice that this drop-down list contains the same unit styles as the main Units dialog box (Format ➤ Units...).

The Units drop-down list also offers the Architectural (stacked) option. This option produces stacked fractions in dimensions. Choose this option if you prefer stacked fractions. You can always make changes to individual dimensions later if you change your mind.

Every dimension style setting has an equivalent system variable. See Appendix D for more on system variables that are directly associated with dimensions.

4. In the Zero Suppression button group just below the Units list, click on 0 Inches to turn off this checkbox. If you leave it turned on, indications of 0 inches will be omitted from the dimension text. (In architectural drawings, 0 inches are shown as in this dimension: 12'-0".)

5. Click on OK to close the Primary Units dialog box.

You have set up Architecture's dimension unit style to show dimensions in feet and inches, rather than inches and decimal inches.

Setting the Height for Dimension Text

Along with the unit style, you will want to adjust the style that is used for the dimension text. The Text button group of the Annotation dialog box lets you select a text style from the Style drop-down list. You can also adjust the height in case you prefer a slightly smaller or larger height than the default style offers. The height now shows 3/16". Change it to 1/8" by following these steps.

1. Highlight the contents of the Height input box.

2. Type **1/8** ↵ to make the text height 1/8" high.

3. Click on OK to return to the Dimension Styles dialog box.

To find out more about the Annotation dialog box and its options, see Appendix D.

Setting the Location of Dimension Text

AutoCAD's default setting for the placement of dimension text puts the text in line with the dimension line, as shown in the example at the top of Figure 9.1. However, we want the new Architectural style to put the text above the dimension line, as is done at the bottom of Figure 9.1. To do that, you will use the dimension style Format options.

1. In the Dimension Styles dialog box, click on the Format... button. The Format dialog box appears.

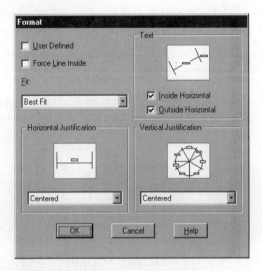

2. In the Vertical Justification box that occupies the lower-right area of the dialog box, open the drop-down list and choose Above. The graphic changes to show you what this format will look like in your dimensions.

3. In the Text box (upper-right corner of the dialog box), click on the Inside Horizontal and Outside Horizontal checkboxes to turn them both off. This forces the dimension text to be aligned with the dimension line. The graphic shows you the effect of these settings on your dimensions.

4. Now click OK to return to the Dimension Style dialog box.

Choosing an Arrow Style and Setting the Dimension Scale

Next, you will want to specify a different type of arrow for your new dimension style. For linear dimension in architectural drawings, a diagonal line or "tick" mark is typically used, rather than an arrow.

In addition, you will want to set the scale for the graphical components of the dimension, such as the arrows and text. Recall from Chapter 8 that text must be scaled up in size in order to appear at the proper size in the final output of the drawing. Dimensions, too, must be scaled so they look right when the drawing is plotted. For both the arrow and scale settings, you will use the Geometry settings.

1. In the Dimension Styles dialog box, click on the Geometry… button. The Geometry dialog box appears.

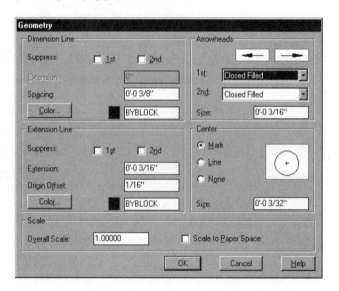

2. In the Arrowheads group, open the first pull-down list and choose Architectural Tick. The graphic shows you what the arrow looks like.

NOTE   See Appendix D for details on how you can create your own arrowheads.

---

3. In the Scale group, locate the Overall Scale input box at the lower-left of the dialog box, and change this value to 48. This is the scale factor for a 1/4" scale drawing.

TIP   Here's a simple way to figure out scale factors: Divide 12 by the decimal equivalent of the inch scale. So for 1/4", divide 12 by 0.25 to get 48. For 1/8", divide 12 by 0.125 to get 96. For 1 1/2", divide 12 by 1.5 to get 8, and so on. For engineering scales, multiply the scale of the drawing by 12. For example, for a scale of 1"=10' scale, multiply the 10 by 12 to get 120.

---

4. In the Dimension Line group, change the Extension value to 1/8. This will cause the dimension extension line to extend beyond the architectural tick 1/8", a typical arrangement for architectural dimensions.

5. Click on OK here and then again at the Dimension Style dialog box. Now you're ready to add architectural dimensions.

TIP   As with other dialog boxes in AutoCAD, you can cycle through options by clicking on the graphic that is displayed in a button group. For example, you can click on the arrowhead graphics to cycle through the different arrowheads that are available.

In a way similar to text styles, the most recently created dimension style becomes the default current style, so when you start dimensioning in the exercises in this chapter, you will be using the architectural style you just created. To switch to another style, open the Dimension Style dialog box again, and then select the style from the Current drop-down list.

In this section, we've introduced you to the various dialog boxes that let you set the appearance of a dimension style. We haven't been able to discuss every option, so if you want to learn more about the other dimension style options, consult Appendix D. There you'll find descriptions of all the items in the Dimension Styles dialog box, plus reference material covering the system variables associated with each option.

TIP   If your application is strictly architectural, you may want to make these same dimension style changes to the Acad.dwt template file, or create a set of template files specifically for architectural drawings of differing scales.

Drawing Linear Dimensions

The most common type of dimension you'll be using is the *linear dimension*, which is an orthogonal dimension measuring the width and length of an object. AutoCAD offers three dimensioning tools for this purpose: Linear (Dimlinear), Continue (Dimcont), and Baseline (Dimbase). These options are readily accessible from the Dimensioning tool palette.

Finding the Dimension Toolbar

Before you apply any dimension, you'll want to open the Dimension toolbar. This toolbar contains nearly all the commands necessary to draw and edit your dimensions.

Right-click on any toolbar; then at the Toolbar dialog box, click on Dimension from the list of toolbars. The Dimension toolbar appears. Click OK to exit the Toolbar dialog box.

The Dimension commands are also available from the Dimension pull-down menu.

TIP   To help keep your screen organized, you may want to dock the Dimension toolbar to the right side of the AutoCAD window. See Chapter 1 for more on docking toolbars.

Now you're ready to begin dimensioning.

Placing Horizontal and Vertical Dimensions

Let's start by looking at the basic dimensioning tool, Linear. The Linear Dimension button (the Dimlinear command) on the Dimension toolbar accommodates both the horizontal and vertical dimensions.

In this exercise, you'll add a vertical dimension to the right side of the Unit plan.

1. To start either a vertical or horizontal dimension, click on Linear Dimension from the Dimension toolbar, or enter **Dli** ↵ at the command prompt. You can also choose Dimension ➣ Linear from the pull-down menu.

2. The prompt First extension line origin or RETURN to select is asking you for the first point of the distance to be dimensioned. An extension line is the line that connects the object being dimensioned to the dimension line. Use the Endpoint Osnap override and pick the upper-right corner of the entry, at the coordinate 29'-0", 30'-10".

> **NOTE**
>
> Notice that the prompt in step 2 gives you the option of pressing ↵ to select an object. If you do this, you are prompted to pick the object you wish to dimension, rather than the actual distance to be dimensioned. We'll look at this method later in this chapter.

3. At the Second extension line origin prompt, pick the lower-right corner of the living room, at coordinate 29'-0", 6'-10".

4. In the next prompt,

   (Mtext/Text/Angle/Horizontal/Vertical/Rotated):

   the dimension line is the line indicating the direction of the dimension and containing the arrows or tick marks. Move your cursor from left to right, and you see a temporary dimension appear. This allows you to visually select a dimension line location.

> **NOTE**
>
> In step 4, you have the option to append information to the dimension's text or change the dimension text altogether. You'll see how later in this chapter.

5. Enter @4~'<0 ↵ to tell AutoCAD you want the dimension line to be 4' to the right of the last point you selected. (You could pick a point using your cursor, but this doesn't let you place the dimension line as accurately.) After you've done this, the dimension is placed in the drawing, as shown in Figure 9.2.

FIGURE 9.2:

The dimension line added to the Unit drawing

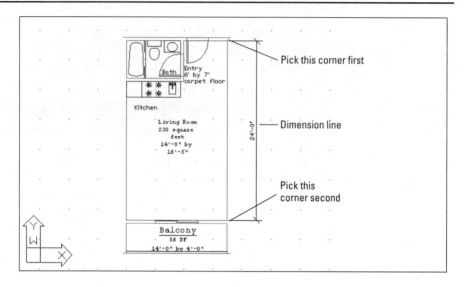

Continuing a Dimension

You will often want to input a group of dimensions strung together in a line. For example, you may want to continue dimensioning the balcony and have the continued dimension aligned with the dimension you just entered. To do this, you use the Continue option found in both the Dimension toolbar and the Dimension pull-down menu.

1. Click on the Continue Dimension option from the Dimension toolbar, or enter **Dco** ⏎. You can also choose Dimension ➤ Continue from the pull-down menu.

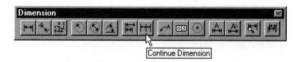

2. At the Second extension line origin or RETURN to Select prompt, pick the upper-right corner of the balcony at coordinate 29'-0", 6'-5". See the top image of Figure 9.3 for the results.

3. Pick the right end of the rail on the balcony, at coordinate 29'-0", 2'-8". See the bottom image of Figure 9.3 for the results.

4. Press ⏎ twice to exit the command.

FIGURE 9.3:

The dimension string continued and completed

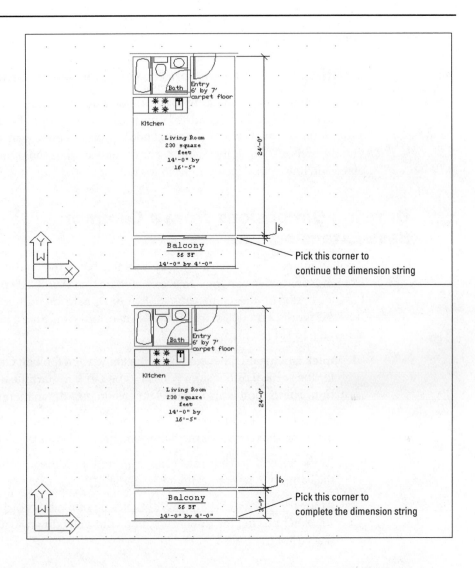

TIP

If you find you've selected the wrong location for a continued dimension, you can click on the Undo tool or press **U** ↵ to back up your dimension.

The Continue Dimension option adds a dimension from where you left off. The last drawn extension line is used as the first extension line for the continued dimension. AutoCAD will keep adding dimensions as you continue to pick points, until you press ↵.

Continuing a Dimension from a Previous Dimension

If you need to continue a string of dimensions from an older linear dimension, instead of the most recently added one, press ↵ at the Specify a second exten-sion line origin or (<select>/Undo) prompt you saw in step 2 of the previous exercise. Then, at the Select continued dimension prompt, click on the extension line from which you wish to continue.

Drawing Dimensions from a Common Base Extension Line

Another method for dimensioning objects is to have several dimensions originate from the same extension line. To accommodate this, AutoCAD provides the Baseline option on the Dimension toolbar or Dimension pull-down menu. To see how this works, you will start another dimension—this time a horizontal one—across the top of the plan.

1. Click on Linear Dimension from the Dimension toolbar. Or, just as you did for the vertical dimension, you can type **Dli** ↵ to start the horizontal dimension. This option is also on the Dimension pull-down menu.

2. At the First extension line... prompt, use the endpoint Osnap to pick the upper-left corner of the bathroom, near coordinate 15'-0", 30'-10".

3. At the Second extension line... prompt, pick the upper-right corner of the bathroom, near coordinate 22'-6", 30'-10".

4. At the Dimension line... prompt, pick a point near coordinate 22'-5", 32'-10". After placing the dimension, pan your view down so it looks similar to Figure 9.4.

TIP   Since you usually pick exact locations on your drawing as you dimension, you may want to turn on the Running Osnaps to avoid the extra step of selecting Osnaps from the Osnap pop-up menu.

FIGURE 9.4:

The bathroom with horizontal dimensions

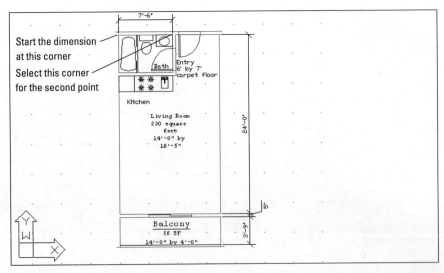

Now you're all set to draw another dimension continuing from the first extension line of the dimension you just drew.

5. Click on Baseline Dimension option from the Dimension toolbar. Or you can type **Dba** ↵ at the command prompt to start a baseline dimension.

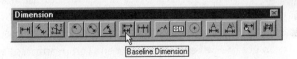

6. At the Second extension line... prompt, click on the upper-right corner of the entry, as shown in Figure 9.5.

7. Press ↵ twice to exit the Baseline Dimension command.

8. Pan your view down so it looks similar to Figure 9.5.

FIGURE 9.5:

The overall width dimension

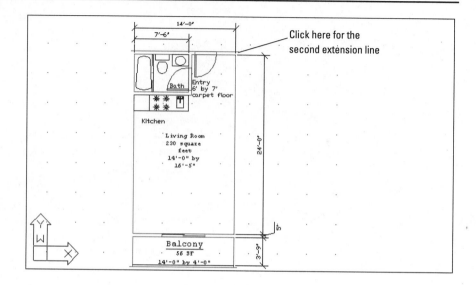

In this example, you see that the Baseline Dimension option is similar to the Continue Dimension option, except that Baseline allows you to use the first extension line of the previous dimension as the base for a second dimension.

Continuing from an Older Dimension   You may have noticed in step 7 that you had to press ↵ twice to exit the command. As with Continue Dimension, you can draw baseline dimension from an older dimension by pressing ↵ at the `Specify a second extension line origin (<select>/Undo)` prompt. You then get the `Select base dimension` prompt, at which you can either select another dimension or press ↵ again to exit the command.

Editing Dimensions

As you begin to add more dimensions to your drawings, you will find that AutoCAD will occasionally place a dimension text or line in an inappropriate location, or you may need to make a modification to the dimension text. In this section, you'll take an in-depth look at how dimensions can be modified to suit those special circumstances that always crop up.

Appending Data to Dimension Text

So far in this chapter, you've been accepting the default dimension text. You can append information to the default dimension value, or change it entirely if you need to. At the point when you see the temporary dimension dragging with your cursor, you enter **T** ↵. Then, by using the less than (<) and greater than (>) symbols, you can add text either before or after the default dimension or replace the symbols entirely to replace the default text. The Properties button on the Object Properties toolbar lets you modify existing dimension text in a similar way. Let's see how this works by changing an existing dimension's text in your drawing.

1. Click on the Properties tool in the Object Properties toolbar.

2. Next, click on the last horizontal dimension you added to the drawing at the top of the screen.

TIP   With the Dimension Edit tool you can append text to several dimensions at once.

TIP   You can also use the Multiline Text Editor (**Ed** ↵ or Modify ➢ Object ➢ Text) to edit the dimension text.

3. Press ↵. The Modify Dimension dialog box appears.

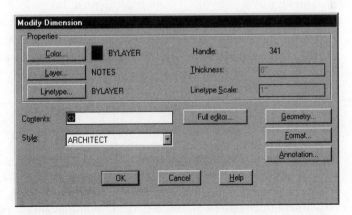

4. Click on the Contents input box, move the cursor behind the <> sign, and then type **to face of stud**.

5. Click on OK. The dimension changes to read "14'-0' to face of stud." The text you entered is appended to the dimension text.

6. Because you don't really need the new appended text for the tutorial, click on the Undo button in the Standard toolbar to remove the appended text.

TIP

Place your appended text in front of the <> symbols if you want to add text to the beginning of the dimension text. You can also replace the dimension text entirely by replacing the <> sign in the Contents input box with new text. If you want to restore a dimension that has been modified, delete everything in the Contents input box including space. Or include a space to leave the dimension text blank.

NOTE

In this exercise, you were only able to edit a single dimension. To append text to several dimensions at once, you need to use the Dimension Edit tool. See the *Making Changes to Multiple Dimensions* sidebar for more on this command.

You can also have AutoCAD automatically add a dimension suffix or prefix to all dimensions, instead of just a chosen few, by using the Annotation option in the Dimension Styles dialog box. See Appendix D for more on this feature.

Besides appending text to a dimension, the Modify Dimension dialog box lets you modify a dimension's other properties. Take a look at the Modify Dimension dialog box in step 3. Notice that it offers the Geometry, Format, and Annotation buttons. These buttons open the same dialog boxes you saw in the beginning of this chapter. Use these buttons to make changes to the formatting of individual dimensions.

Making Changes to Multiple Dimensions

The Dimension Edit tool offers a quick way to edit existing dimensions. It adds the ability to edit more than one dimension's text at one time. One common use would be to change a string of dimensions to read Equal, instead of showing the actual dimensioned distance. The following example shows an alternative to the Properties tool for appending text to a dimension.

1. Click on the Dimension Edit tool in the Dimension toolbar, or type **Ded** ↵.

2. At this prompt:

   `Dimension Edit (Home/New/Rotate/Oblique)<Home>:`

   type **N** ↵ to use the New option. The Multiline Text Editor appears showing the <> brackets in the text box.

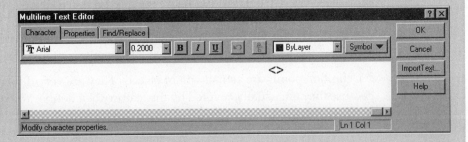

3. Click on the space behind or in front of the <> brackets, and then enter the text you want to append to the dimension. Or you can replace the brackets entirely to replace the dimension with your text.

4. Click OK.

5. At the `Select object` prompt, pick the dimensions you wish to edit. The `Select object` prompt remains, allowing you to select several dimensions.

6. Press ↵ to finish your selection. The dimension changes to include your new text or to replace the existing dimension text.

Dimedit is useful in editing dimension text, but you can also use this command to make graphical changes to the text. Here is a listing of the other Dimedit options:

- **Home** moves the dimension text to its standard default position and angle.

- **Rotate** allows you to rotate the dimension text to a new angle.

- **Oblique** skews the dimension extension lines to a new angle. See *Skewing Dimension Lines* later in this chapter.

Locating the Definition Points

AutoCAD provides the associative dimensioning capability to automatically update dimension text when a drawing is edited. Objects called *definition points* are used to determine how edited dimensions are updated.

The definition points are located at the same points you pick when you determine the dimension location. For example, the definition points for linear dimensions are the extension line origin and the intersection of the extension line/dimension line. The definition points for a circle diameter are the points used to pick the circle and the opposite side of the circle. The definition points for a radius are the points used to pick the circle, plus the center of the circle.

Definition points are actually point objects. They are very difficult to see because they are usually covered by the feature they define. You can, however, see them indirectly using grips. The definition points of a dimension are the same as the dimension's grip points. You can see them simply by clicking on a dimension. Try the following:

1. Make sure the Grips feature is turned on (see Chapter 2 to refresh your memory on the Grips feature).

2. Click on the longest of the three vertical dimensions you drew in the earlier exercise. You will see the grips of the dimension, as shown in Figure 9.6.

FIGURE 9.6:

The grip points are the same as the definition points on a dimension

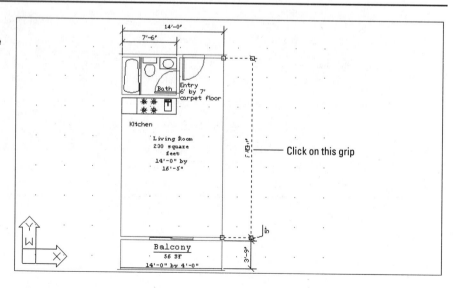

Making Minor Adjustments to Dimensions Using Grips

The definition points, whose location you can see through their grips, are located on their own unique layer called Defpoints. Definition points are displayed regardless of whether the Defpoints layer is on or off. To give you an idea of how these definition points work, try the following exercises, which show you how to directly manipulate the definition points.

1. With the grips visible, click on the grip near the dimension text.

TIP Since the Defpoints layer has the unique feature of being visible even when turned off, you can use it as a layer for laying out your drawing. While Defpoints is turned off, you can still see objects assigned to it, but the objects won't plot.

2. Move the cursor around. Notice that when you move the cursor vertically, the text moves along the dimension line. When you move the cursor horizontally, the dimension line and text move together, keeping their parallel orientation to the dimensioned floor plan.

NOTE Here the entire dimension line moves, including the text. In a later exercise, you'll see how you can move the dimension text independently of the dimension line.

3. Enter @9~'<0 ↵. The dimension line, text, and the dimension extensions move to the new location to the right of the text (see Figure 9.7).

TIP If you need to move several dimension lines at once, select them all at the command prompt; then Shift + click on one set of dimension-line grips from each dimension. Once you've selected the grips, click on one of the hot grips again. You can then move all the dimension lines at once.

FIGURE 9.7:

Moving the dimension
line using its grip

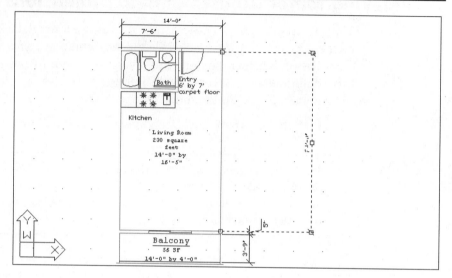

In step 3 of the last exercise you saw that you can specify an exact distance
for the dimension line's new location, by entering a relative polar coordinate.
Cartesian coordinates work just as well. You can even use object snaps to relocate
dimension lines. Next, try moving the dimension line back using the Perpendicular Osnap.

1. Click on the grip at the bottom of the dimension line.

2. Shift + click the right mouse button and choose Perpendicular from the
   Osnap pop-up menu.

3. Place the cursor on the vertical dimension line that dimensions the balcony
   and click on it.

4. The selected dimension line moves to align with the other vertical dimension, back to its original location.

Changing Style Settings of Individual Dimensions

In some cases, you will have to make changes to an individual dimension's style
setting in order to edit that dimension. For example, if you try to move the text of
a typical linear dimension, you'll find that the text and dimension lines are insep-
arable. You need to make a change to the dimensions style setting that controls

how AutoCAD locates dimension text in relation to the dimension line. This section describes how you can make changes to the style settings of individual dimensions to facilitate changes in the dimension.

TIP   If you need to change the dimension style of a dimension to match that of another, you can use the Match Properties tool. See the *How to Quickly Match a Hatch Pattern and Other Properties* sidebar in Chapter 6 for details on how to use this tool.

Moving a Fixed Dimension Text

You may have noticed that AutoCAD automatically placed the wall dimensions 5" dimension text away from the dimension line. This is done to avoid crowding the dimension between the extension lines. In some instances, you will want to manually move a dimension text away from the dimension line, but as you saw in an earlier exercise, this cannot be done with the current settings.

In the next exercise, you will make a change to a single dimension's style settings. Then you'll use grips to move the dimension text away from the dimension line.

1. Press Esc twice to cancel the grip selection from the previous exercise.

2. Click on Properties from the toolbar and then click on the vertical dimension that measures the main room—the 24'-0" dimension—and press ⌐ to finish your selection. The Modify Dimension dialog box appears. This dialog box contains the same three buttons—Geometry..., Format..., and Annotation...—that are in the Dimension Styles dialog box.

3. Click on Format.... The same Format dialog box appears that you saw in the early part of this chapter.

4. At the Format dialog box, choose Leader from the Fit drop-down list.

5. While still in the Format dialog box, change the Vertical Justification group setting to Centered. We'll explain why in the following paragraphs.

6. Click on OK here and then again at the Modify Dimension dialog box.

7. Now click on the 24'-0" dimension to display its grips.

8. Make sure Ortho mode is off, and then click on the grip at the center of the dimension text and move the dimension text above and to the left of its current location, as shown in the top image of Figure 2.8. The dimension text is now horizontal and shows a leader from the text to the dimension line.

In the Format dialog box, the Leader option in the Fit pull-down list lets you move the dimension text independently of the dimension line. It also causes a leader to be drawn from the dimension line to the text. I asked you to change the Vertical Justification option to Centered because otherwise the leader line will be drawn as an underline beneath the dimension text.

In the previous exercise, you changed the format setting of a single dimension *after* it was placed. These settings can be made a standard part of your Architectural dimension style. To do this, choose Format from the Dimension Style dialog box, and then choose Leader from the Fit drop-down list. In doing so, you will be able to move the text of all new dimensions you might add later. However, don't change the Vertical Justification setting to Centered because this will cause all dimensions to appear centered on the dimension line—a format appropriate for mechanical drawings, but not for architectural drawings. For existing dimensions, you will have to use the Properties command as shown in the next exercise.

Both the Fit and Vertical Justification settings can be made using system variables. See Appendix D for more on these settings.

TIP
To change an existing dimension to the current dimension style, use the Dimension Update tool. Click on Dimension Update from the Dimension toolbar, or choose Dimension Update from the pull-down menu. Then select the dimensions you want to change. Press ↵ when you are done selecting dimension. The selected dimensions will be converted to the current style.

Rotating a Dimension Text

Once in a while, a dimension text works better if it is kept in a horizontal orientation, even if the dimension itself is not horizontal. If you find you need to rotate dimension text, here's the way to do it.

1. First, click on the Undo button twice in the toolbar or type **U** ↵ ↵ to return the 24'-0" dimension to its original location.

2. Click on the Dimension Text Edit tool in the Dimension toolbar.

NOTE You can also use the Dimension Edit tool (Dimedit command) in the Dimension toolbar to rotate the dimension text. Click on dimension Edit or type Ded ⏎, R ⏎, enter the rotation angle, and then select the dimension text.

3. At the Select object prompt, click on the 24'-0" dimension text again.

4. Type **A** ⏎.

5. At the Enter text angle prompt, type **45** ⏎ to rotate the text to a 45° angle.

TIP You can also choose Dimension ➢ Align Text ➢ Angle, select the dimension text, and then enter an angle. A 0° angle will cause the dimension text to return to its default angle.

The Dimension Text Edit tool (Dimtedit command) also allows you to Align the dimension text to either the left or right side of the dimension line. This is similar to the Alignment option in the Multiline Text Editor that controls text justification.

Now, for the last operation, you will move the text located next to its associated dimension line, aligning it with the other dimensions in the string.

1. Undo the last exercise. You don't really want the dimension text at an angle.

2. Click on the 5" dimension, so that its grips are displayed.

3. Click on the grip at the center of the dimension text and move the cursor around. Notice that the dimension text follows the cursor, and a leader line extends from the dimension text to the dimension line.

4. Click on a point above and to the left of the original dimension text location (see the bottom image of Figure 9.8). The dimension text moves to its new location. The dimension itself remains highlighted, telling you that it is still available for editing.

5. Now save your drawing. You will use this drawing in its current condition in later chapters.

NOTE

You can use the Home option of the Dimension Text Edit tool, or Dimension ➤ Align Text, to move a dimension text back to its original location.

FIGURE 9.8:

Moving the dimension text using grips

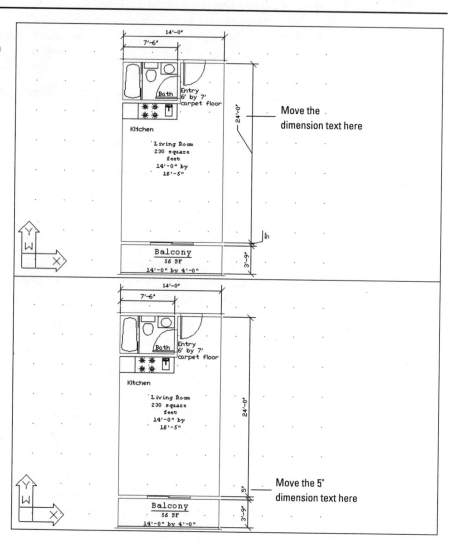

You may want to make other adjustments to the dimension text, such as its location along the dimension line and its rotation angle.

As you have seen in this section, the Grips feature is especially well suited to editing dimensions. With grips, you can stretch, move, copy, rotate, mirror, and scale dimensions.

Modifying the Dimension Style Settings for Groups of Dimensions

In the *Moving a Fixed Dimension Text* section, you used the Properties button on the toolbar to facilitate the moving of the dimension text. You can also use the Dimension ➤ Override option (Dimoverride command) to accomplish the same thing. The Override option allows you to make changes to an individual dimension's style settings. The advantage to Override is that it allows you to affect changes to groups of dimensions, not just one dimension. Here's an example showing how Override can be used in place of the Properties button in the first exercise of the *Moving a Fixed Dimension Text* section.

1. Press the Esc key twice to make sure you are not in the middle of a command. Then choose Dimension ➤ Override from the pull-down menu.

2. At the next prompt:

   Dimension variable to override (or Clear to remove overrides):

   type **Dimfit** ⏎.

3. At the Current value <3> prompt, enter **4** ⏎. This has the same affect as selecting Leader from the Fit pop-up list of the Format dialog box.

4. The Dimension variable to override... prompt appears again allowing you to enter another dimension variable. Press ⏎ to move to the next step.

5. At the Select object prompt, select the dimension you want to change. You can select a group of dimensions if you want to change several dimensions at once. Press ⏎ when you are done with your selection. The dimension settings will be changed for the selected dimensions.

As you can see from this example, Dimoverride requires that you know exactly which dimension variable to edit in order to make the desired modification. In this case, setting the Dimfit variable to 4 will let you move the dimension text independently of the dimension line. If you find the Dimoverride command useful, consult Appendix D to find which system variable corresponds to the Dimension Style dialog box settings.

Editing Dimensions and Other Objects Together

Certainly it's helpful to be able to edit a dimension directly using its grips. But the key feature of AutoCAD's dimensions is their ability to *automatically* adjust themselves to changes in the drawing. As long as you include the dimension's definition points when you select objects to edit, the dimensions themselves will automatically update to reflect the change in your drawing.

To see how this works, try moving the living room closer to the bathroom wall. You can move a group of lines and vertices using the Stretch command and the Crossing option.

1. Click on Stretch from the Modify palette, or type **S** ↵ and then **C** ↵. You will see the following prompt:

   ```
   At the Select objects to stretch by crossing-window or -polygon...
   Select objects: C
   First corner:
   ```

2. Pick a crossing window, as illustrated in Figure 9.9. Then press ↵ to confirm your selection.

FIGURE 9.9:

The Stretch crossing window

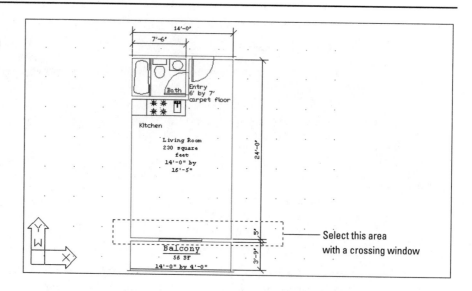

434

3. At the Base point prompt, pick any point on the screen.

4. At the New point prompt, enter **@2'<90** to move the wall 2' in a 90° direction. The wall moves, and the dimension text changes to reflect the new dimension, as shown in Figure 9.10.

5. When you are done reviewing the results of this exercise, exit the file without saving it.

TIP

In some situations, you may find that a crossing window selects objects other than those you want to stretch. This frequently occurs when many objects are close together at the location of a vertex you want to stretch. To be more selective about the vertices you move and their corresponding objects, use a standard window instead of a crossing window to select the vertices. Then pick the individual objects whose vertices you wish to move.

FIGURE 9.10:

The moved wall, with the updated dimensions

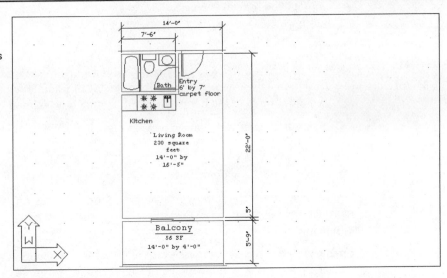

When you selected the crossing window corners, you included the definition points of both vertical dimensions. This allowed you to move the dimension extension lines along with the wall, thereby updating the dimensions automatically.

Understanding the Stretch Command

The tool you used for moving the wall and the dimension line extensions is the Stretch command. This is one of the most useful, yet least understood commands offered by AutoCAD. Think of Stretch as a vertex mover: Its sole purpose is to move the vertices (or endpoints) of objects.

Stretch actually requires you to do two things: select the objects you want to edit, and then select the vertices you wish to move. The crossing window and the Cpolygon window are convenient ways of killing two birds with one stone because they select objects and vertices in one operation. But when you want to be more selective, you can click on objects and window vertices instead. For example, consider the exercise in this chapter where you moved a wall with the Stretch command. If you wanted to move the walls but not the dimension-line extensions, you would do the following:

1. Click on Stretch from the Modify toolbar or from the Modify pull-down menu. You may also type **S** ↵.

2. At the Select object prompt, enter **W** ↵ (Window) or **WP** ↵ (Window Polygon).

3. Window the vertices you wish to move. Since the Window and Window Polygon selection options select objects completely enclosed within the window, most of the items you want to stretch will already be selected.

4. Click on the vertical walls to include them in the set of objects to be edited.

5. Press ↵ to finish your selection.

6. Indicate the base point and second point for the stretch.

You could also use the Remove selection option and click on the dimensions to deselect them in the previous exercise. Then, when you enter the base and second points, the walls would move but the dimensions would stay in place.

Stretch will stretch only the vertices included in the last window, crossing window, crossing polygon, or window polygon (see Chapter 2 for more on these selection options). Thus, if you had attempted to window another part of your drawing in the wall-moving exercise, nothing would have moved. Before Stretch will do anything, objects need to be highlighted (selected) and their endpoints windowed.

The Stretch command is especially well suited to editing dimensioned objects, and when you use it with the Crossing Polygon (CP) or Window Polygon (WP) selection options, you have substantial control over what gets edited.

You can also use the Mirror, Rotate, and Stretch commands with dimensions. The polar arrays will also work, and Extend and Trim can be used with linear dimensions.

When editing dimensioned objects, be sure you select the dimension associated with the object being edited. As you select objects, using the Crossing (C) or Crossing Polygon (CP) selection options will help you include the dimensions. For more on these selection options, see the *Other Selection Options* sidebar in Chapter 2.

TIP If you have some dimension text that overlaps a hatch pattern, and the hatch pattern obscures the text, you can use the Wipeout bonus tool on the Bonus Standard toolbar to mask out portions of the hatch. If a hatch pattern or solid fill completely covers a dimension, you can use the Draworder command to have AutoCAD draw the dimension over the hatch or solid fill. See Chapter 19 for more on the Bonus tools and Chapter 13 for more on the Draworder command.

Using Osnap while Dimensioning

WARNING There is a drawback to setting a running Osnap mode: When your drawing gets crowded, you may end up picking the wrong point by accident. However, you can easily toggle the running Osnap mode off by double-clicking on the OSNAP label in the status bar.

You may find that when you pick intersections and endpoints frequently, as during dimensioning, it is a bit inconvenient to use the Osnap pop-up menu. In situations where you know you will be using certain Osnaps frequently, you can use running Osnaps. You can do so in the following two ways:

- Click on Tools ➢ Object Snap Settings. In the Osnap Settings dialog box, make sure the Running Osnap tab is selected and then select the desired default Osnap mode. You can pick more than one mode, for instance Intersection, Endpoint, and Midpoint, so that whichever geometry you happen to be nearest will be the point selected.

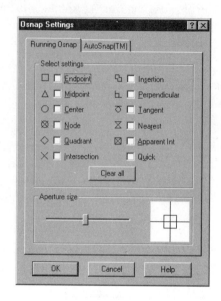

- Another way of accomplishing this is to type **-osnap** ↵ at the command prompt, and then enter the name of the Osnap modes you want to use. If you want to use more than one mode, enter their names separated by commas; for example:

  ```
  endpoint,midpoint,intersect
  ```

  Once you've designated your Running Osnaps, the next time you are prompted to select a point, the selected Osnap modes will be automatically activated. You can still override the default settings using the Osnap pop-up menu (Shift + click the right mouse button). You can toggle the Running Osnaps on or off by double-clicking on the OSNAP label in the status bar, or by pressing F3. The toggle feature is especially helpful in crowded drawings where you may accidentally select an Osnap location while panning or zooming or selecting points for other operations.

Dimensioning Nonorthogonal Objects

So far, you've been reading about how to work with linear dimensions. You can also dimension nonorthogonal objects, such as circles, arcs, triangles, and trapezoids. In this section you will practice dimensioning nonorthogonal objects by drawing an elevation of a window in the set of plans for your studio apartment building. You'll start by drawing the window itself.

1. Open a new file called Window.

2. Set the file up as an architectural drawing at a scale of 3"=1'-0" on an 8 ½×11" sheet.

3. Click Polygon from the Draw toolbar, or type **Pol** ↵.

4. At the Number of sides... prompt, enter 6 ↵.

5. At the Edge/<center of polygon> prompt, pick the center of the polygon at coordinate 22,18.

TIP   You can turn on the Snap mode to help you locate points for this exercise.

---

6. Enter C ↵ at the Inscribe in circle/circumscribe... prompt to select the Circumscribe option. This tells AutoCAD to place the Polygon outside the temporary circle used to define the polygon.

7. At the Radius of circle prompt, you will see the hexagon drag along with the cursor. You could pick a point with your mouse to determine its size.

8. Enter 8 ↵ to get an exact size for the hexagon.

9. Draw a circle with a radius of 7" using 22,18 as its center. Your drawing will look like Figure 9.11.

FIGURE 9.11:

The window frame

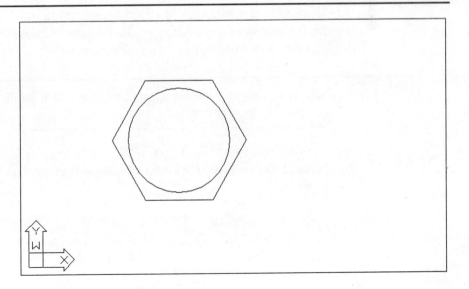

Dimensioning Nonorthogonal Linear Distances

Now you will dimension the window. The unusual shape of the window prevents you from using the horizontal or vertical dimensions you've used already. However, the Dimension ➤ Aligned option will allow you to dimension at an angle.

1. Start by setting the dimension scale to 4. Normally, you would use the Geometry button of the Dimension Style dialog box to set the dimension scale. A shortcut to do this is by typing **Dimscale** ⏎ **4** ⏎. This will change the scale factor of the current dimension style to 4.

2. Click on the Aligned Dimension tool from the Dimension toolbar. You can also enter **Dal** ⏎ to start aligned dimension. You can also select Dimension ➤ Aligned.

3. At the First extension line origin or RETURN to select prompt, press ⏎. You could have picked extension line origins as you did in earlier examples, but using the ⏎ will show you firsthand how the Select option works.

4. At the Select object to dimension prompt, pick the upper-right face of the hexagon near coordinate 2'-5", 1'-10". As the prompt indicates, you can also pick an arc or circle for this type of dimension.

TIP

Just as with linear dimensions, you can enter T ⏎ at step 5 to enter alternate text for the dimension.

---

5. At the Dimension line location (Text/Angle) prompt, pick a point near coordinate 34,26. The dimension appears in the drawing as shown in Figure 9.12.

FIGURE 9.12:

The aligned dimension
of a nonorthogonal line

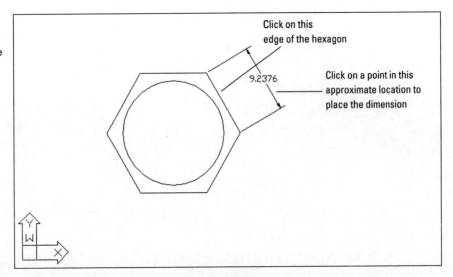

Next, you will dimension a face of the hexagon. Instead of its actual length, however, you will dimension a distance at a specified angle—the distance from the center of the face.

1. Click on Linear Dimension from the Dimension toolbar.

2. At the `First extension line origin or RETURN to select` prompt, press ↵.

3. At the `Select object to dimension...` prompt, pick the lower-right face of the hexagon near coordinate 30,16.

4. At the `Dimension line location (Text/Angle/Horizontal/Vertical/Rotated)` prompt, type **R** ↵ to select the rotated option.

5. At the `Dimension line angle <0>` prompt, enter **30** ↵.

6. At the `Dimension line location` prompt, pick a point near coordinate 35,8. Your drawing will look like Figure 9.13.

FIGURE 9.13:

A linear dimension
using the Rotated
option

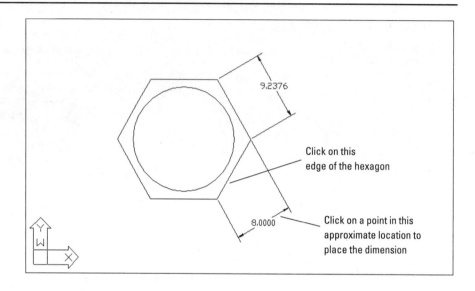

Dimensioning Radii, Diameters, and Arcs

To dimension circular objects, you use another set of options from the Draw ➤
Dimensioning menu.

1. Click on Angular Dimension from the Dimension toolbar. Or you can enter
   Dan ⏎ or choose Dimension ➤ Angular from the pull-down menu to start
   the angular dimension.

2. At the Select arc, circle, line, or RETURN prompt, pick the upper-
   left face of the hexagon near coordinate 15,22.

3. At the Second line prompt, pick the top face at coordinate 21,26.

4. At the Dimension line arc location (Mtext/Text/Angle) prompt,
   notice that as you move the cursor around the upper-left corner of the hexagon, the dimension changes as shown in the top image of Figure 9.14.

5. Pick a point near coordinate 21,23. The dimension is fixed in the drawing (see the bottom image of Figure 9.14).

TIP If you need to make subtle adjustments to the dimension line or text location, you can do so using grips, after you have placed the angular dimension.

FIGURE 9.14:

The angular dimension added to the window frame

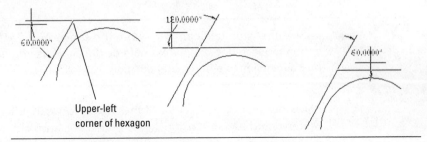

Upper-left
corner of hexagon

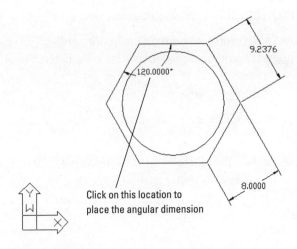

Click on this location to
place the angular dimension

Now try the Diameter option, which shows the diameter of a circle.

1. Click Diameter Dimension from the Dimension toolbar. Or you can enter **Ddi** ↵ to start the diameter dimension.

2. At the `Select arc or circle` prompt, pick the circle.

3. At the `Dimension line location (Mtext/Text/Angle)` prompt, you will see the Diameter dimension drag along the circle as you move the cursor (see the top image of Figure 9.15).

NOTE   If the dimension text can't fit within the circle, AutoCAD gives you the option to place dimension text outside the circle as you drag the temporary dimension to a horizontal position.

4. Place the cursor at the center of the circle. Notice that the dimension text is centered and the dimension arrow points in a horizontal direction as shown in the bottom image of Figure 9.15.

5. With the text centered, click on the mouse.

The Radius Dimension tool on the Dimension toolbar gives you a radius dimension just as Diameter provides a circle's diameter.

Figure 9.16 shows a radius dimension on the outside of the circle, but you can place it inside in a manner similar to the Diameter dimension. The Center Mark tool on the Dimension toolbar just places a cross mark in the center of the selected arc or circle.

FIGURE 9.15:

Dimension showing the diameter of a circle

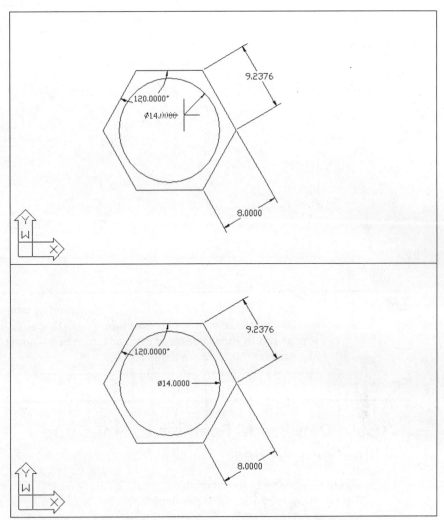

FIGURE 9.16:

A radius dimension shown on the outside of the circle

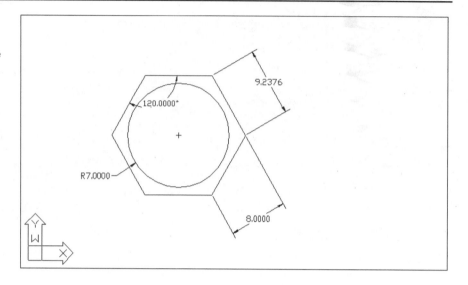

TIP   You can alter the format of diameter dimensions by changing the Dimtix and Dimtofl dimension variable settings. For example, to have two arrows appear across the diameter of the circle, turn both Dimtix and Dimtofl on. See Appendix D for more details.

Using Dimension Families to Fine Tune Dimension Styles

In the first part of this chapter, you set up an architectural dimension style. If you try to draw a radial or diameter dimension, or a leader with this style, you will get an architectural tick mark instead of an arrow pointing to the circle. This can be quite annoying since you would have to change the current dimension style every time you wanted to draw a different type of dimension or add a leader note.

AutoCAD offers the *dimension family* to help you set up each different type of dimension to have their own settings. When you create a new style, it is a "parent" style by default. You can set up a "child" style for radial, diameter, or other types of dimensions. You can use different arrows, text formats, and scales for each child style you set up.

For example, you can have the Architect style as the parent style, and then create a child style for radius dimensions. This child would be set up to use a filled arrow for radial dimensions. The next time you add a radial dimension, an arrow will be used instead of an architectural tick mark. Here are the specific steps to take to set up a child dimension style.

1. Open the Dimension Style dialog box.

2. Select the dimension style to which you want to add a child family member.

3. In the Family button group, click on the type of dimension you wish to change. The options are Linear, Radial, Angular, Diameter, Ordinate, and Leader. Each of these Family options controls the type of dimension of the same name.

4. Modify the child style to your needs (for example, select a standard arrow from the Geometry dialog box).

5. Click Save to save the child.

The next time you draw the type of dimension associated with the child dimension style, AutoCAD will automatically use the child settings, instead of the parent settings. Note that the child settings will inherit the parent settings, but modifications to the parent settings will not affect the child settings. For example, if you change the scale factor for the parent the child scale factor will not change.

Adding a Note with an Arrow

Finally, there is the Dimension ➤ Leader option, which allows you to add a note with an arrow pointing to the object the note describes.

1. Click on Leader from the Dimension toolbar, or enter **Le** ↵, or select Dimension ➤ Leader from the Pull-down menu.

2. At the Leader start prompt, pick a point near the top-left edge of the hexagon at coodinate 16,24.

3. At the To point prompt, enter **@6<110** ↵.

4. At the `To point (Format/Annotation/Undo)<Annotation>` prompt, you can continue to pick points just as you would draw lines. For this exercise, however, press ↵ to finish drawing leader lines.

5. At the `Annotation (or RETURN for options)` prompt, type `Window frame` ↵ ↵ as the label for this leader. Your drawing will look like Figure 9.17.

FIGURE 9.17:

The leader with a note added

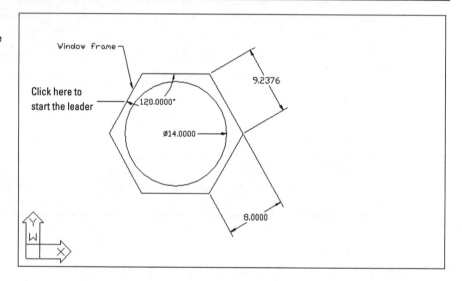

In this exercise, you used the default Annotation option in step 4 to add the text for the note. The Format option in this prompt lets you control the graphic elements of the leader. When you select the Format option by typing **F** ↵, you get the following prompt:

`Spline/STraight/Arrow/None/<Exit>:`

Choose Spline to change the leader from a series of line segments to a spline curve (see Figure 9.18). Often a curved leader shows up better than straight lines do. The STraight option changes the leader line to straight lines. None suppresses the arrowhead altogether, and Arrow restores it.

FIGURE 9.18:

FIGURE 9.18:

The Leader format options

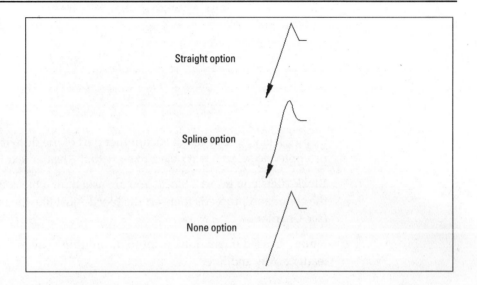

Straight option

Spline option

None option

Using Multiline Text with Leaders

You also have the option to add Multiline text at the leader. Take another look at step 5 in the previous exercise. To add multiline text, you would press ↵ at the `Annotation (or RETURN for options)` prompt in this step. The next prompt to appear is

`Tolerance/Copy/Block/None/<Mtext>:`

Press ↵ again, and AutoCAD opens the Multiline Text Editor. From there, the Leader command acts just like the Mtext command (see Chapter 8 for more on Mtext) by opening the Mtext dialog box.

> **TIP** The notes and leader act like a single object which you can easily edit using grips.

The other options in the `Annotation` prompt are as follows:

Tolerance lets you insert a tolerance symbol. A dialog box opens, where you specify the tolerance information (see *Adding Tolerance Notation* in this chapter and Appendix D for more on the Tolerance feature).

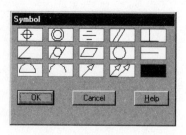

Copy lets you copy text from another part of the drawing. You are prompted to select a text object to copy to the leader text location.

Block lets you insert a block. You are asked for a block name, and then the command proceeds to insert the block—just like the Insert command (see Chapter 3).

None is used if you don't want to do anything beyond drawing the leader arrow and line.

TIP

Just as with other dimensions, and objects in general, you can modify any property of a leader, including its text, using the Properties tool in the Object Properties toolbar. You can, for example, change a straight leader to a spline leader.

Skewing Dimension Lines

At times, you may find it necessary to force the extension lines to take on an angle other than 90° to the dimension line. This is a common requirement of isometric drawings, where most lines are at 30° or 60° angles instead of 90°. To facilitate nonorthogonal dimensions like these, AutoCAD offers the Oblique option.

1. Choose Dimension ➤ Oblique, or type **Ded** ↵ **O** ↵. You can also select Dimension Edit tool from the Dimension toolbar, and then type **O** ↵.

2. At the Select object prompt, pick the aligned dimension at the upper-right of the drawing and press ↵ to confirm your selection.

3. At the Enter obliquing angle (RETURN for none) prompt, enter **60** for 60°. The dimension will skew so that the extension lines are at 60°, as shown in Figure 9.19.

4. Now exit AutoCAD. You are done with the tutorials in this chapter.

FIGURE 9.19:

A dimension using the Oblique option

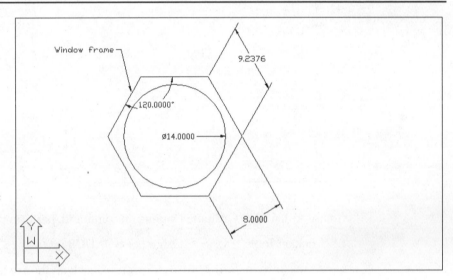

Applying Ordinate Dimensions

In mechanical drafting, *ordinate dimensions* are used to maintain the accuracy of machined parts by establishing an origin on the part. All major dimensions are described as x or y coordinates of that origin. The origin is usually an easily locatable feature of the part, such as a machined bore or two machined surfaces. Figure 9.20 shows a typical application of ordinate dimensions. In the lower-left, note the two dimensions whose leaders are jogged. Also note the origin location in the upper-right.

FIGURE 9.20:

A drawing using ordinate dimensions

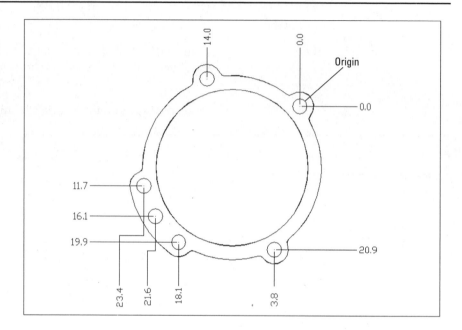

To use AutoCAD's Ordinate Dimension command, perform the following steps.

1. Click on Tools ➤ UCS ➤ Origin, or type **UCS** ↵ **Or** ↵.

2. At the Origin point <0,0,0> prompt, click on the exact location of the origin of your part.

3. Toggle the Ortho mode on.

4. Click on Ordinate Dimension from the Dimension. You can also enter **Dor** ↵ to start the ordinate dimension.

5. At the Select feature prompt, click on the item you want to dimension.

NOTE The direction of the leader will determine whether the dimension will be of the Xdatum or the Ydatum.

6. At the `Leader endpoint (Xdatum/tdatum)` prompt, indicate the length and direction of the leader. Do this by positioning the rubber-banding leader perpendicular to the coordinate direction you want to dimension, and then clicking on that point.

In steps 1 and 2, you used the UCS feature to establish a second origin in the drawing. The Ordinate Dimension tool then uses that origin to determine the ordinate dimensions. You will get a chance to work with the UCS feature in Chapter 16.

You may have noticed options in the Command window for the Ordinate Dimension tool. The Xdatum and Ydatum options force the dimension to be of the x or y coordinate no matter what direction the leader takes. The Mtext option opens the Multiline Text Editor, allowing you to append or replace the ordinate dimension text. The Text option lets you enter a replacement text directly through the Command window.

TIP As with all other dimensions, you can use grips to make adjustments to the location of ordinate dimensions.

If you turn Ortho mode off, the dimension leader will be drawn with a jog to maintain orthogonal (look back at Figure 9.20).

Adding Tolerance Notation

In mechanical drafting, tolerances are a key part of a drawing's notation. They specify the allowable variation in size and shape that a mechanical part can have. To help facilitate tolerance notation, AutoCAD provides the Tolerance command, which offers common ISO tolerance symbols together with a quick way to build a standard *feature control* symbol. Feature control symbols are industry standard symbols used to specify tolerances. If you are a mechanical engineer or drafter, AutoCAD's tolerance notation options will be a valuable tool. However, a full discussion of tolerances requires a basic understanding of mechanical design and drafting and is beyond the scope of this book.

To use the Tolerance command, choose Tolerance from the Dimension toolbar, or type **Tol** ↵ at the command prompt, or select Dimension ➤ Tolerance… from the pull-down menu.

The Symbol dialog box appears.

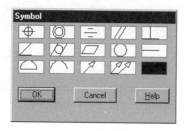

The top image of Figure 9.21 shows what each symbol in the Symbol dialog box represents. The bottom image shows a sample drawing with a feature symbol used on a cylindrical object.

Once you select a symbol, you then see the Geometric Tolerance dialog box. This is where you enter tolerance and datum values for the feature control symbol. You can enter two tolerance values and three datum values. In addition, you can stack values in a two-tiered fashion.

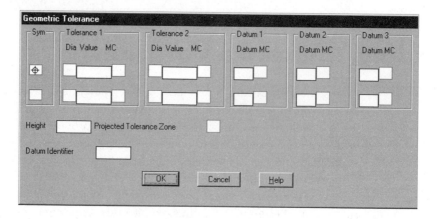

FIGURE 9.21:

The tolerance symbols

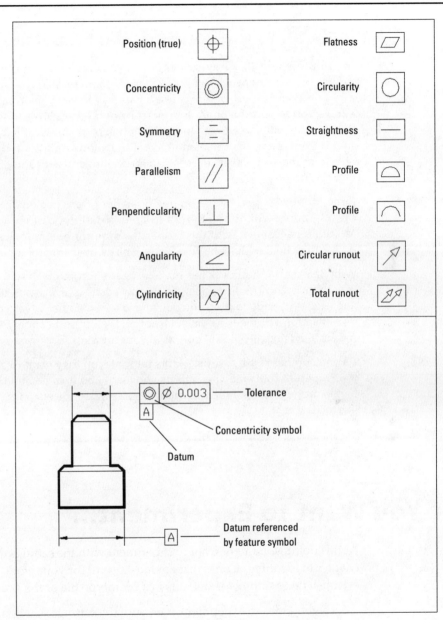

Understanding the Power of the Properties Tool

In both this and the previous chapter, you have made frequent use of the Properties tool in the Object Properties toolbar. By now, you may have recognized that the Properties tool is like a gateway to editing virtually any object. It allows you to edit the general properties of layer, color, and line type assignments. And when used with individual objects, it allows you to edit properties that are unique to the selected object. For example, through this tool, you are able to change a spline leader with an arrow into one with straight line segments and no arrow.

If the Modify Properties dialog box does not offer specific options to edit the object, then it will offer a button to open a dialog box that will. If you edit a Multiline text object with the Properties tool, for example, you will have the option to open the Multiline Text Editor. The same is true for dimension text.

With Release 14, Autodesk has made a clear effort to make AutoCAD's interface more consistent. The Text editing tools now edit text of all types, single line, multiline, and dimension text, so you don't have to remember which command or tool you need for a particular object. Likewise, the Properties tool offers a powerful means to editing all types of objects in your drawing.

As you continue with the rest of this tutorial, you may want to experiment with the Properties tool with new objects you learn about. In addition to allowing you to edit properties, the Properties tool can show you the status of an object, much like the List tool.

If You Want to Experiment...

At this point, you might want to experiment with the settings described in this chapter to identify the ones that are most useful for your work. You can then establish these settings as defaults in a prototype file or the Acad.dwt file.

It's a good idea to experiment even with the settings you don't think you will need often—chances are you will have to alter them from time to time.

As an added exercise, try the steps shown in Figure 9.22. This exercise will give you a chance to see how you can update dimensions on a drawing that has been scaled down.

FIGURE 9.22:

A sample mechanical drawing with dimensions

Add the dimension shown here to the latch drawing you did in Chapter 2.

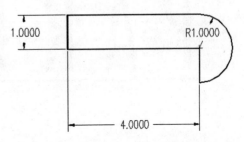

Next, scale the entire drawing down.

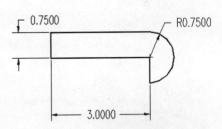

PART III

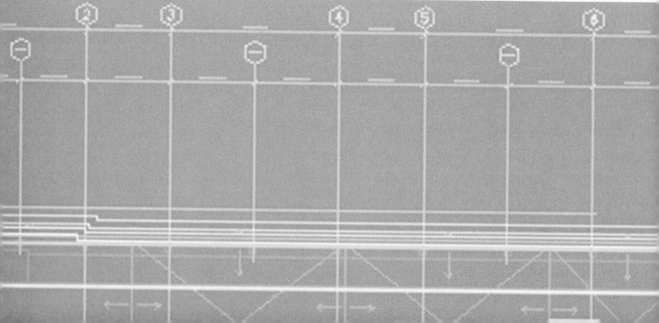

Becoming an Expert

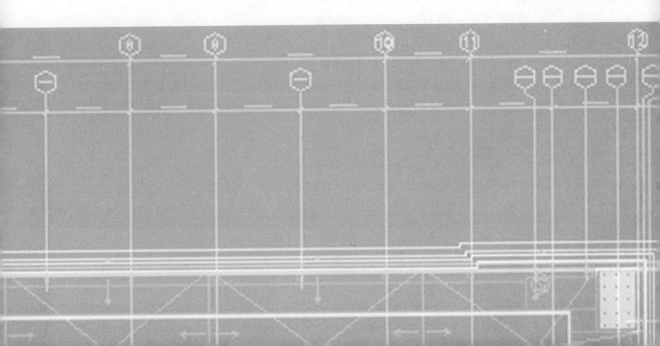

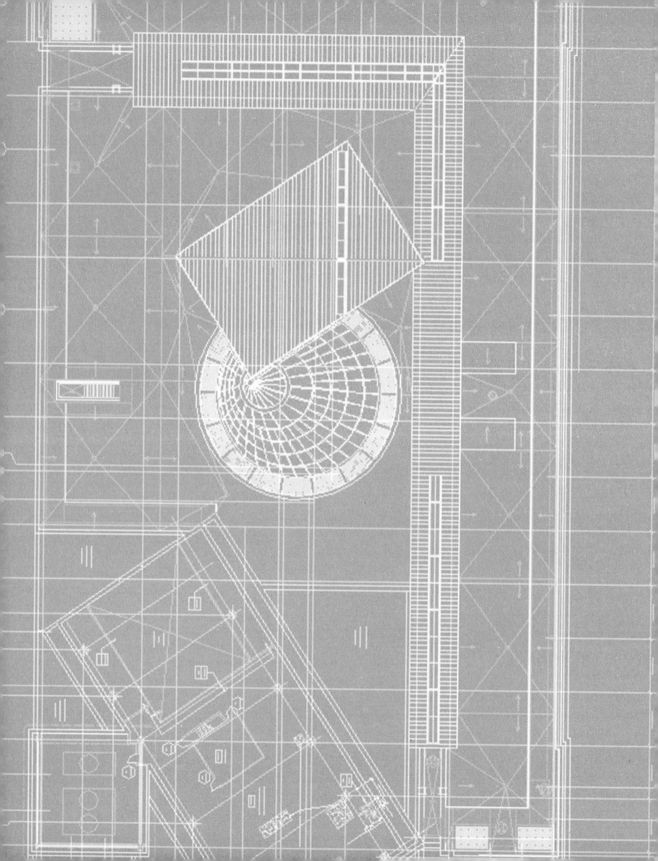

Storing and Linking Data with Graphics

- ■ Creating Attributes

- ■ Editing Attributes

- ■ Extracting and Exporting Attribute Information

- ■ Accessing External Databases

- ■ Linking Objects to a Database

Attributes are unique to computer-aided design and drafting; nothing quite like them exists in traditional drafting. Because of this, they are often poorly understood. Attributes enable you to store information as text that you can later extract to use in database managers, spreadsheet programs, and word processors. By using attributes, you can keep track of virtually any object in a drawing, or maintain textual information within the drawing that can be queried.

Keeping track of objects is just one way of using attributes. You can also use them in place of text objects in situations where you must enter the same text, with minor modifications, in many places in your drawing. For example, if you are drawing a schedule that contains several columns of information, you can use attributes to help simplify your data entry.

Attributes can also be used where you anticipate global editing of text. For example, suppose a note that refers to a part number occurs in several places. If you think you will want to change that part number in every note, you can make the part a block with an attribute. Later, when you know the new part number, you can use the global editing capability of the Attribute feature to change the old part number for all occurrences in one step.

TIP   You can even set up a default value for the attribute, such as *hollow core*, or *hc*. With this value in place, you only have to enter a value when it deviates from the default.

In this chapter you will use attributes for one of their more common functions: maintaining lists of parts. In this case, the parts are doors. We will also describe how to import these attributes into a database management program. As you go through these exercises, think about the ways attributes can help you in your particular application.

Creating Attributes

Attributes depend on blocks. You might think of an attribute as a tag attached to a block, with the tag containing information about the block. For example, you could have included an attribute definition with the door drawing you created in Chapter 2. If you had, then every time you subsequently inserted the door you would have been prompted for a value associated with that door. The value could be a number, a height or width value, a name, or any type of text information you want. When you insert the block, you are prompted for an attribute value. Once you enter a value, it is stored as part of the block within the drawing database. This value can be displayed as text attached to the door, or it can be made invisible. The value can be changed at any time. You can even specify what the prompts say in asking you for the attribute value.

However, suppose you don't have the attribute information when you design the door. As an alternative, you can add the attribute to a *symbol* that is later placed by the door when you know enough about the design to specify what type of door goes where. The standard door type symbol suits this purpose nicely because it is an object that can be set up and used as a block independent of the actual door block.

NOTE A door type symbol is a graphic code used to indicate special characteristics of the associated door. The code refers to a note on another drawing or in a set of written specifications.

In the following exercises, you will create a door type symbol with attributes for the different values normally assigned to doors, namely size, thickness, fire rating, material, and construction.

Adding Attributes to Blocks

In this exercise, you will create a door type symbol, which is commonly used to describe the size, thickness, and other characteristics of any given door in an architectural drawing. The symbol is usually a circle, hexagon, or diamond, with a number in it. The number is usually cross-referenced to a schedule that lists all the door types and their characteristics.

While in this exercise you will be creating a new file containing attribute definitions, you can also include such definitions in blocks you create using the Make Block tool (Block command) or in files you create using the Wblock command. Just create the attribute definitions, then include them with the Block or Wblock selections.

1. Create a new file and call it **S-door** (for symbol-door). Since the symbol will fit in the default limits of the drawing, you don't have to change the limits setting.

Since this is a new drawing, the circle is automatically placed on layer 0. Remember that objects in a block that are on layer 0 will take on the color and line type assignment of the layer on which the block is inserted.

2. Draw a circle with a radius of 0.125 and with its center at coordinate 7,5.

3. Next, zoom into the circle so it is about the same size as shown in Figure 10.1.

4. If the circle looks like an octagon, Choose View ➤ Regen, or type **Re** ↵ to regenerate your drawing.

5. Choose Draw ➤ Block ➤ Define Attributes…, or type **At** ↵. The Attribute Definition dialog box appears.

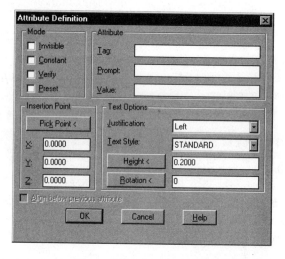

6. Click on the input box labeled Tag in the Attribute group. Enter **d-type**.

The Attribute Tag is equivalent to the field name in a database; it can be up to 31 characters long but it cannot contain spaces. If you plan to use the attribute data in a database program, check that program's manuals for other restrictions on field names.

7. Press the Tab key or click on the input box labeled Prompt, and enter
    Door type. Here you enter the text for the prompt that will appear when
    you insert the block containing this attribute. Often the prompt is the same
    as the tag, but it can be anything you like. Unlike the tag, the prompt can
    include spaces.

Use a prompt that gives explicit instructions so the user will know exactly
what is expected. Consider including an example within the prompt.
(Enclose the example in brackets to imitate the way AutoCAD prompts
often display defaults.)

8. Click on the input box labeled Value. This is where you enter a default value
    for the door type prompt. Enter a hyphen.

If an attribute is to contain a number that will later be used for making
sorts in a database, use a default such as 000 to indicate the number of
digits required. The zeros may also serve to remind the user that values
less than 100 must be preceded by a leading zero, as in 099.

9. Click on the Justification pull-down list, and then highlight Middle. This will
    allow you to center the attribute on the circle's center. You might notice sev-
    eral other options in the Text Options group. Since attributes appear as text,
    you can apply the same settings to them as you would to single line text.

10. Double-click on the input box next to the button labeled Height <, and then
    enter **0.125**. This will make the attribute text 0.125 inches high.

11. Check the box labeled Verify in the Mode group. This option instructs
    AutoCAD to verify any answers you give to the attribute prompts at inser-
    tion time (you'll see later in this chapter how Verify works).

12. Click on the button labeled Pick Point < in the Insertion Point group. The
    dialog box closes momentarily to let you pick a location for the attribute.

13. Using the Center Osnap to pick the center of the circle. You need to place the
    cursor on the circle, not the circle's center, to obtain the center using the
    Osnap. The dialog box reappears.

14. Click on OK. You will see the attribute definition at the center of the circle (see Figure 10.1).

FIGURE 10.1:

The attribute inserted in the circle and the second attribute added

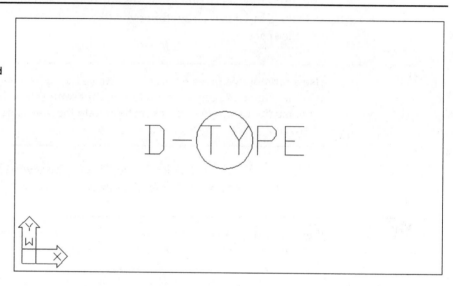

You have just created your first attribute definition. The attribute definition displays its tag in all uppercase letters to help you identify it. When you later insert this file into another drawing, you will see that the tag turns into the value you assign to it when it is inserted. If you only want one attribute, you can stop here and save the file. The next section shows you how you can quickly add several more attributes to your drawing.

Changing Attribute Specifications

Next, you will add a few more attribute definitions, but instead of using the Attribute Definition dialog box, you will make an arrayed copy of the first attribute, and then edit the attribute definition copies. This method can save you time when you want to create several attribute definitions that have similar characteristics. By making copies and editing them, you'll also get a chance to see firsthand how to make changes to an attribute definition.

1. Click on Array Modify toolbar, or type **Ar** ↵.

2. At the `Select objects` prompt, click on the attribute definition you just created, and then press ↵.

3. At the `Rectangular or Polar array (<R>/P)` prompt, type **R** ↵.

4. At the `Number of Rows` prompt, enter 7 ↵.

5. At the `Number of Columns` prompt, press ↵.

6. At the `Distance between Rows` prompt, enter **-.18** ↵. This is about 1.5 times the height of the attribute definition. Be sure to include the minus sign. This will cause the array to be drawn downward.

7. Issue a Zoom Extents or use the Zoom Realtime tool to view all the attributes.

Now you are ready to modify the copies of the attribute definitions.

1. Click on the Properties button on the Object Properties toolbar.

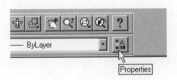

TIP   The Text Edit tool (**Ed** ↵ or Modify ➤ Object ➤ Text) lets you edit the tag, prompt, and default value of an attribute definition. However, it doesn't let you change an attribute definition's *mode*.

---

2. At the `Select Object to Modify` prompt, click on the attribute definition just below the original and then press ↵. The Modify Attribute Definition dialog box appears.

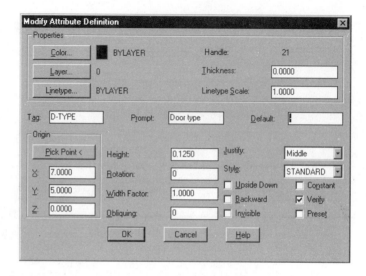

3. Click on the Invisible checkbox in the lower-right portion of the dialog box. This will cause this attribute to be invisible when the file is later inserted.

4. Double-click on the input box labeled Tag, and then enter **d-size**.

5. Press Tab to move to the Prompt input box, and then type **Door size**.

6. Press Tab a second time to move to the Default input box, and then enter 3'-0".

7. Click on OK. You will see the attribute definition change to reflect the new tag.

8. Continue to edit the rest of the attribute definitions using the attributes settings listed in Table 10.1. Also make sure all but the original attributes have the Invisible option turned on.

9. After you have modified all the attributes, use the Draw ➤ Block ➤ Base option to change the base point of this drawing to center of the circle. Use the Center Osnap to get the exact center.

10. Now you have finished creating your door type symbol with attributes. Save the S-door.

TABLE 10.1: Attributes for the door type symbol (make sure the invisible option is checked)

Tag	Prompt	Default
D-number	Door number	-
D-thick	Door thickness	-
D-rate	Fire rating	-
D-matrl	Door material	-
D-const	Door construction	-

When you later insert a file or block containing attributes, the attribute prompts will appear in the order that their associated definitions were created. If the order of the prompts at insertion time is important, you can control it by editing the attribute definitions so their creation order corresponds to the desired prompt order.

Understanding Attribute Definition Modes

In the Attribute Definition dialog box, you saw several checkboxes in the Mode group. I've briefly described what two of these modes do, but below is a list describing all of the modes together in one place for your reference. You won't be asked to use any of the other modes in this tutorial, so the following set of descriptions is provided in case they might be useful for your work.

Invisible   controls whether the attribute is shown as part of the drawing.

Constant   creates an attribute that does not prompt you to enter a value. Instead, the attribute simply has a constant, or fixed, value you give it during creation. Constant is used in situations where you know you will assign a fixed value to an object. Once they are set in a block, constant values cannot be changed using the standard set of attribute editing commands.

Verify   causes AutoCAD to review the attribute values you enter at insertion time and asks you if they are correct.

Continued on next page

Preset causes AutoCAD to automatically assign the default value to an attribute when its block is inserted. This saves time because a preset attribute will not prompt you for a value. Unlike the Constant option, you can edit an attribute that has the Preset option turned on.

You can have all four modes on, all four off, or any combination of modes. With the exception of the Invisible mode, none of these modes can be altered once the attribute becomes part of a block. Later in this chapter we will discuss how to make an invisible attribute visible.

Inserting Blocks Containing Attributes

In the last section, you created a door type symbol at the desired size for the actual plotted symbol. This means that whenever you insert that symbol, you have to specify an x and y scale factor appropriate to the scale of your drawing. This allows you to use the same symbol in any drawing, regardless of its scale. (You could have several door type symbols, one for each scale you anticipate using, but this would be inefficient.)

1. Open the Plan file you created in earlier exercises. Or you can use the f10a-plan.dwg file from the companion CD-ROM.

2. Use the View ➤ Named Views… to restore the view named First.

3. Be sure the Ceiling and Flr-Pat layers are off. Normally in a floor plan the door headers are not visible, and they will interfere with the placement of the door reference symbol.

4. Click the Insert Block or type **I** ↵ to open the Insert dialog box.

5. At the Insert dialog box, click on the File button.

6. Locate the S-door file in the file list and double-click on it.

7. Click on OK.

8. Insert the symbol in the doorway of the lower-left unit near coordinate 41'-3", 72'-4".

9. At the X Scale Factor prompt, enter **96**.

10. Press ↵ at the Y Scale Factor prompt, and again at the Rotation Angle prompt.

11. At the Door Type <-> prompt, enter **A** ↵. Note that this prompt is the prompt you created. Note also that the default value is the hyphen you specified.

NOTE   Attribute data is case sensitive, so text you enter in all capital letters, will be stored in all capital letters.

---

12. At the Door Size <3'-0"> prompt, press ↵ to accept the default. This is also a prompt you created.

13. At the Door Number <-> prompt, enter **116** ↵. Continue to enter the values for each prompt as shown in Table 10.2.

14. When you have finished entering the values, the prompts repeat themselves to verify your entry (because you selected Verify from the Modes group of the Attribute Definition dialog box). You can now either change an entry or just press ↵ to accept the original entry.

15. Now you've finished and the symbol appears. The only attribute you can see is the one you selected to be visible: the door type.

TIP   If the symbol does not appear, go back to the s-door.dwg file and make sure you have set the base point to the center of the circle.

---

16. Add the rest of the door type symbols for the apartment entry doors by copying or arraying the door symbol you just inserted. You can use the previously saved views to help you get around the drawing quickly. Don't worry that the attribute values won't be appropriate for each unit. I'll show you how to edit the attributes in a later section of this chapter.

TABLE 10.2: Attribute values for the typical studio entry door

Prompt	Value
Door type	A
Door number	Same as room number
Door thickness	1 3/4"
Fire rating	20 min.
Door material	Wood
Door construction	Solid core

As a review exercise, you'll now create another file for the apartment number symbol (shown in Figure 10.2). This will be a rectangular box with the room number that you will place in each studio apartment.

1. Save the Plan file and then open a new file called **S-apart** (for symbol apartment).

2. Give the apartment number symbol attribute the tag name **R-number**, the prompt **Room number**, a default value of **000**, and a text height of **0.125** inches.

3. Make the base point of this drawing the lower-left corner of the rectangle.

4. Save S-apart.

5. Open the Plan file again and insert the apartment number symbol (using an x-scale factor of **96**) into the lower-left unit. Give this attribute the value of **116**.

6. Copy or array the room number symbol so that there is one symbol in each of the units. You'll learn how to modify the attributes to reflect their proper values in the following section, *Editing Attributes*. Figure 10.3 shows what the view should look like once you've entered the door symbols and apartment numbers.

FIGURE 10.2:

The apartment number symbol

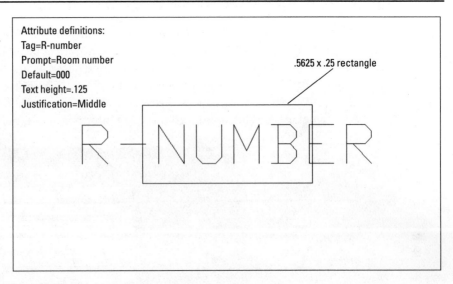

FIGURE 10.3:

An overall view of the plan with door symbols and apartment numbers added

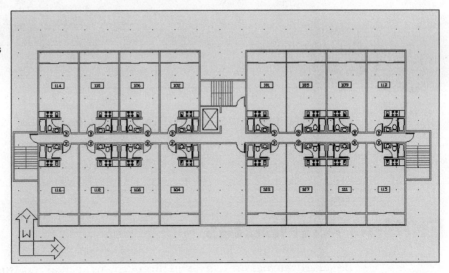

Using a Dialog Box to Answer Attribute Prompts

You can set up AutoCAD to display an Enter Attributes dialog box (instead of individual prompts) for entering the attribute values at insertion time. Because this dialog box allows you to change your mind about a value before confirming your entry, the dialog box allows greater flexibility than individual prompts when entering attributes. You can also see all the attributes associated with a block at once, making it easier to understand what information is required for the block.

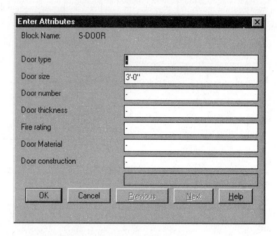

To turn this feature on, do the following.

1. Enter **Attdia** ⏎ at the command prompt.

2. At the New value for ATTDIA <0> prompt, type **1** ⏎.

Attributes set with the Preset mode on will also appear in the dialog box and are treated no differently from other non-constant attributes.

Editing Attributes

Because drawings are usually in flux even after actual construction or manufacturing begins, you will eventually have to edit previously entered attributes. In the example of the apartment building, many things can change before the final set of drawings is completed.

Attributes can be edited individually (one at a time) or they can be edited globally (meaning you can edit several occurrences of a particular attribute tag all at one time). In this section you will make changes to the attributes you have entered so far, using both individual and global editing techniques, and you will practice editing invisible attributes.

Editing Attributes One at a Time

AutoCAD offers an easy way to edit attributes one at a time through a dialog box. The following exercise demonstrates this feature.

1. Use the View ➤ Named View option to restore the First view.

2. Choose Modify ➤ Object ➤ Attribute ➤ Single, or enter **Ate** ↵ at the command prompt.

3. At the Select Block prompt, click on the apartment number attribute in the unit just to the right of the first unit in the lower-left corner. A dialog box appears, showing you the value for the attribute in an input box. Note that the value is already highlighted and ready to be edited.

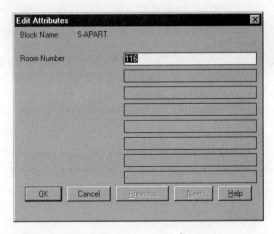

4. Type **112** and then click on OK to make the change.

5. Do this for each room number, using Figure 10.4 to assign room numbers.

> **TIP**
>
> The Edit Attribute option is useful for reviewing attributes as well as editing them because both visible and invisible attributes are displayed in the dialog box.

FIGURE 10.4:

Apartment numbers for one floor of the studio apartment building

Editing Several Attributes in Succession

You can take advantage of the Tab key and the spacebar to quickly edit a series of attributes. In a dialog box, the Tab key moves you to the next option. In AutoCAD, the spacebar reissues the previous command. By combining these two tools, you can make quick work of editing attributes. The following steps describe the process.

1. Choose Modify ➢ Object ➢ Attribute ➢ Single, or enter **Ate** ↵ at the command prompt to start the attribute editing process.

2. Select the first attribute you want to edit.

3. At the Edit Attribute dialog box, enter the new value for the attribute. The old attribute value should already be highlighted. For blocks with multiple attributes, you may need to press the Tab key until you get to the value you want to edit.

4. After entering the new attribute value, press the Tab key to advance to the OK button.

5. Press the spacebar twice—once to accept the OK button, and again to re-issue the Attribute Edit command.

6. Click on the next attribute you want to edit and repeat the process.

If you are comfortable with the keyboard, you can get into a rhythm of selecting and editing attributes using these steps, especially if the block contains only one attribute.

Making Minor Changes to an Attribute's Appearance

Eventually, there will be situations where you will want to make a change to an attribute that doesn't involve its value, such as moving the attribute's location relative to the block it's associated with, or changing its color, its angle, or even its text style. To make these types of changes, you must use the Attedit command. Here's how to do it.

1. Choose Modify ➤ Object ➤ Attribute ➤ Global, or type **Attedit** ↵ at the command prompt.

2. At the Edit Attributes One at a Time? <Y> prompt, press ↵ to accept the default Y.

> **TIP**
>
> If you just want to change the location of individual attributes in a block, you can move attributes using grips. Click on the block to expose the grips and then click on the grip connected to the attribute. Or if you've selected several blocks, shift + click on the attribute grips; then move the attributes to their new location. They will still be attached to their associated blocks.

3. At the Block Name Specification <*> prompt, press ↵. Optionally, you can enter a block name to narrow the selection to specific blocks.

4. At the Attribute Tag Specification <*> prompt, press ↵. Optionally, you can enter an attribute tag name to narrow your selection to specific tags.

5. At the Attribute Value Specification <*> prompt, press ↵. Optionally, you can narrow your selection to attributes containing specific values.

6. At the Select Attributes prompt, you can pick the set of blocks that contain the attributes you wish to edit. Once you press ↵ to confirm your

selection, one of the selected attributes becomes highlighted, and an "x" appears at its base point (see Figure 10.5).

FIGURE 10.5:

Close-up of attribute with x

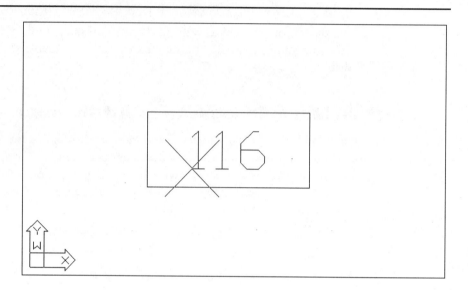

7. At the Value/Position/Height/Angle/Style/Layer/Color/Next <N>: prompt, you can enter the option that best describes the attribute characteristic you wish to change. After you make the change, the prompt returns, allowing you to make another change to the attribute. If you press ⏎ to accept the default, N, another attribute highlights with an x at its base.

8. The Value/Position/Height... prompt appears again, allowing you to make changes to the next attribute.

9. This process repeats until all the attributes have been edited or until you press Esc.

TIP
At some point you may find that an attribute would function better as a single-line text object. A bonus tool called Explode Attribute to Text is available in the Bonus Text Tools toolbar. See Chapter 19 for more information on this bonus tool.

Making Global Changes to Attributes

There will be times when you'll want to change the value of several attributes in a file to be the same value. You can use the Edit Attribute Globally option to make any global changes to attribute values.

Suppose you decide you want to change all the entry doors to a type designated as B, rather than A. Perhaps door type A was an input error, or type B happens to be better suited for an entry door. The following exercise demonstrates how this is done.

1. Use the View Control dialog box (View ➤ Named Views…) to restore the view named Fourth. Pan your view down so you can see the door reference symbol for all the rooms in this half of the drawing.

2. Choose Modify ➤ Object ➤ Attribute ➤ Global, or type **Attedit** ↵ at the command prompt.

3. At the Edit Attributes One at a Time? <Y> prompt, enter **N** ↵ for No. You will see the message Global edit of attribute values. This tells you that you are in the global edit mode.

4. At the Edit Only Attributes Visible On Screen? <Y> prompt, press ↵. As you can see from this prompt, you have the option to edit all attributes, including those out of the view area. You'll get a chance to work with this option later in the chapter.

5. At the Block Name Specification <*> prompt, press ↵. Optionally, you can enter a block name to narrow the selection to specific blocks.

6. At the Attribute Tag Specification <*> prompt, press ↵. Optionally, you can enter an attribute tag name to narrow your selection to specific tags.

7. At the Attribute Value Specification <*> prompt, press ↵. Optionally, you can narrow your selection to attributes containing specific values.

8. At the Select Attributes prompt, select the door type symbols for units 103 to 115.

WARNING   When you are editing attributes, make sure you click the attribute itself and not other graphic components of the block containing the attribute.

9. At the `String to Change` prompt, enter **A** ↵.

10. At the `New String` prompt, enter **B** ↵. The door type symbols all change to the new value.

In step 8 above, you are asked to select the attributes to be edited. AutoCAD limits the changes to those attributes you select. If you know you need to change every single attribute in your drawing, you can do so by answering the series of prompts in a slightly different way, as in the following exercise.

1. Try the same procedure again, but this time enter **N** at the `Edit Only Attributes Visible On Screen` prompt (step 4 in the previous exercise). The message Drawing must be regenerated afterwards appears. The display will flip to text mode.

2. Once again, you are prompted for the block name, the tag, and the value (steps 5, 6, and 7 in the previous exercise). Respond to these prompts as you did before. Once you have done that, you get the message 16 attributes selected. This tells you the number of attributes that fit the specifications you just entered.

3. At the `String to Change` prompt, enter **A** ↵ to indicate you want to change the rest of the A attribute values.

4. At the `New String` prompt, enter **B** ↵. A series of Bs appear, indicating the number of strings that were replaced.

WARNING   If the Regenauto command is off, you must regenerate the drawing to see the change.

TIP   If you find that this method for globally editing attributes is too complex, AutoCAD offers the Global Attribute Edit bonus tool in the Bonus Text Tool toolbar. See Chapter 19 for details.

You may have noticed in the last exercise that the `Select Attribute` prompt is skipped and you go directly to the `String to change` prompt. AutoCAD assumes that you want it to edit every attribute in the drawing, so it doesn't bother asking you to select specific attributes.

Using Spaces in Attribute Values

At times, you may want the default value to begin with a blank space. This enables you to specify text strings more easily when you edit the attribute. For example, you may have an attribute value that reads *3334333*. If you want to change the first 3 in this string of numbers, you have to specify **3334** when prompted for the string to change. If you start with a space, as in _3334333 (I'm only using an underline here to represent the space; it doesn't mean you type an underline character), you can isolate the first 3 from the rest by specifying _3 as the string to change (again, type a space instead of the underline).

You must enter a backslash character (\) before the space in the default value to tell AutoCAD to interpret the space literally, rather than as a press of the spacebar (which is equivalent to pressing ↵).

Making Invisible Attributes Visible

Invisible attributes, such as those in the door reference symbol, can be edited globally using the tools just described. You may, however, want to be a bit more selective about which invisible attribute you want to modify. Or you may simply want to make them temporarily visible for other editing purposes. This section describes how you can make invisible attributes visible.

1. Enter **Attdisp** ↵.

TIP   You may also use the Windows menu to change the display characteristics of attributes. Choose Options ➢ Display ➢ Attribute Display, and then click on the desired option on the cascading menu.

---

2. At the Normal/ON/OFF <Normal> prompt, enter **ON** ↵. Your drawing will look like Figure 10.6. If Regenauto is turned off, you may have to issue the Regen command. At this point, you could edit the invisible attributes individually, as in the first attribute-editing exercise. For now, set the attribute display back to normal.

3. Enter **Attdisp** ↵ again; then at the Normal/ON/OFF prompt, enter **N** ↵ for normal.

NOTE   You get a chance to see the results of the On and Normal options. The Off option will make all attributes invisible, regardless of the mode used when they were created.

FIGURE 10.6:

The drawing with all the attributes visible (door type symbols are so close together that they overlap)

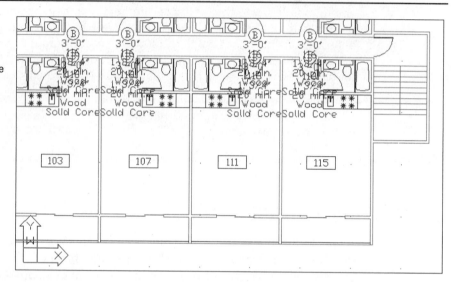

Because the attributes were not intended to be visible, they appear to overlap each other and cover other parts of the drawing when they are made visible. Just remember to turn them back off when you are done reviewing them.

Redefining Blocks Containing Attributes

Finally, you should be aware that attributes act differently from other objects when included in redefined blocks. Normally, blocks that have been redefined change their configuration to reflect the new block definition. But if a redefined block contains attributes, the attributes will maintain their old properties. This means that the old attribute position, style, and so on, do not change even though you may have changed them in the new definition.

Fortunately, AutoCAD offers a tool specifically designed to let you update blocks with attributes. The following describes how you would go about updating attribute blocks.

1. Before you use the command to redefine an attribute block, you must first create the objects and attribute definitions that are going to make up the new replacement attribute block. The simplest way to do this is to explode a copy of the attribute block you wish to update. This ensures that you have the same attribute definitions in the updated block.

2. Make your changes to the exploded attribute block.

WARNING Before you explode the attribute block copy, be sure that it is at a 1-to-1 scale. This is important, because if you don't use Explode, you could end up with all of your new attributes blocks at the wrong size. Also be sure you use some marker device, such as a line, to locate the insertion point of the attribute block *before* you explode it.

3. Type **Attredef** ↵.

4. At the Name of Block W to Redefine prompt, enter the appropriate name.

5. At the Select Objects for New Block prompt, select all the objects, including the attribute definitions, you want to include in the revised attribute block.

6. At the Insertion Base Point of New Block prompt, pick the same location as used for the original block.

   Once you pick the insertion point, AutoCAD will take a few seconds to update the blocks. The amount of time will vary depending on the complexity of the block and the number of times the block occurs in the drawing. If you include a new attribute definition with your new block, it too will be added to all the updated blocks, with its default value. Attribute definitions that are deleted from your new definition will be removed from all the updated blocks.

Common Uses for Attributes

Attributes are an easy way to combine editable text with graphic symbols without resorting to groups or separate text and graphic elements. One of the more common uses of attributes is in column grid symbols. Attributes are well suited for this purpose because they maintain their location in relation to the circle or hexagon shape usually used for grid symbols, and they can be easily edited.

Continued on next page

The illustration in this sidebar shows a portion of the San Francisco Main Library with a typical set of grid symbols. Each symbol contains an attribute similar to the one you created earlier for the room numbers. Other symbols in the figure are also blocks with attributes for text.

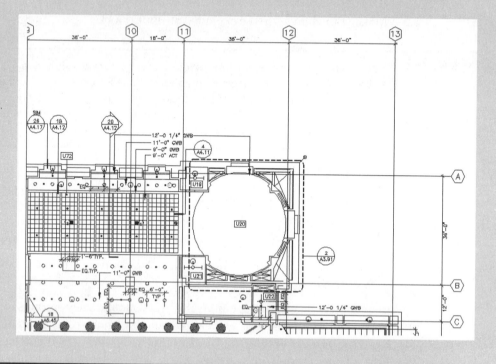

Extracting and Exporting Attribute Information

Once you have entered the attributes into your drawing, you can extract the information contained in them and use it in other programs. You may, for example, want to keep track of the door information in a database manager. This is especially useful if you have a project that contains thousands of doors, such as a large hotel.

TIP   If you simply want to get a count of blocks in your drawing, check out the Count Blocks utility I've included on the companion CD-ROM for just that purpose. See Appendix C for details.

The first step in extracting attribute information is to create a template file using a text editor like Windows Notepad. The template file used with attributes is an ASCII text file containing a list of the attributes you wish to extract and their characteristics. You can also extract information about the block an attribute is associated with. The block's name, x and y coordinates, layer, orientation, and scale are all available for extraction.

NOTE   Don't confuse this attribute template file with the drawing template file you use to set up various default settings.

Determining What to Extract

In the template file, for every attribute you wish to extract, you must give the attribute's tag name followed by a code that determines whether the attribute value is numeric or text, and how many spaces to allow for the value. If it is a numeric value, you must indicate how many decimal places to give the number. If you are familiar with database management programs, you'll know these are typical variables you determine when you set up a database.

WARNING   You cannot have a blank line anywhere in the template file because AutoCAD will reject it. Also, the last line in the file must end with an ⏎, or your data will not extract.

For example, to get a list of rooms containing the B door type, you would create a text file with the following contents:

```
D-ROOM N005000
D-TYPE C001000
```

The first item on each line (D-ROOM and D-TYPE in this example) is the tag of the attribute you want to list. This is followed by at least one space, and then a code that describes the attribute. This code may look a little cryptic at first glance. The following list describes how the code is broken down from left to right:

- The first character of the code is always a C or an N to denote a character (C) or numeric (N) value.

- The next three digits are where you enter the number of spaces the value will take up. You can enter any number from 001 to 999, but you must enter zeros for null values. The D-ROOM example shows the value of *005* for five spaces. The two leading zeros are needed because AutoCAD expects to see three digits in this part of the code.

- The last three digits are for the number of decimal places to allow if the value is numeric. For character values, these must always be zeros. Once again, AutoCAD expects to see three digits in this part of the code, so even if there are no decimal digits for the value, you must include *000*.

Now you will use the Windows Notepad application to create a template file. If you like, you can use any Windows word processor that is capable of saving files in the ASCII format.

1. In Windows 95/NT, locate and start up the Notepad application from the Accessories program group.

2. Enter the following text as it is shown. Press ↵ at the end of *each* line, including the last.

   ```
   D-NUMBER C005000
   D-THICK C007000
   D-RATE C010000
   D-MATRL C015000
   D-CONST C015000
   ```

3. When you have finished entering these lines of text, click on File ➤ Save, and then enter **Door.txt** for the file name. For ease of access, you should save this file to your current default directory, or the \AutoCAD 14\ directory.

4. Close the Notepad, and return to AutoCAD.

You've just completed the setup for attribute extraction. Now that you have a template file, you can extract the attribute data.

Text Editor Line Endings

It is very important that the last line of your file end with a single ⏎. AutoCAD will return an error message if you either leave the ⏎ off or have an extra ⏎ at the end of the file. Take care to end the line with an ⏎ and don't add an extra one. If the extraction doesn't work, check to see if there isn't an extra ⏎ at the end of the file.

Extracting Block Information Using Attributes

I mentioned that you can extract information regarding blocks, as well as attributes. To do this you must use the following format.

```
BL:LEVEL        N002000
BL:NAME         C031000
BL:X            N009004
BL:Y            N009004
BL:Z            N009004
BL:NUMBER       N009000
BL:HANDLE       C009000
BL:LAYER        C031000
BL:ORIENT       N009004
BL:XSCALE       N009004
BL:YSCALE       N009004
BL:ZSCALE       N009004
BL:XEXTRUDE     N009004
BL:YEXTRUDE     N009004
BL:ZEXTRUDE     N009004
```

WARNING A template file containing these codes must also contain at least one attribute tag, because AutoCAD must know which attribute it is extracting before it can tell what block the attribute is associated with. The code information for blocks works the same as for attributes.

I have included some typical values for the attribute codes in this example. The following list describes what each line in the above example is used for.

LEVEL returns the nesting level.

NAME returns the block name.

X returns the X coordinate of the insertion point.

Y   returns the Y coordinate of the insertion point.

Z   returns the Z coordinate of the insertion point.

NUMBER   returns the order number of the block.

HANDLE   returns the blocks handle. If no handle exists, a 0 is returned.

LAYER   returns the layer the block is inserted on.

ORIENT   returns the insertion angle.

XSCALE   returns the X scale.

YSCALE   returns the Y scale.

ZSCALE   returns the Z scale.

XEXTRUDE   returns the block's X extrusion direction.

YEXTRUDE   returns the block's Y extrusion direction.

ZEXTRUDE   returns the block's Z extrusion direction.

Performing the Extraction

AutoCAD allows you to extract attribute information from your drawing as a list in one of three different formats:

- CDF (comma-delimited format)
- SDF (space-delimited format)
- DXF (data exchange format)

Using the CDF Format

The CDF format can be read by many popular database management programs, as well as programs written in BASIC. This is the format you will use in this exercise.

1.   Type **Ddattext** ↵. The Attribute Extraction dialog box appears.

2. If it isn't already selected, click on the radio button labeled Comma Delimited File (CDF).

3. Click on the Template File... button. Then, using the Template File dialog box, locate and select the Door.txt file you created earlier.

TIP
You can select file names of existing template and output files by clicking on the Template File or Output File buttons in the Attribute Extraction dialog box. The File dialog box appears, allowing you to select files from a list.

4. Click on the Output File button. Then, using the File dialog box, enter the name Plan.txt for your output file and place it in the \Program Files\ AutoCAD 14 directory.

5. Click on OK at the Attribute Extraction dialog box. The message "16 records in extract file" appears.

NOTE
You may have noticed the Select Objects< button in the Attribute Extraction dialog box. When you click on this button, the dialog box temporarily closes to let you single out attributes to extract by picking their associated blocks from the display.

AutoCAD has created a file called Plan.txt that contains the extracted list. Let's take a look at its contents.

1. Open the Notepad application (Start ➢ Programs ➢ Accessories ➢ Notepad).

2. Choose File ➤ Open to open `Plan.txt` from the current directory. (In this exercise, the template file is located in the `\Program Files\AutoCAD 14` directory.) You will get the following list:

```
'116','1 3/4"','20 MIN','WOOD','SOLID CORE'
'114','1 3/4"','20 MIN','WOOD','SOLID CORE'
'112','1 3/4"','20 MIN','WOOD','SOLID CORE'
'110','1 3/4"','20 MIN','WOOD','SOLID CORE'
'108','1 3/4"','20 MIN','WOOD','SOLID CORE'
'106','1 3/4"','20 MIN','WOOD','SOLID CORE'
'102','1 3/4"','20 MIN','WOOD','SOLID CORE'
'104','1 3/4"','20 MIN','WOOD','SOLID CORE'
'107','1 3/4"','20 MIN','WOOD','SOLID CORE'
'105','1 3/4"','20 MIN','WOOD','SOLID CORE'
'101','1 3/4"','20 MIN','WOOD','SOLID CORE'
'103','1 3/4"','20 MIN','WOOD','SOLID CORE'
'111','1 3/4"','20 MIN','WOOD','SOLID CORE'
'109','1 3/4"','20 MIN','WOOD','SOLID CORE'
'113','1 3/4"','20 MIN','WOOD','SOLID CORE'
'115','1 3/4"','20 MIN','WOOD','SOLID CORE'
```

Since you picked the comma delimited format (CDF), AutoCAD placed commas between each extracted attribute value (or *field,* in database terminology).

NOTE Notice that the individual values are enclosed in single quotes. These quotes delimit character values. If you had specified numeric values, the quotes would not have appeared. Also note that the fields are in the order they appear in the template file.

The commas are used by some database management programs to indicate the separation of fields in ASCII files. This example shows everything in uppercase letters because that's the way they were entered when I inserted the attribute blocks in my own working sample. The extracted file maintains the case of whatever you enter for the attribute values.

Using Other Delimiters with CDF   Some database managers require the use of other symbols, such as double quotes and slashes, to indicate character values and field separation. AutoCAD allows you to use a different symbol in place of the single quote or comma. For example, if the database manager you use requires double-quote delimiters for text in the file to be imported, you can add the statement:

```
c:quote "
```

to the template file to replace the single quote with a double quote. A line from an extract file using *c:quote "* in the template file would look like this:

```
"115","1 3/4" ","20 MIN","WOOD","SOLID CORE"
```

Notice that the single quote (') is replaced by a double quote ("). You can also add the statement:

```
c:delim /
```

to replace the comma delimiter with the slash symbol. A line from an extract file using both *c:quote "* and *c:delim /* in the template file would look like this:

```
"115"/"1 3/4" "/"20 MIN"/"WOOD"/"SOLID CORE"
```

Here the comma is replaced by a forward slash. You can add either of these statements to the beginning or end of your template file.

Using the SDF Format

Like the CDF format, the space delimited format (SDF) can be read by most database management programs. This format is the best one to use if you intend to enter information into a word-processed document because it leaves out the commas and quotes. You can even import it into an AutoCAD drawing using the method described in Chapter 8. Now let's try using the SDF option to extract the same list we extracted a moment ago using CDF.

1. Type **Ddattext** ↵ at the command prompt.

2. At the Attribute Extraction dialog box, use the same template file name, but for the attribute extract file name, use **Plan-SDF.txt** to distinguish this file from the last one you created.

3. Click on the SDF radio button, and then click on OK. You will see a message that reads "16 records in extract file."

4. After AutoCAD has extracted the list, use the Windows Wordpad to view the contents of the file. You will get a list similar to this one:

```
116 1 3/4" 20 MIN WOOD SOLID CORE
114 1 3/4" 20 MIN WOOD SOLID CORE
```

```
112 1 3/4" 20 MIN WOOD SOLID CORE
110 1 3/4" 20 MIN WOOD SOLID CORE
108 1 3/4" 20 MIN WOOD SOLID CORE
106 1 3/4" 20 MIN WOOD SOLID CORE
102 1 3/4" 20 MIN WOOD SOLID CORE
104 1 3/4" 20 MIN WOOD SOLID CORE
107 1 3/4" 20 MIN WOOD SOLID CORE
105 1 3/4" 20 MIN WOOD SOLID CORE
101 1 3/4" 20 MIN WOOD SOLID CORE
103 1 3/4" 20 MIN WOOD SOLID CORE
111 1 3/4" 20 MIN WOOD SOLID CORE
109 1 3/4" 20 MIN WOOD SOLID CORE
113 1 3/4" 20 MIN WOOD SOLID CORE
115 1 3/4" 20 MIN WOOD SOLID CORE
```

This format shows text without any special delimiting characters.

5. Now save the Plan.dwg file for future chapters.

Using the DXF Format

The third file format is the data exchange format (DXF). There are actually two methods for DXF extraction. The Attribute Extraction dialog box you saw earlier offers the DXF option. This option extracts only the data from blocks containing attributes. Choose the File ➤ Export option; then select .DXF from the List Files of Type drop-box to convert an entire drawing file into a special format for data exchange between AutoCAD and other programs (for example, other PC CAD programs). I will discuss the DXF format in more detail in Chapter 14.

NOTE As an alternate, you can choose File ➤ Export, then at the Export Data dialog box, choose DXX Extract (*.DXX) from the List File of Type drop-down list. Enter a name for the extracted data file in the File Name input box, and then click OK. Finally, in the drawing editor, select the attributes you want to extract. The DXX format is a subset of the DXF format.

Using Extracted Attribute Data with Other Programs

You can import any of these lists into any word-processing program that accepts ASCII files. They will appear as shown in our examples.

As I mentioned earlier, the extracted file can also be made to conform to other data formats.

Microsoft Excel

Excel has no specific requirements for the formatting of AutoCAD extracted data. Use File ➢ Open from the Excel pull-down menu, and then select the .TXT file type from the File dialog box. Excel then opens a very simple to use import tool that steps you through import process. You can choose the delimiting method, whether each field is a character, date, or other type of data, and other formatting options.

If you are a database user familiar with Microsoft Visual Basic, you will want to look at the sample Visual Basic utility supplied with AutoCAD. It shows how you can use VBA to export attribute data directly from AutoCAD to Excel without having to create a template file or perform an export using the Ddattext command. You can find the sample program in the \sample\axtiveX\ExtAttr directory. See Chapter 20 for more on this and other useful VBA-related utilities.

Microsoft Access

Like Excel, you can open the exported attribute data directly in Access. First create a new database table. You can then use the File ➢ Get External Data ➢ Import option from the Access pull-down menu, and then choose Text Files from the Files of Type drop-down list. After selecting the attribute extracted file, Access offers an easy to use import tool that steps you through the process of importing the file. You can specify field and record names, as well as the delimiting method.

If you plan to update the attribute data file on a regular basis, you can have the file linked, instead of imported (File ➢ Get External Data ➢ Link Tables). A linked file is best suited for situations where you want to read the data without changing it. You can generate reports, link the attribute data to other databases, perform searches, or sort the attribute data.

As with Excel, if you are an Visual Basic user, you can add controls to enhance your attribute data link to Access.

Accessing External Databases

AutoCAD offers a way to access an external database from within AutoCAD—the *AutoCAD SQL Extension* (*ASE*). (SQL stands for Structured Query Language. It is a standard by which databases are organized.) With the ASE, you can read and manipulate data from external database files. You can also use ASE to *link* parts of your drawing to an external database. There are numerous reasons for doing this. The most obvious is to keep inventory on parts of your drawing. If you are an interior designer doing office planning, you can link inventory data from a database to your drawing, with a resulting decrease in the size of your drawing file. If you are a facilities manager, you can track the movement of people and facilities using AutoCAD linked to a database file.

In this section I specifically avoid the more complex programming issues of database management systems, and I do not discuss the SQL language on which much of ASE is based. Still, you should be able to make good use of ASE with the information provided here. We'll also be departing from our Studio Apartment example to make use of an office plan example that has already been created by Autodesk.

In these exercises I do assume that you are somewhat familiar with databases. For example, I will frequently refer to something called a *table*. A table is a SQL term referring to the row-and-column data structure of a typical database file. For the sake of this tutorial, you can think of a table as a dBASE database file. Other terms I'll use are *rows*, which are the records in a database, and *columns*, which refer to the database fields.

Finally, it is *very* important that you follow the instructions in these beginning exercises carefully. If anything is missed in the beginning, later exercises will not work properly.

Database Managers and AutoCAD

Chances are, you are already familiar with at least one database program. ASE provides support for dBASE, ODBC, and Oracle databases. Many other database and spreadsheet applications can read and write to at least one of these database formats. If you are a Windows user, you can use Microsoft Excel to create database files for use with AutoCAD ASE.

Setting Up ASE to Locate Database Files

ASE doesn't create new database files. You must use existing files or create them before you use ASE. In the first set of exercises below, you will use two files that come with AutoCAD. The two files are Employee.dbf and Inventry.dbf and they are located in the \AutoCAD 14\sample\Dbf subdirectory. The contents of the first of these database files are shown in Figure 10.7.

FIGURE 10.7:

The contents of the Employee.dbf dBASE III file

EMP_ID	LAST_NAME	FIRST_NAME	DEPT	TITLE	ROOM	EXT
1000	Meredith	Dave	Sales	V.P.	101	8600
1001	Williams	Janice	Sales	Western Region Mgr.	102	8601
1003	Smith	Jill	Sales	Central Region Mgr.	104	8603
1004	Nelson	Kirk	Sales	Canadian Sales Mgr.	109	8640
1005	Clark	Karl	Sales	Educational Sales Mgr.	106	8605
1006	Wilson	Cindy	Accounting	Accountant	109	8606
1007	Ortega	Emilio	Accounting	Accountant	109	8607
1008	Benson	Adam	Accounting	Accountant	109	8608
1009	Rogers	Kevin	Accounting	Accountant	109	8609
1011	Thompson	Frank	Engineering	Mechanical Engineer	123	8611
1012	Simpson	Paul	Engineering	Mechanical Engineer	124	8612
1013	Debrine	Todd	Engineering	Design Engineer	125	8613
1014	Frazier	Heather	Engineering	Application Engineer	126	8614
1016	Taylor	Patrick	Engineering	Software Engineer	128	8616
1017	Chang	Yuan	Engineering	Software Engineer	129	8617
1018	Dempsy	Phil	Engineering	Application Engineer	112	8618
1019	Kahn	Jenny	Engineering	Programmer	113	8619
1020	Moore	George	Engineering	Programmer	114	8620
1021	Price	Mark	Engineering	Software Engineer	115	8621
1022	Quinn	Scott	Engineering	Software Engineer	116	8622
1023	Sanchez	Maria	Engineering	Mechanical Engineer	117	8623
1024	Ross	Ted	Engineering	Application Engineer	118	8624
1025	Saunders	Terry	Engineering	Software Engineer	119	8625
1026	Fong	Albert	Engineering	Programmer	120	8626

Before you start to work with databases, you must tell AutoCAD about your database *environment*. The environment consists of a database management application and its associated directory paths, user access information, and the database tables for that particular database.

If you have installed the full version of AutoCAD, then you are already set up to proceed with the tutorial in the next section. AutoCAD has already included information about the sample database environment. But you will still want to know the method for setting up AutoCAD to recognize a database environment, so that in the future you can access other databases besides those in this sample. To do this, you use the External Database Configuration application that comes with AutoCAD.

Knowing Your Database Structure

Before you actually use the External Database Configuration program, you will want to make sure you are familiar with the way your database files are organized and how that organization relates to the database nomenclature. You will need to know three terms: *catalog*, *schema*, and *tables*.

To help explain these terms, we'll set up a database environment using the sample database files that come with AutoCAD. These files, `computer.dbf`, `employee.dbf` and `inventry.dbf`, are located in AutoCAD subdirectory called `\DBF`. They are known as the tables of the database, while the directory that contains them is the schema. The directory path that leads to the schema, `\AutoCAD 14\sample`, is known as the catalog. As you will see, catalogs and schemas need names, so if you are setting up a database to work with AutoCAD, you may want to start thinking of a meaningful name for these components of your database.

Configuring AutoCAD for the External Database

Now let's use this example to set up AutoCAD's database configuration.

1. From the Windows 95/NT Desktop, choose Start ➤ Programs ➤ AutoCAD R14 ➤ External Database Configuration.

2. The External Database Configuration dialog box appears.

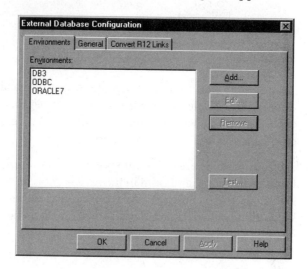

3. Click on Add to create a new environment. (The environment you will be working with in the following tutorial is the DB3 environment that already appears in the Environment list.) The Select DBMS for New Environment dialog box appears.

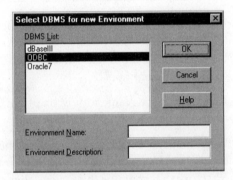

4. Select the type of database you are using from the list. In this example, click on dBaseIII.

5. Enter **Tutorial** in the Environment Name input box.

6. Click OK. The Environment dialog box appears.

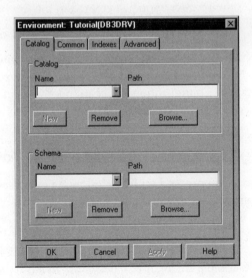

WARNING The configuration of the Environment dialog box will be different depending on the type of database you select in step 4. To see more on the ODBC environment settings, see Appendix A.

7. In the Catalog button group, click on Browse; then in the Browse dialog box, locate and select the `\Program Files\AutoCAD 14\Sample` directory that is the parent to the actual subdirectory that contains the database tables. Click OK to continue.

8. Enter **Cat** in the Name input box of the Catalog button group, and then click on the New button.

9. In the Schema button group, click on the Browse button; then in the Browse dialog box, locate and select the `\Program Files\AutoCAD 14\Sample\Dbf` directory that contains the tables. Click OK to continue.

10. Enter **Catfiles** in the Name input box of the Schema button group, and then click New. Remember these names as you will use them when you open the database from AutoCAD.

11. Click on New, and then click on OK. You will see the name of the database environment you just created in the Environments list box.

12. Click OK to exit the External Database Configuration dialog box.

Now you can access your database from AutoCAD using the environment, catalog, and schema name you have just set up. Other options in the External Database Configuration application let you set up user names and passwords so you can restrict access to the databases, or include indexes for the databases.

Loading the External Database Toolbar

Before you proceed with the following exercises, you will want to open the External Database toolbar.

1. Start AutoCAD if it isn't already open.

2. Right-click on any toolbar, and then click on External Database from the Toolbar dialog box. Click Close to close the toolbar dialog box.

Opening a Database from AutoCAD

Now you're ready to access your database files directly from AutoCAD. In the following exercise, you'll take the first step by making a connection between a database table and AutoCAD.

1. Open the ASEsmp.dwg file from \Program Files\AutoCAD 14\Sample directory. You can also find a copy of this file on the companion CD-ROM of this book.

WARNING   If ASE does not initialize, be sure that the \Program Files\AutoCAD 14\ Support directory is included in the Support option of the Environment settings. This option can be found by clicking on Tools ➤ Preferences; then at the Preferences dialog box, click on the tab labeled Files. The Support subdirectory should be listed in the Support Files Search Path listing. Be sure to close and restart AutoCAD after making the environment change.

2. Click on the Administration button on the External Database toolbar, or type **Aad** ↵.

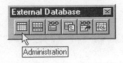

The Administration dialog box appears.

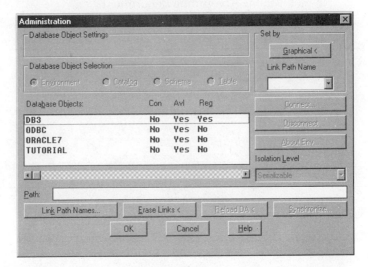

3. Click on TUTORIAL from the Database Objects list. Notice that the Environment button is automatically selected.

4. Click on the Connect button to the right of the list. The Connect to Environment dialog box appears.

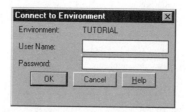

5. Because the user name and password are not important to this tutorial, click on OK.

6. Click on the Catalog button in the Database Object Selection group, and then click on CAT, which appears in the Database Objects list.

7. Click on the Schema button, and then click on CATFILES from the list.

8. Click on the Table button, and then click on Employee from the list.

9. Finally, click on OK. You've just linked to the Employee.dbf file.

Finding a Record in the Database

Now that you are connected to the database, suppose you want to find the record for a specific individual. You might already know that the individual you're looking for is in the Accounting department.

1. Click on the Rows button on the External Database Toolbar, or type **Aro** ↵.

The Rows dialog box appears.

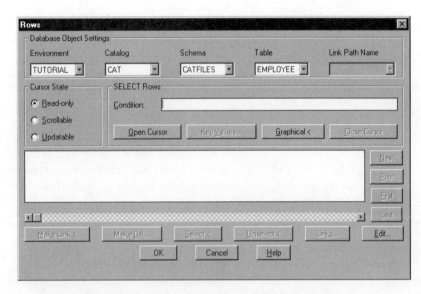

2. Click on the Condition input box and type **dept='Accounting.'** Make sure you include the single quotes.

3. Click on the Scrollable radio button in the Cursor State group, and then click on the Open Cursor button below the Conditions input box. The first item that fulfills the Conditions criteria appears in the list box.

4. Click on the Next button to view the next row that meets the search criteria.

5. Click on Last to view the last row (the one with Kevin Rogers' name).

6. Click on OK to close the dialog box.

You can also click on Open Cursor without entering anything in the input box in step 2. This essentially tells ASE to select all the rows in the current database table. You would then be able to scan the entire table. To exit the list, you choose Close cursor or simply exit the Rows dialog box.

You've just seen how you can locate and view a record in a database. If you wanted to edit or delete that record, you would have clicked on the Updatable radio button in step 3, instead of the Scrollable button. You could then make changes to the database item shown in the list box by clicking on the Edit button. The Edit button then opens another dialog box that allows you to edit individual items in a record. In the following section, you'll use the Edit Row dialog box, not to change a record, but to add one.

The ability to access databases in this way can help you connect AutoCAD graphic data with database information. For example, you may want to keep track of tenant information in your studio apartment building. As you will see later, you can actually link graphics to database records so you can quickly access data regarding a particular tenant. Another application might be generating a bill of materials for a mechanical project, where records in the database relate to parts in a mechanical assembly.

Adding a Row to a Database Table

Now let's get back to our office example. Suppose you have a new employee who will need to be set up in an office. The first thing you will want to do is add his or her name to the database. Here's how it's done.

1. Click on the Rows button on the External Database toolbar, or enter **Aro** ↵.

2. Click on the Updatable button in the Cursor State group, and then click on the Edit button toward the lower-right corner of the dialog box. The Edit Row dialog box appears.

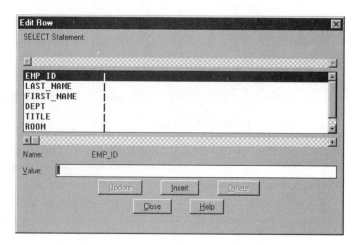

3. Enter the following data in the dialog box. To add an item, highlight the item in the list, and then add the information in the input area at the bottom of the dialog box. After you type in each item, press ↲ to move to the next item.

```
EMP_ID  2000
LAST_NAME  Ryan
FIRST_NAME  Roma
DEPT  Creative Resources
TITLE  Producer/Lyricist
ROOM  122
EXT  8888
```

4. When you've finished entering the list, click on Insert, and then click on Close.

5. Click on OK at the Rows dialog box. You've just added a row to the database and it is the current one.

Linking Objects to a Database

So far, you've looked at ways you can access an external database file. You can also *link* specific drawing objects to elements in a database. But before you can link your drawing to data, you must *register* the table (i.e., database file) to which you want to link, and then create a *link path*.

Registering a table is a way of naming a group of links between your drawing and the database file. You can register a table numerous times, allowing you to set up several different sets of links. For example, you may want to create a set of links between the Names column of your database table and the desks in your office plan. In another instance, you may want to link the phone extension numbers of the same database file to the room numbers in your office plan. To identify these different sets of links, you create a link path name, which is really just a name you give to each set of links.

Now let's see how you can create a link to the database by linking your new employee to one of the vacant rooms.

Creating a Link

In the following set of exercises, you will link an AutoCAD object to a record in the Employee database table.

1. Click on the Administration button on the External Database toolbar.

2. With the Employee table selected, click on the Link Path Names button in the lower-left corner of the dialog box. The Link Path Names dialog box appears.

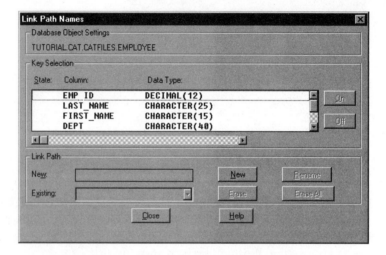

3. Click on the item labeled LAST_NAME in the Key Selection group; then click on the On button to the right. The word "ON" appears next to the name.

4. Repeat step 3 for the item labeled ROOM, which is further down the list.

5. Type **r-number** in the New input box in the Link Path group.

6. Click on New to the right of the New input box. The name R-NUMBER appears in the Existing pop-up list and the message "Registered Successfully" appears in the lower-left corner. At this point, you could select another set of items from the list and create another link path name.

7. Click Close and you return to the Administration dialog box. Click on OK to exit this dialog box.

You've just registered the Employee table and created a link path name for the LAST_NAME and ROOM fields. You can create other link paths that include other fields.

Now you are ready to add a link to room 122. The first step is to locate the record that is associated with room 122.

1. Zoom into the area shown in Figure 10.8.

FIGURE 10.8:

Enlarging your view of room 122

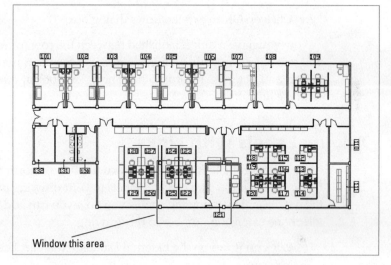

Window this area

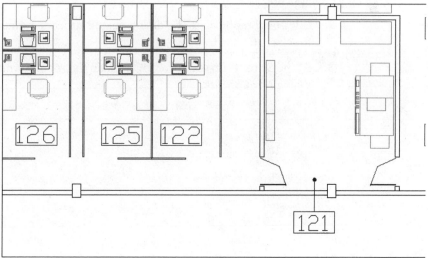

2. Click on Rows on the External Database toolbar.

3. Click on the Conditions input box, and then type **ROOM='122'**.

4. Click on Open Cursor. The record for room 122 appears in the list.

5. Click on the button labeled Make Link <. The dialog box temporarily disappears.

6. Click on the room number (122) and the phone in the upper-left corner of the room. Once you've done this, press ⏎ to return to the Rows dialog box.

7. Click on OK to exit the Rows dialog box.

Now you have a link established between the row for room 122 in the database and two objects in your drawing. Later, you can continue to build links between objects and database records, but for now, let's look at other things you can do with the link.

Adding Labels with Links

Once you've got a link established, you use it to perform a variety of editing tasks. For example, you can add labels to your drawing based on information in the database. The following shows you how you can add the employee name and telephone extension number to the drawing.

1. Click on Rows on the External Database toolbar. The Rows dialog box appears.

2. Click on Graphical <. The dialog box disappears momentarily, allowing you to select an object.

3. At the Select Object prompt, click on the room number (122). The Links dialog box appears.

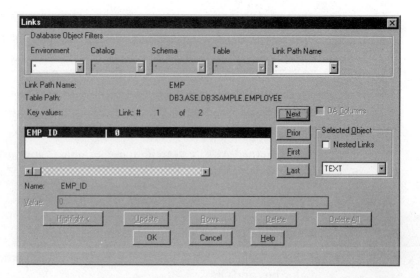

4. Click on the Link Path Name drop-down list and select R-NUMBER.

5. Click OK. The Rows dialog box appears again and displays the record information that is linked to the number.

6. Now click on Make DA. The Make Displayable Attribute dialog box appears.

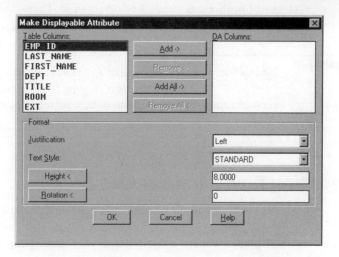

> **WARNING** The *DA* in *Make DA* stands for Displayable Attribute. Don't confuse this with the attributes we've discussed earlier in this chapter. They are not the same.

This dialog box shows two lists. The one on the left shows the items in the database record. The one on the right holds the records you want displayed in the drawing as labels. Right now the DA Columns list is empty.

7. Highlight the LAST_NAME item in the Table Columns list, and then click on the Add -> button. The item is copied into the DA Columns list.

8. Repeat step 7 for the item labeled TITLE in the Table Columns list, and then press OK. The dialog box disappears, and the Left Point prompt appears along with the point selection cursor.

9. Pick a point just below and to the left of the chair in office 122. The Rows dialog box appears.

10. Click on OK. The Rows dialog box closes and you see a new label with the employee's name and title. This new label is also linked to the record in your database.

You may have noticed the Format group in the Make Displayable Attribute dialog box in step 6. These items allow you to control the graphic characteristics of the label, such as justification, style, height, and rotation. There is also a button labeled Add All. This copies all the columns from the Table Columns list to the DA Column list.

> **WARNING** If a table is modified outside of AutoCAD, you must use the Synchronize button in the Administration dialog box to resynchronize the links between your drawing and the database the next time you open the linked drawing file.

Updating Rows and Labels

Chances are the contents of your database will change frequently. In the following exercise, you will get to change a database row and update one of the labels you just placed in your drawing. You will start by quickly setting the current row by selecting an object.

1. Click on Rows on the External Database toolbar. Then at the dialog box, click on the Updatable radio button in the Cursor State group.

2. Click on Graphical<. The dialog box closes and the Select Object prompt appears.

3. Click on the label you just entered. The current row is now set to the one for your employee.

4. Click on the Edit button. Then at the Edit Row dialog box, highlight TITLE.

5. Change the Value input box to read **Chief Designer**, and then press ↵. The ↵ is important; without it the Update button is not activated.

6. Click on Update; then click Close to return to the Rows dialog box.

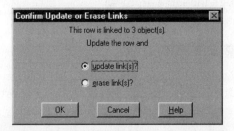

7. Click OK at the Rows dialog box. The label now reflects the change you made in the database.

You have just edited a row in the database and updated the room label at the same time.

Finding and Selecting Graphics through the Database

You've just seen how you can use links to add and update labels to your drawing. Links can also help you find and select objects in a drawing that are linked to a database. The next exercise shows, in a simplified way, how this works.

1. Click on Rows on the External Database toolbar; then type **room ='122'** into the Condition input box in the Select Rows group.

2. Click on Open Cursor. Once again, you see the familiar record we've been working with.

3. Click on Select <. The dialog box temporarily disappears, and you see all the items linked to this record highlighted in the drawing.

4. Press ↵ to return to the Rows dialog box, and then click on OK. The objects linked to the selected record remain highlighted.

Once these steps have been taken, you can use the Previous Object Selection option to select those objects that were highlighted in step 3.

In this example, you only selected objects in one office. However, you can create a record called Vacant, and then link all the vacant offices to this one record. When a new employee is hired, you can then quickly locate all the vacant rooms in the floor plan to place the new employee. If you continue to link each database record with rooms in the drawing, you can then later locate a person's room through the same process.

Deleting a Link

Earlier, you had to change a link that connected a room number and telephone in the drawing to an employee's database record. This next exercise shows you how you can delete the link to the telephone.

1. Click on Rows on the External Database toolbar. Then at the dialog box, click on Graphical <.

2. Click on the phone in room 122. The row assigned to that label is now the current row. The Links dialog box appears.

3. Click on the Environment drop-down list and pick Tutorial.

4. Click OK.

5. At the Rows dialog box, click Links.

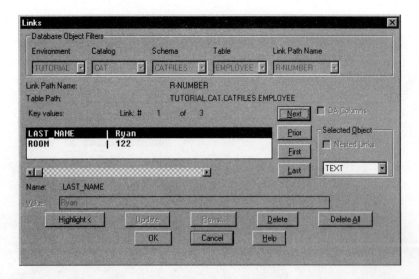

The Key Values list box shows the key values that were selected when you first created the link path name. Above the upper-right side of the list, you see the statement Link: # 1 of 3. This tells you which object link in the drawing you are currently working with.

1. To see which object #1 is, click on the Highlight < button. The dialog box disappears and the drawing shows the room number 122 highlighted.

2. Press ↵, and then click on the Next button to the right of the list. You are now on link #2.

3. Click on Highlight < to visually check that link #2 is in fact the telephone.

4. Press ↵ to return to the Links dialog box.

5. Click on the Delete button at the bottom of the dialog box. The link between the record and the telephone are deleted.

6. Click OK, then OK again at the Rows dialog box.

Filtering Selections and Exporting Links

There are two options you didn't get a chance to try. They are Object Selection and Export Links. Object Selection offers a way to select objects based on a combination of graphical and database criteria. For example, suppose you want to select all the chairs of a certain description from one region of your office plan.

Assuming you have already created links between your database table and your drawing, you could do the following steps.

1. Click on the Select Objects button on the External Database toolbar, or type **Ase** ↵.

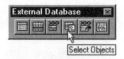

The Select Objects dialog box appears.

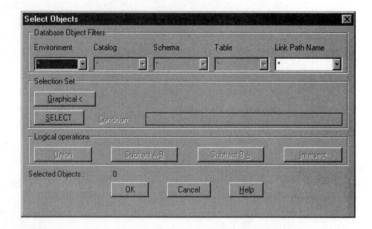

2. Select the appropriate environment, catalog, schema, and table. Under the Conditions input box, enter the search criteria for the chairs.

3. Under the Logical Operations group, choose the Intersect button, and then choose Graphical <. The dialog box temporarily disappears to allow you to select objects.

4. Using a window, select the area in the drawing that includes the chairs you want, and then press ↵.

5. Click OK to exit the dialog box. You can now use the Previous Selection option to select the specified chairs in the area you selected.

The Export Links feature lets you export information on the links between your drawing and your database. This can be useful when you are preparing reports from your database application because database applications are unaware of the number of links that occur to your drawing. Once you export link information, you can then incorporate that information into your report. The exported information lists the object handles and the associated linked database value. Here's a description of how the Export Link function works.

1. Click on the Export Links button on the External Database toolbar, or type **Aex** ↵. You are then asked to select an object.

2. Select the objects that contain the links you wish to export. The Export Links dialog box appears.

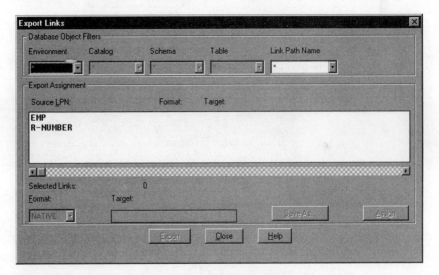

3. You can, at this point, reduce the scope of the link information you will export by selecting a specific environment, catalog, schema, table, or link path name.

4. Select a link path name from the list box.

5. Select Native under the Format pull-down list, and then enter a file name in the Target input box. This will be the name given to the table you want to create.

6. Click on Assign to assign the format and target to the link path name.

7. Choose Export to complete the export process.

You can export multiple link path names by repeating steps 3 through 6, before completing step 7.

Using SQL Statements

For those who are more familiar with SQL, AutoCAD offers a way that lets you access and manipulate database information with a greater degree of control. The SQL Editor can be accessed by clicking on the SQL Editor tool on the External Database toolbar, or by typing **Asq** ↵.

The SQL dialog box appears.

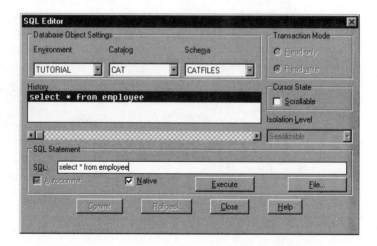

You can then enter a SQL statement in the edit box and click on Execute. Results of your query are displayed in the SQL Cursor dialog box.

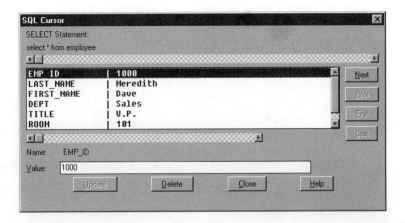

Where to Go from Here

You've seen how you can access and link your drawing to a database. I hope that in this brief tutorial, you can find the information you will need to develop your own database needs.

If you understand SQL, you can take advantage of it to perform more sophisticated searches. You can also expand the functionality of the basic ASE package included with AutoCAD. These topics are, unfortunately, beyond the scope of this book. For more detailed information about ASE and SQL, refer to the *AutoCAD SQL Extension* reference manual.

If You Want to Experiment...

Attributes can be used to help automate data entry into drawings. To demonstrate this, try the following exercise.

Create a drawing file called **Record** with the attribute definitions shown in Figure 10.9. Note the size and placement of the attribute definitions as well as the new base point for the drawing. Save and exit the file, and then create a new drawing called **Schedule** containing the schedule shown in Figure 10.10. Use the Insert command and insert the Record file into the schedule at the point indicated. Note that you are prompted for each entry of the record. Enter any value you like for each prompt. When you are done, the information for one record is entered into the schedule.

FIGURE 10.9:

The Record file with attribute definitions

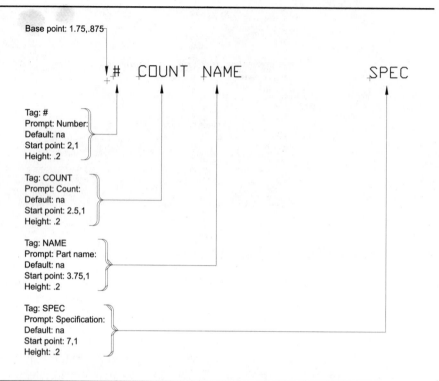

FIGURE 10.10:

The Schedule drawing with Record inserted

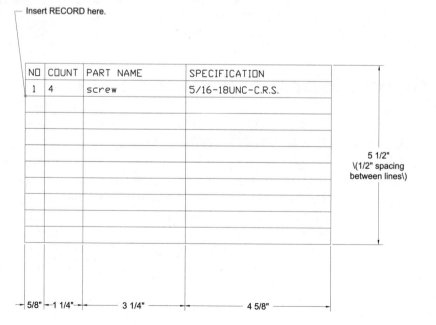

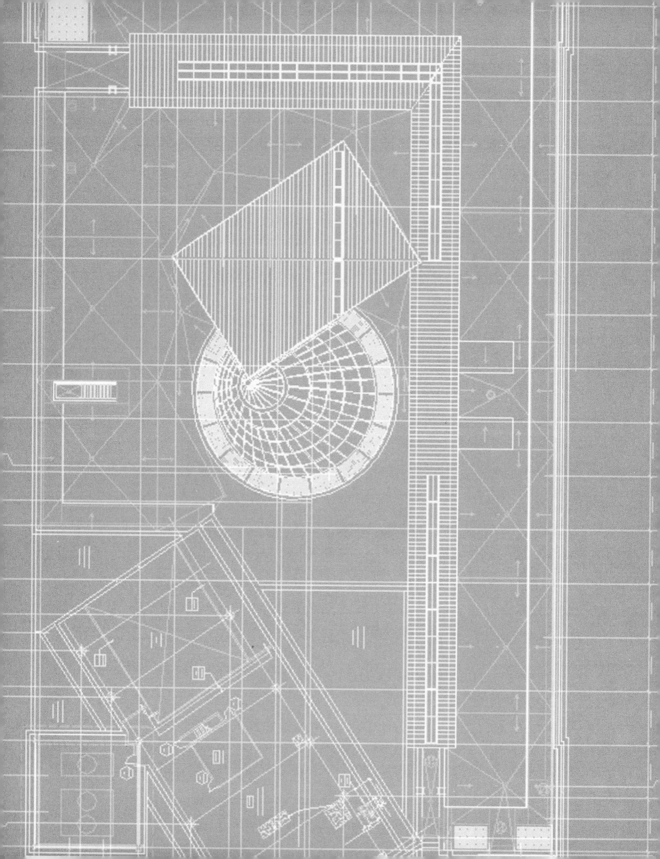

Working with Preexisting Drawings and Raster Images

- Tracing, Scaling, and Scanning Drawings

- Importing and Tracing Raster Images

- Importing PostScript Images

At times you will want to turn a hand-drafted drawing into an AutoCAD drawing file. It may be that you are modifying a design you created before you started using AutoCAD, or that you are converting your entire library of drawings for future AutoCAD use. Or perhaps you want to convert a sketch into a formal drawing. This chapter discusses three ways to enter a hand-drafted drawing: tracing, scaling, and scanning. Each of these methods of drawing input has its advantages and disadvantages.

Tracing, Scaling, and Scanning Drawings

Tracing with a digitizing tablet is the easiest method, but a traced drawing usually requires some cleaning up and reorganization. If dimensional accuracy is not too important, tracing is the best method for entering existing drawings into AutoCAD. It is especially useful for drawings that contain irregular curves, such as the contour lines of a topographical map.

TIP   Even if you don't plan to trace drawings into AutoCAD, you still should read the tracing information because some of the information presented here will help your everyday editing tasks.

Scaling a drawing is the most flexible method because you don't need a tablet to do it and generally you are faced with less clean up afterward. Scaling also affords the most accurate input of orthogonal lines because you can read dimensions directly from the drawing and enter those same dimensions into AutoCAD. The main drawback with scaling is that if the drawing does not contain complete dimensional information, you must constantly look at the hand-drafted drawing and measure distances with a scale. Also, irregular curves are difficult to scale accurately.

Scanning offers some unique opportunities with Release 14, especially if you have a lot of RAM and a fast hard drive. Potentially, you can scan a drawing and save it on your computer as an image file, and then import the image into AutoCAD and trace over it. You still need to perform some clean up work on the traced drawing, but because you can see your tracing directly on your screen, you have better control and you won't have quite as much cleaning up to do as you do when tracing from a digitizer.

There are also vectorizing programs that will automatically convert an image file into a vector file of lines and arcs. These programs may offer some help, but will require the most cleaning up of the options presented here. Like tracing, scanning is best used for drawings that are difficult to scale, such as complex topographical maps containing more contours than are practical to trace on a digitizer, or non-technical line art, such as letterhead and logos.

Tracing a Drawing

The most common method for entering a hand-drafted drawing into AutoCAD is tracing with a digitizer. If you are working with a large drawing and you have a small tablet, you may have to cut the drawing into pieces that your tablet can manage, trace each piece, and then assemble the completed pieces into the large drawing. However, the best solution is to have a large tablet.

The following exercises are designed for a 5"×5" or larger tablet. The sample drawings are small enough to fit completely on this size of tablet. You can use either a stylus or a puck to trace them, but the stylus will offer the most natural feel because it is shaped like a pen. A puck has crosshairs that you have to center on the line you want to trace, and this requires a bit more dexterity.

NOTE   If you don't have a digitizing tablet, you can use scaling to enter the utility room drawing used in this section's tracing exercise. (You will insert the utility room into your apartment building plan in Chapter 12.)

Reconfiguring the Tablet for Tracing

When you first installed AutoCAD, you configured the tablet to use most of its active drawing area for AutoCAD's menu template. Because you will need the tablet's entire drawing area to trace this drawing, you now need to reconfigure the tablet to eliminate the menu. Otherwise, you won't be able to pick points on the drawing outside the 4"×3" screen pointing area AutoCAD normally uses (see Figure 11.1).

TIP   You can save several different AutoCAD configurations that can be easily set using the Preferences dialog box. See Appendix B.

FIGURE 11.1:

The tablet's active drawing area

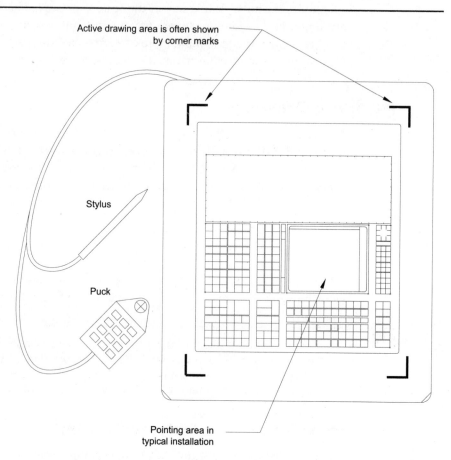

Active drawing area is often shown by corner marks

Stylus

Puck

Pointing area in typical installation

Here are the steps to follow.

1. Start AutoCAD and create a new file called **Utility**.

2. Set up the file as a 1/4"=1'-scale architectural drawing on an 8 ½ × 11" sheet (limits set to 0,0 for the lower-left corner and 528,408 for the upper-right corner).

3. Choose Tools ➤ Tablet ➤ Configure, or type **Ta** ⏎ **CFG** ⏎.

4. At the Enter number of tablet menus desired (0-4) prompt, enter **0** ⏎.

NOTE   When selecting points on the tablet, take care not to accidentally press the pick button twice, as this will give you erroneous results. Many tablets have sensitive pick buttons that can cause problems when you are selecting points.

5. At the Do you want to respecify the Fixed Screen Pointing Area? prompt, enter **Y** ↵.

6. At the Digitize lower left corner of screen pointing area prompt, pick the lower-left corner of the tablet's active drawing area.

NOTE   On some tablets, a light appears to show you the active area; other tablets use a permanent mark, such as a corner mark. AutoCAD won't do anything until you have picked a point, so you don't have to worry about picking a point outside this area.

7. At the Digitize upper right corner of screen pointing area prompt, pick the upper-right corner.

8. At the Do you want to specify the Floating Screen pointing area <N> prompt, press ↵.

Now as you move your stylus or puck you will notice a difference in the relationship between your hand movement and the screen cursor. The cursor moves more slowly and it is active over more of the tablet surface.

Calibrating the Tablet for Your Drawing

Now make a photocopy of Figure 11.2, which represents a hand-drafted drawing of a utility room for your apartment building. Place the photocopied drawing on your tablet so that it is aligned with the tablet and completely within the tablet's active drawing area (see Figure 11.3).

FIGURE 11.2:

The utility room
drawing

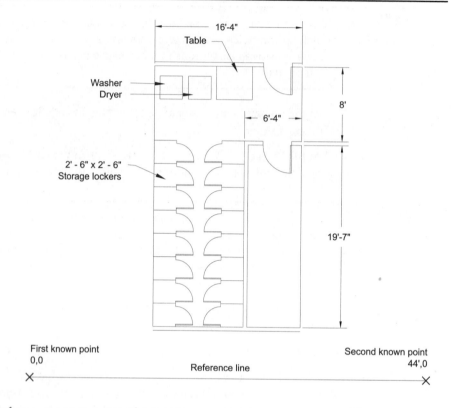

Before you can trace anything into your computer, you must calibrate your tablet. This means you must give some points of reference so AutoCAD can know how distances on the tablet relate to distances in the drawing editor. For example, you may want to trace a drawing that was drawn at a scale of 1/8"=1'-0". You will have to show AutoCAD two specific points on this drawing, as well as where those two points should appear in the drawing editor. This is accomplished by using the Tablet command's Cal option.

NOTE　　When you calibrate a tablet, you are setting ratios for AutoCAD; for example, 2 inches on your tablet equals 16 feet in the drawing editor.

FIGURE 11.3:

The drawing placed on the tablet

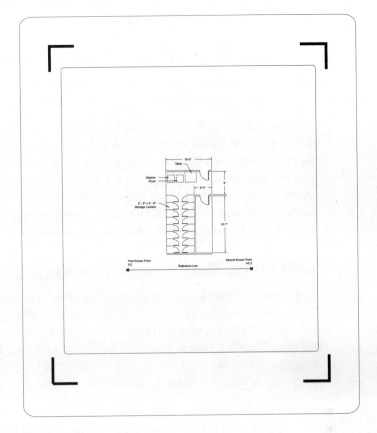

In Figure 11.2, we have already determined the coordinates for two points on a reference line.

1. Choose Tools ➤ Tablet ➤ Calibrate, or enter **Tablet** ↵ **Cal** ↵ at the command prompt.

2. The message "Digitize point #1" appears, asking you to pick the first point for which you know the absolute coordinates. Pick the X on the left end of the reference line.

3. At the Enter coordinates for point #1 prompt, enter **0,0** ↵. This tells AutoCAD that the point you just picked is equivalent to the coordinate 0,0 in your drawing editor.

4. Next, the `Digitize point #2:` prompt asks you to pick another point for which you know the coordinates. Pick the X on the right end of the reference line.

5. At the `Enter coordinates for point #2` prompt, enter **44',0** ⤶.

6. At the `Digitize point #3 (or RETURN to end)` prompt, press ⤶. The tablet is now calibrated.

The word "Tablet" appears on the status bar to tell you that you are in Tablet mode. While in Tablet mode, you can trace the drawing but you cannot access the menus in Windows with some digitizers. (Check your digitizer manual for further information.) If you want to pick a menu item, you must toggle the Tablet mode off by using the F4 function key. Or you can enter commands through the keyboard. (If you need some reminders of the keyboard commands, type **Help** ⤶, and click on Commands from the Help dialog box to get a list.)

Calibrating More than Two Points

In step 6 of the previous exercise, you bypassed the prompt that offered you the chance to calibrate a third point. In fact, you can calibrate as many as 31 points. Why would anyone want to calibrate so many points? Often the drawing or photograph you are trying to trace will be distorted in one direction or another. For example, blueline prints are usually stretched in one direction because of the way prints are rolled through a print machine.

NOTE This section is not crucial to the tutorial and can be skipped for now. You may want to just skim through it and read it more carefully later on.

You can compensate for distortions by specifying several known points during your calibration. For example, we could have included a vertical distance on the utility room drawing to indicate a distance in the y-axis. You could have then picked that distance and calibrated its point. AutoCAD would then have a point of reference for the Y distance as well as the X distance. If you calibrate only two points, as you did in the previous exercise, AutoCAD will scale X and Y distances equally. Calibrating three points causes AutoCAD to scale X and Y distances separately, making adjustments for each axis based on their respective calibration points.

Now suppose you want to trace a perspective view of a building, but you want to "flatten" the perspective so that all the lines are parallel. You can calibrate the four corners of the buildings facade to stretch out the narrow end of the perspective view to be parallel with the wide end. This is a limited form of what cartographers call *rubber-sheeting*, where various areas of the tablet are stretched by specific scale factors.

When you select more than two points for calibration, you will get a message similar to that shown in Figure 11.4. Let's take a look at the parts of this message.

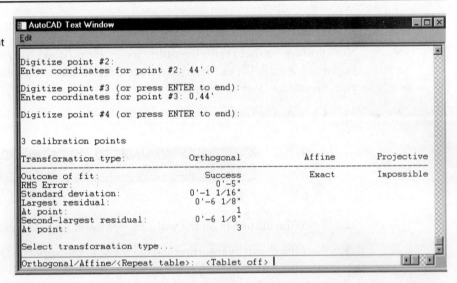

In the text window, you see the labels "Orthogonal," "Affine," and "Projective." These are the three major types of calibrations or transformation types. The orthogonal transformation scales the x- and y-axes using the same values. Affine scales the x- and y-axes separately and requires at least three points. The projective transformation stretches the tablet coordinates differently, depending on where you are on the tablet. It requires at least four calibration points.

Just below each of these labels you will see either "Success," "Exact," or "Impossible." This tells you whether any of these transformation types are available to you. Because this example shows what you see when you pick three points, you get Impossible for the projective transformation.

The far-left column tells you what is shown in each of the other three columns.

Finally, the prompt at the bottom of the screen lets you select which transformation type to use. If you calibrate four or more points, the projective transformation is added to the prompt. The Repeat Table option simply refreshes the table.

Take care when you calibrate points on your tablet. Here are a few things to watch out for when calibrating your tablet:

- Use only known calibration points.

- Try to locate calibration points that cover a large area of your image.

- Don't get carried away. Try to limit calibration points to only those necessary to get the job done.

Tracing Lines from a Drawing

Now you are ready to trace the utility room. If you don't have a digitizer, you can skip this exercise. We've included a traced file on the companion CD-ROM that you can use for later exercises.

1. Click on the Line button on the Draw toolbar, or type **L** ↵.

2. Trace the outline of all the walls except the storage lockers.

3. Add the doors by inserting the Door file at the appropriate points and then mirroring them. The doors may not fit exactly, but you'll get a chance to make adjustments later.

4. Trace the washer and, because the washer and dryer are the same size, copy the washer over to the position of the dryer.

TIP Once a tablet has been calibrated, you can trace your drawing from the tablet, even if the area you are tracing is not displayed in the drawing editor.

At this point, your drawing should look something like the top image of Figure 11.5—a close facsimile of the original drawing, but not as exact as you might like. Zoom in to one of the doors. Now you can see the inaccuracies of tracing. Some of the lines are crooked, and others don't meet at the right points. These inaccuracies are caused by the limited resolution of your tablet, coupled with the lack of steadiness in the human hand. The best digitizing tablets have an accuracy of 0.001 inch, which is actually not very good when you are dealing with tablet distances of 1/8" and smaller. In the following section, you will clean up your drawing.

NOTE   The raggedness of the door arc is the result of the way AutoCAD displays arcs when you use the Zoom command; see Chapter 6 for details.

FIGURE 11.5:

The traced drawing, and a close-up of the door

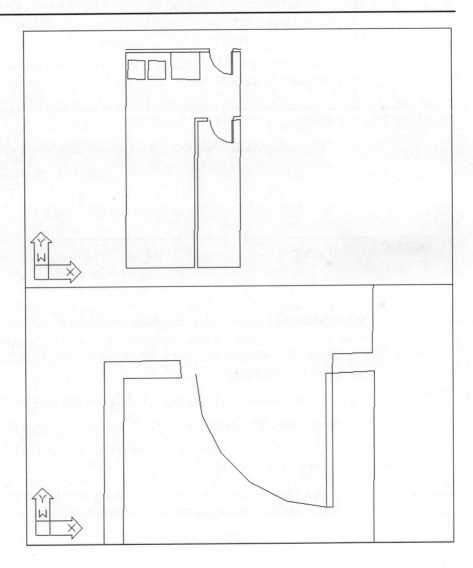

Cleaning Up a Traced Drawing

In this section, you'll reposition a door jamb, straighten some lines, adjust a dimension, and add the storage lockers to the utility room. If you didn't have a chance to digitize your own Utility file, use the file 11a-util.dwg from the companion CD-ROM to do the following exercises.

Moving the End of a Wall   In Figure 11.5, one of the door jambs is not in the right position (the bottom image gives you the best look). In this next exercise, you will fix this by repositioning a group of objects while keeping their vertices intact, using the Grips feature.

1. Pick a crossing window enclosing the door jamb to be moved (see the top image of Figure 11.6).

2. Click on one of the grips at the end of the wall, and then Shift + click on the other grip. You should have two hot grips at the door jamb.

3. Click on the lower of the two hot grips, and drag the corner away to see what happens (see the bottom image of Figure 11.6).

4. Use the Endpoint Osnap to pick the endpoint of the arc. The jamb repositions itself, and all the lines follow (see Figure 11.7).

> **NOTE**
>
> If AutoCAD doesn't respond in the way we've described here, make sure the Verb/Noun selection setting and the Grips feature are both turned on.

Straightening Lines   Another problem in this drawing is that some of the lines are not orthogonal. To straighten them, you use the Change command, together with the Ortho mode. In the following exercise, you'll use the Change command keyboard shortcut.

1. Press the Esc key to clear any grip selections that may be active.

2. Toggle the Ortho mode on.

3. Type -Ch ↵ at the command prompt to start this operation. Make sure you include the minus sign.

4. At the object selection prompt, pick the four lines representing the walls just left of the door, and press ↵ to confirm your selection.

5. At the Properties/<Change point> prompt, click on the corner of where the two walls meet. The four lines straighten out, as shown in Figure 11.8.

6. Once the lines have been straightened, use the Fillet tool in the Modify toolbar to join the corners.

FIGURE 11.6:

A window crossing the door jamb, and the door jamb being stretched

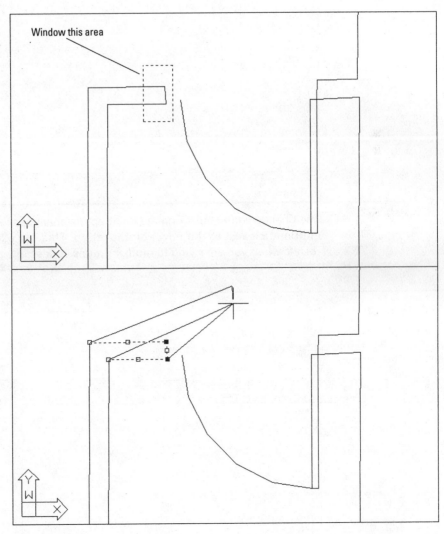

Window this area

FIGURE 11.7:

The repositioned
door jamb

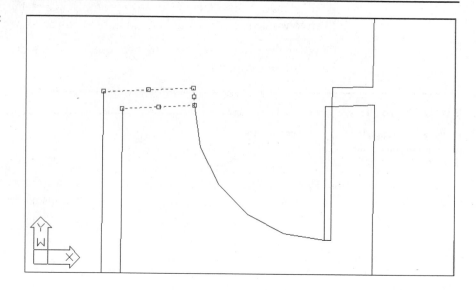

WARNING The Change command's Change Point option changes the location of the endpoint closest to the new point location. This can cause erroneous results when you are trying to modify groups of lines.

FIGURE 11.8:

The lines after using
the Change Point
option of the Change
command

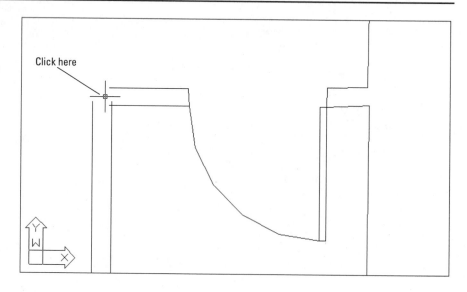

As you have just seen, you can use the Change command to quickly straighten a set of lines. When used carefully, this command can be a real time saver.

WARNING   Be aware that the Change command moves the nearest endpoints of selected lines to the new location. This can cause unpredictable results in some situations (see Figure 11.10). Also note that Change does not affect polyline line segments.

In addition to straightening lines, you can use Change to align a set of lines to another line. For example, when used with the Perpendicular Osnap, several lines can be made to align at a perpendicular angle to another line. However, this only works with the Ortho mode on.

You also can extend several lines to be perpendicular to a nonorthogonal line. To do so, you have to rotate the cursor to that line's angle (see the top image Figure 11.9), using the Snap and system variable. (You can also use the Snap Angle input box in the Tools ➤ Drawing Aids dialog box to rotate the cursor.) Then use the process just described to extend or shorten the other lines (see the bottom image of Figure 11.9).

When changing several lines to be perpendicular to another line, you must carefully choose the new endpoint location. Figure 11.10 shows what happens to the same line work shown in the top image of Figure 11.9 when perpendicular reference is placed in the middle of the set of lines. Some lines are straightened to a perpendicular orientation, while others have the wrong endpoints aligned with the reference line.

Before moving on to the next section, use the Change command to straighten the other lines in your drawing. Start by straightening the corner to the right of the door in Figure 11.8.

1. Issue the Change command again.

2. Select the four lines that represent the walls to the right of the door, and then press ↵.

3. Click on a point near the corner.

4. Chances are, the two vertical lines are not aligned. Move the top line so that it aligns with the lower one. You can use the Perpendicular Osnap to help with the alignment.

5. Use the Change command on each of the other corners until all the walls have been straightened. You can also use Change in a similar way to straighten the door jambs.

6. Once you've straightened the lines, use the Fillet tool on the Modify toolbar to join the corners end to end.

FIGURE 11.9:

You can use the Change command to quickly straighten a set of non-parallel lines and to align their end-points to another reference line.

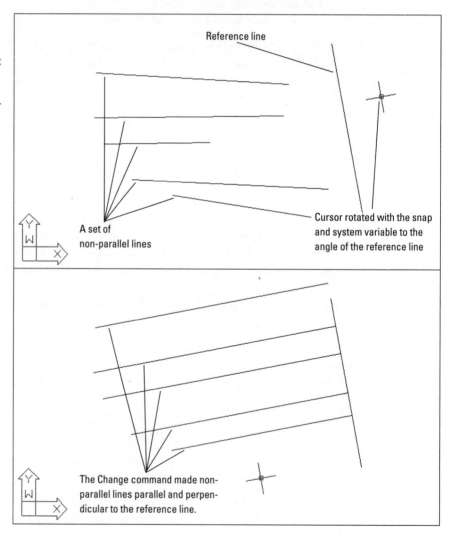

Reference line

A set of non-parallel lines

Cursor rotated with the snap and system variable to the angle of the reference line

The Change command made non-parallel lines parallel and perpendicular to the reference line.

FIGURE 11.10:

The results of the Change command can be unpredictable if the endpoint location is too close to the lines being changed.

Reference line placed in the middle at non-parallel lines

TIP

When using Fillet to join lines, you can issue the Fillet command, and then type **C** ⏎ and enclose the two lines you wish to fillet with a crossing window.

Adjusting the Room Size The overall interior dimension of the original utility room drawing is 16'-4"×28'-0". Chances are the dimensions of the drawing you traced will vary somewhat from these. You will need to adjust your drawing to fit these dimensions.

1. Draw a horizontal line 16'-4" long from the left wall; then draw a vertical line 28' long from the bottom wall line, as shown in Figure 11.11.

2. Use the two lines you drew in step 1 to adjust the walls to their proper positions (see Figure 11.11). You can use either the Grips feature or click Stretch from the Modify toolbar.

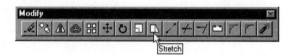

3. Choose Draw ➤ Block ➤ Base, or type **Base** ↵. Then make the upper-left corner of the utility room the base point, near coordinate 13',30'.

4. To add the storage lockers, begin by drawing one 30" x 30" locker accurately.

5. Use the Mirror and Array commands to create the other lockers. Both of these commands are available on the Modify toolbar. (For entering objects repeatedly, this is actually a faster and more accurate method than tracing. If you traced each locker, you would also have to clean up each one.)

Finally, you may want to add the dimensions and labels shown earlier in Figure 11.2.

1. Create a layer called Notes to contain the dimensions and labels.

2. Set the Dimscale dimension setting to 48 before you start dimensioning. This can be done by clicking on Dimension Style from the Dimensioning toolbar, opening the Geometry dialog box, and then entering 48 in the Overall Scale input box (see Chapter 9 for details on this process).

> **NOTE** You can also set the Dimscale dimension setting by typing **Dimscale** ⏎, and then entering the desired scale of 48.

3. Set the text height to 6".

4. When you are done, save the file and exit AutoCAD.

FIGURE 11.11:

The walls stretched to the proper dimensions

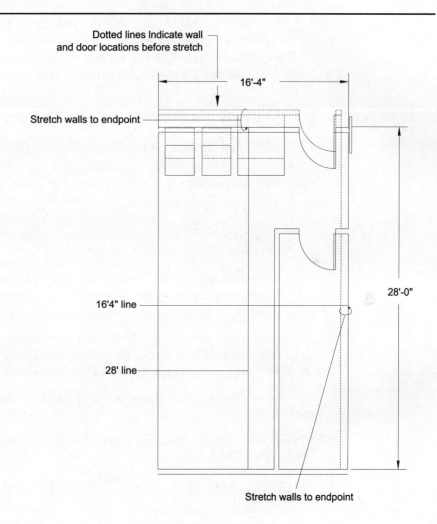

Working Smarter with Digitizers

In the first exercise of this chapter, you traced an entire drawing; however, you could have just traced the major lines with the Ortho mode on, and then used the Offset command to draw the wall thickness. Fillet and Trim (see Chapter 5) could then be used to clean up the drawing where lines cross or where they don't meet.

If you are a civil engineer, you would take a different approach. In laying out a road, for instance, you might first trace in the center lines, and then use the Offset option on the Modify toolbar to place the curb and gutter. You could trace curved features using arcs (just to see what the radius of the curve is), and then redraw the arc accurately, joining straight line segments. The digitizer can be a great tool if it is used with care and a touch of creativity.

Scaling a Drawing

When a hand-drafted drawing is to scale, you can read the drawing's own dimensions or measure distances using an architect's or engineer's scale, and then enter the drawing into AutoCAD as you would a new drawing using these dimensions. Entering distances through the keyboard is slower than tracing, but you don't have to do as much clean up because you are entering the drawing accurately. If the paper drawing has a column grid, input the grid first, and then use the grid as a reference for other dimensions.

When a drawing contains a lot of curves, you'll have to resort to a different scaling method, which is actually an old drafting technique for enlarging or reducing a drawing. The following steps show you how it works.

1. First, draw a grid in AutoCAD to the same proportions as your hand-drafted drawing; that is, if your hand-drafted drawing is 40" by 30", make a 40" by 30" drawing in AutoCAD with grids spaced at 1/4" intervals.

2. Plot this grid on translucent media and place it over the original paper drawing.

3. Place points on the plotted grid where the curves of the original drawing intersect the grid lines of the plot.

4. Finally, copy those intersection points from the plotted grid to the AutoCAD file of the grid.

5. Once you have positioned these points in your AutoCAD file, you can connect them to form the curves by using AutoCAD spline curves.

This method is somewhat time-consuming and not very accurate, but it will work in a pinch. If you plan to enter many drawings containing curves, it's best to purchase a tablet and trace them, or consider scanning or using a scanning service.

Scanning a Drawing

No discussion of drawing input can be complete without mentioning scanners. Imagine how easy it would be to convert an existing library of drawings into AutoCAD drawing files by simply running them through a scanning device. Unfortunately, scanning drawings is not quite that simple.

In scanning, the drawing size can be a problem. Desktop scanners are generally limited to an 8½×14" sheet size. Many low-cost handheld scanners will scan a 22"×14" area. Larger-format scanners are available but more expensive.

Once the drawing is scanned and saved as a file, you have two paths to importing it into AutoCAD. One path is to convert the scanned image into AutoCAD objects such as lines, arcs, and circles. This requires special software and is usually a fairly time-consuming process. Finally, the drawing usually requires some clean up, which can take even longer than cleaning up a traced drawing. The poorer the condition of the original drawing, the more clean up you'll have to do.

Another path is to import a scanned image directly into AutoCAD and then use some or all of the scanned image in combination with AutoCAD objects. You can trace over the scanned image using the standard AutoCAD tools and then discard the image when you are done, or you can use the scanned image as part of your AutoCAD file. With Release 14's ability to import raster images, you can, for example, import a scanned image of an existing paper drawing, and then mask off the area you wish to edit. You can then draw over the masked portions to make the required changes.

Whether a scanner can help you depends on your application. If you have drawings that would be very difficult to trace—large, complex topographical maps, for example—a scanner may well be worth a look. You don't necessarily have to buy one; some scanning services offer excellent value. And if you can accept the quality of a scanned drawing before it is cleaned up, you can save a lot of time. On the other hand, a drawing composed mostly of orthogonal lines and notes may be more easily traced by hand with a large tablet or entered directly by using the drawing's dimensions.

Scanning can be an excellent document management tool for your existing paper drawings. You might consider scanning your existing paper drawings for archiving purposes. You can then use portions or all of your scanned drawings later, without committing to a full-scale, paper-to-AutoCAD scan conversion.

Importing and Tracing Raster Images

If you have a scanner and you would like to use it to import drawings and other images into AutoCAD, you can use AutoCAD's raster image import capabilities. There are many reasons for wanting to import a scanned image. In architectural plans, a vicinity map is frequently used to show the location of a project. With the permission of its creator, you can scan a map into AutoCAD and incorporate it into a cover sheet. That cover sheet may also contain other images, such as photographs of the site, computer renderings and elevations of the project, and company logos.

Another use for importing scanned images is to use the image as a reference to trace over. The first part of this section will show you how you might accomplish this task.

The Insert ➤ Raster Image… option in the pull-down menu opens the Image dialog box, which in turn allows you to import a full range of raster image files.

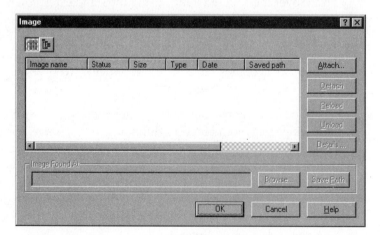

If you read Chapter 6, then this dialog box should look familiar. It looks and works just like the External Reference dialog box. The similarities are more than just cosmetic. Just like External References, raster images are loaded when the current file is open but they are not stored as part of the current file when the file is saved. This helps keep file sizes down, but it also means that you need to keep track of inserted raster files. You will need to make sure that they are kept together with the AutoCAD files in which they are inserted.

Tips for Importing Raster Images

When you scan a document into your computer, you get a raster image file. Unlike AutoCAD files, raster image files are made up of a matrix of colors that form a picture. Vector files, like those produced by AutoCAD, are made up of lines, arcs, curves, and circles. The two formats, raster and vector, are so different that it is difficult to accurately convert one format to the other. It is easier to trace a raster file in AutoCAD than it is to try to have some computer program make the conversion for you.

But even tracing a raster image file can be difficult if the image is of poor quality. Here are a few points you should consider if you plan to use raster import for tracing drawings:

- Scan in your drawing using a grayscale or color scanner, or convert your black-and-white scanned image to grayscale using your scanner software.

- Use a paint program or your scanner software to clean up unwanted gray or spotted areas in the file before importing into AutoCAD.

- If your scanner software or paint program has a de-speckle or de-spot routine, use it. It can help clean up your image and ultimately reduce the raster image file size.

- Scan at a reasonable resolution. Remember that the human hand is usually not more accurate than a few thousandths of an inch, so scanning at 150 to 200 dpi may be more than adequate.

- If you plan to make heavy use of raster import, upgrade your computer to the fastest processor you can afford and don't spare the memory.

The raster import commands can incorporate paper maps or plans into 3D AutoCAD drawings for presentations. I know of one architectural firm that produces some very impressive presentations with very little effort, by combining 2D scanned images with 3D massing models for urban design studies. (A massing model is a model that shows only the rough outline of buildings without giving too much detail. They show the general scale of a project without being too fussy.) Raster images do not, however, appear in perspective views.

TIP AutoCAD offers a "suitcase" utility that will collect AutoCAD files and their related support files, such as raster images, external references, and fonts, into any folder or drive that you specify. See Chapter 19 for details.

Another similarity between Xrefs and imported raster images is that you can clip a raster image so that only a portion of the image is displayed in your drawing. Portions of a raster file that are clipped will not be stored in memory, so your system won't get bogged down, even if the raster file is huge.

NEW! The following exercise gives you step by step instructions on importing a raster file. It will also give you a chance to see how scanned resolution translates into an image in AutoCAD. This is important for those readers interested in scanning drawings for the purpose of tracing over them.

1. Create a new file called `Rastertrace`.

2. Set up the file as a 1/4"=1'-scale architectural drawing on an 8½×11" sheet (limits set to 0,0 for the lower -left corner and 528,408 for the upper-right corner).

3. Choose View ➢ Zoom ➢ All to make sure the entire drawing limits are displayed on the screen.

4. Draw a line across the screen from coordinates 0,20' to 60',20'. You will use this line in a later exercise.

5. Click on Insert ➢ Raster Image…, or type **Im** ↵ to open the Image dialog box.

6. Click on the Attach button in the upper-right of the dialog box. The Select file to attach dialog box appears. This is a typical AutoCAD File dialog box complete with a preview window.

7. Locate and select the `Raster1.jpg` file from the companion CD-ROM. Notice that you can see a preview of the file in the right side of the dialog box.

8. Click Open. The Attach Image dialog box appears. Click OK.

9. Press ↵ at the Insertion Point prompt to accept the 0,0 coordinates.

10. At the Scale Factor prompt, use the cursor to scale the image so it fills about half the screen, as shown in Figure 11.12.

TIP   You can bypass the Image dialog box and go directly to the Attach Image dialog box by entering **lat** ↵ at the command prompt.

The Image Dialog Box Options

The Attach Image dialog box you saw above in step 7 helps you manage your imported image files. It is especially helpful when you have a large number of images in your drawing. Like the External Reference dialog box, you can temporarily unload images (to help speed up editing of AutoCAD objects) reload, detach, and relocate raster images files. Refer to *Other External Reference Options* in Chapter 6 for a detailed description of these options.

FIGURE 11.12:

Manually scaling the
raster image

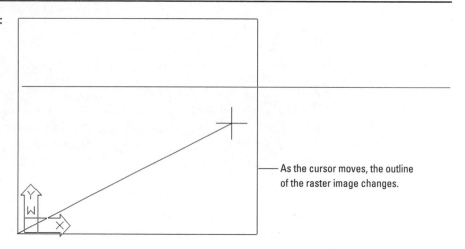

As the cursor moves, the outline
of the raster image changes.

Scaling a Raster Image

The Raster1.jpg from the companion CD-ROM file is a scanned image of
Figure 11.2. It was scanned as a gray scale image at 100 dpi. This shows that you
can get a reasonable amount of detail at a fairly low scan resolution.

Now suppose you wanted to trace over this image to start an AutoCAD drawing. Try the following steps to see how you might begin the process.

1. Choose View ➤ Zoom ➤ Extents.

2. Click on Scale from the Modify toolbar.

3. Click on the edge of the raster image to select it. A crosshatch will appear
    across the image to tell you that it is selected.

4. Press ↵ to finish your selection.

5. At the Base Point prompt, click on the X in the lower-left corner of the image—the one you used in the first exercise to calibrate your digitizing tablet.

6. At the Scale factor>/Reference prompt, enter **R** ↵ to use the Reference option.

7. At the Reference Length prompt, type @ ↵. This tells AutoCAD that you want to use the last point selected as one end of the reference length. Once you enter the @ symbol, you'll see a rubber-banding line emanating from the X.

8. At the Second Point prompt, click on the X at the lower-right corner of the image.

9. At the New Length prompt, enter **44'** ↵. The image enlarges. Remember that this reference line is 44 feet in length relative to the utility room plan.

The image is now scaled properly for the plan it portrays. You can proceed to trace over the image. You can also place the image on its own layer and turn it off from time to time to check your trace work.

Controlling Object Visibility and Overlap with Raster Images

With the introduction of raster image support, AutoCAD inherits a problem fairly common to programs that use them. Raster images will obscure other objects that were placed before the raster image. The image you imported in the last exercise, for example, obscures the line you drew when you first opened the file. In most cases, this overlap may not be a problem, but there will be situations where you will want AutoCAD vector objects to overlap an imported raster image. An example of this would be a civil engineering drawing showing an AutoCAD drawing of a new road superimposed over an aerial view of the location for the road.

Paint and page-layout programs usually offer a "to front" and "to back" tool to control the overlap of objects and images. AutoCAD offers the Draworder command. Here's how it works.

1. Choose View ➢ Zoom ➢ Extents to get an overall view of the image.

2. Choose Tools ➢ Display Order ➢ Bring Above Object.

3. At the `Select object` prompt, select the horizontal line you drew when you first opened the file.

4. You could go on to select other objects. Press ↵ to finish your selection.

5. At the `Select Reference Object` prompt, click on the edge of the raster image of the Utility room.

The drawing regenerates and the entire line appears, no longer obscured by the raster image.

The Draworder command you just used actually offers four options. On the pull-down menu, these options are:

Tools ➢ Display Order ➢ Bring to Front   places an object or set of objects at the top of the draw order for the entire drawing. The effect is that the objects are completely visible.

Tools ➢ Display Order ➢ Send to Back   places an object or set of objects at the bottom of the draw order for the entire drawing. The effect is that the objects may be obscured by other objects in the drawing.

Tools ➢ Display Order ➢ Bring Above Object   places an object or set of objects above another object in the draw order. This has the effect of making the first set of objects appear above the second selected object.

Tools ➢ Display Order ➢ Bring Under Object   places an object or set of objects below another object in the draw order. This has the effect of making the first set of objects appear underneath the second selected object.

You can also use the **Dr** ↵ keyboard shortcut to issue the Draworder command. If you do this, you see this prompt:

```
Above object/Under object/Front/<Back>:
```

You must then select the option by entering through the keyboard the capitalized letter of the option.

Although we've discussed the Display order tools in relation to raster images, they can also be invaluable in controlling visibility of line work in conjunction with hatch patterns and solid fills. See Chapter 13 for a detailed discussion of the display order tools and solid fills.

TIP
Under certain conditions, the draw order of external reference files may not appear properly. If you encounter this problem, open the Xref file and make sure the draw order is correct. Then use the Wblock command to export all its objects to a new file. Use the new file as for the external reference instead of the original external reference.

Clipping a Raster Image

NEW!
In Chapter 6, you saw how you can clip an External Reference object so that only a portion of it appears in the drawing. You can also clip imported raster images in the same way. Just as with Xrefs, you can create a closed outline of the area you want to clip, or you can specify a simple rectangular area. In the following exercise, you'll try out the Imageclip command to control the display of the raster image.

1. Choose Modify ➤ Object ➤ Image Clip, or type **Icl** ↵.

2. At the Select Image to Clip prompt, click on the edge of the raster image.

3. At the ON/OFF/Delete/<New boundary> prompt, press ↵ to create a new boundary.

4. At the Polygonal/<Rectangular> prompt, enter **P** ↵ to draw a polygonal boundary.

5. Select the points shown in the top image of Figure 11.13, and then press ↵ when you are done. The raster image is clipped to the boundary you created, as shown in the continued image of Figure 11.13.

As the prompt in step 3 indicates, you can turn the clipping off or on, or delete an existing clipping boundary through the Image Clip option.

Once you have clipped a raster image, you can adjust the clipping boundary using its grips.

1. Click on the boundary edge of the raster image to expose its grips.

2. Click on a grip in the upper-right corner, as shown in the continued image of Figure 11.13.

3. Drag the grip up and to the right, and then click on a point. The image adjusts to the new boundary.

FIGURE 11.13:

Adjusting the boundary of a clipped image

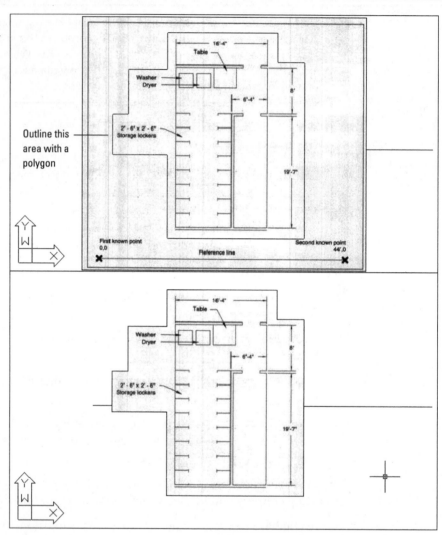

In addition to hiding portions of a raster image that may be unimportant to you, clipping an image file will reduce the amount of RAM the raster image uses during your editing session. AutoCAD will only load the visible portion of the image into RAM. The rest is ignored.

FIGURE 11.13:
CONTINUED

Adjusting the boundary
of a clipped image

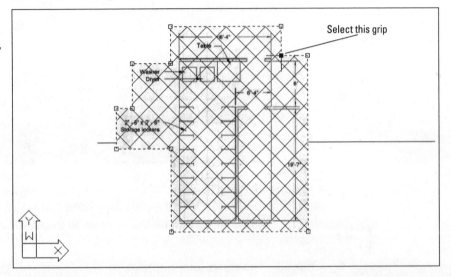

TIP

The Wipeout tool in the Bonus Standard toolbar can also mask out a portion of a raster image. This is useful if you want to hide portions of a raster image that may make it difficult to view overlapping AutoCAD objects such as text or dimensions. Wipeout can also be useful as a general masking tool for AutoCAD objects. See Chapter 19 for details on how this tool works.

Adjusting Brightness, Contrast, and Strength

NEW!

AutoCAD offers a tool that allows you to adjust the brightness, contrast, and strength of a raster image. Try making some adjustments to the raster image of the utility room in the following exercise.

1. Choose Modify ➢ Object ➢ Image ➢ Adjust, or type **Iad** ↵.

2. At the Select Image to Adjust prompt, click on the edge of the raster image. The Image Adjust dialog box appears.

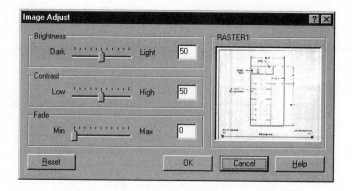

3. Click and drag the Fade slider to the right so that it is near the middle of the slider scale. Or enter 50 in the Fade input box that is just to the right of the slider. Notice how the sample image fades to the AutoCAD background color as you move the slider.

4. Click OK. The raster image appears faded.

You can adjust the brightness and contrast using the other two sliders in the Image Adjust dialog box. The Reset button resets all the settings to their default value.

By using the Image Adjust option in conjunction with image clipping, you can create special effects. Figure 11.14 shows an aerial view of downtown San Francisco. This view consists of two copies of the same raster image. One copy serves as a background, which was lightened using the same method demonstrated in the previous exercise. The second copy is the darker area of the image with a triangular clip boundary applied. You might use this technique to bring focus to a particular area of a drawing you are preparing for a presentation.

Figure 11.14 also contains AutoCAD text and line objects drawn over the image. The text labels make use of the Wipeout bonus tool to hide their background, making them easier to read. The Draworder command is also instrumental in creating this type of image by allowing you to control which object appears on top of others.

TIP　　If the draw order of objects appears incorrectly after opening a file or performing a pan or zoom, issue a Regen to recover the correct draw order view.

FIGURE 11.14:

Two copies of the same image can be combined to create emphasis on a portion of the drawing.

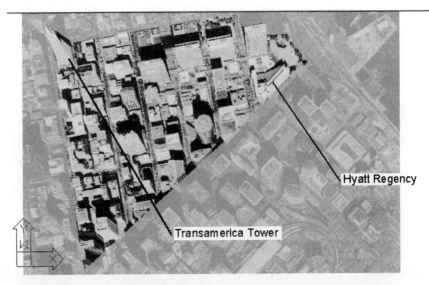

Hyatt Regency

Transamerica Tower

Turning off the Frame, Adjusting Overall Quality, and Transparency

Three other adjustments can be made to your raster image. Frame visibility, image quality, and image transparency.

By default, a raster image will display an outline or frame. In many instances, this frame may detract from your drawing. You can globally turn off image frames by choosing Modify ➤ Object ➤ Image ➤ Frame; then entering On or Off depending on whether you want the frame visible or invisible (see Figure 11.15). You can also type **Imageframe** ↵ **Of** ↵.

> **WARNING**
>
> If you turn off the frame of raster images, you will not be able to select them for editing. You can use this to your advantage if you don't want a raster image to be moved or otherwise edited. To make a raster image selectable, turn on the image frame setting.

If your drawing doesn't require the highest-quality image, you can set the image quality to Draft mode. You might use Draft mode when you are tracing an image, or when the image is already of a high quality. To set the image quality, choose Modify ➤ Object ➤ Image ➤ Quality, and then enter **H** for high quality or **D** for Draft mode. In Draft mode, your drawing will regenerate faster.

A raster image with the frame on (top) and off (bottom)

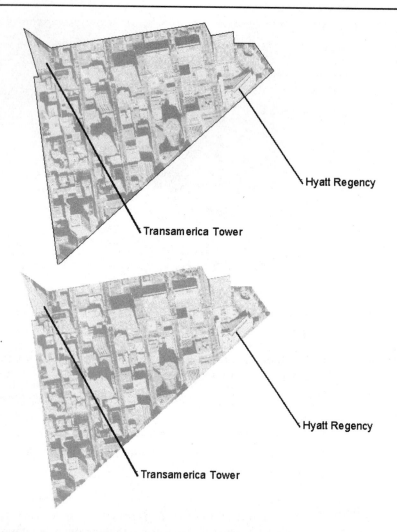

Hyatt Regency

Transamerica Tower

Hyatt Regency

Transamerica Tower

The High mode softens the pixels of the raster image giving the image a smoother appearance. The Draft mode displays the image in a "raw," pixelated state. If you look carefully at the regions between the building and its shadow in the top image of Figure 11.16, you will see that it appears a bit jagged. The bottom image of Figure 11.16 uses the High setting to soften the edges of the building.

A close up of a raster image with quality set to high (top) and draft (bottom)

Finally, you can control the transparency of raster image files that allow transparent pixels. Some file formats, such as the CompuServe GIF 89a format, allow you to set a color in the image to be transparent (usually the background color). Most image-editing programs support this format because it is a popular one used on Web pages.

By turning on the Transparency setting, objects normally obscured by the background of a raster image may show through. Choose Modify ➤ Object ➤ Image ➤ Transparency, and then select the raster image that you wish to make transparent. Enter On or Off depending on whether you want the image to be transparent or not. Unlike the Frame and Quality options, Transparency works on individual objects rather than globally.

> **TIP**
> If you want quick access to the Transparency setting, along with other raster image settings, the Properties tool in the Object Properties toolbar offers many of the same adjustments described in this section. You can access the Image Adjust dialog box, hide or display clipped areas, or hide the entire raster image.

Importing PostScript Images

In addition to raster import, you can use the built-in PostScript import feature to import PostScript files. This feature can be accessed by choosing Insert ➤ Encapsulated PostScript or by typing **Import** ↵ ↵. The Import File dialog box lets you easily locate the file to be imported. Select Encapsulated PostScript (.eps) from the List Files of Type pull-down list, and then browse to find the file you want. Once you select a file, the rest of the program works just like the raster import commands. You are asked for an insertion point, a scale, and a rotation angle. Once you've answered all the prompts, the image appears in the drawing.

> **TIP**
> AutoCAD supports Drag and Drop for many raster file formats, including PostScript .eps.

You can make adjustments to the quality of imported PostScript files by using the Psquality system variable (enter **Psquality** ↵). This setting takes an integer value in the range -75 to 75, with 75 being the default. The absolute value of this setting is taken as the ratio of pixels to drawing units. If, for example, Psquality is set to 50 or -50, then Psin will convert 50 pixels of the incoming PostScript file into 1 drawing unit. You use negative values to indicate that you want outlines of filled areas rather than the full painted image. Using outlines can save drawing space and improve readability on monochrome systems or systems with limited color capability.

Finally, if Psquality is set to 0, only the bounding box of the imported image is displayed in the drawing. Though you may only see a box, the image data is still incorporated into the drawing and will be maintained as the image is exported (using Psout).

Another system variable you will want to know about is Psdrag, which controls how the imported PostScript image appears at the insertion point prompt. Normally, Psdrag is set to 0, so Psin displays just the outline (bounding box) of the imported file as you move it into position. To display the full image of the imported PostScript file as you locate an insertion point, you can set Psdrag to 1. Access Psdrag from the pull-down menus by choosing File ➤ Options ➤ PostScript Display.

TIP
If you need PostScript fonts in your .eps output files, you can use AutoCAD fonts as substitutes. AutoCAD will convert fonts with specific code names to PostScript fonts during the .eps export process. See Appendix B for details.

If You Want to Experiment...

If you want to see firsthand how the PostScript import and export commands work, you can try the following exercise.

1. Open the Plan file.

TIP
This sequence of steps is a quick way to convert a 3D model into a 2D line drawing. You may want to make note of this as you work through the later chapters on 3D.

2. Choose File ➤ Export to open the Export Data dialog box. Select Encapsulated PostScript (.eps) in the List Files of Type pull-down list. You can also

type **Psout** ↵ at the command prompt. This will open the Create PostScript File dialog box and allow you to select or enter a file name.

3. Click the Options button. The Export Options dialog box appears.

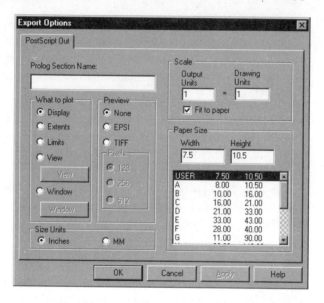

This dialog box offers options similar to the Plot Configuration dialog box.

4. Select the desired area to plot, sheet size, scale, and units from the dialog box; then click OK.

5. At the File dialog box, click on Save to accept the suggested PostScript file name of Plan.eps.

6. Click on Save in the Export Data box.

TIP

You may notice that arcs, circles, and curves are not very smooth when you use this method to export, and then import, PostScript files. To improve the appearance of arcs and curves, specify a large sheet size at the Enter the Size or Width,Height (in Inches) <USER> prompt.

---

7. Choose Insert ➤ Encapsulated PostScript... to open the Select PostScript File dialog box.

8. Locate and select the Plan.eps file. You will be prompted for Insertion point and Scale factor. Position and size the image as required. The file then appears in your drawing.

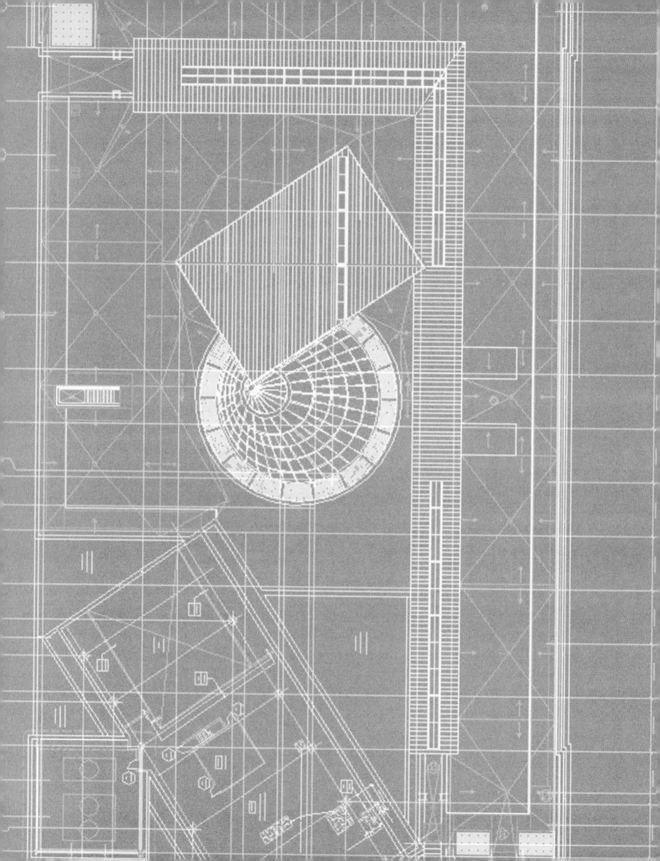

CHAPTER

TWELVE

12

Advanced Editing Methods

- Editing More Efficiently

- Using Grips to Simplify Editing

- Using External References (Xrefs)

- Switching to Paper Space

- Advanced Tools: Selection Filter and Calculator

Because you may not know all of a project's requirements when it begins, you usually base the first draft of a design on projected needs. As the plan goes forward, you make adjustments for new requirements as they arise. As more people enter the project, additional design restrictions come into play and the design is further modified. This process continues throughout the project, from first draft to end product.

In this chapter you will review much of what you've already learned. Throughout the process, you will look at some techniques for setting up drawings to help manage the continual changes a project undergoes. You will also be introduced to new tools and techniques you can use to minimize duplication of work. AutoCAD can be a powerful timesaving tool if used properly. In this chapter, we'll examine methods of harnessing that power.

Editing More Efficiently

The apartment building plan you've been working on is currently incomplete. For example, you need to add the utility room you created in Chapter 11. In the real world, this building plan would also undergo innumerable changes as the project developed. Wall and door locations would change, and more notes and dimensions would be added. However, in the space of this book's tutorials, we can't develop these drawings to full completion. But, we can give you a sample of what is in store while using AutoCAD on such a project.

In this section, you will add a closet to the Unit plan (you will update the Plan file later in this chapter). In the editing you've already done, you've probably found that you use the following commands frequently: Move, Offset, Fillet, Trim, Grips, and the Osnap overrides. Now you will learn some ways to shorten your editing time by using them more efficiently.

Quick Access to Your Favorite Commands

As you continue to work with AutoCAD, you'll find that you use a handful of commands 90 percent of the time. You can collect your favorite commands into a single toolbar using AutoCAD's toolbar customization feature. This way, you can have ready access to your most frequently used commands. Chapter 21 gives you all the information you need to create your own custom toolbars.

Editing an Existing Drawing

First, let's look at how you can add a closet to the Unit plan. You'll begin by copying existing objects to provide the basis for the closet.

1. Open the Unit file.

2. Make Wall the current layer by trying the following: Click on the Make Object Layer Current button on the Object Properties toolbar, and then click on a wall line.

3. Make sure the Notes and Flr-pat layers are frozen. This will keep your drawing clear of objects you won't be editing.

4. If they are not already on, turn on Noun/Verb Selection and the Grips feature.

5. Click on the right-side wall, and then click on its midpoint grip.

6. Enter **C** ↵ to start the Copy mode; then enter **@2'<180**↵ (see Figure 12.1).

7. Press the Esc key to exit the Grip mode.

8. Zoom in to the entry area shown in Figure 12.2.

9. Click Offset from the Modify toolbar, or type **O** ↵.

10. At the Offset distance or through prompt, use the Nearest Osnap and pick the outside wall of the bathroom near the door, as shown in Figure 12.2.

11. At the Second point prompt, use the Perpendicular Osnap override and pick the other side of that wall (see Figure 12.2).

12. Click on the copy of the wall line you just created, and then on a point to the left of it.

13. Press ↵ to exit the Offset command.

FIGURE 12.1:

Copying the wall to start the closet

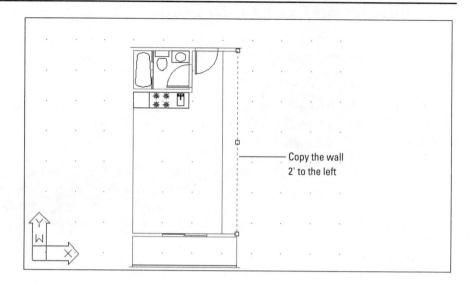

Copy the wall
2' to the left

FIGURE 12.2:

Using an existing wall as a distance reference for copying

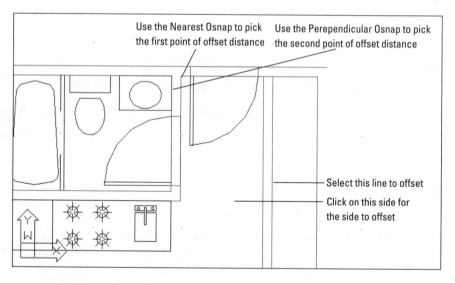

Use the Nearest Osnap to pick the first point of offset distance

Use the Perependicular Osnap to pick the second point of offset distance

Select this line to offset

Click on this side for the side to offset

In steps 9 and 10 of the previous exercise, you determined the offset distance by selecting existing geometry. If you know you want to duplicate a distance, but don't know what that distance is, you can often use existing objects as references.

Next, use the same idea to copy a few more lines for the other side of the closet.

1. Click to highlight the two horizontal lines that make up the wall at the top of your view.

2. Shift + click on the midpoint grips of these lines (see Figure 12.3).

3. Click again on one of the midpoint grips, and then enter **C** ↵ to select the Copy option.

4. Enter **B** ↵ to select a base point option.

5. Use the upper-right corner of the bathroom for the base point, and the lower-right corner of the kitchen as the second point.

6. Press Esc twice to clear the grip selection.

FIGURE 12.3:

Adding the second closet wall

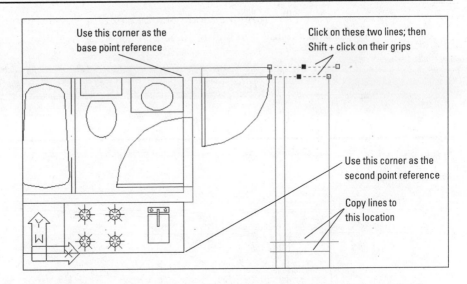

 **NOTE**   In these exercises, you are asked to enter the grip options through the keyboard. This can be a quicker method to access the copy and base grip options. You can also right-click on your mouse and select the Copy and Base options from the pop-up menu.

Now you've got the general layout of the closet. The next step is to clean up the corners. First, you'll have to do a bit of prep work and break the wall lines near the wall intersections, as shown in Figure 12.4.

1. Click on Break from the Modify toolbar. This tool creates a gap in a line, arc, or circle.

2. Click on the vertical wall to the far right at a point near the location of the new wall (see Figure 12.4).

3. Click on the vertical line again near the point you selected in step 2 to create a small gap, as shown in Figure 12.4.

4. Use the Break tool again to create a gap in the horizontal line at the top of the unit, near the door, as shown in Figure 12.4.

5. Click Fillet from the Modify toolbar, or type **F** ↵ and join the corners of the wall as shown in Figure 12.5.

FIGURE 12.4:

Breaking the wall lines

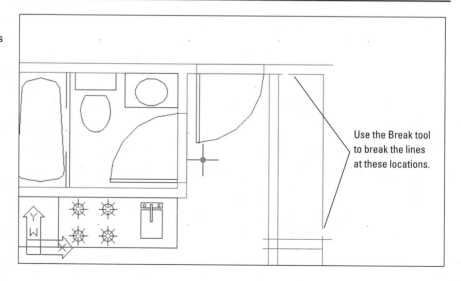

Use the Break tool to break the lines at these locations.

FIGURE 12.5:

Filleting the corners

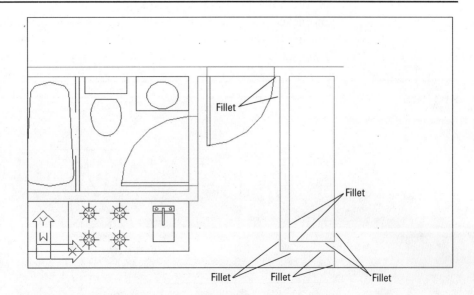

In steps 2 and 3 above, you didn't have to be too exact about where to pick the break points because Construct ➤ Fillet takes care of joining the wall lines exactly. Now you are ready to add the finishing touches.

1. At the closet door location, draw a line from the midpoint of the interior closet wall to the exterior (see the top image of Figure 12.6). Make sure this line is on the Jamb layer.

2. Offset the new line 3' in both directions. These new lines are the closet door jambs.

3. Erase the first line you drew at the midpoint of the closet wall.

4. Click on Trim from the Modify toolbar, or type **Tr** ↵.

5. Click on the two jambs, and then press ↵.

6. Type **F** ↵ to invoke the Fence Selection option; then click on a point to the left of the wall, as shown in the bottom image of Figure 12.6.

7. As you move the cursor, you see a rubber-banding line from the last point you picked. Click on a point to the right of the closet wall so the rubber-banding line crosses over the two wall lines, as shown in the top image of Figure 12.6.

FIGURE 12.6:

Constructing the closet door jambs

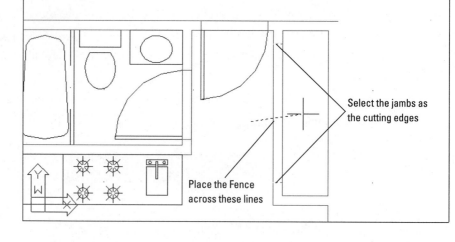

First, draw this line...

...then, offset above and below to these locations

Select the jambs as the cutting edges

Place the Fence across these lines

8. Press ↵ to finish your Fence selection. The wall lines trim back to the jambs.

9. Press ↵ again to exit the Trim command.

10. As shown in Figure 12.7, add door headers and the sliding doors and assign these objects to their appropriate layers.

FIGURE 12.7:

The finished closet

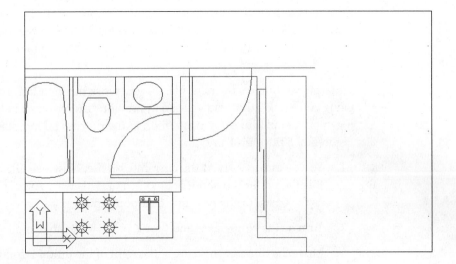

11. Use File ➤ Save to save the file. If you used the file from the companion CD-ROM, use File ➤ Save As and save the file under the name **Unit**.

TIP You can use the Match Properties tool to make a set of objects match the layer of another object. Click Match Properties from the Standard toolbar, select the objects whose layer you want to match, and then select the objects you want to assign to the objects layer. See Chapter 6 for more on the Match Properties tool.

In this exercise, you used the Fence selection to select the objects you wanted to trim. You could have selected each line individually by clicking on them, but the fence option offered you a quick way to select a set of objects without having to be too precise about where they are selected. You'll get a closer look at the Fence selection option a bit later in this chapter.

This exercise also shows that it's easier to trim lines back and then draw them back in than to try to break them precisely at each jamb location. At first this may seem counterproductive, but trimming the lines and then drawing in headers actually takes fewer steps and is a less tedious operation than some other routes. And the end result is a door that is exactly centered on the closet space.

Building on Previously Drawn Objects

Suppose your client decides your apartment building design needs a few one-bedroom units. In this exercise, you will use the studio unit drawing as a basis for the one-bedroom unit. To do so, you will double the studio's size, add a bedroom, move the kitchenette, rearrange and add closets, and move the entry doors. In the process of editing this new drawing, you will see how you can build on previously drawn objects.

Start by setting up the new file. As you work through this exercise, you'll be using commands that you've seen in previous exercises, so I won't bother describing every detail. But do pay attention to the process taking place, as shown in Figures 12.8 through 12.12.

1. You've already saved the current Unit file. Now use File ➤ Save As to save this file under the name of Unit2.dwg. This way, you can use the current file as the basis for the new one-bedroom unit.

2. Turn on the Notes layer and type **Z** ↵ **A** ↵ to get an overall view of the drawing.

3. Move the dimension string at the right of the unit, 14'-5" further to the right, and copy the unit the same distance to the right. Your drawing should look like Figure 12.8.

FIGURE 12.8:

The copied unit

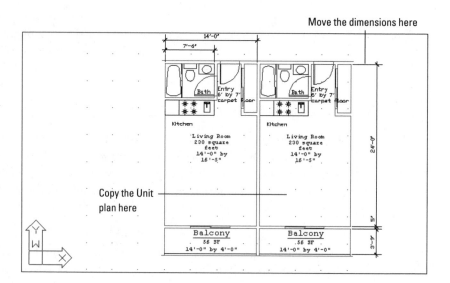

4. Now erase the bathroom, kitchen, door, closet, room labels, and wall lines, as shown in Figure 12.9.

NOTE   Although you could be more selective in step 4 about the objects you erase, and then add line segments where there are gaps in walls, this is considered bad form. When editing files, it's wise to keep lines continuous rather than fragmented. Adding line segments increases the size of the drawing database and slows down editing operations.

FIGURE 12.9:

Objects to be erased

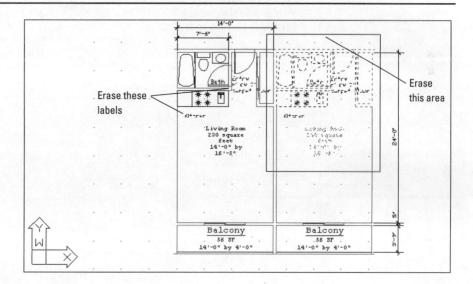

Using the Tracking Feature

The living room of this one-bedroom unit will be on the right side. You will want to move the Living Room label from the left half to the right half. Normally, you would probably just move the label without worrying about accuracy, but we'll use this opportunity to show how the Tracking feature works. In the next exercise, you will place the Living Room label in the center of the living room area.

1. Click on the Living Room label in the unit to the left.

2. Click on the top-center grip in the label, as shown in the top image of Figure 12.10.

FIGURE 12.10:

Using the Tracking feature to move the Living Room label to the center of the new living room

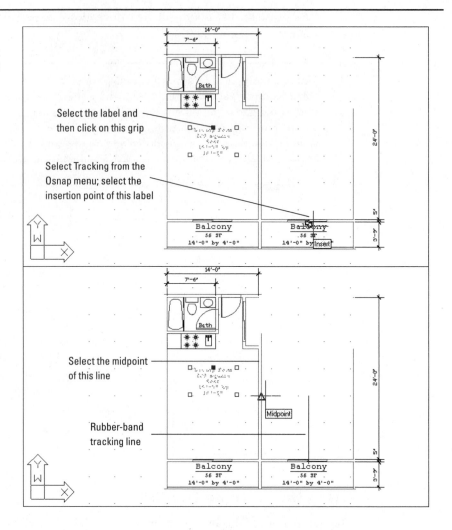

3. Shift + right-click the mouse to open the Osnap menu.

4. Select Tracking.

5. Shift + right-click again, and then select Insert from the Osnap menu.

6. Click on the insertion point of the Balcony label of the unit to the right, as shown in the top image of Figure 12.10. Notice a rubber-banding line emanating from the selected insertion point, as shown in the bottom image of Figure 12.10.

7. Shift + right-click again and select Midpoint.

8. This time, click on the midpoint of the vertical wall between the two units as shown in the bottom image of Figure 12.10. Notice that the rubber-banding line now emanates from a point that represents the intersection of the text insertion point and the midpoint of the wall.

9. Press ↵. The text moves to the middle of the unit to the right.

Tracking works by allowing you to select points that are aligned orthogonally, like the insertion point of the balcony text and the midpoint of the wall in the previous exercise. The following example shows how you can use Tracking to move the endpoint of a line to align with the endpoint of another line.

1. Click on the line at the top-right side of the unit to expose its grips, as shown in the top image of Figure 12.11.

2. Click on the grip at the right end of the line.

3. As in the previous exercise, select Tracking from Osnap menu.

4. Open the Osnap menu again and select Endpoint.

5. Select the rightmost Endpoint of the short line at the bottom-right corner of the unit, as shown in the top image of Figure 12.11.

6. Select Perpendicular from the Osnap menu, and then click on the horizontal line you selected in step 1 (see the bottom image of Figure 12.11).

7. Press ↵ to exit the Tracking mode.

8. Press the Esc key twice to clear the grip selection.

9. Move the kitchen to the opposite corner of the unit, as shown in the top image of Figure 12.12.

10. Click on the Move tool and select the closet area, as shown in Figure 12.12.

11. Move the closet down 5'-5", as shown in the bottom image of Figure 12.12. You can use the corners of the bathroom as reference points.

FIGURE 12.11:

Stretching a line using the Tracking function

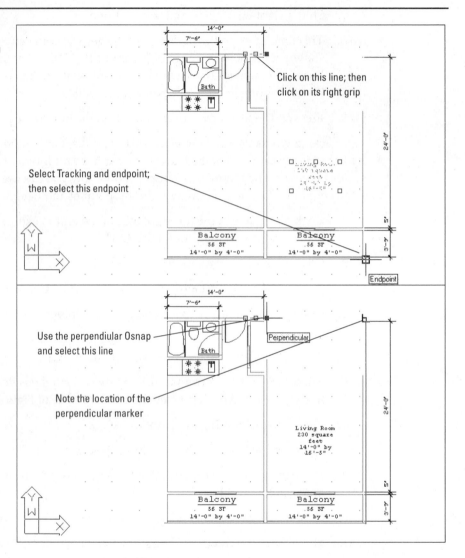

TIP

You may have noticed that while in Tracking mode, you always see a rubber-banding line from the last point selected. Remember that the point from which the rubber-banding line emanates is the point AutoCAD will select when you press ↵ to exit the Tracking mode.

FIGURE 12.12:

Moving the closet and kitchen

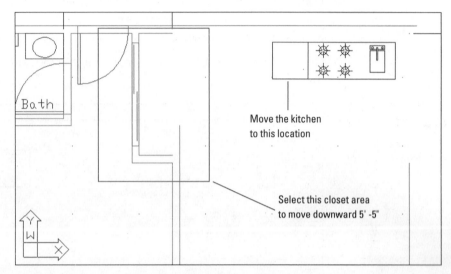

Move the kitchen
to this location

Select this closet area
to move downward 5' -5"

Working with the Fence Selection Option

Next, you'll work on finishing the new bedroom door and entry. Once again, you will get a chance to work with the Fence selection option. Fence is a great tool for selecting locations on objects that would otherwise be difficult to select. With Fence, you can select objects by crossing over them with a rubber-banding line. It's like selecting objects by crossing them out. In addition, the point at which the rubber-banding line crosses the object is equivalent to a pick point. This is important when using commands that respond differently depending on where objects are selected. The following exercise shows how Fence can be helpful in selecting objects in tight spaces.

1. Copy the existing entry door downward, including header and jambs (see Figure 12.13). Use the Endpoint override to locate the door accurately.

2. Clean up the walls by adding new lines and filleting others, as shown in Figure 12.14.

TIP   Use the midpoint of the door header as the first axis endpoint.

3. Mirror the door you just copied so it swings in the opposite direction.

4. Use Stretch (click on Stretch from the Modify toolbar) to move the entry door a distance of 8' to the right, as shown in Figure 12.15. Remember to use a crossing window to select the objects and endpoints you want to stretch.

5. Once you've moved the entry door, mirror it in the same way you mirrored the other door.

FIGURE 12.13:

Using an existing door to create a door opening

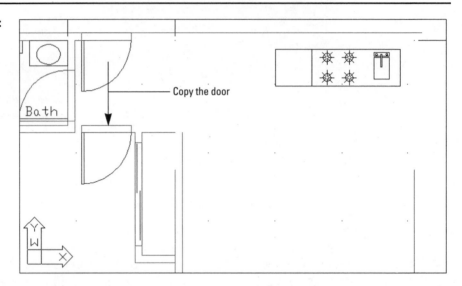

FIGURE 12.14:

Cleaning up the wall

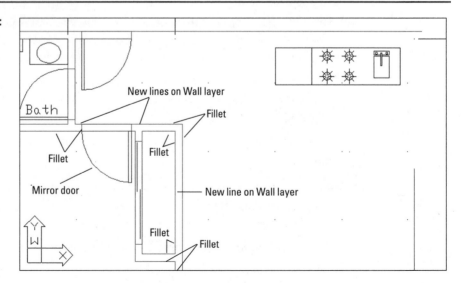

FIGURE 12.15:

Moving the door

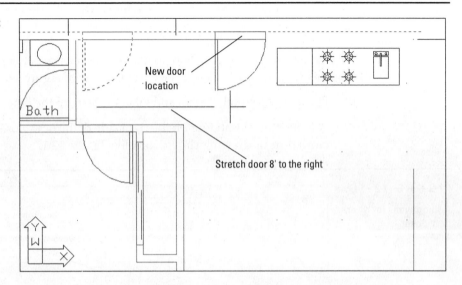

New door location

Stretch door 8' to the right

Bath

In the foregoing exercise, you once again used parts of a previous drawing instead of creating new parts. In only a few instances are you adding new objects.

1. Now set the view of your drawing so it looks similar to Figure 12.16.

2. Click Extend from the Modify toolbar, or type **Ex** ↵ at the command prompt.

3. At the `Select boundary edge(s)… Select object` prompt, pick the wall at the bottom of the screen, as shown in Figure 12.16, and press ↵. Just as with Trim, Extend requires that you first select a set of objects to define the boundary of the extension, and then select the objects you wish to extend.

4. At the `Select object to extend:` prompt, you need to pick the two lines just below the closet door. To do this, first enter **F** ↵ to use the Fence selection option.

5. At the `First Fence point` prompt, pick a point just to the left of the lines you want to extend.

6. Make sure the Ortho mode is off. Then at the `Undo/<Endpoint of line>` prompt, pick a point to the right of the two lines, so the fence crosses over them (see the top image of Figure 12.16).

7. Press ↵. The two lines extend to the wall.

8. Press ↵ again to exit the Extend command.

9. Click trim, and then select the two lines you just extended.

10. Press ↵ to finish your selection.

11. Type **F↵**, and then pick two points to place a fence between the endpoints of the two selected lines (see the bottom image of Figure 12.16).

12. Use a combination of Trim and Fillet to clean up the other walls.

13. Add another closet door on the right side of the new closet space you just created. Your drawing should look like Figure 12.17.

FIGURE 12.16:

Adding walls for a second closet

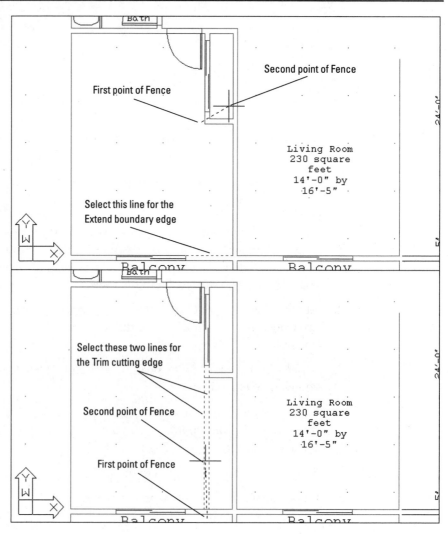

The second closet

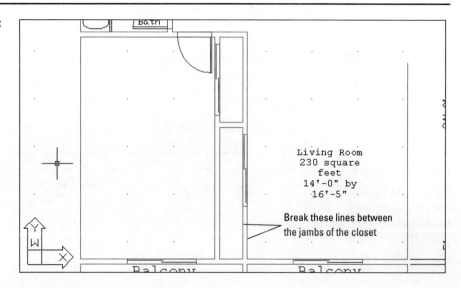

The Extend tool works just like the Trim tool: you first select the boundary objects, and then you select the objects you want to modify. Here again, you used the Fence selection option to select the object to extend. In this situation, the Fence option is crucial because it may be more difficult to select the lines individually.

TIP　　The Trim and Extend tools do not allow you to trim or extend objects in a block. Fortunately, Release 14 offers two bonus utilities on the Bonus Standard Toolbar that will let you select trim and extend boundary objects from within a block. See Chapter 19 for details.

Using Grips to Simplify Editing

Throughout this book, I've shown you ways of using the Grips feature to edit drawings. When and how you use them will really depend on your preference, but there are situations where grip editing makes more sense. Here you'll explore some very basic situations where grips can be useful.

Now, suppose you want to change the location and orientation of the kitchen. In this exercise, you will use the Grips feature to do just that.

1. Set up a view similar to the one in Figure 12.18.

2. Add the horizontal line at the top of the kitchen, as shown in Figure 12.18.

3. Fillet the new line with the vertical wall line to the right of the unit.

4. Click on the kitchen.

5. Click on the grip in the upper-left corner to make it a hot grip. The grip changes from hollow to solid.

FIGURE 12.18:

Finishing the kitchen wall and selecting the kitchen rotation base point

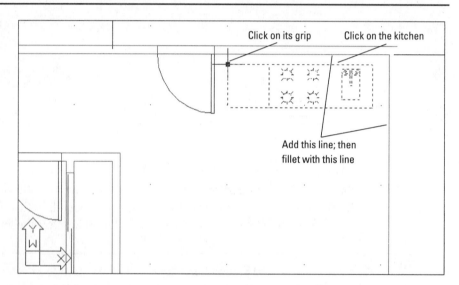

6. Right-click on the mouse and then choose Rotate from the pop-up menu. (You can also press the ↵ key two times until you see the *** ROTATE *** message at the prompt.)

TIP

Remember that the spacebar acts the same as the ↵ key for most commands, including the Grips... modes.

7. Enter -90.

8. Click on the kitchen grip again; then, using the Endpoint Osnap, click on the upper-right corner of the room.

9. Press the Esc key twice to clear the grip selection. Your drawing should look like Figure 12.19.

FIGURE 12.19:

The revised kitchen

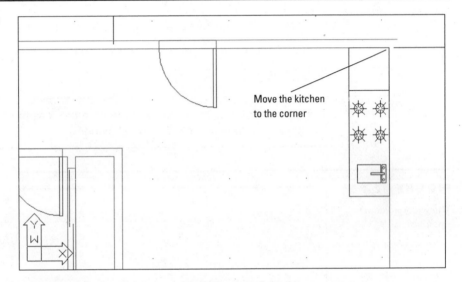

Move the kitchen to the corner

Because the kitchenette is a block, its grip point is the same as its insertion point. This makes the kitchenette block—as are all blocks—a great candidate for grip editing. Remember that the door, too, is a block.

Displaying Grips of Objects within a Block

You can set up AutoCAD to display the grips on all the entities within a block. This allows you to use those grips as handles for any of the grip operations such as Move, Rotate, or Scale. However, you cannot edit individual objects within the block.

To display all the grips within a block, type **Gripblock** ↵ **1** ↵. You can also turn on the *Enable Grips Within a Block* option in the Grips dialog box (Tools ➢ Grips).

Now suppose you want to widen the entrance door from 36" to 42". Try the following exercise involving a door and its surrounding wall.

1. Use a crossing window to select the door jamb to the left of the entry door, as shown in Figure 12.20.

2. Shift + click on both of the door jamb's corner grips.

3. Click on the bottom corner grip again. It is now a hot grip.

4. At the ** Stretch ** prompt, enter **@6<180**. The door should now look like Figure 12.20.

NOTE The Stretch hot grip command will ignore a block as long as you do not include its insertion point in the stretch window.

FIGURE 12.20:

The widened door opening

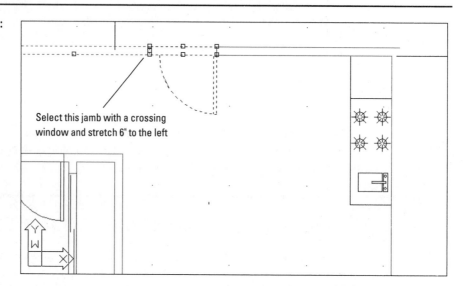

Select this jamb with a crossing window and stretch 6" to the left

Notice that in step 4 you didn't have to specify a base point to stretch the grips. AutoCAD assumes the base to be the original location of the selected hot grip (the grip selected in step 3).

Now you can enlarge the door using the Grips command's Scale function. Scale allows you to change the size of an object or a group of objects. You can change the size visually, by entering a scale value, or by using an object for reference. In this exercise, you will use the current door width as a reference.

1. Press the Esc key twice to clear your selection set.

2. Click on the door, and then on the door's grip point at the hinge side.

3. Right-click the mouse and select Scale.

4. At the `<Scale factor>/Base point/Copy/Undo/Reference/eXit` prompt, enter **R** ↵ to select the Reference option.

5. At the `Reference length <0'-1">` type @ ↵ to indicate that you want to use the door insertion point as the first point of the reference length.

6. At the `Second point` prompt, click on the grip at the endpoint of the door's arc at the wall line (see the top image in Figure 12.21). Now as you move the cursor, the door changes in size relative to the distance between the grip and the end of the arc.

7. At the `<New length>/Base point/Copy/Undo/Reference/eXit` prompt, use the Endpoint Osnap again and click on the door jamb directly to the left of the arc endpoint. The door enlarges to fit the new door opening (see the bottom image in Figure 12.21).

8. To finish this floor plan, zoom out to get the overall view of the unit, turn on the Flr-pat layer, and then erase the floor pattern in the bedroom area just below the bathroom.

9. Save the file.

You could have used the Modify ➤ Scale option to accomplish the operation performed in the above exercise with the Scale hot-grip command. The advantage to using grips is that you don't need to use the Osnap to select exact grip locations, thereby reducing the number of steps you must take to accomplish this task.

In the next section, you will update the Plan file to include the revised studio apartment and the one-bedroom unit you have just created (see Figure 12.22). You will be making changes such as these throughout the later stages of your design project. As you have seen, AutoCAD's ability to make changes easily and quickly can ease your work and help you test your design ideas more accurately.

FIGURE 12.21:

The enlarged door

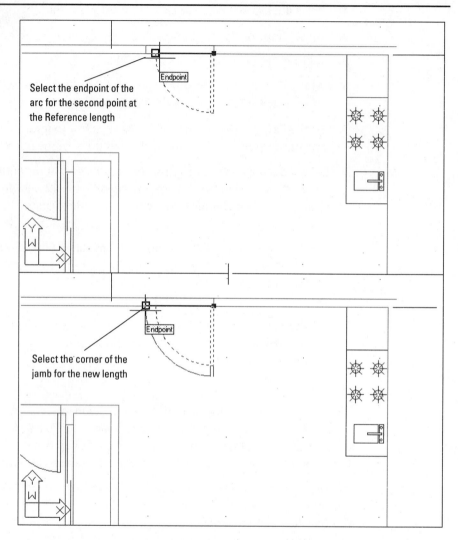

FIGURE 12.22:

The finished one-bedroom unit

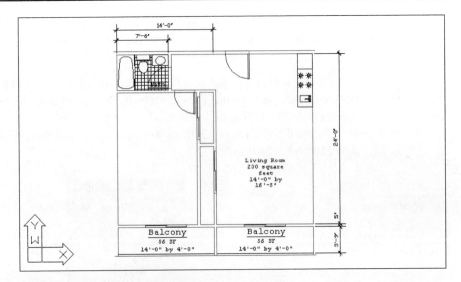

Singling Out Proximate Objects

In Chapter 3 we mentioned that you will encounter situations where you need to select an object that is overlapping or very close to another object. Often in this situation, you end up selecting the wrong object. To help you select the exact object you want, AutoCAD offers the Selection Cycling tool and the Object Selection Settings dialog box.

Selection Cycling

Selection cycling lets you cycle through objects that overlap until you select the one you want. To use this feature, hold down the Ctrl key and click on the object you want to select. If the first object highlighted is not the one you want, click again, but this time don't hold down the Shift key. When several objects are overlapping, just keep clicking until the right object is highlighted and selected. When the object you want is highlighted, press ↵, and then go on to select other objects or press ↵ to finish the selection process. You may want to practice using selection cycling a few times to get the hang of it. It can be a bit confusing at first, but once you've gotten accustomed to how it works, selection cycling can be an invaluable tool.

Object Sorting

If you are a veteran AutoCAD user, you may have grown accustomed to clicking on the most recently created object of two overlapping objects. With Release 12,

AutoCAD introduced user definable controls that set the method of selecting overlapping objects. These controls changed the way AutoCAD selected overlapping objects. You didn't always get to the most recently drawn object when you clicked on overlapping objects.

If you prefer the pre-Release 12 way that AutoCAD offered the most recently drawn object, you can use the Object Sort Method dialog box to revert to the old selection method. This dialog box is buried in the Object Selection Settings dialog box. To get there, click on Options ➢ Selection…, and then click on the Object Sort Method… button.

This dialog box lets you set the sort method for a variety of operations. If you enable any of the operations listed, AutoCAD will use the pre-Release 12 sort method for that operation. You will probably not want to change the sort method for object Snaps or Regens. But by checking Object Selection, you can control which of two overlapping lines are selected when you click on them. For plotting and for PostScript output, you can control the overlay of screened or hatched areas.

These settings can also be controlled through system variables. See Appendix D for details.

NOTE When you use the Draworder command (the Tools ➢ Display Order options), all the options in the Object Sort Method dialog box are turned on.

Using External References (Xrefs)

I mentioned in Chapter 6 that careful use of blocks, external references, and layers can help you improve your productivity. In this section you will see firsthand how to use these features to help reduce design errors and speed up delivery of an accurate set of drawings. You do this by controlling layers in conjunction with blocks and external referenced files (Xrefs) to create a common drawing database for several drawings.

Preparing Existing Drawings for Cross-Referencing

In Chapter 6 we discussed how you can use Xrefs to assemble one floor of the apartment. In this section you will explore the creation and use of Xrefs to build multiple floors, each containing slightly different sets of drawing information. By doing so, you will learn how Xrefs allow you to use a single file in multiple drawings to save time and reduce redundancy. You'll see that by sharing common data in multiple files, you can reduce your work and keep the drawing information consistent.

You'll start by creating the files that you will use later as Xrefs.

1. Open the Plan file. If you didn't create the Plan file, you can use the `12a-plan.dwg` file from the companion CD-ROM (see Figure 12.23).

FIGURE 12.23:

The overall plan

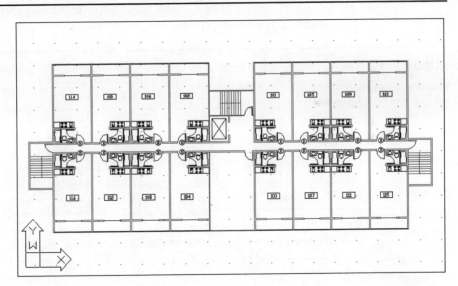

2. Turn off the Notes layer to get a clear, uncluttered view of the individual unit plans.

3. Use the Wblock command (enter **W** ↵ at the command prompt) and write the eight units in the corners of your plan to a file called **Floor1.dwg** (see Figure 12.24). When you select objects for the Wblock, be sure to include the door symbols for those units. Use 0,0 for the Wblock insertion base point.

FIGURE 12.24:

Units to be exported to the Floor1 file

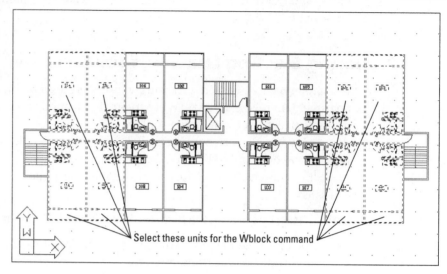

Select these units for the Wblock command

4. Using Figure 12.25 as a guide, insert Unit2 into the corners where the other eight units were previously.

FIGURE 12.25:

Insertion information for Unit2

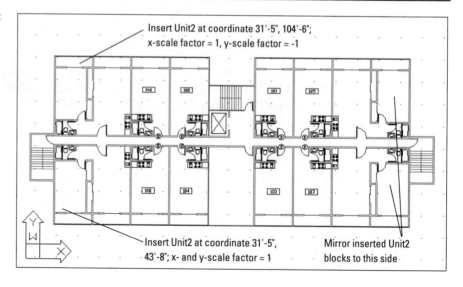

Insert Unit2 at coordinate 31'-5", 104'-6"; x-scale factor = 1, y-scale factor = -1

Insert Unit2 at coordinate 31'-5", 43'-8"; x- and y-scale factor = 1

Mirror inserted Unit2 blocks to this side

NOTE If you didn't create the Unit2 file from earlier in this chapter, you can use the Unit2.dwg file from the companion CD-ROM.

5. Once you've accurately placed the corner units, use the Wblock command to write these corner units to a file called Floor2.dwg. Again, use the 0,0 coordinate as the insertion base point for the Wblock.

6. Now use File ➤ Save As to turn the remaining set of unit plans into a file called Common.dwg.

You've just created three files: Floor1, Floor2, and Common. Each of these files contains unique information about the building. Next, you'll use the Xref command to re-combine these files for the different floor plans in your building.

Assembling External References to Build a Drawing

Next, you will create composite files for each floor, using external references of only the files needed for the individual floors. You will use the Attach option of the Xref command to insert all the files you exported from the Plan file.

1. Close the Common.dwg file, open a new file, and call it **Xref-1**.

2. Set up this file as an architectural drawing 18"×24" with a scale of 1/8"=1'. The upper-right corner limits for such a drawing are 2304, 1728.

3. Set Ltscale to 96.

4. Open the Reference toolbar by right-clicking on a toolbar, and then selecting Reference from the Toolbars dialog box.

5. Close the Toolbars dialog box.

6. Click on External Reference Attach from the Reference toolbar, or type **Xa↵**.

The Select File to Attach dialog box appears.

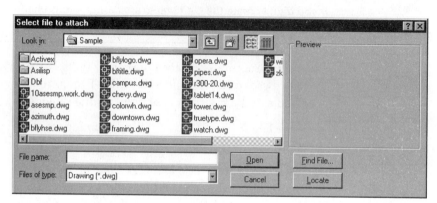

7. Locate and select the Common.dwg file.

8. At the Attach Xref dialog box, make sure the Specify On-Screen checkbox is not checked, and then enter 0,0 in the At input box just to the left of the checkbox.

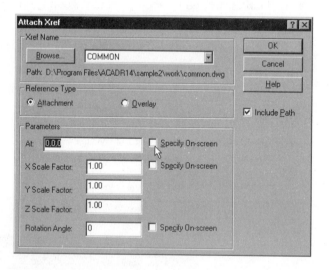

NOTE Because the insertion points of all the files are the same, namely 0,0, they will fit together perfectly when they are inserted into the new files.

9. Click OK. The Common.dwg file appears in the drawing.

10. Click External Reference Attach again, and then click the browse button to insert the Floor1 file.

11. Repeat step 10 to insert the `Col-grid.dwg` file as an Xref. The `Col-grid.dwg` file can be found on the companion CD-ROM. You now have the plan for the first floor.

12. Save this file.

Now use the current file to create another file representing a different floor.

1. Use File ➤ Save As to save this file as `Xref-2.dwg`.

2. Click on the External Reference tool in the Reference toolbar or type **Xr** ↵.

3. At the External Reference dialog box, highlight Floor1 in the list of Xref, and then click Detach.

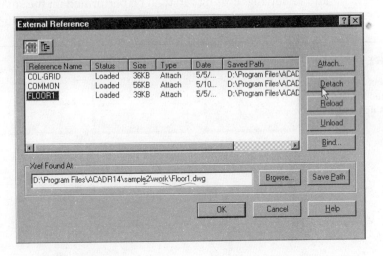

4. Click on Attach; then at the Attach Xref dialog box, click Browse.

5. Locate and select `Floor2.dwg`.

6. In the Attach Xref dialog box, make sure the At option is set to 0,0, just as you did in step 8 in the previous exercise.

7. Click OK. The Floor2 drawing appears in place of Floor1.

WARNING   If you move an external reference file after you have inserted it into a drawing, AutoCAD may not be able to find it later when you attempt to open the drawing. If this happens, you can use the Browse option in the External Reference dialog box to tell AutoCAD the new location of the external referenced file.

Now when you need to make changes to Xref-1 or Xref-2, you can edit the individual external referenced files that they comprise. Then, the next time you open either Xref-1 or Xref-2, the updated Xrefs will automatically appear in their most recent forms.

External references do not need to be permanent. As you saw in the previous exercise, you can attach and detach them easily at any time. This means, if you need to get information from another file—to see how well an elevator core aligns, for example—you can temporarily external reference the other file to quickly check alignments, and then detach it when you are done.

Think of these composite files as final plot files that are only used for plotting and reviewing. Editing can then be performed on the smaller, more manageable external referenced files. Figure 12.26 diagrams the relationship of these files.

FIGURE 12.26:

Diagram of external referenced file relationships

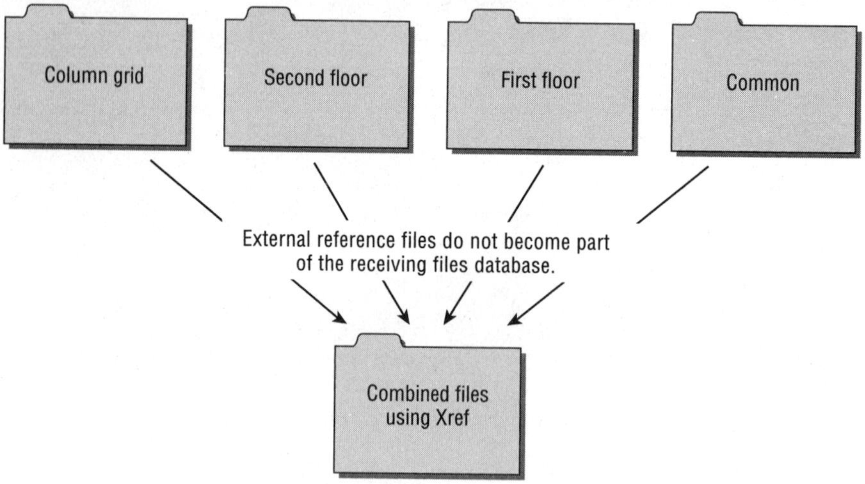

The combinations of external references are limited only by your imagination, but avoid multiple external references of the same file.

TIP

Because Xref files do not become part of the file they are referenced into, you must take care to keep Xref files in a location where AutoCAD can find them when the referencing file is opened. This can be a minor annoyance when you need to send files to others outside your office. To help you keep track of external references, AutoCAD offers the Pack 'n Go tool in the Bonus Standard toolbar. See Chapter 19 for details.

Updating Blocks in External References

There are several advantages to using external reference files. Because the Xrefs don't become part of the drawing file's database, the referencing files remain quite small. Also, because Xref files are easily updated, work can be split up among several people in a workgroup environment or on a network. For example, in our hypothetical apartment building, one person can be editing the Common file while another works on Floor1, and so on. The next time the composite Xref-1 .dwg or Xref-2.dwg file is opened, it will automatically reflect any new changes made in the external referenced files. Now let's see how to set this up.

1. Open the Common.dwg file.

2. Next, you will update the Unit plan you edited earlier in this chapter. Click on Insert Block from the Draw toolbar.

3. At the Insert dialog box, click on the File button, and then locate and select Unit.dwg. Then click on Open here, and again in the Insert dialog box.

4. At the warning message, click on OK.

5. At the Insertion point prompt, press Esc.

6. Enter **RE** ⏎ to regenerate the drawing. You will see the new Unit plan in place of the old one (see Figure 12.27). You may also see all the dimensions and notes for each unit.

7. If the Notes layer is on, use the Layer & Linetype Properties dialog box or the layer drop-down list to turn it off.

FIGURE 12.27:

The Common file with the revised Unit plan

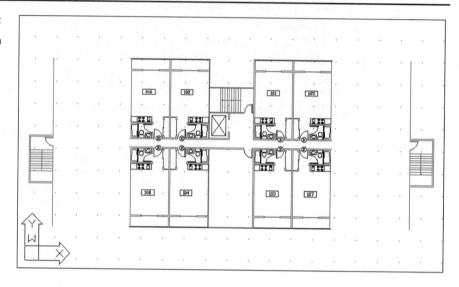

8. Using Insert Block in the Draw toolbar again, replace the empty room across the hall from the lobby, with the utility room you created in Chapter 11 (see Figure 12.28). If you didn't create the utility room drawing, use the Utility .dwg file from the companion CD-ROM.

FIGURE 12.28:

The utility room installed

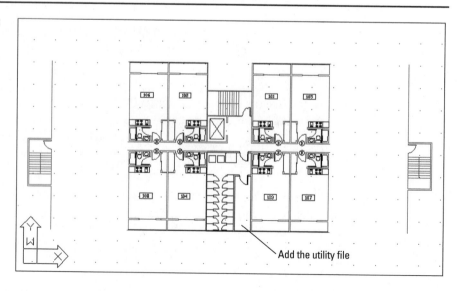

Add the utility file

9. Save the Common file.

10. Now open the Xref-1 file. You will see the utility room and the typical units in their new form. Your drawing should look like the top image of Figure 12.29.

11. Open Xref-2. You see that the utility room and typical units are updated in this file as well (see the bottom image of Figure 12.29).

FIGURE 12.29:

The Xref-1 file with the units updated

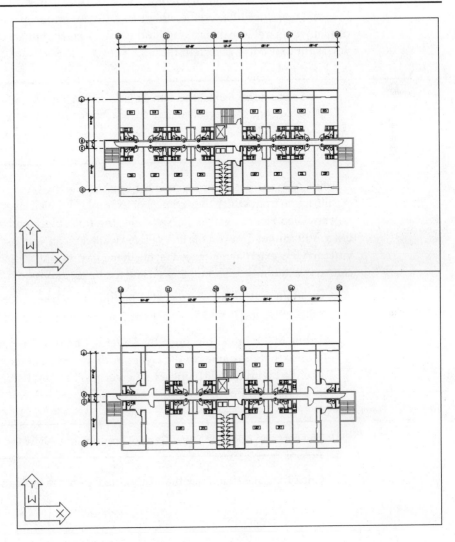

If this were a typical manually drafted project, someone would have had to make changes to both plans shown in Figure 12.29, duplicating a great deal of work.

Importing Named Elements from External References

In Chapter 5 we discussed how layers, blocks, line types, and text styles—called *named elements*—are imported along with a file that is inserted into another. External reference files, on the other hand, do not import named elements. You can, however, review their names and use a special command to import the ones you want to use in the current file.

TIP

You can set the Visretain system variable to 1 to force AutoCAD to remember layer settings of external referenced files. You can also use the Layer Manager bonus utility to save layer settings for later recall. The Layer Manager is described in detail in Chapter 19.

AutoCAD renames named elements from Xref files by giving them the prefix of the file name from which they come. For example, the Wall layer in the Floor1 file will be called Floor1 | wall in the Xref-1 file; the Toilet block will be called Floor1 | toilet. You cannot draw on the layer Floor | wall, nor can you insert Floor1 | toilet; but you can view external referenced layers in the Layer Control dialog box, and you can view external referenced blocks using the Insert dialog box.

Next, you'll look at how AutoCAD identifies layers and blocks in external referenced files, and you'll get a chance to import a layer from an Xref.

1. While in the Xref-1 file, open the Layer & Linetype Properties dialog box. Notice that the names of the layers from the external referenced files are all prefixed with the file name and the vertical bar (|) character. Exit the Layer & Linetype properties dialog box.

NOTE

You can also open the Layer Control pop-up list to view the layer names.

---

2. Click External Reference Bind from the Reference toolbar, or enter **Xb** ↵.

The Xbind dialog box appears.

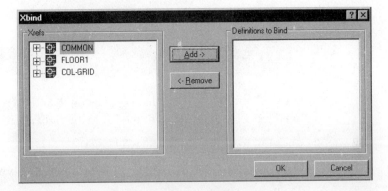

You see a listing of the current Xrefs. Each listing shows a plus sign to the left. This list box follows the Microsoft Windows 95 format for expandable lists, much like the directory listing in the Windows Explorer.

3.   Click on the plus sign next to the FLOOR1 Xref listing. The list expands to show the types of elements available to bind.

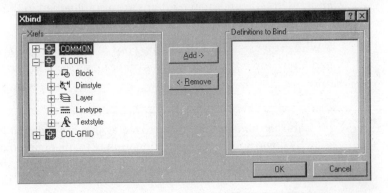

4.   Now click on the plus sign next to the Layer listing. The list expands further to show the layers available for binding.

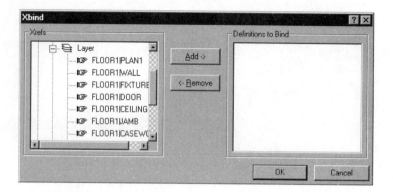

5. Locate Floor1 | wall in the listing, click on it, and then click on the Add button. Floor1 | wall is added to the list to the right: Definitions to Bind.

6. Click OK to bind the Floor1 | wall layer.

7. Now open the Layer & Linetype Properties dialog box.

8. Scroll down the list and look for the Floor1 | wall layer. You will not find it. In its place is a layer called Floor1$0$wall.

As you can see, when you use Xbind to import a named item, such as the Floor1 | wall layer, the vertical bar (|) is replaced by two dollar signs surrounding a number, which is usually zero. (If for some reason the imported layer name Floor1$0$wall already exists, then the zero in that name is changed to 1, as in *Floor1$1$wall*.) Other named items are also renamed in the same way, using the 0 replacement for the vertical bar.

While you used the Xbind dialog box to bind a single layer, you can also use it to bind multiple layers, as well as other items from Xrefs attached to the current drawing.

TIP   You can bind an entire Xref to a drawing, converting it into a simple block. By doing so, you have the opportunity to maintain unique layer names of the Xref being bound, or merge the Xref's similarly named layers with those of the current file. See Chapter 6 for details.

Nesting External References and Using Overlays

External references can be nested. For example, the Common.dwg file created in this chapter might use the Unit.dwg file as a external reference rather than an inserted block, and you would still get the same result in the Xref-1.dwg file. That is, you would see the entire floor plan, including the unit plans, when you open Xref-1.dwg. In this situation, Unit.dwg is nested in the Common.dwg file, which is in turn external referenced in the Xref-1.dwg file.

Though nested Xrefs can be helpful, you will want to take care in using external references in this way. For example, you might create an external reference using the Common.dwg file in the Floor1.dwg file as a means of referencing walls and other features of the Common.dwg file. You might also reference the Common.dwg file into the Floor2.dwg file for the same reason. Once you do this, however, you will have three versions of the Common plan in the Xref-1.dwg file, because each Xref now has Common.dwg attached to it. And because AutoCAD would dutifully load Common.dwg three times, Xref-1.dwg would occupy substantial computer memory, slowing your computer down when you edit the Xref-1.dwg file.

To avoid this problem, you can use the Overlay option of the Attach Xref dialog box. An overlayed external reference cannot be nested. For example, if you use the Overlay option when inserting the Common.dwg file into the Floor1.dwg and Floor2.dwg files, the nested Common.dwg file would be ignored when you opened the Xref-1.dwg file, thereby eliminating the redundant occurrence of Common.dwg. In another example, if you use the Overlay option to import the Unit.dwg file into the Common.dwg file and then attach the Common.dwg into Xref-1.dwg as an Xref, you would not see the Unit plan in Xref-1.dwg. The nested Unit.dwg drawing would be ignored.

Switching to Paper Space

Your set of drawings for this studio apartment building would probably include a larger-scale, more detailed drawing of the typical Unit plan. You already have the beginnings of this drawing in the form of the Unit file.

As you have seen, the notes and dimensions you entered into the Unit file can be turned off or frozen in the Plan file so they don't interfere with the graphics of the drawing. The Unit file can be part of another drawing file that contains more detailed information on the typical unit plan at a larger scale. To this new drawing you can add other notes, symbols, and dimensions. Whenever the Unit file is altered, you update its occurrence in the large-scale drawing of the typical unit as well as in the Plan file (see Figure 12.30). The units are thus quickly updated, and good correspondence is ensured among all the drawings for your project.

FIGURE 12.30:

Relationship of drawing files in a project

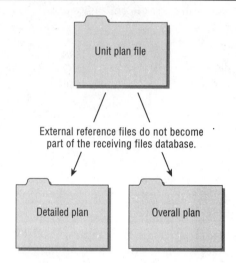

Now suppose that you want to combine drawings having different scales in the same drawing file—for example, the overall plan of one floor plus an enlarged view of one typical unit. This can be accomplished by using the Paper Space mode first discussed in Chapter 6. First, let's see how to get into Paper Space.

Understanding Model Space and Paper Space

So far, you've looked at ways to help you get around in your drawing while using a single view. This single view representation of your AutoCAD drawing is called the *Model Space* display mode. You also have the capability to set up multiple views of your drawing, called *floating viewports*. Floating viewports can be created by using the *Paper Space* display mode.

To get a clear understanding of these two modes, imagine that your drawing is actually a full-size replica or model of the object you are drawing. Your computer screen is your window into a "room" where this model is being constructed, and the keyboard and mouse are your means of access to this room. You can control your window's position in relation to the object through the use of pan, zoom, view, and other display-related commands. You can also construct or modify the model by using drawing and editing commands. Think of this room as your Model Space.

So far, you have been working on your drawings by looking through a single "window" into Model Space. Now suppose you have the ability to step back and add windows with different views looking into your Model Space. The effect is as if you have several video cameras in your Model Space "room," each connected to a different monitor. You can view all your windows at once on your computer screen, or enlarge a single window to fill the entire screen. Further, you can control the shape of your windows and easily switch from one window to another. This is what Paper Space is like.

Paper Space lets you create and display multiple views of Model Space. Each view window, called a *viewport*, acts like an individual virtual screen. One viewport can have an overall view of your drawing, while another can be a close-up. Layer visibility can also be controlled individually for each viewport, allowing you to display different versions of the same area of your drawing. You can move, copy, and stretch viewports, and even overlap them.

NOTE   Another type of viewport called the *Tiled* viewport can be set up in Model Space. We discuss this type of viewport in Chapter 16.

Perhaps one of the more powerful features of Paper Space is that you can plot several views of the same drawing on one sheet of paper. You can also include graphic objects such as borders and notes that appear only in Paper Space. In this function, Paper Space acts very much like a page-layout program such as Quark or Adobe PageMaker. You can "paste up" different views of your drawing and then add borders, title blocks, general notes, and other types of graphic and textural data. Figure 12.31 shows the Plan drawing set up in Paper Space mode to display several views.

FIGURE 12.31:

Different views of the same drawing in Paper Space

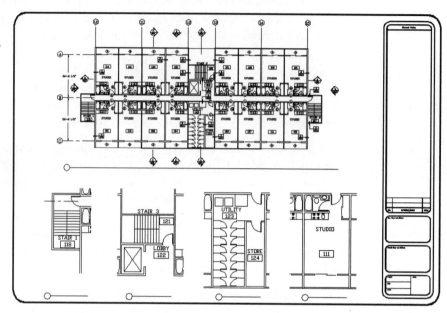

Taking a Tour of Paper Space

Your gateway to Paper Space is the Tilemode system variable. When Tilemode is set to 1 (On), the default setting, you are in Model Space. When it is set to 0 (Off), you are in Paper Space. This system variable is neatly packaged in the pull-down menu as View ➤ Model Space (tiled) and View ➤ Paper Space. Let's start with the basics of entering Paper Space.

1. If it isn't already open, open the Xref-1 file, making sure your display shows all of the drawing.

2. Click on View ➤ Paper Space, or enter Tilemode ↵ 0 ↵. You can also double-click on the word "TILE" in the status bar. Your screen goes blank and your UCS icon changes to a triangular shape. Also note the word "PAPER" replacing TILE in the status bar; this tells you at a glance that you are in Paper Space.

NOTE   A third option, View ➤ Model Space (Floating) switches you to Paper Space, and then places you in a Model Space window. You'll learn about floating Model Space later in this chapter.

The new UCS icon tells you that you are in Paper Space. But where did your drawing go? Before you can view it, you must create the windows, or *viewports*, that let you see into Model Space. But before you do that, let's explore Paper Space.

1. Click on Data ➤ Drawing Limits, or enter Limits ↵ at the command prompt. Then note the default value for the lower-left corner of the Paper Space limits. It is 0'-0", 0'-0".

2. Press ↵ and note the current default value for the upper-right corner of the limits. It is 1'-0", 9", which is the standard default for a new drawing. This tells us that the new Paper Space area is 12" wide by 9" high—an area quite different from the one you set up originally in this drawing.

3. Click on Data ➤ Drawing Limits again.

4. At the ON/OFF prompt, press ↵.

5. At the upper-right corner prompt, enter **42,30** ↵ to designate an area that is 42" × 30".

6. Click on View ➤ Zoom ➤ All.

Now you have your Paper Space set up. The next step is to create viewports so you can begin to paste up your views.

7. Click on View ➤ Floating Viewports ➤ 3 Viewports, or type **Mv** ↵ **3** ↵.

8. At the Horizontal/Vertical/Above/Below/Left/<Right> prompt, enter **A** ↵ for Above. This option creates one large viewport along the top half of the screen, with two smaller viewports along the bottom.

9. At the Fit/<first point> prompt, enter **F** ↵ for the Fit option. Three rectangles appear in the formation, shown in Figure 12.32. Each of these is a viewport to your Model Space. The viewport at the top fills the whole width of the drawing area; the bottom half of the screen is divided into two viewports.

FIGURE 12.32

The newly created viewports

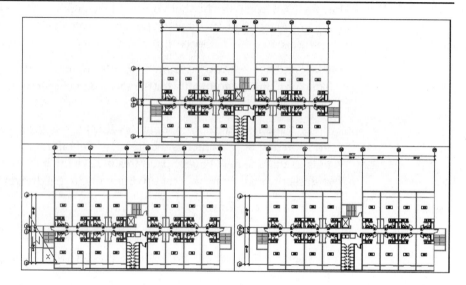

Now suppose you need to have access to the objects within the viewports in order to adjust their display and edit your drawing.

10. Click on View ➤ Model Space (Floating). This gives you control over Model Space even though you are in Paper Space. (You can also enter **MS** ↵ as a keyboard shortcut to entering Model Space mode.)

    The first thing you notice is that the UCS icon changes back to its L-shaped arrow form. It also appears in each viewport, as if you had three AutoCAD windows instead of just one.

11. Move your cursor over each viewport. Notice that in one of the viewports the cursor appears as the AutoCAD crosshair cursor, while in the other viewports it appears as an arrow pointer. The viewport that shows the AutoCAD cursor is the active one; you can pan and zoom, as well as edit objects in the active viewport.

TIP   If your drawing disappears from a viewport, you can generally retrieve it by using View ➤ Zoom ➤ Extents (**Zoom** ↵ **E** ↵).

12. Click on the lower-left viewport to activate it.

13. Click on View ➤ Zoom ➤ Window and window the elevator area.

14. Click on the lower-right viewport and use View ➤ Zoom ➤ Window to enlarge your view of a typical unit. You can also use the Pan Realtime and Zoom Realtime tools.

When you use View ➤ Floating Model, the UCS icon again changes shape—instead of one triangular-shaped icon, you have three arrow-shaped ones, one for each viewport on the screen. Also, as you move your cursor into the currently active viewport, the cursor changes from an arrow into the usual crosshair. Another way to tell which viewport is the active one is by its double border.

You can move from viewport to viewport even while you are in the middle of most commands. For example, you can issue the Line command, then pick the start point in one viewport, then go to a different viewport to pick the next point, and so on. To activate a different viewport, you simply click on it (see Figure 12.33). You can also switch viewports by entering Ctrl+R.

> **WARNING** You cannot move between viewports while in the middle of the Snap, Zoom, Vpoint, Grid, Pan, Dview, or Vplayer commands.

FIGURE 12.33:

The three viewports, each with a different view of the plan

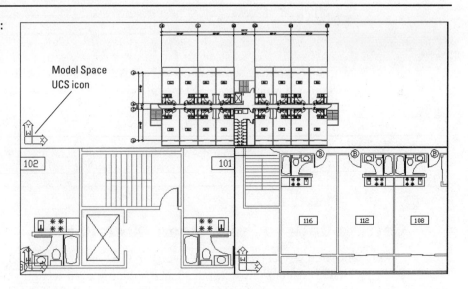

Your current view of the viewports is a bit constricted. Take the following steps to give yourself some room and to view a bit more of the Paper Space work area.

1. Choose View ➤ Paper Space, or type **PS** ↵. You can also double-click on the word "MODEL" in the status bar.

2. Use the Zoom Realtime tool to zoom the Paper Space view back just a bit so it looks like Figure 12.34.

FIGURE 12.34:

The view of Paper Space after zooming out

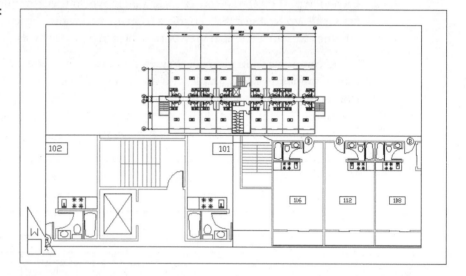

This brief exercise shows that you can use the Zoom tool in Paper Space just as you would in Model Space. All the display-related commands are available including Pan Realtime.

NOTE   Unlike prior versions of AutoCAD, zooms and pans in Paper Space do not trigger Regens.

Getting Back to Full-Screen Model Space

Once you've created viewports, you can then re-enter Model Space through the viewport using View ➤ Model Space (Floating). But what if you want to quickly get back into the old familiar full-screen Model Space you were in before you entered Paper Space? The following exercise demonstrates how this is done.

1. Click on View ➤ Tiled Model Space, or enter **Tm** ↵ **1** ↵. Your drawing returns to the original full-screen Model Space view—everything is back to normal.

2. Click on View ➤ Paper Space, or enter **Tm** ↵ **0** ↵. You are back in Paper Space. Notice that all the viewports are still there when you return to Paper Space. Once you've set up Paper Space, it remains part of the drawing until you delete all the viewports.

You may prefer doing most of your drawing in Model Space and using Paper Space for setting up views for plotting. Since viewports are retained, you won't lose anything when you go back to Model Space to edit your drawing.

Working with Paper Space Viewports

Paper Space is intended as a page-layout or composition tool. You can manipulate viewports' sizes, scale their view independently of one another, and even set layering and line-type scale independently. Let's try manipulating the shape and location of viewports, using the Modify command options.

1. Click on the bottom edge of the lower-left viewport to expose its grips (see the top image of Figure 12.35)

2. Click on the upper-right grip, and then drag it to the location shown in the top image of Figure 12.35.

3. Press the Esc key and then erase the lower-right viewport by clicking on Erase in the modify toolbar. Then click on the bottom edge of the viewport.

4. Move the lower-left viewport so it is centered in the bottom half of the window, as shown in the bottom image of Figure 12.35.

FIGURE 12.35:

Stretching, erasing, and moving viewports

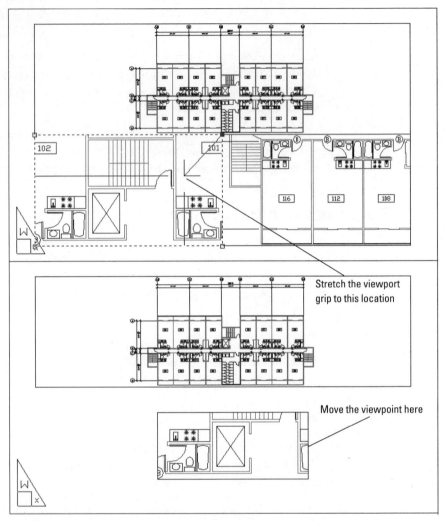

Stretch the viewport grip to this location

Move the viewpoint here

In this exercise, you clicked on the viewport edge to select it for editing. If, while in Paper Space, you attempt to click on the image within the viewport, you will not select anything. Later you will see, however, that you can use the Osnap modes to snap to parts of the drawing image within a viewport.

Viewports are recognized as AutoCAD objects, so they can be manipulated by all the editing commands just like any other object. In the foregoing exercise you moved, stretched, and erased viewports. Next, you'll see how layers affect viewports.

1. Create a new layer called **Vport**.

2. Use the Properties button on the toolbar to change the viewport borders to the Vport layer.

3. Finally, turn off the Vport layer. The viewport borders will disappear.

A viewport's border can be assigned a layer, color, or line type. If you put the viewport's border on a layer that has been turned off or frozen, that border will become invisible, just like any other object on such a layer. Making the borders invisible is helpful when you want to compose a final sheet for plotting. Even when turned off, the active viewport will show a heavy border around it when you switch to floating model, and all the viewports will still display their views.

Disappearing Viewports

As you add more viewports to a drawing, you may discover that some of them blank out, even though you know you haven't turned them off. Don't panic. AutoCAD limits the number of viewports that display their contents at any given time to 48. (A viewport that displays its contents is said to be active.) This limit is provided because too many active viewports can bog down a system.

If you are using a slow computer with limited resources, you can lower this limit to 2 or 3 to gain some performance. Then only two or three viewports will display their contents. (All viewports that are turned on will still plot, however, regardless of whether their contents are visible or not.) Zooming into a blank viewport will restore its visibility thereby allowing you to continue to work with enlarged Paper Space views containing only a few viewports.

The Maxactvp system variable controls this value. Type **Maxactvp** and then enter the number of viewports you want to have active at any given time.

Scaling Views in Paper Space

Paper Space has its own unit of measure. You have already seen how you can set the limits of Paper Space independently of Model Space. When you first enter Paper Space, regardless of the area your drawing occupies in Model Space, you are given limits that are 12 units wide by 9 units high. This may seem incongruous at first, but if you keep in mind that Paper Space is like a paste-up area, then this difference of scale becomes easier to comprehend. Just as you might paste up photographs and maps representing several square miles onto an 11"×17 " board, so can you use Paper Space to paste up views of scale drawings representing city blocks or houses. Only in AutoCAD, you have the freedom to change the scale and size of the objects you are pasting up.

> **NOTE**
>
> While in Paper Space, you can edit objects in a Model Space viewport, but to do so, you must use View ➢ Floating Model Space. You can then click on a viewport, and then edit within that viewport. While in this mode, objects that were created in Paper Space cannot be edited. View ➢ Paper Space brings you back to the Paper Space environment.

If you want to be able to print your drawing at a specific scale, then you must carefully consider scale factors when composing your Paper Space paste-up. Let's see how to put together a sheet in Paper Space and still maintain accuracy of scale.

1. Click on View ➢ Floating Model Space, or enter **MS** ↵, to return to Model Space. This will allow us to manipulate the views of each viewport.

2. Click on the top view to activate it.

3. Click on View ➢ Zoom ➢ Scale, or enter **Z** ↵ **S** ↵.

4. At the All/Center/Dynamic/Extents… prompt, enter **1/96xp** ↵. The xp suffix appended to the 1/96 tells AutoCAD that the current view should be scaled to 1/96 of the Paper Space scale. You get the 1/96 by taking the inverse of the drawing's scale factor, 96.

5. Click on the lower viewport.

6. Choose View ➢ Zoom ➢ Scale again and enter **1/24xp** ↵ at the All/Center/ Dynamic prompt. Your view of the unit will be scaled to 1/4"=1' in relation to Paper Space (see Figure 12.36).

FIGURE 12.36:

Paper Space viewport views scaled to 1/8" = 1' and 1/2"=1'

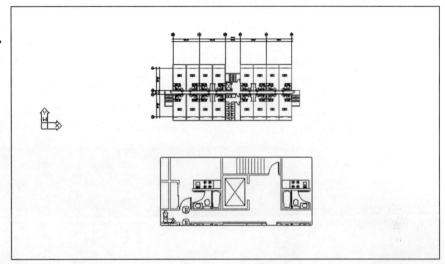

It's easy to adjust the width, height, and location of the viewports so that they display only the parts of the unit you want to see; just go back to the Paper Space mode and use the Stretch, Move, or Scale commands to edit any viewport border. The view within the viewport itself will remain at the same scale and location, while the viewport changes in size. You can move and stretch viewports with no effect on the size and location of the objects within the view.

If you have a situation where you need to overlay one drawing on top of another, you can overlap viewports. Use the Osnap overrides to select geometry within each viewport, even while in Paper Space. This allows you to align one viewport on top of another at exact locations.

You can also add a title block in Paper Space at a 1:1 scale to frame your viewports, and then plot this drawing from Paper Space at a scale of 1:1. Your plot will appear just as it does in Paper Space, at the appropriate scale.

WARNING While working in Paper Space, pay close attention to whether you are in Paper Space or floating Model Space mode. It is easy to accidentally perform a pan or zoom within a floating Model Space viewport when you intend to pan or zoom your Paper Space view. This can cause you to lose your viewport scaling or alignment with other parts of the drawing. It's a good idea to save viewport views using View ➤ Named Views in case you happen to accidentally change a viewport view.

Setting Layers in Individual Viewports

Another unique feature of Paper Space viewports is their ability to freeze layers independently. You could, for example, display the usual plan information in the overall view of a floor but show only the walls in the enlarged view of one unit.

You control viewport layer visibility through the Layer & Linetype Properties dialog box. You may have noticed that there are three sun icons for each layer listing.

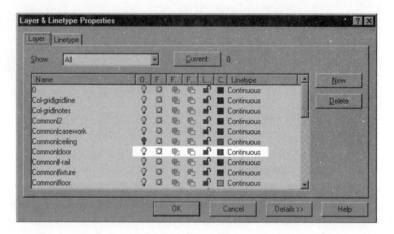

You're already familiar with the sun icon farthest to the left. This is the Freeze/Thaw icon that controls the freezing and thawing of layers globally. Just to the right of that icon is a sun icon with a transparent rectangle. This icon controls the freezing and thawing of layers in individual viewports. The next exercise shows you first hand how it works.

1. Activate the lower viewport.

2. Open the Layer & Linetype Properties dialog box.

3. In the Common | Wall layer listing, move your cursor over the icon that shows a transparent rectangle over a sun. You will see a tool tip describing its purpose: Freeze/Thaw in current viewport.

WARNING   The Cur VP and New VP options in the Layer Control dialog box cannot be used while you are in tiled Model Space.

4. Click on the sun with the transparent rectangle icon. The sun changes into a snowflake telling you that the layer is now frozen for the current viewport.

5. Click on OK. The active viewport will regenerate, with the wall layer of the Common Xref made invisible in the current viewport. However, the Walls remain visible in the other viewport (see Figure 12.37).

FIGURE 12.37:

The drawing editor with the Wall layer turned off in the active viewport

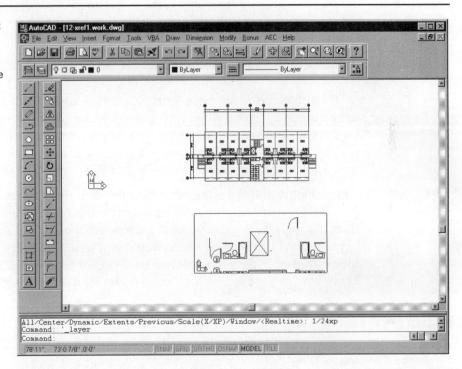

You might have noticed the other similar looking sun icon next to the one you used in the previous exercise. This icon shows an opaque rectangle over the sun.

This other icon controls layer visibility in any new viewports you might create next, rather than controlling existing viewports.

If you prefer, you can also use the Layer Control pop-up list in the toolbar to freeze layers in individual viewports. Select the layer from the list, and then click on the same sun icon with the small rectangle below it. Now save and exit the Xref-1 file.

Masking Out Parts of a Drawing

In Chapter 6 we described a method for using 3D Faces to hide floor patterns under equipment or furniture in a floor layout. You can use a similar method to hide irregular-shaped areas in a Paper Space viewport. This would be desirable for plotting site plans, civil plans, or floor plans that require portions of the drawing to be masked out. Or you may want to mask part of a plan that is overlapped by another to expose dimension or text data.

This section concludes the apartment building tutorial. Although you haven't drawn the complete building, you've already learned all the commands and techniques you need to do so. Figure 12.38 shows you a completed plan of the first floor; to complete your floor plans and get some practice using AutoCAD, you may want to add the symbols shown in this figure to your Plan file.

Since buildings like this one often have the same plans for several floors, the plan for the second floor can also represent the third floor. Combined with the first floor, this will give you a three-level apartment building. This project might also have a ground-level garage, which would be a separate file. The Col-grid.dwg file can be used in the garage file as a reference for dimensions. The other symbols can be blocks stored as files that can be retrieved in other files.

FIGURE 12.38:

A completed floor of the apartment building

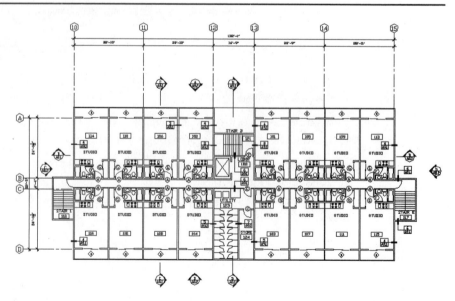

Paper Space and the San Francisco Main Library Project

The San Francisco Main Library project made extensive use of Paper Space. As I've shown you in earlier chapter, the library project used multiple instances of the same file to show different types of information. Paper Space was instrumental in enabling the CAD specialists to manage large amounts of drawing data. One floor plan drawing served as the basis for several sheets including floor plans, reflected ceiling plans, equipment plans, exit plans, and others.

The top image of the two graphics in this sidebar shows a Paper Space view of a drawing from the San Francisco Main Library construction document set. This particular sheet shows the floor pattern layout of some of the main circulation areas.

The title block is inserted in Paper Space as a block, rather than as an Xref. This was done because each drawing has unique drawing title information that is kept as attribute data in the title block. The attributes can be easily updated from a dialog box.

The plan drawings are Xrefs inserted into Model Space with Paper Space viewports displaying selected areas. The viewport borders are turned on in this view to show how they are arranged. These borders are turned off when the drawing is plotted.

Notice that the grid reference symbols are in their own viewport adjacent to the main enlarged floor plan. These adjacent grid viewports display portions of the drawing that are actually some distance away from the floor plan shown in the main viewport. The second image in this sidebar shows the overall floor plan with the viewport areas outlined. Here you can see that the column grid symbols are actually at the edge of the drawing. This example shows how viewports helped the creator of this drawing re-use existing data. If a change is made to the overall plan including the column grids, the enlarged plan of the entry is automatically updated.

Continued on next page

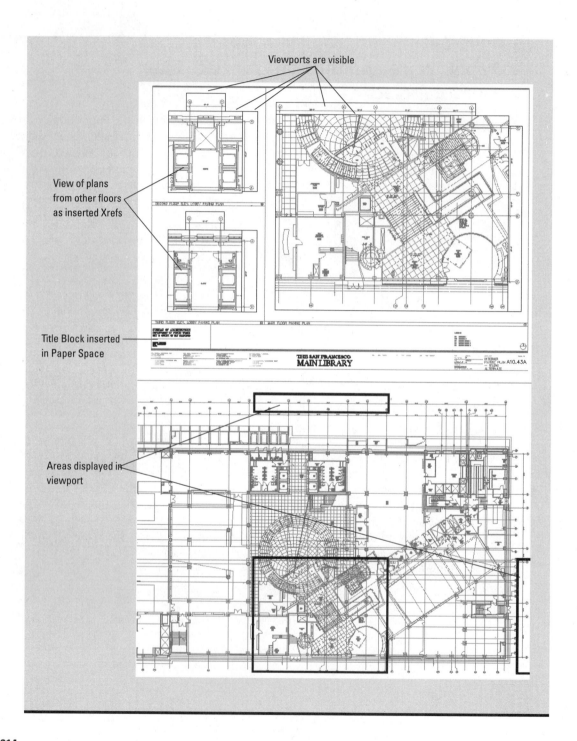

Viewports are visible

View of plans
from other floors
as inserted Xrefs

Title Block inserted
in Paper Space

THE SAN FRANCISCO
MAIN LIBRARY

Areas displayed in
viewport

Line-Type Scales and Paper Space

As you have seen from previous exercises, drawing scales have to be carefully controlled when creating viewports. Fortunately, this is easily done by choosing View ➤ Zoom ➤ Scale, and then entering the scale factor followed by **.xp**. While Paper Space offers the flexibility of combining different scale images in one display, it also adds to the complexity of your task in controlling that display. Your drawing's line type scale, in particular, needs careful attention.

In Chapter 4 you saw how you had to set the line-type scale to the scale factor of the drawing in order to make the line type visible. If you intend to plot that same drawing from Paper Space, you will have to set the line-type scale back to 1 to get the line types to appear correctly. This is because AutoCAD faithfully scales line types to the current unit system. Remember that Paper Space units differ from Model Space units. So when you scale a Model Space image down to fit within the smaller Paper Space area, the line types remain scaled to the increased line-type scale settings. In the case of that Chapter 4 example, line types are scaled up by a factor of 48. This causes noncontinuous lines to appear as continuous in Paper Space because you only see a small portion of a greatly enlarged noncontinuous line type.

The *Psltscale* system variable allows you to determine how line-type scales are applied to Paper Space views. You can set Psltscale so that the line types will appear the same regardless of whether you view them directly in tiled Model Space, or through a viewport in Paper Space. By default, this system variable is set to 1. This causes AutoCAD to scale all the line types uniformly across all the viewports in Paper Space. You can set Psltscale to 0 to force the viewports to display line types exactly as they appear in Model Space.

This setting can also be controlled in the Linetype tab of the Layer & Linetype Properties dialog box. There you will see a setting called Use Paper Space Units for Scaling in the lower-right corner. When this is checked, Psltscale is set to 1. When it is unchecked, Psltscale is set to 0.

Dimensioning in Paper Space

At times, you may find it more convenient to add dimensions to your drawing in Paper Space rather than directly on your objects in Model Space. There are several dimension settings you will want to know about that will enable you to do this.

To have your dimensions produce the appropriate values in Paper Space, you need to have AutoCAD adjust the dimension text to the scale of the viewport from which you are dimensioning. You can have AutoCAD scale dimension values so they correspond to a viewport zoom-scale factor. The following steps show you how this setting is made.

1. Open the Dimension Style dialog box.

2. Click on the Annotation button.

3. Click on the Units... button in the Annotation dialog box.

4. In the Linear input box of the Scale group, enter the inverse of the scale factor of the viewport you intend to dimension. For example, if the viewport is scaled to a 1/24xp scale, enter **24**. (If the Linear box is grayed out, remove the check from the Paper Space Only checkbox.)

5. Click on the Paper Space Only checkbox so a check appears there.

6. Click OK, and then click OK again at the Annotation dialog box.

7. Click on the Geometry button in the Dimension Styles dialog box.

8. Click on the Scale to Paper Space checkbox to place a check there. This forces the dimension objects to be scaled to Paper Space units.

9. Click OK, and then click OK to exit the Dimension Style dialog box.

You are ready to dimension in Paper Space. Remember that you can snap to objects in a floating viewport so you can add dimensions as you normally would in Model Space.

WARNING While AutoCAD offers the capability of adding dimensions in Paper Space, you may want to refrain from doing so until you have truly mastered AutoCAD. Because Paper Space dimensions won't be visible in Model Space, it is easy to forget to update your dimension when your drawing changes. Dimensioning in Paper Space can also create confusion for others editing your drawing at a later date.

Other Uses for Paper Space

The exercises presented in this section should give you a sense of how you work in Paper Space. We've given examples that reflect the more common uses of

Paper Space. Remember that it is like a page layout portion of AutoCAD—separate yet connected to Model Space through viewports.

You needn't limit your applications to floor plans. Interior and exterior elevation, 3D models, and detail sheets can all take advantage of Paper Space. When used in conjunction with AutoCAD raster import capabilities, Paper Space can be a powerful tool for creating large format presentations.

Advanced Tools: Selection Filter and Calculator

Before ending this chapter, you will want to know about two other tools that are extremely useful in your day-to-day work with AutoCAD: Selection Filters and the Calculator. I've saved the discussion of these tools for this chapter because you won't really need them until you've become accustomed to the way AutoCAD works. Chances are you've already experimented with some of AutoCAD's menu options not yet discussed in the tutorial. Many of the pull-down menu options and their functions are self-explanatory. Selection Filters and the Calculator, however, do not appear in any of the menus and require some further explanation.

We'll start with Selection Filters.

Filtering Selections

Suppose you need to take just the walls of your drawing and isolate them in a separate file. One way to do this would be to turn off all the layers except the Wall layer; then you could use the Wblock command and select the remaining walls, using a window to write the wall information to a file. Filters can simplify this operation by allowing you to select groups of objects based on their properties.

1. Open the Unit file.

2. Start the Wblock command by clicking on File ➢ Export. In the Create Drawing File dialog box, enter **unitwall.dwg** in the File input box, and click OK.

3. Press ↵ at the prompt for a block name, and then enter **0,0** at the Insertion base prompt.

4. At the object selection prompt, type 'Filter ↵. The Object Selection Filters dialog box appears.

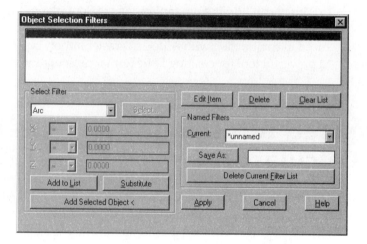

5. Open the drop-down list in the Select Filter button group.

6. Scroll down the list and find and highlight the Layer option.

7. Click on the Select... button next to the pop-up list to get a list of layers, highlight Wall, and then click OK.

8. At the Object Selection Filters dialog box, click on the Add to List button toward the bottom of the Select Filter button group. Layer = Wall is added to the list box.

9. Click on Apply. The dialog box closes.

10. Type all ↵ to select everything in the drawing. Only the objects assigned to the Wall layer are selected. You'll see a message in the Command window indicating how many objects were found and how many were filtered out.

11. Press ↵ and you'll see the message Exiting Filtered selection. 14 found.

12. Press ↵ again to complete the Wblock command. All the walls are written out to a file called **Unitwall**.

In this exercise, you filtered out a layer using the command. Once a filter is designated, you then select the group of objects you want AutoCAD to filter through. AutoCAD finds the objects that match the filter requirements and passes those objects to the current command.

As you've seen from the previous exercise, there are many options to choose from in this utility. Let's take a closer look.

Working with the Object Selection Filters Dialog Box

To use the Object Selection Filters dialog box, you first select the criteria for filtering from the pull-down list. If the criteria you select is a named item (layers, line types, colors, or blocks), you can then click on the Select button to choose specific items from a list. If there is only one choice, the Select button is grayed out.

Once you've determined what to filter, you must add it to the list by clicking on the Add to List button. The filter criteria then appears in the list box at the top of the dialog box. Once you have something in the list box, you can then apply it to your current command or to a later command. AutoCAD will remember your filter settings, so if you need to re-select a filtered selection set, you don't have to redefine your filter criteria.

Saving Filter Criteria

If you prefer, you can preselect a filter criteria. Then, at any `Select objects` prompt, you can click on Selection Filters from the toolbar (or type **'Filter ⏎**), highlight the appropriate filter criteria in the list box, and click on Apply. The specifications in the Object Selection Filters dialog box remain in place for the duration of the current editing session.

You can also save a set of criteria by entering a name in the input box next to the Save As button and then clicking the button. The criteria list data is saved in a file called `Filter.nfl`. You can then access the criteria list at any time by opening the Current pop-up list and choosing the name of the saved criteria list.

Filtering Objects by Location

Notice the X, Y, and Z pull-down lists just below the main Select Filters pull-down list. These lists become accessible when you select a criteria that describes a geometry or a coordinate (such as an arc's radius or center point). You can use these lists to define filter selections even more specifically, using greater than (>), less than (<), equal to (=), or not equal to (!=) comparisons (called *relational operators*).

For example, suppose you want to grab all the circles whose radii are greater than 4.0 units. To do this, choose Circle Radius from the Select Filters pop-up list.

Then in the X list, select the >. Enter **4.0** in the input box to the right of the X list, and click on Add to List. You see the item:

```
Circle Radius > 4.0000
```

added to the list box at the top of the dialog box. You have used the > to indicate a circle radius greater than 4.0 units.

Creating Complex Selection Sets

There will be times when you will want to create a very specific filter list. For instance, say you need to filter out all the door blocks on the layer Floor2 *and* all arcs with a radius equal to 1. To do this, you use the *grouping operators* found at the bottom of the Select Filter pull-down. You'll need to build a list as follows:

```
** Begin OR
** Begin AND
Entity = Block
Layer = Floor2
** End AND
** Begin AND
Entity = Arc
Arc Radius = 1.0000
** End AND
** End OR
```

Notice that the Begin and End operators are balanced; that is, for every Begin OR or Begin AND, there is an End OR or an End AND.

This list may look rather simple, but it can get confusing—mostly because of the way we normally think of the terms *and* and *or*. If a criteria is bounded by the AND grouping operators, then the objects must fulfill *both* criteria before they are selected. If a criteria is bounded by the OR grouping operators, then the objects fulfilling *either* criteria will be selected.

Here are the steps to build the list shown just above.

1. In the Select Filter pull-down list, choose **Begin OR, and click on Add to List. Then do the same for **Begin AND.

2. Click on Block from the Select Filters list, and then on Add to List.

3. For the layer, click on Layer from the Select Filter list. Then click Select..., choose the layer name, and click Add to List.

4. In the Select Filter list, choose **End AND and click on Add to List. Then do the same for **Begin AND.

5. Select Arc from the Select Filter list and click Add to List.

6. Select Arc Radius from the Select Filter list, and enter **1.0** in the input box next to the X pop-up. Be sure the = shows in the X pull-down, and then click on Add to List.

7. Choose **End AND and click on Add to List. Then do the same for **End OR.

If you make an error in any of the above steps, just highlight the item, select an item to replace it, and click on the Substitute button instead of the Add to List button. If you only need to change a value, click on Edit Item near the center of the dialog box.

Finding Geometry with the Calculator

Another useful AutoCAD tool is the geometry Calculator. Like most calculators, it adds, subtracts, divides, and multiplies. If you enter an arithmetic expression such as 1 + 2, the calculator returns 3. This is useful for doing math on-the-fly, but the Calculator does much more than arithmetic, as you will see in the next examples.

Finding the Midpoint between Two Points

One of the most common questions heard from AutoCAD users is, "How can I locate a point midway between two objects?" You can draw a construction line between the two objects, and then use the Midpoint override to select the midpoint of the construction line. The Calculator offers another method that doesn't require drawing additional objects.

In the following exercise, you start a line midway between the center of an arc and the endpoint of a line. Draw a line and an arc and try this out.

1. Start the Line command, and at the From point prompt, type 'Cal ↲.

2. At the >> Expression prompt, enter **(end + cen)/2** ↲.

3. At the >> Select entity for END snap prompt, the cursor turns into a square. Place the square on the endpoint of a line and click on it.

4. At the >> Select entity for CEN snap prompt, click on an arc. The line will start midway between the arc's center and the endpoint of the line.

TIP

Typing the Calculator expressions may seem a bit too cumbersome to use on a regular basis, but if you find you could use some of its features, you can create a toolbar macro to simplify the Calculators use. See Chapter 21 for more on customizing toolbars.

Using Osnap Modes in Calculator Expressions

In the foregoing exercise, you used Osnap modes as part of arithmetic expressions. The Calculator treats them as temporary placeholders for point coordinates until you actually pick the points (at the prompts shown in steps 3 and 4 above).

The expression:

```
(end + cen)/2
```

finds the average of two values. In this case, the values are coordinates, so the average is the midpoint between the two coordinates. You can take this one step further and find the centroid of a triangle using this expression:

```
(end + end + end)/3
```

Note than only the first three letters of the Osnap mode are entered in Calculator expressions. Table 12.1 shows what to enter in an expression for Osnap modes.

TABLE 12.1: The Geometry Calculator's Osnap modes

Calculator Osnap	Meaning
End	Endpoint
Ins	Insert
Int	Intersection
Mid	Midpoint
Cen	Center
Nea	Nearest
Nod	Node

TABLE 12.1 CONTINUED: The Geometry Calculator's Osnap modes

Calculator Osnap	Meaning
Qua	Quadrant
Per	Perpendicular
Tan	Tangent
Rad	Radius of object
Cur	Cursor pick

I've included two items in the table that are not really Osnap modes, though they work similarly when they are used in an expression. The first is Rad. When you include Rad in an expression, you get the prompt:

```
Select circle, arc or polyline segment for RAD function:
```

You can then select an arc, polyline arc segment, or circle, and its radius is used in place of Rad in the expression.

The other item, Cur, prompts you for a point. Instead of looking for specific geometry on an object, it just locates a point. You could have used Cur in the previous exercise in place of the End and Cen modes, to create a more general purpose midpoint locator as in the following form:

```
(cur + cur)/2
```

Since AutoCAD does not provide a specific tool to select a point midway between two other points, the form shown here would be useful as a custom toolbar macro. You'll learn how to create macros in Chapter 19.

Finding a Point Relative to Another Point

Another common task in AutoCAD is starting a line at a relative distance from another line. The following steps describe how to use Calculator to start a line from a point that is 2.5" in the x-axis and 5.0" in the y-axis from the endpoint of another line.

1. Start the Line command. At the First point prompt, enter **'Cal** ⏎.

2. At the >> Expression prompt, enter **end + [2.5,5.0]** ⏎.

3. At the >> Select entity for END snap prompt, pick the endpoint. The line starts from the desired location.

In this example, you used the Endpoint Osnap mode to indicate a point of reference. This is added to Cartesian coordinates in square brackets, describing the distance and direction from the reference point. You could have entered any coordinate value within the square brackets. You could also have entered a polar coordinate in place of the Cartesian coordinate, as in the following:

```
end + [5.59<63]
```

You don't have to include the @, because the Calculator assumes you want to add the coordinate to the one indicated by the Endpoint Osnap mode. Also, it's not necessary to include every coordinate in the square brackets. For example, to indicate a displacement in only one axis, you can leave out a value for the other two coordinates, as in the following examples:

```
[4,5] = [4,5,0]  [,1] = [0,1,0]
[,,2] = [0,0,2]
[] = [0,0,0]
```

Adding Feet and Inch Distances On-the-Fly

One of the more frustrating situations you may have run across is having to stop in the middle of a command to find the sum of two or more distances. Say you start the Move command, select your objects, and pick a base point. Then you realize you don't know the distance for the move, but you do know that the distance is the sum of two values—unfortunately, one value is in feet and the other is in inches. Usually in this situation you would have to reach for pen and paper (or, if you've got one, a foot and inch calculator), then figure out the distance, and then return to your computer to finish the task. AutoCAD's Geometry Calculator puts an end to this runaround.

The following shows you what to do if you want to move a set of objects a distance that is the sum of 12 ' 6 " -5/8" and 115- 3/4".

1. Issue the Move command, select objects, and pick a base point.

2. At the Second point prompt, start the Calculator.

3. At the >> Expression: prompt, enter:

```
[@12'6" + 115-3/4" < 45]
```

Then press ↵, and the objects move into place at the proper distance.

> **WARNING** You must always enter an inch symbol (") when indicating inches in the Calculator.

In this example, you are mixing inches and feet, which under normal circumstances is a time-consuming calculation. Notice that the feet-and-inch format follows the standard AutoCAD syntax (no space between the feet and inch values). The coordinate value in square brackets can have any number of operators and values, as in the following:

```
[@4 * (22 + 15) - (23.3 / 12) + 1 < 13 + 17]
```

This expression demonstrates that you can also apply operators to angle values.

Guidelines for Working with the Calculator

You may be noticing some patterns in the way expressions are formatted for the Calculator. Here are some guidelines to remember:

- Coordinates are enclosed in square brackets.
- Nested or grouped expressions are enclosed in parentheses.
- Operators are placed between values, as in simple math equations.
- Object snaps can be used in place of coordinate values.

Table 12.2 lists all the operators and functions available in the Calculator. You may want to experiment with these other functions on your own.

TABLE 12.2: The Geometry Calculator's functions

Operator/Function	What It Does	Example
+ or -	Add or subtract numbers or vectors	2 - 1 = 1 [a,b,c] + [x,y,z] = [a+x, b+y, c+z]
* or /	Multiply or divide numbers or vectors	2 * 4.2 = 8.4 a*[x,y,z] = [a*x, a*y, a*z]
^	Exponentiation of a number	3^2 = 9
sin	Sine of angle	sin (45) = 0.707107
cos	Cosine of angle	cos (30) = 0.866025

TABLE 12.2 CONTINUED: The Geometry Calculator's functions

Operator/Function	What It Does	Example
tang	Tangent of angle	tang (30) = 0.57735
asin	Arcsine of a real number	asin (0.707107) = 45.0
acos	Arccosine of a real number	acos (0.866025) = 30.0
atan	Arctangent of a real number	atan (0.57735) = 30.0
ln	Natural log	ln (2) = 0.693147
log	Base-10 log	log (2) = 0.30103
exp	Natural exponent	exp (2) = 7.38906
exp10	Base-10 exponent	exp10 (2) = 100
sqr	Square of number	sqr (9) = 81.0
abs	Absolute value	abs (~-3.4) = 3.4
round	Rounds to nearest integer	round (3.6) = 4
trunc	Drops decimal portion of real number	trunc (3.6) = 3
r2d	Converts radians to degrees	r2d (1.5708) = 90.0002
d2r	Converts degrees to radians	d2r (90) = 1.5708
pi	The constant pi	3.14159

The Geometry Calculator is capable of much more than the typical uses you've seen here and extend beyond the scope of this text. Still, the processes described in this section will be helpful as you use AutoCAD. If you want to know more about the Calculator, consult the *AutoCAD Command Reference* and the *User's Guide* that comes with Release 14.

If You Want to Experiment...

You may want to experiment further with Paper Space to become more familiar with it. Try the following exercise. In it you will add two more viewports using the View ➤ Viewports (Floating) options (Mview and Copy commands. In the process, you'll find that editing Paper Space views requires frequent shifts from Model Space to Paper Space and back.

1.   Open the Xref1 file you used for the earlier Paper Space exercise.

2.   If you aren't already in Paper Space, type **Pspace** ↵.

3.   Turn on the Vport layer and Stretch the lower viewport so that it occupies the lower-right third of the screen (see the top image of Figure 12.39).

4.   Switch to floating Model Space and click on the lower viewport.

5.   Pan the view so the entire stair is displayed.

6.   Return to Paper Space to create a new viewport.

7.   Choose View ➤ Floating Viewports ➤ 1 Viewport, or type **Mview** ↵.

8.   At the OFF/ON/Hideplot prompt, pick the lower-left corner of the screen.

9.   At the Other corner prompt, size the viewport so that it is similar to the viewport on the right, as shown in the bottom image of Figure 12.39.

10.   At the command prompt, type **Mspace** ↵ to switch over to Model Space.

11.   Pick the lower-left viewport.

12.   Type **Regen** ↵. Notice that only the current viewport regenerates.

13.   Use the Zoom and Pan commands to display the stairway at the far left of the floor plan.

14.   Return to Paper Space and copy the new viewport to the right.

15.   Return to Model Space and pan the view to display the stairway to the far right of the floor plan.

16.   Return to Paper Space to resize the viewports to display only the stairs, as in the continued image of Figure 12.39.

FIGURE 12.39:

Creating new viewports in Paper Space

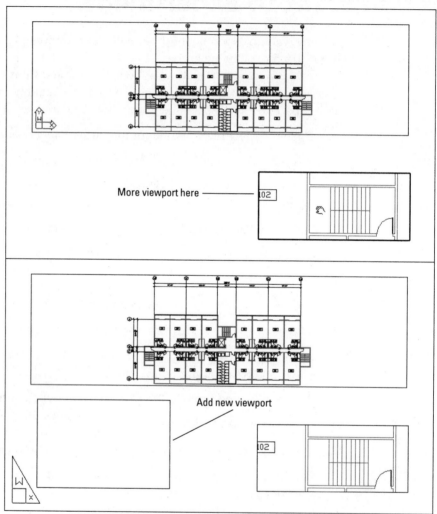

**FIGURE 12.39
CONTINUED:**

Creating new viewports
in Paper Space

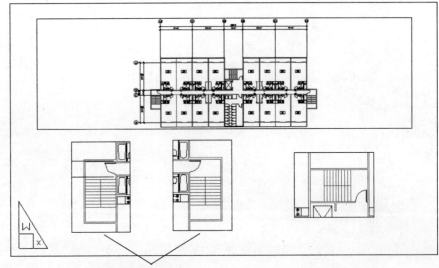

Copy viewport and change
view to show other stair

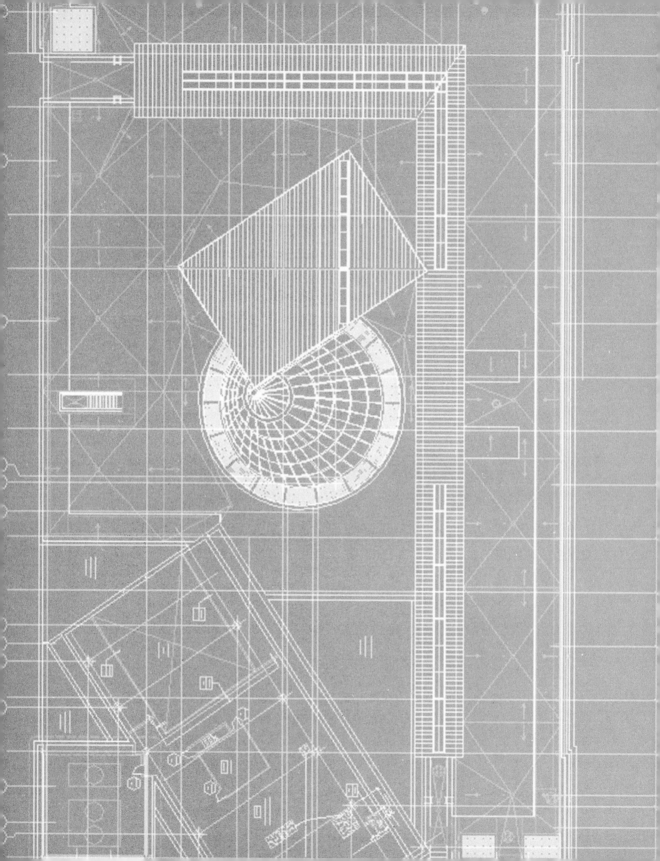

CHAPTER

THIRTEEN

Drawing Curves and Solid Fills

13

So far in this book, you've been using basic lines, arcs, and circles to create your drawings. Now it's time to add polylines and spline curves to your repertoire. Polylines offer many options for creating forms, including solid fills. Spline curves are perfect for drawing smooth, nonlinear objects. The Splines are true *NURBS* curves. NURBS stands for Non-Uniform Rational B-Splines.

Introducing Polylines

Polylines are like composite line segments and arcs. A polyline may look like a series of line segments, but it acts like a single object. This characteristic makes polylines useful for a variety of applications, as you'll see in the upcoming exercises.

Drawing a Polyline

First, to introduce you to the polyline, you will begin a drawing of the top view of the joint in Figure 13.1.

FIGURE 13.1:

A sketch of a
metal joint

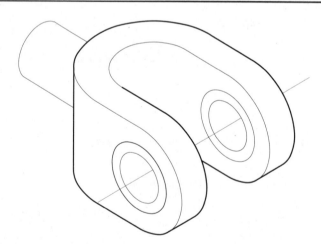

1. Open a new file and save it as **Joint2d**. Don't bother to make special setting changes, as you will do this drawing with the default settings.

2. Click the Polyline tool on the Draw toolbar, or type **Pl** ↵.

3. At the `From point` prompt, enter a point at coordinate 3,3 to start your polyline.

4. At the prompt:

   `Arc/Close/Halfwidth/Length/Undo/Width/<Endpoint of line>`

   enter **@3<0** ↵ to draw a horizontal line of the joint.

> **NOTE** You can draw polylines just as you would with the Line command. Or you can use the other Pline options to enter a polyline arc, specify polyline thickness, or add a polyline segment in the same direction as the previously drawn line.

5. At the `Arc/Close/Halfwidth...` prompt, enter **A** ↵ to continue your polyline with an arc.

> **NOTE** The Arc option allows you to draw an arc that starts from the last point you selected. Once selected, the Arc option offers additional options. The default Save option is the endpoint of the arc. As you move your cursor, an arc follows it in a tangent direction from the first line segment you drew.

6. At the prompt:

   `Angle\CEnter\CLose\Direction\Halfwidth\Line\Radius\`
   `Second pt\Undo\Width\<Endpoint of arc>:`

   enter **@4<90** ↵ to draw a 180° arc from the last point you entered. Your drawing should now look like Figure 13.2.

7. Continue the polyline with another line segment. To do this, enter **L** ↵.

8. At the `Arc\Close\Halfwidth...` prompt, enter **@3<180** ↵. Another line segment continues from the end of the arc.

9. Press ↵ to exit Pline.

You now have a sideways, U-shaped polyline that you will use in the next exercise to complete the top view of your joint.

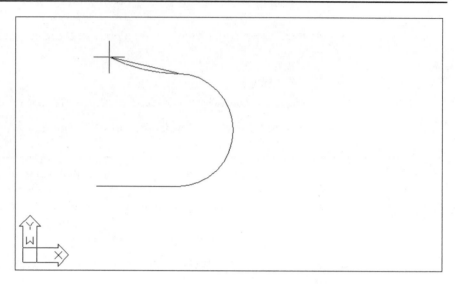

Polyline Options

Let's pause from the tutorial to look at some of the Polyline options you didn't use.

Close   draws a line segment from the last endpoint of a sequence of lines to the first point picked in that sequence. This works exactly like the Close option for the Line command.

Length   enables you to specify the length of a line that will be drawn at the same angle as the last line entered.

Halfwidth   creates a tapered line segment or arc by specifying half its beginning and ending widths (see Figure 13.3).

Width   creates a tapered line segment or arc by specifying the full width of the segment's beginning and ending points.

Undo   deletes the last line segment drawn.

If you want to break down a polyline into simple lines and arcs, you can use the Explode option on the Modify toolbar, just as you would with blocks. Once a polyline is exploded, it becomes a set of individual line segments or arcs.

FIGURE 13.3:

Tapered line segment
and arc created with
Halfwidth

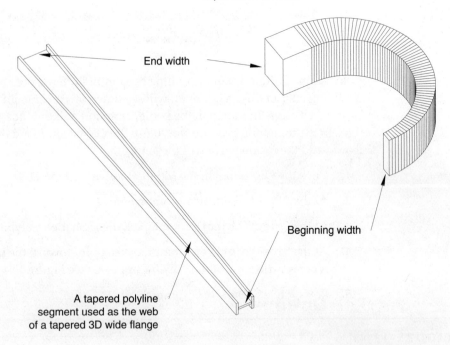

A tapered arc used to
represent a 3D duct

End width

Beginning width

A tapered polyline
segment used as the web
of a tapered 3D wide flange

To turn off the filling of solid polylines, click Tools ➢ Drawing Aids, then at the
Drawing Aids dialog box, remove the check from the Solid Fill option. (The Display
options are explained in detail later in this chapter in the section on solid fills.)

NOTE The Fillet tool on the Modify toolbar can be used to fillet all the vertices of
a polyline composed of straight line segments. To do this, click Fillet, and
then set your fillet radius. Click Fillet again, type **P** ↵ to select Polyline
option, and then pick the polyline you want to fillet.

Editing Polylines

You can edit polylines with many of the standard editing commands. To change the
properties of a polyline, click the Properties tool on the Object Properties toolbar
(Ddmodify). The Stretch command on the Modify toolbar can be used to displace

vertices of a polyline, and the Trim, Extend, and Break commands on the Modify toolbar also work with polylines.

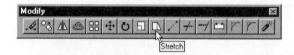

In addition, there are many editing capabilities offered only for polylines. For instance, later in this chapter you will see how you can smooth out a polyline using the Curve Fit option in the Pedit command and the Modify Polyline dialog box. In the following exercise, you'll use the Offset command on the Modify toolbar to add the inside portion of the joint.

1. Click the Offset tool in the Modify toolbar, or type **O** ↵.

2. At the Offset distance prompt, enter **1**.

3. At the Select object prompt, pick the U-shaped polyline you just drew.

4. At the Side to offset prompt, pick a point toward the inside of the U. A concentric copy of the polyline appears (see Figure 13.4).

5. Press ↵ to exit the Offset command.

FIGURE 13.4:

The offset polyline

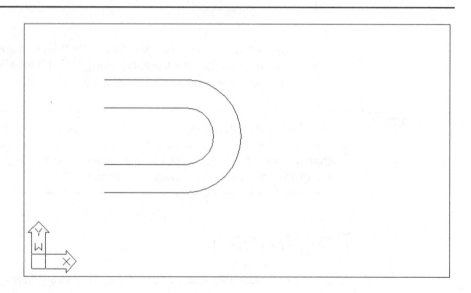

The concentric copy of a polyline made with Construct ➤ Offset can be very useful when you need to draw complex parallel curves like the ones in Figure 13.5.

FIGURE 13.5:

Sample complex curves drawn by using offset polylines

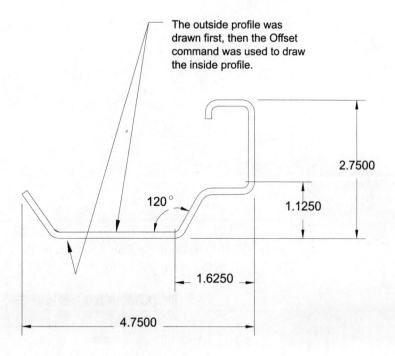

The outside profile was drawn first, then the Offset command was used to draw the inside profile.

Next, complete the top view of the joint.

1. Connect the ends of the polylines with two short line segments (see Figure 13.6).

WARNING The objects to be joined must touch the existing polyline exactly endpoint to endpoint, or else they will not join. To ensure that you place the endpoints of the lines exactly on the endpoints of the polylines, use the Endpoint Osnap override to select each polyline endpoint.

FIGURE 13.6:

The joined polyline

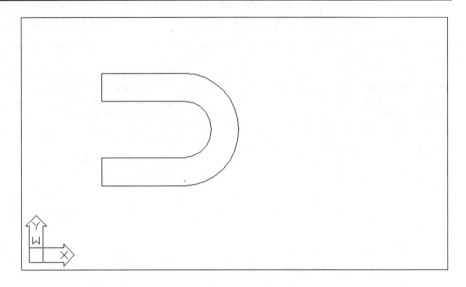

2. Choose Modify ➢ Object ➢ Polyline, or type **Pe** ↵. You can also choose Edit Polyline from the Modify II toolbar.

3. At the Select polyline prompt, pick the outermost polyline.

4. At the Close/Join/Width… prompt, enter **J** ↵ for the Join option.

5. At the Select objects prompt, select all the objects you have drawn so far.

6. Once all the objects are selected, press ↵ to join them all into one polyline. It appears that nothing has happened, though you will see the message "4 segments added to polyline in the Command window." The 4 segments in the message refers to the 4 objects in your drawing.

7. Press ↵ again to exit the Pedit command.

8. Click the drawing to expose its grips. The entire object is hightlighted, telling you that all the lines have been joined into a single polyline.

By using the Width option under Edit Polyline, you can change the thickness of a polyline. Let's change the width of your polyline, to give some thickness to the outline of the joint.

1. Click the Edit Polyline tool from Modify toolbar again.

2. Click the polyline.

3. At the Close/Join/Width... prompt, enter **W** ⏎ for the Width option.

4. At the Enter new width for all segments prompt, enter **.03** ⏎ for the new width of the polyline. The line changes to the new width (see Figure 13.7), and you now have a top view of your joint.

5. Press ⏎ to exit the Pedit command.

6. Save this file.

FIGURE 13.7:

The polyline with a new thickness

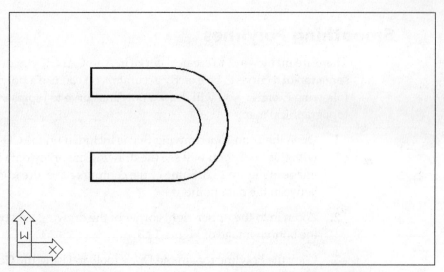

Now here's a brief look at a few of the Pedit options you didn't try firsthand:

Close   connects the two endpoints of a polyline with a line segment. If the polyline you selected to be edited is already closed, this option changes to Open.

Open   removes the last segment added to a closed polyline.

Spline/Decurve   smooths a polyline into a spline curve (discussed in detail later in this chapter).

Edit Vertex   lets you edit each vertex of a polyline individually (discussed in detail in the next section).

Fit   turns polyline segments into a series of arcs.

Ltype Gen   controls the way non-continuous line types pass through the vertices of a polyline. If you have a fitted or spline curve with a non-continuous line type, you will want to turn this option on.

TIP

You can change the thickness of regular lines and arcs by using Pedit to change them into polylines, and then using the Width option to change their width.

Smoothing Polylines

There are many ways to create a curve in AutoCAD. If you don't need the representation of a curve to be exactly accurate, you can use a polyline curve. In the following exercise, you will draw a polyline curve to represent a contour on a topographical map.

1. Open the Topo.dwg drawing that is included on the CD-ROM that comes with this book. You will see the drawing of survey data shown in the top image of Figure 13.8. Some of the contours have already been drawn in between the data points.

2. Zoom in to the upper-right corner of the drawing, so your screen looks like the bottom image of Figure 13.8.

3. Click the Polyline tool in the Draw toolbar. Using the Center Osnap, draw a polyline that connects the points labeled "254.00." Your drawing should look like the continued image of Figure 13.8.

FIGURE 13.8:

The Topo.dwg drawing shows survey data portrayed in an AutoCAD drawing. Notice the dots indicating where elevations were taken. The actual elevation value is shown with a diagonal line from the point.

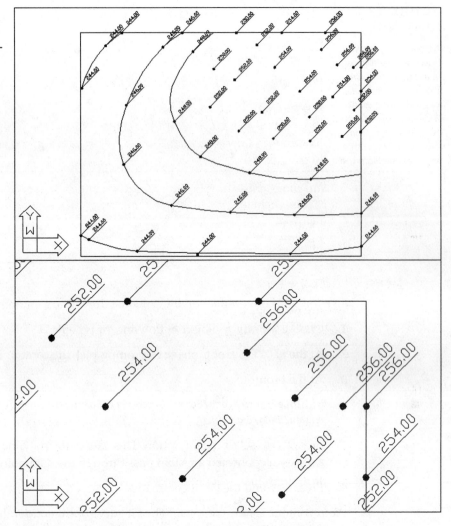

4. When you have drawn the polyline, press ↵.

TIP

If Running Osnaps are not set, you can double-click the OSNAP label in the status bar to open the Osnap Settings dialog box. From there, you can select Center to turn on the Center Running Osnaps dialog box. See Chapter 3 for more on this dialog box.

**FIGURE 13.8:
CONTINUED**

The Topo.dwg drawing
shows survey data por-
trayed in an AutoCAD
drawing. Notice the
dots indicating where
elevations were taken.
The actual elevation
value is shown with a
diagonal line from the
point.

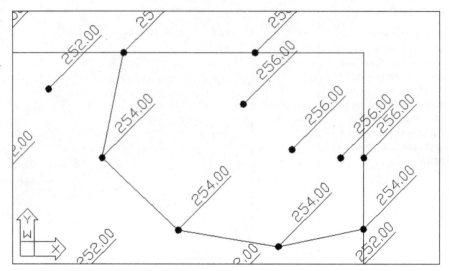

Next you will convert the polyline you just drew into a smooth contour line.

1. Choose Modify ➤ Object ➤ Polyline, or type **Pe** ↵.

2. At the PEDIT Select objects prompt, pick the contour line you just drew.

3. At the prompt:

    ```
    Close/Join/Width/Edit vertex/Fit/Spline/Decurve/Ltype
    gen/Undo/Exit:
    ```

    press **F** ↵ to select the Fit option. This causes the polyline to smooth out into
    a series of connected arcs that pass through the data points.

4. Press ↵ to end the Pedit command.

Your contour is now complete. The Fit curve option under the Pedit command
causes AutoCAD to convert the straight-line segments of the polyline into arcs.
The endpoints of the arcs pass through the endpoints of the line segments, and
the curve of each arc depends on the direction of the adjacent arc. This gives the
effect of a smooth curve. Next, you'll use this polyline curve to experiment with
some of the editing options unique to the Pedit command.

Turning Objects into Polylines and Polylines into Splines

There may be times when you will want to convert regular lines, arcs, or even circles into polylines. You may want to change the width of lines, or join lines together to form a single object such as a boundary. Here are the steps to take to convert lines, arcs, and circles into polylines.

1. Choose Modify ➢ Object ➢ Polyline. You can also type **Pe** ↵ at the command prompt.

2. At the Select polyline prompt, pick the object you wish to convert. If you want to convert a circle to a polyline, you must first break the circle (Break option on the Modify toolbar) so that it becomes an arc of approximately 359°.

3. At the prompt:

   Object selected is not a polyline. Do you want to turn it into one? <Y>

   press ↵ twice. The object is converted into a polyline.

If you have a polyline you would like to turn into a true spline curve, do the following:

1. Choose Modify ➢ Object ➢ Polyline, or type **Pe** ↵. Select the polyline you want to convert.

2. Type **S** ↵ to turn it into a polyline spline; then type **X** ↵ to exit the Pedit command.

3. Click the Spline tool in the Draw Toolbar or type **Spl** ↵. You can also select Draw ➢ Spline from the pull-down menu

4. At the Object/<Enter first point> prompt, type **O** ↵ for the Object option.

5. At the Select object prompt, click the polyline spline. Though it may not be apparent at first, the polyline is converted into a true spline.

You can also use the Spline Edit tool (Modify ➢ Object ➢ Spline or **Spe** ↵) on a polyline spline. If you do, the polyline spline is automatically converted into a true spline.

Editing Vertices

One of the Pedit options we haven't yet discussed, Edit Vertex, is almost like a command within a command. Edit Vertex has numerous suboptions that allow you to fine-tune your polyline by giving you control over its individual vertices. We'll discuss this command in depth in this section.

To access the Edit Vertex options, follow these steps.

1. First, turn off the Data and Border layers to hide the data points and border.

2. Issue the Pedit command again. Then select the polyline you just drew.

3. Type **E** ↵ to enter the Edit Vertex mode. An X appears at the beginning of the polyline, indicating the vertex that will be affected by the Edit Vertex options.

WARNING When using Edit Vertex, you must be careful about selecting the vertex to be edited. Edit Vertex has six options, and you often have to exit the Edit Vertex operation and use Pedit's Fit option to see the effect of Edit Vertex's options on a curved polyline.

Edit Vertex Suboptions

Once you've entered the Edit Vertex mode of the Pedit command, you have the option to perform the following functions:

- Break the polyline between two vertices

- Insert a new vertex

- Move an existing vertex

- Straighten a polyline between two vertices

- Change the Tangent direction of a vertex

- Change the width of the polyline at a vertex

These functions are presented in the form of the prompt:

```
Next/Previous/Break/Insert/Move/Regen/Straighten/Tangent/Width/
eXit <N>:
```

We'll examine each of the options presented in this prompt in the rest of this section, starting with the Next and Previous options.

Next and Previous   The Next and Previous options enable you to select a vertex for editing. When you started the Edit Vertex option, an X appeared on the selected polyline to designate its beginning. As you select Next or Previous, the X moves from vertex to vertex to show which one is being edited. Let's try this out.

1. Press ↵ a couple of times to move the X along the polyline. (Because Next is the default option, you only need to press ↵ to move the X.)

2. Type **P** ↵ for Previous. The X moves in the opposite direction. Notice that now the default option becomes P.

TIP
> To determine the direction of a polyline, note the direction the X moves in when you use the Next option. Knowing the direction of a polyline is important for some of the other Edit Vertex options discussed below.

Break   The Break option breaks the polyline between two vertices.

1. Position the X on one end of the segment you want to break.

2. Enter **B** ↵ at the command prompt.

3. At the Next/Previous/Go/Exit <N> prompt, use Next or Previous to move the X to the other end of the segment to be broken.

4. When the X is in the right position, pick Go from the Edit Vertex menu or enter **G** ↵, and the polyline will be broken (see Figure 13.9).

NOTE
> You can also use the Break and Trim options on the Modify toolbar to break a polyline anywhere, as you did when you drew the toilet seat in Chapter 3.

Insert   Next, try the Insert option, which inserts a new vertex.

1. Type **X** ↵ to temporarily exit the Edit Vertex option. Then type **U** ↵ to undo the break.

2. Type **E** ↵ to return to the Edit Vertex option, and position the X before the new vertex.

3. Press ↵ to advance the X marker to the next point.

4. Enter **I** ↵ to select the Insert option.

5. When the prompt Enter location of new vertex appears, along with a rubber-banding line originating from the current X position (see Figure 13.10), pick a point indicating the new vertex location. The polyline is redrawn with the new vertex.

FIGURE 13.9:

How the Break option works

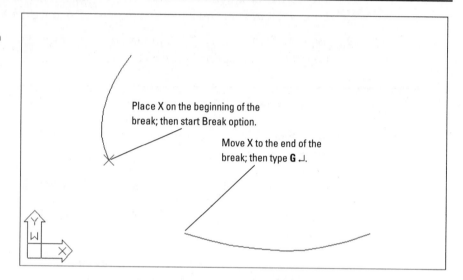

Place X on the beginning of the break; then start Break option.

Move X to the end of the break; then type **G** ↵.

FIGURE 13.10:

The new vertex location

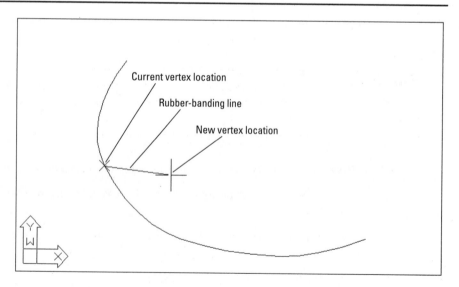

Current vertex location

Rubber-banding line

New vertex location

Notice that the inserted vertex appears between the currently marked vertex and the *next* vertex, so this Insert option is sensitive to the direction of the polyline. If the polyline is curved, the new vertex will not immediately be shown as curved (see the top image of Figure 13.11). You must smooth it out by exiting the Edit Vertex option and then using the Fit option, as you did to edit the site plan (see the bottom image of Figure 13.11). You can also use the Stretch command (on the Modify toolbar) to move a polyline vertex.

FIGURE 13.11:

The polyline before and after the curve is fitted

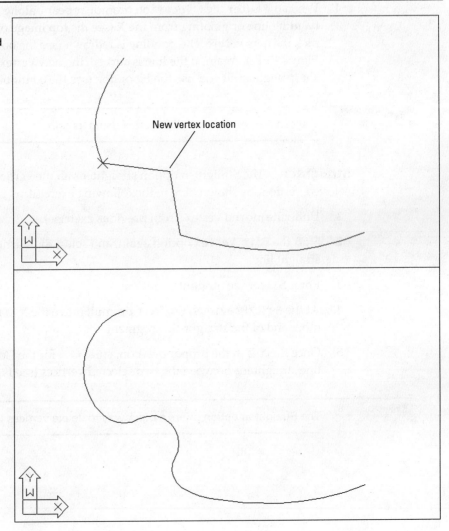

New vertex location

Move   In this brief exercise, you'll use the Move option to move a vertex.

1. Undo the inserted vertex by exiting the Edit Vertex option (X ↵) and typing **U** ↵.

2. Restart the Edit Vertex option, and use the Next or Previous option to place the X on the vertex you wish to move.

3. Enter **M** ↵ for the Move option.

4. When the `Enter new location` prompt appears, along with a rubber-banding line originating from the X (see the top image of Figure 13.12), pick the new vertex. The polyline is redrawn (see the bottom image of Figure 13.12). Again, if the line is curved, the new vertex appears as a sharp angle until you use the Fit option (see the continued of 13.12).

> **TIP**   You can also move a polyline vertex using its grip.

Straighten   The Straighten option straightens all the vertices between two selected vertices, as shown here in the following exercise.

1. Undo the moved vertex (from previous exercise).

2. Start the `Edit Vertex` option again, and select the starting vertex for the straight line.

3. Enter **S** ↵ for the Straighten option.

4. At the `Next/Previous/Go/Exit` prompt, move the X to the location for the other end of the straight-line segment.

5. Once the X is in the proper position, enter **G** ↵ for the Go option. The polyline straightens between the two selected vertices (see Figure 13.13).

> **TIP**   The Straighten option offers a quick way to delete vertices from a polyline.

FIGURE 13.12:

Picking a new location
for a vertex, with the
polyline before and
after the curve is fitted

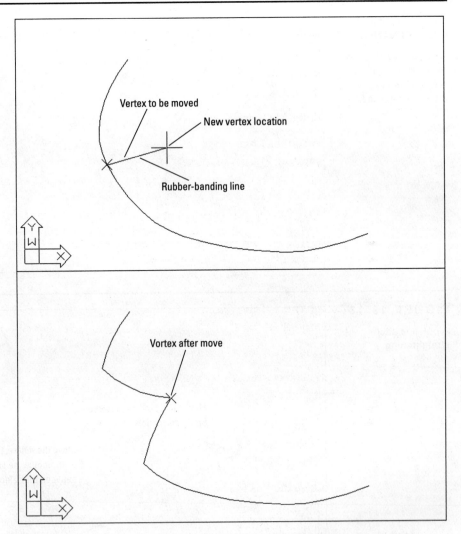

FIGURE 13.12:
CONTINUED

Picking a new location
for a vertex, with the
polyline before and
after the curve is fitted

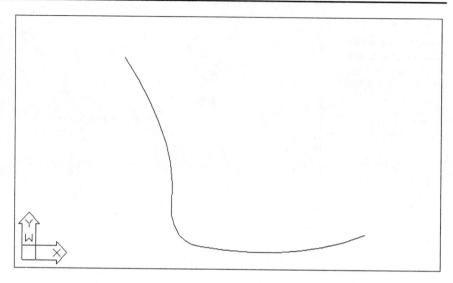

FIGURE 13.13:

A polyline after
straightening

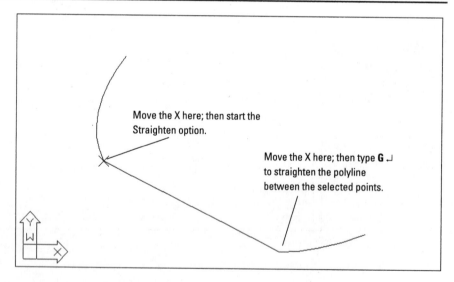

Move the X here; then start the
Straighten option.

Move the X here; then type **G** ⏎
to straighten the polyline
between the selected points.

Tangent   Next is the Tangent option, which alters the direction of a curve on a curve-fitted polyline.

1. Undo the straightened segment from the previous exercise.

2. Restart the Edit Vertex option, and position the X on the vertex you wish to alter.

3. Enter **T** ↲ for the Tangent option. A rubber-banding line appears (see the top image of Figure 13.14).

4. Point the rubber-banding line in the direction for the new tangent, and click the mouse. An arrow appears, indicating the new tangent direction (see the bottom image of Figure 13.14).

Don't worry if the polyline shape does not change. You must use Fit to see the effect of Tangent (see the continued image of Figure 13.14).

Width Finally, try out the Width option. Unlike the Pedit command's Width option, Edit Vertex/Width enables you to alter the width of the polyline at any vertex. Thus you can taper or otherwise vary polyline thickness.

1. Undo the tangent arc from the previous exercise.

2. Return to the Edit Vertex option, and place the X at the beginning vertex of a polyline segment you want to change.

3. Type **W** ↲ to issue the Width option.

4. At the `Enter starting width` prompt, enter a value, 1' for example, indicating the polyline width desired at this vertex.

5. At the `Enter ending width` prompt, enter the width, 2' for example, for the next vertex.

Again (as with Tangent), don't be alarmed if nothing happens after you enter this Width value. To see the result, you must exit the Edit Vertex command (see Figure 13.15).

NOTE The Width option is useful when you want to create an irregular or curved area in your drawing that is to be filled in solid. This is another option that is sensitive to the polyline direction.

FIGURE 13.14:

Picking a new tangent direction

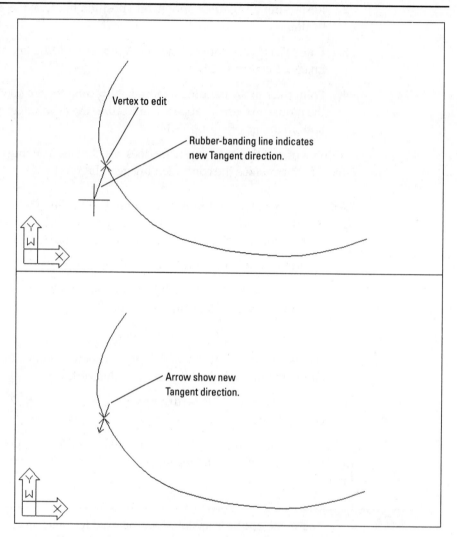

FIGURE 13.14:
CONTINUED

Picking a new tangent
direction

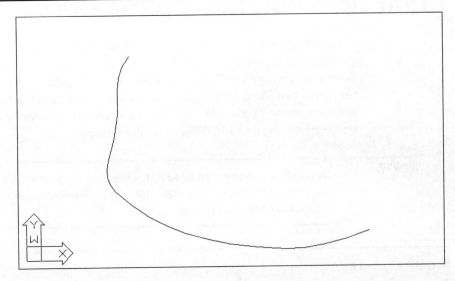

FIGURE 13.15:

A polyline with the
width of one segment
increased

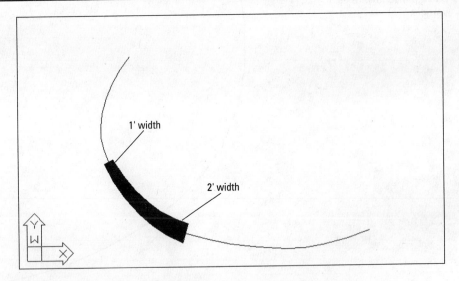

As you have seen throughout these exercises, you can use the Undo option to reverse the last Edit Vertex option used. And you can use the Edit option to leave Edit Vertex at any time. Just enter **X** ↵, and this brings you back to the Pedit Close/Join/Width... prompt.

Creating a Polyline Spline Curve

The Pedit command's Spline option (named after the spline tool used in manual drafting) offers you a way to draw smoother and more controllable curves than those produced by the Fit option. A polyline spline does not pass through the vertex points as a fitted curve does. Instead, the vertex points act as weights pulling the curve in their direction. The polyline spline only touches its beginning and end vertices. Figure 13.16 illustrates this concept.

NOTE   A polyline spline curve does not represent a mathematically true curve. See *Using True Spline Curves* later in this chapter to learn how to draw a more accurate spline curve.

FIGURE 13.16:

The polyline spline curve pulled toward its vertices

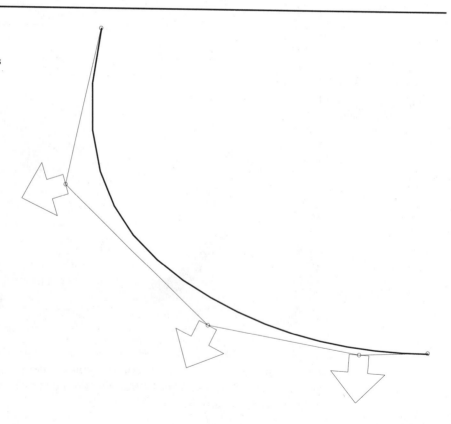

Let's see how using a polyline spline curve might influence the way you edit a curve.

1. Undo the width changes you made in the previous exercise.

2. To change the contour into a polyline spline curve, choose Modify ➢ Object ➢ Polyline.

3. Then pick the polyline to be curved.

4. At the Close\Join\Width... prompt, enter **S** ↵. Your curve will change to look like Figure 13.17.

5. Press ↵ to exit Edit Polyline.

FIGURE 13.17:

A spline curve

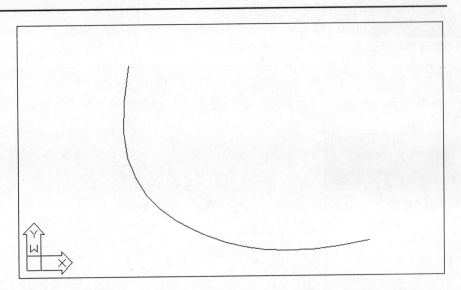

The curve takes on a smoother, more graceful appearance. It no longer passes through the points you used to define it. To see where the points went and to find out how spline curves act, do the following:

1. Make sure the Noun/Verb Selection mode and the Grips feature are turned on.

2. Click the curve. You'll see the original vertices appear as grips (see the top image of Figure 13.18).

FIGURE 13.18:

The fitted curve changed to a spline curve, with the location of the second vertex and the new curve

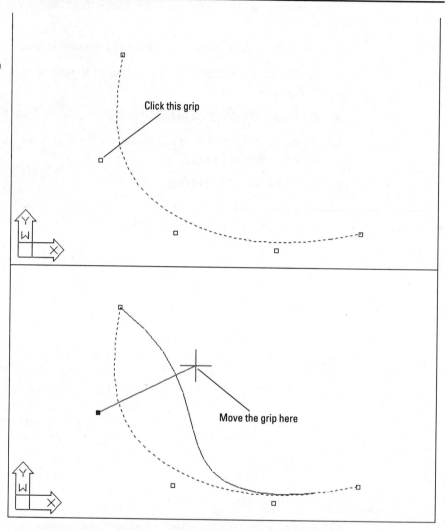

3. Click the grip that is second from the top of the curve, as shown in the bottom image of Figure 13.18, and move the grip around. Notice how the curve follows, giving you immediate feedback on how the curve will look.

4. Pick a point as shown in the continued image of Figure 13.18. The curve is fixed in its new position.

FIGURE 13.18:
CONTINUED

The fitted curve
changed to a spline
curve, with the location
of the second vertex
and the new curve

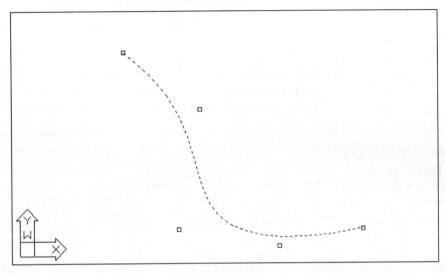

Using True Spline Curves

So far, you've been working with polylines to generate spline curves. The advantage to using polylines for curves is that they can be enhanced in other ways. You can modify their width, for instance, or join several curves together. But at times you will need a more exact representation of a curve. The Spline object, created with Draw ➤ Spline, offers a more accurate model of spline curves, as well as more control over its shape.

Drawing a Spline

The next exercise demonstrates the creation of a spline curve.

1. Undo the change made in the last two exercises.

2. Turn the Data layer on so you can view the data points.

3. Adjust your view so you can see all the data points with the elevation of 250.00 (see Figure 13.19).

4. Click the Spline tool on the Draw toolbar, or type **Spl** ↵.

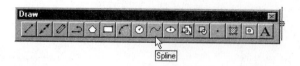

5. At the Object/<Enter first point> prompt, use the Center Osnap to start the curve on the first data point in the lower-right (see Figure 13.19). The prompt changes to Close/Fit Tolerance/<Enter point>.

FIGURE 13.19:

Starting the Spline curve at the first data point

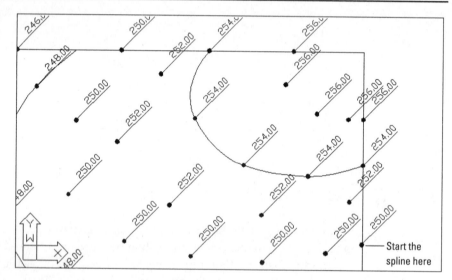

6. Continue to select the 250.00 data points until you reach the last one. Notice that as you pick points, a curve appears, and bends and flows as you move your cursor.

7. Once you've selected the last point, press ↵. Notice that the prompt changes to Enter start tangent. Also, a rubber-banding line appears from the first point of the curve to the cursor. As you move the cursor, the curve adjusts to the direction of the rubber-banding line. Here, you can set the tangency of the first point of the curve (see the top image of Figure 13.20).

8. Press ↵. This causes AutoCAD to determine the first point's tangency based on the current shape of the curve. A rubber-banding line appears from the last point of the curve. As with the first point, you can indicate a tangent direction for the last point of the curve (see bottom image of Figure 13.20).

9. Press ↵ to exit the Spline command without changing the endpoint tangent direction.

FIGURE 13.20:

The last two prompts of the Spline command let you determine the tangent direction of the spline.

Rubber-banding line indicates tangent direction.

Rubber-banding line indicates tangent direction.

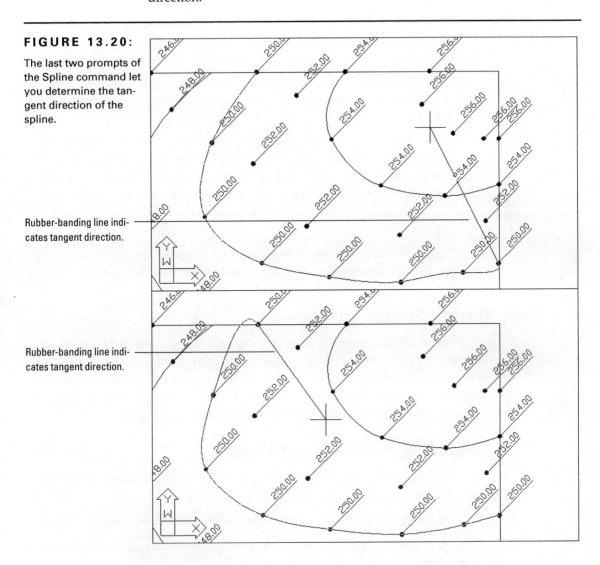

You now have a smooth curve that passes through the points you selected. These points are called the *control points*. If you click the curve, you'll see the grips appear at the location of these control points, and you can adjust the curve simply by clicking the grip points and moving them. (You may need to turn off the data layer to see the grips clearly.)

TIP   See Chapter 2 for more detailed information on grip editing.

You may have noticed two other options—Fit Tolerance and Close—as you were selecting points for the spline in the last exercise. Here is a description of these options.

Fit Tolerance   lets you change the curve so that it doesn't actually pass through the points you pick. When you select this option, you get the prompt Enter Fit Tolerance <0.0000>. Any value greater than 0 will cause the curve to pass close to, but not through the points. A value of 0 causes the curve to pass through the points. (You'll see how this works in a later exercise.)

Close   lets you close the curve into a loop. If you choose this option, you are prompted to indicate a tangent direction for the closing point.

Fine-Tuning Spline Curves

Spline curves are different from other types of objects, and many of the standard editing commands won't work on splines. AutoCAD offers the Modify ➤ Object ➤ Spline option (Splinedit command) for making changes to splines. The following exercise will give you some practice with this command. You'll start by focusing on Splinedit's Fit Data option, which lets you fine-tune the spline curve.

Controlling the Fit Data of a Spline

The following exercise will demonstrate how the Fit Data option lets you control some of the general characteristics of the curve.

1. Choose Modify ➤ Object ➤ Spline, or type **Spe** ↵ at the command prompt.

2. At the Select Spline prompt, select the spline you drew in the previous exercise.

3. At the prompt:

    Fit Data/Close/Move Vertex/Refine/rEverse/Undo/eXit <X>:

    type **F** ↵ to select the Fit Data option.

> **NOTE** The Fit Data option is similar to the Edit Vertex option of the Pedit command, in that Fit Data offers a subset of options that let you edit certain properties of the spline.

Controlling Tangency at the Beginning and End Points

4. At this prompt:

   ```
   Add/Close/Delete/Move/Purge/Tangents/toLerance/Exit <X>
   ```

   type **T** to select the Tangents option. Move the cursor, and notice that the curve changes tangency through the first point, just as it did when you first created the spline (Figure 13.20).

5. Press ↵. You can now edit the other endpoint tangency.

6. Press ↵ again. You return to the Add/Close/Delete... prompt.

Adding New Control Points Now add another control point to the spline curve.

7. At the Add/Close/Delete... prompt, type **A** ↵ to access the Add option.

8. At the Select point prompt, click the second grip point from the bottom end of the spline (see the top image of Figure 13.21). A rubber-banding line appears from the point you selected. That point and the next point are highlighted. The two highlighted points tell you that the next point you select will fall between these two points. You also see the Enter new point prompt.

9. Click a new point. The curve changes to include that point. In addition, the new point becomes the highlighted point, indicating that you can continue to add more points between it and the other highlighted point (see the bottom image of Figure 13.21).

10. Press ↵. The Select point prompt appears, allowing you to select another point if you so desire.

11. Press ↵ again to return to the Add/Close/Delete... prompt.

FIGURE 13.21:

Adding a new control point to a spline

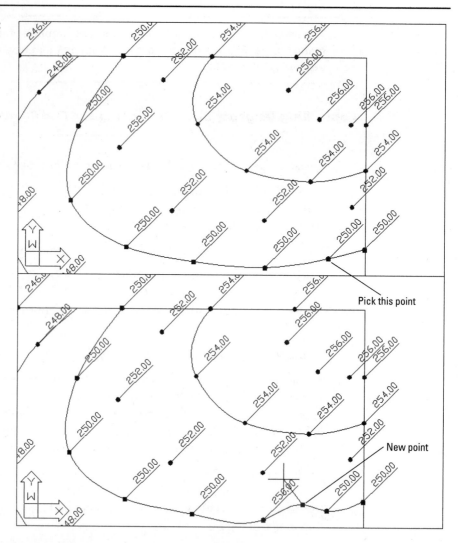

Adjusting the Spline Tolerance Setting   Before we end our examination of the Fit Data options, let's look at how Tolerance works.

1. At the Add/Close/Delete... prompt, type **L** ↵ to select the Tolerance option. This option sets the tolerance between the control point and the curve.

2. At the Enter fit tolerance <0.0000>: prompt, type **30** ↵. Notice how the curve no longer passes through the control points, except for the beginning and endpoints (see Figure 13.22). The fit tolerance value you enter determines the maximum distance away from any control point the spline can be.

3. Type **X** ↵ to exit the Fit Data option.

FIGURE 13.22:

The spline after setting the control point tolerance to 30

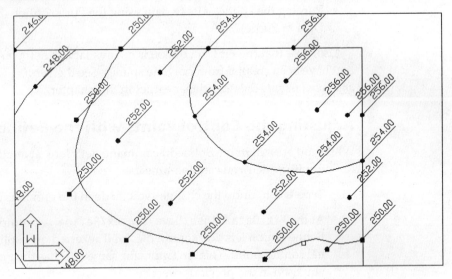

You've seen how you can control many of the shape properties of a spline through the Fit Data option. Here are descriptions of the other Fit Data options you didn't try in these exercises:

Delete   removes a control point in the spline.

Close   lets you close the spline into a loop.

Move   lets you move a control point.

Purge   deletes the fit data of the spline, thereby eliminating the Fit Data option for the purged spline. (See *When* Can't *You Use Fit Data?* just below.)

When *Can't* You Use Fit Data?   The Fit Data option of the Splinedit command offers many ways to edit a spline; however, this option is not available to all spline curves. When you invoke certain of the other Splinedit options, a spline curve will lose its fit data, thereby disabling the Fit Data option. These operations are as follows:

- Fitting a spline to a tolerance (Spline/Fit Tolerance) and moving its control vertices.

- Fitting a spline to a tolerance (Spline/Fit Tolerance) and opening or closing it.

- Refining the spline.

- Purging the spline of its fit data using the Purge option (Splinedit ➤ Fit Data ➤ Purge).

Also, note that the Fit Data option is not available when you edit spline curves that have been created from polyline splines. See the *Turning Objects into Polylines and Polylines into Splines* sidebar earlier in this chapter.

Adjusting the Control Points with the Refine Option

While you are still in the Splinedit command, let's look at another of its options, Refine, with which you can fine-tune the curve:

1. Type **U** ↵ to undo the changes you made in the previous exercise.

2. At the Fit Data/Close/Move Vertex/Refine... prompt, type **R** ↵. The Refine option lets you control the "pull" exerted on a spline by an individual control point. This isn't quite the same effect as the Fit Tolerance option you used in the previous exercise.

3. At the prompt:

   Add Control Point/Elevate Order/Weight/Exit <X>:

   type **W** ↵. The first control point is highlighted.

4. At the next prompt:

   Next/Previous/Select Point/Exit/<Enter new weight><1.0000> <N>:

   press ↵ three times to move the highlight to the fourth control point.

5. Type **25** ↵. The curve not only moves closer to the control point, it also bends around the control point in a tighter arc (see Figure 13.23).

FIGURE 13.23:

The spline after increasing the Weight value of a control point

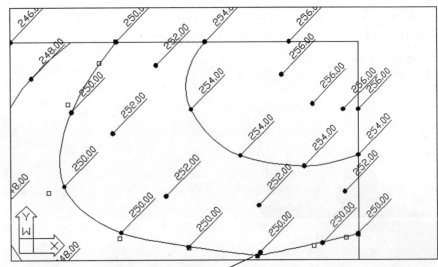

Spline is closer and tighter

You can use the Weight value of Splinedit's Refine option to pull the spine in tighter. Think of it as a way to increase the "gravity" of the control point, causing the curve to be pulled closer and tighter to the control point.

Continue your look at the Splinedit command by adding more control points—without actually changing the shape of the curve. You do this using Refine's Add Control Point and Elevate Order options.

1. Type **1** ↲ to return the spline to its former shape.

2. Type **X** ↲ to exit the Weight option; then type **A** ↲ to select the Add Control Point option.

3. At the `Select a point on the spline` prompt, click the second-to-last control point toward the top end of the spline (see the top image of Figure 13.24). The point you select disappears and is replaced by two control points roughly equidistant from the one you selected (see the bottom image of Figure 13.24). The curve remains unchanged. Two new control points now replace the one control point you selected.

4. Press ↲ to exit the Add control point option.

5. Now type **E** ↲ to select the Elevate Order option.

6. At the `Enter new order <4>` prompt, type **6** ↲. The number of control points increases, leaving the curve itself untouched.

7. Type **X** ↵ twice to exit the Refine option and then the Splinedit command.

FIGURE 13.24:

Adding a single control point using the Refine option

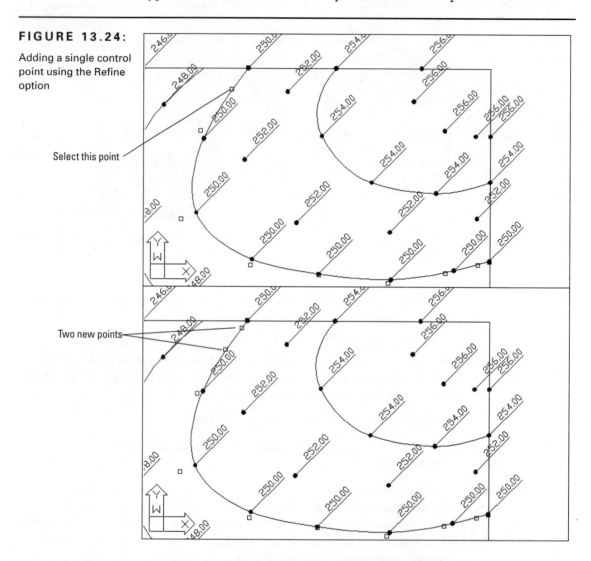

You would probably never edit contour lines of a topographical map in quite the way these exercises have shown. But by following this tutorial you have explored all the potential of the AutoCAD's spline object. Aside from its usefulness for drawing contours, it can be a great tool for drawing free-form illustrations. It is also an excellent tool for mechanical applications, where precise, nonuniform curves are required, such as drawings of cams or sheet metal work.

Marking Divisions on a Curve

Perhaps one of the most difficult things to do in manual drafting is to mark regular intervals on a curve. AutoCAD offers the Divide and Measure commands to help you perform this task with speed and accuracy.

The use of Divide and Measure are discussed here in conjunction with polylines, but you can use these commands on any object except blocks and text.

Dividing Objects into Segments of Equal Length

Divide can be used to divide an object into a specific number of equal segments. For example, suppose you needed to mark off the contour you've been working on in this chapter into nine equal segments. One way to do this is to first find the length of the contour by using the List command, and then sit down with a pencil and paper to figure out the exact distances between the marks. But there is another, easier way.

Divide will place a set of point objects on a line, arc, circle, or polyline, marking off exact divisions. This next exercise shows how it works.

1. Open the file called 13a-divd.dwg from the companion CD-ROM. This is a file similar to the one we have been discussing in the prior exercises.

2. Choose Draw ➢ Point ➢ Divide, or type **Div** ↵.

3. At the Select objects to divide prompt, pick the spline contour line.

4. The <Number of segments>/Block prompt that appears next is asking for the number of divisions you want on the selected object. Enter **9** ↵.

The command prompt now returns, and it appears that nothing has happened. But AutoCAD has placed several points on the contour indicating the locations of the nine divisions you have requested. To see these points more clearly, follow these steps:

5. Click Format ➢ Point Style. The Point Style dialog box appears.

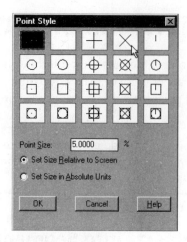

6. Click the X point style in the upper-right side of the dialog box, click the Set Size Relative to Screen radio button, and then click OK.

7. Enter **Re** ↵. A set of Xs appear, showing the nine divisions (see Figure 13.25).

TIP   You can also change the point style by changing the Pdmode system variable. When Pdmode is set to 3, the point appears as an X. See Appendix D for more on Pdmode.

FIGURE 13.25:

Using the Divide and Measure commands on a polyline

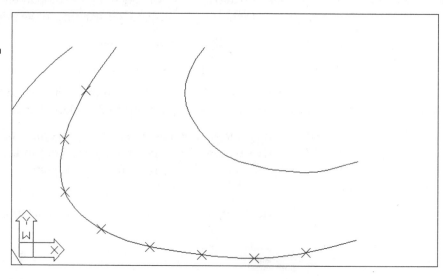

The Divide command uses *Point* objects to indicate the division points. Point objects are created by using the Point command; they usually appear as dots. Unfortunately, such points are nearly invisible when placed on top of other objects. But, as you have seen, you can alter their shape using the Point Style dialog box. You can use these X points to place objects or references to break the object being divided. (Divide does not actually cut the object into smaller divisions.)

TIP
If you are in a hurry, and you don't want to bother changing the shape of the point objects, you can do the following: set the Running Osnaps to Node. Then, when you are in point selection mode, move the cursor over the divided curve. When the cursor gets close to a point object, the Node Osnap marker will appear.

Dividing Objects into Specified Lengths

The Measure command acts just like Divide; however, instead of dividing an object into segments of equal length, Measure marks intervals of a specified distance along an object. For example, suppose you need to mark some segments exactly 5' apart along the contour. Try the following exercise to see how Measure is used to accomplish this task.

1. Erase the X-shaped point objects.

2. Choose Draw ➤ Point ➤ Measure, or type **Me** ↵.

3. At the Select object to measure prompt, pick the contour at a point closest to its lower endpoint. I'll explain shortly why this is important.

4. At the <Segment length>/Block prompt, enter **5'** ↵. The X points appear at the specified distance.

5. Now exit this file.

NOTE
Measure is AutoCAD's equivalent of the divider tool in manual drafting. A divider is a V-shaped instrument, similar to a compass, used to mark off regular intervals along a curve or line.

Bear in mind that the point you pick on the object to be measured will determine where Measure begins measuring. In the last exercise, for example, you picked the contour near its bottom endpoint. If you had picked the top of the contour, the results would have been different because the measurement would have started at the top, not the bottom.

Marking Off Intervals Using Blocks Instead of Points

You can also use the Block option under the Divide and Measure commands to place blocks at regular intervals along a line, polyline, or arc. Here's how to use blocks as markers:

1. First be sure the block you want to use is part of the current drawing file.

2. Start either the Divide or Measure command.

3. At the `Number of segments:` prompt, enter **B**.

4. At the `Block Name to Insert:` prompt, enter the name of a block.

5. At the `Align Block with Object? <Y>` : prompt, press ⏎ if you wish the blocks to follow the alignment of the selected object. (Entering **N** ⏎ causes each block to be inserted at a 0 angle.)

6. At the `Number of Segments:` prompt, enter the number of segments. The blocks appear at regular intervals on the selected object.

One example of using Divide's or Measure's Block option is to place a row of sinks equally spaced along a wall. Or you might use this technique to make multiple copies of an object along an irregular path defined by a polyline. In civil projects a fence line can be indicated by using Divide or Measure to place Xs along a polyline.

Sketching with AutoCAD

No discussion of polylines would be complete without mentioning the Sketch command. Though AutoCAD isn't a sketch program, you *can* draw "freehand" using the Sketch command. With Sketch, you can rough in ideas in a free-form way, and later overlay a more formal drawing using the usual lines, arcs, and circles. You can use sketch with a mouse, but it makes more sense to use this command with a digitizing tablet that has a stylus. The stylus affords a more natural way of sketching.

Freehand Sketching with AutoCAD

Here's a step-by-step description of how to use Sketch.

1. Make sure the Ortho and Snap modes are turned off. Then type **Skpoly** ↵ **1** ↵. This sets the Sketch command to draw using polylines.

2. Type **Sketch** ↵ at the command prompt.

3. At the Record increment prompt, enter a value that represents the smallest line segment you will want Sketch to draw. This command approximates a sketch line by drawing a series of short line segments. So the value you enter here determines the length of those line segments.

4. At the Sketch. Pen eXit Quit Record Erase Connect prompt, press the pick button and then start your sketch line. Notice that the message "<Pen down>" appears, telling you that AutoCAD is recording your cursor's motion.

> **NOTE** You can also start and stop the sketch line by pressing the **P** key.

5. Press the pick button to stop drawing. The message "<Pen up>" tells you AutoCAD has stopped recording your cursor motion. As you draw, notice that the line is green. This indicates that you have drawn a temporary sketch line and have not committed the line to the drawing.

6. A line drawn with Sketch is temporary until you use Record to save it, so turn the sketch line into a polyline now by typing **R**.

7. Type **X** ↵ to exit the Sketch command.

Here are some of the other Sketch options we weren't able to cover in this brief description:

Connect   allows you to continue a line from the end of the last temporary line drawn. Type **C** and then move the cursor to the endpoint of the temporary line. AutoCAD automatically starts the line, and you just continue to draw. This only works in the <Pen up> mode.

Period (.)   allows you to draw a single straight-line segment by moving the cursor to the desired position and then pressing the period key. This only works in the <Pen up> mode.

Record, **Erase**, **Quit**, and **Exit**   control the recording of lines and exiting from the Sketch command. Record is used to save a temporary sketched line; once a line has been recorded, you must edit it as you would any other line. With Erase you can erase temporary lines before you record them. Quit ends the Sketch command without saving unrecorded lines. On the other hand, the Exit option on the Sketch menu automatically saves all lines you have drawn, and then exits the Sketch command.

Filling In Solid Areas

You have learned how to create a solid area by increasing the width of a polyline segment. But suppose you want to create a simple solid shape or a very thick line. AutoCAD provides the Solid, Trace, and Donut commands to help you draw simple filled areas. The Trace command acts just like the Line command (with the added feature of drawing wide line segments), so only Solid and Donut are discussed here.

TIP   You can create free-form solid filled areas using the new Solid hatch pattern. Create an enclosed area using any set of objects, and then use the Hatch tool to apply a solid hatch pattern to the area. See Chapter 6 for details on using the Hatch tool.

Drawing Solid Filled Areas

In the past, AutoCAD users used hatch patterns to fill in solid areas—and that was a great way to fill an irregular shape. However, hatches tended to increase the size of a file dramatically, thereby increasing loading and regeneration time. Autodesk has completely changed the way Release 14 handles hatches, so they don't use nearly the amount of memory they once did. You can even use a new, predefined hatch pattern called Solid to create a memory efficient solid fill of an irregular-shaped area.

Here is a short exercise to demonstrate how to use it.

1.   Open file 13a-htch.dwg from the companion CD-ROM.

2.   Click hatch from the Draw toolbar.

3.   At the Boundary Hatch dialog box, click the Pick Points button.

4. Click the area bounded by the border and contour line in the upper-right corner of the drawing, as shown in the top image of Figure 13.26. Then press ↵. You have the option here to click more areas if you so desire.

5. Back at the Boundary Hatch dialog box, click the Pattern button.

6. At the Hatch pattern palette dialog box, click SOLID from the list at the left.

7. Click OK, and then Click Apply. A solid fill is applied to the selected area, as shown in the bottom image of Figure 13.26.

FIGURE 13.26:

Locating the area to fill, and the final result of the solid hatch

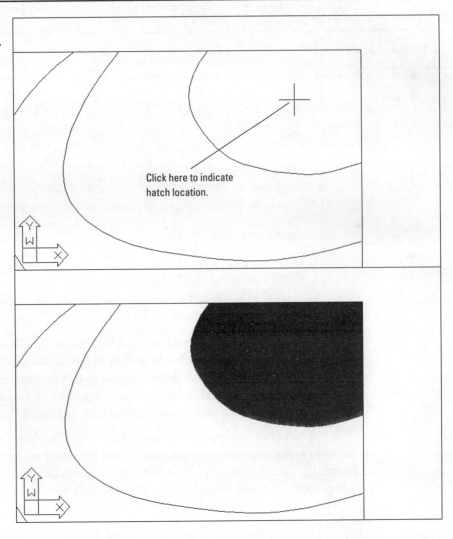

Click here to indicate hatch location.

Overlapping Solid Lines and Shaded Fills

If you use a raster plotter or laser printer that can convert solid areas into screened or gray-shaded areas, you may encounter the problem of shading areas overlapping lines and hiding them. This problem may not be apparent until you actually plot the drawing; it frequently occurs when a gray shaded area is bounded by lines (see Figure 13.27).

The left side of Figure 13.27 shows how shading or solid fills can cover line work. The outline of the walls is obscured by the shading. The right side of Figure 13.27 shows how the drawing was intended to be displayed and printed.

FIGURE 13.27:

Problems that occur with overlapping lines and gray areas

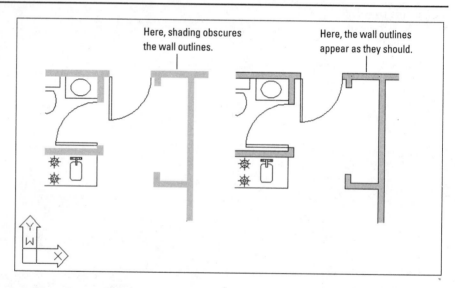

Here, shading obscures the wall outlines.

Here, the wall outlines appear as they should.

Most other graphics programs have specific tools to handle this overlapping difficulty. These tools are commonly named Move To Front or Move To Back, indicating that you move an object in front of or behind another object. AutoCAD offers the Draworder command to perform the same function as the Move to Back and Move to Front tools of other programs.

To force an object to appear above another, choose Tools ➢ Display Order ➢ Bring To Front, and then select the object that you want to have overlap all the others. Or use Tools ➢ Display Order ➢ Send to Back to place an object behind other objects. You can also select specific objects to overlay or underlap using the

Tools ➤ Display Order ➤ Bring Above Object and Send Under Object options. If you would like more detailed instructions on how to use Draworder, see *Controlling Object Visibility and Overlap with Raster Images* in Chapter 11.

Drawing Filled Circles

If you need to draw a thick circle like an inner tube, or a solid filled circle, perform the following steps.

1. Choose Draw ➤ Donut, or type **Do** ↵ at the command prompt.

2. At the `Inside diameter` prompt, enter the desired diameter of the donut "hole." This value determines the opening at the center of your circle.

3. At the `Outside diameter` prompt, enter the overall diameter of the circle.

4. At the `Center of doughnut` prompt, click the desired location for the filled circle. You can continue to select points to place multiple donuts (see Figure 13.28).

5. Press ↵ to exit this process.

FIGURE 13.28:

Drawing wide circles using the Donut command

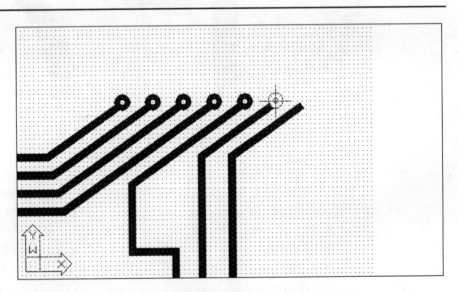

If you need to fill only a part of a circle, such as a pie slice, you can use the Donut command to draw a full, filled circle, and then use the Trim or Break options on the Modify toolbar to cut out the portion of the donut you don't need.

Toggling Solid Fills On and Off

Once you have drawn a solid area with the Pline, Solid, Trace, or Donut commands, you can control whether the solid area is actually displayed as filled in. Open the Drawing Aids dialog box by choosing Tools ➢ Drawing Aids..., or by typing **Rm** ↵. If the Solid Fill checkbox does not show a checkmark, thick polylines, solids, traces, and donuts appear as outlines of the solid areas (see Figure 13.29).

NOTE   You can shorten regeneration and plotting time if solids are not filled in.

FIGURE 13.29:

Two polylines with the Fill option turned on (top) and turned off (bottom)

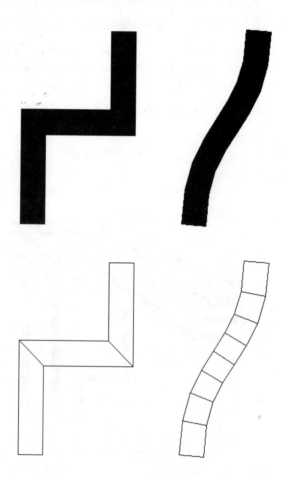

WARNING   If Regenauto is turned off, you will have to issue the Regen command to display the effects of the Fill command.

The Drawing Aids Solid Fill option is an easy-to-remember way to control the display of solid fills. Or you can enter **Fill** ⏎ at the command prompt; then, at the ON/OFF <ON> prompt, enter your choice of **on** or **off**.

If You Want to Experiment...

There are many valuable uses for polylines beyond those covered in this chapter. I encourage you to become familiar with this unique object so you can take full advantage of AutoCAD.

To further explore the use of polylines, try the following exercise, further illustrated in Figure 13.30. It will give you an opportunity to try out some of the options discussed in this chapter that weren't included in exercises.

1. Open a new file called **PART13**. Set the Snap mode to .25 and be sure the Snap mode is on. Use the Pline command to draw the object shown at step 1 of figure 13.30. Draw it in the direction indicated by the arrows and start at the upper-left corner. Use the Close option to add the last line segment.

2. Start the Pedit command, select the polyline, and then type **E** ⏎ to issue the Vertex option. At the Next/Previous/Break prompt, press return until the X mark moves to the first corner shown in the figure to the right. Enter an **S** for the Straighten option. At the Next/Previous/Go prompt, press return twice to move the X to the other corner shown in the figure. Press **G** for Go to straighten the polyline between the two selected corners.

3. Press return twice to move the X to the upper-right corner, and then enter **I** for Insert. Pick a point as shown in the figure. The polyline changes to reflect the new vertex. Enter an **X** to exit the Edit Vertex option, and then press return to exit the Pedit command.

4. Start the Fillet command and use the Radius option to set the fillet radius to .30. Press return to start the Fillet command again, but this time use the Polyline option and pick the polyline you just edited. All the corners fillet to the .30 radius. Add the .15 radius circles as shown in the figure and exit the file with the End command.

FIGURE 13.30:

Drawing a simple plate
with curved edges

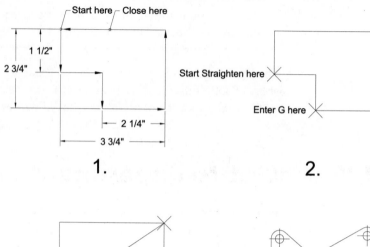

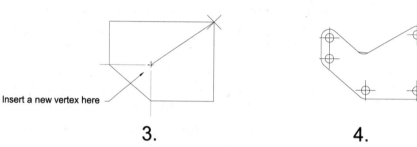

1.

2.

3.

4.

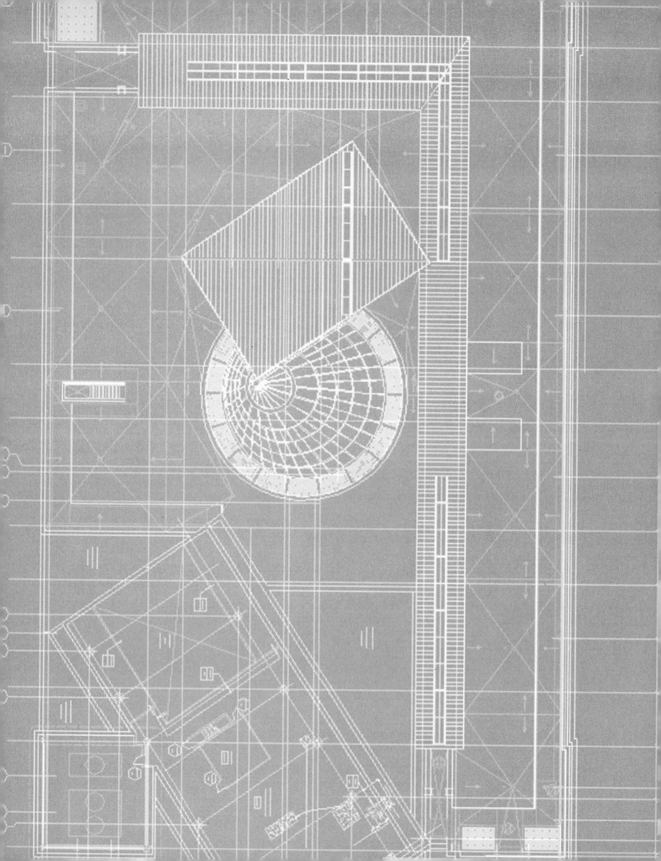

CHAPTER

FOURTEEN

14

Getting and Exchanging Data from Drawings

- Getting Information about a Drawing

- Exchanging CAD Data with Other Programs

- Using AutoCAD Drawings in Desktop Publishing

- Combining Data from Different Sources

AutoCAD drawings contain a wealth of data. In them you can find graphic information such as distances and angles between objects, as well as precise areas and the properties of objects. But as you become more involved with AutoCAD, you will find that you also need data of a different nature. For example, as you begin to work in groups, the various settings in a drawing become important. Statistics on the amount of time you spend on a drawing are needed when you are billing computer time. As your projects become more complex, file maintenance requires a greater degree of attention. To take full advantage of AutoCAD, you will want to exchange much of this data with other people and other programs.

In this chapter, you will explore the ways in which all types of data can be extracted from AutoCAD and made available to you, your coworkers, and other programs. First, you will discover how to get specific data on your drawings. Then you will look at ways to exchange data with other programs—such as word processors, desktop-publishing software, and even other CAD programs.

Getting Information about a Drawing

AutoCAD can instantly give you precise information about your drawing, such as the area, perimeter, and location of an object; the base point, current mode settings, and space used in a drawing; and the time at which a drawing was created and last edited. In this section you will practice extracting this type of information from your drawing, using the tools found in the Tools ➤ Inquiry option's cascading menu.

TIP   To find absolute coordinates in a drawing, use the ID command. Choose Tools ➤ Inquiry ➤ ID point, or type **ID** ↵. At the ID Point prompt, use the Osnap overrides to pick a point, and its x, y, and z coordinates will be displayed on the prompt line.

Finding the Area or Location of an Object

Architects, engineers, and facilities planners often need to know the square-foot area of a room or a section of a building. A structural engineer might want to find the cross-sectional area of a beam. In this section you will practice determining the areas of both regular and irregular objects.

First you will find out the square-foot area of the living room and entry of your studio unit plan.

1. Start AutoCAD and open the Unit file you created earlier, or use the 14a-unit.dwg file from the companion CD-ROM.

2. Zoom into the living room and entry area so you have a view similar to Figure 14.1.

3. Choose Tools ➤ Inquiry ➤ Area, or type **Area** ↵ at the command prompt. You can also click and drag List from the Standard toolbar, and then select Area.

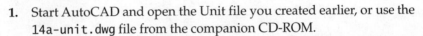
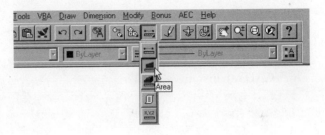

4. Using the Endpoint Osnap, start with the lower-left corner of the living room and select the points indicated in Figure 14.1. You are indicating the boundary of the entry and living room area.

5. When you have come full circle to the eighth point shown in Figure 14.1, press ↵. You get the message

    ```
    Area = 39570.00 sq in (274.7917 sq ft), Perimeter = 76'-0"
    ```

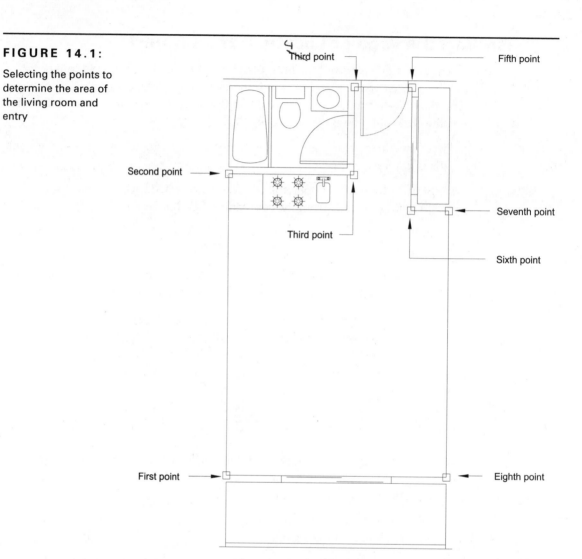

FIGURE 14.1:

Selecting the points to determine the area of the living room and entry

There is no limit to the number of points you can pick to define an area, so you can obtain the areas of very complex shapes.

Using Boundary

Using the Object option of the Area command, you can also select circles and polylines for area calculations. Using this option in conjunction with another AutoCAD utility called Boundary, you can quickly get the area of a bounded space. You will recall from the discussion on hatch patterns in Chapter 6 that a region polyline is drawn when you use the Boundary Hatch (Bhatch) function; Boundary works similarly. Where Bhatch generates a hatch pattern that conforms to the outline of a boundary, Boundary generates a polyline outline without adding the hatch. The following steps show you how to use it.

1. Set the current layer to Floor.

2. Turn off the door and fixture layers. Also make sure the ceiling layer is turned on. You want the boundary to follow the interior wall outline, so you need to turn off any objects that will affect the outline, such as the door and kitchen.

3. Choose Draw ➣ Boundary..., or type **bo** ↵. The Boundary Creation dialog box appears.

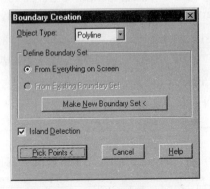

WARNING There is one caveat to using Boundary: You must be sure the area you are trying to define has a continuous border. If there are any gaps at all, no matter how small, Boundary will give you an error message.

4. Click on the Pick Points < button. The dialog box closes.

5. At the Select internal point prompt, click on the interior of the unit plan. The outline of the interior is highlighted (see Figure 14.2).

FIGURE 14.2:

Once you select a point on the interior of the plan using Boundary, an outline of the area is highlighted and sur-rounded by a dotted line.

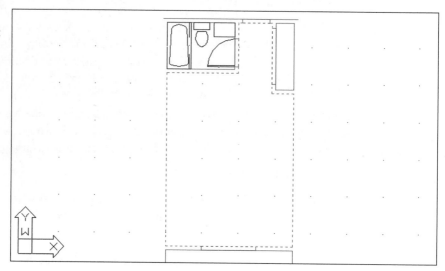

6. Press ↵. Boundary draws an outline of the floor area using a polyline. Since the current layer is Floor, the boundary is drawn on the floor layer and given the default cyan color of the layer.

7. Choose Tools ➤ Inquiry ➤ Area again, or type **Area** ↵ at the command prompt; and then enter **O** ↵ for the Object option.

8. Click on the boundary; when it is highlighted, press ↵. You get the same Area… message you got in the previous exercise.

> **TIP**
>
> If you need to recall the last area calculation value you received, you can enter **'Setvar** ↵ **Area** ↵. The area will be displayed in the prompt. Enter **'Perimeter** ↵, and you get the last perimeter calculated.

The Boundary command creates a polyline that conforms to the boundary of an area. This feature, combined with the ability of the Area command to find the area of a polyline, makes short work of area calculations.

Finding the Area of Complex Shapes

The Boundary command works fine as long as the area does not contain *islands* that you do not want included in the area calculation. An island is a closed area within a larger area within which you are attempting to hatch or create a boundary. In the case of the Flange part, the islands are the two circles at the lower end of the part.

For areas that do contain islands, you must enlist the aid of the other Area command options: Object, Add, and Subtract. Using Add and Subtract, you can maintain a running total of several separate areas being calculated. This gives you flexibility in finding areas of complex shapes.

The exercise in this section guides you through the use of these options. First, you'll look at how you can keep a running tally of areas. For this exercise, you will use a flange shape that contains circles. This shape is composed of simple arcs lines and circles.

1. Exit the Unit file, and open the file named Flange.dwg from the companion CD-ROM (see Figure 14.3). Don't bother to save changes in the Unit file.

2. Choose Draw ➤ Boundary....

3. At the Boundary Dialog box, click on Pick Points.

4. Click on the interior of the flange shape. Notice that the entire shape is highlighted, including the circle islands.

5. Press ↵.

FIGURE 14.3:

A flange to a mechanical device

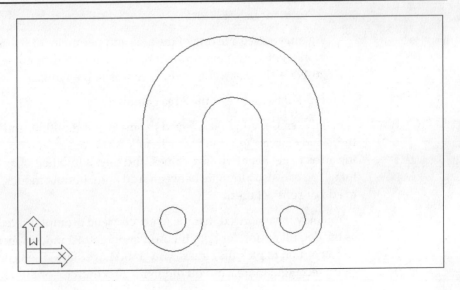

You now have a polyline outline of the shape. As you saw in the previous exercise, the polyine will aid you in quickly obtaining the area. Now let's continue by using the Area command's Add and Subtract options.

1. Choose Tools ➢ Inquiry ➢ Area.

2. Type **A** ↵ to enter the ADD mode, and then **O** ↵ to select an Object.

3. Click on the outline of the flange. You see the message:

   ```
   Area = 27.7080, Perimeter = 30.8496
   Total area = 27.7080
   ```

4. Press ↵ to exit the Add mode.

5. Type **S** ↵ to enter the Subtract mode, and then type **O**↵ to select an object.

6. Click on one of the circles. You see the message:

   ```
   Area = 0.6070, Perimeter = 2.7618
   Total area = 27.1010
   ```

   This shows you the area and perimeter of the selected object, and a running count of the total area of the flange outline minus the circle.

7. Click on the other circle. You see the message:

   ```
   Area = 0.6070, Perimeter = 2.7618
   Total area = 26.4940
   ```

   Again, you see a listing of the area and perimeter of the selected object along with a running count of the total area, which now shows a value of 26.4940. This last value is the true area of the flange.

8. Press ↵ twice to exit the Area command.

In the exercise, you first selected the main object outline and then subtracted the island objects. You don't have to follow this order; you can start by subtracting areas to get negative area values, and then add other areas to come up with a total. You can also alternate between Add and Subtract modes, in case you forget to add or subtract areas.

You may have noticed that the Area command prompt offered <first point> as the default option for both the Add and Subtract modes. Instead of using the Object option to pick the circles, you could have started selecting points to indicate a rectangular area, as you did in the first exercise of this chapter.

It is important to remember that whenever you press ↲ while selecting points for an area calculation, AutoCAD automatically connects the first and last points and returns the area calculated. If you are in the Add or Subtract mode, you can then continue to select points, but the additional areas will be calculated from the *next* point you pick.

As you can see from these exercises, it is simpler to first outline an area with a polyline, wherever possible, and then use the Object option to add and subtract area values of polylines.

In this example, you obtained the area of a mechanical object. However, the same process works for any type of area you want to calculate. It can be the area of a piece of property on a topographical map, or the area of a floor plan. For example, you can use the Object option to find an irregular area like the one shown in Figure 14.4, as long as it is a polyline.

FIGURE 14.4:

The site plan with an area to be calculated

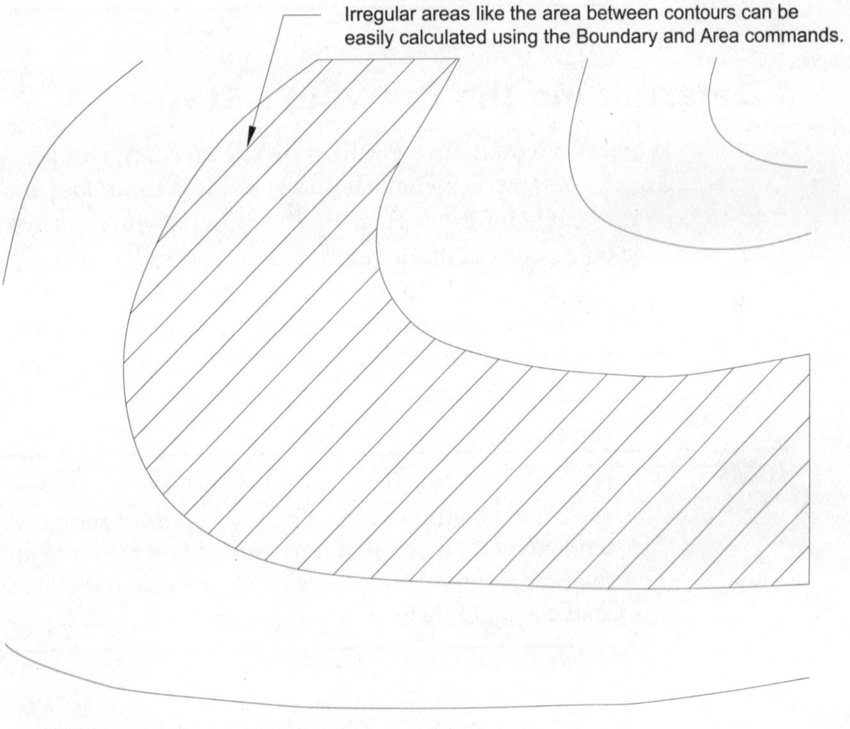

Irregular areas like the area between contours can be easily calculated using the Boundary and Area commands.

Recording Area Data in a Drawing File

Once you find the area of an object, you'll often need to record it somewhere. You can write it down in a project log book, but this is easy to overlook. A more dependable way to store area information is to use *attributes*.

For example, in a building project, you can create a block that contains attributes for the room number, room area, and the date when the room area was last taken. You might make the area and date attributes invisible, so only the room number appears. This block could then be inserted into every room. Once you find the area, you can easily add it to your block attribute with the Ddate command. In fact, such a block could be used with any drawing in which you wished to store area data. See Chapter 10 for more on Attributes.

TIP   Appendix C describes an AutoLISP program on your companion CD-ROM that lets you easily record area data in a drawing file.

Determining the Drawing's Status

When you work with a group of people on a large project, keeping track of a drawing's setup becomes crucial. The Status command enables you to obtain some general information about the drawing you are working on, such as the base point, current mode settings, and workspace or computer memory use. Status is especially helpful when you are editing a drawing someone else has worked on, because you may want to identify and change settings for your own style of working. When you select Tools ➤ Inquiry ➤ Status, you get a list like the one shown in Figure 14.5.

NOTE   If you have problems editing a file created by someone else, the difficulty can often be attributed to a new or different setting you are not used to working with. If you find that AutoCAD is acting in an unusual way, use the Status command to get a quick glimpse of the file settings before you start calling for help.

FIGURE 14.5:

The Status screen of
the AutoCAD Text
Window

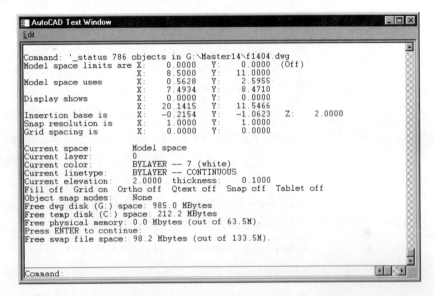

Here is a brief description of each item on the status screen. Note that some of the items you see listed on your screen will vary somewhat from what we've shown here, but the information applies to virtually all situations except where noted.

(number) **entities in G:\Master14\f1404.dwg**   The number of entities or objects in the drawing.

Model space limits are   The coordinates of the Model Space limits (see Chapter 3 for more details on limits).

Model space uses   The area the drawing occupies; equivalent to the extents of the drawing.

**Over: If present, means that part of drawing is outside the limit boundary.

Display shows   The area covered by the current view.

Insertion base, Snap resolution, and Grid spacing lines   The current default values for these mode settings.

Current space   Model Space or Paper Space.

Current layer   The current default layer.

Current color   The color assigned to new objects.

Current linetype   The line type assigned to new objects.

Current elevation/thickness   The current default z coordinate for new objects, plus the default thickness of objects; these are both 3D-related settings (see Chapter 15 for details).

Fill, Grid, Ortho, Qtext, Snap, and Tablet   The status of these options.

Object snap modes   The current default Osnap setting.

Free dwg disk (drive:)   The amount of space available to store drawing-specific temporary files.

Free temp disk (drive:)   The amount of space you have left on your hard drive for AutoCAD's resource temporary files.

Free physical memory   The amount of free RAM available.

Free swap file space   The amount of Windows swap file space available.

> **NOTE**   When you are in Paper Space, the Status command displays information regarding the Paper Space limits. See Chapter 12 for more on Model Space and Paper Space.

In addition to being useful in understanding a drawing file, Status is an invaluable tool for troubleshooting. Frequently, problems can be isolated by a technical support person using the information provided by the Status command.

> **NOTE**   For more information on memory use, see Appendix A.

Keeping Track of Time

The Time command allows you to keep track of the time spent on a drawing, for billing or analysis purposes. You can also use Time to check the current time and find out when the drawing was created and most recently edited. Because the AutoCAD timer uses your computer's time, be sure the time is set correctly in DOS.

To access the Time command, enter **Time** ↵ at the command prompt, or select Tools ➤ Inquiry ➤ Time. You get a message like the one in Figure 14.6.

FIGURE 14.6:

The Time screen in the
AutoCAD Text Window

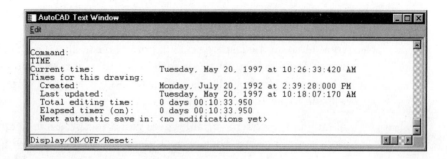

The first three lines tell you the current date and time, the date and time the drawing was created, and the last time the drawing was saved or ended.

The fourth line shows the total time spent on the drawing from the point that the file was opened. This elapsed timer lets you time a particular activity, such as changing the width of all the walls in a floor plan or redesigning a piece of machinery. You can turn the elapsed timer on or off, or reset it, by entering **on, off,** or **reset** at the prompt shown as the last line of the message. The last line tells you when the next automatic save will be.

Getting Information from System Variables

If you've been working through this book's ongoing studio apartment building tutorial, you'll have noticed occasional mentions of a *system variable* in conjunction with a command. You can check the status or change the setting of any system variable while you are in the middle of another command. To do this, you simply type an apostrophe ('), followed by the name of the system variable, at the command prompt.

For example, if you have started to draw a line, and you suddenly decide you need to rotate your cursor 45°, you can do the following steps.

1. At the To point prompt, enter **'snapang**.

2. At the New value for Snapang prompt, enter a new cursor angle. Once you have entered an angle value, you are returned to the Line command with the cursor in its new orientation.

You can also recall information such as the last area or distance calculated by AutoCAD. Because the Area system variable duplicates the name of the Area command, you need to choose Tools ➤ Inquiry ➤ Set Variables, and then type **Area** ↵ to read the last area calculation. You can also type **'Setvar** ↵ **Area** ↵ . The choose Tools ➤ Inquiry ➤ Set Variables option also lets you list all the system variables and their status, as well as access each system variable individually by entering a question mark (?).

Many of the system variables give you direct access to detailed information about your drawing. They also let you fine-tune your drawing and editing activities. In Appendix D you'll find all the information you need to familiarize yourself with the system variables available. Don't feel that you have to memorize them all at once; just be aware that they are available.

NOTE   Many of the dialog box options you have been using throughout this book, such as the options found in the Preferences dialog box, are actually system variable settings.

Keeping a Log of Your Activity

At times you may find it helpful to keep a log of your activity in an AutoCAD session. A log is a text file containing a record of your activities in AutoCAD. It may also contain notes to yourself or others about how a drawing is set up. Such a log can help you determine how frequently you use a particular command, or it can help you construct a macro for a commonly used sequence of commands.

The following exercise demonstrates how you can save and view a detailed record of an AutoCAD session using the Log feature.

1. Click on tools ➤ Preferences…. Then at the Preferences dialog box, click on the tab labeled General at the top of the dialog box. A new set of options appears.

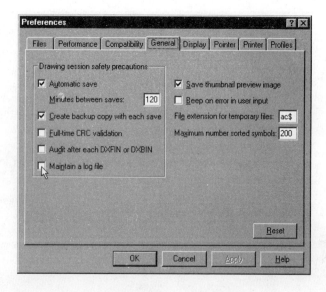

TIP

As a shortcut, you can quickly turn the Maintain a Log File feature on and off by typing **Logfileon** ↵ and **Logfileoff** ↵ at the command prompt in AutoCAD.

2. Click on the checkbox labeled Maintain a Log File in the Drawing Session Safety Precautions group, and then click on OK

3. Click on Tools ➤ Inquiry ➤ Status.

4. Return to the General tab of the Preferences dialog box, and then click on the Maintain a Log File checkbox again to remove the X.

5. Click OK to exit the dialog box.

6. Switch over to the Program Manager and start the Notepad application, or any text editor.

7. With the text editor, open the file called Acad.log in the \Program Files\ AutoCAD 14 directory. This is the file that stores the text data from the command prompt whenever the Log File option is turned on. You must turn off the Log File feature before you can actually view this file in AutoCAD.

Since Acad.log is a standard text file, you can easily send it to other members of your workgroup, or print it out for a permanent record.

Easy Access to the Acad.log File

If you want to have easy access to the Acad.log file, place a shortcut to it in your AutoCAD Release 14 program group. Here's how it's done:

1. Open the Windows Explorer and locate and highlight the Acad.log file.

2. Right-click on the Acad.log file.

3. At the pop-up menu, select Create Shortcut. A new file named Shortcut to Acad.log is created.

4. Shift + click and drag this Shortcut file to the Desktop. (A Shift + click on a file moves the file instead of making a copy.)

5. Right-click on the Start button.

6. Click on the Open option in the pop-up menu. The Start Menu window appears.

7. Double-click on the Programs icon in the Start Menu window. The Programs Window appears.

8. Adjust your view of the Programs window so you can see the AutoCAD Release 14 program group icon.

9. Click and drag the Shortcut to Acad.log file into the AutoCAD Release 14 program group icon.

Once this is done, you can open the Acad.log file by choosing Start ➤ Programs ➤ AutoCAD R14 ➤ Shortcut to Acad.log from the Windows 95 or NT 4 Start menu. Note that you cannot access this file while AutoCAD is open and the Log file feature is turned on.

Capturing and Saving Text Data from the AutoCAD Text Window

If you are working in groups, it is often quite helpful to have a record of the status, editing time, and system variables for particular files readily available to other group members. It is also convenient to keep records of block and layer information, so you can see if a specific block is included in a drawing or what layers are normally on or off.

You can use the Windows Clipboard to capture and save such data from the AutoCAD Text Window. The following steps show you how it's done.

1. Move the arrow cursor to the command prompt at the bottom of the AutoCAD window.

2. Right-click on the mouse. A pop-up menu appears.

3. Click on Copy History. The content of the text window is copied to the clipboard.

By default, the text window stores 400 lines of text. You can change this number by changing the options in the Text Window group in the Display tab of the Preferences dialog box.

If you only want to copy a portion of the text window to the clipboard, perform the following steps.

1. Press the F2 function key to open the text window.

2. Using the I-beam text cursor, highlight the text you wish to copy to the clipboard.

3. Right-click on your mouse, and then click on Copy from the pop-up menu. You can also click on Edit ➢ Copy from the text window's menu bar. The highlighted text is copied to the clipboard.

4. Open a Notepad or another word processor file and paste the information.

You may notice three other options on the pop-up menu: Paste to CmdLine, Paste, and Preferences…. Paste to CmdLine offers a way to capture data, such as layer, linetype, block names, or even commands, and paste them into the command prompt window. The Paste option will paste the first line of the contents of the clipboard into the command line or input box of a dialog box. This can be useful for entering repetitive text or for storing and retrieving a frequently used command. Preferences… will open the Preferences dialog box.

TIP

Items copied to the clipboard from the AutoCAD Text Window can be pasted into dialog box input boxes. This can be a quick way to transfer layer, line type, or other named items from the text window into dialog boxes.

Recovering Corrupted Files

No system is perfect. Eventually, you will encounter a file that is corrupted in some way. AutoCAD offers two tools that can frequently salvage a corrupted file: Audit and Recover. Audit allows you to check a file that you are able to open, but you suspect has some problem. Recover allows you to open a file that is so badly corrupted that AutoCAD is unable to open it in a normal way. You can access these tools from the File ➤ Utilities cascading menu. The functions of the these options are described here.

Audit   checks the current file for any errors and displays the results in the text window.

Recover   attempts to recover damaged or corrupted AutoCAD files. The current file is closed in the process as Recover attempts to open the file to be recovered.

More often than not, these tools will do the job, though they aren't a panacea for all file corruption problems. In the event that you cannot recover a file even with these tools, make sure your computer is running smoothly and that other systems are not faulty.

Exchanging CAD Data with Other Programs

AutoCAD offers many ways to share data with other programs. Perhaps the most common type of data exchange is to simply share drawing data with other CAD programs. In this section, you'll look at how you can export and import CAD drawings using the .dxf file format. You'll also look at how you can use bitmap graphics, both to and from AutoCAD, through the Windows clipboard.

Other types of data exchange involve text, spreadsheets, and databases. I cover database links in Chapter 10, but here we'll look at how you can include text, spreadsheet, and database files in a drawing or include AutoCAD drawings in other program files using a Windows feature called Object Linking and Embedding.

Using the .dxf File Format

A .dxf file is a DOS text file containing all the information needed to reconstruct a drawing. It is often used to exchange drawings created with other programs.

Many micro-CAD programs, including some 3D perspective programs, can generate or read files in .dxf format. You may want to use a 3D program to view your drawing in a Perspective view, or you may have a consultant who uses a different CAD program that accepts .dxf files. There are many 3D rendering programs that read .dxf files, on both the IBM PC and compatibles and on Apple Macintosh computers. Most 2D drafting programs also read and write .dxf files.

You should be aware that not all programs that read .dxf files will accept all the data stored therein. Many programs that claim to read .dxf files will "throw away" much of the .dxf file's information. Attributes are perhaps the most commonly ignored objects, followed by many of the 3D objects, such as meshes and 3D faces. But .dxf files, though not the most perfect medium for translating data, have become something of a standard.

NOTE   AutoCAD no longer supports the IGES (Initial Graphics Exchange Specification) standard for CAD data translation.

Exporting .dxf Files

To export your current drawing as a .dxf file, try the following exercise:

1. Choose File ➤ Export. The Export Data dialog box appears.

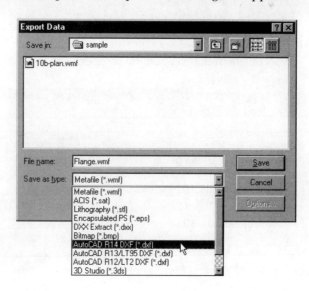

NOTE You can also Click on File ➤ Export..., and then enter the name of your export file, including the .dxf extension. AutoCAD will skip the prompt in step 3 and proceed to create the .dxf file.

2. Click on the Save as Type drop-down list. You then have the option to export your drawing under a number of formats, including three different .dxf formats.

3. Select the appropriate .dxf format, and then enter a name for your file. You do not have to include the .dxf file name extension.

4. Select a Folder for the file, and then click Save.

In step 2, you can select from the following .dxf file formats:

- AutoCAD R14 DXF

- AutoCAD R13/LT 95 DXF

- AutoCAD R12/LT 2 DXF

Choose the format appropriate to the program you are exporting to. In most cases, the safest choice is AutoCAD R12/LT 2 DXF if you are exporting to another CAD program, though AutoCAD will not maintain the complete functionality of Release 14 for such files.

Once you've selected a .dxf format from the Save as Type drop-down list, you can set more detailed specifications by clicking on the Options button in the Export Data dialog box. Doing so opens the Export Options dialog box.

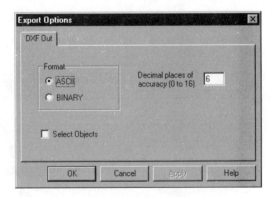

Here you have the following options:

Format lets you choose between ASCII (plain text) or binary file formats. Most other programs will accept ASCII, so it is the safest choice. Some programs will accept binary .dxf files, which have the advantage of being more compact than the ASCII format.

Select Objects lets you select specific objects within the drawing for export. You are given the option to select objects after you have closed the Export Options dialog box and have selected Save from the Export Data dialog box.

Decimal places of accuracy allows you to determine the accuracy of the exported file. Keeping this value low will help reduce the size of the export file, particularly if it is to be in the ASCII format. Some CAD programs do not support the high accuracy of AutoCAD, so using a high value here may have no significance.

TIP   You can also type **Dxfout** ↵ at the command prompt to open the Create DXF file dialog box. This is a standard Windows file dialog box that includes the options button described here. This dialog box displays only .dxf file formats in the Save as Type drop-down list.

Opening or Importing .dxf Files

Some offices have standardized their CAD drawings on the .dxf file format. This is most commonly seen in offices that use a variety of CAD software besides AutoCAD. Release 14 lets you open .dxf files directly, as if they were .dwg files. Here's how it's done.

1. Choose File ➤ Open.

2. At the Select File dialog box, choose .dxf from the Files of Type drop-down list.

3. Locate and select the .dxf file you wish to open.

You can also import .dxf files into an open file, provided the .dxf file does not contain blocks or other named elements that do not exist in the current file.

1. Type **Dxfin** ↵ from the command prompt. The Select .DXF File dialog box appears. This is a typical Windows-style file dialog box.

2. Locate and select the .dxf file you wish to import.

3. Double-click on the file name to begin importing it.

If the import drawing is large, AutoCAD may take several minutes.

Exchanging Files with Earlier Releases

One persistent dilemma that has plagued AutoCAD users is how to exchange files between earlier versions of the program. In the past, if you upgraded your AutoCAD, you would find that you were locked out from exchanging your drawings with people using earlier versions. Release 12 alleviated this difficulty by making Release 12 files compatible with Release 11 files.

With Release 13, we had a file structure that was radically different from earlier versions of AutoCAD. Fortunately, you can still exchange files with earlier versions of the program, using the Save as Type drop-down list in the Save Drawing As dialog box.

However, you don't get something for nothing. While you can make a "round trip" from Release 14 to Release 13 and back without losing any drawing data, there are certain things you will lose when you save a Release 14 file in Release 12 format. Bear these considerations in mind when you use Save As to save a file to Release 12:

- Splines become polyline splines.

- 3D Solids become polylines representing the wireframe of the solid.

- Multilines become polylines.

- Line types with embedded shapes are separated into lines and shapes. Dimension styles are not completely translated.

- Line styles are not completely translated.

- TrueType fonts are not supported in Release 12 or earlier versions.

When you save a drawing as a Release 12 file, you will receive a message telling you how the file is being modified to accommodate the limited Release 12 format. You may want to use the LogfileonO command to store this conversion message for future reference.

Using AutoCAD Drawings in Desktop Publishing

As you probably know, AutoCAD is a natural for creating line art, and because of its popularity, most desktop-publishing programs are designed to import AutoCAD drawings in one form or another. Those of you who employ desktop-publishing software to generate user manuals or other technical documents will probably want to be able to use AutoCAD drawings in your work. In this section, we will examine ways to output AutoCAD drawings to formats that most desktop-publishing programs can accept.

There are two methods for exporting AutoCAD files to desktop-publishing formats: raster export and vector file export.

Exporting Raster Files

In some cases, you may only need a rough image of your AutoCAD drawing. You can export your drawing as a raster file that can be read in virtually any desktop-publishing and word-processing program. Here are the steps for accessing this feature:

1. Click on Tools ➢ Preferences to open the Preferences dialog box.

2. Click on the Printer tab. You will see a list of printer configuration options.

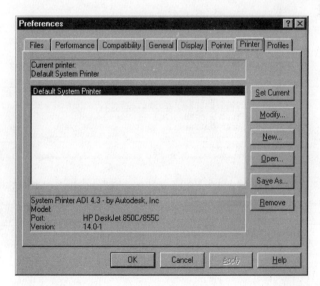

3. Click on New to see a listing of printer options in the Add a Printer dialog box.

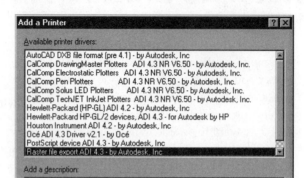

4. Click on the option that reads "Raster file export ADI 4.3 - by Autodesk Inc." You may also add a description for this selection in the Add a Description input box.

5. Click OK. The AutoCAD Text Window appears with a display of raster size options.

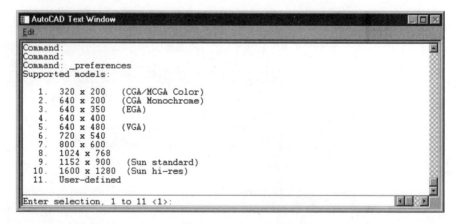

6. Select a size you want to work with by typing its number and pressing ⏎. If you are uncertain about what size you want, you can select any size at first, and then come back and add another version of the Raster File Export option for a different raster image size.

7. Once you've selected a size, you are shown a list of file formats:

   1. `Microsoft Windows Device-independent Bitmap (.BMP)`
   2. `TrueVision TGA Format`
   3. `Z-Soft PCX Format`
   4. `TIFF (Tag Image File Format)`

8. Select a format by entering its number followed by ↵. You are then presented with a list of color options. The following list is offered when you select option 4, the .tiff format:

   1. `Monochrome`
   2. `Color - 16 colors`
   3. `Color - 256 colors`

9. Select the color option you desire. If you select an option other than monochrome, you then get the following message:

   ```
   You can specify the background color to be any of AutoCAD's
   256 standard colors.  The default of 0 selects a black screen
   background.
   Enter selection, 0 to 255 <0>:
   ```

10. As the message tells you, you can determine the background color of your raster images. The default 0 gives you a black background. Enter 7 for a white background, or enter another color number. Once you've entered a color, you see the following message:

    ```
    Sizes are in Inches and the style is landscape
    Plot origin is at (0.00,0.00)
    Plotting area is 640.00 wide by 480.00 high (MAX size)
    Plot is NOT rotated
    Hidden lines will NOT be removed
    Plot will be scaled to fit available area

    Do you want to change anything? (No/Yes/File) <N>:
    ```

NOTE The color numbers are based on the standard AutoCAD color index that you see when you select colors for objects or layers.

11. The options presented here are the same as those presented in a more understandable way in the Plot Configuration dialog box. You have the

opportunity to change them when you are ready to create your raster file, so press ↵ to accept the default, No. You return to the Preferences dialog box.

12. Click OK. You now have a printer option that will generate a raster file of your drawing (rather than print or plot your drawing).

When you are ready to create a raster file, proceed as if you were to plot your file. Then at the Print/Plot Configuration dialog box, select the raster output option from the Device and Default Selection dialog box (see Chapter 7 for details on using the Print/Plot dialog box).

The range of raster output options is quite comprehensive. Chances are, if you need raster output from AutoCAD, at least one of the available options should fill your needs.

Exporting Vector Files

If you need to preserve the accuracy of your drawing, or if you wish to take advantage of TrueType or PostScript fonts, you really have no choice but to use either the .dxf or PostScript vector formats.

For vector format files, .dxf is the easiest to work with; and with TrueType support, .dxf can preserve font information between AutoCAD and desktop-publishing programs that support the .dxf format. PostScript is a raster/vector hybrid file format that AutoCAD supports; unfortunately, Release 14 has dropped direct PostScript font support. However, you can still use substitute fonts to stand in for PostScript fonts. These substitute fonts will be converted to true PostScript fonts when AutoCAD exports the drawing. You won't actually see the true results of your PostScript output until you actually print your drawing out on a PostScript printer.

We've already covered .dxf file export in the *Using the .dxf File Format* section of this chapter, so we'll concentrate on PostScript in this section.

TIP   If you are a circuit board designer or drafter, you may want to use the PostScript Out option to output your layout to PostScript typesetting devices. This will save time and file size since this option converts AutoCAD entities into true PostScript descriptions.

PostScript Output

AutoCAD is capable of exporting to the Encapsulated PostScript file format (.eps). You actually have two ways of obtaining PostScript output. You can use the File ➤ Export option from the menu bar, or you can install a PostScript printer driver and plot your drawing to an .eps file. In the *If You Want to Experiment* section of Chapter 11, I've described the steps for using File ➤ Export to export .eps files. To set up AutoCAD to plot your drawing to an .eps file, follow the same steps described in the previous *Exporting Raster Files* section, but in step 4, select the option that reads "PostScript device ADI 4.3 - by Autodesk Inc" instead of the Raster file driver.

WARNING   AutoCAD does not preserve font information when creating .eps files from the printer option.

PostScript Font Substitution

I mentioned earlier that AutoCAD will substitute its own fonts with PostScript fonts when a file is exported to an .eps file using the Export Data dialog box. If your work involves PostScript output, you will want to know these font names in order to make the appropriate substitution. Table 14.1 shows a listing of AutoCAD font names and their equivalent PostScript names.

To take advantage of AutoCAD's ability to translate fonts, you need to create AutoCAD fonts that have the names listed in the first column of Table 14.1. You then need to use those fonts when creating text styles in AutoCAD. Then AutoCAD will convert the AutoCAD fonts into the corresponding PostScript fonts.

Creating the AutoCAD fonts can be simply a matter of copying and renaming existing fonts to those listed in Table 14.1. For example, you could make a copy of the Romans.shx font and name it Agd.shx. Better yet, if you have the PostScript .pfb file of the font, you can compile it into an AutoCAD font file and re-name the compiled file appropriately. By compiling the .pfb file, you will get a close approximation of its appearance in AutoCAD. See the *Using PostScript Fonts* sidebar in Chapter 8 for a description on how to compile PostScript fonts.

TABLE 14.1: A listing of AutoCAD font file names and their corresponding PostScript fonts

AutoCAD Font Name	PostScript Font Name	AutoCAD Font Name	PostScript Font Name
agd	AvantGarde-Demi	agdo	AvantGarde-DemiOblique
agw	AvantGarde-Book	agwo	AvantGarde-BookOblique
bdps	Bodoni-Poster	bkd	Bookman-Demi
bkdi	Bookman-DemiItalic	bkl	Bookman-Light
bkli	Bookman-LightItalic	c	Cottonwood
cibt	CityBlueprint	cob	Courier-Bold
cobo	Courier-BoldOblique	cobt	CountryBlueprint
com	Courier	coo	Courier-Oblique
eur	EuroRoman	euro	EuroRoman-Oblique
fs	FreestyleScript	ho	Hobo
hv	Helvetica	hvb	Helvetica-Bold
hvbo	Helvetica-BoldOblique	hvn	Helvetica-Narrow
hvnb	Helvetica-Narrow-Bold	hvnbo	Helvetica-Narrow-BoldOblique
hvno	Helvetica-Narrow-Oblique	hvo	Helvetica-Oblique
lx	Linotext	ncb	NewCenturySchlbk-Bold
ncbi	NewCenturySchlbk-BoldItalic	nci	NewCenturySchlbk-Italic
ncr	NewCenturySchlbk-Roman	par	PanRoman
pob	Palatino-Bold	pobi	Palatino-BoldItalic
poi	Palatino-Italic	por	Palatino-Roman
rom	Romantic	romb	Romantic-Bold
romi	Romantic-Italic	sas	SansSerif
sasb	SansSerif-Bold	sasbo	SansSerif-BoldOblique
saso	SansSerif-Oblique	suf	SuperFrench

TABLE 14.1 CONTINUED: A listing of AutoCAD font file names and their corresponding PostScript fonts

AutoCAD Font Name	PostScript Font Name	AutoCAD Font Name	PostScript Font Name
sy	Symbol	te	Technic
teb	Technic-Bold	tel	Technic-Light
tib	Times-Bold	tibi	Times-BoldItalic
tii	Times-Italic	tir	Times-Roman
tjrg	Trajan-Regular	vrb	VAGRounded-Bold
zcmi	ZapfChancery-MediumItalic	zd	ZapfDingbats

If you are using PostScript fonts not listed in Table 14.1, you can add your own AutoCAD-to-PostScript substitution by editing the `Acad.psf` file. This is a plain text file that contains the font substitution information as well as other PostScript translation data.

TIP The HPGL plot file format is another vector format you can use to export your AutoCAD drawings. Use the method described earlier in *Exporting Raster Files* to add the HPGL plotter driver to your printer/plotter configuration.

Combining Data from Different Sources

Imagine being able to import and display spreadsheet data into an AutoCAD drawing. Further imagine that you could easily update that spreadsheet data, either from directly within the drawing or remotely by editing the source spreadsheet document. With a little help from a Windows feature called *Object Linking and Embedding,* or OLE, such a scenario is within your grasp. The data is not limited to spreadsheets; it could be a word-processed document, a database report, or even a sound or video clip.

To import data from other applications, you use the Cut and Paste feature found in virtually all Windows programs. You cut the data from the source document then paste it into AutoCAD.

When you paste data into your AutoCAD file, you have the option to have it *linked* to the source file or to *embed* it. If you link it to the source file, then the pasted data will be updated whenever the source file is modified. This is similar to an AutoCAD cross-referenced file (see Chapter 12 for more on cross-referenced files).

You can also paste data into AutoCAD without linking it; then it is considered an embedded object. You can still open the application associated with the data by double-clicking on it, but the data is no longer associated with the source file. This is similar to a drawing inserted as a block where changes in the source drawing file have no effect on the inserted block.

Let's see firsthand how OLE works. The following exercise shows how to link an Excel spreadsheet into AutoCAD. You will need a copy of Excel for Windows 95/NT, but if you have another application that supports OLE, you can follow along.

1. Open the file called 14a-plan-xls.dwg from the companion CD-ROM. This is a copy of the plan you may have created in earlier exercises.

2. Open the Excel spreadsheet called 14a-plan.xls, also from the companion CD-ROM.

3. In Excel, highlight the door data, as shown in Figure 14.7, by clicking on cell A1 and dragging to cell G17.

4. Choose Edit ➤ Copy. This places a copy of the selected data into the Windows Clipboard.

5. Switch to AutoCAD, either by clicking on a visible portion of the AutoCAD window, or by clicking on the AutoCAD button in the Taskbar at the bottom of the Windows Desktop.

6. Choose Edit ➤ Paste Special.... The Paste Special dialog box appears.

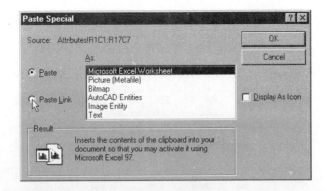

The Excel spreadsheet

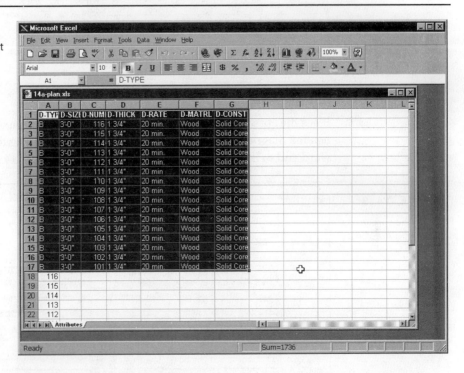

7. Click on the Paste Link radio button to tell AutoCAD you want this paste to be a link. Notice that the list of source types changes to show only one option: Microsoft Excel Worksheet.

8. Click OK. The spreadsheet data appears in the drawing (see Figure 14.8).

FIGURE 14.8:

The AutoCAD drawing with the spreadsheet pasted

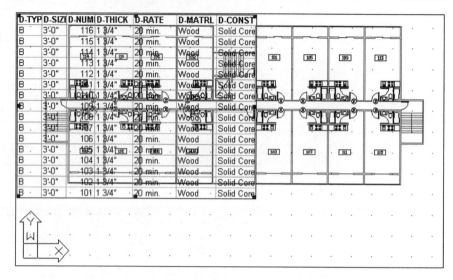

D-TYP	D-SIZE	D-NUM	D-THICK	D-RATE	D-MATRL	D-CONST
B	3'-0"	116	1 3/4"	20 min.	Wood	Solid Core
B	3'-0"	115	1 3/4"	20 min.	Wood	Solid Core
B	3'-0"	114	1 3/4"	20 min.	Wood	Solid Core
B	3'-0"	113	1 3/4"	20 min.	Wood	Solid Core
B	3'-0"	112	1 3/4"	20 min.	Wood	Solid Core
B	3'-0"	111	1 3/4"	20 min.	Wood	Solid Core
B	3'-0"	110	1 3/4"	20 min.	Wood	Solid Core
B	3'-0"	109	1 3/4"	20 min.	Wood	Solid Core
B	3'-0"	108	1 3/4"	20 min.	Wood	Solid Core
B	3'-0"	107	1 3/4"	20 min.	Wood	Solid Core
B	3'-0"	106	1 3/4"	20 min.	Wood	Solid Core
B	3'-0"	105	1 3/4"	20 min.	Wood	Solid Core
B	3'-0"	104	1 3/4"	20 min.	Wood	Solid Core
B	3'-0"	103	1 3/4"	20 min.	Wood	Solid Core
B	3'-0"	102	1 3/4"	20 min.	Wood	Solid Core
B	3'-0"	101	1 3/4"	20 min.	Wood	Solid Core

9. Place the cursor on the upper-left corner of the spreadsheet so that a double-headed diagonal arrow appears, and then click and drag the corner downward and to the right to make the size shown in Figure 14.9.

FIGURE 14.9:

Resizing the spreadsheet within AutoCAD

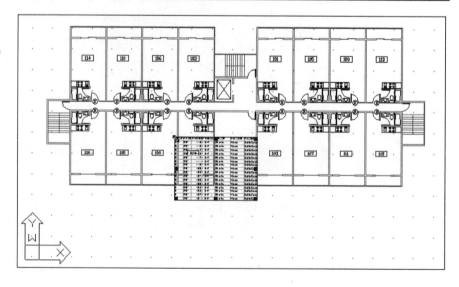

10. Place the cursor over the spreadsheet data so it looks like a cross, and then click and drag the spreadsheet to the lower-right corner of the drawing.

11. Zoom into the spreadsheet so you can read its contents clearly.

As you saw in steps 8 and 9, you can re-size a pasted object using the corner or side grips. The corner grips will maintain the original proportion of the inserted object.

You now have a linked object inserted into the AutoCAD drawing. You can save this file and send it off to someone else, along with the pasted document, 14a-plan.xls, and the other person will be able to open the AutoCAD file and view the drawing with the spreadsheet.

WARNING   Objects that are pasted into AutoCAD are maintained within AutoCAD until you use Erase to delete them. They act like other AutoCAD objects where layers are concerned. One limitation to Pasted objects is that they will not appear in prints or plots unless you use the Windows System printer or plotter.

Now let's see how the link feature works by making some changes to the spreadsheet data.

1. Go back to Excel by clicking on the Excel button in the Windows toolbar.

2. Click on the cell just below the column heading D-RATE.

3. Change the cell's contents by typing **No Rating** ↵.

4. Go back to AutoCAD and notice that the corresponding cell in the inserted spreadsheet has changed to reflect the change you made to the original document. Since you inserted the spreadsheet as a linked document, OLE updates the pasted copy whenever the original source document changes.

5. Now close both the Excel spreadsheet and AutoCAD drawing.

Editing Links

Once you've pasted an object with links, you can control the link by selecting Edit ➤ OLE Links... (Olelinks). If there are no linked objects in the drawing, this option does nothing, otherwise it opens the Links dialog box.

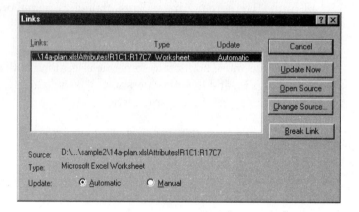

The following list describes the options available in this dialog box:

Cancel does just that. It cancels the link between a pasted object and its source file. Once this option is used, changes in the source file have no effect on the pasted object. This is similar to using the Bind option in the Xref command.

Update Now updates an object's link when the Manual option is selected.

Open Source opens the application associated with the object and lets you edit it.

Change Source... lets you change the object's link to a different file. When you select this option, AutoCAD opens the Change Link dialog box, which lets you select another file of the same type. For example, if you are editing the link to a sound file, the Change Link dialog box will display files with the .wav file extension.

Automatic and **Manual** radio buttons control whether linked objects are updated automatically or manually.

Break Link disconnects the link between the inserted data and the source document. The inserted data then becomes embedded, rather than linked.

Adding Sound, Motion, and Photos to Your Drawings

You've already seen how you can include scanned images in AutoCAD drawings through the Raster Image tools. Through Object Linking and Embedding, you can also include sound files, video clips, and animation. Imagine how you might be able to enhance your AutoCAD files with these types of data. You can include voice annotation or, if the file is to go to a client, an animated walk-through of your building or mechanical design. The potential for this feature is enormous.

Options for Embedding Data

If you don't need to link the imported data to its source, the Paste Special dialog box lets you convert the imported data to a number of other formats. Here is a brief description of each format that is available:

Picture (Metafile)   imports the data as vector or bitmap graphics, whichever is appropriate. If applicable, text is also maintained as text, though not editable within AutoCAD.

Bitmap   imports the data as a bitmap image, closely reflecting the appearance of the data as it appears on your computer screen in the source application.

AutoCAD Entities   converts the data into AutoCAD objects such as lines, arcs and circles. Text is converted into AutoCAD single-line text objects.

Image Entity   converts the data into an AutoCAD raster image. You can then edit it using the raster image-related tools found in the Modify ➢ Object ➢ Image cascading menu of the menu bar. See Chapter 11 for more on how to use raster images.

Text   converts the data into AutoCAD multiline text objects.

The options you see in the Paste Special dialog box will depend on the type of data being imported. You saw how the Microsoft Excel Worksheet option maintains the imported data as a Microsoft worksheet. If the contents of the clipboard come from another program, you will be offered that program as a choice in place of Excel.

NOTE

The Edit ➤ Paste option will embed OLE data objects into AutoCAD, as will the Paste From Clipboard tool in the Standard toolbar.

Using the Clipboard to Export AutoCAD Drawings

Just as you can cut and paste data into AutoCAD from applications that support OLE, you can also cut and paste AutoCAD images to other applications. This can be useful as a way of including AutoCAD images into word-processed documents, spreadsheets, or desktop-publishing documents. It can also be useful in creating background images for visualization programs such as 3D Studio, or paint programs such as Fractal Painter.

NOTE

If you cut and paste an AutoCAD drawing to another file using OLE, then send the file to someone using another computer, they must also have AutoCAD installed before they can edit the pasted AutoCAD drawing.

The receiving application does not need to support OLE, but if it does, then the exported drawing can be edited with AutoCAD and will maintain its accuracy as a CAD drawing. Otherwise, the AutoCAD image will be converted to a bitmap graphic.

To use the Clipboard to export an object or set of objects from an AutoCAD drawing, use the Edit ➤ Copy option. You are then prompted to select the objects you want to export. If you want to simultaneously export and erase objects from AutoCAD, choose Edit ➤ Cut.

If you want the AutoCAD image to be linked to AutoCAD, use Edit ➤ Copy Link. You won't be prompted to select objects. The current visible portion of your drawing will be exported. If you want the entire drawing to be exported, use View ➤ Zoom ➤ Extents before using the Copy Link option. Otherwise, set up AutoCAD to display the portion of your drawing you want exported, before using Copy Link.

In the receiving application, choose Edit Paste ➤ Special. You'll see a dialog box similar to AutoCAD's Paste Special dialog box. Select the method for pasting your AutoCAD image, and then click OK. If the receiving application does not have a Paste Special option, choose Edit ➤ Paste. The receiving application will convert the image into a format it can accept.

TIP You can copy multiple viewport views from Paper Space into the Clipboard using the Edit ➤ Copy Link option.

If You Want to Experiment...

With a little help from a Visual Basic macro and OLE, you can have Excel extract attribute data from a drawing, and then display that data in a spreadsheet imported into AutoCAD. The following exercise uses a Visual Basic macro embedded in the 14a-plan.xls file you used in an earlier exercise.

1. Open the 14a-plan-xls.dwg file in AutoCAD again.

2. Open the 14a-plan.xls file in Excel.

3. Repeat the exercise in the *Combining Data from Different Sources* section of this chapter, but stop before exiting the two files.

4. In AutoCAD, choose Modify ➤ Object ➤ Attribute ➤ Single, and then click on the door symbol in room 115.

5. Change the Fire Rating Attribute value to 1 hour, and then click OK.

6. Go to Excel, and then choose Tools ➤ Macro ➤ Macros.

7. At the Macros dialog box, highlight the Extract macro, and then click Run. Excel will take a moment to extract the attribute data from the open file; then it will display the data in the spreadsheet.

8. Return to AutoCAD and check the Fire Rating Value for room 115 in the imported spreadsheet. It reflects the change you made in the attribute in step 4.

9. Close both the files.

The macro you used in the Excel file is a small sample of what can be done using AutoCAD's implementation of Visual Basic Automation. You'll learn more about VBA in Chapter 20.

In this chapter, you have seen how AutoCAD allows you to access information ranging from the areas of objects to information from other programs. You may never use some of these features, but knowing they are there may at some point help you to solve a production problem.

You've just completed Part III of our tutorial. If you've followed the tutorial from the beginning, this is where you get a diploma. You have reached Expert status in 2D drawing and have the tools to tackle any drawing project thrown at you. You only need to log in some time on a few real projects to round out your experience.

From now on, you won't need to follow the book's chapters in order. If you're interested in 3D, go ahead and continue to Part IV, where you'll get thorough instructions on 3D drawing and imaging with AutoCAD. Otherwise, you can skip to Part V to become a full-fledged AutoCAD power-user.

Also, don't miss the appendices and the CD-ROM—they are packed with information that will answer many of your specific questions or problems. Of course, the entire book is a ready reference to answer questions as they arise or to refresh your memory about specific commands.

Good luck!

PART IV

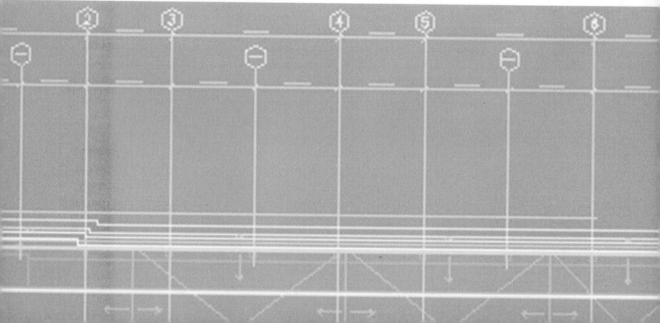

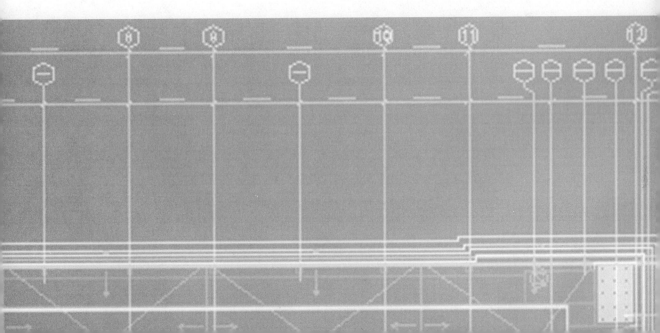

Modeling
and Imaging in 3D

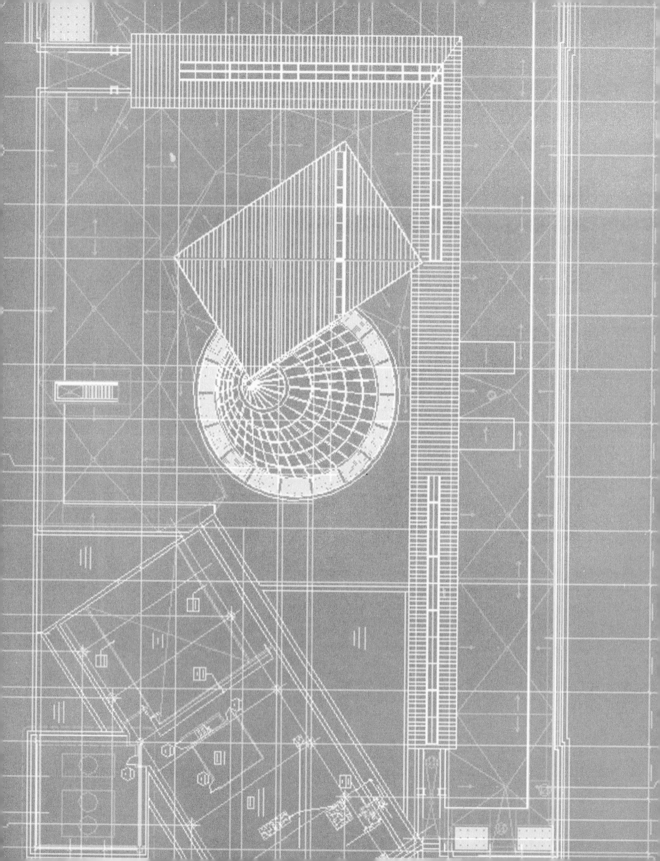

CHAPTER
FIFTEEN

15

Introducing 3D

- Creating a 3D Drawing

- Viewing a 3D Drawing

- Visualizing Your Model

- Getting the 3D Results You Want

- Drawing 3D Surfaces

- Creating and Using Slides

Viewing an object in three dimensions lets you have a sense of its true shape and form. It also helps you conceptualize the design, which results in better design decisions. Finally, using three-dimensional objects helps you communicate your ideas to those who may not be familiar with the plans, sections, and side views of your design.

A further advantage to drawing in three dimensions is that you can derive 2D drawings from your 3D model, which might otherwise take considerably more time with standard 2D drawing methods. For example, you could model a mechanical part in 3D and then quickly derive its top, front, and right-side views using the techniques discussed in this chapter.

AutoCAD offers two methods for creating 3D models: *surface modeling* and *solid modeling*. In this chapter, you will be introduced to surface modeling. You'll get a chance to explore solid modeling in Chapter 18.

With surface modeling, you use two types of objects. One is called a 3D Face, which you will learn about later in this chapter. The other is the standard AutoCAD set of objects you've been using all along, but with a slight twist. By changing the thickness property of objects, you can create 3D surfaces. These surfaces, along with some 3D editing tools, let you create virtually any 3D form you may need.

In this chapter, you will use AutoCAD's 3D capabilities to see what your studio apartment looks like from various angles.

Creating a 3D Drawing

By now, you should be aware that AutoCAD objects have properties that can be manipulated to set color, line type, and layer assignments. Another property called *thickness* lets you turn two dimensional objects into 3D forms. For example, to draw a cube, you first draw a square, and then change the thickness property of the square to some value greater than zero (see Figure 15.1). This thickness property is a value given as a z coordinate. Imagine that your screen's drawing area is the drawing surface. A z coordinate of 0 is on that surface. A z coordinate greater than 0 is a position closer to you and above that surface. Figure 15.2 illustrates this concept.

FIGURE 15.1:

How to create a cube
using extrusion

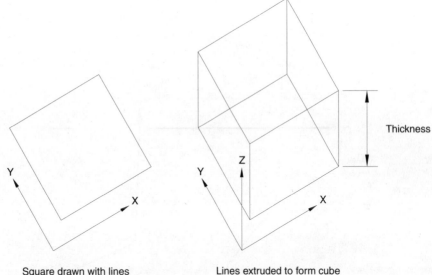

Square drawn with lines   Lines extruded to form cube

When you draw an object with thickness, you don't see the thickness until you view the drawing from a different angle. This is because normally your view is perpendicular to the imagined drawing surface. At that angle, you cannot see the thickness of an object because it projects toward you—just as a sheet of paper looks like a line when viewed from one end. Thus, to view an object's thickness, you must change the angle at which you view your drawing.

Another object property related to 3D is *elevation*. You can set AutoCAD so that everything you draw has an *elevation*. By default, objects have a zero elevation. This means that objects are drawn on the imagined 2D plane of Model Space, but you can set the z coordinate for your objects so that whatever you draw is above or below that surface. An object with an elevation value other than 0 rests not *on* the imagined drawing surface but *above* it (or *below* it if the z coordinate is a negative value). Figure 15.3 illustrates this concept.

FIGURE 15.2:

The z coordinate in relation to the x and y coordinates

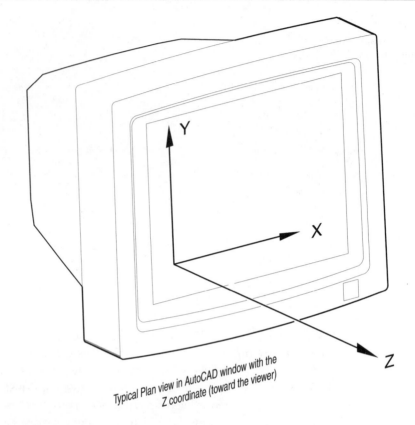

Typical Plan view in AutoCAD window with the Z coordinate (toward the viewer)

Changing a 2D Plan into a 3D Model

In this exercise, you will turn the 2D Unit drawing into a 3D drawing by changing the properties of the wall lines. You will also learn how to view the 3D image.

1. Start AutoCAD and open the Unit file or use 15a-unit.dwg from the companion CD-ROM.

2. Set the current layer to Wall, and turn off all the other layers except Jamb.

3. Turn on the grid (if it isn't on already). Your screen should look like Figure 15.4.

FIGURE 15.3:

Two identical objects at
different z coordinates

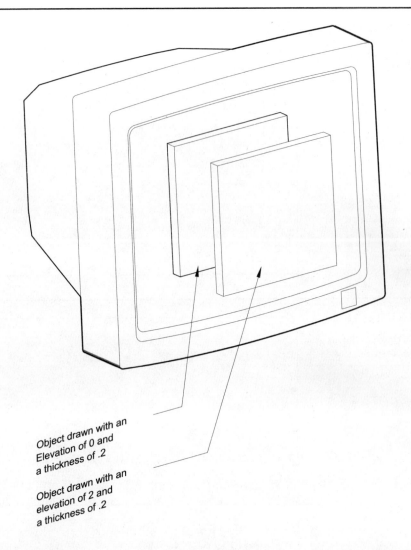

Object drawn with an
Elevation of 0 and
a thickness of .2

Object drawn with an
elevation of 2 and
a thickness of .2

4. Click on View ➤ 3D Viewpoint ➤ SW Isometric. Your view now looks as if
   you are standing below and to the left of your drawing, rather than directly
   above it (see Figure 15.5). The UCS icon helps you get a sense of your new
   orientation. The grid also shows you the angle of the drawing surface.

FIGURE 15.4:

The Plan view of the walls and door jambs

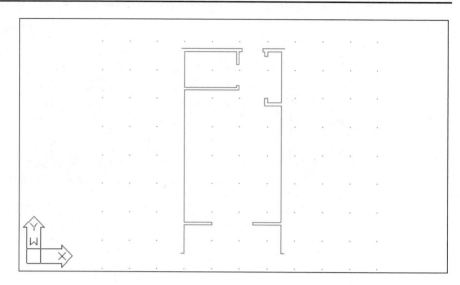

FIGURE 15.5:

A 3D view of the floor plan

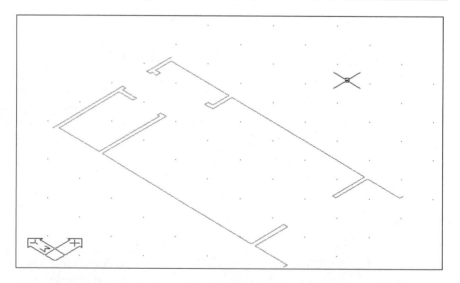

5. Click on the Properties button on the Object Properties toolbar.

6. At the Select object prompt, use a crossing window to pick the entire drawing and press ↵.

7. At the Change Properties dialog box, double-click on the Thickness input box, enter **8'**, and click on OK. The walls and jambs now appear to be 8' high.

Figure 15.6 shows the extruded wall lines. You are able to see through the walls because this is a *Wireframe view*. A Wireframe view shows the volumes of a 3D object by showing the lines representing the intersections of surfaces. Later we will discuss how to make an object's surfaces opaque in order to facilitate a particular point of view for a drawing.

In step 4, you were able to quickly obtain a 3D view from a set of 3D View options. You'll learn more about these options as you progress through this chapter.

NOTE   Notice that when you extruded the walls, the interior bathroom walls did not change with the others. This is because those walls are part of a block. You must redefine the block to change the thickness of the objects it contains.

FIGURE 15.6:

The wall lines, extruded (Wireframe view)

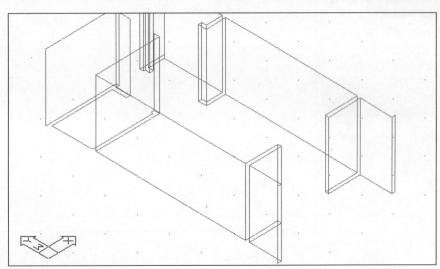

Next you will change the elevation of the door headers by moving them in the z-axis using grips.

1. First, zoom out a bit to get all of the drawing in view, as shown in Figure 15.7. You can use the Pan and Zoom tools in this 3D view as you would in a 2D view.

2. Turn on the Ceiling layer. The door headers appear as lines on the floor where the door openings are located.

3. Click on the two magenta lines representing the header over the balcony door. As you do so, notice that your cursor's shape conforms to the 3D view.

4. Shift + click on the midpoint grips of these two lines.

5. Click again on one of the hot grips.

6. At the ** STRETCH ** prompt, enter @0,0,7' ↵. (Don't forget to indicate feet for the 7.) The lines move to a new position 7' above the floor (see Figure 15.7).

FIGURE 15.7:

The header lines at the new elevation

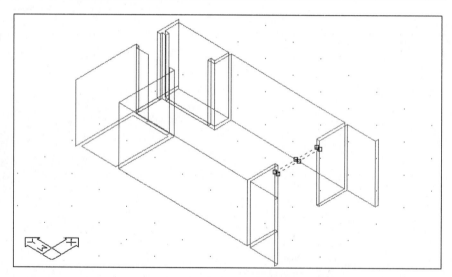

7. Click on the Properties button on the Object Properties toolbar and change the thickness of the header to 1' using the Thickness input box. Click on OK.

8. Click on the four lines representing the door header for the closet and entry.

9. Repeat steps 3 through 7. Your drawing will look like Figure 15.8.

10. Use the View Control dialog box (choose View ➤ Named Views...) to create a new view under the name of 3D.

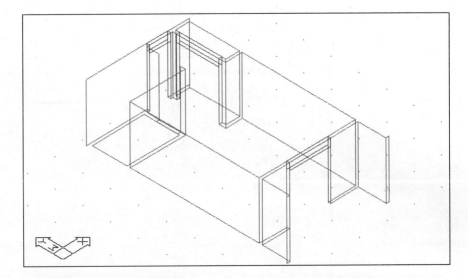

You could have used the Move command to move the lines to their new elevation, entering the same @0,0,7' at the Second point prompt for Move. Because you must select objects to edit them using grips, with Move you save a step by not having to select the lines a second time for the Properties tool.

Creating a 3D Object

Though you may visualize a design in 3D, you will often start sketching it in 2D and later generate the 3D views. When you know from the start what the thickness and height of an object will be, you can set these values so that you don't have to extrude the object later. The following exercise shows you how to set elevation and thickness before you start drawing.

1. Choose Format ➤ Thickness.

2. Enter 12" ↵ at the New Current Thickness prompt. Now as you draw objects, they will appear 12".

3. Draw a circle representing a planter at one side of the balcony (see Figure 15.9). Make it 18" in diameter. The planter appears as a 3D object with the current thickness and elevation settings.

FIGURE 15.9:

The planter

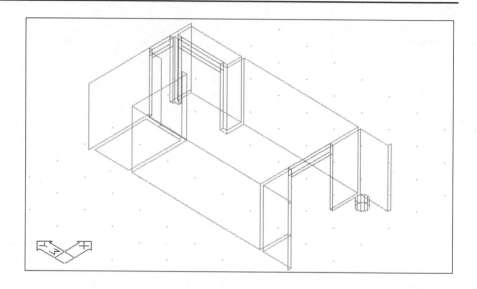

> **TIP**
>
> If you use the same thickness and elevation often, you can even create a template file with these settings so they are readily available when you start your drawings. The command for setting thickness and elevation is Elev. You can also use the Elevation and Thickness system variables to set the default elevation and thickness of new objects.

Having set the thickness setting to 12, everything you draw will have a thickness of 12 inches until you change it back to zero or some other setting.

> **NOTE**
>
> You can also change the default elevation from 0 to some other positive or negative value. To do this, you type **Elev** ↵ and then enter the elevation you want. You are then prompted for a thickness as well.

Giving objects thickness and modifying their elevation is a very simple process, as you have seen. With these two properties, you can create nearly any three-dimensional form you need. Next you will discover how to control your view of your drawing.

Viewing a 3D Drawing

Your first 3D view of a drawing is a Wireframe view. It appears as if it were an open model made of wire; none of the sides appear solid. This section describes how to manipulate this Wireframe view so you can see your drawing from any angle. This section will also describe how, once you have selected your view, you can view the 3D drawing as a solid object with the hidden lines removed. It will cover methods for saving views for later recall.

Finding Isometric and Orthogonal Views

First, let's start by looking at some of the viewing options available. You used one option already to get the current 3D view. That option, View ➤ 3D Viewpoint ➤ SW Isometric, brings up an Isometric view from a south-west direction, where north is the same direction as the y-axis. Figure 15.10 illustrates the three other Isometric View options: SE Isometric, NE Isometric, and NW Isometric. In Figure 15.10, the cameras represent the different viewpoint locations. You can get an idea of their location in reference to the grid and UCS icon shown in the figure.

FIGURE 15.10:

This diagram shows the viewpoints for the four Isometric views available from the View pull-down menu.

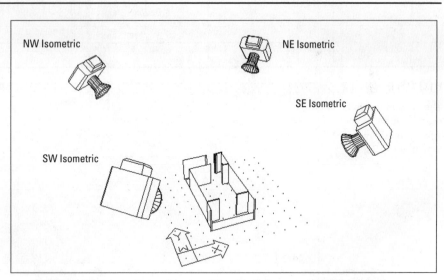

NW Isometric

NE Isometric

SE Isometric

SW Isometric

Another set of options available on the View ➤ 3D Viewpoint cascading menu are Top, Bottom, Left, Right, Front, and Back. These are Orthogonal views that show the sides, top, and bottom of the model, as shown in Figure 15.11. In this figure, the cameras once again show the points of view.

To give you a better idea of what an Orthogonal view looks like, Figure 15.12 shows the view that you see when you choose View ➤ 3D Viewpoint ➤ Right. It is a side view of the unit.

FIGURE 15.11:

This diagram shows the six viewpoints of the Orthogonal view options on the View ➤ 3D Viewpoint cascading menu.

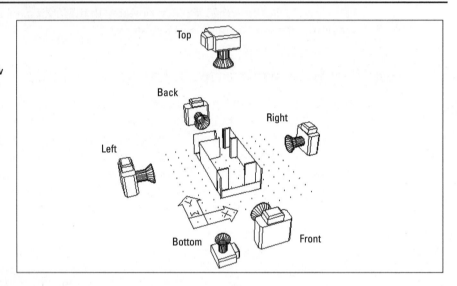

FIGURE 15.12:

The view of the unit model you see when you choose View ➤ 3D Viewpoint ➤ Right

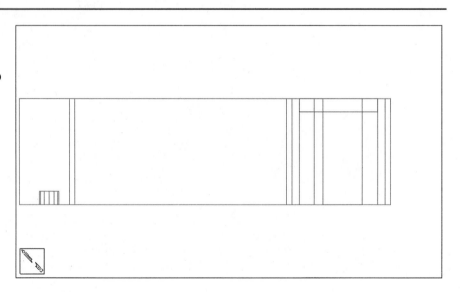

When you use any of the View options described here, AutoCAD will attempt to display the extents of the drawing. You can then use the Pan and Zoom tools to adjust your view.

If you find you use these view options frequently, you may want to open the Viewpoint toolbar.

This toolbar offers quick, single-click access to all the options discussed in this section. To open it, right-click on any toolbar, and then click on Viewpoint in the Toolbars dialog box.

Using a Dialog Box to Select 3D Views

You now know that you can select from a variety of "canned" viewpoints to view your 3D model. You can also fine-tune your view by indicating an angle from the drawing's x-axis and from the floor plane using the Viewpoint Presets dialog box. The following steps show you how it works.

1. Click on View ➤ 3D Viewpoint ➤ Select…, or type **Vp** ↵. The Viewpoint Presets dialog box appears (see Figure 15.13). The square dial to the left lets you select a viewpoint location in degrees relative to the x-axis. The semicircle to the right lets you select an elevation for your viewpoint.

2. Click on the area labeled 135 in the upper-left of the square dial. Then click on the area labeled 60 in the right-hand semicircle. Notice that the pointer moves to the angle you've selected and the input boxes below the graphic change to reflect the new settings.

3. Click on OK. Your view changes according to the new settings you just made.

Other settings in this dialog box let you determine whether the selected view angles are relative to the World Coordinate System or to the current User Coordinate System (UCS is discussed in Chapter 16). You can also go directly to a Plan view by clicking on Set to Plan View button.

There are a couple of features of the Viewpoint Presets dialog box that are not readily apparent. First of all, you can select the exact angle indicated by the label of either graphic by clicking anywhere inside the outlined regions around the pointer (see Figure 15.13). For example, in the graphic to the left, click anywhere in the region labeled 90° to set the pointer to 90° exactly.

You can set the pointers to smaller degree increments by clicking within the pointer area. For example, if you click in the area just below the 90° region in the left graphic, the pointer will move to that location. The angle will be slightly greater than 90°.

FIGURE 15.13:

The Viewpoint Presets dialog box

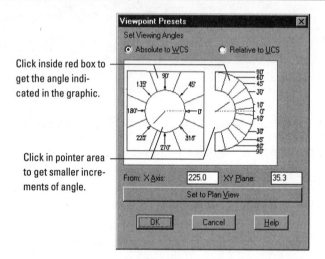

Click inside red box to get the angle indicated in the graphic.

Click in pointer area to get smaller increments of angle.

If you want to enter an exact value from the x-axis or x-y plane, you can do so by entering an angle value in the input boxes provided. You can obtain virtually any view you want using the options offered in this dialog box.

NOTE Three other options—Rotate, Tripod, and Vector—are also available in the View pull-down menu. These options are somewhat difficult to use and duplicate the functions described here so we're not including them in our discussion. If you'd like to learn more about these options, consult the AutoCAD Help system and look up the Vpoint command. You can also check out the *AutoCAD 14 Instant Reference* on the Companion CD-ROM.

Visualizing Your Model

From time to time, you will want to get an idea of how your model looks with hidden lines removed. This is especially true of complex 3D models. Frequently, object intersections and shapes are not readily apparent until you can see what object lies in front of others.

AutoCAD provides two helpful viewing commands, both on the Tools menu, for this situation. First, the Hide command allows you to quickly view your drawing with hidden lines removed. You can then assess where surfaces are and get a better feel for the model. Hide is also an option at plot time, allowing you to create hard copy line drawings of a 3D model. You can then render the hard copy using manual techniques if you want.

The second command, Shade, lets you add a sense of solidity to the image by adding color to surfaces. Shade has a variety of options for controlling how colors are applied. Unfortunately, you cannot plot a view generated by the Shade command. You can, however, store the view as a Slide file for independent viewing.

Let's begin by looking at the Hide command; we'll discuss the Shade command following Hide.

Loading the Render Toolbar

Both Hide and Shade are located on the Render toolbar. Choose View ➤ Toolbars, and then click on Render on the Toolbar dialog box. The Render toolbar will appear.

Click on Close to close the Toolbars dialog box.

Removing Hidden Lines

Hide is perhaps the easiest of all the AutoCAD commands to use. Try the following to see a Hidden-Line view of your model.

1. Restore the view you saved earlier with the name 3D.

2. Click on the Hide button on the Render toolbar, or enter **Hi** ↵ at the command prompt. You can also choose View ➢ Hide.

AutoCAD will display this message:

```
Regenerating drawing
```

You'll also see a graphic bar in the status bar showing the progress of the hidden-line removal. When AutoCAD is done, the image appears with hidden lines removed (see Figure 15.14).

FIGURE 15.14:

A unit in our apartment building with hidden lines removed

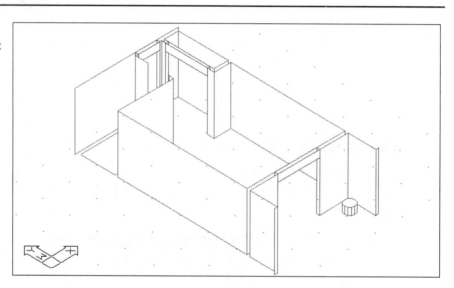

TIP

You can also plot a view with hidden lines removed by checking the Hide Lines checkbox in the Plot Configuration dialog box before you start your plot. Using the Hide Lines option will generally add only a few minutes to your plot time.

This Hidden-Line view will remain until your drawing is regenerated. Note that you cannot use the View command to save a Hidden-Line view. You can, however, save this view as a Slide.

NOTE   Hide does not hide text objects, unless the text objects have a thickness.

Although it did not take much time to perform a hidden-line removal on this drawing, the more complex the 3D drawing, the longer the Hide command will take. But even the most complex model you create will not take much more than several minutes.

Shading Your 3D Model

If you're used to looking at Wireframe 3D images, the Hide command is usually good enough to give you an idea of how your model looks. But when you want to get an even better visualization of the form your model is taking on, it's time for the Shade command. To see how it works, try the following exercise.

1. Open the Viewpoint Presets dialog box by choosing View ➤ 3D Viewpoint ➤ Select....

2. Enter **244** in the From X Axis input box and **34** in the XY Plane input box, and then click OK. This changes the view so you have a different line of sight to each wall surface.

3. Choose View ➤ Shade ➤ 16 Color Filled. Just as with the Hide command, AutoCAD displays a message telling you that it is regenerating the drawing. In a short time, the Shaded view appears.

4. Choose View ➤ Shade ➤ 256 Color Edge Highlight. Notice that this time the color of the vertical surfaces is varied to help differentiate their orientation (see Figure 15.15).

5. Now try View ➤ Shade ➤ 256 color. Now only the surfaces appear, with no edges showing.

FIGURE 15.15:

The Unit plan shaded using the 256 Color Edge Highlighted option

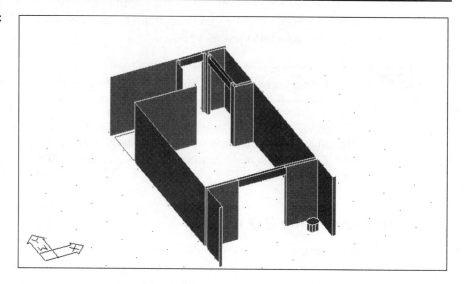

In step 2, you changed your view slightly so your line of sight to the various walls was at a different angle. Had you not changed your view, the Shade command would have shaded all the walls with the same intensity in steps 4 and 5. This is because Shade renders a view as if a light source emanates from the same direction as the viewer. Thus, when all the walls are at the same angle to the view, they all receive and reflect the same amount of light. With the model slightly turned, however, light then reflects off each surface differently.

In this exercise, each option you selected from the pull-down menu generated a different view. The Shade tool in the Render toolbar will repeat the last Shade option selected from the pull-down menu.

This tool can help you if you want quick access to the Shade command.

There is a third method for visualizing your model that allows you to place varying light sources in your drawing. The AutoCAD rendering functions on the Render toolbar let you adjust light reflectance of surfaces, smooth out faceted surfaces such as spheres and cylinders, and place light sources accurately. You'll get a chance to work with the rendering functions in Chapter 16. For now, let's look at some other factors that affect how a 3D model will look when it is shaded or when hidden lines are removed.

TIP   A system variable, Shadedif, influences the contrast of colors among different surfaces. A higher Shadedif number increases contrast; a lower number decreases contrast. The value can range from 0 to 100, with a default setting of 70. You may want to experiment with this setting on your own.

Getting the 3D Results You Want

Working in 3D is tricky because you can't see exactly what you are drawing. You must alternately draw and then hide or shade your drawing from time to time to see exactly what is going on. Here are a few tips on how to keep control of your 3D drawings.

Making Horizontal Surfaces Opaque

To make a horizontal surface appear opaque, you must draw it with a wide polyline, a solid hatch, or a 3D Face. For example, consider a table: You might represent the tabletop with a rectangle and give it the appropriate thickness, but the top would appear to be transparent when the lines were hidden. Only the sides of the tabletop would become opaque. To make the entire tabletop opaque, and the tabletop is an irregular shape, you can use a Solid Hatch or an object called a Region. We'll discuss Regions in Chapter 18.When the lines are hidden, the tabletop appears to be opaque (see Figure 15.16).

When a circle is used as an extruded form, the top surface appears opaque when you use the Hide command. Where you want to show an opening at the top of a circular volume, as in a circular chimney, you can use two 180° arcs (see Figure 15.17).

FIGURE 15.16:

One table using lines for the top, and another using a solid fill

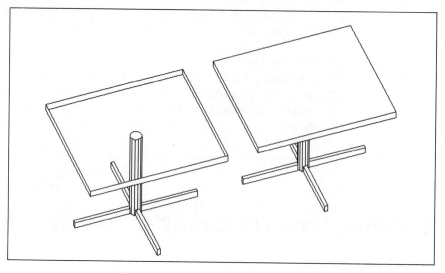

FIGURE 15.17:

A circle and two joined arcs

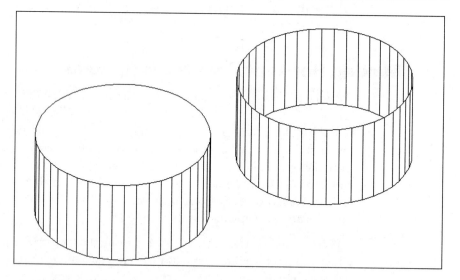

TIP Another type of surface object is the Region. Regions, like Solid Hatches, can create irregular-shaped surfaces. See Chapter 18 for more information on Region.

For complex horizontal surfaces, you can use a combination of wide polylines, solids, and 3D Faces to create them. For example, a sidewalk on a street corner would use a donut for the rounder corner, and solids or 3D Faces at either side for the straight portion of the sidewalk. It's okay to overlap surfaces to achieve the effect you want.

Setting Layers Carefully

Bear in mind that the Hide command hides objects that are obscured by other objects on layers that are turned off. For example, if a couch in the corner of the studio unit is on a layer that is off when you use Hide, the lines behind the couch are hidden even though the couch does not appear in the view (see Figure 15.18). You can, however, freeze any layer containing objects that you do not want affected by the hidden-line removal process. You can also use AutoCAD's Solid Modeler (described in Chapter 18) to draw complex 3D surfaces with holes.

Drawing 3D Surfaces

In your work with 3D so far in this chapter, you have simply extruded existing forms, or you have set AutoCAD to draw extruded objects. But extruded forms have their limitations. Using just extruded forms, it's hard to draw diagonal surfaces in the z-axis. AutoCAD provides the 3DFace object to give you more flexibility in drawing surfaces in three-dimensional space. The 3DFace produces a 3D surface where each corner can be given an x, y, and z value. By using 3D Faces in conjunction with extruded objects, you can create a 3D model of just about anything. When you view these 3D objects in a 2D Plan view, you will see them as 2D objects showing only the x and y positions of their corners or endpoints.

Using Point Filters

Before you start working with 3D surfaces, you should have a good idea of what the z coordinate values are for your model. The simplest way to construct surfaces in 3D space is to first create some layout lines to help you place the endpoints of 3D Faces.

FIGURE 15.18:

A couch hiding a line, when the layer is turned on (top) and turned off bottom)

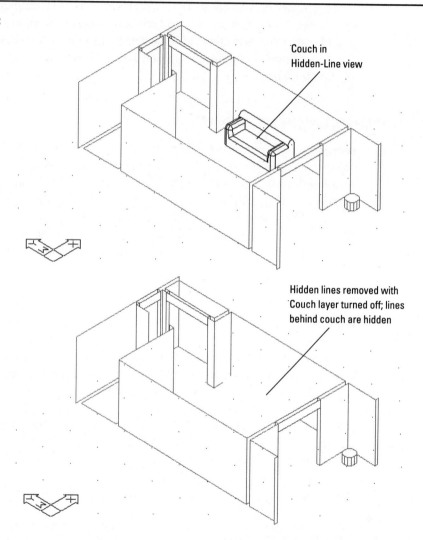

Couch in
Hidden-Line view

Hidden lines removed with
Couch layer turned off; lines
behind couch are hidden

AutoCAD offers a method for 3D point selection, called *filtering*, that simplifies the selection of z coordinates. Filtering allows you to enter an x, y, or z value by picking a point on the screen and telling AutoCAD to use only the x, y, or z value of that point, or any combination of those values. If you don't specify a z coordinate, the current elevation setting is assumed.

In the following exercises, let's imagine you decide to add a new two-story unit to your apartment design. You will add a stair rail to the studio apartment to access that second floor. In doing this, you will practice using 3D Faces and filters. You'll start by doing some setup, so you can work on a copy of the Unit file and keep the old Unit plan for future reference.

1. Restore the view you saved earlier as a 3D view, using View ➤ Named Views....

2. Save the Unit file, and then use File ➤ Save As to create a drawing called **Unitloft** from the current file. (You can also use the Unitloft.dwg file supplied on the companion CD-ROM.)

3. Choose Format ➤ Thickness and set the Thickness to 0.

4. Set the current layer to Wall.

Now you are ready to lay out your stair rail.

1. Click on Line on the Draw toolbar.

2. At the From Point prompt, Shift + click the right-mouse button to bring up the Osnap menu; then pick Point Filters ➤ .xy. As an alternate, you may enter **.xy** ↵ instead of using the Osnap menu. By doing this you are telling AutoCAD that you are going to first specify the x and y coordinates for this beginning point, and then later indicate the z coordinate.

NOTE   Notice the .X, .Y, and .Z options on Object Snap menu (Shift + right-click). These are the 3D filters. By picking one of these options as you select points in a 3D command, you can filter an x, y, or z value, or any combination of values, from that selected point. You can also enter filters through the keyboard.

---

3. At the From Point: .xy of prompt, pick a point along the same axis as the bathroom wall, 3'- 6" from the right-side wall of the unit near coordinate 25'- 6",25'-5". This will be the first line at the bottom of the stair rail. (You don't need to be too exact because we are just practicing.)

4. At the (need Z) prompt, enter **9'** ↵ (the z coordinate).

5. At the to point prompt, pick .xy again from the Osnap menu, or enter **.xy** ↵.

6. Enter **@12' <270**.

7. At the (need Z): prompt, enter **0** ↵.

8. Press ↵ to end the Line command. Your drawing should look like Figure 15.19.

FIGURE 15.19:

3D view of the stair rail

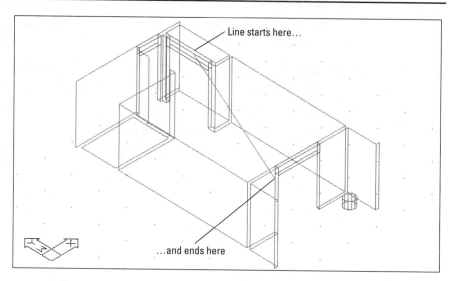

Line starts here...

...and ends here

Filters can also be used in a 2D drawing to select an x or y component of an object to which you want to align a point.

Now you will copy the line vertically to draw the top of the stair rail.

1. Click on the Copy Objects button on the Modify toolbar.

2. Select the 3D line you just drew, and press ↵.

3. At the Base Point prompt, pick any point on the screen.

4. At the Second Point prompt, enter **.xy** ↵, and then enter **@** ↵. This tells AutoCAD that your second point will maintain the x,y coordinates of the first point.

5. At the (need Z) prompt, enter **3'6"** ↵ to place the copy 3'-6" on the z-axis. A copy of the 3D line appears 3'-6" above the original.

In step 4 you specified that the second point used the same x and y coordinates of the base point, so you only needed to enter the z value for the second point. In the earlier exercise, you used a relative coordinate to move door headers to a position 7' higher than their original location. You could have used the same method here to copy the line vertically, but in this exercise you got a chance to see how the point filter works.

Creating Irregular 3D Surfaces

Sometimes you will want to draw a solid surface so that when you remove hidden lines, objects will appear as surfaces rather than wireframes. If you were to continue drawing the side of the stair rail using lines, the side of the stair rail would appear transparent. So the next step is to fill in the side using 3D Faces.

TIP   It generally makes life easier to first draw a wireframe of your object using lines, and then use their endpoints to fill in the surfaces.

Loading the Surfaces Toolbar

The 3DFace command and AutoCAD's 3D shapes are located on the Surfaces toolbar. Right-click on any toolbar to open the Toolbars dialog box, and then click on the Surfaces checkbox. Click Close in the Toolbars dialog box to close it.

Adding a 3D Face

Now that you've opened the Surfaces toolbar, you can begin to draw 3D Faces.

1. Zoom in to the two lines you just created, so you have a view similar to Figure 15.20.

FIGURE 15.20:

Zooming in to the stair rail lines

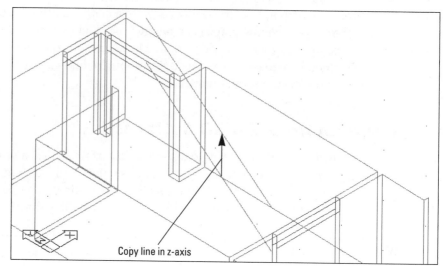

Copy line in z-axis

2. Click on the 3D Face button on the Surfaces toolbar, or type **3f** ↵.You can also choose Draw ➤ Surfaces ➤ 3D Face.

3. At the First Point prompt, use the Osnap overrides to pick the first of the four endpoints of the 3D lines you drew. Be sure the Ortho mode is off.

TIP

The Running Osnap mode can help you select endpoints quickly in this exercise. See Chapter 3 if you need help remembering how to set up the Running Osnap mode.

4. As you continue to pick the endpoints, you will be prompted for the second, third, and fourth points.

NOTE

With the 3DFace command, you pick four points in a circular fashion, as shown in Figure 15.21. Once you've drawn one 3D Face, you can continue to add more by selecting more points.

5. When the Third point prompt appears again, press ↵ to end the 3DFace command. A 3D Face appears between the two 3D lines. It is difficult to tell if they are actually there until you use the Hide command, but you should see vertical lines connecting the endpoints of the 3D lines. These vertical lines are the edges of the 3D Face (see Figure 15.21).

FIGURE 15.21:

The 3D Face

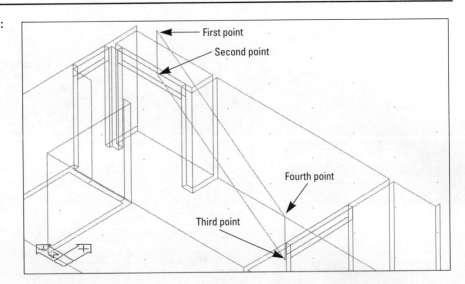

> **NOTE**
>
> When the Third point prompt reappears, you can draw more 3D Faces if you like. The next 3D Face will use the last two points selected as the first two of its four corners—hence the prompt for a third point.

6. Copy the 3D Face you just drew 5" horizontally in the 0 angle direction.

7. Use the 3DFace command to put a surface on the top and front side of the rail, as demonstrated in the top and middle image of Figure 15.22.

8. Use the Intersection Osnap override to snap to the corners of the 3D Faces.

9. Use the Hide command on the Render toolbar to get a view that looks like the bottom image of Figure 15.22.

10. Copy the three 3D Faces you just created 3' horizontally in the 0 angle direction.

FIGURE 15.22:

The top and front faces of the stair rail, and the stair rail with the hidden lines removed

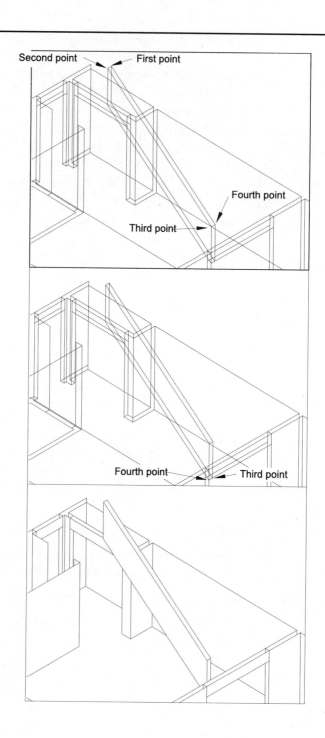

Now you can save the `Unitloft.dwg` file.

Hiding Unwanted Surface Edges

When using the 3DFace command, you are limited to drawing surfaces with four sides. You can, however, create more complex shapes by simply joining several 3D Faces. Figure 15.23 shows an odd shape constructed of three joined 3D Faces. Unfortunately, you are left with extra lines that cross the surface as shown in the top image of Figure 15.23; but you can hide those lines by using the Invisible option under the 3DFace command, in conjunction with the Splframe variable.

FIGURE 15.23:

Hiding the joined edge of multiple 3D Faces

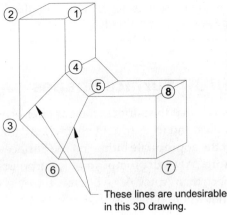

Drawing an odd-shaped surface using 3d Face generates extra lines. The numbers in the drawing to the left indicate the sequence of points selected to create the surface.

These lines are undesirable in this 3D drawing.

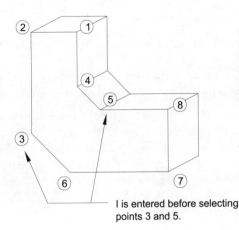

By drawing the same surface using the I option before selecting the appropriate points, the unwanted lines will be hidden. This drawing indicates where the I option is issued in the point-selection sequence.

I is entered before selecting points 3 and 5.

To make an edge of a 3D Face invisible, start the 3DFace command as usual. While selecting points, just before you pick the first point of the edge to be hidden, enter **I** ↵ as shown in the bottom image of Figure 15.23. When you are drawing two 3D Faces sequentially, only one edge needs to be invisible to hide their joining edge.

You can make invisible edges visible for editing by setting the Splframe system variable to 1. Setting Splframe to 0 will cause AutoCAD to hide the invisible edges. Bear in mind that the Splframe system variable can be useful in both 3D and 2D drawings.

TIP
The Edge option on the Surfaces toolbar lets you change an existing visible 3D Face edge to an invisible one. Click on the Edge button and then select the 3D Face edge to be hidden.

Using Predefined 3D Surface Shapes

You may have noticed that the Surfaces toolbar offers several 3D surface objects, such as cones, spheres, and torus (donut-shaped). All are made up of 3D Faces. To use them, click on the appropriate button on the Surfaces toolbar. When you select an object, AutoCAD will prompt you for the points and dimensions that define that 3D object; then AutoCAD will draw the object. This provides quick access to shapes that would otherwise take substantial time to create.

Things to Watch Out for When Editing 3D Objects

You have seen how you can use the Copy command on 3D lines and 3D Faces. You can also use the Move and Stretch commands on 3D lines, 3D Faces, and 3D shapes to modify their z coordinate values—but you have to be careful with these commands when editing in 3D. Here are a few tips to keep in mind:

- The Scale command will scale an object's z coordinate value, as well as the standard x and y coordinates. (Click and drag the Resize button on the Modify toolbar and select Scale on the flyout.) Suppose you have an object with an elevation of two units. If you use the Scale command to enlarge that object by a factor of 4, the object will have a new elevation of 2 units times 4, or 8 units. If, on the other hand, that object has an elevation of 0, its elevation will not change, because 0 times 4 is still 0.

- Array, Mirror, and Rotate (on the Modify toolbar) can also be used on 3D lines, 3D Faces, and 3D shapes, but these commands won't affect their z coordinate values. Z coordinates can be specified for base and insertion points, so take care when using these commands with 3D models.

- Using the Move, Stretch, and Copy commands (on the Modify toolbar) with object snaps can produce some unpredictable and unwanted results. As a rule, it is best to use point filters when selecting points with Osnap overrides. For example, to move an object from the endpoint of one object to the end-point of another on the same z coordinate, invoke the .XY point filter at the Base Point and Second Point prompts before issuing the endpoint over-ride. Proceed to pick the endpoint of the object you want; then enter the z coordinate, or just pick any point to use the current default z coordinate.

- When you create a block, the block will use the UCS that is active at the time the block is created to determine its own Local Coordinate System. When that block is later inserted, it will orient its own coordinate system with the current UCS. (UCS is discussed in more detail in Chapter 16.)

Turning a 3D View into a 2D AutoCAD Drawing

There are many architectural firms that use AutoCAD 3D models to study their designs. Once a specific part of a design is modeled and approved, they convert the model into 2D elevations, ready to plug into their elevation drawing.

At the end of Chapter 11, I describe a method you can use to convert a 3D model into a 2D AutoCAD drawing. If you need more accuracy in the conversion, config-ure the AutoCAD Plotter for an ADI Plotter. Set it up to plot a .dxb file. Your plots will then generate .dxb files, which you can import using the Insert ➤ Drawing Exchange Binary option in the menu bar. This opens the Select DXB File dialog box from which you can select the appropriate .dxb file.

Creating and Using Slides

Three-dimensional graphics are often handy for presentations, and 3D AutoCAD images are frequently used for that purpose, as well as for producing drafted 2D drawings. You may want to show off some of your 3D work directly from the computer screen. However, if your drawings are complicated, your audience may get impatient waiting for the hidden lines to be removed. Fortunately, AutoCAD provides two commands that let you save a view from your screen in a form that will display quickly.

The Mslide and Vslide commands will save a view as a file on disk. Such a view is called a *Slide*. You can display a Slide any time you are in the AutoCAD drawing editor. Slides display at redraw speed, no matter how complex they may be. This means you can save a Slide of a Hidden-Line view of your 3D drawing and recall that view quickly at any time.

Slides can also be used for reference during editing sessions, instead of panning, zooming, or viewing. A Slide cannot be edited, however, nor will it be updated when you edit the drawing.

Creating Slides

In the following exercise, you will make a few Slides of the Unit file.

1. Open the Unit file and click on the Hide button on the Render toolbar to get a Hidden-Line view of the unit.

2. Type **Mslide** ↵ at the command prompt.

3. At the File dialog box, click on Save to accept the default file name, Unit.sld. (The default Slide name is the same name as the current drawing, with the extension .sld.) The actual drawing file is not affected.

4. Zoom in to the bathroom, and use Mslide to save another view called **Unitbath**, this time without the hidden lines removed.

5. When the File dialog box appears, highlight the File input box at the bottom of the dialog box, enter **Unitbath** ↵, and click OK.

Viewing Slides

Now that you've saved two views, let's see how to view them.

1. Zoom back to the previous view and then type **Vslide** ↵.

2. At the File dialog box, locate and select Unitbath.dwg and click on Save. The Slide of the bathroom appears. You can move the cursor around the

view and start commands in the normal way, but you cannot edit or obtain information from this Slide.

3. Start Vslide again.

4. This time, click on Save at the dialog box to accept the default Slide file name, Unit. The 3D view of the unit appears with its hidden lines removed. Because Slides display at redraw speed, you don't have to wait to view the unit without its hidden lines.

NOTE Any command that performs a redraw will also return you to the current drawing.

5. Click on View ➤ Redraw View to return to the drawing being edited.

6. Open the Plan file and use the Vslide command to view the Unitbath Slide again. As you can see, you are able to call up the Slide from any file, not just the one you were in when you created the Slide.

7. Now create a Slide of the Plan file and call it **Plan1**.

Next, you'll get to see how you might automate a Slide presentation using the Slides you just created.

Automating a Slide Presentation

As mentioned in Chapter 7, Script (Tools ➤ Run Script…) can be used to run a sequence of commands automatically. Let's create a Script file to automatically show the Slides you made in the last exercise.

A Script file is really nothing more than a list of "canned" AutoCAD commands and responses. In this example, you'll add the Delay command, whose sole function is to pause a Script for a specific length of time.

1. Open a new file called **Show**.

2. Use a text editor like the Windows notepad to create a file called **Show.scr**, and enter the following lines into this file, pressing ↵ at the end of each line:

```
vslide
unit
delay 3000
vslide
```

```
unitbath
delay 3000
vslide
Plan1
```

These lines are a sequence of predetermined instructions to AutoCAD that can be played back later. Save this file in the same place where your Slide files are located. When you play this Script file, each line is entered at the AutoCAD command prompt, just as you would enter it through the keyboard. Notice that the Vslide command is executed before each Slide, which is then followed by the line delay 3000, which tells AutoCAD to pause roughly 3,000 milliseconds after each Vslide command is issued (you can substitute another value if you like). If no delay is specified, the next Slide will come up as soon as the previous Slide is completed.

You can also have the Slides repeat themselves continuously by adding the Rscript command at the very end of the Show.scr file. You may want to do this in a presentation intended for casual viewing, such as an exhibit in a display area with people passing through. To stop a repeating Script, press the Backspace key.

Now try playing the Script.

1. Return to AutoCAD, and then click Tools ➣ Run Script…, or enter **Script** ↵.

2. At the Select Script File dialog box, highlight and pick the file you just created (Show.scr) from the file list, and then click OK.

The Slides you saved will appear on the screen in the sequence in which you entered them in the Show.scr file.

Creating a Slide Library

You can group Slide files together into one file to help keep your Slides organized—for example, by project or by drawing type. Slide libraries also save disk space, since they often require less space than the total consumed by the individual Slide files.

Slide files are also used to create custom dialog boxes that show sample views of objects. Examples of such dialog boxes are the Hatch Pattern palette and the 3D Objects dialog box, which is displayed when you select Draw ➣ Surfaces ➣ 3D Surfaces.

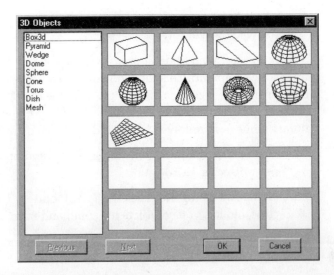

The tool you use to create a Slide library is the Slidelib.exe utility that comes with AutoCAD. This utility can be found in the \support subdirectory of AutoCAD R14. To create a Slide library, follow these steps.

1. Use a word processor and make a list of the Slides you want to include in the library. For the Slides you created earlier, it would look like the following:

   ```
   unit
   unitbath
   plan1
   ```

   Notice that you do not include the .sld extension in the file names in your list.

2. Save this list as a plain text file, with an appropriate name. For this example, call it **Slide1.lst**. Be sure it is saved in the same directory as your Slide files.

3. Locate the Slidelib.exe program, you should find it in \support subdirectory. Be sure your Slidelib.exe file is in the same directory as your Slide list file and Slide files.

   Do not include the file name extension; the Slidelib utility program automatically adds the file extension .slb. For example, if you use Plans as the library name in step 4, a Slide library file called Plans.slb is created.

4. Open a DOS window and go to your AutoCAD \Support subdirectory.

5. At the DOS prompt, enter **slidelib Myslides < slide1.lst** ↵. A file named Myslides.slb will be created. The library name can be any legal DOS file

name, but don't use file names over eight characters long, such as those allowed by Windows 95.

Now let's test your Slide library. To view a Slide from a Slide library, you use the Vslide command. This time, however, you will specify the file name differently. Instead of picking a Slide name from the dialog box, you must enter the name at the prompt line in a special format. The name must be entered with the library name first, followed by the individual Slide name in parentheses.

1. Open a new temporary file called **Temp**, and at the AutoCAD command prompt, enter **Vslide** ↵.

2. At the File dialog box, click the Type It button. This causes the dialog box to close and lets you complete the command from the command line.

3. At the `Slide file< current file name>` prompt, enter **Myslides(plan1)** ↵. The Slide will appear in the drawing area.

WARNING   If you placed the Slide library file in a directory other than the current one, be sure you enter the directory name before the Slide library name in step 3.

To use Slide libraries from Scripts, you use the Slide library and Slide name following the Vslide command, as in the following example:

```
vslide
myslides(unit)
delay 3000
vlside
myslides(unitbath)
delay 3000
vslide
myslides(plan1)
delay 3000
rscript
```

You've seen how you can save and display 3D views quickly and how you can automate a presentation of Slides using Scripts. With these tools, you can create an impressive, fast-paced presentation.

If You Want to Experiment...

Architects traditionally use 3D models made from cardboard or "chipboard" to help others visualize their ideas. And if you've ever taken a class in architectural design, chances are you've had to make such a model yourself. 3D modeling on a computer is faster and a lot more fun than creating a physical chipboard model, and in some cases it can show you things that a physical model cannot.

The following exercise is really just for fun. It shows you how to do a limited form of animation, using View ➢ 3D Viewpoint, the Mslide command, and Scripts.

1. Open the Unit plan.

2. Do a hidden-line removal; then use Mslide to create a Slide called **V1**.

3. Click and drag the Inquiry button on the Object Properties toolbar, and then select Locate Point on the flyout. Pick a point in the center of the floor plan. This marks the view center for the next step.

4. Enter **Vpoint** ↵ **R** ↵ at the command prompt.

5. At the Enter angle at XY plane prompt, enter **235** ↵; at the next prompt, press ↵.

6. Do another hidden-line removal, and use Mslide again to create a Slide called **V2**.

7. Repeat steps 4 through 6, but this time increase by 10 the angle value you entered at step 5 (to **245**). At step 6, increase the Slide name by 1 (to **V3**).

8. Keep repeating steps 4 through 6, increasing the angle value by 10 each time and increasing the Slide file name by 1. Repeat these steps at least five more times.

9. Use a text editor to create a Script file called **Animate.scr,** containing the following lines, pressing ↵ at the end of each line:

```
Vslide v1
Vslide v2
Vslide v3
Vslide v4
Vslide v5
Vslide v6
Vslide v7
```

```
Vslide v8
Rscript
```

10. Return to AutoCAD. At the command prompt, enter **Script** ↵ and click on Animate at the File dialog box. Then click OK and watch the show.

11. Press Esc or Backspace to end the show.

You might also want to try creating an animation that moves you completely around the Unit plan.

Here's another suggestion for experimenting: To practice drawing in 3D, turn the kitchen of your 3D Unit drawing into a 3D object. Make the cooking top 30" high and add some cabinet doors.

Have fun!

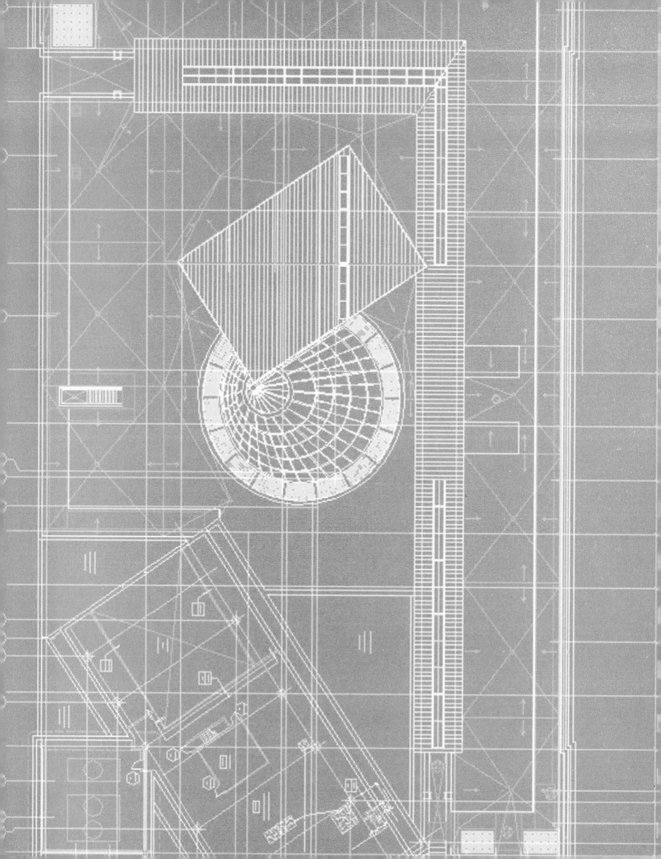

CHAPTER
SIXTEEN

16

Using Advanced 3D Features

- Mastering the User Coordinate System (UCS)

- Creating Complex 3D Surfaces

- Other Surface Drawing Tools

- Editing a Mesh

- Moving Objects in 3D Space

- Viewing Your Model in Perspective

AutoCAD's extended set of tools for working with 3D drawings lets you create 3D objects with few limitations on shape and orientation. This chapter focuses on the use of these tools, which help you easily generate 3D forms and view them in both the Perspective and Orthogonal modes.

Mastering the User Coordinate System

The User Coordinate System (UCS) allows you to define a custom coordinate system in 2D and 3D space. In fact, you've been using a special UCS called the World Coordinate System all along.

By now you are familiar with the L-shaped icon in the lower-left corner of the AutoCAD screen, containing the letters *W*, *X*, and *Y*. The W indicates that you are currently in what AutoCAD calls the World Coordinate System (WCS); the X and Y indicate the positive directions of the x- and y-axes. WCS is a global system of reference from which you can define other User Coordinate Systems.

It may help to think of these AutoCAD User Coordinate Systems as different drawing surfaces, or two-dimensional planes. You can have several User Coordinate Systems at any given time. By setting up these different UCSs, you are able to draw as you would in the WCS in 2D, yet draw a 3D image. Let's say you want to draw a house in 3D with doors and windows on each of its sides. You can set up a UCS for each of the sides; then you can move from UCS to UCS to add your doors and windows (see Figure 16.1). Within each of these UCSs, you draw your doors and windows as you would in a typical 2D drawing. You can even insert elevation views of doors and windows that you have created in other drawings.

In this chapter you will be experimenting with a number of different views and UCSs. All of the commands you will use are available both at the command line and also via the menu bar. Additionally, a number of the UCS commands can be accessed from the UCS toolbar.

FIGURE 16.1:

Different User
Coordinate Systems in
a 3D drawing

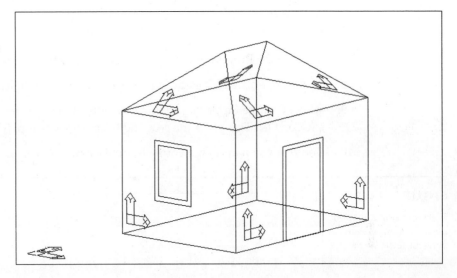

Defining a UCS

In the first set of exercises, you will draw a chair that you can later add to your 3D
Unit drawing. In drawing this chair, you will be exposed to the use of the UCS, as
well as to some of the other 3D capabilities available in AutoCAD.

Begin the chair by drawing the seat and legs.

1. Start AutoCAD and open a new file called **Barcelon**.

2. Set up your drawing as an architectural drawing with a scale of 1"=1'-0" on
   an 8½×11" sheet. You will want to set the upper-right corner of the limits to
   132×102.

3. Choose View ➢ Zoom ➢ All or type **Z** ↵ **A** ↵.

4. To draw the seat of the chair, click Rectangle on the Draw toolbar. Draw a
   rectangle measuring 20" in the x-axis and 30" in the y-axis. Position the rectangle so the lower-left corner is at the coordinate 2'-0", 2'-0" (see the top
   image of Figure 16.2).

5. To draw the back of the chair, draw another rectangle 17" in the x-axis and
   30" in the y-axis, just to the right of the previous rectangle (see the top image
   of Figure 16.2).

6. Click on View ➤ 3D Viewpoint ➤ SW Isometric. This gives you a 3D view from the lower-left of the rectangles, as shown in the bottom image of Figure 16.2.

7. Click on the Properties button on the Object Properties toolbar.

8. At the Select objects prompt, select the two rectangles.

9. At the Change Properties dialog box, enter **3** in the Thickness input box and click on OK. This gives the seat and back a thickness of 3".

10. Zoom out a bit and give yourself some room to work.

FIGURE 16.2:

The chair seat (top) and back (bottom) in Plan and Isometric views

Notice that the UCS icon appears in the same plane as the current coordinate system. The icon will help you keep track of which coordinate system you are in. Now you can see the chair components as 3D objects.

Next, you will define a UCS based on one side of the seat. Before you do that, open the UCS toolbar.

1. Right-click on any toolbar.

2. At the Toolbars dialog box, locate UCS and click on the checkbox.

3. Close the Toolbars dialog box.

To define a new UCS, you will use the three-point method. This lets you define the plane of the UCS based on three points. Several other options are available to help you define, save, restore, and delete a UCS. We will look at these options later in this chapter.

1. Click on the 3 Point UCS tool on the UCS toolbar. You may also choose Tools ➤ UCS ➤ 3 Point, or type **UCS** ↵ **3** ↵. This option allows you to define a UCS based on three points that you select.

NOTE   Remember, it helps to think of a UCS as a drawing surface situated on the surface of the object you wish to draw or edit.

2. At the Origin point <0,0,0> prompt, use the Endpoint Osnap to pick the bottom of the lower-left corner of the rectangle representing the seat (see label 1 in Figure 16.3). This is the origin point of your UCS.

3. At the next prompt, Point on positive portion of the X axis <2'-1",2'- 0",0'- 0">, use the Endpoint Osnap to pick the bottom of the lower-right corner of the rectangle (see label 2 in Figure 16.3). (The default

value for the prompt in this step, 2'-1",2'-0",0'-0", indicates the positive direction of the x-axis of the current coordinate system.)

4. At the next prompt: `Point on positive - Y portion of the UCS X-Y plane <2'- 0",2'-0",2'-1">` pick the top of the left-hand corner of the rectangle, just above the corner you picked for the origin of the UCS (see label 3 in Figure 16.3). The screen regenerates, and both the cursor and the UCS icon change to indicate your new UCS.

NOTE   The prompts in steps 3 and 4 are asking you for the direction of the x-axis (step 3) and of the y-axis (step 4) in your new UCS.

FIGURE 16.3:

Selection points to define a new UCS

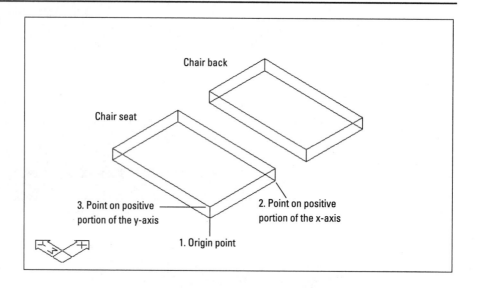

5. Now that you have defined a UCS, you may want to save it so that you can return to it in a later editing session. Click on Named UCS from the UCS toolbar, or choose Tools ➤ UCS ➤ Named UCS. You can also type **UC** ↵. The UCS Control dialog box appears.

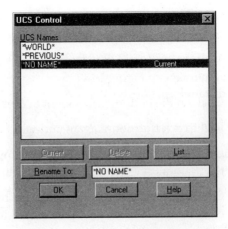

6. Click on the item labeled *NO NAME* in the list of UCS names.

7. In the input box to the right of the Rename button, enter **3dsw**.

8. Click on the Rename button. The current UCS is renamed to 3DSW.

9. Click OK to exit the dialog box.

From now on, you can open the UCS Control dialog box, click on 3DSW from the UCS names list, and then click the Current button whenever you want to return to this UCS. You'll get a chance to use the Current button in *Creating a Complex 3D Surface* later in this chpater.

Working in a UCS

Next, you will want to arrange the seat and back and draw the legs of the chair. Your UCS is oriented so that you can easily adjust the orientation of the chair components to their proper orientation. As you work through the next exercise, notice that while you are manipulating 3D objects, you are really using the same tools you've used to edit 2D objects.

1. Click on the seat back to expose its grips.

2. Click on the bottom grip, as shown in the first image of Figure 16.4.

3. Right-click the mouse to open the Grip Edit pop-up menu.

4. Select Rotate from the menu. Notice how the seat back now rotates with the movement of the cursor. Take a moment to play with this rotation as it may

take a while to grow accustomed to it. Since this is an Isometric view, you can get an optical illusion effect.

5. Type **80** ↵ to rotate the seat back 80 degrees. Your view will look like the bottom image of Figure 16.4.

6. Click on the bottom grip shown in the bottom image of Figure 16.4.

7. Right-click the mouse again and select Move.

8. Using the Endpoint Osnap, click the top corner of the chair seat, as shown in the bottom image of Figure 16.4, to join the chair back to the seat.

9. Click on both the chair seat and back; then click on the bottom-corner grip of the seat, as shown in the continued image of Figure 16.4.

10. Right-click the mouse; then at the Grip Edit pop-up menu, click on Rotate.

11. Enter **-10** ↵ to rotate both the seat and back a minus 10 degrees. Press the Esc key twice to clear the grips. Your chair will look like Figure 16.5.

The new UCS orientation enabled you to use the grips to adjust the chair seat and back. All of the grip rotation in the previous exercise was confined to the plane of the new UCS. Mirroring and scaling will also occur in relation to the current UCS.

Now to finish the chair seat and back, add a 3D Face to their top and bottom surfaces.

1. Click on the 3D Face button on the Surfaces toolbar, or choose Draw ➤ Surfaces ➤ 3D Face, to draw a surface over the top sides of the chair seat and back. Start the 3D Face in the leftmost corner of the seat and work in a counterclockwise fashion.

NOTE   To display the Surfaces toolbar, right-click on any toolbar, and then choose Surfaces from the Toolbars dialog box. If you need some help with the 3DFace command, see Chapter 15.

2. Add the 3D Faces to the bottom of the chair seat and to the chair back, as shown in Figure 16.6.

FIGURE 16.4:

Moving the components of the chair into place

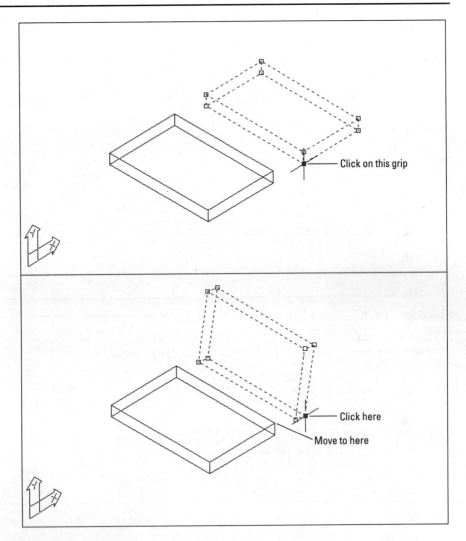

FIGURE 16.4:
CONTINUED

Moving the compo-
nents of the chair into
place

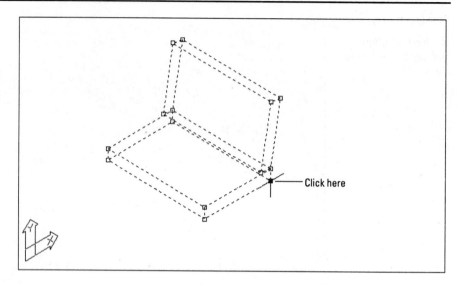

FIGURE 16.5:

The chair after rotating
and moving the com-
ponents into place

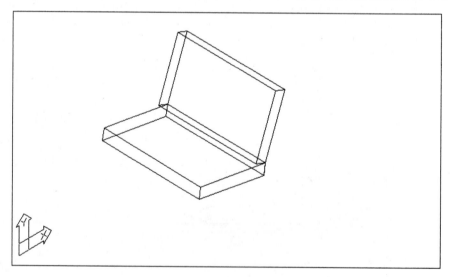

FIGURE 16.6:

The 3D view of your drawing so far, showing where to pick points for the 3D Face

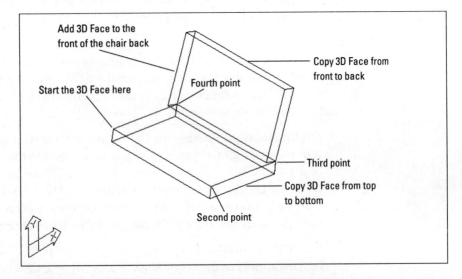

Normally, when picking points for 3D Faces, it doesn't matter where you start selecting points. But for the purpose of this tutorial, you selected points for the seat's 3D Face starting at the leftmost corner and working in a counterclockwise fashion. The way you create the chair seat will influence the action of some UCS command options that you'll use later in this chapter.

Controlling the UCS Icon

So far, you have used only the UCS 3 Point option (View ➤ Set UCS ➤ 3 Point) to create other coordinate systems. There are several other options available to allow easy creation of and access to the UCS function. In the following section, *Using Viewports to Aid in 3D Drawing*, you will want to set the UCS icon to show the current UCS origin location as well as its orientation.

1. Make sure your view is similar to the one in Figure 16.6.

2. Click on View ➤ Display ➤ UCS Icon ➤ Origin, or type **Ucsicon** ⏎ **OR** ⏎. Do this now in your current drawing, and the UCS icon will move to a location below the chair.

Now, whenever a new UCS is defined, the UCS icon will shift its location to show you not only the orientation of the UCS but also its origin. This will be useful in later exercises.

The View ➤ Display ➤ UCS Icon cascading displays two options: On and Origin. These two options actually represent the On, Off, Origin, and Noorigin options of the Ucsicon command. Let's take a moment to look at all the options offered by the Ucsicon command:

Origin/Noorigin   makes the UCS icon appear at the location of the current UCS's 0,0,0 origin point (Origin), or places it in the lower-left corner of the AutoCAD window (Noorigin). If the UCS's origin is off the screen while the Origin option is active (shown by a checkmark in the menu), the UCS icon appears in the screen's lower-left corner. (This is the option you used just above as View ➤ Display ➤ UCS Icon ➤ Origin.)

On /Off   controls whether the UCS icon is displayed or not. These options appear as the single View ➤ Display ➤ UCS Icon➤ On. When this option is checked, it is on. When this option is checked, the icon is displayed; when it is not checked, the icon is turned off.

In addition, there are two other settings you will want to know about that do not appear on the menu:

All   lets you set the UCS icon's appearance in all the viewports on your screen at once. This option has no significance if you only have one viewport on the screen. To use this option, type **UCSicon ↵ A ↵**.

UCSFollow   is a system variable that, when set to 1, will cause the display to always show a Plan view of the current UCS.

Using Viewports to Aid in 3D Drawing

In Chapter 12, you were introduced to AutoCAD's floating viewports in Paper Space. In this next section, you will use *tiled* viewports to see your 3D model from several sides at the same time. This is helpful in both creating and editing 3D drawings because it allows you to refer to different portions of the drawing without having to change views. Tiled viewports are created directly in Model Space.

1. Click on View ➤ Tiled Viewports ➤ 3 Viewports.

2. At the Horizontal/Vertical/Above/Below/Left <Right> prompt, press ↵ to accept the default Right option. This causes the right viewport to occupy half the screen, while the left half is divided into two smaller viewports.

WARNING   Unlike floating viewport, you cannot plot multiple views from a set of tiled viewports.

Now you see three of the same images in each viewport. Each viewport can display a different view of your drawing. In step 2, the prompt gives you the option to divide the screen horizontally in three equal viewports (Horizontal) or vertically into three equal viewports (Vertical). Above, Below, and Left each divide the screen into unequally sized viewports, with the option name indicating where the larger of the three viewports is placed.

1. Click on the upper-left viewport to activate it. Then click on View ➤ 3D Viewpoint ➤ Plan View ➤ World UCS, or type **Plan** ↵ **W** ↵. (The W is the World option of the Plan command—it sets your view up as a Plan view of the WCS.) The view changes to a Plan view of your chair.

2. Use the Zoom Realtime tool to zoom back a bit so the chair doesn't fill the viewport (see Figure 16.7).

3. Click on the lower-left viewport.

4. Click on View ➤ 3D Viewpoint ➤ Plan View ➤ Current UCS to get a Plan view of the current UCS. The side view of your chair will appear in this viewport.

5. Again, zoom out a bit so the image of the chair doesn't fill the viewport (see Figure 16.7).

6. Switch to the 3D view on the right and enlarge it to get a better look at the chair in 3D. You should have a screen similar to Figure 16.7.

FIGURE 16.7:

Three viewports,
each displaying a
different view

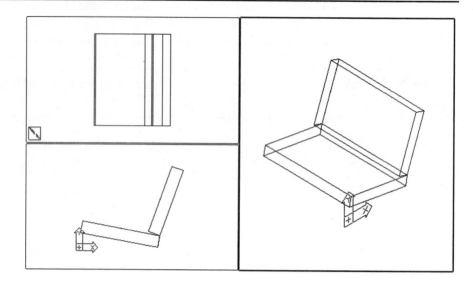

Adding the Legs

Now let's finish off the chair by adding legs.

1. Go to the side view of the chair and move the chair seat and back vertically in the y-axis 8.5 inches. Make sure you select all the lines and 3D Faces for the move. You may have to pan the view down so that all of the chair is displayed.

2. Next, draw two curved polylines, as shown in Figure 16.8. You may have to adjust your view so you can draw the legs more easily. You don't have to be absolutely perfect about placing or shaping these lines.

3. Use the grips of the polylines to adjust their curve, if necessary.

4. Use Modify ➤ Object ➤ Polyline to give the polylines a width of 0.5".

5. Use the Properties tool on the Object Properties toolbar to open the Modify Polyline dialog box and give the polylines a thickness of -2" (minus 2 inches). Notice that as you draw and edit a polyline, it appears in both the Plan and 3D views.

NOTE Polylines are the best objects to use for 3D because you can generate complex shapes easily by giving the polylines thickness and width.

FIGURE 16.8:

Drawing the legs of the chair

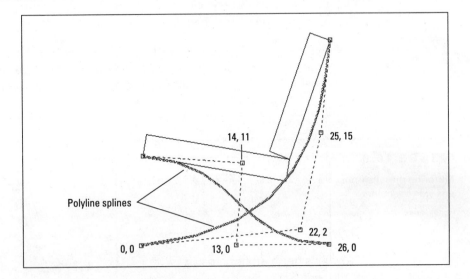

6. Click on the Plan view of the chair in the upper-left viewport.

7. Click on the Named UCS tool on the UCS toolbar, or choose Tools ➤ UCS ➤ Named UCS.

8. At the UCS Control dialog box, click on *WORLD*, click on the Current button, and finally on OK.

9. Toggle the Ortho mode on, and then click on Mirror on the Modify toolbar.

10. Click on the two polylines representing the chair legs. You can use any viewport to select the chair legs, but make sure you click on the upper-left viewport after selecting the legs; then press ↵.

11. At the First point of mirror line prompt, use the Midpoint Osnap and select the midpoint of the chair seat, as shown in Figure 16.9.

12. At the second point, pick any location to the right of the point you selected, so that the rubber-banding line is exactly horizontal.

13. Press ↵ at the Delete old object prompt. The legs are mirrored to the opposite side of the chair. Your screen should look similar to Figure 16.9.

NOTE Notice that the broken-pencil UCS icon has shifted to the viewport in the lower-left corner. This icon tells you that the current UCS is perpendicular to the plane of that view.

FIGURE 16.9:

Mirroring the legs from one side to another

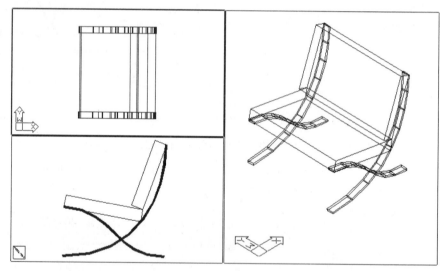

Your chair is now complete. Let's finish up by getting a better look at it.

1. Click on the viewport to the right.

2. Click on View ➤ Tiled Viewports ➤ 1 Viewport. The 3D view fills the screen in preparation for the next set of exercises.

3. Choose View ➤ Hide to get a view of your chair with the lines hidden, as shown in Figure 16.10.

FIGURE 16.10:

The chair in 3D with hidden lines removed

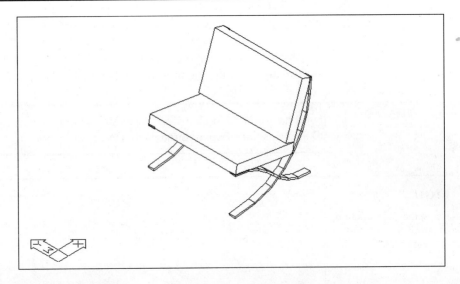

Controlling the UCS

There are a number of other ways to define a UCS. You can, for example, use the 3D Face of your chair as the definition for a UCS. In the following set of exercises, you will get some practice moving your UCS around. Learning how to move effortlessly between UCSs is crucial to your mastering the creation of 3D models, so you'll want to pay special attention to the command options shown in these procedures. These options are accessible from either the Tools ➢ UCS cascading menu or the UCS toolbar.

UCS Based on Object Orientation

You can define a UCS based on the orientation of an object. This is helpful when you want to work on a predefined object to fill in detail on its surface plane.

1. Click on the Object UCS tool on the UCS toolbar, or choose Tools ➢ UCS ➢ Object. You can also type **UCS ↵ OB ↵**.

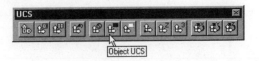

2. At the Select object to align UCS prompt, pick the 3D Face used to define the top surface of the chair seat. Because the 3D Face and the polyline outline of the seat share a common edge, you may need to use the Selection Cycling feature to pick the 3D Face. The UCS icon shifts to reflect the new coordinate system's orientation (see Figure 16.11).

TIP If you have a Hidden-Line view, selection cycling will not work for picking 3D Faces. Issue a Regen to return to a Wireframe view.

FIGURE 16.11:

Using the Object option of the UCS command to locate a UCS

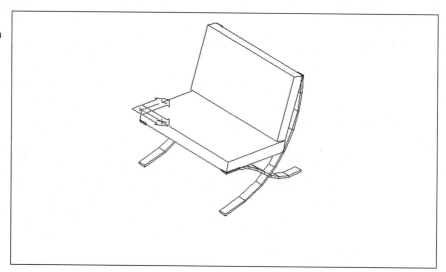

Orientation of the UCS Origin   Remember earlier in the chapter when you drew the 3D Face for the seat in a specific way? Well, the location of the UCS origin and its orientation are dependent on how that 3D Face was created. If you had drawn it other than as instructed, the UCS you defined using the Object option in the above exercise would not have been generated as described.

Table 16.1 describes how an object will determine the orientation of a UCS.

TABLE 16.1: Effects of objects on the orientation of an UCS

Object Type	UCS Orientation
Arc	The center of the arc establishes the UCS origin. The x-axis of the UCS passes through the pick point on the arc.
Circle	The center of the circle establishes the UCS origin. The x-axis of the UCS passes through the pick point on the circle.
Dimension	The midpoint of the dimension text establishes the origin of the UCS origin. The x-axis of the UCS is parallel to the x-axis that was active when the dimension was drawn.
Line	The endpoint nearest the pick point establishes the origin of the UCS, and the x-z plane of the UCS contains the line.
Point	The point location establishes the UCS origin. The UCS orientation is arbitrary.
2D Polyline	The starting point of the polyline establishes the UCS origin. The x-axis is determined by the direction from the first point to the next vertex.
Solid	The first point of the solid establishes the origin of the UCS. The second point of the solid establishes the x-axis.
Trace	The direction of the trace establishes the x-axis of the UCS with the beginning point setting the origin.
3D Face	The first point of the 3D Face establishes the origin. The first and second points establish the x-axis. The plane defined by the face determines the orientation of the UCS.
Shapes, Text, Blocks, Attributes, and Attribute Definitions	The insertion point establishes the origin of the UCS. The object's rotation angle establishes the x-axis.

UCS Based on an Offset Orientation

There may be times when you want to work in a UCS that has the same orientation as the current UCS but is offset. For example, you may be making a drawing of a building that has several parallel walls offset with a sawtooth effect (see Figure 16.12). You can easily hop from one UCS to another parallel UCS by using the Origin option.

FIGURE 16.12:

Using the Origin option
to shift the UCS

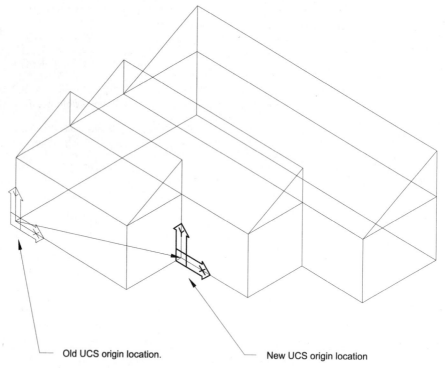

Old UCS origin location.   New UCS origin location

1. Click on the UCS Origin tool on the UCS toolbar, or choose Tools ➤ UCS ➤
    Origin. You can also type **UCS** ↵ **O** ↵.

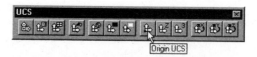

2. At the Origin point <0,0,0> prompt, pick the bottom end of the chair leg,
    just below the current UCS origin. The UCS icon shifts to the end of the leg,
    with its origin at the point you picked (see Figure 16.13).

FIGURE 16.13:

FIGURE 16.13:

Moving the origin of
the UCS

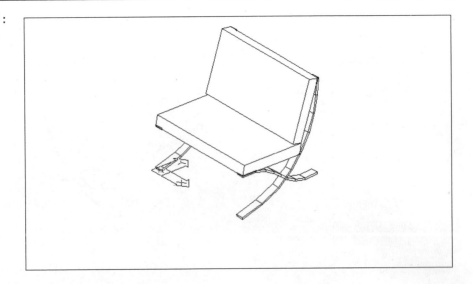

UCS Rotated Around an Axis

Now suppose you want to change the orientation of the x-, y-, or z-axis of the current UCS. You can accomplish this by using the X, Y, or X Axis Rotate options of the UCS command. Let's try rotating the UCS about the z-axis to see how this works.

1. Click on the Z Axis Rotate UCS tool on the UCS toolbar, or choose Tools ➢ UCS ➢ Z Axis Rotate. You can also type **UCS** ⏎ **Z** ⏎. This will allow you to rotate the current UCS about the z-axis.

2. At the Rotation angle about Z axis <0> prompt, enter **90** for 90°. The UCS icon rotates to reflect the new orientation of the current UCS (see Figure 16.14).

FIGURE 16.14:

Rotating the UCS about
the z-axis

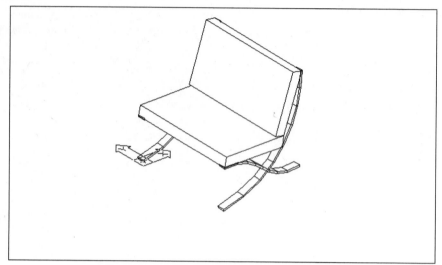

Similarly, the X and Y Axis Rotate options allow you to rotate the UCS about the current x- and y-axis, respectively, just as you did for the z-axis above.

Finally, you can skew the UCS by using the Z Axis Vector option. This is useful when you need to define a UCS based on a z-axis determined by two objects.

1. Click on the Z Axis Vector UCS tool on the UCS toolbar, or choose Tools ➤ UCS ➤ Z Axis Vector. You can also type **UCS** ↵ **ZA** ↵.

2. At the Origin point <0,0,0> prompt, press ↵ to accept the default, which is the current UCS origin. You can shift the origin point at this prompt if you like.

3. At the next prompt:

   Point on positive portion of Z-axis <0'-0", 0'- 0", 0'-1">:

   use the Endpoint Osnap override and pick the other chair leg end, as shown in Figure 16.15. The UCS twists to reflect the new z-axis of the UCS.

WARNING Because your cursor location is in the plane of the current UCS, it is best to pick a point on an object using either the Osnap overrides or the coordinate filters.

FIGURE 16.15:

Picking points for the Z Axis Vector option

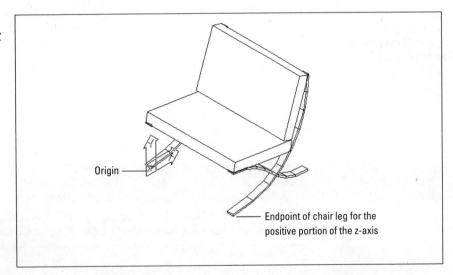

Origin

Endpoint of chair leg for the positive portion of the z-axis

Orienting a UCS in the View Plan

Finally, you can define a UCS in the current view plane. This is useful if you want to quickly switch to the current view plane for editing or for adding text to a 3D view.

Click on the View UCS tool on the UCS toolbar, or choose View ➤ Set UCS ➤ View. You can also type **UCS** ↵ **V** ↵. The UCS icon changes to show that the UCS is aligned with the current view.

AutoCAD uses the current UCS origin point for the origin of the new UCS. By defining a view as a UCS, you can enter text to label your drawing, as you would in a technical illustration. Text entered in a plane created in this way will appear normal (see Figure 16.16).

FIGURE 16.16:

Adding text to a 3D view using the View option of the UCS command

Now we've finished our tour of the UCS command. Set the UCS back to the World Coordinate System and save the `Barcelon.dwg` file.

Creating Complex 3D Surfaces

In the previous example, you drew a chair composed of objects that were mostly straight lines or curves with a thickness. All the forms in that chair were defined in planes perpendicular to each other. At times, however, you will want to draw objects that do not fit so easily into perpendicular or parallel planes. The following exercise demonstrates how you can create more complex forms using some of AutoCAD's other 3D commands.

Laying Out a 3D Form

In this next group of exercises, you will draw a butterfly chair. This chair has no perpendicular or parallel planes to work with, so you will start by setting up some points that you will use for reference only. This is similar in concept to laying out a 2D drawing. You will construct some temporary 3D lines that you will use for reference. These temporary lines will be your layout. These points will define the major UCSs needed to construct the drawing. As you progress through the drawing construction, notice how the reference points are established to help create the chair.

1. If it isn't open already, open the Barcelon drawing, and then use File ➤ Save As to save the file under the name **Btrfly**.

2. Choose View ➤ 3D Viewpoints ➤ Plan View ➤ World UCS; then choose View ➤ Zoom ➤ All to display the overall area of the drawing.

NOTE   You will draw the butterfly chair almost entirely while viewing it in 3D. This approach is useful when you are creating complex shapes.

3. Erase the entire contents, and then make sure you are in the WCS by choosing Tools ➤ UCS ➤ World.

4. Click Rectangle on the Draw toolbar. Draw a rectangle 20" square with its first corner at coordinate 36, 36.

5. Use the Offset tool to offset the square 4" out, so you have two concentric squares with the outer square measuring 28".

6. Move the larger of the two squares, the 28" square, to the left 2". Your screen should look similar to Figure 16.17.

7. Choose View ➤ 3D Viewpoint ➤ SW Isometric. This will give you a view from the lower-left side of the rectangles.

8. Zoom out so the rectangles occupy about a third of the drawing area window.

FIGURE 16.17:

Setting up a layout for a butterfly chair

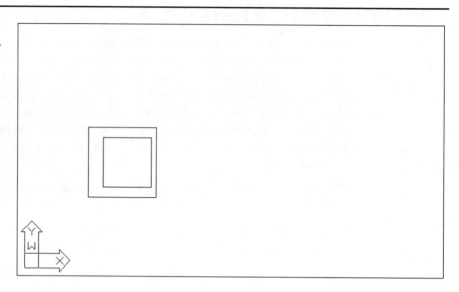

Now you need to move the outer rectangle in the z-axis so that its elevation is 30".

1. Click on the outer rectangle, and then click on one of its grips.

2. Right-click to open the Grip Edit pop-up menu.

3. Select Move, and then enter **@0,0,30** ↵. This tells AutoCAD to move the rectangle a 0 distance in both the x- and y-axis, and 30" in the z-axis.

4. Pan your view downward so it looks similar to Figure 16.18.

5. Use the Line tool and draw lines from the corners of the outer square to the corners of the inner square, as shown in Figure 16.18. Use the Endpoint Osnap to select the exact corners of the squares. This is the layout for your chair—not yet the finished product.

Spherical and Cylindrical Coordinate Formats

In the foregoing exercise, you used relative Cartesian coordinates to locate the second point for the Move command. For commands that accept 3D input, you can also specify displacements by using the *Spherical* and *Cylindrical Coordinate* formats.

FIGURE 16.18:

The finished chair layout

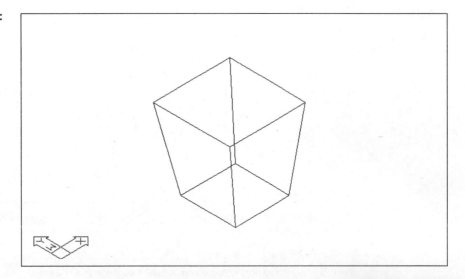

The Spherical Coordinate format lets you specify a distance in 3D space while specifying the angle in terms of degrees from the x-axis of the current UCS and degrees from the x-y plane of the current UCS (see the top image of Figure 16.19). For example, to specify a distance of 4.5" at a 30° angle from the x-axis and 45° from the x-y plane, you'd enter **@4.5<30<45**. This is the direct distance, followed by a < symbol; then the angle from the x-axis of the current UCS followed by another <symbol; then the angle from the x-y plane of the current UCS. To use the spherical coordinate format to move the rectangle in the exercise, you would enter **@30<0<90** at the Second point prompt.

The Cylindrical Coordinate format, on the other hand, lets you specify a location in terms of a distance in the plane of the current UCS and a distance in the z-axis. You also specify an angle from the x-axis of the current UCS (see the bottom image of Figure 16.19). For example, to locate a point that is a distance of 4.5" in the plane of the current UCS, at an angle of 30° from the x-axis, and a distance of 3.3" in the z-axis, you'd enter **@4.5<30,3.3**. This is the distance of the displacement as it relates to the plane of the current UCS, followed by the < symbol; then the angle from the x-axis, followed by a comma; then the distance in the z-axis. Using the cylindrical format to move the rectangle, you would enter **@0<0,30** at the Second point prompt.

FIGURE 16.19:

The spherical and cylindrical coordinate formats

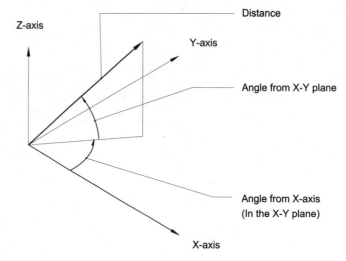

[Distance] < [Angle from X-axis] < [Angle from X-Y plane]

The Spherical Coordinate Format

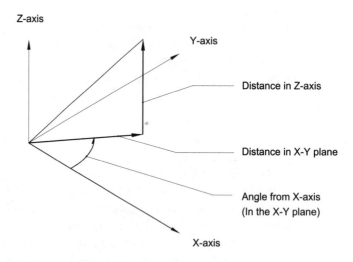

[Distance in X-Y plane] < [Angle from X-axis] , [Distance in Z-axis]

The Cylindrical Coordinate Format

Using a 3D Polyline

Now you will draw the legs for the butterfly chair, using a 3D polyline. This is a polyline that can be drawn in 3D space.

1. Choose Draw ➤ 3D Polyline, or type **3p** ↵.

2. At the First point prompt, pick a series of points, as shown in Figure 16.20, using the Endpoint and Midpoint Osnap.

TIP   This would be a good place to use the Running Osnap feature.

---

3. Draw another 3D polyline in the mirror image of the first (see Figure 16.20).

4. Erase the rectangles and connecting lines that make up the frame.

FIGURE 16.20:

Using 3D polylines to draw the legs of the butterfly chair

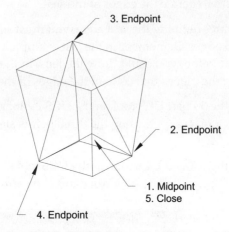

3. Endpoint

Draw a polyline in the sequence shown to the left. Use the Osnap overrides indicated in the figure.

2. Endpoint

1. Midpoint
5. Close

4. Endpoint

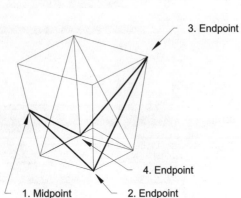

3. Endpoint

Repeat the process for the other part of the chair legs.

4. Endpoint

1. Midpoint
5. Close

2. Endpoint

> **WARNING** All objects, with the exception of lines, 3D Faces, 3D Meshes, and 3D polylines, are restricted to the plane of your current UCS. The Pline command can only be used to draw polylines in one plane, but the 3DPoly command allows you to create a polyline in three dimensions. Three-dimensional polylines cannot, however, be given thickness or width.

Creating Curved 3D Surface

Next, you will draw the seat of the chair. The seat of a butterfly chair is usually made of canvas and drapes from the four corners of the chair legs. You will first define the perimeter of the seat using arcs, and then use the Edge Surface tool on the Surfaces toolbar to form the shape of the draped canvas. Edge Surface creates a surface based on four objects defining the edges of that surface. In this example, you will use arcs to define the edges of the seat.

To draw the arcs defining the seat edge, you must first establish the UCSs in the planes of those edges. Remember in the last example you created a UCS for the side of the chair before you could draw the legs. In the same way, you must create a UCS defining the planes that contain the edges of the seat.

1. Click on the 3 Point UCS tool on the UCS toolbar, or choose Tools ➤ UCS ➤ 3 Point, to create a UCS using the three points shown in the top image of Figure 16.21.

2. Click on the Named UCS tool on the UCS toolbar, or choose Tools ➤ UCS ➤ Named UCS…. The UCS Control dialog box appears.

3. Highlight the *NO NAME* item in the list box; in the input box, change the name to **Front**.

AutoCAD will convert the UCS names to all capital letters.

4. Click on the Rename To button, and then on OK. The new current UCS is now named Front.

5. Define a UCS for the side of the chair as shown in the middle image of Figure 16.21, and use the UCS Control dialog box to rename this UCS **Side**, just as you did for Front in steps 1 through 4. Remember that you renamed the *No Name* UCS.

6. Repeat these steps again for a UCS for the back of the chair, named **Back**. Use the bottom image of Figure 16.21 for reference.

7. Open the UCS Control dialog box again and highlight FRONT.

8. Click on the Current button below the list, and then on OK. This activates Front as the current UCS.

WARNING Don't skip step 8. If you do, you will not get the results you want when you start picking the arc's endpoints in step 9. AutoCAD only draws arcs in the current UCS. Remember: Only lines, 3D polylines, and other 3D objects can be drawn in three-dimensional space. All other objects can be drawn only in the current UCS.

9. Choose Draw ➤ Arc ➤ Start, End, Direction.

10. Draw the arc defining the front edge of the chair (see Figure 16.22). Use the Endpoint Osnap override to pick the top endpoints of the chair legs as the endpoints of the arc. (If you need help with the Arc command, refer to Chapter 3.)

11. Repeat steps 7 through 10 for the UCS named Side, and then again for the UCS named Back—each time using the top endpoints of the legs for the endpoints of the arc.

FIGURE 16.21:

Defining and saving
three UCSs

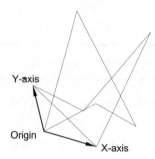

Set up the Front UCS

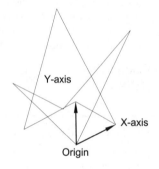

Set up the Side UCS

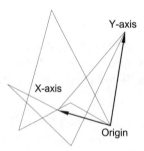

Set up the Back UCS

FIGURE 16.22:

Drawing the seat edge using arcs

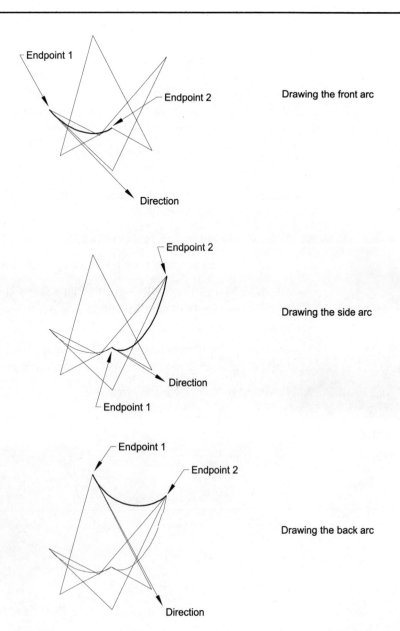

Endpoint 1

Endpoint 2

Direction

Drawing the front arc

Endpoint 2

Direction

Endpoint 1

Drawing the side arc

Endpoint 1

Endpoint 2

Drawing the back arc

Direction

Next, you will mirror the side-edge arc to the opposite side. This will save you from having to define a UCS for that side.

1. Click on the Named UCS tool on the UCS toolbar, and use the UCS Control dialog box to make the World UCS (*WORLD*) current. The reason for doing this is that you want to mirror the arc along an axis that is parallel to the plane of the WCS. Remember that you must go to the coordinate system that defines the plane you wish to work in.

2. Click on the arc you drew for the side of the chair (the one drawn on the Side UCS).

3. Click on the midpoint grip of the arc in the Side UCS; then right-click on the mouse and select Mirror.

4. Enter **C** ↵ to select the Copy option.

5. Enter **B** ↵ to select a new base point for the mirror axis.

6. At the Base point prompt, use the Intersect Osnap to pick the intersection of the two lines in the Front plane.

7. Next, use the Intersection override to pick the intersection of the two legs in the Back plane. Refer to Figure 16.23 for help. The arc should mirror to the opposite side, and your chair should look like Figure 16.24.

8. Press Esc twice to clear the grips.

FIGURE 16.23:

Mirroring the arc defining the side of the chair seat

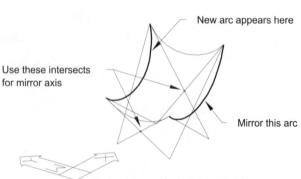

New arc appears here

Use these intersects for mirror axis

Mirror this arc

First, set the current UCS to World

FIGURE 16.24:

Your butterfly chair
so far

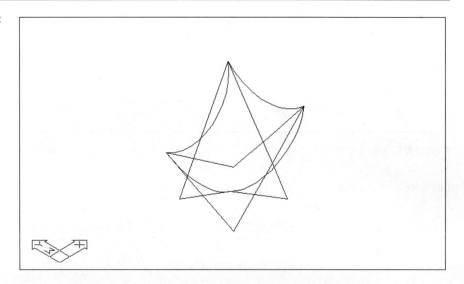

Finally, let's finish off this chair by adding the mesh representing the chair seat.

1. Click on the Edge Surface button on the Surfaces toolbar, or enter **Edgesurf** ↵ at the command prompt.

NOTE
To display the Surfaces toolbar, choose Tools ➤ Toolbars ➤ Surfaces.

2. At the Select edge 1 prompt, pick the arc on the Front UCS.

3. At the Select edge 2 prompt, pick the next arc on the Side UCS.

WARNING
For the command to work properly, the arcs—or any set of objects—used to define the boundary of a mesh with the Edge Surface option must be connected exactly end-to-end.

4. Continue to pick the other two arcs in succession. (The arcs must be picked in a circular fashion, not crosswise.) A mesh will appear, filling the space between the four arcs. Your chair is now complete.

5. Use View ➤ Hide to get a better view of the butterfly chair. You should have a view similar to Figure 16.25.

6. Save this file.

FIGURE 16.25:

The completed butter-fly chair

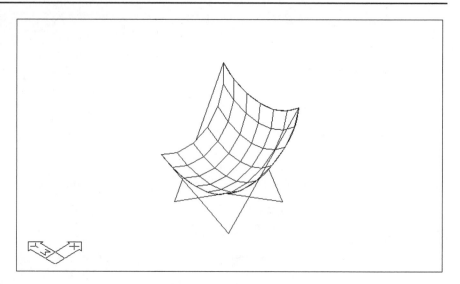

At this point, you've been introduced to a few of the options on the Surfaces toolbar. You'll get a chance to use these later in this chapter. Next, you'll learn how to edit mesh objects like the Butterfly chair's seat.

Adjusting the Settings That Control Meshes

As you can see, the seat in our butterfly chair is made up of rectangular segments. If you want to increase the number of segments in the mesh (to get a look like that in Figure 16.26), you can change the Surftab1 and Surftab2 system variables. Surftab1 controls the number of segments along edge 1, the first edge you pick in the sequence; and Surftab2 controls the number of segments along edge 2. AutoCAD refers to the direction of edge 1 as *m* and the direction of edge 2 as *n*. These two directions can be loosely described as the x- and y-axes of the mesh, with m being the x-axis and n being the y-axis.

See Chapters 13 and 14 and Appendix D for more on system variables.

In Figure 16.26 the setting for Surftab1 is 24, and for Surftab2 the setting is 12. The default value for both settings is 6. If you would like to try different Surftab settings on the chair mesh, you must erase the existing mesh, change the Surftab settings, and then use the Edge Surface tool again to define the mesh.

FIGURE 16.26:

The butterfly chair with different Surftab settings

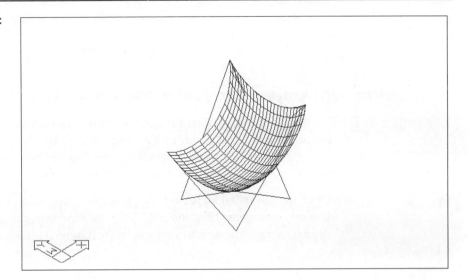

Creating a 3D Mesh by Specifying Coordinates

If you need to draw a mesh like the one in the previous example, but you want to give exact coordinates for each vertex in the mesh grid, you can use the 3DMesh command. Suppose you have data from a survey of a piece of land; you can use 3DMesh to convert your data into a graphic representation of its topography. Another use of 3DMesh is to plot mathematical data to get a graphic representation of a formula.

Because you must enter the coordinate for each vertex in the mesh, 3DMesh is better suited in scripts or AutoLISP programs, where a list of coordinates can be applied automatically to the 3DMesh command in a sequential order. See Chapter 19 and the *ABCs of AutoLISP*, which is on the companion CD-ROM for more on AutoLISP.

Other Surface Drawing Tools

In the last example, you used the Edge Surface tool to create a 3D surface. There are several other 3D surface commands available that allow you to generate complex surface shapes easily.

TIP
All the objects described in this section, along with the meshes described earlier, are actually composites of 3D Faces. This means these 3D objects can be exploded into their component 3D Faces, which in turn can be edited individually.

Using Two Objects to Define a Surface

The Ruled Surface tool on the Surfaces toolbar draws a surface between two 2D objects, such as a line and an arc or a polyline and an arc. This command is useful for creating extruded forms that transform from one shape to another along a straight path. Let's see firsthand how this command works.

1. Open the file called Rulesurf.dwg from the companion CD-ROM. It looks like the top image of Figure 16.27. This drawing is of a simple half circle drawn using a line and an arc. Ignore the diagonal blue line for now.

2. Move the line between the arc endpoints 10" in the z-axis.

3. Now you are ready to connect the two objects with a 3D surface. Click on the Ruled Surface button on the Surfaces toolbar, or choose Draw ➤ Surfaces ➤ Ruled Surface.

4. At the Select first defining curve prompt, place the cursor toward the right end of the arc and click on it.

5. At the Select second defining curve prompt, move the cursor toward the right end of the line and click on it, as shown in the bottom image of Figure 16.27. The surface will appear as shown in Figure 16.28.

WARNING   The position you use to pick the second object will determine how the surface is generated.

FIGURE 16.27:

Drawing two edges for the Ruled Surface option

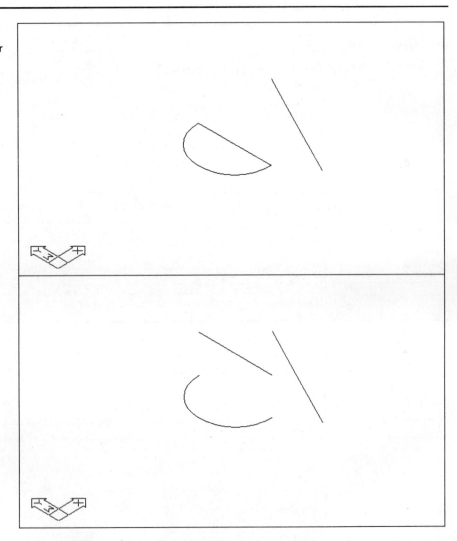

The location you use to select the two objects for the Ruled Surface is important. We asked you to select specific locations on the arc and line so that the ruled surface is generated properly. Had you selected the opposite end of the line, for example, your result would look more like Figure 16.29. Notice that the segments defining the surface cross each other. This crossing effect is caused by picking the defining objects near opposite endpoints. The arc was picked near its lower end, and the line was picked toward the top end. At times you may actually want this effect.

FIGURE 16.28:

The Rulesurf surface

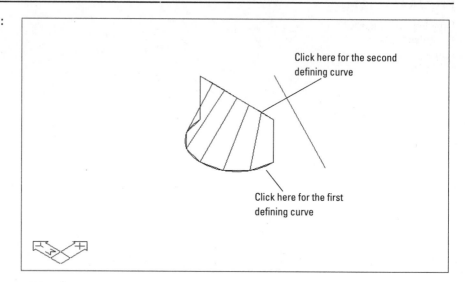

Click here for the second
defining curve

Click here for the first
defining curve

FIGURE 16.29:

The ruled surface
redrawn by using dif-
ferent points to select
the objects

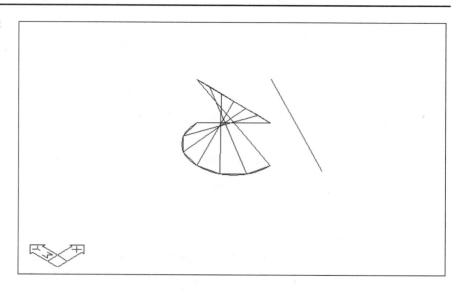

Extruding an Object along a Straight Line

The Tabulated Surface tool also uses two objects to draw a 3D surface, but instead of drawing the surface between the objects, Tabulated Surface extrudes one object in a direction defined by a direction vector. The net result is an extruded shape the length and direction of the direction vector. To see what this means firsthand, try the following exercise.

1. While still in the Rulesurf drawing, click on the Undo button in the Standard toolbar to undo the Ruled Surface from the previous exercise.

2. Click on Tabulated Surface from the Surface toolbar, or choose Draw ➤ Surfaces ➤ Tabulated Surfaces.

3. At the Path curve prompt, click on the arc.

4. At the Select Direction Vector prompt, click on the lower end of the blue line farthest to the right. The arc is extruded in the direction of the blue line, as shown in Figure 16.30.

The direction vector can be any object, but AutoCAD will only consider the object's two endpoints when extruding the path curve. Just as with the Ruled Surface, the point at which you select the direction vector object affects the outcome of the extrusion. If you had selected a location near the top of the blue line, the extrusion would have gone in the opposite direction from the exercise.

Since the direction vector can point in any direction, the Tabulated Surface tool allows you to create an extruded shape that is not restricted to a direction perpendicular to the object being extruded.

The path curve defining the shape of the extrusion can be an arc, circle, line, or polyline. You can use a curve fitted polyline or a spline polyline to create more complex shapes, as shown in Figure 16.31.

FIGURE 16.30:

Extruding an arc using
a line to indicate the
extrusion direction

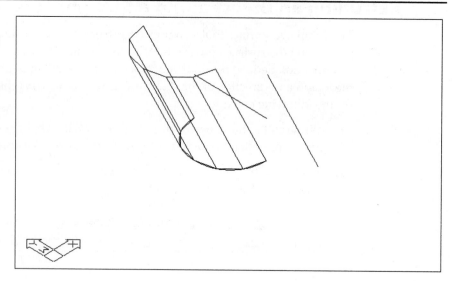

FIGURE 16.31:

Some samples of other
shapes created using
Ruled Surfaces and
Tabulated Surfaces

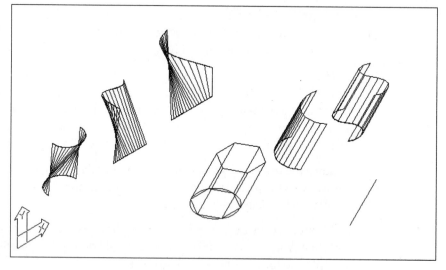

If you want to increase the number of facets in either the Ruled Surface or Tabulated Surface, set the Surftab1 system variable to the number of facets you desire.

Extruding a Circular Surface

The Revolved Surface tool allows you to quickly generate circular extrusions. Typical examples are vases or tea cups. The following exercise shows how the Revolved Surface tool is used to draw a pitcher. You'll use an existing drawing that has a profile of the pitcher already drawn.

1. Open the `Pitcher.dwg` file from the companion CD-ROM. This file contains a polyline profile of a pitcher as well as a single line representing the center of the pitcher (see the top image of Figure 16.32). The profile and line have already been rotated to a position that is perpendicular to the WCS. The grid is turned on so you can better visualize the plane of the WCS.

2. Click on the Revolved Surface button on the Surfaces Toolbar.

3. At the `Select Path Curve` prompt, click on the polyline profile, as shown in the top image of Figure 16.32.

4. At the `Select Axis of Revolution` prompt, click near the bottom of the vertical line representing the center of the vase, as shown in the top image of Figure 16.32.

5. At the `Start angle <0>` prompt, press ↵ to accept the 0 start angle.

6. At the `Included angle (+=ccw, -=cw) <Full circle>` prompt, press ↵ to accept the Full Circle default. The pitcher appears, as shown in the bottom image of Figure 16.32.

FIGURE 16.32:

Drawing a pitcher
using the Revolved
Surface tool

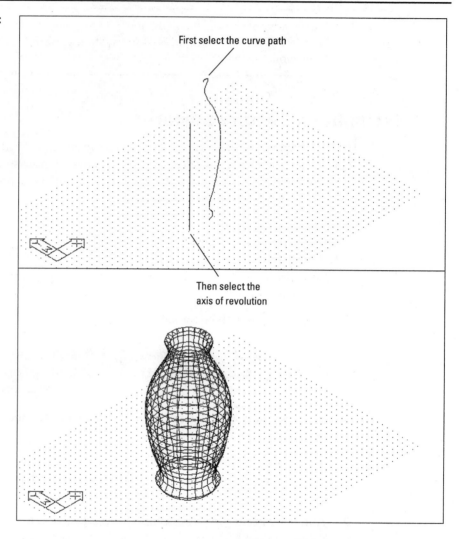

First select the curve path

Then select the
axis of revolution

Notice that the pitcher is made up of a faceted mesh, like the mesh that is created by the Edge Surface tool. Just as with the Edge Surface tool, you can set the number of facets in each direction using the Surftab1 and Surftab2 system variable settings. Both Surftab1 and Surftab2 were already set to 24 in the Pitcher.dwg file, so the pitcher shape would appear fairly smooth.

You may have noticed that in steps 5 and 6 of the previous exercise you have a few options. In step 6, you can specify a start angle. In this case, you accepted the 0 default. Had you entered a different value, 90 for example, then the extrusion would have started in the 90-degree position relative to the current WCS. In step 7, you have the option of specifying the angle of the extrusion. Had you entered 180, for example, your result would have been half the pitcher. You can also specify the direction of the extrusion by specifying a negative or positive angle.

Editing a Mesh

Once you've created a mesh surface with either the Edge Surface or Revolved Surface tool, you can make modifications to it. For example, suppose you wanted to add a spout to the pitcher you created in the previous exercise. You can use grips to adjust the individual points on the mesh to reshape the object. Here, you must take care how you select points. The UCS will become useful for editing meshes, as shown in the following exercise.

1. Zoom into the area shown in the top image of Figure 16.33.

2. Click on the pitcher mesh to expose its grips.

3. Shift + click on the grips shown in the bottom image of Figure 16.33.

4. Click on the grip shown in the continued image of Figure 16.33 and slowly drag the cursor to the left. As you move the cursor, notice how the lip of the pitcher deforms.

5. When you have the shape of a spout similar to the bottom image of Figure 16.33, select that point. The spout will be fixed in the new position.

You can refine the shape of the spout by carefully adjusting the position of other grip points around the edge of the pitcher. Later, when you render the pitcher, you can apply a smooth shading value so that the sharp edges of the spout are smoothed out.

Adding a spout to the
pitcher mesh

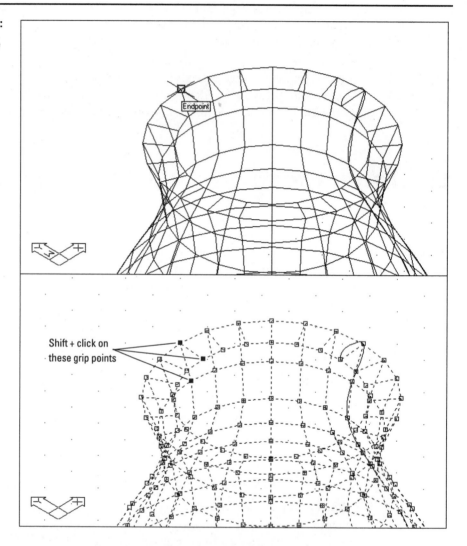

This exercise shows how easy it is to make changes to a mesh by moving individual grip locations. You will want to know, however, that when you move mesh
grips manually (as opposed to entering coordinates), their motion is restricted to a
plane that is perpendicular to the current UCS. You can use this restriction to your
advantage. For example, if you want to move the spout downward at a 30 degree
angle, you can rotate the UCS so it is tipped at a 30 degree angle in relation to the
top of the pitcher, and then edit the mesh grips as you did in the previous exercise.

**FIGURE 16.33:
CONTINUED**

Adding a spout to the
pitcher mesh

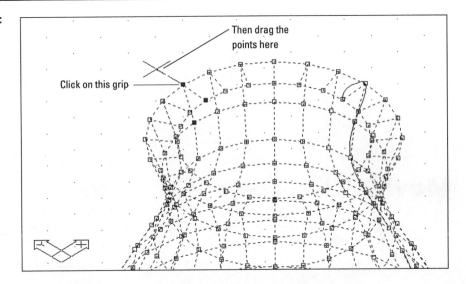

Another option would be to specify a *relative* coordinate as opposed to selecting a point. By specifying a coordinate, such as @.5<50, you would not have to move the UCS. Using this method, however, removes you from the spontaneity of being able to select a point visually.

Other Mesh Editing Options

You can use Modify ➤ Object ➤ Polyline to edit meshes in a way similar to editing polylines. When you choose this option and pick a mesh, you get this prompt:

```
Edit vertex/Smooth surface/Desmooth/Mclose/Nclose/Undo/eXit <X>:
```

Here are descriptions of these options:

Edit vertex   allows you to relocate individual vertices in the mesh.

Smooth surface   is similar to the Spline option for polylines. Rather than having the mesh's shape determined by the vertex points, Smooth surface adjusts the mesh so that mesh vertices act as control points that pull the mesh—much as a spline frame pulls a spline curve.

TIP   You can adjust the amount of pull the vertex points exert on a mesh by using Smooth surface in conjunction with the Surftype system variable.

Desmooth   reverses the effects of Smooth surface.

Mclose and **Nclose**   allow you to close the mesh in either the m or n direction. When either of these options is used, the prompt line will change, replacing Mclose or Nclose with Mopen or Nopen, allowing you to open a closed mesh.

The Edit Polyline tool in the Modify II toolbar performs the same function as Modify ➤ Object ➤ Polyline.

Moving Objects in 3D Space

AutoCAD provides two utilities for moving objects in 3D space: Align and 3D Rotate. Both of these commands are found on the Rotate flyout of the Modify toolbar. They help you perform some of the more common moves associated with 3D editing.

Aligning Objects in 3D Space

In mechanical drawing you often create the parts in 3D, and then show an assembly of the parts. The Align option can greatly simplify the assembly process. The following exercise describes how Align works.

1. Choose Modify ➤ 3D Operation ➤ Align, or type **Al** ↵.

2. At the Select objects prompt, select the 3D source object you want to align to another part. (The *source object* is the object you want to move.)

3. At the 1st source point prompt, pick a point on the source object that is the first point of an alignment axis—such as the center of a hole or the corner of a surface.

4. At the 1st destination point prompt, pick a point on the destination object to which you want the first source point to move. (The *destination object* is the object with which you want the source object to align.)

5. At the 2nd source point prompt, pick a point on the source object that is the second point of an alignment axis—such as another center point or other corner of a surface.

6. At the 2nd destination point prompt, pick a point on the destination object indicating how the first and second source points are to align in relation to the destination object.

7. At the 3rd source point prompt, you can press ↵ if two points are adequate to describe the alignment. Otherwise, pick a third point on the source object that, along with the first two points, best describes the surface plane you want aligned with the destination object.

8. At the 3rd destination point prompt, pick a point on the destination object that, along with the previous two destination points, describes the plane with which you want the source object to be aligned. The source object will move into alignment with the destination object.

Figure 16.34 gives some examples of how the Align utility works.

FIGURE 16.34:

Aligning two 3D objects

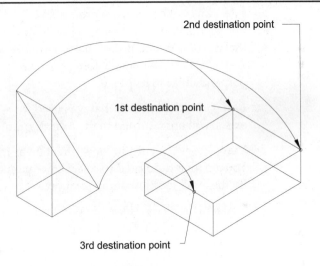

2nd destination point

1st destination point

3rd destination point

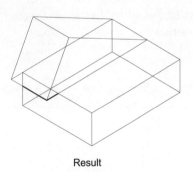

Result

Rotating an Object in 3D

If you just want to rotate an object in 3D space, the Modify ➤ 3D Operation ➤ Rotate 3D option on the menu bar can simplify the operation. Once you've selected this option and selected the objects you want to rotate, you get the following prompt:

```
Axis by Entity/Last/View/Xaxis/YAxis/Zaxis/<2points>
```

This prompt is asking you to describe the axis of rotation. Here are descriptions of the options presented in the prompt:

Entity allows you to indicate an axis by clicking on an object. When you select this option, you are prompted to pick a line, circle, arc, or 2D polyline segment. If you click on a line or polyline segment, the line is used as the axis of rotation. If you click on a circle, arc, or polyline arc segment, AutoCAD uses the line passing through the center of the circle or arc and perpendicular to its plane.

Last uses the last axis that was used for a 3D rotation. If no previous axis exists, you are returned to the Axis... prompt.

View uses the current view direction as the direction of the rotation axis. You are then prompted to select a point on the view direction axis to specify the exact location of the rotation axis.

Xaxis/Yaxis/Zaxis uses the standard x-, y-, or z-axis as the direction for the rotation axis. You are then prompted to select points on the x-, y-, or z-axis to locate the rotation axis.

<2points> uses two points you provide as the endpoints of the rotation axis.

This completes our look at creating and editing 3D objects. You have had a chance to practice using nearly every type of object available in AutoCAD. You might want to experiment on your own with the predefined 3D shapes offered on the Surfaces toolbar. In the next section, you'll discover how you can generate perspective views.

Viewing Your Model in Perspective

So far, your views of 3D drawings have been in *parallel projection*. This means parallel lines appear parallel on your screen. Though this type of view is helpful while constructing your drawing, you will want to view your drawing in true perspective from time to time, to get a better feel for what your 3D model actually looks like.

There's really only one command that offers perspective views in AutoCAD, but that one command, called Dview, is a complex one. With this in mind, you may want to begin these exercises when you know you have an hour or so to complete them all at one sitting.

If you are ready now, let's begin!

1. Open the `Barcelon.dwg` file you created in the earlier part of this chapter, or use the copy of the `Barcelon.dwg` file on the companion CD-ROM. Be sure you are in the World Coordinate System. Choose View ➤ 3D Viewpoint ➤ Plan View ➤ World UCS, or type **Plan** ↵. This will display a Plan view of the chair.

2. Use View ➤ Zoom ➤ All to get an overall view of the drawing.

3. Click on View ➤ 3D Dynamic View, or enter **Dv** ↵ at the command prompt.

4. At the `Select object` prompt, pick the chair seat and back. You will use these objects as references while using the Dview command.

5. Next you will see a fairly lengthy prompt:

   ```
   CAmera/TArget/Distance/POints/PAn/Zoom/TWist/CLip/Hide/Off/
   Undo/<eXit>:
   ```

   at which you can select the appropriate option. (These options are discussed in the remaining exercises in this chapter.) Then the screen will change to show only the objects you selected.

Dview allows you to adjust your Perspective view in real time. For this reason, you are asked to select objects that will allow you to get a good idea of your view without slowing the real time display of your model. If you had selected the whole chair, view selection would be slower because the whole chair would have to be dragged during the selection process. For a file as small as this chair, it isn't a big problem; but for larger files, you will find that selecting too many objects can bog down your system.

Setting Up Your Perspective View

AutoCAD uses the analogy of a camera to help determine your Perspective view. As with a camera, your Perspective view is determined by the distance from the object, camera position, view target, and camera lens type.

Follow these steps to determine the camera and target positions.

1. At the DVIEW prompt, enter **PO** ↵ for the Points option.

2. At the `Enter target point <current point>` prompt, pick the center of the chair. This will allow you to adjust the camera target point, which is the point at which the camera is aimed.

3. At the `Enter camera point <current point>` prompt, pick the lower-left corner of the screen. This places the camera location (the position from which you are looking) below and to the left of the chair, on the plane of the WCS (see Figure 16.35).

WARNING   When selecting views in this set of exercises using Dview and its options, be sure you click the mouse/pick button as indicated in the text. If you press the ↵ key (or click the ↵ button on the mouse), your view will return to the default orientation, which is usually the last view selected.

FIGURE 16.35:

The target and camera points

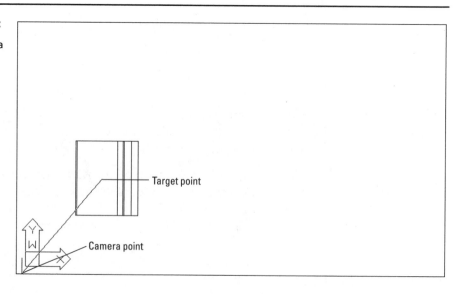

Your view now changes to reflect your target and camera locations, as shown in Figure 16.36. The Dview prompt returns, allowing you to further adjust your view.

FIGURE 16.36:

The view with the camera and target positioned

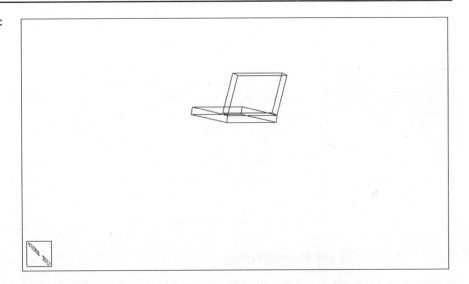

If you like, you can press ↵ at the Select object prompt without picking any object, and you will get the default image, a house, to help you set up your view (see Figure 16.37). Or you can define a block and name it **Dviewblock**. Dviewblock should be defined in a one-unit cubed space. AutoCAD will search the current drawing database, and if it finds Dviewblock, AutoCAD will use it as a sample image to help you determine your Perspective view.

NOTE   Make Dviewblock as simple as possible, but without giving up the detail necessary to distinguish its orientation.

FIGURE 16.37:

The default sample
image used with Dview

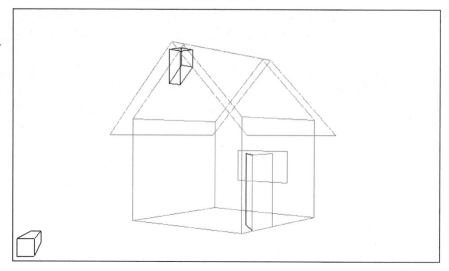

Adjusting Distances

Next, you will adjust the distance between the camera and target.

1. At the DVIEW prompt, enter **D** ↵ for the Distance option. A slide bar appears at the top of the screen.

NOTE   The Distance option actually serves two functions: aside from allowing you to adjust your camera to target distance, it also turns on the Perspective view mode. The Off option of Dview changes the view back to a parallel projection.

---

2. At the New camera/target distance <current distance> prompt, move your cursor from left to right. The chair appears to enlarge and reduce. You can also see that the position of the diamond in the slide bar moves. The slide bar gives you an idea of the distance between the camera and the target point in relation to the current distance.

3. As you move the diamond, you see lines from the diamond to the 1× value (1× being the current view distance). As you move the cursor toward the 4× mark on the slide bar, the chair appears to move away from you. Move the cursor toward 0×, and the chair appears to move closer.

4. Move the cursor further to the left; as you get to the extreme left, the chair appears to fly off the screen. This is because your camera location has moved so close to the chair that the chair disappears beyond the view of the camera—as if you were sliding the camera along the floor toward the target point. The closer to the chair you are, the larger and farther above you the chair appears to be (see Figure 16.38).

FIGURE 16.38:

The camera's field of vision

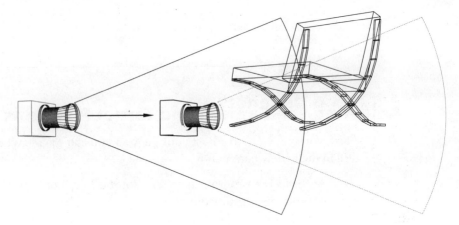

5. Adjust your view so it looks like Figure 16.39. To do this, move the diamond to between 1× and 4× in the slide bar.

6. When you have the view you want, click the mouse/pick button. The slide bar disappears and your view is fixed in place. Notice that you are now viewing the chair in perspective.

FIGURE 16.39:

The Perspective view of
the chair after using the
Distance option

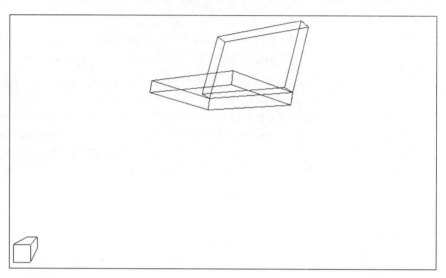

Adjusting the Camera and Target Positions

Next, you will want to adjust your view so you can see the whole chair. You are
still in the Dview command.

1. At the DVIEW prompt, enter **TA** ↵ for the Target option. The chair will temporarily disappear from view.

NOTE
Using Dview's Target option is like standing in one location while moving
the camera angle around.

2. When you see the following prompt:

   `[T]oggle angle in/Enter angle from X-Y plane <.00>:`

   move your cursor very slowly in a side-to-side motion. Keep the cursor centered vertically or you may not be able to find the chair. The chair moves in
   the direction of the cursor in an exaggerated manner. The sideways motion
   of the cursor simulates panning a camera from side to side across a scene
   (see Figure 16.40).

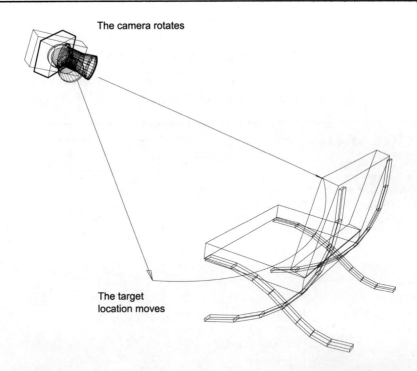

FIGURE 16.40:

Adjusting the target option is like panning your camera across a scene

The camera rotates

The target location moves

3. Center the chair in your view, and then move the cursor slowly up and down. The chair moves in the opposite direction to the cursor. The up-and-down motion of the cursor simulates panning a camera up and down.

TIP If you lose your view of the chair but remember your camera angle, you can enter it at the Enter angle in X-Y plane prompt to help relocate your view.

4. Enter **Ta** ↵. You will see the prompt:

   ```
   Toggle angle in/Enter angle from XY plane <-35.2644>:
   ```

   At this prompt, you can enter a value representing the vertical angle between the camera and the target point.

5.   Press ↵ to accept the default. This fixes the vertical motion of the target location to its current default location. However, you can still move the target horizontally. Here you can enter an angle value representing the angle between the camera and target in a horizontal plane.

6.   Position the view of the chair so it looks like Figure 16.41, and click the mouse/pick button. You've now fixed the target position.

FIGURE 16.41:

While in the Dview Target option, set up your view so it looks like this figure

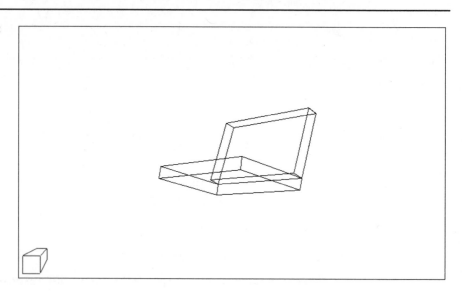

In steps 4 and 5 above, I mentioned that you could enter an angle value indicating either the vertical or horizontal angle to the target. Once you enter that value (or just press ↵), the angle becomes fixed in either the vertical or horizontal direction. Then, as you move your cursor, the view's motion will be restricted to the remaining unfixed direction. In the exercise, you fixed the vertical angle, and then visually selected a horizontal angle. If instead, you would prefer to "fix" the horizontal angle and visually adjust the vertical, you can enter **Ta** ↵ **T** ↵ ↵ at the Dview prompt.

Changing Your Point of View

Next, you will want to adjust the camera location to one that is higher in elevation.

1.   At the Dview prompt, enter **CA** ↵ to select the Camera option.

NOTE   Using Dview's's Camera option is like changing your view elevation while constantly looking at the chair.

2. At the following prompt:

    ```
    [T]oggle angle in/Enter angle from XY plane <11>:,
    ```

    move your cursor slowly up and down. As you move the cursor up, your view changes as if you were rising above the chair (see Figure 16.42). If you know the vertical angle you want, you could enter it now.

FIGURE 16.42:

While in the Camera option, moving the cursor up and down is like moving your camera location up and down in an arc.

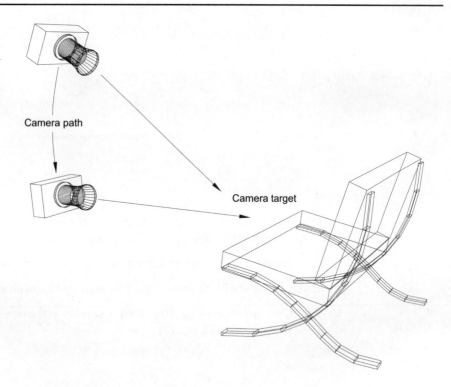

Camera path

Camera target

3. Move the cursor down so you have a view that is roughly level with the chair, and then move the cursor from side to side. Your view changes as if you were walking around the chair, viewing it from different sides (see Figure 16.43).

FIGURE 16.43:

Moving the cursor from side to side is like walking around the target position.

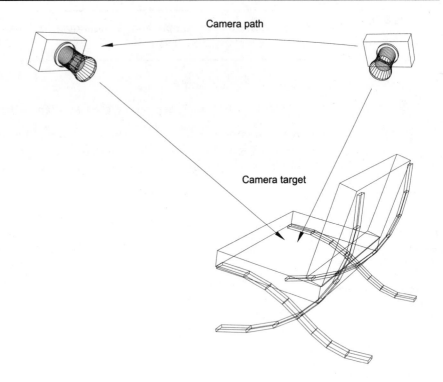

4. When you are ready, enter **T** ↵ to choose the [T]oggle angle in/Enter angle from XY plane option. The prompt changes to

   [T]oggle angle from/Enter angle in XY plane from x axis <-144>:

   If you know the horizontal angle you want, you can enter it now.

5. Position your view of the chair so it is similar to the one in Figure 16.44, and click the mouse/pick button.

FIGURE 16.44:

Set up your camera location so you have a view similar to this one

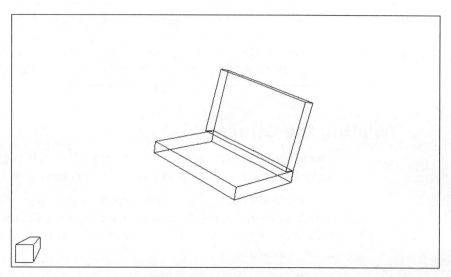

In steps 2 and 4, we mentioned that you could enter an angle value indicating either the vertical or horizontal angle to the camera. Once you indicate a value, either by entering a new one or by pressing ↵, the angle becomes fixed in either the vertical or horizontal direction. Then, as you move your cursor, the view's motion will be restricted to the remaining unfixed direction.

Using the Zoom Option as a Telephoto Lens

The Zoom option of Dview allows you to adjust your view's cone of vision, much like a telephoto lens in a camera. You can expand your view to include more of your drawing, or narrow the field of vision to focus on a particular object.

1. At the Dview prompt, enter **Z** ↵ for the Zoom option. Move your cursor from side to side, and notice that the chair appears to shrink or expand. You also see a slide bar at the top of the screen, which lets you see your view in relation to the last Zoom setting, indicated by a diamond. You can enter a value for a different focal length, or you can visually select a view using the slide bar.

2. At the Adjust Lens Length <50.000mm> prompt, press ↵ to accept the 50.000mm default value.

NOTE When you don't have a Perspective view (obtained by using the Distance option) and you use the Zoom option, you will get the Adjust zoom scale factor <1> prompt instead of the Adjust lenslength prompt. The Adjust zoom... prompt acts just like the standard Zoom command.

Twisting the Camera

The Twist option lets you adjust the angle of your view in the view frame—like twisting the camera to make your picture fit diagonally across the frame.

1. At the Dview prompt, enter **TW** ↵ for the Twist option. Move your cursor, and notice that a rubber-banding line emanates from the view center; the chair also appears to rotate, and the coordinate readout changes to reflect the twist angle.

2. At the New view twist <0> prompt, press ↵ to keep the current 0° twist angle.

3. Press ↵ again to exit the Dview command, and the drawing regenerates, showing the chair in perspective (see Figure 16.45).

4. Choose View ➤ Hide to see a hidden line Perspective view.

FIGURE 16.45:

A Perspective view of the chair

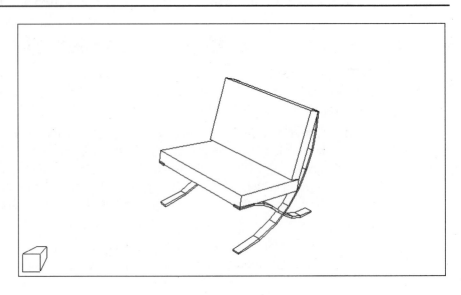

In the next section, you will look at one special Dview option—Clip—that lets you control what is included in your 3D views.

Using Clip Planes to Hide Parts of Your View

At times, you may want a view that would normally be obscured by objects in the foreground. For example, if you try to view the interior of your Unit drawing, the walls closest to the camera obscure your view. The Dview command's Clip option allows you to eliminate objects in either the foreground or the background, so you can control your views more easily. In the case of the apartment unit, you can set the Clip/Front option to delete any walls in the foreground that might obscure your view of its interior (see Figure 16.46).

FIGURE 16.46:

A view of an apartment unit interior using the Clip/Front plane

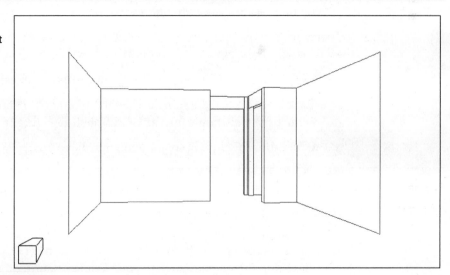

1. Open the 16a-unit.dwg file from the companion CD-ROM. You see a view similar to the one in Figure 16.46, but the walls between the interior of the unit and the balcony obscure the interior. Next you will the Dview's Clip option to hide the walls in the foreground.

2. Click on View ➤ 3D Dynamic View, or enter **Dv** ⏎ at the command prompt. Then select all of the drawing.

3. While still in the Dview command, enter **CL** ⏎ for the Clip option.

4. At the Back/front<off> prompt, enter **F** ↵ for the Front option. A slide bar appears at the top of the screen.

5. As you move the diamond on the slide bar from left to right, the walls in the foreground begin to disappear, starting at the point closest to you. Moving the diamond from right to left brings the walls back into view. You can select a view either by using the slide bar or by entering a distance from the target to the Clip plane.

6. At the Eye/<distance from target>< current distance>: prompt, move the slide bar diamond until your view looks similar to Figure 16.47. Then click the mouse/pick button to fix the view.

7. To make sure the Clip plane is in the correct location, preview your perspective view with hidden lines removed. Enter **H** ↵ at the Dview prompt. The drawing regenerates, with hidden lines removed.

There are several other Dview Clip options that let you control the location of the Clip plane. These options are described as follows:

Eye   places the Clip plane at the position of the camera itself.

Back   operates in the same way as the **Front** option, but it clips the view behind the view target instead of in front (see Figure 16.47).

Off   turns off any Clip planes you may have set up.

You've now completed the Dview command exercises and should now have a better understanding of how Dview can be used to get exactly the image you want.

If you like, you can use View ➤ Named Views to save your Perspective views. This is helpful when you want to construct several views of a drawing to play back later as part of a presentation. You can also use the Hide and Shade options on the Tools pull-down menu to help you visualize your model.

FIGURE 16.47:

Effects of the Clip planes

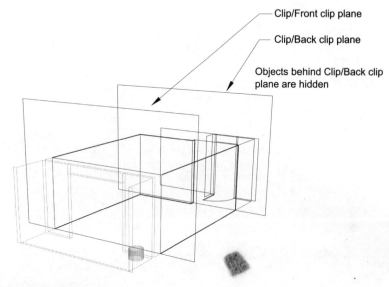

Clip/Front clip plane

Clip/Back clip plane

Objects behind Clip/Back clip plane are hidden

Objects in Clip/Front of front clip plane are hidden

TIP

The quickest and easiest way to establish a Perspective view is to first use the Viewpoint Presets dialog box to set up your 3D view orientation; then start Dview, and use the Distance option right off the bat to set your camera-to-target distance. Once this is done, you can easily use the other Dview options as needed, or exit Dview to see your Perspective view.

If You Want to Experiment...

You've covered a lot of territory in this chapter, so it may be a good idea to play with these commands to help you remember what you've learned. Try the exercise shown in Figure 16.48.

FIGURE 16.48:

Drawing a 3D over-stuffed couch

Rotate the WCS 90 degrees in the x-axis, then draw the shape shown to the right using a spline curve polyline.

Use the Vpoint command to get a 3D view of the shape.

Return to the WCS and then copy the shape in the y-axis so it looks similar to this view. Add arcs connecting the bottom endpoints of the shapes.

Make two more copies of the shape and rotate them so they are oriented as shown to the right.

Add more arcs to the endpoints of these new shapes.

Set the Surftab1 system variable to 12 and the Surftab2 system variable to 24.

Use the Edgesurf command to create the mesh forming the couch back and arms.

Mirror the meshes to create the arms for the other side.

Draw some cushions and add them to your couch.

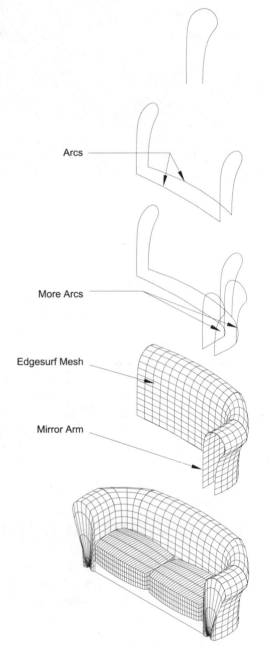

Arcs

More Arcs

Edgesurf Mesh

Mirror Arm

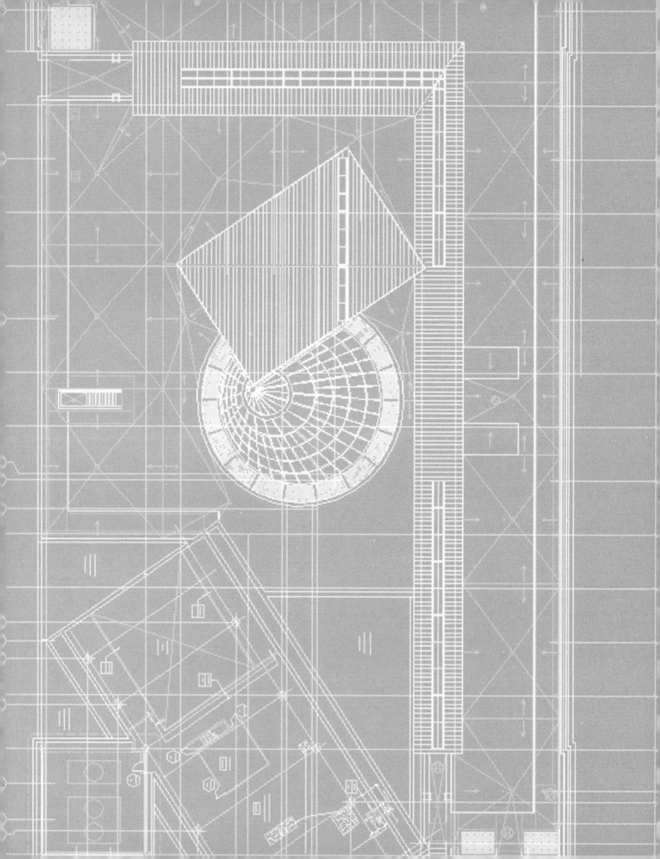

CHAPTER
SEVENTEEN

17

3D Rendering in AutoCAD

- Things to Do before You Start
- Creating a Quick Study Rendering
- Adding a Background Scene
- Effects with Lighting
- Adding Reflections and Detail with Ray Tracing
- Creating and Adjusting Texture Maps
- Adding Landscape and People
- Other Rendering Output Options
- Improving Your Image and Editing

Just a few years ago, it took the power of a workstation to create the kind of images you will create in this chapter. Today, you can render not just a single image, but several hundred images to build computer animations. And with the explosion of game software, the Internet, and virtual reality, real-time walk-through sessions of 3D computer models are nearly as commonplace as word processors.

In this chapter, you'll learn how you can use rendering tools in AutoCAD to produce rendered still images of your 3D models. With these tools, you can add materials, control lighting, and even add landscaping and people to your models. You also have control over the reflectance and transparency of objects, and you can add bitmap backgrounds to help set the mood.

NOTE   Prior to Release 14, these rendering tools were sold as a separate add-on product called AutoVision.

Things to Do before You Start

You will want to take certain steps before you start working with the rendering tools so you won't run into problems later. First, make sure you have a lot of free disk space on the drive where Windows is installed. Having 100 megabytes of free disk space will ensure that you won't exceed your RAM capacity while rendering. This may sound like a lot, but remember, you are attempting to do with your desktop computer what only workstations were capable of a few years ago. Also, make sure there is plenty of free disk space on the drive where your AutoCAD files are kept.

Creating a Quick Study Rendering

Throughout this chapter, you will work with a 3D model that was created using AutoCAD's solid modeling tools (you'll learn more about solid modeling in Chapter 18). The model is of two buildings on a street corner. You'll start by creating a basic rendering using the default settings in the Render dialog box.

1. Open the Facade3.dwg file from the companion CD-ROM.

2. Open the Render toolbar from the Toolbar dialog box.

3. Choose View ➤ Render ➤ Render..., or click on the Render tool in the Render toolbar.

The Render dialog box appears. In time, you will become intimately familiar with this dialog box.

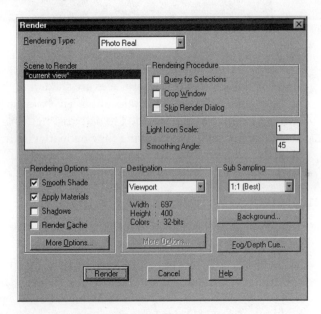

4. Click on the Render button. AutoCAD will take a minute or two to render the current view. While it's working, you will see messages in the Command window showing you the progress of the rendering. When AutoCAD is done, the model appears as a surface shaded model (see Figure 17.1).

FIGURE 17.1:

The Facade model
rendered using all the
default settings

When you render a model without any special settings, you get what is called a
Z buffer shaded model. The surfaces are shaded in their color and the light source
is, by default, from the camera location. This view is much like a hidden line
removed view with color added to help distinguish surface orientation. You can
actually get a similar view using the Shade tool in the standard AutoCAD Render
toolbar.

Simulating the Sunlight Angle

The ability to add a sunlight source to a drawing is one of AutoCAD's key features. This is a frequently used tool in the design of buildings in urban and subur-
ban settings. Neighboring building owners will want to know if your project will
cast darkening shadows over their homes or workplaces. The Sun option lets you
accurately simulate the sun's location in relation to a model and its surrounding
buildings. AutoCAD also lets you set up multiple light sources other than the sun.

So let's add the sun to our model to give a better sense of the buildings form
and relationship to its site.

1. Choose View ➤ Render➤ Lights, or click on Lights from the Render toolbar.

TIP

Whenever you are creating a new Light or other object in the Rendering tool, you usually have to give it a name first, before you can do anything else.

2. In the Lights dialog box, choose Distant Light from the drop-down list next to the New button toward the bottom left.

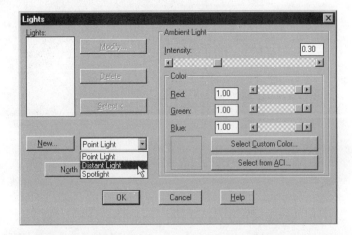

3. Click on the New button. The New Distant Light dialog box appears.

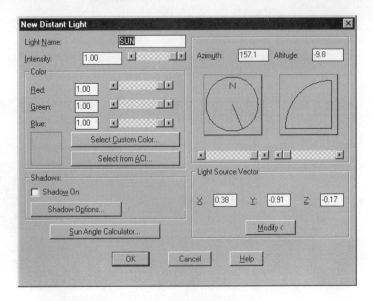

4. Type **SUN**. The word "SUN" appears in the Light Name input box toward the top of the dialog box. This dialog box lets you control various aspects of the light source, such as color and location.

5. Because we want to simulate the sun in this example, click on the button labeled Sun Angle Calculator.... The Sun Angle Calculator dialog box appears.

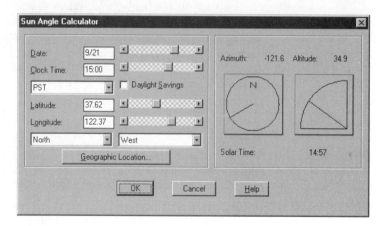

Notice that you have options for setting the date and time to determine the exact location of the sun. In addition, you have the option to indicate where true polar north is in relation to your model. AutoCAD assumes polar north is at the 90 degree position in the WCS.

6. One important factor for calculating the sun angle is finding your location on the earth. Click on the Geographic Location... button. The Geographic Location dialog box appears.

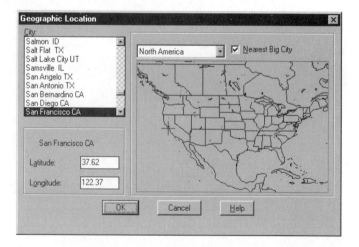

Here you can tell AutoCAD where your building is located in the world.

7. For the sake of this tutorial, let's suppose the Facade model is a building in San Francisco, California, USA. Select North America from the drop-down list above the map.

8. Locate and select San Francisco CA in the scrolling list to the left of the map. Notice that the Latitude and Longitude input boxes below the list change to reflect the location of San Francisco. For locations not listed, you can enter values manually in those input boxes.

9. Now click OK to return to the Sun Angle Calculator dialog box. Set the Date for 9/21 and the time for 14:00 hours. Notice that the graphic to the right of the dialog box adjusts to show the altitude and azimuth angle of the sun for the time you enter.

10. Click OK, and then click OK again at the Lights dialog box.

11. Choose View ➣ Render➣ Render, or click on Render from the Render tool-bar. Then click on the Render button in the Render dialog box. Your model will be shaded to reflect the sun's location (see Figure 17.2).

FIGURE 17.2:

The Facade model with the sun light source added

Notice that the building itself looks darker than before, and that the ground plane is lighter. Remember that in the first rendering, the light source is the same as the camera location, so the wall facing you receives more direct light. In this last rendering, the light source is at a glancing angle, so the surface appears darker.

I mentioned that you can set the direction of polar north. This is accomplished by clicking on the North Location button in the Lights dialog box. When selected, this button opens the North Location dialog box, shown in Figure 17.3. With this dialog box, you can set true north in any of three ways. You can click on the graphic to point to the direction, use the slide bar at the bottom to move the arrow of the graphic and adjust the value in the input box, or enter a value directly into the input box. You also have the option to indicate which UCS is used to set the north direction. For example, you may have already set a UCS to point to the true north direction. You only need to select the UCS from the list and leave the angle at 0.

FIGURE 17.3:

The North Location dialog box

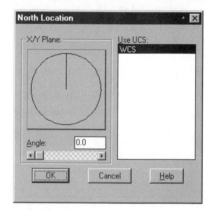

Improving the Smoothness of Circles and Arcs

You might notice that at times when using the Render, Hide, or Shade tools, solid or region arcs appear segmented rather than curved. This may be fine for producing layouts or backgrounds for hand-rendered drawings, but for final plots, you will want arc and circles to appear as smooth curves. You can adjust the accuracy of arcs in your hidden, rendered, or shaded views through a setting in the Preferences dialog box.

The Rendered Object Smoothness setting in the Performance tab of the Preferences dialog box can be modified to improve the smoothness of arcs. Its default setting is .5, but you can increase this to as high as 10 to smooth out faceted curves. In the Facade3.dwg model, you can set Rendered Object Smoothness to 1.5 to render the arch in the entry as a smooth arc instead of a series of flat segments. This setting can also be adjusted using the Facetres system variable.

Adding Shadows

There is nothing like adding shadows to a 3D rendering to give the model a sense of realism. AutoCAD offers three methods for casting shadows. The default method is called Volumetric Shadows. This method takes a considerable amount of time to render more complex scenes. When using AutoCAD's Ray Trace option (described later in this chapter), shadows will be generated using the Ray Trace method. The third method, called Shadow Maps, offers the best speed but requires some adjustment to get good results. Shadow Maps offers a soft-edge shadow. While shadow maps are generally less accurate than the other two methods, the soft-edge option offers a level of realism not available in the other two methods.

In the following exercise, you will use the Shadow Map method. It requires the most amount of adjustments and yields a faster rendering.

1. Choose View ➣ Render ➣ Lights, or click on Lights from the Render toolbar.

2. At the Lights dialog box, make sure SUN is highlighted, and then click Modify.... The Modify Distant Light dialog box appears.

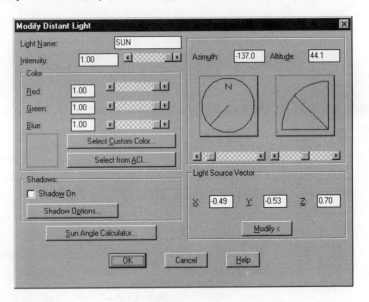

3. Click on the Shadow On checkbox, and then click on the Shadow Options... button. The Shadow Options dialog box appears.

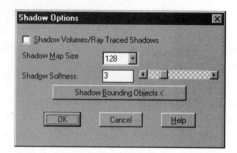

4. In the Shadow Map Size input box, select 512 from the drop-down list. This is the actual number of pixels used to create the shadow map.

5. Click on the Shadow Bounding Objects... button. The dialog box temporarily disappears to allow you to select objects from the screen. This option allows you to select the objects you want to cast shadows.

6. Select the entire Facade building. Don't select any of the building next to it. When you are done, press ↵. The Shadow Options dialog box reappears.

7. Click OK to close the dialog box, and then click OK at the Modify Distant Light dialog box. It may take several seconds before the dialog box closes.

8. When you get to the Lights dialog box, click OK to close it.

9. Click on the Render button on the Render toolbar.

10. At the Render dialog box, check the Shadows checkbox, and then click on the Render button. After a minute or two, the model appears rendered with shadows (see Figure 17.4).

Don't panic if the shadows don't appear correct. The Shadow Map method needs some adjustment before it will give the proper shadows. The default settings are appropriate for views of objects from a greater distance than our current view. The following exercise will show you what to do for "close-up" views.

1. Open the Render dialog box again, and then click on the button labeled More Options. The Photo Real Render Options dialog box appears.

2. In the Depth Map Shadow Control group, change the Minimum Bias value from 2 to .1.

3. In the same group, change the Maximum Bias value from 4 to .2.

4. Click OK to close the dialog box, and then click Render. Your next rendering will show more accurately drawn shadows (see Figure 17.5).

FIGURE 17.4:

The Facade model rendered with shadows using the Shadow Map method

FIGURE 17.5:

The Rendered view with the Shadow bias settings revised

The shadow still looks a bit rough. You can further refine the shadow's appearance by increasing the Shadow Map Size to greater than 512. This setting can be found in the Shadow Options dialog box in step 4 of the exercise just before the last one. Figure 17.6 shows the same rendering with the Shadow Map Size set to 1024. As you increase the map size, you also increase render time and the amount of RAM required to render the view. If you don't have enough free disk space, you may find that AutoCAD will refuse to render the model. You will then either have to free up some disk space or decrease the map size.

FIGURE 17.6:

The Rendered view with the Shadow Map Size set to 1024

Notice that the shadow has a soft edge. You can control the softness of the shadow edge using the Shadow Options dialog box you saw in the exercise before the last one. The Shadow Softness input box and slide bar let you sharpen the shadow edge by decreasing the value or soften it by increasing the value. The soft shadow is especially effective for renderings of building interiors or scenes where you are simulating artificial light.

Adding Materials

The rendering methods you've learned so far can be of enormous aid in your design effort. Simply being able to see how the sun affects your design can be of enormous help in selling your ideas or helping get plans through a tough planning board review. But the look of the building is still somewhat cartoonish. You can further enhance the rendering by adding materials to the objects in your model.

Let's suppose you want a granitelike finish to appear on the Facade model. You will also want the building next to the Facade model to appear as a glass tower. The first step to adding materials is to acquire the materials from AutoCAD's materials library.

1. Choose View ➢ Render➢ Materials...., or click on Materials from the Render toolbar.

The Materials dialog box appears.

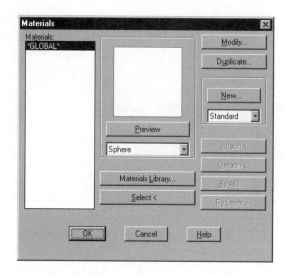

2. Click on the Materials Library... button in the middle of the dialog box. The Materials Library dialog box appears.

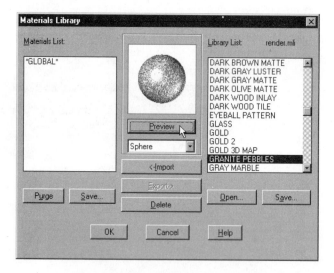

3. In the Library List box, find and select Granite Pebbles so it is highlighted. This is the material you will assign to the facade.

4. Click on the Preview button in the middle of the dialog box. A view of the material appears on a sphere giving you an idea of what the material looks like.

5. Click on the Import button. Notice that Granite Pebbles now appears in the Materials List box to the left. This list box shows the materials you've transferred to your drawing.

6. Now locate Glass in the Library list to the right and select it. Click the Preview button again to see what it looks like. Notice that the preview shows a transparent sphere showing some reflected light. You may notice a textured effect caused by the low color resolution of the AutoCAD display.

7. Click on the Import button again to make Glass available in the drawing; then click OK to exit the Materials Library dialog box.

Once you've acquired the materials, you will have to assign them to objects in your drawing.

1. In the Materials dialog box, highlight the Granite Pebbles item shown in the list to the left, and then click on the Attach< button in the right half of the dialog box. The dialog box temporarily disappears allowing you to select the objects you want to appear as Granite Pebbles.

2. Click on the Facade model, including the steps, columns, and arched entrance, and then press ↵. After a moment, the Materials dialog box appears again.

3. Click on Glass from the Materials list.

4. This time you'll assign a material based on its layer. Click on the By Layer... button to the right of the dialog box. The Attach by Layer dialog box appears.

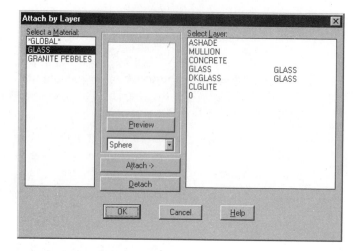

5. Shift + click on Glass and Dkglass from the Select Layer list to the right, and then click on the Attach button. Notice that the word "Glass" now appears next to the layer names you selected, indicating that the Glass material is now associated with those layers.

6. Click OK to exit the Attach by Layer dialog box; then click OK again to exit the Materials dialog box.

7. Now render your model. You may want to take a break at this point, as the rendering will take a few minutes. When AutoCAD is done, your rendering will look like Figure 17.7.

FIGURE 17.7:

The Facade model with the glass and granite pebbles materials added

Adjusting the Materials' Appearance

The Facade model looks more like it has an Army camouflage paint job instead of a granite finish. Also, the glass of the office tower is a bit too transparent. Fortunately, you can make several adjustments to the materials. You will want to reduce the scale of the granite pebbles material so it is in line with the scale of the model. You will also want to darken the glass material so it looks more like the tinted glass used in modern office buildings. You'll start with the granite pebbles.

1. Choose View ➤ Render ➤ Materials....

2. At the Materials dialog box, select Granite Pebbles from the Materials list, and then click on the Modify button. The Modify Granite Material dialog box appears.

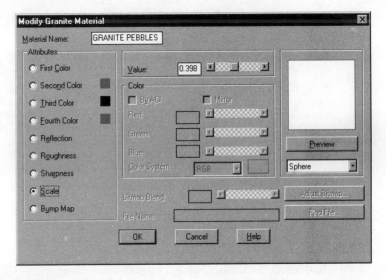

3. Click on the Scale radio button in the Attributes button group in the left-hand side of the dialog box.

4. Change the Value input box near the top of the dialog box from .398 to .010. This will reduce the scale of the material.

5. Click on OK to return to the Materials dialog box.

The Modify Granite Materials dialog box offers a variety of options that let you control reflectivity, roughness, color, transparency, and, of course, scale. The Help button on the Modify Granite Material dialog box will give a brief description of these options. As you'll see when you continue with the next exercise, not all materials have the same options.

1. Select Glass from the Materials list, and then click on the Modify... button again. The Modify Standard Material dialog box appears.

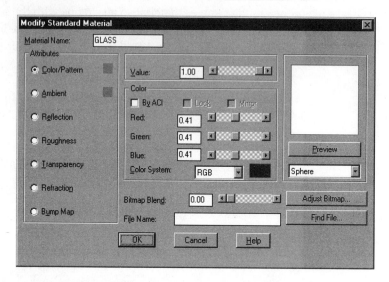

Notice that this dialog box offers a slightly different set of Attributes options from those offered in the Modify Granite Materials dialog box you edited in the previous exercise.

2. Select the Transparency radio button in the Attributes button group, and then adjust the Value option downward to .55. This will have the effect of darkening the glass.

3. Select the Color/Pattern radio button; then, in the Color button group, adjust the red value to 69, the Green value to 60, and the Blue to .58. This will give the glass a bronze tint.

4. Select Cube from the drop-down list just below the Preview button, and then click on the Preview button to get a preview of the color settings.

5. Click on OK in both the Modify Standard Material and Materials dialog box to exit them.

6. Render the view with the new material settings. After a few minutes, your view will look something like Figure 17.8.

The Facade model after modifying the material settings

There are four basic types of materials: Standard, Marble, Granite, and Wood. Each type has its own set of characteristics that you can adjust. You can even create new materials based on one of the four primary types of materials. Now let's continue by making another adjustment to the material settings.

The granite surface of the Facade is a bit too strong. You can reduce the graininess of the granite by further editing in the Modify Granite Material dialog box.

1. Click on Materials from the Render toolbar, and then select Granite Pebbles from the Materials list, and then choose Modify....

2. At the Modify Granite Material dialog box, click on the Sharpness Attribute radio button. Then set the value input box to .20.

3. Click OK, and then click OK again at the Materials dialog box.

4. Choose View ➢ Render ➢ Render, and then click on the Render button of the Render dialog box. Your rendering appears after a few minutes with a softer granite surface (see Figure 17.9).

FIGURE 17.9:

The rendered image with a softer granite surface

Adding a Background Scene

You could continue by adding and adjusting materials to the other parts of model, but let's try dressing up our view by including a sky. To do so, we need to set up the background.

1. Open the Render dialog box, and then click on the button labeled Background. The Background dialog box appears.

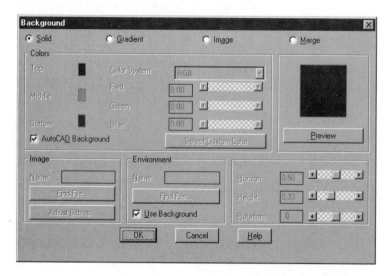

2. In the row of radio buttons across the top, find and click on Image. Notice that several of the options near the bottom of the dialog box are now available.

3. Click on the Find File... button at the bottom left of the dialog box. The Background Image dialog box appears.

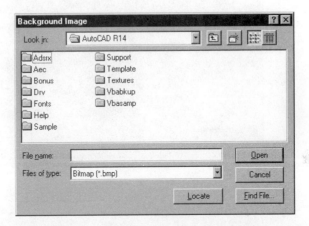

This is a typical AutoCAD file dialog box.

4. Use the Background Image dialog box to locate the Sky.tga file. It can be found in the \Textures subdirectory of the \AutoCAD R14 directory.

5. Once back at the Background Image, click on Preview to see what the file looks like. Sky.tga is a bitmap image of a blue sky with clouds.

6. Click OK. Then, once back at the Render dialog box, click on Render. The background appears behind the model, as shown in Figure 17.10.

I chose to add a bitmap image for a background, but you can use other methods to generate a background. For example, you might prefer to use a gradient shade or color for the background. This can help give a sense of depth to the image (see Figure 17.11). You can, of course, add a single color to the background if you prefer.

To create a Gradient background, select the Gradient radio button at the top of the Background dialog box. You can then adjust the color for the top, middle, and bottom third of the background. AutoCAD automatically blends the three colors from top to bottom to create the gradient colors.

FIGURE 17.10:

The Facade model rendered with a sky bitmap image for a background

FIGURE 17.11:

The Facade model with a gradient color background

Effects with Lighting

Up to now, you've only used one light source, called a Distant Light, to create a sun. You have two other light sources available to help simulate light: point-light sources and spotlights. This section will show you some examples of how you can use these types of light sources, along with some imagination, to perform any number of visual tricks with them.

Simulating the Interior Lighting of an Office Building

Our current rendering shows a lifeless-looking office building. It's missing a sense of activity. You might notice that when you look at glass office buildings, you can frequently see the ceiling lights from the exterior of the building—provided the glass isn't too dark. In a subtle way, those lights lend a sense of life to a building.

To help improve the image, you'll add some ceiling lights to the office building. We've already supplied the lights in the form of square 3D Faces arrayed just at the ceiling level of each floor, as shown in Figure 17.12.

FIGURE 17.12:

The 3D Face squares representing ceiling light fixtures

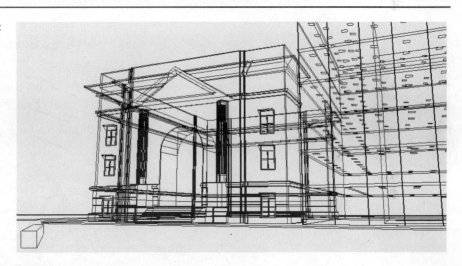

In this section, we'll show you how to make them appear illuminated.

1. Start by assigning a reflective material to the squares. Choose View ➤ Render ➤ Materials ➤, and then click on the Materials Library button.

2. At the Materials Library dialog box, locate and select White Plastic from the List at the right, and then click on Import.

3. Click on OK to exit the Materials Library dialog box. Then at the Materials dialog box, highlight White Plastic in the list to the left and click on the By Layer button.

4. In the Attach By Layer dialog box, make sure White Plastic is highlighted in the Select a Material list to the left; then click on the Clglite layer in the Select Layer list to the right.

5. Click on the Attach> button. The word White Plastic will appear next to the Clglite layer name in the Select Layer list.

6. Click OK to exit the Attach By Layer dialog box, and then click OK to exit the Materials dialog box.

You now have a reflective, white material assigned to the ceiling fixtures. But the reflective material alone will not give the effect of illuminated lights. You need a light source that can be reflected by the fixtures giving the impression of illumination. For this, you'll use a point-light source.

1. Choose View ➣ 3D Viewpoint ➣ SE Isometric to get an Isometric view of the model.

2. Zoom into the base of the office building so your view is similar to Figure 17.13.

3. Choose View ➣ Render➣ Lights…. Then at the Lights dialog box, select Point Light from the New drop-down list; then click on the New button.

4. At the New Point Light dialog box, enter **Point1** for the light name; then enter **300** in the Intensity input box.

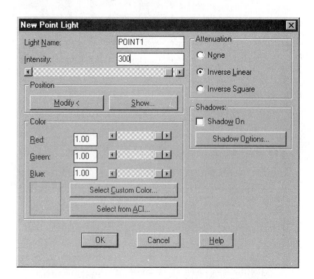

5. Click on the Modify... button, and then select a point at the very center of the office building base, as shown in Figure 17.13.

Selecting the point-light source location in the SW Isometric view

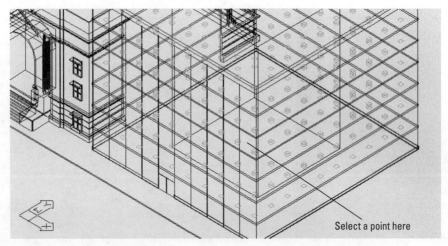

Select a point here

6. Click on OK to exit the New Point Light dialog box, and then click on OK in the Lights dialog box.

7. Choose View ➤ Named Views.... Then at the Named Views dialog box, select 3DFront and click the Restore button.

8. Click OK to exit the Named Views dialog box.

9. Go ahead and render the view. After a minute, you will have a Rendered view similar to Figure 17.14.

The new point light in conjunction with the 3D Face light fixture adds a sense of life and depth to the office building. Notice that despite the fact that the light is located inside the box representing the office core, the light manages to strike all the lights of all the floors as if the floors and core were transparent. Since you didn't turn on the Shadow feature for the point-light source, its light passes through all the objects in the model.

There is even light falling on the granite facade building illuminating the inside of the arched entrance. This shows that with careful use of lighting, you can bring out some of the detail in the facade model that might otherwise get lost with the distant light source.

Of course, you can use point-light sources in a more traditional way, representing light bulbs or other nondirectional light sources. But by playing with light source location and shadow, you can create effects to help enhance your rendering.

FIGURE 17.14:

The Rendered view with ceiling lights

Simulating a Night Scene with Spotlights

Spotlights are lights that are directed. They are frequently used to provide emphasis and are usually used for interior views or product presentations. In this exercise, you'll set up a night view of the facade model using spotlights to illuminate the facade.

You'll start by setting up a view to help place the spotlights. Once they are placed, you make some adjustments to them to get a view you want.

1. Choose View ➤ 3D Viewpoint Presets ➤ SE Isometric; then zoom into the Facade so your view looks similar to Figure 17.15.

2. Choose View ➤ Render ➤ Lights .... Then at the Lights dialog box, select Spotlight from the New drop-down list.

3. Click New. Then at the New Spotlight dialog box, enter **Spot-L**. This designates a spotlight you will place on the left side of the facade.

4. Enter **400** in the Intensity input box. Then click on the Modify< button.

5. At the `Enter Target Location` prompt, use the Nearest Osnap and select the point on the window, as indicated in Figure 17.15.

6. At the `Enter Light Location` prompt, select the point indicated in Figure 17.15. Once you've selected the light location, you return to the New Spotlight dialog box. You can, in the future, adjust the light location if you choose.

7. Click OK. Then at the Lights dialog box, click on New again to create another spotlight.

8. This time, enter **Spot-R** for the name. Set the intensity to **400** as before.

9. Click on the Modify button and select the target and light locations indicated in Figure 17.16.

10. Click OK to exit the New Spotlight dialog box, and then click OK again at the Lights dialog box. You now have two spotlights on your building.

11. Choose View ➤ Named Views... and restore the 3DFront view.

12. Render the model (you should know how this is done by now). Your view will look similar to Figure 17.17.

FIGURE 17.15:

Selecting the points for the first spotlight

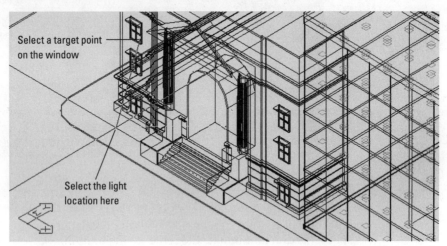

Select a target point on the window

Select the light location here

FIGURE 17.16:

Selecting the points for the second spotlight

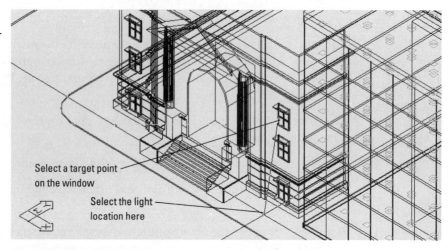

Select a target point on the window

Select the light location here

FIGURE 17.17:

The Rendered view of the model with the spotlights

The Rendered view has a number of problems. First, the sunlight source needs to be turned off. Second, the spotlights are too harsh. We can also see that the spotlights don't illuminate the center of the building, so you'll need to add some lighting at the entrance. We'll solve these problems in the next section.

Controlling Lights with Scenes

The first problem we face is how to turn off the sun. You can set the sunlight intensity value to zero using the Modify Distant Light dialog box. Another way is to set up a scene. AutoCAD lets you combine different lights and views into named scenes. These scenes can then be quickly selected at render time so you don't have to adjust lighting or views every time you want a specific setup. Here's how it works.

1. Choose View ➤ Render ➤ Scene, or click on Scene from the Render toolbar.

You will see the Scenes dialog box.

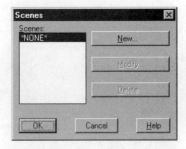

2. Click on New. The New Scene dialog box appears.

3. Enter **NIGHT** for the scene name. The name appears in the Scene Name input box.

4. Select 3DFRONT from the Views list and then Shift + click on SPOT-L, SPOT-R, and POINT1 from the Lights list.

5. Click OK. Notice that now you have NIGHT listed in the Scenes list in the Scenes dialog box.

6. Click on New again, and then type **DAY**.

7. Select 3DFRONT from the Views list, and SUN and POINT1 from the Lights list. Then click OK. You now have two scenes set up.

8. Click OK, and then open the Render dialog box. Notice that you have DAY and NIGHT listed in the Scene list box in the upper left of the Render dialog box.

9. Select Night, and then click on the Render button. Your view will look like Figure 17.18.

FIGURE 17.18:

Rendering the Night scene

We now see that without the sunlight source, our view is considerably darker. Let's continue by adding a few more light sources and adjusting some existing ones.

1. Choose View ➢ 3D Viewpoint Presets ➢ SE Isometric, and then zoom into the office building so your view looks similar to Figure 17.19.

2. Open the Lights dialog box, select Point Light from the New drop-down list, and click New.

3. Enter the name **Point2**, and then give this new point light an intensity value of **500**.

4. Click on the Modify< button, and place the Point2 light in the center of the office building in the same location as Point1.

5. Click OK; then create another point-light source called **Point3** and give it an intensity of **150**.

6. Click on the Modify< button, adjust your view so it looks similar to Figure 17.20, and then place the light in the Facade entrance, as shown in Figure 17.20. Use the .X, .Y, and .Z point filters to select the location of the light.

7. Click OK. Then at the Light dialog box, select the Spotlight from the list and click on Modify.

8. At the Modify Spotlight dialog box, change the Falloff value in the upper right to **80**.

9. Click OK, and then repeat steps 7 and 8 for the SPOT-R spotlight.

10. Click OK at the Modify Spotlight dialog box.

11. At the Light dialog box, increase the Ambient light intensity to **50**, and then click OK.

FIGURE 17.19:

Adding another point-light source to the office building

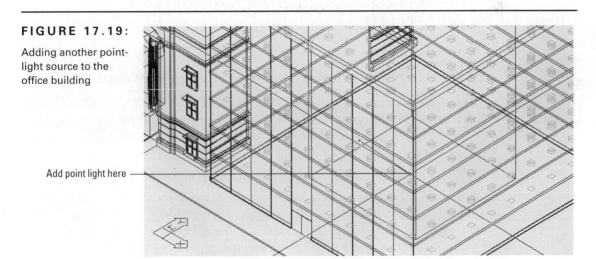

Add point light here

FIGURE 17.20:

Adding a point-light source for the entrance to the facade

Use the .Z point filter and pick this endpoint

Use the .Y point filter and pick this midpoint

Use the .X point filter and pick this midpoint

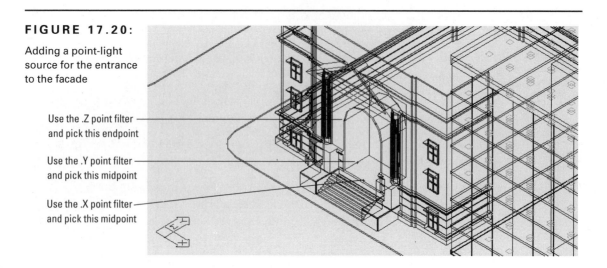

You've got the new lights installed and the spotlights adjusted. Before you render your scene, you need to include the new lights in the scene you set up for the night rendering.

1. Choose View ➤ Render➤ Scene.

2. Highlight Night in the Scenes list, and then click on the Modify... button.

3. Shift + click on Point2 and Point3 in the Lights list, and then Alt + click on Point1 to de-select it.

4. Click OK at both the Modify Scene and Scenes dialog box.

5. Choose Render and make sure Night is selected in the Scene list.

6. Click on the Render button. Your view will look similar to Figure 17.21.

The new rendering is brighter. You can also see the effects of an increased falloff for the spotlights. They don't have the sharp edge they had in the first night rendering, and the light is spread in a wider radius, illuminating more of the lower portion of the facade.

You also see another byproduct of using the Scene tools. You didn't have to return to the 3DFront view to render the model. Since the 3DFront view is included in the scene information, AutoCAD automatically rendered the model from that view when the Night scene was selected. If you were to issue the Regen command now, you would see that AutoCAD still maintains the SE Isometric view.

FIGURE 17.21:

The night rendering with added lights and an increased falloff area for the spotlights

Adding Reflections and Detail with Ray Tracing

You've been gradually building up the detail and realism in your renderings by adding light and materials. In this section, you'll learn how using a different rendering method can further enhance your 3D models. Up until now, you've been using the standard AutoCAD rendering method. Ray Tracing can add interest to a rendering, especially where reflective surfaces are prominent in a model. In this section, you'll use the Ray Tracing method to render your model after making a few adjustments to the glass material.

What Is Ray Tracing?

To make a long, complicated story short, Ray Tracing simulates the way light works. And it does it in somewhat of a reverse way. Ray Tracing analyses the light path to each pixel of your display, tracing the light or "ray" from the pixel to the light origin as it bounces off objects in your model. Ray Tracing takes into account the reflectivity and, in the case of glass, the refraction of light as it is affected by objects in the model. Because more objects in a model offer more surfaces to reflect

Continued on next page

light, Ray Tracing becomes more time consuming as the number of objects increase. Also, since each pixel is analyzed, a greater image size increases the render time geometrically. For example, by doubling the width and height of the view size, you are essentially increasing the number of pixels by four times.

AutoCAD offers Ray Tracing as an option for rendering both shadows and the entire scene. The Ray Trace options offer greater accuracy in exchange for slow rendering time. If you choose to select ray traced shadows, for example, you can expect at least a fourfold increase in rendering time. Rendering an entire scene can increase rendering time by an order of magnitude.

Needless to say, if you are in a time crunch, you will want to save Ray Tracing just for the essential final renderings. Use Renders or other rendering options for study rendering or for situations that don't require the accuracy of Ray Tracing.

Assigning a Mirror Attribute to Glass

Glass is a complex material to model in computer renderings. The AutoCAD standard rendering method simply gives glass a transparency with some "highlight" reflection. But glass has both a refractive and reflective attribute that makes it difficult to model. Because Ray Tracing models the way light works, it is especially well suited to rendering views that contain large areas of glass.

To demonstrate what Ray Tracing can do, you'll use it to render the facade model that happens to contain an office building with a typical glass exterior. You'll start by making an adjustment to the glass material to make it appear more reflective.

1. Choose View ➤ Render ➤ Materials, and then at the Materials dialog box, highlight Glass in the list box and click on the Modify button.

2. Click on the Reflection radio button in the Attribute button group.

3. Click on the Mirror checkbox in the Color button group, and then click on OK to close the Modify Standard Materials dialog box.

4. Click OK again at the Materials dialog box, and then open the Render dialog box.

5. Choose Photo Raytrace from the Rendering Type list box near the top of the dialog box.

6. Click on the More Options button. Then at the More Options dialog box, set the Minimum Bias setting to **.1** and the Maximum Bias setting to **.2**. Whenever you change the rendering type, you must re-set these settings. AutoCAD does not automatically transfer these settings to different rendering types.

7. Click OK, and then select Day from the Scene list. Next, click on the Background... button.

8. In the Background dialog box, make sure the Use Background checkbox is checked in the Environment button group; then click on the OK button. This tells AutoCAD to reflect the background image in the glass.

9. Click on the Render button. Your view will look similar to Figure 17.22.

FIGURE 17.22:

The Facade model rendered with the Raytrace method

The sky bitmap used as a background is faintly reflected in the glass of the office building. The office building has also become brighter from the reflection. Also notice the secondary reflection of the interior ceiling on the west interior wall of the office.

The brightness of the office building is a bit overwhelming, so you will want to adjust the glass material to tone it down.

1. Choose View ➢ Render ➢ Materials; then with the Glass material highlighted, select Modify.

2. At the Modify Standard Materials dialog box, make sure the Color/Pattern radio button is selected; then set the Value setting in the Color button group to **.20**. This will help darken the office building.

3. Click OK to close the Modify Standard Materials dialog box, and then Click OK at the Materials dialog box.

4. Render the scene again. Your view will look something like Figure 17.23.

FIGURE 17.23:

The rendering with a lower Color/Pattern setting for the Glass material

You can further reduce the brightness of the office building by reducing the intensity value of the point-light source you added early in this chapter.

Getting a Sharp, Accurate Shadow with Ray Tracing

In the beginning of this chapter, we showed you how to use the Shadow Map method for casting shadows. Shadow maps offer the feature of allowing a soft-edge shadow in exchange for accuracy. For exterior views, you may prefer a sharper shadow. The Facade example loses some detail using the Shadow Map method; in particular, the grooves in the base of the building disappear. By switching to the Ray Trace method for casting shadows, you can recover some of this detail.

1. Choose View ➤ Render ➤ Lights…. Then from the Lights list, select Sun and click on Modify….

2. At the Modify Distant Light dialog box, click on the Shadow Options... button.

3. At the Shadow Options dialog box, click on Shadow Volumes/Ray Trace Shadows checkbox to place a checkmark there.

4. Click OK at all the dialog boxes to exit them and return to the AutoCAD view.

5. Render the view using the Photo Ray Trace rendering type. Your view will look like Figure 17.24.

FIGURE 17.24:

The Facade model using the Shadow Volumes/Ray Trace Shadows option

Notice that you can now see the rusticated base clearly. The shadows also appear sharper, especially around the surface detail of the Facade model.

Creating and Adjusting Texture Maps

You've already seen how you can assign a material to an object by adding the granite pebbles and glass materials to the buildings in the Facade3.dwg file. Many of these materials make use of bitmap image files to simulate textures. You can create your own surface textures or use bitmaps in other ways to help enhance your rendering. For example, you can include a photograph of existing buildings that may exist within the scene you are rendering.

Figure 17.25 shows a bitmap image that was scanned into the computer and edited using a popular paint program. Now imagine that this building is across the street from the Facade model, and you want to include it in the scene to show its relationship to your building.

FIGURE 17.25:

A photographic image of a building that was scanned into a computer and saved as a bitmap file

The following exercise will show you how it's done.

1. Click on Redraw from the Standard toolbar, and then adjust your view so it looks like the top image of Figure 17.26.

2. Draw a line 133-feet long, as shown in the top image of Figure 17.26.

3. Change the thickness of the line to **80'** using the Properties tool.

4. Choose View ➤ Render ➤ Materials. Then at the Materials dialog box, click on New. Notice that the New Standard Materials dialog box is the same as the dialog box for the Glass material. The settings are not the same, however.

5. Enter **build1** for the material name.

6. Make sure the Color/Pattern radio button is selected, and then click on the Find File button in the lower-right corner of the dialog box.

7. Click on the List Files of Type drop-down list. Notice that you have several file types from which to choose.

8. Choose GIF from the list, and then locate the `Market2.gif` file. This file comes with the other sample files from the companion CD-ROM.

9. Choose Open to exit this dialog box. Then click OK at the New Standard Material dialog box.

10. At the Materials dialog box, make sure Build1 is selected in the materials list, and then click on the Attach button.

11. Select the line you added in step 1, and then press ↵.

12. Click OK to exit the Materials dialog box, and then render the scene. Your view will looks like the bottom image of Figure 17.26.

FIGURE 17.26:

Adding a bitmap image of a building to your rendering

Add line with Thickness

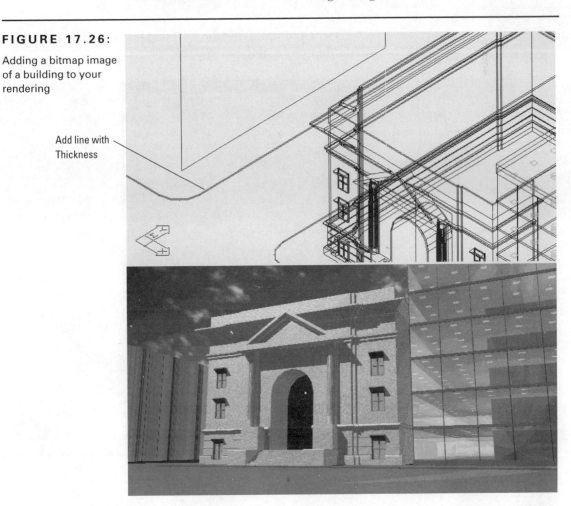

The bitmap image does not appear properly in the Rendered view. Instead, it looks like a vertical streak of colors. When you see this streaking, you know your bitmap image or material is not properly aligned with the object to which it is attached. The following exercise introduces you to the tools you need to properly align a bitmap image to an object.

1. Redraw the screen. Then choose View ➤ Render ➤ Mapping..., or click on Mapping from the Rendering toolbar.

2. At the Select object prompt, select the extruded line you created in the last exercise. The Mapping dialog box appears.

3. Click on the Adjust Coordinates... button. The Adjust Planar Coordinates dialog box appears.

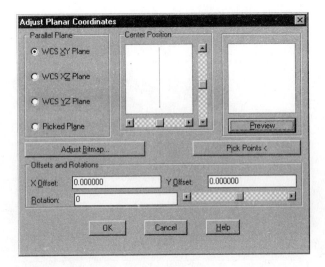

Notice the rectangle in the area labeled Center Position. This shows the relationship of the bitmap image to the object to which it has been assigned. All you can see is a vertical line.

4. Click on the WCS YZ Plane radio button. The plane defined by the y- and z-axes is parallel to the surface on which you want the bitmap to appear.

5. Click on the Preview button. Now you can see how the bitmap will appear on the vertical surface. You now need to adjust the positioning of the bitmap.

6. First you will want to increase the size of the bitmap in relation to the surface so the image of the building completely covers the surface. To do this, you will need one other dialog box. Click on the Adjust Bitmap button. The Adjust Object Bitmap Placement dialog box appears (see the top image of Figure 17.27).

7. Enter .95 in the Scale input box to the left of the U, and then enter .76 in the Scale input box to the left of the V. The U is the horizontal direction scale and the V is the vertical direction scale.

8. Click on the Preview button to view the effect of the scaling. Notice that the image is larger but still not centered vertically.

9. Use the Vertical Offset sliders to move the outer rectangle in the graphic upward so it looks like the bottom image of Figure 17.27, and then click on the Preview button again. Now the image fits within the rectangle.

10. Click OK at each of the dialog boxes to close them, and then render the model. Your view will look like Figure 17.28.

The Adjust Object
Bitmap Placement
dialog box

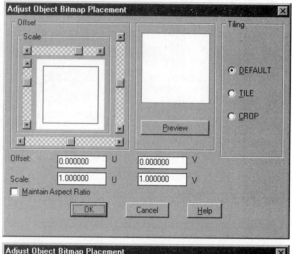

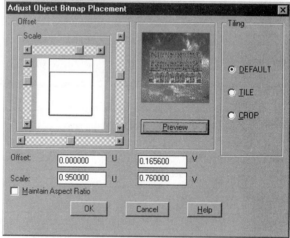

Notice that the image of the building across the street now appears correctly and no longer looks like vertical streaks. Neither are there any odd blank spaces on the building. As you have seen in the previous exercise, the Adjust Object Bitmap Placement dialog box allows you to stretch the image vertically or horizontally in case the image is distorted and it needs to be fitted to an accurately drawn object.

FIGURE 17.28:

The Rendered view with the bitmap image adjusted

Another option is to use a paint program to refine the bitmap image before it is used in AutoCAD. AutoCAD attempts to place the bitmap accurately on a surface, so if the bitmap is fairly clean and doesn't have any extra blank space around the edges, you can usually place it on an object without having to make any adjustments other than its orientation.

Adding Landscape and People

There's nothing like adding landscaping and people to a rendering to add a sense of life and scale. Computer images, in particular, need landscape props because they tend to appear cold and somewhat lifeless. AutoCAD offers a set of pre-built landscape objects to help soften the appearance of your rendering. Let's see how we can add a few trees and people to the Facade model.

1. Choose View ➤ Redraw, and then choose View ➤ Render ➤ Landscape New. You can also click on the Landscape New tool from the Render toolbar.

The Landscape New dialog box appears.

2. Click on Quaking Aspen from the Library list, and then click on Preview to view the item.

3. Use the slider just below the Preview button and change the Height value from 20 to **100**, the highest setting.

4. Click on the Position< button, and then click on the point indicated in the top image of Figure 17.29 to place the tree in front of the buildings. You may have to adjust your view.

5. Click on the View Aligned checkbox to de-select this option. We'll explain what this option does later in this section.

6. Click OK. The tree appears as a rectangle with a text label telling you what it is, as shown in the bottom image of Figure 17.29.

7. Copy the tree to the positions indicated in the bottom image of Figure 17.29.

8. Now render the view. You will see a view similar to Figure 17.30.

The trees you added are actually two-dimensional bitmap images. If you view the model from a glancing angle, the trees will begin to look thinner and you will see that they are indeed two-dimensional. Two of the options in the Library New dialog box offer some options to reduce the 2D effect. The View Aligned option we asked you to turn off in step 5 forces the tree to be aligned to your point of view, so you never see the object edge-on. Another option, Crossing Faces, creates two images of the object to appear. Each image is crossed over the other, as shown in Figure 17.31, creating an almost 3D look.

FIGURE 17.29:

Placing the trees in the Facade model

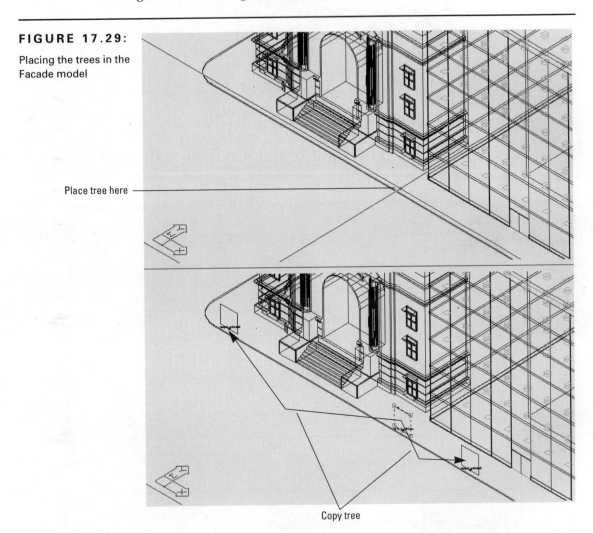

Place tree here

Copy tree

FIGURE 17.30:

The Rendered view of the model with the trees

FIGURE 17.31:

The Crossing Faces option used with a landscape object

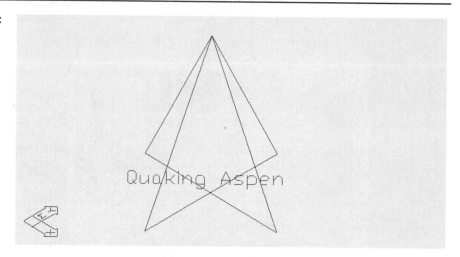

New Object Types in AutoCAD

If you were to use the List tool to find out what the landscape objects were, you would find that that they are called Plant or Person. Does AutoCAD Release 14 have some new object types we don't know about? The answer is maybe.

Release 14 allows third-party developers to add new object types that aren't native to the program itself. This is a fairly revolutionary idea. AutoCAD uses this new capability by adding Plants and People objects. However, there is a problem with adding new object types: you need the third-party application to view and edit the objects you create. When the application is not present, the new objects become what Autodesk calls *Proxies*. Proxies will allow themselves to be edited with a limited set of editing tools. The level of "editability" of proxies is determined by the application that created them.

Where AutoCAD's rendering tools are concerned, the application is always present so you are always able to edit the trees and people.

The ability to add new object types to an AutoCAD drawing has some far-reaching implications. The possibilities for third-party developers are enormous, and you, the end user, will benefit in many ways. The Landscape tool in AutoCAD is an example of what can be done.

There are a few things wrong with this rendering. The trees are too small, and they appear to be shaded on the wrong side. The shadows on the trees don't reflect the location of the Distant Light setting in the model. The street is also unusually empty for a daytime scene. The trees are easily fixed using standard AutoCAD editing tools. You can also add some people using the Landscape New tool in the Render toolbar.

1. Redraw the screen, and then click on one of the trees to expose its grip.

2. Click on the grip at the base of the tree, right-click on the mouse and select Rotate from the pop-up menu.

3. Type **180** ↵ to rotate the tree 180 degrees.

4. Click on the grip again, right-click on the mouse and this time select Scale.

5. Enter **2.4** ↵ to increase the size of the tree by 2.4 times.

6. Repeat steps 1–4 for each of the other trees.

7. Open the Landscape New dialog box again and select People #1 from the list.

8. Change the Height value to 66, and then use the Position button to place the people at the entrance of the Facade building (see Figure 17.32). The people will appear as triangles in the Wireframe view. (Make sure you use the Nearest Osnap override to place the people.)

9. Click OK. Then repeat steps 7 and 8 to place People #2 in front of the office building between the trees (see Figure 17.32).

10. Render the view. Your view will look similar to Figure 17.33.

FIGURE 17.32:

Placing people in the scene

Place People #1 at the midpoint of this line

Place People #2 here

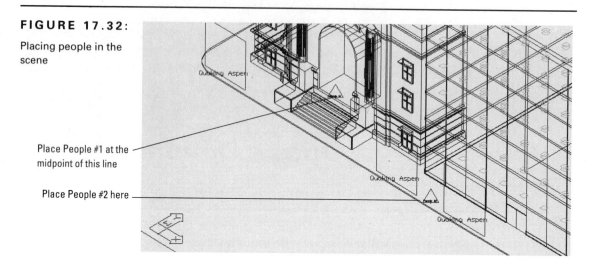

FIGURE 17.33:

The view after rendering with the trees adjusted and people added

The shadows of the trees now match the sun's location, and they are a size better suited to the model. However, notice that the people are not lit very well. This is because when we placed them, we did not turn off the View Align option. Therefore, they are facing your view tilted slightly away from the sun. This has the effect of darkening their image.

You can use View ➤ Render Landscape Edit to change the settings for landscape objects. You will be prompted to select an object. Once you do, you will see the Landscape Edit dialog box, which is identical to the Landscape New dialog box. From there, you can make changes to the settings for the selected landscape object.

Other Rendering Output Options

All through this chapter, you have been rendering to the AutoCAD drawing area. You can also render to a file, which enables you to recall the image at any time in any application, or render to the Render window. From there, you have a number of options in dealing with the rendered image.

Rendering to the Render Window

The Render window lets you control the resolution and color depth of your image. It also lets you save the images you render in the Windows .bmp format. Another advantage of the Render window is that you can render several views and then compare them before you decide which ones to save.

1. Open the Render dialog box, and then select Render Window from the Destination drop-down near the bottom of the dialog box.

2. Click on Render. After a moment the Render window will appear. It will then take a minute or two before the image finishes rendering and appears in the window.

Notice that the image is within its own window. If you render another view, that view will also appear in its own window leaving the previous renderings undisturbed. You can use File ➤ Save in the Render Window to save the file as a .bmp file for later editing or printing, or you can print directly from the Render window. You can also use the Render window to cut and paste the image to another application or to view other files in the .bmp format.

To set the size of renderings, you use the File ➤ Option tool in the Render window. This option opens the Windows Render Options dialog box (see Figure 17.34). Here you can choose from two standard sizes or enter a custom size for your rendering. You can also choose between 8-bit (256 colors) and 24-bit (16 million colors) color depth. Changes to these settings don't take effect until you render another view.

FIGURE 17.34:

The Window Render Options dialog box

Rendering Directly to a File

Rendering to the Render window allows you to view and compare your views before you save them. However, you can only save your views in the .bmp format. If you plan to further edit the image in an image-processing program, this may not be a problem. But if you want to use your image file with a program that requires a specific file format, you may want to render directly to a file. Here's how it's done.

1. Open the Render dialog box, and then select File from the Destination group in the lower middle of the dialog box.

2. Choose More Options... at the bottom of the Destination group. The File Output Configuration dialog box appears.

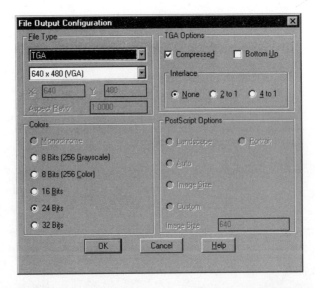

3. Click on the File Type drop-down list to see the options. You can save your image in .gif, .tga, .tif, .pcx, or even PostScript format. There are also several other formats available. You might also notice the other options available in the dialog box, such as color depth, resolution, and compression. Not all these options are available for all the file types. For example, .gif is limited to 256 colors, so the other color options will not apply to .gif files.

4. Click on OK to return to the Render dialog box, and then click on the Render button. The Rendering File dialog box appears, prompting you for a file name for your image.

5. Enter **Facade1**. AutoCAD will add the file name extension for you.

6. Click OK and AutoCAD proceeds to render to the file.

As AutoCAD renders to the file, it tells you how much of the image has been rendered in the command line.

Improving Your Image and Editing

There will be times when you will be rushing to get a rendering done and won't want to wait for each trial rendering to become visible. AutoCAD offers several tools that can save you time by limiting the resolution or area being rendered. Suppose you just want to render the area where you've added a tree to make sure its in the right location. The following exercise will show you how this is done.

1. Choose View ➤ Named Views..., and then restore the 3DFront view.

2. Open the Render dialog box and set the Destination option to Viewport.

3. Click on the Crop Window checkbox to activate this option, and then click on the Render button.

4. You are prompted to `Pick Crop Window to Render`. Select the area shown in Figure 17.35, indicated by the rubber-banding square. Once you select the window, AutoCAD renders only the area you selected.

FIGURE 17.35:

Selecting the Crop window

Crop window —

The Crop Window option is a working tool and is not available when File or Render Window are selected as destinations.

You can also select specific objects to be included in the rendering by checking the Query for Selection checkbox in the Render dialog box. This option asks you to select a set of objects before it proceeds to render. You can render to all three destination options with Query for Selection turned on.

If you want to get a quick rendering with a reduced resolution to check composition, you can use the Sub Sampling option drop-down list. Try the following exercise to see how it works.

1. Open the Render dialog box, and then open the Sub Sampling drop-down list.

2. Choose 3:1 from the list, make sure the Crop Window option is unchecked, and then click on the Render button. Your view will render faster, but will look a bit crude (see Figure 17.36).

FIGURE 17.36:

A Rendered view with the Sub Sampling option set to 3:1

The different ratios in the Sub Sampling option tell you how many pixels are being combined to reduce the resolution of the image. For example, 3:1 will combine three pixels into one to reduce the resolution to a third of the original.

Smoothing Out the Rough Edges

The Sub Sampling option increases the jagged appearance of your rendering because of the reduced resolution. For your final rendering, you can actually improve the smoothness of edges and thereby increase the apparent resolution by using the Anti-Aliasing option in the Render dialog box. This option performs a kind of computer trick that reduces the jagged appearance of object edges. Anti-Aliasing blends the color of two adjacent contrasting colors. This gives the effect of smoothing out the "stair-step" appearance of a computer generated image. The improvement to your rendering can be striking. Try the following exercise to see firsthand what Anti-Aliasing can do.

1. Open the Render dialog box, and then click on the More Options... button.

2. In the Raytrace Rendering Options dialog box, click on the Medium radio button in the Anti-Aliasing button group, and then click OK.

3. Select 1:1 from the Sub Sampling drop-down list, and then click on the Render button. The rendering will take several minutes, so you may want to take a break at this point. When the rendering is done, it will look similar to Figure 17.37.

FIGURE 17.37:

A rendering with the Anti-Aliasing setting set to Medium

Notice that the edges of the buildings are much smoother. You can also see that the vertical mullions of the office building are more clearly defined. One negative point is that the texture effect of the Facade model has been reduced. You may have to increase the scale value for the Granite Pebbles material setting to bring the texture back.

As you can see from this exercise, you trade off rendering speed for a cleaner image. You will want to save the higher anti-aliasing settings for your final output.

If You Want to Experiment...

In this chapter, you've participated in a guided tour of AutoCAD's rendering tools and have seen the main features of this product. Because of space considerations, I didn't go into the finer details of many of its features, but you do have the basic knowledge from which to build your rendering skills. Without too much effort, you can adapt much of what you've learned here to your own projects. If you need more detailed information, you can use the Help button found on all the Render dialog boxes.

Computer rendering of 3D models is a craft that takes some time to master. You will want to take some time to experiment with these rendering tools to see firsthand the types of results you can expect. You might want to try different types of views like an Isometric or Elevation view, the latter of which is shown in Figure 17.38. With a bit more detail added, this rendered elevation could fit nicely into a set of renderings for a presentation.

FIGURE 17.38:

An Elevation view of the Facade model

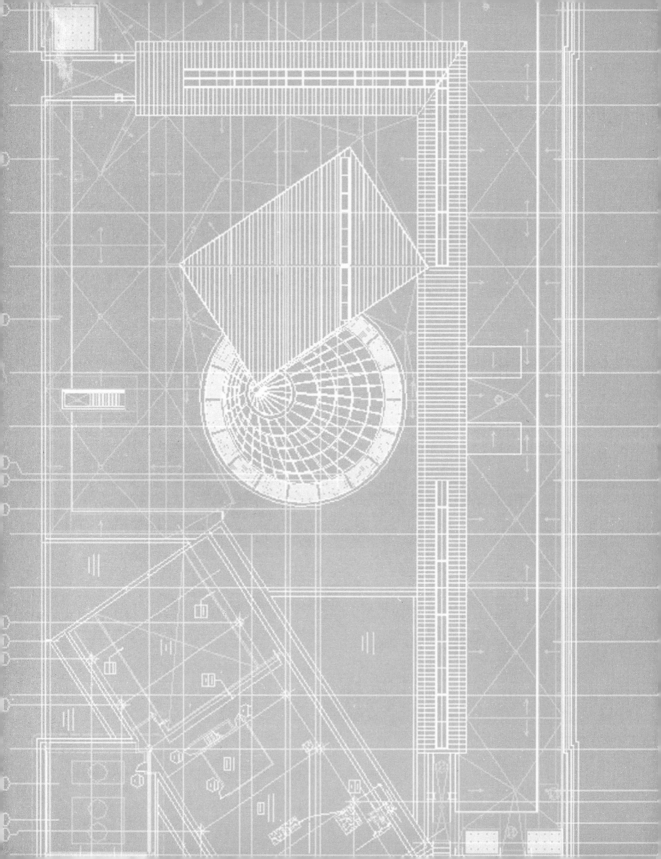

Mastering 3D Solids

- Understanding Solid Modeling

- Creating Solid Forms

- Creating Complex Primitives

- Editing Solids

- Enhancing the 2D Drawing Process

- Finding the Properties of a Solid

- Taking Advantage of Stereolithography

18

So far, you have been creating 3D models according to a method called *surface modeling*: As you drew, you used 3D Faces to give your models form and the appearance of solidity. But there is another method that you can use to create 3D computer models: *solid modeling*.

With surface models, drawing a simple cube requires several steps; with solids, you can create a cube with one command. Having created a solid model, you can assign materials to it and have the computer find physical properties of the model, such as weight and center of mass. It is easier to create models by using solid modeling, and there are many advantages to the technique, especially in mechanical design and engineering.

Solid modeling was once thought to require more computational power than most personal computers could offer, but with today's microcomputer hardware, solid modeling is well within the reach of most PC users. AutoCAD offers built-in solid modeling functions, which you will explore in this chapter.

Understanding Solid Modeling

Solid modeling is a way of defining 3D objects as solid forms rather than as wireframes with surfaces attached. When you create a 3D model using solid modeling, you start with the basic forms of your model—cubes, cones, and cylinders, for instance. These basic solids are called *primitives*. Then, using more of these primitives, you begin to add to or subtract from your basic forms. For example, to create a model of a tube, you first create two solid cylinders, one smaller in diameter than the other. Then you align the two cylinders so they are concentric, and you tell AutoCAD to subtract the smaller cylinder from the larger one. The larger of the two cylinders then becomes a tube whose inside diameter is that of the smaller cylinder, as shown in Figure 18.1.

Several primitives are available for modeling solids in AutoCAD (see Figure 18.2).

FIGURE 18.1:

Creating a tube using
solid modeling

Create two cylinder primitives,
one for the outside diameter
and one for the inside diameter.

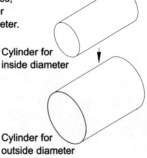

Cylinder for
inside diameter

Cylinder for
outside diameter

Superimpose the cylinder
for the inside diameter onto
the cylinder for the outside
diameter.

Use the Subtract command
to subtract the inside
diameter cylinder from
the outside diameter cylinder.

These shapes—box, wedge, cone, cylinder, sphere, and donut (or *torus*)—can be joined in one of four ways to produce secondary shapes. The first three, demonstrated in Figure 18.3 using a cube and a cylinder as examples, are called *Boolean operations*. (The name comes from the nineteenth-century mathematician George Boole.) The following list describes the three joining methods:

1. **Intersection** uses only the intersecting region of two objects to define a solid shape.

2. **Subtraction** uses one object to cut out a shape in another.

3. **Union** joins two primitives so they act as one object.

FIGURE 18.2:

The solids primitives

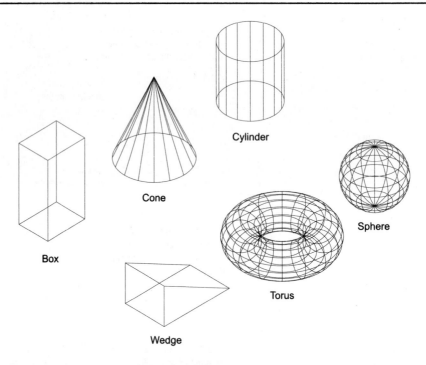

A fourth option, *Interference*, lets you find exactly where two or more solids coincide in space—similar to the results of a Union. You can have AutoCAD either show you the shape of the coincident space or create a solid based on the coincident space's shape.

Joined primitives are called *composite solids*. You can join primitives to primitives, composite solids to primitives, and composite solids to other composite solids.

Now let's take a look at how these concepts let us create models in AutoCAD.

FIGURE 18.3:

The intersection, sub-
traction, and union of a
cube and a cylinder

A solid box and a
solid cylinder are
superimposed.

The intersection of the
primitives creates a solid
cylinder with the ends skewed.

The cylinder subtracted
from the box creates
a hole in the box.

The union of the two
primitives creates a
box with two round pegs.

Creating Solid Forms

In this section, you will begin to draw the object shown in Figure 18.4. In the
process, you will explore the creation of solid models by creating primitives and
then setting up special relationships between them.

FIGURE 18.4:

This steel bracket was
created in and rendered
in AutoCAD.

Displaying the Solids Toolbar

All of the commands you will use to create the solids primitives, and many of the
commands you can use for editing solids, are accessible on the Solids toolbar.
Choose Tools ➢ Toolbars ➢ Solids, or click on Solids on the Tools flyout on the
Standard toolbar. The Solids toolbar will appear.

Now you're ready to begin creating basic solids.

Creating Primitives

Primitives are the basic building blocks of solid modeling. At first, it may seem
limiting to have only six primitives to work with, but consider the varied forms
you can create with just a few two-dimensional objects. Let's begin by creating
the basic mass of our steel bracket.

1. Open a new file called **Bracket.**

2. Set the Snap spacing to **0.5** (using Tools ➢ Drawing Aids…), and turn on the
    grid and the Snap mode.

3. Turn on the dynamic coordinate readout by pressing F6. You'll use the readout to help guide you in selecting points in the exercises that follow.

4. Click on the Box button on the Solids toolbar, or enter **BOX** ↵. You may also choose Draw ➤ Solids ➤ Box.

5. At the Center/<Corner of box><0,0,0> prompt, pick a point at coordinate 3,2.5.

6. At the Cube/Length/<Other corner> prompt, enter @7,4 ↵ to create a box with a length of 7 and a width of 4.

7. The Height prompt that appears next is asking for the height of the box in the z-axis. Enter **1** ↵.

   You've now drawn your first primitive, a box that is 7" long by 4" wide by 1" deep. Now, let's change the view so we can see the box more clearly. Use the Vpoint command to shift your view so you are looking at the WCS from the lower left.

8. Open the Viewpoint Presets dialog box (choose View ➤ 3D Viewpoint ➤ Select…), and then enter **225** in the From X Axis input box and **19.5** in the XY Plane input box.

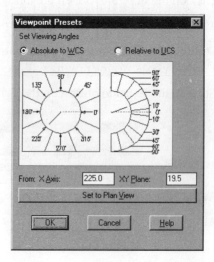

9. Click OK, and then adjust your view so it looks similar to Figure 18.5.

FIGURE 18.5:

The first stage of the bracket

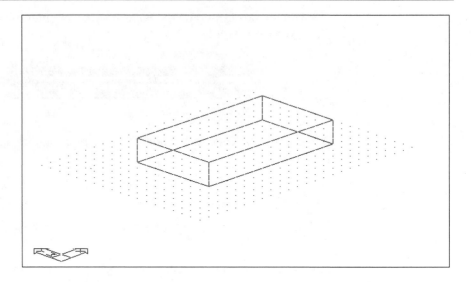

Turning a 2D Polyline into a 3D Solid

Now let's add another box to form the lower lip of the bracket. This time, you'll create a box primitive from a polyline.

1. Click on the Polyline tool on the Draw toolbar.

2. At the From point prompt, start the polyline from the coordinate .5,2.5.

3. Continue the polyline around to create a rectangle that is 1" in the x-axis and 3" in the y-axis. Your drawing will look like Figure 18.6.

4. Click on the Extrude button on the Solids toolbar, or type **EXT** ↵.

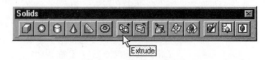

5. At the Select objects prompt, pick the polyline and press ↵.

6. At the Path/<Height of extrusion> prompt, type **1** ↵.

7. At the Extrusion taper angle <0> prompt, press ↵ to accept the default taper of 0°. (You'll get to see what the Taper option does in a later exercise.) The polyline now extrudes in the z-axis to form a bar, as shown in Figure 18.7.

8. Type **R** ↵ to redraw the screen.

FIGURE 18.6:

The polyline drawn in place

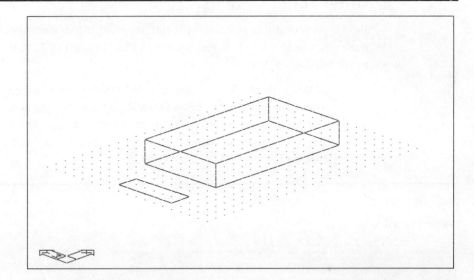

FIGURE 18.7:

The converted polyline box

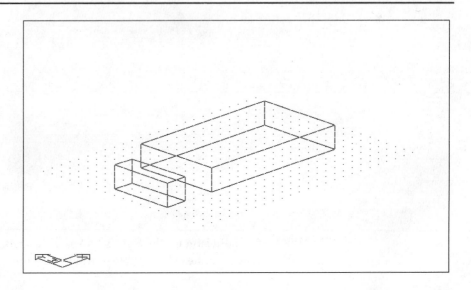

You've now drawn two box primitives using the Box and the Extrude options on the Solids toolbar. Just for variety's sake, we had you create the smaller box by converting a polyline into a solid, but you could just as easily have used Box for that as well. Extrude will convert polylines, circles, and traces into solids. (Regular lines, 3D lines, 3D Faces, and 3D polylines cannot be extruded.)

Other Solids Options

Before you continue, let's examine the commands for primitives that you haven't had a chance to use yet. Refer to Figures 18.8 through 18.11 to understand the terms used with these other primitives.

> **CONE ↵ (Cone icon on the Solids toolbar)** draws a circular cone or a cone with an elliptical base. Drawing a circular cone is much like drawing a circle, with an added prompt asking for a height. The Ellipse option acts like the Ellipse command (on the Draw toolbar), with an additional prompt for height.

FIGURE 18.8:

Drawing a solid cone

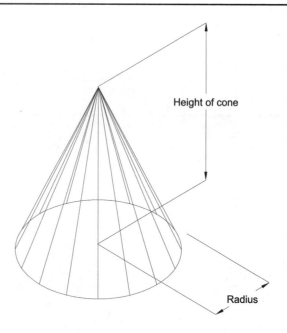

> **SPHERE ↵ (Sphere icon on the Solids toolbar)** acts like the Circle command, but instead of drawing a circle it draws a sphere.

FIGURE 18.9:

Drawing a solid sphere

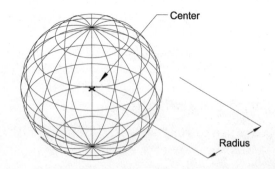

TORUS ↵ **(Torus icon on the Solids toolbar)** creates a torus (a donut-shaped solid). You are prompted for two diameters or radii, one for the diameter or radius of the torus and another for the diameter or radius of the tube portion of the torus.

FIGURE 18.10:

Drawing a solid torus

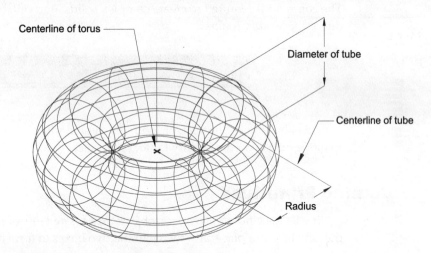

WEDGE ↵ **(Wedge icon on the Solids toolbar)** creates a wedge-shaped solid. This command acts much like the Box command you used to draw the bracket. You have the choice of defining the wedge by two corners or by its center and a corner.

FIGURE 18.11:

Drawing a solid wedge

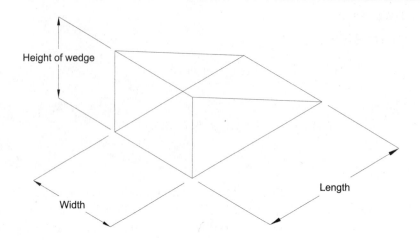

In the following exercises you will be creating and combining solid primitives. The commands required to create complex solids are available on the Explode flyout of the Modify toolbar.

To use the Union, Subtract, or Intersect commands, click and drag on the Explode button on the Modify toolbar and select the desired command option.

Joining Primitives

Now let's see how the two box objects you created are joined. First you'll move the new box into place, and then join the two boxes to form a single solid.

1. Start the Move command, pick the smaller of the two boxes, and then press ↵.

2. At the Base point prompt, use the Midpoint Osnap override and pick the middle of the back edge of the smaller box, as shown in the top image of Figure 18.12.

3. At the Second point prompt, pick the middle of the bottom edge of the larger box, as shown in the bottom image of Figure 18.12.

FIGURE 18.12:

Moving the smaller box

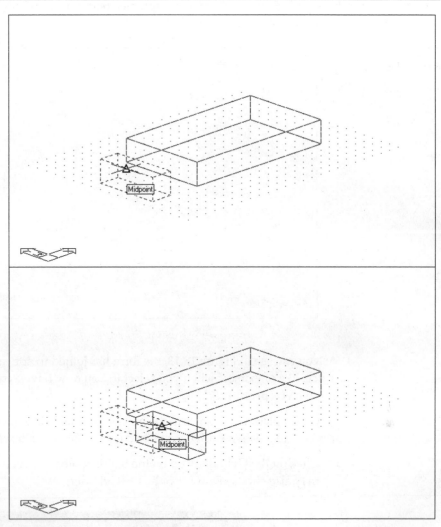

4. Choose Modify ➤ Boolean ➤ Union, or type **Uni** ↵. You may also click on Union in the Modify II toolbar.

5. At the Select object prompt, pick both boxes and press ↵. Your drawing now looks like Figure 18.13.

FIGURE 18.13:

The two boxes joined

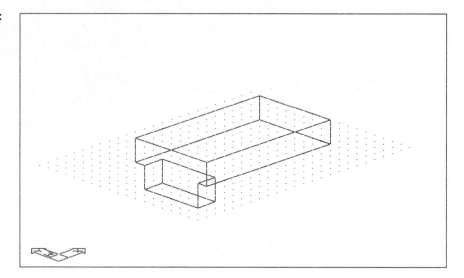

As you can see in Figure 18.13, the form has joined to appear as one object. It also acts like one object when you select it. You now have a composite solid made up of two box primitives.

Now let's place some holes in the bracket. In this next exercise, you will discover how to create negative forms to cut portions out of a solid.

1. Click on the Cylinder icon on the Solids toolbar, or type **Cylinder** ↵. You may also choose Draw ➢ Solids ➢ Cylinder.

2. At the Ellipse/<center point> prompt, pick a point at the coordinate 9,5.5.

3. At the Diameter/<radius> prompt, enter **.25**.

NOTE

As with the Circle command, you can enter **D** to specify a diameter or enter a radius value directly.

4. At the Center of other end/<Height> prompt, enter **1.5** ⏎. The cylinder is drawn.

5. Copy the cylinder two inches in the negative direction of the y-axis, so your drawing looks like Figure 18.14.

FIGURE 18.14:

The cylinders added to the drawing

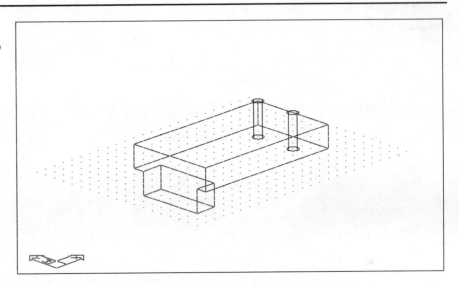

You now have the cylinder primitive, but you still need to define its relationship to the composite solid you created from the two boxes.

1. Choose Modify ➤ Boolean ➤ Subtract, or type **Su** ⏎. You may also click on Subtract from the Modify II toolbar.

2. At the `Select solids and regions to subtract from...` `Select objects` prompt, pick the composite solid of the two boxes and press ↵.

3. At the `Solids and regions to subtract...` `Select objects` prompt, pick two of the cylinders and press ↵. The cylinder has now been subtracted from the bracket.

4. To view the solid, choose View ➤ Hide. You'll see a Hidden-Line view of the solid, as shown in Figure 18.15.

FIGURE 18.15:

The bracket so far, with hidden lines removed

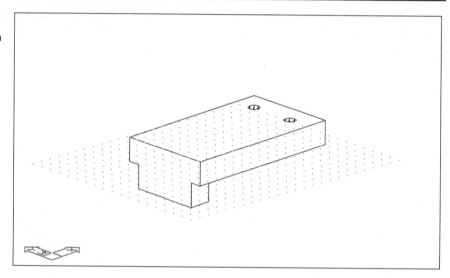

As you've learned in the earlier chapters in Part IV, Wireframe views, such as the one in step 3, are somewhat difficult to decipher. Until you use the Hide command (step 4), you cannot tell for sure that the subtracted cylinder is in fact a hole. Using the Hide command frequently will help you keep track of what's going on with your solid model.

In step 3 of the previous exercise, you may have noticed that the cylinders changed shape to conform to the depth of the bracket. You'll also recall that we asked you to draw the cylinder at a height of 1.5", not 1", which is the thickness of the bracket. Having drawn the cylinder taller than needed, you can see that when AutoCAD performed the subtraction, it ignored the portion of the cylinder that doesn't affect the bracket. AutoCAD will always discard the portion of a primitive that isn't used in a Subtract operation.

Creating Complex Primitives

As you learned earlier, you can convert a polyline into a solid by using the Extrude option on the Solids toolbar. This process lets you create more complex primitives. In addition to the simple straight extrusion you've already tried, you can also extrude shapes into curved paths, or you can taper an extrusion.

Tapering an Extrusion

Next, you'll take a look at how you can taper an extrusion to create a fairly complex solid with little effort.

1. Draw a 3"×3" closed polyline at the top of the current solid. Start at the back-left corner of the bracket at coordinate 3.5,3,1, and then draw the 3"×3" closed polyline to fit in the top of the composite solid, as shown in Figure 18.16.

WARNING   Remember to use the Close option to create the last side of the box.

---

2. Click on Fillet on the Modify toolbar. At the Polyline/Radius/Trim/ <Select first line> prompt, type **R** ↵ to set the radius of the fillet.

3. At the prompt for the fillet radius, type **.5** ↵.

4. At the command prompt, press ↵ to again issue the Fillet command, and then type **P** ↵ to tell the Fillet command that you want to chamfer a polyline.

5. Click on the polyline. The corners become rounded.

6. Click on the Extrude button on the Solids toolbar, or enter **Ext** ↵ at the command prompt.

7. At the Select object prompt, pick the polyline you just drew and press ↵. (As the prompt indicates, you can pick polylines or circles.)

8. At the Path/<Height of extrusion> prompt, enter **3** ↵.

9. At the Extrusion taper angle from Z <0> prompt, enter **4** for 4° of taper. The extruded polyline looks like Figure 18.17.

FIGURE 18.16:

Drawing the 3"×3" poly-line box

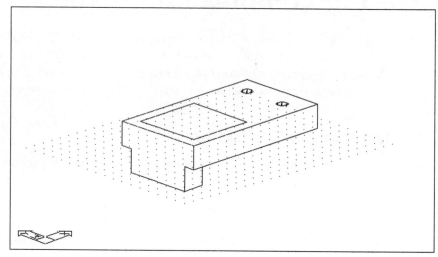

FIGURE 18.17:

The extruded polyline

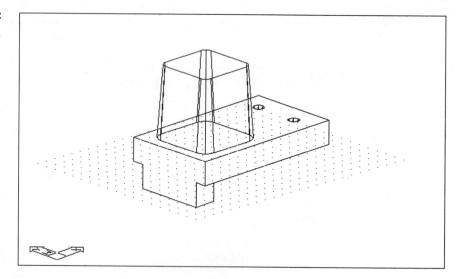

NOTE   In step 9, you can indicate a taper for the extrusion. Specify a taper in terms of degrees from the z-axis, or enter a negative value to taper the extrusion outward. Or press ↵ to accept the default, 0°, to extrude the polyline without a taper.

10. Now join the part you just created with the original solid. Choose Modify ➤ Boolean ➤ Union, and then select the extruded part and the rectangular solid just below it.

Extruding on a Curved Path

As demonstrated in the following exercise, the Extrude command lets you extrude virtually any polyline shape along a path that is defined by a polyline, arc, or 3D polyline.

1. Choose View ➤ Zoom ➤ Extents and turn off the grid.

2. Choose View ➤ Hide. This will help you view and select parts of your model in the following steps.

3. Start by placing the UCS on a vertical plan perpendicular to the back of the bracket. Do this by clicking and dragging on the UCS button on the Standard toolbar and selecting Preset Options on the flyout. You may also choose Tools ➤ UCS ➤ Preset UCS..., or type **Dducsp** ↵. The UCS Orientation dialog box appears.

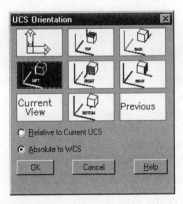

4. Click on the graphic labeled Left, toward the middle left of the dialog box, and then click OK. The UCS will shift over to the back of the bracket, as shown in the top image of Figure 18.18.

TIP The UCS Orientation dialog box is useful for moving from the World Coordinate System to one of the predetermined UCS orientations. However, this dialog box produces unexpected results when used from other UCSs.

5. Start a polyline at the point shown in the top image of Figure 18.18. Use the Midpoint Osnap to make sure you select the midpoint of the vertical corner edge. After you locate the first point, enter the following coordinates:

```
@2<180
@1<270
@2<180
```

When you are done, your drawing should look like the bottom image of Figure 18.18.

6. Click on Fillet from the Modify toolbar, and then type **R** ↵ to set the fillet radius.

7. Enter **.4** ↵ for the fillet radius.

8. Press ↵ to reissue the Fillet command, and then type **P** ↵ to select the Polyline option

9. Click on the polyine you drew on the back side of the solid.

10. Choose Tools ➤ UCS ➤ Y Axis Rotate, and then enter **90** ↵. This will rotate the UCS 90 degrees around the y-axis so the UCS is perpendicular to the front face of the solid.

11. Draw a circle with a 0.35" radius at the location shown in the second image of Figure 18.18.

TIP The Hidden-Line view of the solid in Figure 18.18 shows a lot of extra facets on the curved portion of the model. You can set up AutoCAD so these extra facets don't appear. Open the Preferences dialog box and place a check by the Show Silhouettes in Wireframe option on the Performance tab.

At this point, you've created the components needed to do the extrusion. Next, you'll finish the extruded shape.

1. Click on the Extrude button on the Solids toolbar, click on the circle, and then press ↵.

2. At the Path/<Height of Extrusion> prompt, type **P** ↵ to enter the Path option.

3. At the Select path prompt, click on the polyline curve. AutoCAD will pause a moment and then generate a solid "tube" that follows the path. The

tube may not look like a tube because AutoCAD draws extruded solids such as this with a single line showing its profile.

4. Choose Modify ➤ Boolean ➤ Subtract, and then select the rectangular solid.

5. Press ↵. At the Select object prompt, click on the curved solid and press ↵. The curved solid is subtracted from the tapered solid. Your drawing will look like Figure 18.19.

FIGURE 18.18:

Setting up your drawing to create a curved extrusion

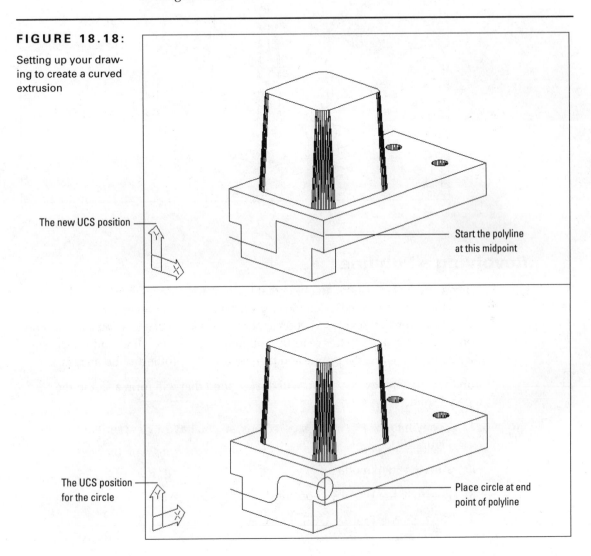

The new UCS position

Start the polyline
at this midpoint

The UCS position
for the circle

Place circle at end
point of polyline

In this exercise, you used a curved polyline for the extrusion path, but you can use any type of 2D or 3D polyline, as well as lines and arcs, for an extrusion path.

FIGURE 18.19:

The solid after subtracting the curve

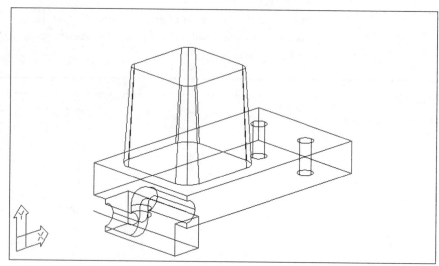

Revolving a Polyline

When your goal is to draw an object that is circular, the Revolve command on the Solids toolbar is designed to let you create a solid that is revolved, or swept in a circular path. Think of Revolve's action as similar to a lathe that lets you carve a shape from a spinning shaft. In this case, the spinning shaft is a polyline, and rather than carving it, you define the profile and then revolve the profile around an axis.

In the following exercise, you will draw a solid that will form a slot in the tapered solid.

1. Zoom in to the top of the tapered box, so you have a view similar to Figure 18.20.

2. Turn the Snap mode off.

3. Return to the WCS by choosing Tools ➤ UCS ➤ World.

4. Next, choose Tools ➤ UCS ➤ Origin.

5. At the Origin prompt, use the Midpoint Osnap override and pick the mid-point of the top surface, as shown in Figure 18.20.

FIGURE 18.20:

An enlarged view of the top of the tapered box and the new UCS location

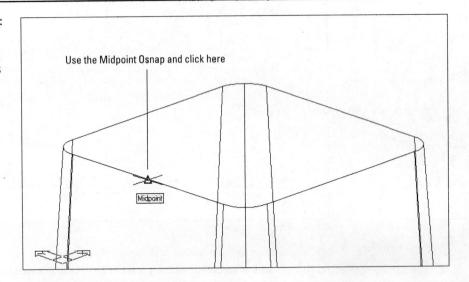

Use the Midpoint Osnap and click here

Midpoint

6. Set the Snap distance to **0.25**, and with the coordinate readout turned on, draw a polyline using the following coordinates:

```
Start at -0.25,0
@0.75<90
@0.75<0
@0.7071<315
@0.5<0
@0.7071<45
@0.75<0
@0.75<270
```

7. When you've finished, type **C** ↵ to close the polyline. AutoCAD will not revolve an open polyline. Your drawing should look like Figure 18.21.

8. Click on the Revolve button on the Solids toolbar, or type **Rev** ↵ at the command prompt.

Solids

Revolve

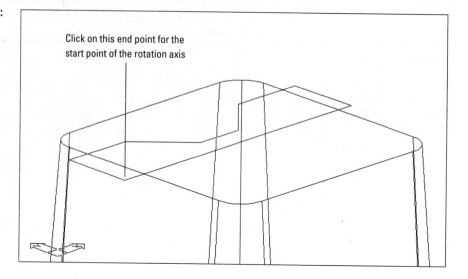

Click on this end point for the
start point of the rotation axis

9. At the Select object prompt, pick the polyline you just drew and press ⏎.

10. When you see the next prompt:

   Axis of revolution - Object/X/t/<Start point of axis>:

   use the Endpoint Osnap override and pick the beginning endpoint of the polyline you just drew.

11. Turn on the Ortho mode (press F8) and turn off the Snap mode (press F9). Then pick a point to the far left of the screen, so the rubber-banding line is parallel with the x-axis of the current UCS.

12. At the Angle of revolution <full circle> prompt, press ⏎ to sweep the polyline a full 360°. The revolved form will appear, as shown in Figure 18.22.

You have just created a revolved solid that will be subtracted from the tapered box to form a slot in the bracket. But before you subtract it, you need to make a slight change in the orientation of the revolved solid.

1. Choose Modify ➤ 3D Operation ➤ Rotate 3D.

2. At the Select objects prompt, select the revolved solid and press ⏎.

3. At this prompt:

   Axis by Entity/Last/View/Xaxis/taxis/Zaxis/<2point>

use the Midpoint Osnap and click on the right-side edge of the top surface, as shown in Figure 18.23.

FIGURE 18.22:

The revolved polyline

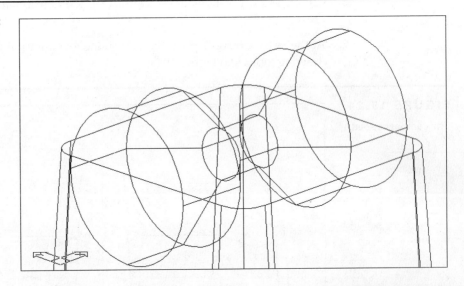

FIGURE 18.23:

Selecting the points to rotate the revolved solid in 3D space

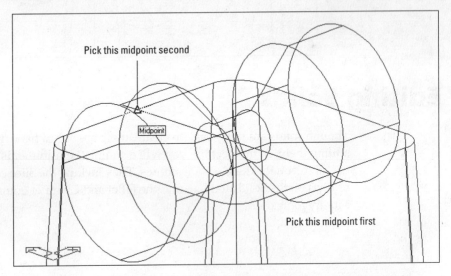

Pick this midpoint second

Midpoint

Pick this midpoint first

4. At the 2nd point on axis prompt, use the Midpoint Osnap again and click on the opposite side of the top surface, as shown in Figure 18.23.

5. At the `<Rotation angle>/Reference:` prompt, type **5** ↵. The solid rotates 5°.

6. Choose Modify ➢ Boolean ➢ Subtract, click on the tapered box, and then press ↵.

7. At the `Select object` prompt, click on the revolved solid and press ↵. Your drawing looks like Figure 18.24.

FIGURE 18.24:

The composite solid

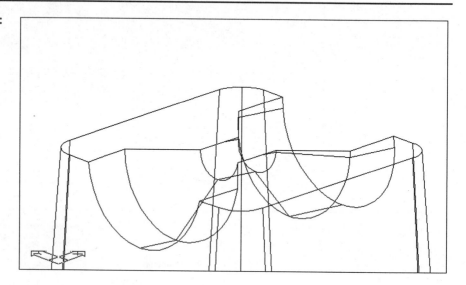

Editing Solids

Though solids are fairly easy to create, there are only a handful of commands for editing them. In this section, you will examine the commands that will be most useful to you for these editing chores. They include the Slice command and its options on the Solids toolbar, and the Fillet and Chamfer commands on the Modify toolbar.

Splitting a Solid into Two Pieces

Unfortunately, although reworking a part of your solid may be a common task for you, there aren't any simple ways to make changes to solids. You can, however, slice a solid into two parts. This action can facilitate the enlargement of solids, or simplify the creation of models by letting you create one monolithic shape to then slice into smaller components. The next exercise shows you how to use the Slice command.

1. Zoom to the previous view and return to the World Coordinate System.

2. Click on the Slice button on the Solids toolbar, or type **Slice** ⏎.

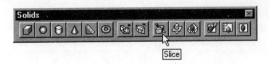

> **NOTE** In step 2, you could select more than one solid. The Slice command would then slice all the solids through the plane indicated in steps 3 and 4.

3. At the `Select object` prompt, click on the part you've been working on and press ⏎.

4. At the next prompt:

   `Slicing plane by Object/Zaxis/View/XY/tZ/ZX/<3points>:`

   type **XY** ⏎. This will let you indicate a slice plane parallel to the x-y plane.

5. At the `Point on XY plane <0,0,0>:` prompt, type **0,0,.5** ⏎. This places the slice plane at the z coordinate of .5 units. You can use the Midpoint Osnap and pick any vertical edge of the rectangular solid.

> **NOTE** If you want to delete one side of the sliced solid, you can indicate the side you want to keep by clicking on it in step 5, instead of entering **B** ⏎.

6. At the `Both sides/<Point on desired side of the plane>` prompt, type **B** ⏎ to keep both sides of the solid. AutoCAD will divide the solid horizontally, one half inch above the base of the part, as shown in Figure 18.25.

The solid sliced through the base

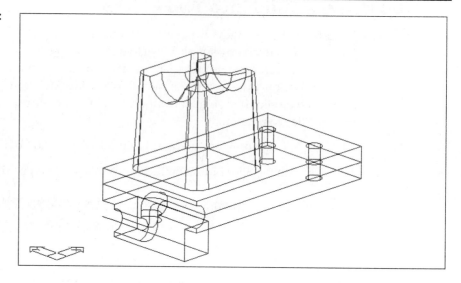

The Slice Options

There were several options in step 3 of the previous exercise that are worth discussing here. Here are descriptions of those options:

Object lets you select an object to define the slice plane.

Zaxis lets you select two points defining the z-axis of the slice plane. The two points you pick will be perpendicular to the slice plane.

View generates a slice plane that is perpendicular to your current view. You are prompted for the coordinate through which the slice plane must pass—usually a point on the object.

<3point> is the default, and lets you select three points defining the slice plane. Normally, you would pick points on the solid.

XY/tZ/ZX pick one of these to determine the slice plane based on the x-, y-, or z-axis. You are prompted to pick a point through which the slice plane must pass.

Rounding Corners with the Fillet Tool

Your bracket has a few sharp corners that you may want to round in order to give the bracket a more realistic appearance. You can use the Construct menu's Fillet and Chamfer commands to add these rounded corners to your solid model.

1. Adjust your view of the model so it looks similar to the top image of Figure 18.26.

2. Click on Fillet on the Modify toolbar.

3. At the `<Select first object>` prompt, pick the edge indicated in the top image of Figure 18.26.

FIGURE 18.26:

Filleting solids

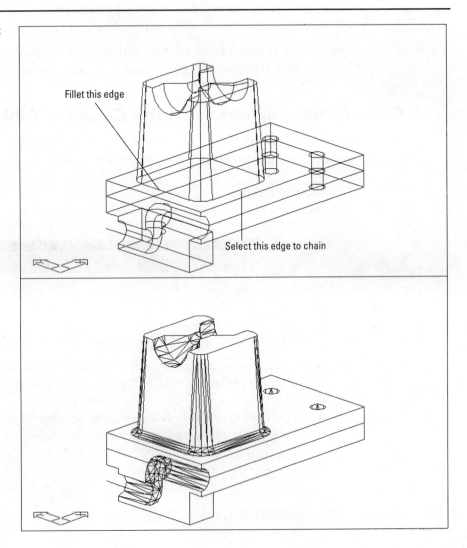

Fillet this edge

Select this edge to chain

4. At the Enter radius prompt, type **.2** ↵.

5. At the Chain/Radius/<Select edge> prompt, type **C** ↵ for the Chain option. Chain lets you select a series of solid edges to be filleted.

6. Select one of the other three edges at the base of the tapered form, and press ↵ when you are done.

7. Choose Hide on the Render toolbar, or type **Hide** ↵, to get a better look at your model, as shown in the bottom image of Figure 18.26.

As you saw in step 5, Fillet acts a bit differently when you use it on solids. The Chain option lets you select a set of edges, instead of just two adjoining objects.

Chamfering Corners with the Chamfer Tool

Now let's try chamfering a corner. To practice using Chamfer, you'll add a countersink to the cylindrical hole you created in the first solid.

1. Type **Regen** ↵ to return to a Wireframe view of your model.

2. Click Chamfer on the Modify toolbar, or type **Cha** ↵.

3. At this prompt:

   Polyline/Distance/Angle/Trim/Method/<select first line>:

   pick the edge of the hole, as shown in Figure 18.27. Notice that the top surface of the solid is highlighted, and the prompt changes to Next/ok. The highlighting indicates the base surface, which will be used as a reference in step 5. (You could also type **N** ↵ to choose the other adjoining surface, the inside of the hole, as the base surface.)

FIGURE 18.27:

Picking the edge to chamfer

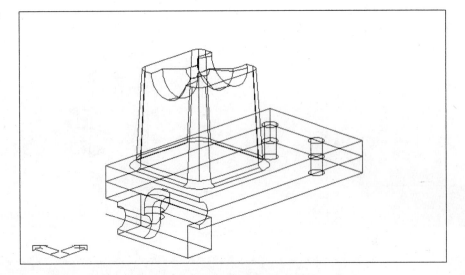

4. Press ↵ to accept the current highlighted face.

5. At the Enter base surface distance prompt, type **.125** ↵. This indicates that you want the chamfer to have a width of .125 across the highlighted surface.

6. At the Enter other surface distance <0.1250> prompt, type **.2** ↵.

7. At the Loop <select edge> prompt, click on the edge of both holes and then press ↵. When it is done, your drawing will look like Figure 18.28.

NOTE The Loop option in step 7 lets you chamfer the entire circumference of an object. You don't need to use it here because the edge forms a circle. Loop is used when you have a rectangular or other polygonal edge you want to chamfer.

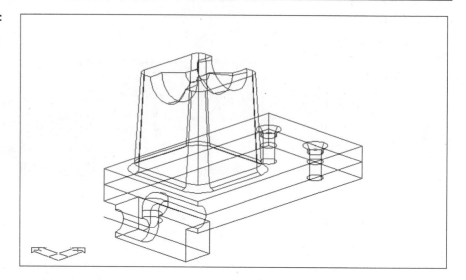

Enhancing the 2D Drawing Process

Using solids to model a part such as the bracket example used in this chapter may seem a bit on the exotic side, but there are definite advantages to modeling in 3D—even if you want to draw the part in only 2D as a page in a set of manufacturing specs.

The following exercises show you how to quickly generate a typical mechanical drawing from your 3D model using Paper Space and the Solids toolbar. You will also examine techniques for dimensioning and including hidden lines.

Drawing a Standard Top, Front, and Right-Side View

One of the more common types of mechanical drawings is the *orthogonal projection*. This style of drawing shows the top, front, and right-side view of an object. Sometimes a 3D image is also added for clarity. You can derive such a drawing within a few minutes, once you have created your 3D solid model. The first step is to select a sheet title block. The title block consists of a border and an area in the lower-right corner for notes and other drawing information.

NOTE   If you need to refresh your memory about using Paper Space, refer to Chapter 12.

Setting Up a File with a Title Block

The first step is to create a file using one of AutoCAD's template files designed for mechanical applications.

1. Save the bracket.dwg file, and then Choose File ➤ New.

2. At the Create New Drawing dialog box, click on the Use a Template button.

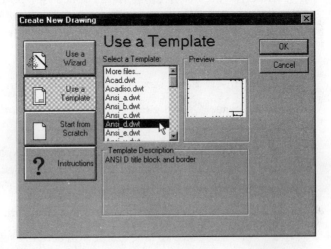

3. From the Select a Template list box, select Ansi_d.dwt, and then click OK. A title block appears, along with a viewport to Model Space.

4. Use File ➤ Save As to save this file as Bracket_title.dwg.

You are now in floating Model Space. Though it may not be obvious at first glance, the title block is in Paper Space and an active Model Space viewport is inside the title block.

WARNING If for some reason you do not see a listing of template files in the Create New dialog box, you will need to setup AutoCAD to look for these files in the right place. Normally, AutoCAD will look in the \Program Files\ AutoCAD R14\Template directory for template files. Check the *Template Drawing File Location* listing in the Files tab of the Preferences dialog box. See C*onfiguring AutoCAD* in Appendix B for details.

Importing the 3D Model

The next step is to insert the Bracket solid model into this drawing. Remember that while you are in a floating Model Space viewport, anything you do affects Model Space. So in the next exercise, you will use the Insert tool to import the Bracket drawing into the Model Space of this new drawing.

1. Choose Insert ➤ Block.

2. At the Insert dialog box, click on the File button.

3. At the Select Drawing File dialog box, locate and select the Bracket.dwg file and click Open.

4. Back at the Insert dialog box, make sure the Explode checkbox in the lower-left corner of the dialog box is checked, and click on the Specify on Screen checkbox to de-select this option.

5. Click OK. The drawing appears in the viewport.

There's one more step to take before you actually set up the Orthogonal views. You will want to make the current viewport display a front view of the bracket. This is easily done with a single menu bar option.

1. Choose View ➤ 3D Viewpoint ➤ Front. The Viewport view changes to show the front view of the model.

2. Choose View ➤ Zoom ➤ Scale, and then type **1xp** ↵ to give the view a 1 to 1 scale. The view is now in proper scale to the title block.

3. Choose View ➤ Paper Space, and then using its grips, re-size the viewport so it is just large enough to display the model, as shown in Figure 18.29. To

expose the viewport grip, click on the inner border of the title block, as shown in Figure 18.29.

4. Move the viewport to a location similar to the one shown in Figure 18.29.

FIGURE 18.29:

Re-sizing the viewport so it is just large enough to contain the view of the bracket

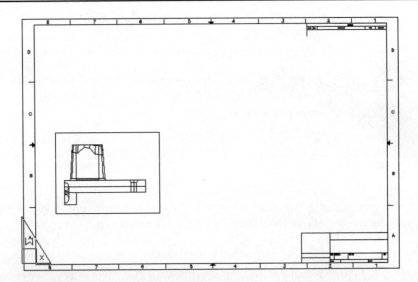

Creating the Orthogonal Views

Now you are ready to create the Orthogonal views. The next part will seem simple compared with the steps you had to take to set up the title block and viewport.

1. Click on Setup View from the Solids toolbar, or choose Draw ➤ Solids ➤ Setup ➤ View.

2. At the Ucs/Ortho/Auxiliary/Section/<Exit> prompt, type **O** ↵.

3. At the Pick Side of Viewport to Project prompt, place the cursor on the right side of the viewport so that a Midpoint Osnap marker appears, as shown in the top image of Figure 18.30. A rubber-banding line appears.

4. At the View Center prompt, click on a point to the right of the viewport at about half the width of the viewport. The right-side view of the bracket appears, as shown in the bottom image of Figure 18.30. You can click again to adjust the horizontal position of the right-side view.

5. Once you're satisfied with the location of the view, press ↵. You don't have to be too precise at this point as you will be able to adjust the view's location later.

6. At the `Clip First Corner` prompt, click on a location below and to the left of the right-side view, as shown in the continued image of Figure 18.30.

7. At the Clip Other Corner prompt, click above and to the right of the view, as shown in the continued image of Figure 18.30.

8. At the `View Name` Prompt, enter **rightside** ↵. Notice that the `Ucs/Ortho/Auxiliary/Section/<Exit>` prompt appears again. This allows you to set up another view.

At this point, you can exit the Setup Profile tool by pressing ↵, but you need another view. Continue with the following steps to create the top view.

9. Type **O** ↵ again, but this time click on the top edge of the front-view viewport.

10. Follow steps 4 through 8 to create a top view. In step 4, click on a point above the viewport instead of to the right.

11. Name this third viewport **Top**.

12. When you return to the `Ucs/Ortho/Auxiliary/Section/<Exit>` prompt, press ↵ to exit the command.

Each new view you create using the Setup View tool is scaled to match the original view from which it is derived. As you saw from step 3, the view that is generated depends on the side of the viewport you select. If you had picked the bottom of the viewport, a bottom view would be generated, which would look the same as the top view until you use the View ➤ Hide option to see it as a Hidden-Line view.

In step 12, you have continued to add views of the left and bottom side, as well as views based on the UCS orientation.

Adding the Orthogonal
views in Paper Space

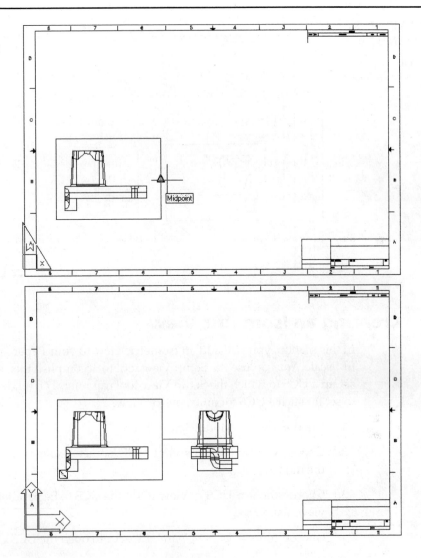

**FIGURE 18.30:
CONTINUED**

Adding the Orthogonal
views in Paper Space

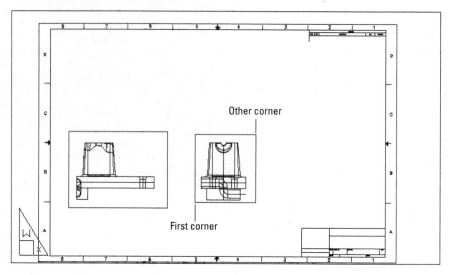

Creating an Isometric View

In this section, you will add an Isometric view to your Paper Space layout at a 1
to 1 scale. You can use the Setup View tool to accomplish this, but you'll need to
set up a UCS to which the Setup View tool can refer. The following explains how
to set up such a UCS for an Isometric view.

1. Choose View ➤ Model Space (Tiled).

2. Choose View ➤ 3D Viewpoint ➤ SE Isometric to get an Isometric view of
   the model.

3. Choose Tools ➤ UCS ➤ View to set the UCS to be parallel to the current
   view plane.

4. Choose Tools ➤ UCS ➤ Named UCS... to open the UCS Control dialog box.

5. Rename the current *NO NAME* UCS to **SWIsometric**.

6. Choose View ➤ Paper Space to return to the Paper Space view of your
   model.

Notice that even though you changed your view in Model Space, the Paper
Space viewports maintain the views as you last left them.

Now you're ready to create a viewport showing the same Isometric view you set up in Model Space.

1. Click Setup View in the Solids toolbar.

2. At the `Ucs/Ortho/Auxiliary/Section/<Exit>` prompt, type **U** ↵.

3. At the `Named/World/?/<Current>` prompt, press ↵ to accept the current UCS.

4. At the `Enter view scale<1.0000>` prompt, press ↵ to accept the scale of 1.

5. At the `View center` prompt, click on a point above and to the right of the original viewport. The Isometric view of the model appears, as shown in Figure 18.31. If you don't like the view's location, you can continue to click on points until the view's location is just where you want it.

6. Press ↵ when you are satisfied with the view's location.

7. At the `Clip First corner` prompt, window the Isometric view to define the viewport border.

8. Name the view **SWIsometric**.

9. Press ↵ to exit the Setup View tool.

FIGURE 18.31:

Adding a viewport for the Isometric view

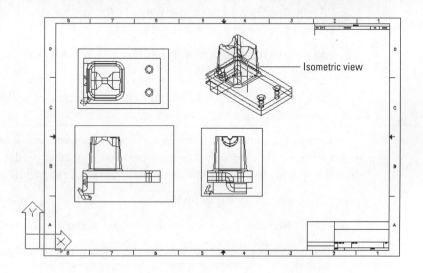

There were a lot of steps involved in creating these views. However, imagine the work involved if you had to create these views manually, and you'll appreciate the power of these few simple tools.

Creating Hidden-Line Views

We aren't quite finished yet. Typically, orthographic projections, such as the top, front, and right-side view, will show the hidden portions of the model with dashed lines. For example, the holes toward the right end of the bracket would be shown dashed in the front view. You could set up the viewports to do a hidden-line removal at plot time, but this would not create the effect you want.

Fortunately, AutoCAD offers the Setup Profile tool to quickly generate a proper Orthographic Projection view of your solid model. Take the following steps to create your first Hidden-Line view.

1. First go to floating Model Space by choosing View ➣ Model Space (Floating).

2. Click on the lower-left viewport.

3. Choose Setup Profile from the Solids toolbar, or choose Draw ➣ Solids ➣ Setup ➣ Profile.

4. Click on both halves of the solid model, and then press ↲.

5. At the `Display hidden profile lines on separate layer?` <Y> prompt, press ↲.

6. At the `Project profile lines onto a plane?` <Y> prompt, press ↲.

7. At the `Delete tangential edges?` <Y> prompt, press ↲. AutoCAD will work for a moment, and then the command prompt will appear with no apparent change to the drawing.

You don't see the effects of the Setup Profile tool yet. You'll need to make the solid model invisible to display the work that was done by the Setup Profile tool. You'll also have to make a few layer changes to get the profile views just right.

1. Choose View ➣ Paper Space.

2. Zoom into the front view so it fills most of the display area.

3. Turn off layer 0 (zero). If it is the current layer, you will get a message telling you that you are about to turn off the current layer. Go ahead and click OK.

You've just turned off the layer of the solid model leaving the profile created by the Setup Profile tool. Notice that you only see an image of the front view.

4. Open the Layer & Linetype tool (click on the Layers tool in the Object Properties toolbar or choose Format ➢ Layer from the menu bar).

5. Select the layer whose name begins with the "PH" prefix.

6. Change its line type to Hidden. You may need to load the hidden-line type.

7. Once you've changed the line type, click OK to exit the Layer & Linetype Properties dialog box. The front view now displays hidden lines properly with dashed lines, as shown in Figure 18.32.

FIGURE 18.32:

The front view after using the Setup Profile tool

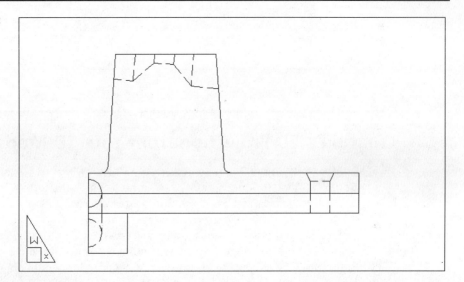

The Setup Profile tool creates a 2D drawing of your 3D model. This 2D drawing is projected onto an imaginary plane that is parallel to the view from which you selected the model while using the Setup Profile tool. To see this clearly, take a look at your model in Model Space.

1. Choose View ➢ Model Space (Tiled).

2. Turn layer 0 back on. You see the projected 2D view next to the 3D model, as shown in Figure 18.33.

FIGURE 18.33:

The projected view next to the 3D solid model

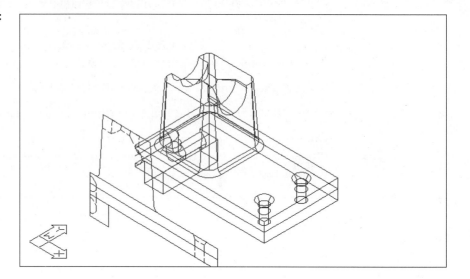

Creating a 2D Projection from Your 3D Model

Another tool on the Solids toolbar creates 2D drawings of 3D solid models. The *Setup Drawing* tool does nearly the same thing as the Setup Profile tool, with some differences. First of all, the Setup Drawing tool only works with viewports that are created by the Setup View tool. It automatically turns off the layer on which the solid model resides. So once it has created a 2D view, you can see the results without having to adjust layer settings. Also, unlike the Setup Profile tool, Setup Drawing leaves the 2D drawing objects as individual objects ready to be edited, instead of turning them into blocks.

Finally, the Setup Drawing tool creates layers whose names offer a better description of their purpose. For example, if you use Setup Drawing to create a 2D drawing of the right-side view, you will get layers entitled Rightside-dim, Rightside-hid, and Rightside-vis. These layer names are derived from the View name from which the 2D drawing is derived. Setup Drawing adds the -dim, -hid, and -vis suffixes to the view name to create the layer name. These suffixes are abbreviations for dimension, hidden, and visible.

Adding Dimensions and Notes in Paper Space

Though I don't recommend adding dimensions in Paper Space for architectural drawings, it may be a good idea for mechanical drawings like the one in this chapter. By maintaining the dimensions and notes separate from the actual model, you keep these elements from getting in the way of your work on the solid model. You also avoid the confusion of having to scale the text and dimension features properly to ensure that they will plot at the correct size.

NOTE See Chapters 8 and 9 for a more detailed discussion of notes and dimensions.

As long as you set up your Paper Space work area to be equivalent to the final plot size, you can set dimension and text to the sizes you want at plot time. If you want text 1/4" high, you set your text styles to be 1/4" high.

To dimension, just make sure you are in Paper Space (View ➤ Paper Space), and then use the Dimension commands in the normal way. However, there is one thing you do have to be careful of: If your Paper Space viewports are set to a scale other than 1 to 1, you must set the Annotation Units option in the Dimension Style dialog box to a proper value. The following steps show you how.

1. Choose Dimension ➤ Styles.

2. At the Dimension Styles dialog box, make sure you have selected the style you want to use, and click on Annotation.

3. In the Annotation dialog box, click on the Units button.

4. In the Scale input box, enter the value by which you want your Paper Space dimensions multiplied. For example, if your Paper Space views are scaled at one-half the actual size of your model, you would enter **2** in this box to multiply your dimensions' values by 2.

TIP To make sure the value you need in step 4 is correct, just determine what scale factor you would need for your Paper Space drawing to get its actual size; that's the value you need to enter.

5. Once you have entered a scale value, make sure the Paper Space Only checkbox is checked. This ensures that your dimension is scaled only while you are adding dimensions in Paper Space. Dimensions added in Model Space are not affected.

You've had to complete a lot of steps to get the final drawing you have now, but, compared to having to draw these views by hand, you have undoubtedly saved a great deal of time. In addition, as you will see later in this chapter, what you have is more than just a 2D drafted image. With what you have created, further refinements are now quite easy.

Drawing a Cross Section

One element of your drawing that is missing is a cross section. AutoCAD will draw a cross section through any part of the solid model. In the following exercise, you will draw such a cross section.

1. First, save your drawing so you can return to this stage (in case you don't want to save the results of the following steps).

2. Choose Tools ➤ UCS ➤ World.

3. Click on the Section tool on the Solids toolbar.

4. At the `Select object` prompt, click on both halves of the solid model and press ↵.

5. At the next prompt:

   `Section plane by Object/Last/Zaxis/View/XY/tZ/ZX/<3points>`

   enter **ZX** ↵. This tells AutoCAD you want to cut the solid in the plane defined by the x- and z-axes.

6. At the `Point on ZX plane` prompt, pick the midpoint of the top-right surface of the solid (see the top image of Figure 18.34). The section cut appears as shown in the bottom image of Figure 18.34.

FIGURE 18.34:

Selecting the point on the z-x plane to define the section-cut outline

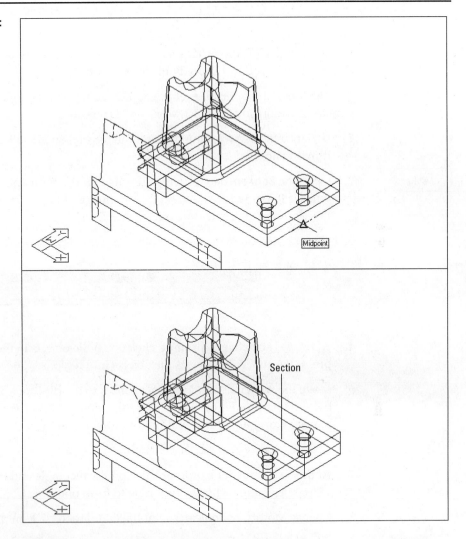

FIGURE 18.34:

Selecting the point on the z-x plane to define the section-cut outline

The section shown in the bottom image of Figure 18.34 is a type of object called a *region*. In the next section, you'll learn how regions share some characteristics with 3D Solids.

Using 3D Solid Operations on 2D Drawings

You can apply of some of the features described in this chapter to 2D drafting by taking advantage of AutoCAD's *region* object. Regions are two-dimensional objects to which you can apply Boolean operations.

Try the following optional exercise, which demonstrates how two Boolean operations, Union and Subtract, work on 2D objects.

1. If you have been working through the tutorial on 3D solids, save the Bracket drawing now.

2. Open the Region.dwg drawing supplied on the companion CD-ROM. You will see the drawing shown in the top image of Figure 18.35. The objects in this drawing are circles and closed polylines.

3. Click on Region in the Draw toolbar, or type **Reg** ↵.

4. At the Select object prompt, click on all the objects in the drawing and press ↵. AutoCAD converts the objects into regions.

5. Move the two circles and the hexagons into the positions illustrated in the bottom image of Figure 18.35. (For this demonstration exercise, you don't have to worry about matching the positions exactly.)

6. Choose Modify ➢ Boolean ➢ Union.

7. At the Select object prompt, click on the rectangle and the two circles. The circles merge with the rectangle to form one object.

8. Choose Modify ➢ Boolean ➢ Subtract, and then click on the newly created region and press ↵.

9. At the next Select object prompt, click on the two hexagons. Now you have a single, 2D solid object in the shape of a wrench, as shown in the continued image of Figure 18.35.

You can use regions to generate complex surfaces that might include holes or unusual bends (see Figure 18.36). Two things to keep in mind:

- Regions act like surfaces; when you remove hidden lines, objects behind the regions are hidden.

- You can explode regions to edit them. (You can't do this with solids.) However, exploding a region causes the region to lose its surfacelike quality, and objects will no longer hide behind its surface(s).

FIGURE 18.35:

Working with regions in the Region.dwg file

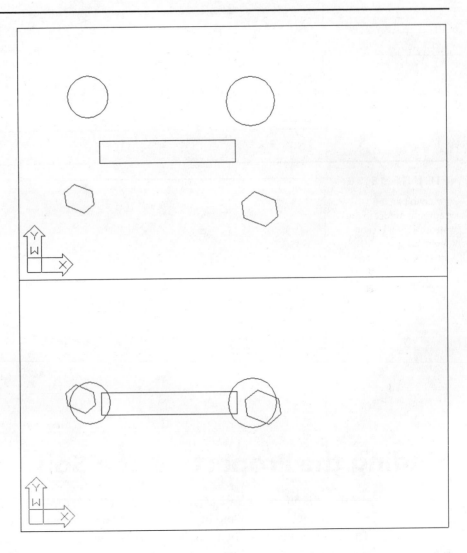

**FIGURE 18.35:
CONTINUED**

Working with regions
in the Region.dwg file

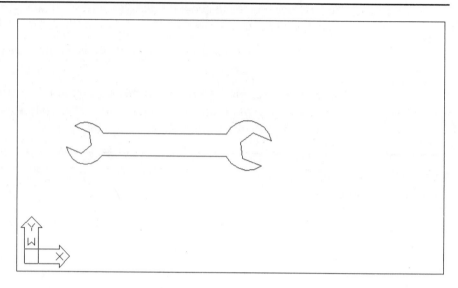

FIGURE 18.36:

You can use the
regional model to cre-
ate complex 2D sur-
faces for use in 3D
surface modeling.

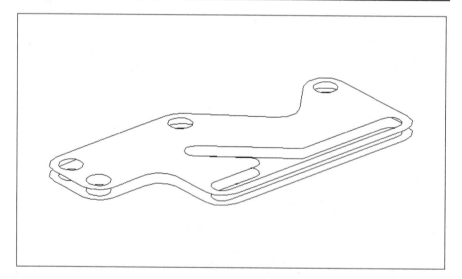

Finding the Properties of a Solid

All of this effort to create a solid model isn't just to create a pretty picture. Once
your model is drawn and built, you can obtain information about its physical
properties. In this section, you will look at a few of the commands that let you
gather such information.

Finding a Model's Mass Properties

You can find the volume, moment of inertia, and other physical properties of your model by using the Massprop command. These properties can also be recorded as a file on disk so you can modify your model without worrying about losing track of its original properties.

1. Open the Bracket drawing you worked on through most of this chapter.

2. Click and drag on the Distance tool on the Standard toolbar. Select Mass Properties on the flyout, or enter **Massprop** ↵.

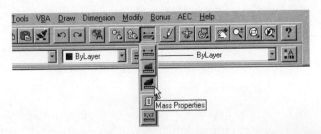

3. At the Select object prompt, select the two halves of the solid model. AutoCAD will calculate for a moment, and then it will display a list of the object's properties, as shown in Figure 18.37.

FIGURE 18.37:

The Mass Properties listing derived from the solid model

```
AutoCAD Text Window                                    _□X
Edit
Command: MASSPROP
Select objects: 1 found

 elect objects: |
──────────────────   SOLIDS   ──────────────────

Mass:                   35.1657
Volume:                 35.1657
Bounding box:       X: 2.9990  --  10.0000
                    Y: 2.5000  --  6.5000
                    Z: 0.4990  --  4.0000
Centroid:           X: 5.5725
                    Y: 4.5055
                    Z: 1.7242
Moments of inertia: X: 886.9826
                    Y: 1318.5188
                    Z: 1924.6475
Products of inertia: XY: 882.4382
                     YZ: 272.9676
                     ZX: 317.4906
Radii of gyration:  X: 5.0222
                    Y: 6.1233
                    Z: 7.3980
Press ENTER to continue:
Principal moments and X-Y-Z directions about centroid:
                    I: 61.3669 along [0.9424 -0.0061 -0.3344]
                    J: 121.9476 along [-0.0229 0.9963 -0.0826]
                    K: 126.0628 along [0.3337 0.0855 0.9388]

Write to a file ? <N>:
Command: |
```

Taking Advantage of Stereolithography

A discussion of solid modeling wouldn't be complete without mentioning *Stereolithography*. This is one of the more interesting technological wonders that has appeared as a byproduct of 3D computer modeling. Stereolithography is a process that generates resin reproductions of 3D computer solid models. It offers the mechanical designer a method of rapidly prototyping designs directly from AutoCAD drawings. The process requires special equipment that will read computer files in a particular format.

AutoCAD supports stereolithography through the Stlout command. This command generates an .stl file, which can be used with *Stereolithograph Apparatus* (*STA*) to generate a model. You must first create a 3D solid model in AutoCAD; then you can proceed with the following steps to create the .stl file.

1. Choose File ➤ Export.

2. At the Export Data dialog box, open the Save as Type drop-down list and select Lithography (*.stl). Click on the Save button.

> **TIP**   You can also type **Stlout** ↵ at the command prompt to bypass steps 1 and 2.

3. At the `Select a single object for STL output` prompt, select a solid or a set of solids, and press ↵. All solids must reside in the positive x, y, and z coordinates of the world coordinate system.

The AutoCAD 3D solids are translated into a set of triangular-faceted meshes in the .stl file. You can use the Facetres system variable to control the fineness of these meshes. See Chapter 17 for more information on Facetres.

If You Want to Experiment...

This chapter has focused on a mechanical project, but you can, of course, use solids to help simplify the construction of 3D architectural forms. If your interest lies in architecture, try drawing the window in Figure 18.38. (Imagine trying to create this window without the solid-modeling capabilities of AutoCAD!)

FIGURE 18.38:

Drawing a window

Using a closed polyline, draw the outline of a window that is 24" wide by 36" high.

Offset the outline by 3.5" toward its center.

Draw several closed polyline rectangles 1" wide to represent the window mullions.

Use the Vpoint command to change your view to one similar to this one.

Use the Extrude command to turn the polylines into solids. Use the thicknesses shown in the drawing to the right.

Use the Subtract command to subtract the inside outline of the frame from the outside.

Use the Union command to join all the solids into one object.

Issue the hide command to view the end product.

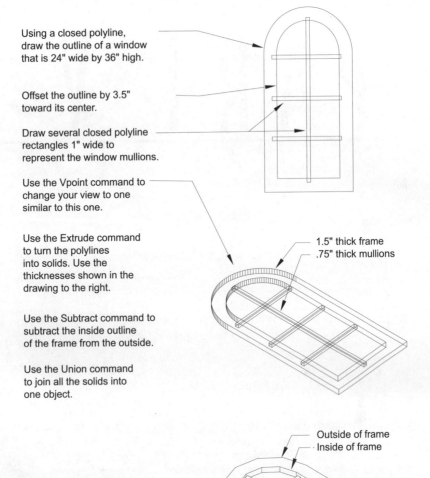

1.5" thick frame
.75" thick mullions

Outside of frame
Inside of frame

PART V

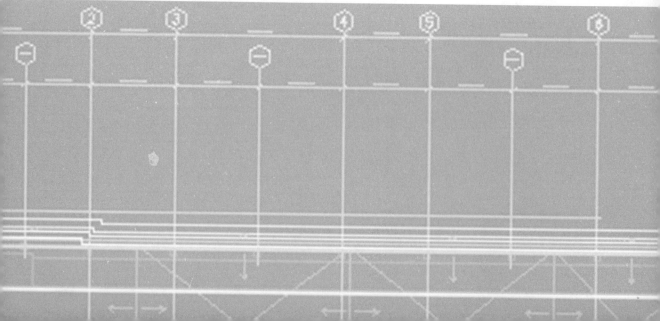

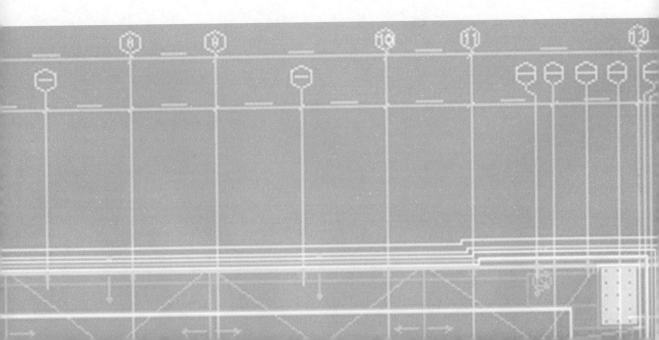

Customization: Taking AutoCAD to the Limit

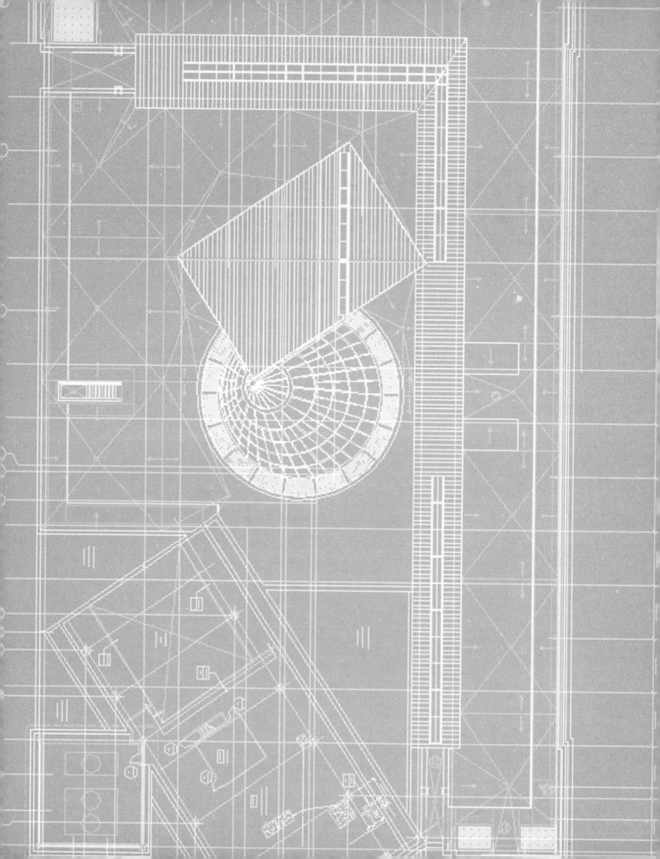

Introduction to Customization

- Enhancements Straight from the Source

- Utilities Available from Other Sources

- Putting AutoLISP to Work

- Loading AutoLISP Programs Automatically

- Creating Keyboard Macros with AutoLISP

- Using Third-Party Software

- Getting the Latest Information from Online Services

- Posting and Accessing Drawings on the Web

AutoCAD offers a wealth of features that you can use to improve your productivity. But even with these aids to efficiency, there are always situations that can use some further automation. In this chapter, you'll be introduced to the different ways AutoCAD can be customized and enhanced with add-on utilities.

First, you'll discover how the AutoCAD Bonus Tools can help boost your productivity. Many of these utilities were created using the programming tools that are available to anyone, namely AutoLISP and VBA. Next, you'll learn how to load and run AutoLISP utilities that are supplied on this book's companion CD-ROM. By doing so, you'll be prepared to take advantage of the many utilities available from user groups and online services. Finally, you'll finish the chapter by taking a look at how third-party applications and the Internet can enhance AutoCAD's role in your workplace.

Enhancements Straight from the Source

If you've followed the tutorial in this book, you've already used a few add-on programs that come with AutoCAD, perhaps without even being aware that they were not part of the core AutoCAD program. In this section we'll introduce you to the AutoCAD Bonus Tools: a set of AutoLISP, ARX, and VBA tools that showcase these powerful customization environments. The best part about the Bonus Tools is that you don't have to know a thing about programming to take advantage of them.

There are so many of these bonus tools that I can't provide step-by-step instructions on all of them. Instead, we will offer a detailed look at some of the more complicated tools and provide shorter descriptions for others. We'll start with the Bonus Layer Tools.

Loading the Bonus Tools

If you installed AutoCAD using the Typical Installation option, you may not have installed the AutoCAD Bonus Tools yet. Fortunately, you can install these utilities separately without having to reinstall the entire program.

Proceed as if you are installing AutoCAD for the first time. When you see the Setup Choices dialog box, choose the Add button to add new components to the current system. You will see an item called Bonus in the Custom Components dialog box that appears next. Place a check in the Bonus checkbox, and then proceed with the installation. When Setup is finished, open AutoCAD and load the Bonus menu. See Chapter 21 for more detailed information on loading menus.

Tools for Managing Layers

In a recent survey of AutoCAD users, Autodesk discovered that one of the most frequently used features in AutoCAD was the Layer command. As a result, the layer controls in Release 14 have been greatly improved. Still, there is room for some improvement. The Bonus Layer Tools offer some shortcuts to controlling layer settings as well as one major layer enhancement called the Layer Manager.

TIP All of the bonus tools discussed in this section have keyboard command equivalents. Check the status bar when selecting these tools from the toolbar or pull-down menu for the keyboard command name.

Saving and Recalling Layer Settings

The Layer Manager lets you save layer settings. This can be crucial when you are editing a file that serves multiple uses, such as a floor plan and reflected ceiling plan. You can, for example, turn layers on and off to set up the drawing for a reflected ceiling Plan view, and then save the layer settings. Later, when you need to modify the ceiling information, you can recall the layer setting to view the ceiling data. The following steps show you how the Layer Manager works.

1. In AutoCAD, open the `14a-unit.dwg` file. Open the Layer & Linetype Properties dialog box and turn on all the layers except the Notes and Flr-pat layer. Your drawing should look similar to the top image of Figure 19.1.

2. Click on the Layer Manager tool in the Bonus Layer.

The Layer Manager dialog box appears.

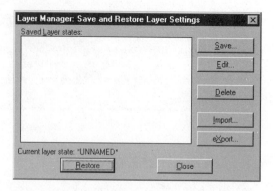

3. Click on the Save button. The Layer State Name dialog box appears.

4. Enter **blank floor plan,** and then click OK. You return to the Layer Manager dialog box. Notice that the name you entered for the layer state appears in the list box.

5. Click on the Close button.

6. Now open the Layer & Linetype Properties dialog box again and turn on the flr-pat and notes layer and turn off the ceiling layer. Your drawing will look like the bottom image of Figure 19.1.

7. Click on the Layer Manager tool again.

8. Click on BLANK FLOOR PLAN from the list, and then click Restore.

9. Click Close. Your drawing reverts to the previous view with the notes and flr-pat layers turned off and the ceiling layer on.

The layer states are saved with the file so you can retrieve them at a later date. As you can see from the Layer Manager dialog box, you have a few other options. Here is a listing of those options and what they do:

Edit... opens the Layer & Linetype Properties dialog box to let you edit the settings for a layer state. Highlight the layer state from the list, and then choose Edit....

Delete deletes a layer state from the list.

Import imports a set of layer states that have been exported using the Export option of this dialog box.

Export saves a set of layer states as a file. By default, the file is given the name of the current file with the .lay file name extension. You can import the layer state file into other files.

FIGURE 19.1:

The view of the
Unit.dwg file before
and after changing
layer settings

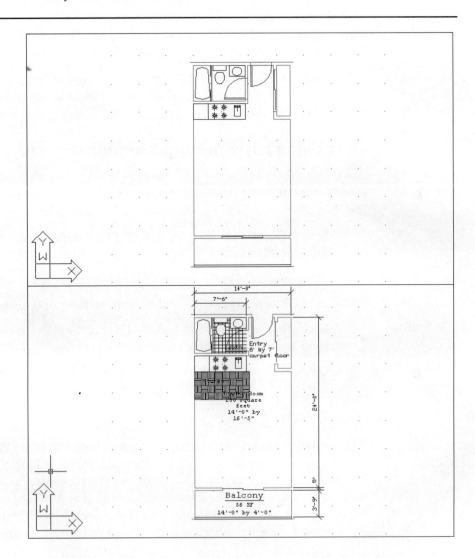

Changing the Layer Assignment of Objects

In addition to the Layer Manager, the Bonus Layer toolbar offers two tools that change the layer assignments of objects. The Match Objects Layer tool is similar to the Match Properties tool, but is streamlined to just operate on layer assignments. After clicking on this tool, you first select the object or objects you wish to change, and then you select an object whose layer you wish to match.

The Change to Current Layer tool changes an object's layer assignment to the current layer. This tool has long existed as an AutoLISP utility and you'll find that you'll get a lot of use from it.

Controlling Layer Settings through Objects

The remaining set of Bonus Layer tools lets you make layer settings by selecting objects in the drawing. The tools in this set are simple to use: just click on the tool, and then select an object. The following list describes what each tool does.

Isolate Objects Layer will turn off all the layers except for the layer of the selected object.

Freeze object Layer will freeze the layer of the selected object.

Turn Objects Layer Off will turn off the layer of the selected object.

Lock Objects Layer will lock the layer of the selected object. A locked layer is one that is visible but cannot be edited.

Unlock Object Layer will unlock the layer of the selected object.

Tools for Editing Text

It seems that we can never have enough text editing features. Even the realm of word processors contains a seemingly innumerable set of tools for setting fonts, paragraphs, tabs, and tables. Some programs even check our grammar. While we're not trying to write the great American novel in AutoCAD, we are interested in getting our text in the right location, at the right size, with some degree of style. This often means using a mixture of text and graphics editing tools.

Release 14 has brought us some great improvements in text handling through an improved text editor. Here are some additional tools that will help ease your way through some otherwise difficult editing tasks.

Masking Text Backgrounds

One problem AutoCAD users frequently face is how to get text to read clearly when it is placed over a hatch pattern or other graphic. The Hatch command will hatch around existing text leaving a clear space behind it. But what about those situations where you must add text *after* a hatch pattern has been created? Or what about those instances where you need to mask behind text that is placed over non-hatch object, such as dimension leaders or raster images?

The Text Mask tool addresses this problem by masking the area behind text with a special masking object called a Wipeout. Try the following exercise on the 14a-unit.dwg file to see firsthand how it works.

1. In the Unit file, make sure the Flr-pat and Notes layer are turned on.

2. Adjust your view so you see the kitchen area as it appears in the top image of Figure 19.2. Notice that the Kitchen label is obscured by the floor's hatch pattern.

3. Choose Text Mask from the Bonus Text Tools toolbar.

You'll see the following message:

```
Initializing...
Loading WIPEOUT for use with TEXTMASK...
Enter offset factor relative to text height <0.35>:
```

4. Here you can enter the amount of space you want around the text as a percentage of the text height. Press ↵ to accept the default.

5. At the Select Text to MASK... prompt, use a window to select the Kitchen text and click on the Living Room text. When you're done selecting text, press ↵. You'll see the message Wipeout created for each object selected, and the text will appear on a clear background, as shown in the bottom image of Figure 19.2.

FIGURE 19.2:

Creating a mask behind text

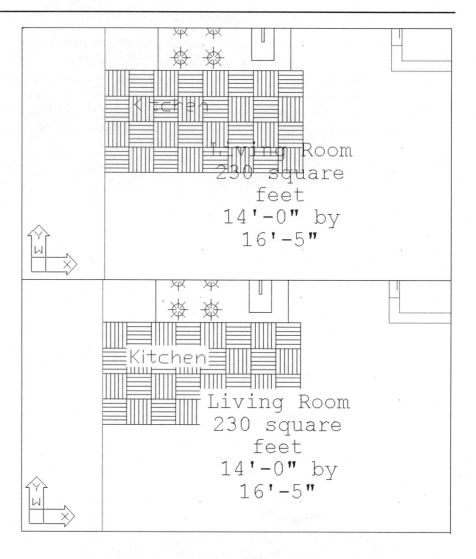

Text Mask creates an object called a Wipeout that masks other objects behind the text. Wipeout is not a standard AutoCAD object; it is a new object created through AutoCAD's programming interface.

The Wipeout object has its own little quirks that you will want to know about. To get a bit more familiar with Wipeout objects, try the following exercise.

1. Click on the Kitchen text. Notice that both the text and the Wipeout object are selected.

2. Click on Move from the Modify toolbar.

3. Move the text and Wipeout object to the right about 12 inches. The text seems to disappear.

4. Type **Re** ↵ to issue a Regen. The text appears once again.

   The text and Wipeout objects are linked so that if you select the text, you automatically select the Wipeout object. Also, the display order of the two objects gets mixed up when you move them so you need to issue a Regen to restore the text's visibility. You can also edit or erase the Wipeout object. There is a description on how to edit Wipeout objects in the *Bonus Standard Tools* section later in this chapter.

Next, you'll look at ways to globally change text objects.

Making Global Changes to Text Objects

Technical drawings often contain repetitive text containing much of the same information. Frequently, an AutoCAD user will create one text object and copy it several times, saving the time it takes to type the text in multiple times. This is a great method for adding text to a drawing, but it also tends to multiply mistakes. Here are two tools that will help you make changes to multiple sets of text objects with a minimum amount of pain.

Changing Multiple Text Items

The Change Multiple Text Items tool lets you change the height, justification, rotation angle, style, and width of a selected set of text. You can also change the text itself if you need to. It's fairly straightforward to use—the following steps will show you how.

1. Click on Change Multiple Text Items from the Bonus Text Tools toolbar.

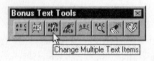

2. Select the text you want to edit, and then press ↵. You will then see this prompt:

   ```
   Height/Justification/Location/Rotation/Style/Text/Undo/Width:
   ```

3. Type in the letter of the option you want, and then proceed to answer the prompts that follow. For example, if you enter **H** ↵ at the prompt, AutoCAD will ask you for a new text height.

4. After entering a new height value, the selected text will change to the new height and the Height/Justification/Location prompt will return, allowing you to make further changes.

NOTE It you've used the Text Mask tool on the text you are changing, the masking Wipeout object will not be affected. See the *Wipeout* section later in this chapter for information on editing Wipeout objects.

The following is a description of each of the options offered by the Change Multiple Text Items tool:

Height lets you change the height of selected text either individually or all at once.

Justification lets you change the justification of the text.

Location lets you move individual text objects to a new location.

Rotation lets you change the rotation angle of the selected text. You can rotate all the text to the same angle or set the text angle individually.

Style lets you assign a new text style to the selected text. You can change the style for all the selected text at once or individually.

Text lets you perform a search and replace on the selected text, or replace each text with new text individually.

Undo will undo the last option you used.

Width lets you change the width factor of the selected text, either all at once or one at a time.

Finding and Replacing Text The Find and Replace Text tool does just what its name says. It locates a particular string of text that you specify and replaces it with another string. Unfortunately, it only works for single-line text objects.

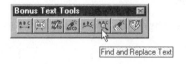

When you click on the Find and Replace Text tool, you are presented with the Find and Replace dialog box.

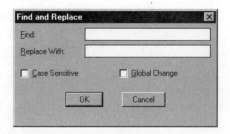

After you've entered a Find and Replace With value, and clicked OK, you are prompted to select objects. You can select any set of single-line text object. Once you make your selection, and if AutoCAD finds the text you specified, you see the second Find and Replace dialog box.

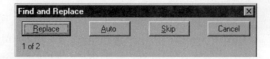

Along with this dialog box, you will see one of the selected text objects highlighted. You can click on any of the options presented in this dialog box to replace the highlighted text, proceed to replace all the text (Auto), skip the highlighted text and move on to the next one, or cancel the Find and Replace tool altogether. If you know you want to replace all the selected text, you can click on the Global Change checkbox in the first dialog box and forego the second dialog box.

Other Bonus Text Tools

We've shown you three of the main text editing tools in the Bonus Text Tools toolbar. There are several more that you may find useful. By now, you should feel comfortable in exploring these tools on your own. The following is a brief description to get you started:

Global Attribute Edit simplifies the global editing of Attribute text.

Text Fit lets you visually stretch or compress text to fit within a given width.

Arc Aligned Text creates text that follows the curve of an arc. If the arc is stretched or changed, the text follows the arc's shape. This is one of the more interesting bonus text tools offering a wide range of settings presented in a neat little dialog box.

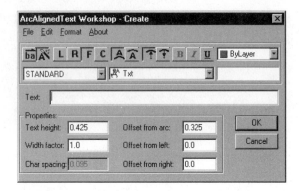

Explode Attributes to Text   explodes blocks containing attributes so that the attribute values are converted into plain single-line text.

Explode Text   converts the individual characters in a text object into polylines. Beware! This tool can take some time while it works.

TIP   If you want text to follow a curved path, take a look at the `Txtpath.lsp` utility from the companion CD-ROM. It draws text on a spline curve to follow virtually any contour you want. (See Appendix C.)

Bonus Standard Tools

The Bonus Standard toolbar seems to be the answer to most AutoCAD users' wish lists. As with many of the bonus tools discussed so far, these tools have been floating around in the AutoCAD user community as AutoLISP utilities. However, some are completely new. We'll start with a look at one tool that has been on my wish list for quite some time.

Wipeout

In Chapter 6 we described two methods for masking hatch patterns behind graphics in a space planning example. A third method is to use the Wipeout tool. Wipeout creates an object called Wipeout, which acts like a mask. If you read the previous section on the Text Mask tool, you've gotten a glimpse at how Wipeout works because the Text Mask tool uses the Wipeout object. The following exercise demonstrates how to use this tool in another application.

Imagine that you've set up a Paper Space layout showing an enlarged view of one of the units of the studio apartment building from this book. You want to show dimensions and notes around the unit, but there are too many other objects in the way. The Wipeout tool can be of great help in this situation. Here's how.

1. Open the 19wipe.dwg file. This is one of the sample files from the companion CD-ROM. When you open this file you will be in Paper Space.

2. While still in Paper Space, zoom in to the typical Unit plan so your view looks similar to Figure 19.3.

3. Create a layer called Wipeout and make it current.

4. Switch to Floating Model Space by choosing View ➤ Model Space (Floating), or by double-clicking on the "PAPER" label in the status bar.

5. Draw the closed polyline shown in Figure 19.3. You don't have to be exact about the shape; you can adjust it later.

6. Click on Wipeout from the Bonus Standard toolbar.

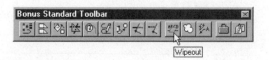

7. At the Wipeout Frame/New <New> prompt, press ↵ to accept the default New option.

8. At the Select a polyline prompt, select the polyline you just drew.

9. At the Erase polyline? Yes/No <No> prompt, enter **Y** ↵ to erase the polyline. The area enclosed by the polyline will be masked out.

FIGURE 19.3:

Adding a polyline to
the enlarged Unit plan

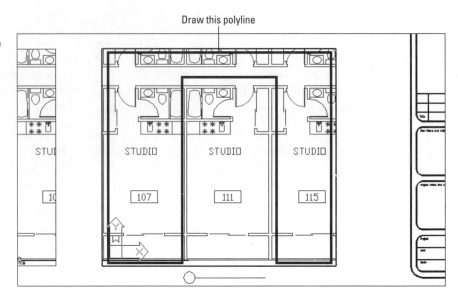

The Wipeout object has a border that can be turned on and off. When visible, you can click on the Wipeout border and use its corner grips to re-shape the area that it covers. You can also erase, move, or copy the Wipeout object using its border. In the example of the Unit plan, you will want to hide the Wipeout border. Take the following steps to turn off the Wipeout border's visibility.

1. Click on the Wipeout button in the Bonus Standard toolbar.

2. At the Frame/New <New> prompt, type **F** ↵.

3. At the OFF/ON <ON> prompt, type **OFF** ↵. The frame disappears.

When the frame is off, you cannot edit the Wipeout object. Of course, you can turn it back on using the Frame option you used in step 2 of the previous exercise. By the way, if you need to edit the Text Mask tool described earlier in this chapter, you use the Frame option presented in the above exercise to turn on the Text Mask border.

With the Wipeout object in place and its border turned off, you can add dimension and notes around the image without having the adjoining graphics interfere with the visibility of your notes. Figure 19.4 shows the Unit plan with the dimensions inserted from the individual Unit plan file.

FIGURE 19.4:

The Unit plan with dimensions added and the viewport border adjusted to hide the graphics beyond the Wipeout object

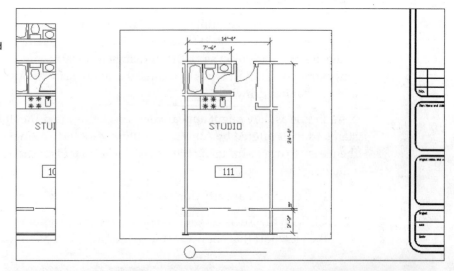

There is one more point I should address here. If you switch to Paper Space and zoom out to view the entire Paper Space drawing, you'll notice that the Wipeout object appears in the overall plan at the top of the screen (see Figure 19.5). Fortunately, you can freeze the Wipeout layer in the viewport with the Overall view to hide the Wipeout object.

FIGURE 19.5:

The Wipeout object as it appears in the overall Plan view

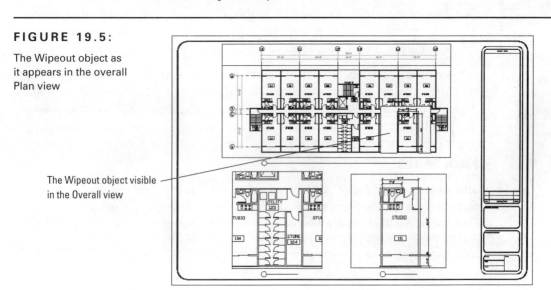

The Wipeout object visible in the Overall view

Revision Cloud

A revision cloud is a cloudlike outline drawn around parts of a drawing that have been revised. They are used to alert the viewer to any changes that have occurred in the design of a project since the drawings were last issued. Revision clouds are fairly common in most types of technical drawings, including architectural, civil, and mechanical drawings.

As simple as they might appear, revision clouds are difficult to draw using the standard tools offered by AutoCAD. But now we have a single tool that makes them easy to draw. Try using the Revision Cloud tool on the 19wipe.dwg file by following these steps.

1. If you haven't already done so, switch your drawing to Paper Space.

2. Click on the Revision Cloud tool. Then click on a point near the right side of the viewport that shows a view of the Unit plan, as shown in Figure 19.6.

3. Move the cursor in a counterclockwise direction to encircle the Unit plan view. As you move the cursor, the cloud is drawn.

4. Bring the cursor full circle back to the point from which you started. When you approach the beginning of the cloud, the revision cloud closes and you exit the Revision Cloud tool.

If you need to change the size of the arcs in the revision cloud, you can do so in step 2 by entering **A** ↵. You can then enter an arc length. Also note that you must draw the cloud in a counterclockwise direction, otherwise the arcs of the cloud will point in the wrong direction.

Pack 'n Go

The Xref feature of AutoCAD has helped streamline the production of large architectural projects. The San Francisco Main Library project, in particular, benefited from Xrefs. But Xrefs also introduce one major problem. When it comes time to send the AutoCAD files to other consultants, you have to figure out which files are external references for other files. In a large project, management of Xrefs can become a major headache.

FIGURE 19.6:

Drawing a Revision cloud

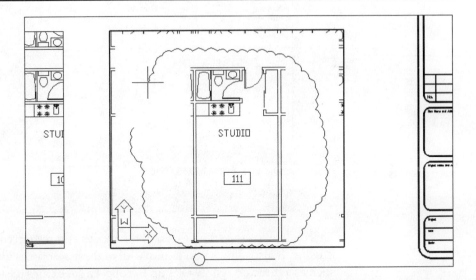

The Pack 'n Go utility is designed to help you manage Xrefs, as well as most other external resources that an AutoCAD drawing may depend on, such as line-type definitions and text fonts. Here's how it works.

1. Click on the Pack 'n Go tool in the Bonus Standard toolbar.

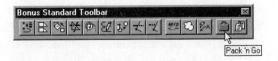

The Pack & Go dialog box appears.

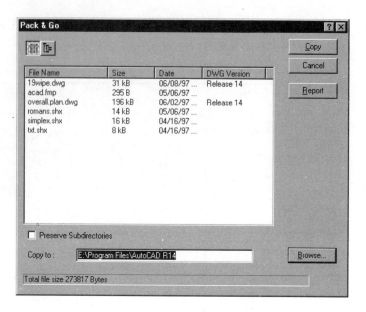

This dialog box shows all external references and resources the current file is using. It also allows you to move all of these resources into one location, such as a directory you've set up to collect a set of files to send to a client or consultant.

2. To choose a location for the copies of your files, click on the Browse button in the lower-right corner of the dialog box. A Browse for Folder dialog box lets you locate and select a folder in which to place your copies.

3. Click Copy to copy all the drawing files and resources to the selected directory.

In addition to the files and resources, Pack 'n Go generates three script files designed to convert the drawing files into any format from Release 12 to Release 14. (See Chapter 15 for more on Script files.)

Another helpful feature of the Pack 'n Go tool is the Report generator. If you click on the Report button in the Pack 'n Go dialog box, a Report dialog box opens providing a written description of the current file and it resources.

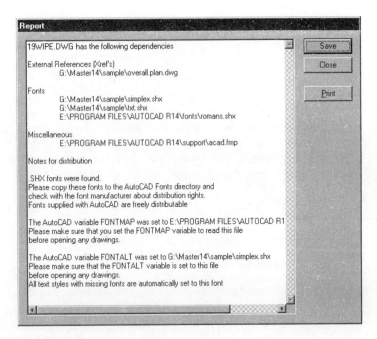

You can save this report as a text file by clicking on the Save button. Such a report can be used as a readme file when sending drawings to clients or consultants.

Using Add-On Utilities on the San Francisco Main Library Project

While the San Francisco Main Library project was a successful use of AutoCAD, it had its ups and downs. Perhaps one of the biggest problems occurred when a large number of AutoCAD drawings had to be transferred between the architects, SMWM, and the CAD specialists, who were producing the drawings, Technical Publications.

As we mentioned in previous chapters, the San Francisco Main Library project made extensive use of the Xref feature in AutoCAD. Xrefs were a great time saver overall, but frequently, the links between the Xref source files and their receiving files were lost when they were transferred from the architect to the CAD specialist. This was the result of the architect and CAD specialist having their own, separate directory structures for the CAD drawings, which tended to confuse Auto-CAD. Extra time was spent reestablishing links between drawings and their Xrefs.

Continued on next page

Had there been a tool like the Pack 'n Go utility, the Xref problems would not have occurred and the project would have gone much more smoothly. Pack 'n Go would have also helped in managing the many different text fonts used on the project.

But despite the minor glitches, the application of AutoCAD in the San Francisco Main Library project was quite successful, due in part to Technical Publications' extensive use of other add-on utilities available at the time. Many of those same utilities can be found in the On-Screen AEC add-on available on the companion CD-ROM, some of which are even duplicated in the Bonus Tools described in this chapter.

Extended Change Properties

When you use the Properties tool with multiple objects, you see a dialog box that lists the properties common to all objects: color, layer, line type, and thickness. At times, this limited range of property options seems restrictive. Now, Release 14 offers the Extended Change Properties tool, which adds a few more properties to those found in the standard Properties dialog box.

When you click on the Extended Change Properties tool and select several objects, you see a slightly different version of the Change Properties dialog box.

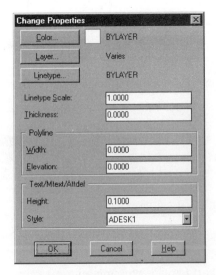

This dialog box offers a few extra options that relate to polylines and text. If you happened to have include either polyines or text in the selection set, you can enter a value to set the width and elevation of polylines or the height and style of text.

Multiple Pedit

If you only want to change the properties of polylines, you may want to use the Multiple Pedit tool.

This tool works exactly like the standard Pedit command (found by choosing Modify ➤ Object ➤ Polyline) with two exceptions: it does not offer the Edit Vertex option and you are not limited to a single polyline. This means that you can select multiple polylines to change their width, curvature, or open/close status. Multiple Pedit also lets you easily convert multiple lines and arcs into polylines.

Perhaps one of the most common uses for this tool is to change the width of a set of lines, arcs, and polylines. If you include lines and arcs in a selection set with this tool, they will be converted into polylines and the specified width will be applied.

Multiple Entity Stretch

The Stretch command has always been limited by the fact that you can only select one set of vertices. The Multiple Entity Stretch tool removes that limitation and makes stretching multiple objects a simpler task. Here's how it works.

1. Click on Multiple Entity Stretch from the Bonus Standard toolbar.

You'll see the following message:

```
Define crossing windows or crossing polygons...
CP(crossing polygon)/<Crossing First point>:
```

2. Start to place crossing windows around the vertices you want to stretch. You may also enter **Cp** ⏎ and proceed to place crossing polygons around the vertices.

3. When you are done selecting vertices, press ⏎.

4. Go ahead and select a base point and second point to move the vertices.

Quick Multiple Trims with Extended Trim

The Extended Trim tool is actually best described by its title in the Bonus pull-down menu: Cookie Cutter Trim. It is capable of trimming a set of objects to a closed shape, such as a circle or closed polyline. You can, for example, use it to cut out a star shape in a crosshatch pattern. You can also trim multiple objects to a line or arc as well. To use it, do the following.

1. Choose Extended Trim from the Bonus Standard toolbar, or select Bonus ➤ Cookie Cutter Trim.

2. Select an object that is to be the trim boundary; that is, the object to which you want to trim.

3. Click on the side of the selected object that you want trimmed.

Extended Trim only allows you to select a single object to trim to, but it trims multiple objects quickly and with fewer clicks of the mouse.

Clipping a Curved Shape with Extended Clip

In Chapters 6 and 11, you saw how you can clip portions of an Xref or raster image so that only a portion of these objects were visible. One limitation to the Xref and Raster clip option is that you can only clip areas defined by straight lines. You cannot, for example, clip an area defined by a circle or ellipse.

Extended Clip is designed for those instances where you absolutely need to clip an Xref, raster image, or block to a curved area. The following steps show you how it works.

1. Create a clip boundary using a curved polyline or circle.

2. Choose Extended Clip from the Bonus Standard toolbar.

3. Click on the boundary.

4. Click on the Xref, block, or image you wish to clip.

5. At the Enter max error distance for resolution of arcs <7/16"> prompt, press ↵. The Xref, block, or image will clip to the selected boundary.

6. You may erase the boundary you created in step 1 or keep it for future reference.

Extended Clip really doesn't clip to the boundary you created, but instead, approximates that boundary by creating a true clip boundary with a series of very short line segments. In fact, the prompt in step 5 lets you specify the maximum allowable distance between the straight line segments it generates and the curve of the boundary you create (see Figure 19.7).

Once you've created a boundary using Extended Clip, you can edit the properties of the boundary using Modify ➣ Object ➣ Clip for Xrefs and blocks, or Modify ➣ Object ➣ Image Clip for raster images.

Extended Clip allows you to set the maximum distance from the your clip boundary and the one it generates.

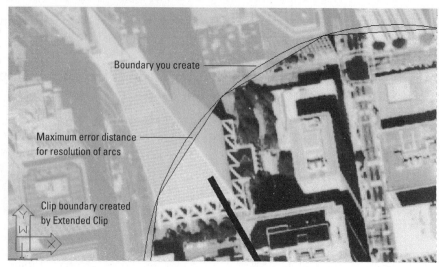

Boundary you create

Maximum error distance for resolution of arcs

Clip boundary created by Extended Clip

Block-Related Tools

Every now and then, you run into a situation where you want to use objects within a block to trim or extend to, or perhaps you may want to copy a part of a block to another part of your drawing. Here are three tools that will let you do these things. They're fairly simple to use, so the following descriptions should be enough to get you started.

Copy Nested Entities   lets you copy single objects within a block. You are only allowed to select objects individually—one click at a time. The copied objects will be placed on the current layer.

Trim to Block Entities   lets you trim to objects in a block. It works just like the standard Trim command with the exception that you must select the objects to trim to individually.

Extend to Block Entities   lets you extend to objects in a block. It also works like its standard counterpart with the exception that you must select the objects you wish to extend to individually.

Miscellaneous Bonus Standard Tools

This last set of tools offers a mixed bag of functions. Try them out at least once. They may fill a need on your wish list.

Quick Leader   draws a leader with text, just like the standard Leader tool in the Dimension toolbar. The main difference is that Quick Leader doesn't ask you as many questions.

Move Copy Rotate   combines these three functions into one tool. It's like a streamlined Grip Edit tool without the grips.

List Xref/Block Entities   will display basic information about an Xref or block.

Tools on the Bonus Pull-Down Menu

All the bonus tools we've discussed so far are available as options in the Bonus pull-down menu. There are some additional options on the pull-down menu you won't see in any of the toolbars. You won't want to miss these additional tools. They can be greatly enhance your productivity on any type of project.

Pop-Up Menu

Pop-up menus are great for providing quick access to frequently used functions. The Popup Menu option in the Bonus pull-down menu lets you turn any pull-down menu into a pop-up menu. So if you find that you use a particular pull-down frequently, give this handy utility a try. Here's how it works.

1. Choose Bonus ➤ Tools ➤ Popup Menu. This places a checkmark next to this option.

2. Now Ctrl + right-click on your mouse. The View menu pops up. You can then select from the View menu as you would if it were open from the menu bar.

3. To select another menu as a pop-up candidate, Alt + click on the right-mouse button. The Pick a Popup Menu dialog box appears.

4. Select the menu you want from the list, and then click OK. From then on, the menu you select will pop up when you Ctrl + click the right-mouse button.

If you don't care for any of the existing pull-down menus, you can create your own pull-down menu, and then turn it into a pop-up menu. See Chapter 21 for more on creating pull-down menus.

Command Alias Editor

Throughout this book, I've been showing you the keyboard shortcuts to the commands of AutoCAD. All of these shortcuts are stored in a file called Acad.pgp in the \Program Files\AutoCAD R14\Support directory. In the past, you had to edit this file with a text editor to modify these command shortcuts (otherwise know as command aliases). But to make our lives simpler, Autodesk has supplied the Command Alias Editor, which automates the process of editing, adding, or removing command aliases from AutoCAD.

In addition, the Command Alias Editor lets you store your own alias definitions in a separate file. You can then recall your file to load your own command aliases. Here's how the Command Alias Editor works.

1. Choose Bonus ➤ Tools ➤ Command Alias Editor…. The AutoCAD Alias Editor dialog box appears.

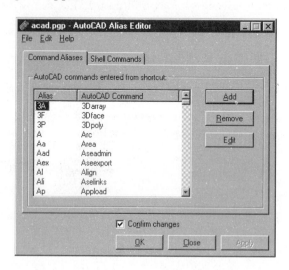

2. As you can see from the button options, you can add a new alias or delete or edit an existing alias. If you click on the Add button, you see the New Command Alias dialog box.

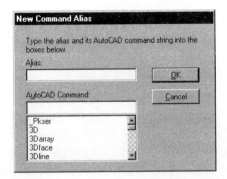

In this dialog box, you enter the desired alias in the Alias input box, and then select the command from the list box below. You can also enter a command or macro name, such as Wipeout, in the input box. When you click on the Edit option in the AutoCAD Alias Editor dialog box, you see a dialog box identical to this one with the input boxes already filled in.

3. When you are done creating or editing an alias, click OK. You return to the AutoCAD Alias Editor dialog box.

4. Click OK to exit the dialog box. You see a warning message.

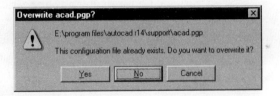

This message is telling you that you are about to overwrite the Acad.pgp file.

5. Click No to leave the Acad.pgp file untouched. You then see the Save As dialog box. You can enter an alternate file name, such as Myalias.pgp, to store your personal set of command aliases.

6. Once you've entered a name and saved your settings, you will see a message telling you that your new settings have taken effect. Click OK to return to AutoCAD.

If you're a veteran AutoCAD user, you may have become accustomed to your own set of command aliases. If so, you may want to leave the original Acad.pgp file alone and create your own .pgp file as I've suggested in step 5. Then, whenever you use AutoCAD, you can open the AutoCAD Alias Editor, and then choose File Open and load your personal .pgp file. From then on, the aliases in your file will supersede those of the standard `Acad.pgp` file.

System Variable Editor

Depending on the type of drawing you are working on, certain AutoCAD settings work better than others. For example, a 3D modeling project may work more smoothly with the Performance settings in the Preferences dialog box set a certain way, while a large 2D plan layout requires an entirely different set of setting. If you find yourself wishing you could store all of AutoCAD's dialog box settings at a given moment in time, then here's the tool for you.

Nearly all of AutoCAD's settings are controlled through system variables. Dialog box options are frequently tied to system variables as well as some command option default settings. The System Variable Editor is a tool that lets you save the current system variable settings to a file for later recall. With this tool, you can save and restore a carefully tuned AutoCAD setup with a few clicks of the mouse, instead of reconstructing individual dialog box or system variable settings. Here's how it works.

1. Choose Bonus ➢ Tools ➢ System Variable Editor…, or type **Sd** ⏎. The System Variable Editor dialog box appears.

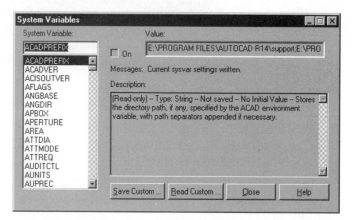

2. You can enter a system variable name or select it from the list box to the left. A description of the system variable is displayed in the Description box.

3. Once you've selected a system variable, you can enter a value for it in the Value input box. An On checkbox is provided for system variables that have

an On/Off state instead of a value. Changes you make to system variables take effect immediately.

4. Finally, the buttons labeled Save Custom… and Read Custom… allow you to save the current state of the system variables to a file. The file will have the .svf file name extension.

If you create a custom .svf file, AutoCAD will automatically save the System Variable settings prior to your changes in .svf file with the name of the current drawing. This is a safety measure in case you've made a terrible blunder in your settings. You can use the Read Custom… button to restore your saved settings. AutoCAD also provides a special .svf file called Defaults.svf in the AutoCAD R14\ Bonus subdirectory. You can open this file from the System Variable Settings dialog box to restore the "factory" default AutoCAD system variable settings.

Dimstyle Export and Dimstyle Import

Most AutoCAD users really only need to set up their dimension styles once, then make minor alteration for drawing scale. You can set up your dimension styles in a template file, then use that template whenever you create new drawings. That way, your dimension styles will already be set up the way you want them.

But frequently, you will receive files that were created by someone else who many not have the same ideas about dimension styles as you do. Normally, this would mean that you would have to re-create your favorite settings in a new dimension style. Now with the Release 14's Bonus Tools, you can export and import dimension styles at any time, saving you the effort of re-creating them. Here's how it works.

1. Open a file from which you wish to export a dimension style.

2. Choose Bonus ➢ Tools ➢ Dimstyle Export…, or enter **Dimex** ↵. The Dimension Style Export dialog box appears.

3. Click on the Browse button at the top of the dialog box to locate and name a file for storing your dimension style. AutoCAD appends the .dim file name extension.

4. Click Open in the Open dialog box. If the file you specified does not exist, AutoCAD will ask you if you want to create it. Click OK to create a new .dim file.

5. Select the name of the dimension style you want to export from the Available Dimension Styles list box.

6. Click on the Full Text Style information radio button to include all the information regarding the associated text style.

7. Click OK. You will see a message in the Command widow telling you that your dimension style was successfully exported.

To import a style you've exported, take the following steps.

1. Open a file into which you want to import a dimension style.

2. Choose Bonus ➤ Tools ➤ Dimstyle Import, or type **Dimim** ↵. The Dimension Style Import dialog box appears.

3. Click the Browse button to open the Open dialog box.

4. Locate and select the dimension style file you saved earlier, and then click Open.

5. Click on either the Keep Existing Style or Overwrite Existing Style radio button to choose which action to take.

6. Click OK.

Options for Selecting Objects, Attaching Data to Objects, and Updating Polylines

This last set of options is less likely to get as much use as the others we've discussed so far, so we've included a brief description of them here without going into too much detail. They're actually fairly easy to use, and you shouldn't have any trouble trying them out.

Get Selection Set   lets you create a selection set based on layer and type of object. You can either enter a layer or object type when prompted to do so, or select a representative object from the screen.

Xdata Attachment   lets you attach extended data to objects. Extended data is usually only used by AutoLISP, ADS, or ARX applications. You are asked to select the object that will receive the data, and then for an application name that serves as a tag to tell others who the data belongs to. You can then select a data type. Once this is done, you can enter your data.

List Entity Xdata   will display extended data that has been attached to an object.

Pline Converter   converts all polylines, except for curve fitted or spline polylines, into the Release 14 lightweight polyline. This only applies to drawings created in an earlier version of AutoCAD. Generally, old polylines are automatically converted when opened by Release 14, but there are some situations where old polylines will persist, such as:

- If the Plinetype system variable is set to any value other than 2.

- If a drawing containing polylines from an older version of AutoCAD is inserted as a block, and then exploded.

- If a third-party application constructs an old-style polyline.

Utilities Available from Other Sources

The utilities listed in the previous section are just a few samples of the many available for AutoCAD. Other sources for AutoLISP utilities are the AutoCAD journals *Cadence* and *Cadalyst*. Both offer sections that list utilities written by readers and editorial staff. If you don't already have a subscription to one of these publications and want to know more about them, their contact information follows:

Cadence
Cadence Design Systems, Inc.
555 River Oaks Parkway
San Jose, CA 95134
1 (800) 746-6233
`http://www.cadence.com`

Cadalyst
Advanstar Communications
859 Willamette Street
P.O. Box 10460
Eugene, OR 97440-2460
`http://www.cadonline.com`

Finally, the companion CD-ROM included with this book contains some freeware and shareware utilities.

Also on the CD-ROM, I have included my own AEC (architecture, engineering, civil) software offering basic architectural utilities, such as a symbols library, automatic door and window insertion program, and reference symbols. If you're using AutoCAD's 3D features, you'll also want to check out the Eye2eye replacement for the Dview command. Eye2eye lets you easily create perspective views using a camera and target object. For more information on what is included on the companion CD-ROM, see Appendix C.

Putting AutoLISP to Work

Most high-end CAD packages offer a macro or programming language to help users customize their systems. AutoCAD has *AutoLISP*, which is a pared-down version of the popular Common LISP artificial intelligence language.

Don't let AutoLISP scare you. In many ways, an AutoLISP program is just a set of AutoCAD commands that help you build your own features. The only difference is that you have to follow a different set of rules when using AutoLISP. But this isn't so unusual. After all, you had to learn some basic rules about using AutoCAD commands, too—how to start commands, for instance, and how to use command options.

If the thought of using AutoLISP is a little intimidating to you, bear in mind that you don't really need substantial computer knowledge to use this tool. In this section, you will see how you can get AutoLISP to help out in your everyday editing tasks, without having to learn the entire programming language.

Other Customization Options

If you are serious about customization, you'll want to know about Autodesk's ObjectARX programming environment that allows Microsoft Visual C++ programmers to develop full applications that work within AutoCAD. ObjectARX allows programmers to create new objects within AutoCAD as well as add functionality to existing objects. ObjectARX is beyond the scope of this book so to find out more, contact your AutoCAD dealer or visit Autodesk's Web site at www.autodesk.com.

If you are familiar with Visual Basic, Release 14 offers Visual Basic ActiveX Automation as part of its set of customization tools. ActiveX Automation offers the ability to create macros that operate across different applications. It also gives you access to AutoCAD objects through an object-oriented programming environment. Automation is a broad subject, so Chapter 20 is devoted to this topic.

Finally, you'll see references to *ADS* as you read through this section. ADS stands for the AutoCAD Development System. It is an older AutoCAD programming environment for C programmers. While it is still supported, it is being phased out and developers using ADS are encouraged to move to ObjectARX.

Loading and Running an AutoLISP Program

Many AutoCAD users have discovered the usefulness of AutoLISP through the thousands of free AutoLISP utilities that are available from bulletin board and online services. In fact, it's quite common for users to maintain a "toolbox" of their favorite utilities on a diskette. But before you can use these utilities, you need to know how to load them into AutoCAD. In the following exercise, you'll load and use a sample AutoLISP utility found on the companion CD-ROM.

1.   Start AutoCAD and open the 14a-unit.dwg file again.

2. Click on Tools ➤ Load Application. The Load AutoLISP, ADS, and ARX Files dialog box appears.

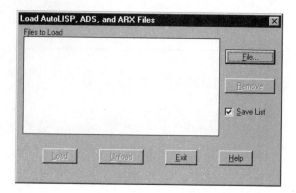

3. Click on the File button.

4. In the Directories list, locate and select the Getarea.lsp file from the companion CD-ROM. It is included among the sample drawing files.

5. Highlight Getarea.lsp and click on the Load button. You will see the message "C:Getarea Loaded."

6. Now enter **getarea** ↵.

7. At the Pick point inside area to be calculated prompt, click inside the Unit plan.

8. At the select location for area note prompt, pick a point just above the door to the balcony. A label appears displaying the area of the room in square feet.

You have just loaded and used an AutoLISP utility. As you saw in the file dialog box, there are several other utilities you can load and try out. You'll be introduced to a few more of these utilities later on in Appendix C, but for now, let's look more closely at the Load AutoLISP, ADS, and ARX Files dialog box.

NOTE   Some of the more popular AutoLISP utilities have become part of the core AutoCAD Program. Two new tools in Release 14—Match Properties and Make Objects Layer Current—have been around as AutoLISP utilities since the earliest releases of AutoCAD.

Working with the Load AutoLISP, ADS, and ARX Files Dialog Box

The Load AutoLISP, ADS, and ARX Files dialog box gives you plenty of flexibility in managing your favorite AutoLISP utilities. As you saw from the previous exercise, you can easily find and select utilities using this dialog box. Once you locate a file, it becomes part of the list, saving you from having to hunt down your favorite utility every time you want to use it.

Even when you exit AutoCAD, the dialog box retains the name of any AutoLISP file you select. This is because, by default, the Save List checkbox in the dialog box is checked. (If you don't want to retain items in the list, turn this option off.)

To remove an item from the list, just highlight it and click on the Remove button. As with any other list box, you can select multiple items and load them all at once.

Loading AutoLISP Programs Automatically

As you become more familiar with the AutoCAD user community, either online or through user groups, you may find yourself building a library of AutoLISP utilities of your own. If that library becomes extensive, you may find it tedious to load each utility one by one from the Load AutoLISP, ADS, and ARX Files dialog box.

If you find yourself in this situation, you can have AutoCAD automatically load all of your utilities for you at start-up time. To do this, you will need to create a file called Acad.1sp, and include some special code in that file. Here's how to create your Acad.1sp file.

WARNING Some third-party AutoCAD products use an Acad.1sp file of their own. Before you try to append any of these products to an existing Acad.1sp file, be sure you have a backup copy of that file in case anything goes wrong.

Use the Windows Notepad text editor to create a file called **Acad.lsp** in your AutoCAD directory. For example, suppose you have three AutoLISP files named

Edge.lsp, xplode.lsp, and Xdata.lsp. To have AutoCAD automatically load them, you would create an Acad.lsp file that contains the following lines:

```
(load "Xdata")
(load "Xplode")
(load "Edge")
```

NOTE   In the Acad.lsp file, each line is entered in the same way you would enter it when you load the utilities from the command prompt. Note that the .lsp extension is not required.

As a final step, you must make sure that AutoCAD can find these files. This means you must include their location in the Files tab of the Preferences dialog box. In particular, they should be included in the Support File Search Path listing.

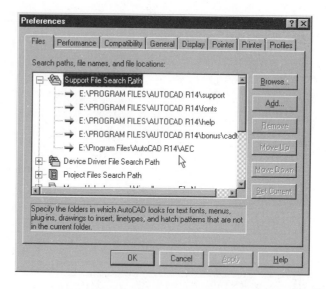

Creating Keyboard Macros with AutoLISP

You can write some simple AutoLISP programs of your own that create what are called *keyboard macros*. Macros—like Script files—are strings of predefined keyboard entries. They are invaluable for shortcuts to commands and options you use frequently. For example, you might find that, while editing a particular drawing, you often use the Break command to break an object at a single point. Here's a way to turn this operation into a macro.

1. Open the Unit file and, at the command prompt, enter the following. Be sure you enter the line exactly as shown here. If you make a mistake while entering this line, you can use the I-beam cursor or arrow keys to go to the location of your error to fix it.

```
(defun C:breakat () (command "_break" pause "f" pause "@")) ↵
```

2. Next, enter **breakat** ↵ at the command prompt. The Break command will start and you will be prompted to select an object.

3. Click on the wall on the right side of the unit.

4. At the Enter First Point prompt, click on a point on the wall where you want to create a break.

5. To see the result of the break, click on the wall again. You will see that it has been split into two lines, as shown in Figure 19.8.

FIGURE 19.8:

With the grips exposed, you can see that the wall is split into two lines.

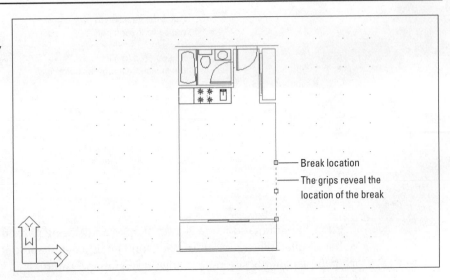

Break location

The grips reveal the location of the break

You've just written and run your first AutoLISP macro! Let's take a closer look at this very simple program (see Figure 19.9). It starts out with an opening parenthesis, as do all AutoLISP programs, followed by the word *DEFUN*. Defun is an

AutoLISP function that lets you create commands; it is followed by the name you want to give the command (*Breakat*, in this case). The command name is preceded by *C:*, telling Defun to make this command accessible from the command prompt. If the C: were omitted, you would have to start Breakat using parentheses, as in (Breakat).

FIGURE 19.9:

Breakdown of the Breakat macro

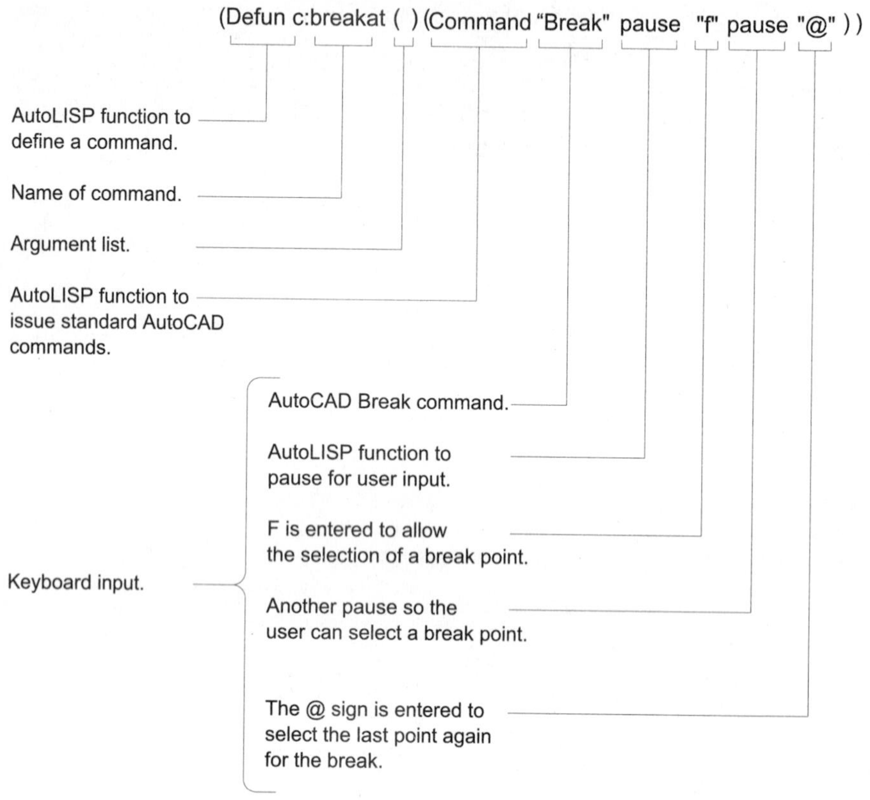

(Defun c:breakat ( ) (Command "Break" pause "f" pause "@"))

AutoLISP function to define a command.

Name of command.

Argument list.

AutoLISP function to issue standard AutoCAD commands.

AutoCAD Break command.

AutoLISP function to pause for user input.

F is entered to allow the selection of a break point.

Keyboard input.

Another pause so the user can select a break point.

The @ sign is entered to select the last point again for the break.

After the command name is a set of open and closing parentheses. This encloses what is called the *argument list*. We won't go into detail about it here; just be aware that these parentheses must follow the command name.

Finally, a list of words follows, enclosed by another set of parentheses. This list starts with the word *command*. Command is an AutoLISP function that tells

AutoLISP that whatever follows should be entered just like regular keyboard input. Only one item in the Breakat macro—the word *pause*—is not part of the keyboard input series. Pause is an AutoLISP function that tells AutoLISP to pause for input. In this particular macro, AutoLISP pauses to let you pick an object to break.

Notice that most of the items in the macro are enclosed in quotation marks. Literal keyboard input must be enclosed in quotation marks in this way. The Pause function, on the other hand, does not require quotation marks because it is a proper function, one that AutoLISP can recognize.

Finally, the program closes with two closing parentheses. All parentheses in an AutoLISP program must be in balanced pairs, so these two parentheses close the opening parenthesis at the start of the Command function as well as the opening parenthesis back at the beginning of the Defun function.

Storing AutoLISP Macros as Files

When you create a program at the command prompt, such as you did with the Breakat macro, AutoCAD remembers it only until you exit the current file. Unless you want to recreate this macro the next time you use AutoCAD, you can save it by copying it into an ASCII text file with a .lsp extension, as shown in the following example, where I've saved the Breakat macro along with some other macros I use often.

Figure 19.10 shows the contents of a file I've named `Keycad.lsp`. This file contains the macro you used above along with several others. The other macros are commands that include optional responses. For example, the third item, `defun c:corner`, would cause AutoCAD to start the Fillet command, enter an **R** ↵ to issue the Radius option, and finally enter a **0** for the fillet radius. Table 19.1 shows the command abbreviations and what they do.

FIGURE 19.10:

The contents of Keycad.lsp

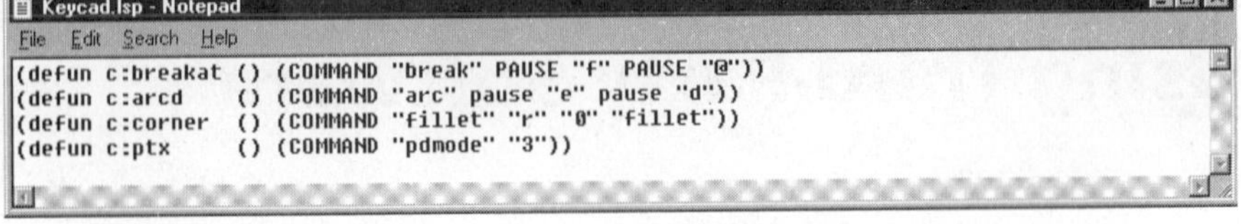

```
Keycad.lsp - Notepad
File  Edit  Search  Help
(defun c:breakat ()  (COMMAND "break" PAUSE "f" PAUSE "@"))
(defun c:arcd     ()  (COMMAND "arc" pause "e" pause "d"))
(defun c:corner   ()  (COMMAND "fillet" "r" "0" "fillet"))
(defun c:ptx      ()  (COMMAND "pdmode" "3"))
```

TABLE 19.1: The shortcut key (command abbreviations) macros provided by the Keycad.1sp file

Abbreviation	Command or Action Taken
Breakat	Breaks an object at a single point
Arcd	Draws an arc using the Start, End, Direction sequence
Corner	Sets the Fillet radius to 0; then starts the Fillet command
ptx	Sets the point style to be in the shape of an X

Use the Windows Notepad application and copy the listing in Figure 19.10. Give this file the name **Keycad.lsp,** and be sure you save it as an ASCII file. Then, whenever you want to use these macros you don't have load each one individually; instead, you load the Keycad.1sp file the first time you want to use one of the macros, and they're all available for the rest of the session.

Once it is loaded, you can use any of the macros contained within it just by entering the macro name. For example, entering **pts** ↵ will set the point style to the shape of an X.

Macros loaded in this manner will be available to you until you exit AutoCAD. Of course, you can have these macros loaded automatically every time you start AutoCAD by including the statement **(load "keycad")** in your Acad.1sp file. That way, you don't have to remember to load it in order to use the macros.

Now that you have some firsthand experience with AutoLISP, I hope these examples will encourage you to try learning more about this powerful tool. If you would like to learn more about AutoLISP, I've included *the ABCs of AutoLISP* on the companion CD-ROM. This 400-page book, converted into an electronic document, is a complete resource for AutoLISP, including tutorials and example programs.

Using Third-Party Software

One of the most significant reasons for AutoCAD's popularity is its strong support for third-party software. AutoCAD is like a chameleon; it can change to suit its environment. Out of the box, AutoCAD may not fulfill the needs of some users. But by incorporating one of the over 300 third-party add-ons, you can tailor AutoCAD to suit your specific needs.

This section discusses a few of the third-party add-ons that are popular today, so you'll know about some of the possibilities open to you while using AutoCAD. This section will give you an idea of the scope of third-party software. For more information on the myriad third-party tools out there, check out the Autodesk Web site at http://www.autodesk.com.

Custom-Tailoring AutoCAD

The needs of an architect are far different from those of a mechanical designer or a civil engineer. Third-party developers have created some specialized tools that help users of specific types of AutoCAD applications.

Many of these tools come complete with libraries of parts or symbols, AutoLISP, ADS, or ARX programs, and menus—all integrated into a single package. These packages offer added functions to AutoCAD that simplify and speed up the AutoCAD user's work. For example, most AEC (architectural or engineering construction) add-ons offer utilities for drawing walls, inserting doors and windows, and creating schedules. These functions can be performed with the stock AutoCAD package but usually require a certain amount of effort. Certainly, if you have the time, you can create your own system of symbols, AutoLISP programs, and menus, and often this is the best way of molding AutoCAD to your needs. However, when users want a ready-made solution, these add-ons are invaluable.

TIP   The companion CD-ROM includes a basic AEC add-on called *On-Screen AEC*. This add-on provides the basic tools for creating architectural CAD drawings, as well as some great utilities for your everyday use.

Specialized third-party add-ons are available for AEC, mechanical, civil engineering, piping, mapping, finite element analysis, numeric control, GIS, and many other applications. They can save you a good deal of frustration and time, especially if you find just the right one for your environment. Like so many things, however, third-party add-ons can't be all things to all people. It is likely that no matter what add-on you purchase, you will find something lacking. When you're considering custom add-ons, make sure that there is some degree of flexibility in the package, so if you don't like something, you can change it or add to it later.

Check with your AutoCAD dealer for information on third-party add-ons. Most AutoCAD dealers carry the more popular offerings. You might also want to get involved with a user group in your area.

Third-Party Product Information on the World Wide Web

The World Wide Web is another good place to start looking for the third-party add-ons. In particular, you will want to take a look at the Autodesk Registered Developers Web site at www.ipc.com/autodesk/. There you'll find the complete *AutoCAD Resource Guide* from ICP, Inc. As of this book's publication, this guide contains listings and information on virtually all the third-party products available for AutoCAD. You can search for products using a variety of criteria.

Autodesk's Own Offerings

Autodesk also offers a wide variety of add-ons to AutoCAD from simple symbols libraries to full-blown, industry-specific applications. There are offerings for architecture, civil, mechanical, mapping, data management, and 3D Visualization. Check out the Autodesk Web site for full details.

Getting the Latest Information from Online Services

There are many resources available for the AutoCAD user. Perhaps the most useful can be found on today's popular online services and in AutoCAD related newsgroups. If you don't already subscribe to one, you would do well to get a modem and explore the AutoCAD newsgroups, departments, or forums on online services.

To start with, check out the two Internet newsgroups that are devoted to AutoCAD users:

- Alt.cad.autocad
- comp.cad.autocad

Both offer a forum for you to discuss your AutoCAD questions and problems with other users. Most Internet browsers let you access newsgroups. For example, you can open a News window from Netscape Communicator by choosing Window ➤ Netscape News. From the Netscape News window, choose File ➤ Add Newsgroup, and then enter the name of the newsgroup into the input box that pops-up. From then on, you can read messages, reply to posted messages, or post your questions.

The Autodesk forum on CompuServe is another excellent source of useful AutoCAD-related information, as well as utilities and troubleshooting tips. You can often get the latest information on new products, updates, bug fixes, and more. To get to the Autodesk forum, click the GO button on the Compuserve button bar, and then enter **ACAD** at the Go dialog box.

Another online service that offers help to AutoCAD users is America Online (AOL). Although it doesn't offer a direct line to Autodesk, there is a forum for AutoCAD users to exchange ideas and troubleshooting tips. AOL also offers a library of AutoCAD-related utilities. To get to the AutoCAD folder in AOL, choose Go To ➤ Keyword. Then at the Keyword dialog box, enter **CAD** and click GO.

Cadalyst and Cadence, the two North American magazines devoted to AutoCAD that I mentioned earlier, both have their own Web sites. Cadalyst is at `http:\\www.cadonline.com`; Cadence is at `http:\\www.cadence.com`. Also check out the Sybex Web site at `http:\\www.sybex.com` for the latest information on more great books on AutoCAD. Finally, check out my own site—`http:\\www.omura.com`—for information concerning this and other books, files, and links to other AutoCAD resources.

Posting and Accessing Drawings on the World Wide Web

The World Wide Web has become a major part of the computer industry. If you're in business, any business, a Web presence is seen as a necessity, even if you don't think anyone will ever use it. But the Web offers AutoCAD users some real, practical benefits through its ability to publish drawings and other documents online. AutoCAD gives you tools that allow you to post drawings on the Web that others can view and download. In the AEC industry in particular, this can mean easier access to documents needed by contractors, engineers, cost estimators, and other involved in the design, bidding, and construction of architectural projects. Suppliers of products can post symbols libraries of their products or even 3D solid models.

In this section, you'll learn about the tools AutoCAD provides for publishing and accessing drawings on the Web. I will assume some knowledge on your part of the HTML format used to create Web pages, and a basic familiarity with browsing the Web and using FTP sites. First, we'll start by showing you how to create a Web-viewable drawing.

Using Your Web Space

Nearly all Internet service providers offer "Web space" as part of their basic package. Web space is an area on your Internet provider's computer reserved for you alone. You can place your Web page documents there for others to view. Of course, along with the Web space you get your own Web address. If you are using the Internet now, but aren't sure whether you can use your Internet account to post Web pages, check with your Internet service provider. You may already have the Web space and not even know it.

Once you've established your Web space, you'll need to know how to post your Web pages. If you need help in this area, Sybex offers *Mastering Web Design* (Sybex, 1997).

Creating a Web-Compatible Drawing

AutoCAD users have been looking for ways to publish their drawings on the Web for some time. The earlier efforts involved capturing bitmap images of drawings and adding them to Web pages. While this is fairly simple to do, this method allowed for only the crudest of images to be displayed. Drawings had to be limited in size and resolution to make them easily accessible. If you wanted to add URL links (clickable areas on an image that opened other documents), you had to delve into the inner workings of Web page design.

URL stands for Uniform Resource Locator and is a standard system for addressing Internet locations on the World Wide Web.

Fortunately, Autodesk has come up with the DWF drawing file format. DWF allows you to easily add vector format images to your Web pages. These images can be viewed using the same pan and zoom tools available in AutoCAD, thereby allowing greater detail to be presented. In addition, you can embed URL links that can open other documents with a single mouse click. These links can be attached to objects or areas in the drawing.

Opening the Internet Utilities Toolbar

Before you get started, make sure the Internet Utilities toolbar is open.

If it isn't, perform the following steps.

1. Right-click on any toolbar.

2. At the Toolbar dialog box, click on the Menu Group drop-down list.

3. Select Inet from the list. The toolbar list will change to show the Internet Utilities.

4. Click on the Internet Utilities checkbox. The Internet Utilities toolbar appears.

If you can't find the Inet menu group in step 3, you need to install the Internet Utilities. You can do so by running the AutoCAD Setup program from the AutoCAD Release 14 CD-ROM.

Installing the Internet Utilities

Start the AutoCAD installation. At the Welcome screen, click Next. At the Setup Choices screen, click on Add. At the Custom Components dialog box, locate Internet in the Components list and click on its checkbox. Click Next. You will see a message telling you where Setup is installing the Internet Utilities and the amount of space it will take. Click Next to proceed with the installation.

Creating a .dwf File

Now you're ready to move ahead. Take the following steps to see how you can save a drawing in the .dwf format.

1. Open the `Plan.dwg` file in AutoCAD. You can use the `12a-plan.dwg` file from the companion CD-ROM if you didn't create the `Plan.dwg` file on your own.

2. Choose File ➤ Export.

3. At the Export Data dialog box, open the Save as Type drop-down list and choose Drawing Web Format (*.dwf). You may need to scroll down the list as this option is at the bottom.

4. Click Save. You've just created a .dwf file.

NOTE   You can also type **Dwfout** ↵ to open a Create DWF File dialog box. This is similar to the one you saw in step 3 but automatically limits the output file to the .dwf format.

In step 3, you may have noticed that the Options button becomes available after you select the .dwf format. When you click on Options, the DWF Export Options dialog box appears.

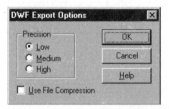

This dialog box lets you set the level of accuracy your exported drawing will offer. The higher the accuracy, the greater the file size, so you don't want to go for the highest level of accuracy unless you really need it. In most cases, you may get by with the low setting. Where your drawing covers a large area, a football stadium for example, you may want to use Medium or High. Make a few sample files and view them through your Web browser to see firsthand which quality level works best.

Now let's continue by adding the .dwf file to a Web page file.

Adding a .dwf File to a Web Page

Creating a .dwf file is simple. Adding it to a Web page is a bit more work. For this section, we'll assume that you are familiar with the creation and editing of HTML documents. HTML stands for Hyper Text Markup Language, but don't let the fancy title scare you. The fundamentals of HTML are really quite easy to learn. If you need to know more about HTML, check out *HTML: No Experience Required* (Sybex, 1997). Now let's proceed with the instructions.

Open your HTML document, either in a word processor or in a Web page creation program, and then insert the following code in the location where you want the .dwf file to appear.

```
<object
 classid ="clsid:B2BE75F3-9197-11CF-ABF4-08000996E931"
 codebase = "ftp://ftp.autodesk.com/pub/autocad/plugin/whip
.cab#version=2,0,0,0"
 width=400
 height=300 >
<param name="Filename"  value="drawingname.dwf">
<param name="View"      value="10000,20000 30000,40000">
<param name="Namedview" value="viewname">
<embed name= drawingname src=" drawingname.dwf"
 pluginspage=http://www.autodesk.com/products/autocad/whip/whip.htm
width=400
 height=300
 view="10000,20000 30000,40000"
 namedview="INITIAL">
</object>
```

This code includes all the data required for both Netscape Communicator and Microsoft Internet Explorer. You'll want to keep the code for both browsers in your HTML file so that users of both browsers can view your drawings.

We're showing some generic code in this example. You'll want to make a few changes to it to make it applicable to your specific .dwf file. The items in italics are the ones you will want to change. Let's look at them one by one so you know exactly how to replace them in your file.

Determining Files and Opening Views

As you scan down the code, you'll see two lines labeled width and height:

```
width=400
  height=300 >
```

These two lines are for the benefit of the Microsoft Internet Explorer. The numeric values in this bit of code determine the size of your drawing in the Explorer window. They describe the width and height in pixels. You can replace the numbers here to whatever value you want, but keep them in a range that will fit neatly in a typical Web page format.

The next set of lines determines the actual file name and opening view for the .dwf file.

```
<param name="Filename"  value="drawingname.dwf">
<param name="View"      value="10000,20000 30000,40000">
<param name="Namedview" value="viewname">
<embed name= drawingname src=" drawingname.dwf"
```

The first three lines shown here are for the Microsoft Internet Explorer. In the first line, replace the italicized letters with your own .dwf file name. You can also specify a URL to a .dwf file at another location, such as `http://www.omura.com/sample.dwf`.

The next two lines describe the view name to which Explorer is to open the .dwf file, or the actual coordinates for the opening view. Use one or the other, but don't use both view parameters.

NOTE   With regard to the view name in the HTML code, AutoCAD will create a view called *Initial* when you create the .dwf file. This view will be of the drawing at the time that the .dwf file is created. You may want to use the Initial view name just to simplify your page creation efforts.

The fourth line is for the benefit of Netscape Communicator. Again, you enter the name of the .dwf file here in place of the *drawingname.dwf* letters. You'll also see "name = *drawingname*." This lets you identify the drawing with Java and JavaScript applications. You can replace the italicized name with your own name. Also, it doesn't have to be the drawing name.

Further down the listing you will see the width, height, and view parameters repeated:

```
width=400
  height=300
  view="10000,20000 30000,40000"
  namedview="viewname">
```

This set of parameters is intended for Netscape Communicator users and should match the data you provide for the Microsoft Internet Explorer in the previous set of lines.

Your Internet Provider Needs to Know...

Finally, whether you are using an Internet provider or an in-house Web server, your server will need to be able to recognize the .dwf file type. You will need to inform your Webmaster that you intend to use the .dwf file in your Web page. They in turn will need to add the MIME type of "drawing/x-dwf" to their Internet server. This registers the .dwf file type with the Internet server software enabling others to view your drawings online.

Viewing Your Web Page

Once you have your HTML file completed, you are ready to view it with a browser. You will need the version 3.0 or higher of either Microsoft Internet Explorer or Netscape Communicator *and* the Autodesk Whip 2.0 driver. This driver can be obtained from the Autodesk Web page. There are separate drivers for the Explorer and Netscape Communicator, so be sure you locate the Whip driver for your browser. These drivers come in the form of installation files that are fairly large. Set aside at least a half an hour of download time.

Once the installation file is downloaded, double click on it and follow the instructions. It will locate your browser automatically, then prompt you for a location for the Whip driver software. Once this is done, you're ready to view your page!

NOTE You may have noticed that the sample HTML code you saw in the previous section included some Web addresses. These addresses allow a viewer without the Whip driver to automatically locate and download the driver when they attempt to view your page.

We've provided a sample page on the companion CD-ROM in case you are in a hurry to see how .dwf files look on a Web page. The following exercise steps you through the opening and viewing of that sample page. This will give you a chance to see just how useful a .dwf file can be.

1. Using the Windows Explorer, locate the `houseplan.html` file from the companion CD-ROM and double-click on it. Your Internet browser will open with a view of a simple floor plan.

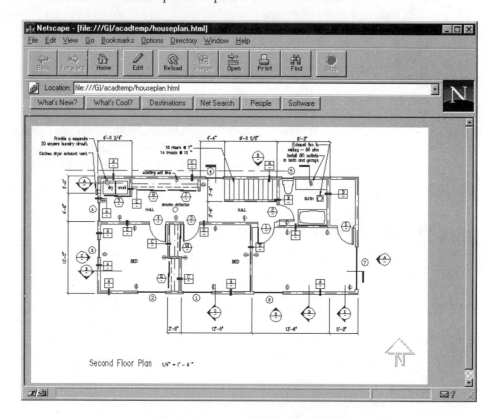

As you move the mouse over the image, you'll see the Pan Realtime hand cursor.

2. Click and drag the Pan Realtime cursor over the image. Notice that it works just like the Pan Realtime tool in AutoCAD.

3. Right-click on the mouse. A pop-up menu appears.

Notice that this menu is also similar to the one you see in AutoCAD, with some additions.

4. Select Zoom from the menu. The cursor changes to the Zoom Realtime cursor.

5. Zoom in on the view as you would in AutoCAD.

6. Adjust your view so you see the lower-left corner of the plan, similar to Figure 19.11.

7. Double-click on the wall reference symbol shown in Figure 19.11. A new page appears showing a wall type detail drawing associated with the symbol you clicked on.

8. Click on the button labeled Back on the Netscape button bar to return to the previous page.

9. Click on the door symbol shown in Figure 19.11. This time you see a page showing the door schedule.

In this example, you saw how you can click on an area of the drawing to get to another drawing. These clickable objects are called URL links. It is possible to set up these URL links to open the actual wall detail associated with the symbol. In the next section, you'll learn how these links were created.

FIGURE 19.11:

Exploring a Web page containing a .dwf file

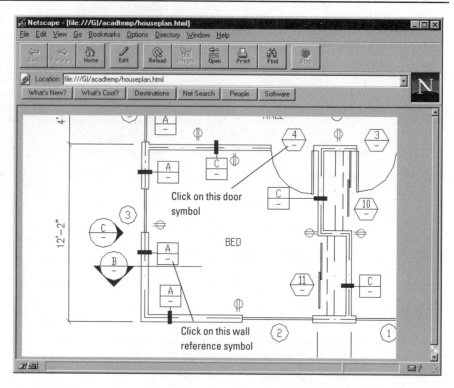

Adding Links to Other Drawings or Web Pages

The first file you opened in your browser in the previous exercise was really not much more than the HTML file you looked at in the previous section. Only the names of files were modified to include the floor plan. The ability to have a clickable object in the plan comes from the .dwf file itself. Before you save your drawing in the .dwf format, you add links to other HTML files while in AutoCAD. The following shows you how links were added to the plan you saw in the previous exercise.

1. In AutoCAD, open the file called houseplan.dwg.

2. Click on Attach URL from the Internet Utilities toolbar.

3. At the URL by (Area/<Objects>) prompt, press a ↵ to assign URLs to objects in the drawing.

4. Click on the Hexagonal door symbols, as shown in Figure 19.12. When you're done, press ↵. (In the sample file you looked at previously, we added a link to all of the hexagonal symbols.)

5. At the Enter URL prompt, enter Doorshc.html, which is the name of the HTML file that contains the Doorsch.dwf file.

6. Choose File ➤ Export and export the current file as a .dwf file.

FIGURE 19.12:

Adding URL links to the Houseplan drawing

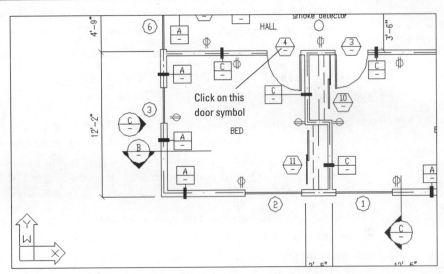

As indicated in the prompt in step 3, you can assign a URL to an area instead of an object by entering **A** ↵, and then selecting a rectangular window to define the area.

TIP

If you place anchors in your HTML files, you can include them in your URL address in step 5. For example, if you place the anchor <A name = "door-1"> </A> in a particular place in the HTML document, you can have your link go directly to that location by including the number sign followed by the anchor name in your URL, as in **Doorsch.html#door-1**.

You don't have to limit your links to HTML files containing AutoCAD drawings. You can link to all sorts of Web documents, even to other sites. For example, in step 5 you could have entered **http://www.autodesk.com** to link the hexagonal door symbols to the Autodesk Web site.

Viewing and Removing Links

A couple of other tools on the Internet Utilities toolbar allow you to view or remove the URLs associated with objects and areas. The List URL tool will display the URL attached to an object or area. The Detach URL tool will clear the URL that is attached to an area or object. If you have difficulty remembering which objects have URLs assigned to them, you can use the Select URL tool to highlight all the objects and areas that have URLs attached to them.

Opening, Inserting, and Saving .dwg Files over the Web

If you find you need to share your AutoCAD drawings with a lot of people, you can post your files on your Web site and allow others to download it. This is typically done through a Web page by assigning a graphic or a string of text to a file. A person viewing your page can then click on the graphic or text to start the download process.

AutoCAD also offers a way to open files directly from a Web page. You'll need to know the name of the file you are downloading, but beyond that, the process is quite simple. Try downloading a sample drawing from my Web page at www.omura.com to see how this process works.

1. First, make the connection to your Internet service provider.

2. With AutoCAD open, choose Open from URL from the Internet Utilities toolbar. The Open DWG from URL dialog box appears.

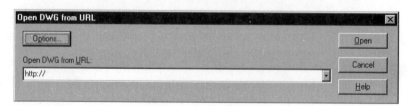

3. Click on the Options… button. The Internet Configuration dialog box appears.

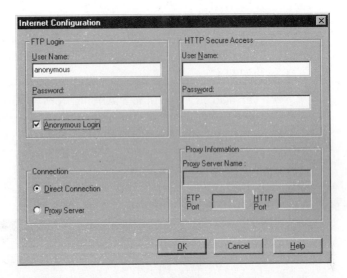

4. Make sure the Anonymous Login checkbox is checked. The anonymous user name is a standard way of accessing Web sites for file transfer where no password is assigned or needed.

5. Click OK to return to the Open DWG from URL dialog box.

6. Enter **www.omura.com/sample.dwg** in the input box. The input box should read http://www.omura.com/sample.dwg when you are done.

7. Click Open. The Remote Transfer in Progress dialog box appears as the file is downloaded. After a minute or two, the file appears in the drawing editor.

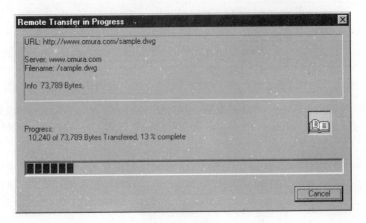

The Insert from URL tool works in exactly the same way as the Open from URL tool. The only difference is that the downloaded file will be inserted into the current file instead of closing the current file and opening the downloaded file.

TIP You can also click and drag a .dwf file from a Web page into AutoCAD to download and open a .dwg file, provided a .dwg file with the same name as the .dwf file exists on the Web site.

If you've already downloaded this file once before, you will get a message telling you that the file already exists in the \Windows\Temp directory.

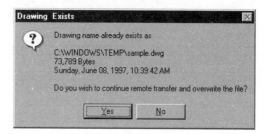

Regardless of whether you use the Open from URL or Insert from URL, AutoCAD saves the downloaded file in the \Windows\Temp directory first before opening it.

Saving a File to a Web or FTP Site

If you have both read and write privileges to a Web or FTP site, you can save files to that site directly from AutoCAD. The first step in doing this is to set up AutoCAD to provide your user name and password. Take the following steps to do this.

1. While in AutoCAD, click on the Configure Internet Host tool in the Internet Utilities toolbar. The Internet Configuration dialog box appears. Notice that this is the same dialog box you opened in step 3 of the previous exercise.

2. Click on the Anonymous Login checkbox to remove the checkmark. This allows you to enter values in the User Name and Password input boxes in the FTP Login group.

3. Enter your user name in the User Name input box and your password in the Password input box, and then click OK.

Let's take a moment to review the Internet Configuration dialog box because this is the one place where problems can occur if settings are incorrect.

If you are an individual user on a single computer connected to an Internet service provider, you would most likely use the Direct Connection option in the Connection group. The Proxy Server option is intended for systems on a company-wide network whose access to the Internet is controlled through a single computer called a proxy server. If you find yourself in this situation, you will have to consult with your network administrator to gain access to the Internet. You can use the Help button in this dialog box to gain further information and to fill out the Proxy Information.

The HTTP Secure Access group should be filled in if you find yourself logging on frequently to Web sites that require password access.

Once your Internet configuration is up and working, you are ready to use the Save to URL tool in the Internet Utilities toolbar to upload a file to your Web site.

1. Choose Save to URL from the Internet Utilities toolbar. The Save DWG to URL dialog box appears.

2. Enter the FTP name of your Web site in the Save DWG to URL input box. Typically, this would the same as your Web site with an *ftp* prefix instead of the usual *www* prefix, and would include the name of the directory where your files are stored. An example might be `ftp://ftp.myips.com/mypublic_dir/sample.dwg`. Remember to include the drawing name at the end.

3. Click OK to save the file to your Web site. You'll see the Remote Transfer in Progress dialog box as the file is being saved.

Getting Help

These Web access features open up a whole new world of possibilities for AutoCAD users. But there are many variables and places where you can encounter problems. AutoCAD offers the Internet Help button on the Internet Utilities toolbar to answer your questions about the Internet Utilities. There you'll find detailed information about the topics covered in this section.

In addition, you will want to check out the `Aipk.html` and `Opening.html` files that come with the Whip2 plug-ins. These documents, located in the

\Program Files\AutoCAD Internet directory, provide tips, tutorials, and ideas on how to use the Internet and World Wide Web with AutoCAD. They even offer animated .gif images and sample pages. Check it out!

If You Want to Experiment...

If you haven't already done so, take a careful look at the readme HTML document that comes with the Whip2 plug-in. It offers some additional information that can be helpful to the first time Web author.

1. Choose Start ➤ Programs ➤ Whip Netscape Plug-in ➤ ReadMe. Or, if you are using the Microsoft Internet Explorer, choose Start ➤ Programs ➤ Whip Explorer Plug-in ➤ ReadMe. Your Internet Browser opens the readme file.

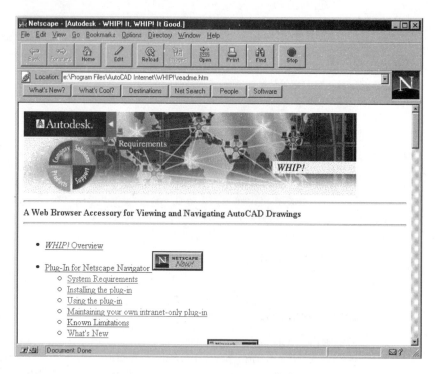

2. Scroll down the file until you see the Publish DWF file for Whip listing.

3. Double-click on the HREF tag topic to find out how to add a URL link to a Web page.

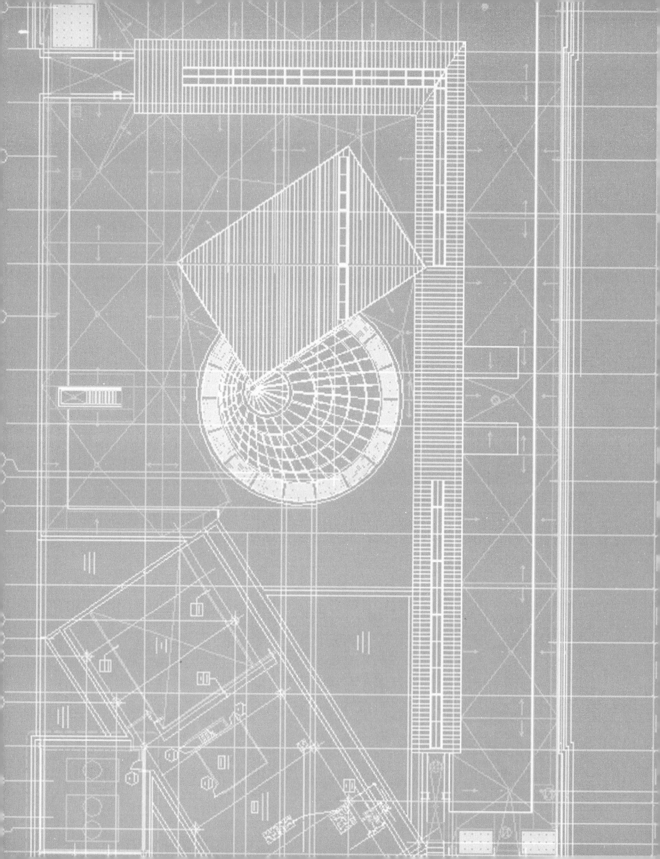

CHAPTER

TWENTY

20

Using ActiveX Automation with AutoCAD

- Understanding ActiveX Automation

- The AutoCAD Object Model

- Automation Techniques

- The AutoCAD VBA Preview

One of the major leaps forward in AutoCAD 14 is the addition of ActiveX Automation server capabilities to AutoCAD itself. This addition makes it possible to automate AutoCAD operations from a wide variety of other applications, including Microsoft Visual Basic, Microsoft Excel, and Microsoft Word. In this chapter, we'll review the basics of ActiveX Automation and investigate the integration of this powerful technique with AutoCAD. We'll also see some examples of using ActiveX Automation, and touch on the AutoCAD Release 14 Preview, VBA Edition.

Unlike the other skills we've covered in this book, ActiveX Automation programming is not done within AutoCAD, but within other programs such as Visual Basic or Excel. So we've departed from the usual tutorial style to provide reference information on this exciting new topic. On the CD-ROM, you'll find all of the examples discussed in this chapter, with the Visual Basic samples, in both source and compiled format, so you can test them even if you don't own a copy of Visual Basic.

What Is ActiveX Automation?

You've seen by now that AutoCAD is an immensely flexible and programmable drawing system. You can control AutoCAD from the command prompt, from menus and toolbars, and from AutoLISP macros and programs. AutoDesk also supplies a set of extensions for controlling AutoCAD from the C++ language. These extensions, called ObjectARX, are designed for use from C++ only and are beyond the scope of this book.

Now, with AutoCAD 14, there's an entirely new way to control AutoCAD—through ActiveX Automation. ActiveX Automation is a Microsoft-created standard, formerly called OLE Automation, that allows one Windows application to control another Windows application through exposed objects. In this chapter, we'll see how you can use an external application to control AutoCAD, and get familiar with the ActiveX Automation capabilities of AutoCAD 14.

If you want to see some immediate examples of ActiveX Automation programming, skip forward to the *Automation Techniques* section. But be sure to come back and read other material in this chapter for an overview of the potential of ActiveX Automation with AutoCAD.

Integrating Applications

AutoCAD is a marvelously flexible application, but like all computer applications, it's specialized in one particular area. AutoCAD's specialty is producing drawings. Despite some capabilities for handling text, numbers, and data storage, AutoCAD isn't a word processor, spreadsheet, or database program—nor should it be. By concentrating their efforts on drawing functionality, the Autodesk developers can produce the best possible drawing application, and let other teams produce the best possible word processors, spreadsheets, and databases.

However, there are times when it would be nice to combine the capabilities of multiple programs. Imagine that you have a complex architectural drawing for an entire building, such as an office building, and you need to produce some custom reports on the number of desks, chairs, and computer workstations the plan includes. Yes, you could figure out a way to do this within AutoCAD itself. But wouldn't it be much easier to somehow use the AutoCAD data within a database program that has a very strong report generator? Or suppose you need to include a summary of lumber board-feet in a document you're preparing in a word processor. Wouldn't you like to be able to read the necessary information from the drawing file you've been working with?

The reason ActiveX Automation was developed is to exploit these synergies between different applications. Windows itself allows multiple applications to execute at the same time; ActiveX Automation allows those applications to communicate among themselves. Each application can decide what information and capabilities it wants to publicize, or expose, to other applications on the system.

NOTE   You'll find references to "OLE Automation" in books about Windows programming. As it's expanded beyond its original roots in the Object Linking and Embedding standard, this technology has been renamed "ActiveX Automation." Whatever you refer to it as, the ideas are the same.

Clients and Servers

Although ActiveX Automation always involves a conversation between two applications, it's not a two-way conversation between equal partners. Every piece of ActiveX Automation programming involves two programs with different roles. The *client* is the application that initiates the conversation. The *server* is the application that responds to the client. ActiveX Automation code runs in the client, while the actions that this code controls are executed by the server. Figure 20.1 shows the relationship between client and server in a typical ActiveX Automation exchange.

FIGURE 20.1:

ActiveX Automation in action

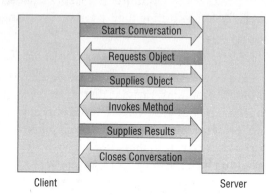

As the figure shows, there are three steps in every ActiveX Automation operation. First, one application decides to start the ActiveX Automation operation. This application automatically becomes the client, and the application it is calling, or *invoking*, becomes the server. We'll see how to program this part of the exchange in a few moments.

After the conversation has started, the client application runs code that contains server commands. It's up to the server application to decide which commands to expose, but the client application chooses which ones to actually use at any given time. ActiveX Automation commands are then passed to the server, which responds to them appropriately.

The client may continue sending commands to the server as long as it cares to do so. The server will faithfully execute each of these commands (assuming that they don't contain syntactical errors) in turn. When it's done controlling the server, the client can explicitly end the conversation, or it can simply stop sending commands.

There are many more ActiveX servers than ActiveX clients available. That's because programming ActiveX server support into an application is a much simpler task than making that application an ActiveX client. However, there are still a wide variety of ActiveX clients from which to choose. Here are a few of the applications you can use to control ActiveX servers, including AutoCAD:

- Visual Basic 4.0 or 5.0

- Excel 95 or 97

- Word 95 or 97

- Access 95 or 97

- PowerPoint 97

NOTE Although the code in this chapter should work in any of these clients, it's all taken from the chapter examples, which are written in Excel 95 or Visual Basic 5.0. The sample code is all included on the companion CD-ROM, but of course you'll have to provide your own copy of one of these ActiveX clients to test it.

Automation Objects

An ActiveX Automation server (such as AutoCAD 14) exposes its functionality by way of *objects*. An object is simply an abstract representation of some piece of the server application. It can be the application itself, a portion of a document managed by the application, or a part of the application's interface such as a toolbar. An object is distinguished from other objects by three things:

- The type, or *class*, of the object

- The *properties* of the object

- The *methods* of the object

The properties of an object are the various characteristics that describe that object. The methods of an object are the various operations that the object can perform. A server application can choose which of the properties and methods of its objects it chooses to make available by way of ActiveX Automation.

For example, one of the objects supplied by AutoCAD as an ActiveX Automation server is a Line object. Not surprisingly, this represents a single line somewhere on an AutoCAD drawing. The properties of a line include a number of things you can set about that line if you're working directly in AutoCAD. A few of the properties of the Line object are:

- Color
- Layer
- StartPoint
- EndPoint
- Thickness

The methods of a line include things you can do with a line in the AutoCAD user interface. Some of the methods of a Line object are:

- Copy
- Erase
- Mirror
- Move
- Rotate

Automation and AutoCAD

Applications vary widely in the extent to which they expose their capabilities via ActiveX Automation. Some, such as Microsoft Excel, allow client applications to manipulate both their data and their interface. You can use ActiveX Automation, for example, to change the contents of a cell on an Excel worksheet or to add an item to an Excel menu. Other applications, such as Microsoft Visual Basic, expose only a few bits of their interface to ActiveX Automation clients.

AutoCAD takes a middle road here. All of the objects on your drawings are available through ActiveX Automation, as are the major factors that control your view of the drawing, such as the size and placement of viewports. But the parts of AutoCAD that do not have direct impact on drawings, such as the location and contents of toolbars, are not exposed to ActiveX Automation clients.

This decision on the part of Autodesk means that you can use ActiveX Automation to manipulate drawings in almost any imaginable way, but you can't use ActiveX Automation to extend the capabilities of the AutoCAD environment itself. You can't, for example, write a utility that stores the locations of AutoCAD toolbars in a database and restores these locations on demand. The information that would be needed to do this simply isn't available to ActiveX clients.

An Automation Sample

Before we go further into a systematic exploration of the ActiveX Automation capabilities of AutoCAD 14, let's take a look at an example of using these capabilities. The file census1.xls, on the companion CD-ROM, demonstrates the basic principles of using Automation with AutoCAD. This is an Excel 95 workbook that contains two worksheets. The worksheet Module1 has code that uses ActiveX Automation to return a list of the objects in an open AutoCAD drawing. Figure 20.2 shows such a census for the r300-20.dwg file that ships with AutoCAD.

FIGURE 20.2:

Census for the
r300-20.dwg sample

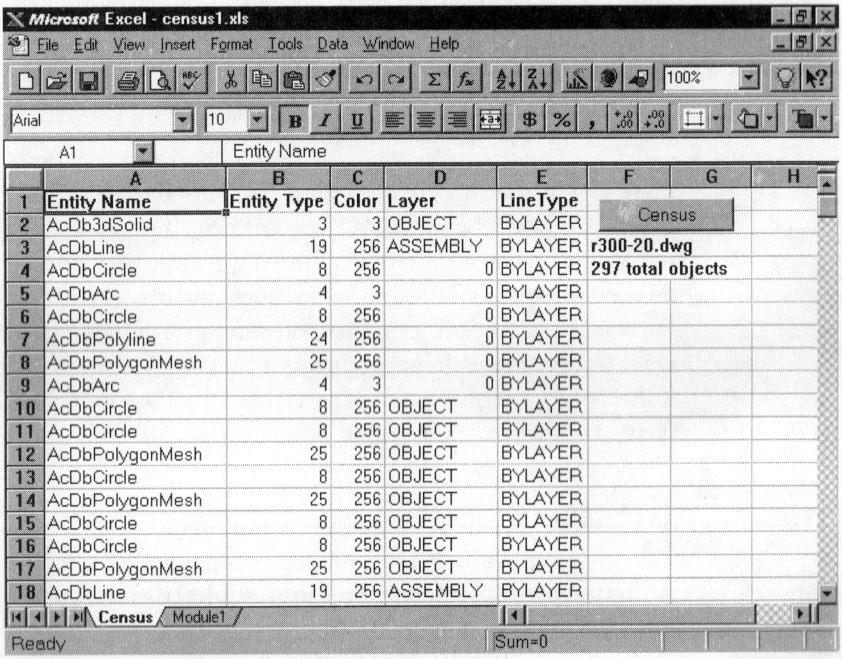

	A	B	C	D	E	F	G	H
1	Entity Name	Entity Type	Color	Layer	LineType	Census		
2	AcDb3dSolid	3	3	OBJECT	BYLAYER			
3	AcDbLine	19	256	ASSEMBLY	BYLAYER	r300-20.dwg		
4	AcDbCircle	8	256		0	BYLAYER	297 total objects	
5	AcDbArc	4	3		0	BYLAYER		
6	AcDbCircle	8	256		0	BYLAYER		
7	AcDbPolyline	24	256		0	BYLAYER		
8	AcDbPolygonMesh	25	256		0	BYLAYER		
9	AcDbArc	4	3		0	BYLAYER		
10	AcDbCircle	8	256	OBJECT	BYLAYER			
11	AcDbCircle	8	256	OBJECT	BYLAYER			
12	AcDbPolygonMesh	25	256	OBJECT	BYLAYER			
13	AcDbCircle	8	256	OBJECT	BYLAYER			
14	AcDbPolygonMesh	25	256	OBJECT	BYLAYER			
15	AcDbCircle	8	256	OBJECT	BYLAYER			
16	AcDbCircle	8	256	OBJECT	BYLAYER			
17	AcDbPolygonMesh	25	256	OBJECT	BYLAYER			
18	AcDbLine	19	256	ASSEMBLY	BYLAYER			

TIP

ActiveX Automation code won't work if AutoCAD is in the middle of a command. For example, if you've chosen LineType from the Format menu, which opens the Layer & LineType Properties dialog box, you'll find that none of the code in this chapter will function. Make sure that all dialogs are closed when you're experimenting with ActiveX Automation code.

Let's review some of the Excel code that created this census. Although it's not our intent to try to teach Excel programming in this book, the basic principles of using ActiveX Automation are the same for any application that uses a version of Visual Basic as its programming language.

TIP

To view the code within the Excel workbook, just click on the "Module1" tab at the bottom of the workbook.

All of the code for this simple example is contained within a single procedure named GetCensus. The procedure starts out by defining some variables to use:

```
Dim oAutoCad As Object
Dim oModelSpace As Object
Dim wksCensus As Worksheet
Dim intI As Integer
```

Here oAutoCad and oModelSpace are variables that will be used to represent objects supplied by AutoCAD (respectively, the AutoCAD application itself and the Model Space of the current drawing), while wksCensus is a variable that will be used to represent the Excel worksheet (an object within the same application as the code), and intI is a simple loop counter. You'll see that every variable has a type: Object, Worksheet, or Integer, in this case. Worksheet is an example of an *early-bound* variable—one whose type is specified when the variable is defined. Object is a *late-bound* variable—one that can hold any sort of object from any application.

WARNING

Although early-bound variables are generally faster than late-bound variables, AutoCAD 14 does not support early-bound variables as an Automation server. You'll have to declare all variables that will hold AutoCAD objects "As Object."

In order to start the conversation with AutoCAD, Excel uses a GetObject statement:

```
Set oAutoCad = GetObject(, "AutoCAD.Application")
```

This tells Excel to open an ActiveX Automation session with an active instance of AutoCAD; that is, one that was opened manually or by some other application before this code was executed. AutoCAD.Application is the class name for

AutoCAD, which uniquely identifies AutoCAD to ActiveX Automation clients. There are other ways to open an Automation session, which we'll see later.

Once Excel is talking to AutoCAD, it retrieves some simple information and places it on the Census worksheet:

```
Set wksCensus = Worksheets("Census")
wksCensus.Range("A2", "E1000").Clear
Set oModelSpace = oAutoCad.ActiveDocument.ModelSpace
wksCensus.Cells(3, 6) = oAutoCad.ActiveDocument.Name
wksCensus.Cells(4, 6) = oModelSpace.Count & " total objects"
```

The first two lines of this block of code create a reference to Excel's own worksheet object and use its Clear method to remove any data that is already on the worksheet. The next line initializes the oModelSpace variable to refer to the Model Space of the active document within AutoCAD; that is, to whatever drawing is loaded. It does this by locating the Model Space within a hierarchy of AutoCAD objects. We'll learn more about this hierarchy in the next section.

The next two lines write the values of AutoCAD properties to particular cells on the worksheet. oAutoCad.ActiveDocument.Name retrieves the Name property of the active document, while oModelSpace.Count retrieves the number of objects within the Model Space. You'll see that properties are referred to by separating them from the name of their parent objects with a single dot.

The main work of the code is done within a loop that visits every object in the drawing's Model Space:

```
For intI = 0 To oModelSpace.Count - 1
    With oModelSpace.Item(intI)
        wksCensus.Cells(intI + 2, 1) = .EntityName
        wksCensus.Cells(intI + 2, 2) = .EntityType
        wksCensus.Cells(intI + 2, 3) = .Color
        wksCensus.Cells(intI + 2, 4) = .Layer
        wksCensus.Cells(intI + 2, 5) = .Linetype
    End With
Next intI
```

TIP If you know AutoLISP, but not Visual Basic, look up "AutoLISP and Automation Comparison" in the AutoCAD Help file. You'll find a handy list of equivalents between the two languages.

The oModelSpace object is a *collection* object, that is, one that contains many other objects. The Count property of the collection tells you how many objects are in that collection. These objects are each assigned a number, starting at zero, so the highest-numbered object is at Count-1. The loop here goes through the entire collection, referring in turn to each object within it. The line of code With oModelSpace .Item(intI) tells Excel that everything until the corresponding End With refers to this particular numbered object within the collection. Each of these objects has properties such as EntityName and EntityType, and Excel retrieves these and writes them out to the worksheet. Our census is complete!

WARNING

This is not production-quality code! In particular, there's no provision for unexpected errors.

The AutoCAD Object Model

Almost every ActiveX Automation server supplies more than one object to clients, and AutoCAD is no exception. AutoCAD exposes about 70 objects to Automation clients, with a total of about 500 methods and properties. The developer needs some organizing principle to help make sense of this overwhelming complexity. This principle is provided by the AutoCAD *object model*. An object model provides a simple framework for understanding the relation of objects to each other and to the overall functionality of the application. In this section we'll investigate this object model to see some of the capabilities of ActiveX Automation in AutoCAD.

TIP

The lists of objects, methods, and properties in this chapter are only partial. For the full AutoCAD object model, refer to the acadauto.hlp file that ships with the product.

The Object Hierarchy

It's convenient to think of the AutoCAD objects as arranged in a hierarchy. Figure 20.3 shows the top portion of this hierarchy, beginning with the AutoCAD Application object.

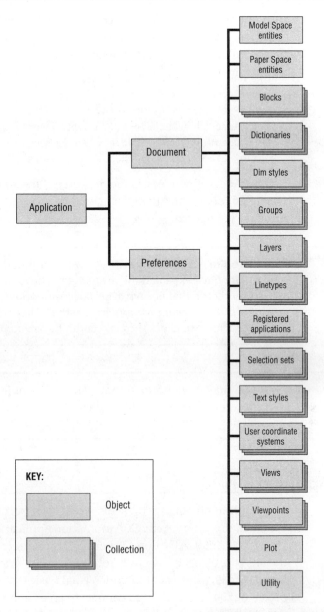

FIGURE 20.3:

Top part of the AutoCAD object hierarchy

Each object in the hierarchy contains the objects beneath it. For example, the Application object contains a Preferences object and a Document object. These are objects themselves, but they may also be referred to by using properties of their parent object. This is a general principle of ActiveX Automation: you retrieve objects by working your way down from the top of the object hierarchy, using the Visual Basic Set keyword to refer to each object as you go. If you need to use both the Document object and the Preferences object in your code, you could do so like this:

```
Dim oAutoCad As Object
Dim oDocument As Object
Dim oPreferences As Object
Set oAutoCad = GetObject(, "AutoCAD.Application")
Set oDocument = oAutoCad.ActiveDocument
Set oPreferences = oAutoCad.Preferences
```

Here, ActiveDocument is the property of the Application object that returns the Document object, and Preferences is the property of the Application object that returns the Preferences object.

WARNING   If you're experienced with ActiveX Automation with other servers, you might have expected the properties to have the same name as the objects they return; that is, oAutoCad.Document would be the correct syntax. Alas, AutoCAD doesn't always follow the usual conventions in this area, so you'll have to check the Help carefully as you return objects.

TIP   You may have noticed that none of the objects in Figure 20.3 refer to drawing objects. You'll find these listed under the *Block* section below, as all drawing objects are only available via a Block object.

Application

The Application object represents AutoCAD itself. It's always the first object your code will use in any ActiveX Automation application, because it's the single object that AutoCAD allows other objects to directly access (without going through the object hierarchy). You can use either the GetObject statement or the CreateObject statement in your Visual Basic code to connect to the Application object. GetObject is used to connect to an existing instance of AutoCAD, while CreateObject launches a new instance of AutoCAD.

Often your client application won't know whether AutoCAD is running or not, and whether the drawing you want to work with is loaded or not. In these circumstances, you can use code similar to this (taken from the AutoCAD Drawing Explorer sample on the companion CD) to put AutoCAD into the state you want:

```
' Connect to AutoCAD and load the requested drawing.
' Start by trying to connect to a running instance
On Error Resume Next
Set oAcad = GetObject(, "AutoCAD.Application")
If Err.Number Then
    ' We couldn't find a running instance, so try to launch
    ' a new instance of AutoCAD
    Err.Clear
    Set oAcad = CreateObject("AutoCAD.Application")
    If Err.Number Then
        ' Couldn't find it, couldn't create it: give up
        MsgBox "Unable to launch AutoCAD session", _
        vbCritical, "AutoCAD Drawing Explorer"
        End
    Else
        ' CreateObject launches an invisible session.
        ' Make it visible.
        oAcad.Visible = True
    End If
End If
On Error GoTo HandleErr
' If we get this far, AutoCAD is open. Now see what
' drawing (if any) is loaded
If oAcad.ActiveDocument.FullName <> txtDrawing Then
    ' Some other drawing is loaded. Save it, and
    ' load the one we want
    oAcad.ActiveDocument.Save
    oAcad.ActiveDocument.Open txtDrawing
End If
```

WARNING Although CreateObject *should* create a completely invisible instance of AutoCAD, there's a bug in AutoCAD 14: floating toolbars in an instance launched in this fashion are visible, whether the application itself is visible or not. Since the AutoCAD object model doesn't allow you to manipulate toolbar visibility, you really have no choice but to make the whole application visible.

Table 20.1 shows some of the methods and properties of the Application object. You shouldn't try to memorize this table (or the others later in the chapter). Rather, they're provided to allow you to familiarize yourself with some of the capabilities that AutoCAD makes available as an ActiveX Automation server.

TABLE 20.1: Application methods and properties

Name	Type	Description
LoadARX	Method	Loads an AutoCAD ARX application
Quit	Method	Closes the current drawing and close AutoCAD
Update	Method	Updates the entire drawing
ActiveDocument	Property	Returns the Document object
Caption	Property	The caption of the AutoCAD window
Top	Property	Top position of the AutoCAD window (pixels from the top of the screen)
Left	Property	Left position of the AutoCAD window (pixels from the left edge of the screen)
Height	Property	Height of the AutoCAD window (pixels)
Width	Property	Width of the AutoCAD window (pixels)
Visible	Property	True if AutoCAD is currently visible

TIP

You can use the AutoCAD Drawing Explorer on the companion CD-ROM to view typical values of many AutoCAD properties.

TIP

Unlike many ActiveX Automation servers, AutoCAD does not attach miscellaneous methods (such as prompting for user input) to either the Application or the Document object. Instead, there's a separate Utility object, described later in this chapter, for this purpose.

Preferences

The Preferences object provides your ActiveX Automation applications with access to just about every option in the AutoCAD Tools ➤ Preferences dialog box. Just as there's only one such dialog box in a session of AutoCAD, each instance of the AutoCAD Application object supplies precisely one Preferences object. This object can be retrieved by using the Application.Preferences property. The properties of the Preferences object tell you what preferences the user has chosen in the AutoCAD Preferences dialog. By assigning new values to these properties, you can actually change those preferences.

> **TIP**
>
> If you change any of the user's preferences, store the old values first and provide a way to reset the changes. This way you can avoid destroying customizations that might have taken the user a long while to set up.

Table 20.2 shows some of the methods and properties of the Preferences object. This object in particular has many properties. The table shows only a few of them to give you some sense of what's available.

TABLE 20.2: Preferences methods and properties

Name	Type	Description
DeleteProfile	Method	Delete an AutoCAD user profile
ExportProfile	Method	Export an AutoCAD user profile
ImportProfile	Method	Import an AutoCAD user profile
ActiveProfile	Property	Current user profile
CustomDictionary	Property	Name of the custom dictionary to use
TempFilePath	Property	Directory AutoCAD uses to store temporary files
CreateBackup	Property	True if AutoCAD should always create backup files
TextFont	Property	Font to use for new text
TextFontSize	Property	Size of new text in points
CursorSize	Property	Cursor size as a percentage of the screen size

> **TIP** Although the Preferences object provides ways to create, save, and change profiles, the AutoCAD object model has no way to enumerate all of the available profiles. If you need this information, you'll have to read it from the Windows registry, under `HKEY_CURRENT_USER\Software\Autodesk\AutoCAD\R14.0\<your serial number>\Profiles`.

Document

Unlike most other ActiveX servers (for example, Microsoft Word, Excel, or PowerPoint), AutoCAD can only open a single document (drawing) at a time. Thus, the object hierarchy includes only one Document object, which represents the loaded drawing (assuming that one is open). This object is returned by the `Application.ActiveDocument` property.

As you might expect, most of the methods of the Document object relate to file manipulation. There are two major classes of properties for this object: *defaults* and *collections*. Defaults, such as ActiveLayer, control the results of subsequent drawing actions. To create new objects on a specific layer, you first need to set the `Document.ActiveLayer` property to that layer, and then create the objects. Collections include groups of other objects that the document keeps track of. For example, there is a Layers collection that includes Layer objects, one for each layer in the drawing. Layers is a collection, but it's also a property of the Document object. To access the collection, you need to use the property:

```
Set oLayers = oAutoCad.ActiveDocument.Layers
```

Table 20.3 shows some of the methods and properties of the Document object.

TABLE 20.3: Document methods and properties

Name	Type	Description
AuditInfo	Method	Checks the integrity of a drawing file and optionally attempt to fix errors
Export	Method	Exports the drawing to a non-AutoCAD format
GetVariable	Method	Gets the value of an AutoCAD system variable
HandleToObject	Method	Returns an object, given its handle

TABLE 20.3 CONTINUED: Document methods and properties

Name	Type	Description
Import	Method	Imports a non-AutoCAD drawing
New	Method	Creates a new drawing
Open	Method	Opens an existing drawing
Regen	Method	Regenerates the entire drawing
Save	Method	Saves the drawing
SaveAs	Method	Saves the drawing under a new name
SetVariable	Method	Sets the value of a system variable
WBlock	Method	Writes a selection set out as a new drawing file
ActiveDimStyle	Property	Default dimension style for new objects
ActiveLayer	Property	Default layer for new objects
ActiveLineType	Property	Default line type for new objects
ActiveSpace	Property	Toggles between Model Space and Paper Space
FullName	Property	Path and file name of the current drawing
Name	Property	File name (only) of the current drawing
ObjectSnapMode	Property	True if Object Snap is on
Saved	Property	True if the document has no unsaved changes

TIP

The HandleToObject method provides an easy way to retrieve objects that you've already worked with, but are located deep in the hierarchy of the drawing, without going through all of the intermediate objects. Handles are discussed in the *Block* section below.

NOTE

The AutoCAD Automation Help file reverses the meaning of Document .Saved.

Block

The Block object represents a single block within the AutoCAD drawing. A block can consist of a single entity or any number of entities. Each block has a name that can be retrieved and a count of the entities under the block. Figure 20.4 shows the bottom portion of the AutoCAD object hierarchy, starting with the Block object.

Note that although the Block object contains many types of entities, there is not a separate collection for each of these types. Rather, the different objects are put together into one heterogeneous collection of entities. You use the Block object's item method, or just the index of the collection, to retrieve any given object that belongs to the Block. For example, given a block containing a single line, you can retrieve the line this way:

```
Set oLine = oBlock.Item(0)
```

The next line of code is equivalent to the last one, since Item is the default property of the Block object:

```
Set oLine = oBlock(0)
```

The different entities within the block can be identified by means of their unique *handle* values. Each of the objects that can be contained in a block has a Handle property, and these properties are unique across all objects in the drawing. You can use the Document object's HandleToObject method (see Table 20.3) to retrieve an object, given its handle.

In addition to any named blocks you might have created, there are two special blocks in every drawing: the ModelSpace and PaperSpace objects. The Model-Space object contains every entity in the drawing's Model Space, while the PaperSpace object contains every entity in the drawing's Paper Space. You can retrieve these special blocks by using properties of the document object:

```
Set oModelSpace = oDocument.ModelSpace
Set oPaperSpace = oDocument.PaperSpace
```

In addition, if you go through all the members of the Document's Blocks collection, you'll find that two of them have the special names "*PAPERSPACE" and "*MODELSPACE." These are copies, of course, of the PaperSpace and ModelSpace objects. If you're trying to carry out some operation on all user-created blocks, you'll want to skip these two blocks.

FIGURE 20.4:

Lower part of the
AutoCAD object
hierarchy

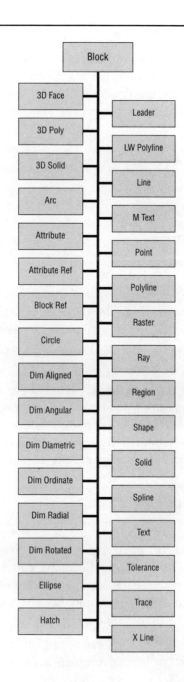

Entity Properties

Each entity you might find in a Block's collection has its own properties. A Line object, for example, has StartPoint and EndPoint properties, while an Arc object has StartAngle, EndAngle, Center, and Radius properties—to name a few. There are some properties common to nearly all entities:

- Color
- EntityName
- EntityType
- Handle
- Layer
- LineType
- Visible

All the other properties are specific to their entity types. If your ActiveX Automation code acts on all entities in a particular Block, you'll need to check the EntityName or EntityType properties of each entity to determine whether it's an appropriate target for your actions.

Covering all of the properties of every entity is beyond the scope of this book. The *Automation Techniques* section later in this chapter shows what you can do with a few selected properties. The AutoCAD Drawing Explorer on the companion CD-ROM will display a small selection of these properties as well. Beyond that, you'll need to refer to the `acadauto.hlp` file.

Dictionary

A Dictionary object represents a single AutoCAD dictionary, which is an arbitrary collection of objects, each associated with a keyword. Don't confuse a Dictionary object with the sort of dictionary you'd use for spell checking; it's a completely different animal. (If you're familiar with Visual Basic, you'll recognize a similarity between AutoCAD dictionaries and VBA collections.)

You can retrieve the objects in a dictionary if you know their keywords. You can also create new dictionaries and add and delete objects from dictionaries. What you can't do is get a complete list of all the objects in a dictionary. You have to know what's in there. Thus, dictionaries are most useful to applications that need to organize their own data, not to applications that are trying to work with data left by other applications.

Table 20.4 shows some of the methods and properties of the Dictionary object.

TABLE 20.4: Dictionary methods and properties

Name	Type	Description
AddObject	Method	Adds an object to an existing dictionary
Delete	Method	Deletes an entire dictionary
GetName	Method	Given an object, retrieve its keyword
GetObject	Method	Given a keyword, retrieve an object
GetXData	Method	Gets the extended data for an object
Remove	Method	Removes an object from a dictionary
Rename	Method	Renames an object in a dictionary
Replace	Method	Replaces an object in a dictionary with a new object
SetXData	Method	Sets the extended data for an object
Name	Property	The name of the dictionary

DimStyle

A DimStyle object represents a set of dimensioning properties that control the appearance of dimensions in your drawing. You can add new DimStyles by using the Add method of the DimStyles collection, but you can't set their properties directly by manipulating the DimStyle object. Rather, you need to change the dimensioning system variables by using the methods of the Document object. So creating and saving a new DimStyle object follows this outline:

1. Use `Document.DimStyles.Add` to create the new object.

2. Use `Document.SetVariable` to change the appropriate system variables.

3. Use `Document.ActiveDimStyle` to make your new object the default for new dimensions.

If you need to change the style on an existing dimension, set the StyleName property of the dimension to the name of a DimStyle object with the styles you desire.

Group and SelectionSet

Both Groups and SelectionSets are collections of entities from a drawing (just as a block is a collection of entities). The difference between the two is mainly in the methods you use to manipulate the objects in the collection. You can think of a Group object as representing the collection created with the AutoCAD Group command, and a SelectionSet object as representing a group of objects selected with a Selection Window or a Selection Fence in the AutoCAD user interface.

Generally, you won't find Group objects to be of very much use in ActiveX Automation applications because there's nothing you can do to the group as a whole. SelectionSet objects provide a nice interface to allow the user to choose entities on screen for your program to work with. There's an example of using a SelectionSet object for this purpose later in this chapter, in the *User Interaction* section.

Layer

A Layer object represents a single layer on your AutoCAD drawing. Once you've added some Layer objects to your drawing, you can control the layer for new objects by setting the ActiveLayer property of the Document object. You can change the layer of a drawing entity simply by assigning the name of a different Layer object to the entity's Layer property.

The properties of a layer (shown in Table 20.5) provide you with the same control you get from the Layer Control on the AutoCAD Object Properties toolbar.

TABLE 20.5: Layer methods and properties

Name	Type	Description
Delete	Method	Deletes an entire layer
Color	Property	Color used to plot objects on the layer
Freeze	Property	True if the layer is frozen

TABLE 20.5 CONTINUED: Layer methods and properties

Name	Type	Description
LayerOn	Property	True if the layer is on
LineType	Property	Default line type for the layer
Lock	Property	True if the layer is locked
Name	Property	Name of the layer

Layers are among the objects with a Color property (drawing entities and Groups also have a Color property). AutoCAD supplies constants for some of the most common colors, but for the most part, you use the number that you'd see in the Select Color dialog box to specify a color. Here's a Visual Basic procedure you can use to translate the common colors into friendlier names:

```
Function TranslateColor(intColor As Integer) As String
    ' Translate an AutoCAD color value to a string
    Select Case intColor
        Case acByBlock
            TranslateColor = "By Block"
        Case acByLayer
            TranslateColor = "By Layer"
        Case acRed
            TranslateColor = "Red"
        Case acYellow
            TranslateColor = "Yellow"
        Case acGreen
            TranslateColor = "Green"
        Case acCyan
            TranslateColor = "Cyan"
        Case acMagenta
            TranslateColor = "Magenta"
        Case acBlue
            TranslateColor = "Blue"
        Case acWhite
            TranslateColor = "White"
        Case 8
            TranslateColor = "Light Gray"
        Case 9
            TranslateColor = "Dark Gray"
```

```
            Case Else
                TranslateColor = "Custom Color #" & CStr(intColor)
        End Select
    End Function
```

LineType

A LineType object represents a single style of line used in objects, and its combination of dots, dashes, and symbols. The Document.ActiveLineType property sets the type of line to be used for new objects in your drawing. LineType objects only have two properties of interest: their Name and their Description, the latter of which is a series of characters representing the line.

WARNING   With most AutoCAD objects, you can use the Add method of the parent collection to create new instances. Unfortunately, because there is no way to edit the properties of a LineType object, this doesn't really do you any good. To add new LineTypes to a drawing, you need to use the LineTypes.Load method to load them from an AutoCAD linetype definition file. To create new line types, you'll need to use the Visual Basic file and string manipulation capabilities to modify a linetype definition file, and then load your new linetype from the file—not a task for the novice.

RegisteredApplication

The RegisteredApplications collection provides an ActiveX Automation equivalent of the AutoLISP regapp function. Before an external application can use AutoCAD extended data, it needs to be registered in the drawing. From an Automation client you can use the RegisteredApplications.Add method to accomplish this. You can also use this collection to list all the applications that are already registered for the current drawing.

TextStyle

A TextStyle object represents a set of formatting properties for a piece of text (which itself is represented by a Text object in the Drawing's collection of entities). You can use the Add method of the TextStyles collection to create a new TextStyle object, and then set its properties. To control the style of newly created text, use the

`Document.ActiveTextStyle` property. To change the style of existing text, set the StyleName property of the Text object to the name of a TextStyle in the drawing.

Table 20.6 shows some of the methods and properties of the TextStyle object.

TABLE 20.6: TextStyle methods and properties

Name	Type	Description
Delete	Method	Deletes the TextStyle from the drawing
FontFile	Property	Path and file name of the font to use
Height	Property	Height of the text in drawing units
LastHeight	Property	Previous value of the Height property
ObliqueAngle	Property	Slant of the text
TextGenerationFlag	Property	Set to acTextFlagBackward for backward text, or acTextFlagUpsideDown for inverted text

UserCoordinateSystem

A UserCoordinateSystem object represents a User Coordinate System (UCS). You define a new UCS by specifying its Origin, X vector, and Y vector; these properties together are sufficient to determine the Z vector of the UCS. You can also retrieve the UCS Matrix for any given UCS, which provides the necessary 4x4 transformation matrix to transform values from the UCS back to the World Coordinate System. Table 20.7 shows some of the methods and properties for the UCS object.

TABLE 20.7: UserCoordinateSystem methods and properties

Name	Type	Description
GetUCSMatrix	Method	Retrieves the transformation matrix for the UCS
Origin	Property	Origin of the UCS
XVector	Property	X vector of the matrix
YVector	Property	Y vector of the matrix

TIP   All coordinates entered through ActiveX Automation are entered in the World Coordinate System (WCS).

View

A View object represents a single 3D view of your drawing. Views don't contain drawing objects. Rather, they are a set of instructions that tell AutoCAD how to portray the drawing objects. Views are used only as input to other objects. You can use a view as an argument to the PlotView method of the Plot object or the SetView method of the Viewport object. This has the effect of defining the view that those other objects use for their own operations.

Table 20.8 shows some of the methods and properties for the UCS object.

TABLE 20.8: View methods and properties

Name	Type	Description
Delete	Method	Deletes the view from the drawing
Center	Property	Starting point of the view line of sight
Direction	Property	Direction vector of the view
Height	Property	Height of the view
Target	Property	Ending point of the view line of sight
Width	Property	Width of the view

Viewport

A Viewport object defines the properties of the on-screen view of your drawing. You select a viewport by setting the Document.ActiveViewport property to the name of a Viewport object. In addition to defining the portion of a drawing that you can see on the screen, a Viewport object provides methods to allow you to zoom in on a portion of the drawing. Table 20.9 lists some of the methods and properties of the Viewport object.

TABLE 20.9: Viewport methods and properties

Name	Type	Description
GetGridSpacing	Method	Gets the grid spacing for this viewport
GetSnapSpacing	Method	Gets the snap spacing for this viewport
SetGridSpacing	Method	Sets the grid spacing for this viewport
SetSnapSpacing	Method	Sets the snap spacing for this viewport
SetView	Method	Chooses the View to associate with this viewport
ZoomAll	Method	Zooms to show the entire drawing
ZoomScaled	Method	Zooms to a particular magnification
Center	Property	Starting point of the viewport line of sight
Direction	Property	Direction vector of the viewport
GridOn	Property	True to show the grid
Height	Property	Height of the viewport
OrthoOn	Property	True to turn Ortho mode on
SnapOn	Property	True to turn Snap mode on
Target	Property	Ending point of the viewport line of sight
UCSIconOn	Property	True to show the UCS icon
Width	Property	Width of the viewport

Plot

Each AutoCAD drawing has precisely one Plot object, retrieved with the PlotObject property of the Document Object. This object is a repository for the settings that control the plotted (or printed) output of the drawing. The methods of the Plot object allow you to trigger a plot from your ActiveX Automation code. Table 20.10 shows some of the methods and properties of the Plot object.

TABLE 20.10: Plot methods and properties

Name	Type	Description
PlotExtents	Method	Plots the portion of the drawing that contains objects
PlotPreview	Method	Displays the Plot Preview dialog box
PlotToDevice	Method	Sends the plot to the specified device
PlotToFile	Method	Sends the plot to the specified file
PlotView	Method	Specifies the view to use for the plot
PlotWithConfigFile	Method	Plots according to the specified configuration file
HideLines	Property	Set to True to remove hidden lines
Origin	Property	Origin of the plot on the paper
PaperSize	Property	Paper size for the plot

WARNING   Because the PlotPreview method displays a dialog box within the AutoCAD interface, it halts all of your code until the user responds. Don't call PlotPreview if the Visible property of the Application object is set to False!

Utility

Designers of Automation models often face the problem of deciding how to expose useful functionality that doesn't seem to be tightly associated with a particular object in the application. AutoCAD's answer to this problem is the Utility object. This is an object with no properties (except for the standard reference back to the Application object) but a host of methods. Table 20.11 lists these methods. You might think of this as the "Miscellaneous" object of AutoCAD.

TABLE 20.11: Methods of the Utility object

Name	Description
AngleFromXAxis	Calculates the angle of a given line from the X axis
AngleToReal	Converts an angle as a string to a real number in a specified unit of measurement
AngleToString	Converts an angle as a real number to a string in a specified unit of measurement
DistanceToReal	Converts a distance as a string to a real number in a specified unit of measurement
EndUndoMark	Marks the end of a group of operations (see StartUndoMark)
GetAngle	Interactively gets an angle from the user (considering the ANGBASE system variable)
GetCorner	Interactively gets the corner of a rectangle from the user
GetDistance	Interactively gets a distance from the user
GetInput	Interactively gets a keyword index from the user (see InitializeUserInput)
GetInteger	Interactively gets an integer from the user
GetKeyword	Interactively gets a keyword from the user (see InitializeUserInput)
GetOrientation	Interactively gets an angle from the user (ignoring the ANGBASE system variable)
GetPoint	Interactively gets a point from the user
GetReal	Interactively gets a real number from the user
GetString	Interactively gets a string from the user
InitializeUserInput	Sets up for a GetXXXX method that can accept keywords
PolarPoint	Gets a point at a specified distance and angle from a given point
RealToString	Converts a distance as a real number to a string in a specified unit of measurement
StartUndoMark	Marks the start of a group of operations (see EndUndoMark)
TranslateCoordinates	Translates a point from one set of coordinates to another

TIP

The GetXXXX methods of the Utility object prompt for their input in the Command window. To prompt the user to select entities from a drawing, use the `SelectionSet.SelectOnScreen` method.

Automation Techniques

As you've seen, the AutoCAD object model is fairly complex. It's also oriented towards drawing, rather than control of the AutoCAD user interface. While the ActiveX Automation control over a drawing is limited mainly by your imagination, it's sometimes difficult to know where to start. In this section, we'll explore a couple of simple ActiveX Automation operations. All of these samples are on the companion CD-ROM. If you're new to ActiveX Automation, you may want to open the samples and single-step through them so you can trace the full flow of the programs.

NOTE

The samples are supplied both as executable programs and as Visual Basic 5.0 source code. You can run the samples and see them in action without having Visual Basic on your computer, but to inspect the source code you'll need Visual Basic.

Creating a Drawing

We've already seen (in the section on the Application object) how to open an existing drawing in AutoCAD. What if you'd like to create a new drawing? This ability comes in handy if your program is designed to be a sort of "Wizard" program, automating the process of getting started with AutoCAD. For example, you might prompt the user for a new drawing name and for a type of drawing, and automatically generate the drawing for them. This is similar to the capability already provided by the Create New Drawing ➤ Use a Template feature of AutoCAD. The difference is that you can take total control of the drawing created by code, and possibly change settings based on user interaction.

This code is extracted from the GridMaker sample application on the companion CD-ROM:

```
' Make sure we have enough information to proceed
    If Len(txtDrawing & "") = 0 Or Len(txtTemplate & "") = 0 Then
        GoTo ExitHere
    End If
    ' Connect to AutoCAD and load the requested drawing.
    ' Start by trying to connect to a running instance
    On Error Resume Next
    Set moAcad = GetObject(, "AutoCAD.Application")
    If Err.Number Then
        ' We couldn't find a running instance, so try to launch
        ' a new instance of AutoCAD
        Err.Clear
        Set moAcad = CreateObject("AutoCAD.Application")
        If Err.Number Then
            ' Couldn't find it, couldn't create it: give up
            MsgBox "Unable to launch AutoCAD session", _
                vbCritical, "AutoCAD Drawing Explorer"
            End
        Else
            ' CreateObject launches an invisible session.
            ' Make it visible.
            moAcad.Visible = True
        End If
    End If
    On Error GoTo HandleErr
    ' If we get this far, AutoCAD is open. Save whatever
    ' drawing is open and create a new drawing. If there
    ' is no drawing open, this command is harmless
    moAcad.ActiveDocument.Save
    ' Create a new document based on the selected template
    Set moDocument = moAcad.ActiveDocument.New(txtTemplate)
    ' Give the drawing a name by calling the SaveAs method
    moDocument.SaveAs (txtDrawing)
```

In this sample, the txtDrawing control contains the name of the drawing to create, and the txtTemplate control contains the name of the template to use for it. Conceptually, the process is fairly simple. First, the code gets a pointer to the running instance of AutoCAD, or, if none can be found, it launches AutoCAD. Then, it saves any document that might be open and uses the New method of the

ActiveDocument to create a new document. Finally, it uses the SaveAs method to assign the selected name to the document.

TIP   Because the Name and FullName properties of the Document object are read-only, the only way to assign a name to a drawing is to use the Document.SaveAs method.

WARNING   AutoCAD Help claims that supplying a template name to the New method is optional. I did not find this to be the case. The New method will only work if you supply a template name.

Drawing a Line

Once you've created or retrieved a drawing using ActiveX Automation, you'll probably want to modify the drawing. We'll demonstrate this process with the GridMaker sample, which generates a series of lines. Figure 20.5 shows Grid-Maker in action, atop an AutoCAD drawing that it has just created. It doesn't look like much, does it? But when you realize that this entire drawing was created automatically, without having to enter the coordinates for any points or even touch the AutoCAD interface with your mouse, it takes on new significance.

Drawing a line is simple. First, you need to define the starting and ending points of the line. In AutoCAD, a point is represented by a three-element array of double-precision floating-point numbers. As you might expect, these three elements represent the X, Y, and Z positions of the point.

Once you've defined two points, you draw the line by calling the AddLine method of the Model Space object (assuming you haven't switched to Paper Space view; the PaperSpace object also contains an AddLine method). This draws the line and returns the Line object to your code. To actually show the line, you need to either regenerate the drawing (using the Document.Regen method), or tell AutoCAD to display the line using its own Update method.

FIGURE 20.5:

Drawing created with
GridMaker

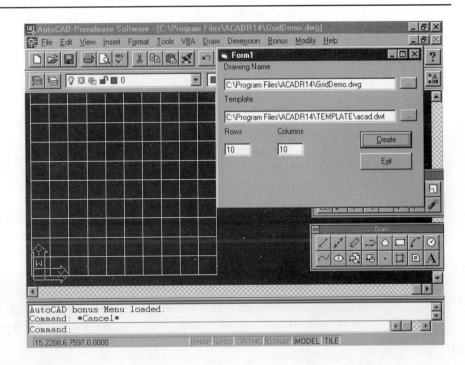

The code in GridMaker simply runs a pair of loops, one to draw the horizontal lines (by holding X constant and varying Y) and one to draw the vertical lines (by holding Y constant and varying X):

```
' Now create the lines
    For intI = 0 To txtRows
        ptStart(0) = 0
        ptStart(1) = intI
        ptStart(2) = 0
        ptEnd(0) = txtColumns
        ptEnd(1) = intI
        ptEnd(2) = 0
        Set oLine = moDocument.ModelSpace.AddLine(ptStart, ptEnd)
        oLine.Update
    Next intI
    For intI = 0 To txtColumns
        ptStart(0) = intI
        ptStart(1) = 0
```

```
                    ptStart(2) = 0
                    ptEnd(0) = intI
                    ptEnd(1) = txtRows
                    ptEnd(2) = 0
                    Set oLine = moDocument.ModelSpace.AddLine(ptStart, ptEnd)
                    oLine.Update
                Next intI
```

TIP   This code uses the Update method on each line as it's created, so that you can actually watch the drawing being created. In a real application, you'd probably want to wait until the end of the process and call Document .Regen instead, so all the drawing is done at once.

User Interaction

The Highlite sample application demonstrates a technique that lets the user of your application select objects on the AutoCAD drawing. This sample shows you how to work with an arbitrary set of AutoCAD drawing objects. When you press the Start Cycling button, AutoCAD prompts you to select objects, and then varies the color of the selected objects so that you get strong visual feedback as to what you selected. When you press Stop Cycling, the objects are returned to their original colors.

You might think you would have to write a tremendous amount of code to handle all of the standard ways of selecting objects: clicking on them, boxing them, and so on. But one of the strengths of ActiveX Automation is that applications can expose such complex behavior as a single method—in this case, the SelectOnScreen method of the SelectionSet object.

To use this method, your code first needs to create a new SelectionSet object, and then call the SelectOnScreen method. You can name your object anything you wish when you create it:

```
' Create a new selection set
    Set moSelSet = moAcad.ActiveDocument. _
     SelectionSets.Add("Highlite")
     ' Get some objects in it
    moSelSet.SelectOnScreen
```

When you call this method, control leaves your code and enters the hands of the end user (your application will wait until the user is done). AutoCAD places the standard Select objects prompt on the command line, and the user can use any of the standard AutoCAD methods to choose the objects to work with. When the user is done, you can query the SelectionSet to see what they chose. For example, here's the code from Highlite that stores the color of each object the user selected so that we can restore it later:

```
' Save the colors of all selected objects
    ReDim maSaveColor(0 To moSelSet.Count - 1)
    For intI = 0 To moSelSet.Count - 1
        maSaveColor(intI) = moSelSet(intI).Color
    Next intI
```

Setting Active Properties

Your application may need to ensure that AutoCAD is in a particular state before you start operating on the contents of the drawing. Conversely, you might want to sense the state of AutoCAD to determine whether it's safe to proceed with some operation. The Active sample application on the companion CD-ROM (see Figure 20.6) demonstrates these techniques by synchronizing its user interface with the selections in AutoCAD.

FIGURE 20.6

The Active Sample

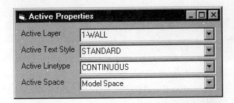

This sample starts out by retrieving lists of available layers, line types, and text styles from AutoCAD, and using them to fill combo boxes. For example, this code provides Active with a list of all of the available AutoCAD layers:

```
' Retrieve the list of layers
    cboLayer.Clear
    For intI = 0 To moDocument.Layers.Count - 1
        cboLayer.AddItem moDocument.Layers(intI).Name
    Next intI
```

To keep the Active interface synchronized with AutoCAD, we must employ a Visual Basic timer. This lets us run some code once a second, so that we can check the current values of the appropriate AutoCAD properties. Using a timer for this is necessary because AutoCAD doesn't notify our program by means of events when the user makes some change. To set the combo box on the Visual Basic form to the current value of the Document.ActiveLayer property in AutoCAD, you need this code:

```
With cboLayer
        For intI = 0 To .ListCount - 1
            If .List(intI) = moDocument.ActiveLayer.Name Then
                .ListIndex = intI
                Exit For
            End If
        Next intI
    End With
```

Finally, to update the property in AutoCAD, we wait until the user selects a new value in the combo box, and use that value to set the property. To do so, we must retrieve an appropriate object and set it into the Document.ActiveLayer property:

```
' Retrieve the layer object we selected
    Set oLayer = moDocument.Layers(cboLayer.Text)
' And set the ActiveLayer property
    Set moDocument.ActiveLayer = oLayer
```

NOTE   As it's written, the Active sample application won't know if you add a new layer, line type, or text style to the AutoCAD drawing. To add this capability, you could add a second timer to the form and use it to refresh the list of available items in the combo boxes, perhaps once every ten seconds.

The AutoCAD VBA Preview

AutoCAD R14 actually ships with two versions on the same CD. The first is the regular version that this whole book is about. The second is the AutoCAD Release 14 Preview, VBA Edition (we'll call it "AutoCAD VBA"). AutoCAD VBA includes, in addition to the usual AutoLISP programming language, a second language: Microsoft Visual Basic for Applications.

To install AutoCAD VBA, run the \acad\vbainst\setup.exe program from your AutoCAD CD. When you've done this, there's a new command available: VBAIDE. When you enter this command, you'll be placed in the VBA development environment, shown in Figure 20.7.

FIGURE 20.7:

The VBA development environment

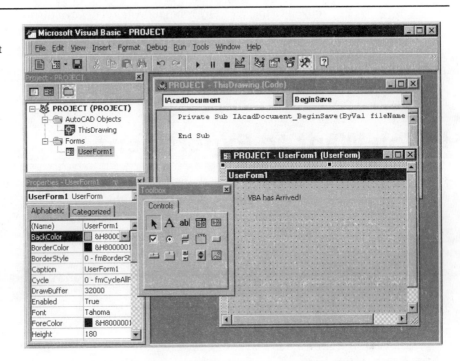

If you've used any other product with VBA 5.0, such as Word 97, Excel 97, or Visio 5.0, you'll feel right at home in this window. If not, don't panic! Because this feature was added relatively late during the creation of AutoCAD R14, we're not able to cover it in depth in the printed version of this book. But you'll find two chapters on VBA coming soon to the Sybex Web site, at http://www.sybex.com.

TIP   AutoCAD VBA has not yet been localized. Even if you've purchased a non-English version of AutoCAD, you'll find that the VBA development environment is presented in English.

WARNING   AutoCAD VBA is currently a preview, not a supported product! If you've installed this version and run into problems, Autodesk technical support won't help you. However, if you're an AutoLISP developer, you should definitely look into VBA; you may find that your applications can be moved to this new environment with relatively little trouble. Autodesk is anxious to receive customer feedback on the potential of VBA in AutoCAD. You can send your comments to vba.support@autodesk.com, with a subject line starting with "VBA:."

If You Want to Experiment...

The code examples in this chapter are designed to show you just some of the possibilities of using ActiveX Automation with AutoCAD. To go further, take a look at the acadauto.hlp file on the AutoCAD CD, which is peppered with short code examples. You'll also need an ActiveX client program such as Visual Basic. Here's a few ideas to get you started thinking:

- Allow the user to specify a group of objects and a layer to which to move them

- Create a list showing the location of all chairs on your office plan

- Select a group of drawings and send them to the plotter one by one

- Extract the blocks from one drawing and recreate them in another

- Create a new drawing layer and use it for backup copies of selected objects

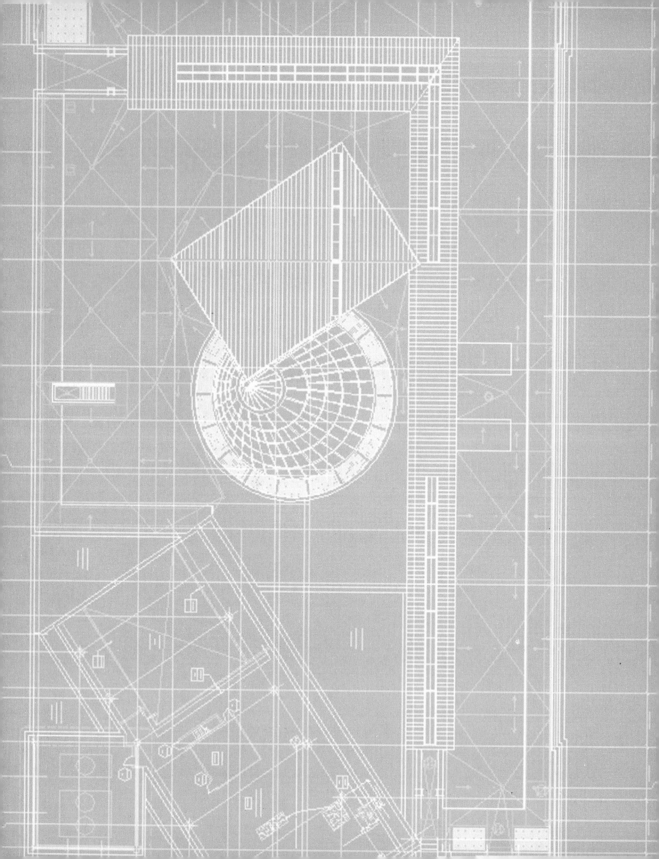

CHAPTER

TWENTY-ONE

21

Integrating AutoCAD into Your Projects and Organization

- Customizing Toolbars

- Adding Your Own Pull-Down Menus

- Creating Custom Line Types and Hatch Patterns

- Supporting Your System and Working in Groups

- Establishing Office Standards and Maintaining Files

- Using Networks and Keeping Records

- Understanding What AutoCAD Can Do for You

AutoCAD offers a high degree of flexibility and customization, allowing you to tailor the software's look and feel to your requirements. In this final chapter, you will examine how you can fit AutoCAD into your work group and office environment.

The first part of the chapter shows how you can adapt AutoCAD to fit your particular needs. You will learn how to customize AutoCAD by modifying its menus, and how to create custom macros for commands that your work group uses frequently.

Then we'll examine some general issues of using AutoCAD in an office. In this discussion you may find help with some problems you have encountered when using AutoCAD in your particular work environment. We'll also discuss the management of AutoCAD projects.

Customizing Toolbars

The most direct way to adapt AutoCAD to your way of working is to customize the toolbars. AutoCAD offers new users an easy route to customization. You can create new toolbars, customize tools, and even create new icons. In this section, you'll discover how easy it is to add features to AutoCAD.

Taking a Closer Look at the Toolbars Dialog Box

Throughout this book, you've used the Toolbars dialog box to open toolbars that are specialized for a particular purpose. The Toolbars dialog box is one of the many entry points to customizing AutoCAD. Let's take a closer look at this dialog box to see what other options it offers besides just opening other toolbars.

1. Right-click on the Draw toolbar. The Toolbars dialog box opens.

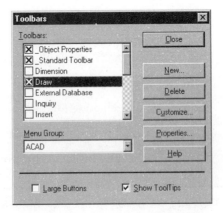

The Toolbars list box shows a listing of all the toolbars available in AutoCAD.

2. Scroll the list box up until you see Inquiry. Highlight it and then click on the Properties... button. The Toolbar Properties dialog box appears.

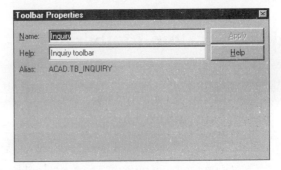

The Name input box controls the title that appears in the toolbars title bar. The Help input box controls the help message that appears in the status line.

3. Click on Close in the Toolbar dialog box to close both dialog boxes.

As you can see from this Toolbar Properties dialog box, you can rename a toolbar and alter its help message, if you choose. Here are brief descriptions of some of the other options in the Toolbars dialog box:

Close   closes the dialog box.

New   lets you create a new toolbar.

Delete   deletes a toolbar from the list.

Customize... opens the Customize Toolbar dialog box from which you can click and drag predefined buttons.

Properties... opens the Toolbar Properties dialog box.

Help displays helpful information about the Toolbar dialog box.

Large Buttons changes all the tools to a larger format.

Show Tooltips controls the display for the tool tips.

You'll get to use most of these other options in the following sections.

NOTE   Typically, AutoCAD stores new toolbars and buttons in the Acad.mns file (see *The Windows Menu Files* sidebar later in this chapter). You can also store them in your custom menu files. Once you've created and loaded your menu file as described in the later section *Adding Your Own Pull-Down Menu*, choose your menu from the Menu Group pull-down list in the New Toolbar dialog box described below.

Creating Your Own Toolbar

You may find that instead of using one toolbar or flyout, you are moving from flyout to flyout from a variety of different toolbars. If you keep track of the tools you use most frequently, you can create your own custom toolbar containing your favorite tools. Here's how it's done.

1. Right-click on an button in any toolbar. The Toolbars dialog box opens.

2. Click on the New button. The New Toolbar dialog box appears.

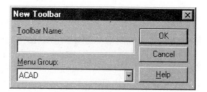

3. Enter **My Toolbar** in the Toolbar Name input box, and then click on OK. A small, blank toolbar appears in the AutoCAD window.

Notice that ACAD.My Toolbar now appears in the Toolbar dialog box list. You can now begin to add buttons to your toolbar.

4. Click on Customize… from the Toolbars dialog box. The Customize Toolbars dialog box appears.

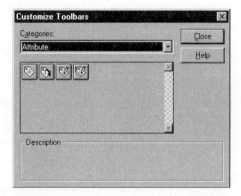

5. Open the Categories pull-down list. Notice that the list contains the main categories of commands.

6. Choose Draw from the list. The list box displays all the tools available for the Draw category. Notice that the dialog box offers several additional arc and circle tools not found in the Draw toolbar.

7. Click on the first tool in the top row: the Line tool. You'll see a description of the tool in the Description box at the bottom of the dialog box.

8. Click and drag the Line tool from the Customize Toolbars dialog box into the new toolbar you just created. The Line tool now appears in your toolbar.

9. Click and drag the Arc Start End Direction tool to your new toolbar.

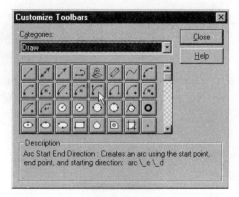

10. Exit the Customize Toolbar dialog box and the Toolbars dialog box.

You now have a custom toolbar with two buttons. You can add buttons from different categories if you like. You are not restricted to buttons from one category.

NOTE   If you need to remove a tool from your toolbar, click and drag it out of your toolbar into the blank area of the drawing. Do this while the Customize Toolbars dialog box is open.

AutoCAD will treat your custom toolbar just like any other toolbar. It will appear when you start AutoCAD and will remain until you close it. You can recall it by the same method described in the first exercise.

Opening Toolbars from the Command Line

You may want to know how to open toolbars using the command line. This can be especially helpful if you want to create toolbar buttons that open other toolbars.

1. Type **-Toolbar** ⤶ at the command prompt (don't forget to include the minus sign at the beginning of the Toolbar command).

2. At the Toolbar Name <All> prompt, enter the name of the toolbar you want to open.

3. At the Show/Hide/Left/Right/Top/Bottom/Float: <Show> prompt, press ⤶. The toolbar appears on the screen.

A typical button macro for opening a toolbar might look like this:

```
^c^cToolbar[space]ACAD.Arc[space][space]
```

Here, the [space] is added for clarity. You would press the spacebar in its place. This example shows a macro that opens the Arc toolbar (ACAD.Arc).

As the prompt in step 3 indicates, you can specify the location of the toolbar by left, right, top, or bottom. Float lets you specify the location and number of rows for the toolbar.

The following list shows the toolbar names available in the standard AutoCAD system. Use the following names with the Toolbar command:

ACAD.TB_OBJECT_PROPERTIES

ACAD.TB_STANDARD

ACAD.TB_DIMENSIONING

ACAD.TB_DRAW

ACAD.TB_EXTERNAL_DATABASE

ACAD.TB_INQUIRY

ACAD.TB_INSERT

ACAD.TB_MODIFY

ACAD.TB_MODIFYII

ACAD.TB_OBJECT_SNAP

ACAD.TB_REFERENCE

ACAD.TB_RENDER

ACAD.TB_SOLIDS

ACAD.TB_SURFACES

ACAD.TB_UCS

ACAD.TB_VIEWPOINT

ACAD.TB_ZOOM

You may notice that the toolbar names in the Toolbars dialog box do not match those shown in this list. You can find the "true" name of a toolbar by highlighting it in the Toolbars dialog box, and then clicking on Properties…. The toolbar's true name is displayed under Alias.

Customizing Buttons

Now let's move on to some more serious customization. Suppose you want to create an entirely new button with its own functions. For example, you may want to create a set of buttons that will insert your favorite symbols. Or you might want to create a toolbar containing a set of tools that open some the other toolbars that are normally "put away."

Creating a Custom Button

In the following set of exercise, you'll create a button that inserts a door symbol. You'll add your custom button to the toolbar you just created.

1. Open the Toolbars dialog box again, and then click on Customize....

2. Select Custom from the drop-down list. The list box now shows two blank buttons, one for a single command and another for flyouts. (The one for flyouts has a small triangle in the lower-right corner.)

4. Click and drag the single command blank button to your new toolbar.

5. Right-click on the blank button in your new toolbar. The Button Properties dialog box appears. This dialog box lets you define the purpose of your custom button.

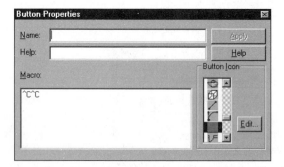

Let's pause for a moment to look at this dialog box. The Name input box lets you enter a name for your button. This name will appear as a tool tip. You must enter a name before AutoCAD will create the new button definition.

The Help input box just below the name lets you add a help message. This message will appear in the lower-left corner of the AutoCAD window when you point to your button.

The Macro area is the focus of this dialog box. Here, you can enter the keystrokes you want to "play back" when you click on this button.

Finally, to the right, you see a scroll bar that lets you scroll through a set of icons. You'll also see a button labeled Edit. When you highlight an icon in the scroll box, and then click on Edit, an Icon Editor tool appears allowing you to edit an existing icon, or create a new icon.

Now let's go ahead and add a macro and new icon to this button.

1. In the Name input box, enter Door. This will be your tool tip for this button.

2. In the Help input box, enter **Inserts a single door**. This will be the help message for this button

3. In the Macro input box, enter the following:

```
^c^cinsert door
```

TIP

You can put any valid string of keystrokes in the Macro input box, including AutoLISP functions. See Chapter 19 or the *ABCs of AutoLISP* on the companion CD-ROM for more on AutoLISP. You can also include pauses for user input using the backslash (\) character. See the *Pausing for User Input* section later in this chapter.

Note that the two ^Cs already appear in the Macro input box. These represent two Cancels being issued. This is the same as pressing the Escape key twice. It ensures that when the macro starts, it cancels any unfinished commands.

You follow the two cancels with the Insert command as it is issued from the keyboard. If you need help finding the keyboard equivalent of a command, consult the *AutoCAD 14 Instant Reference* on the companion CD-ROM, which contains a listing of all the command names.

WARNING

It is important that you enter the exact sequence of keystrokes that follow the command, otherwise your macro may get out of step with the command prompts. This will take a little practice and some going back and forth between testing your button and editing the macro.

After the Insert command, there is a space, and then the name "Door" appears. This is the same sequence of keystrokes you would enter at the command line to insert the door drawing you created in Chapters 2 and 3. You could go on to include an insertion point, scale factor, and rotation angle in this macro, but these options are better left for the time when the door is actually inserted.

Creating a Custom Icon

You have all the essential parts of the button defined. Now you just need to create a custom icon to go with your door button.

1. In the Icon scroll box, scroll down the list until you see a blank icon.

2. Click on the blank icon, and then click on Edit. The Button Editor appears.

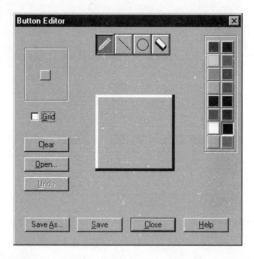

NOTE If you prefer, you can use any of the predefined icons in the scroll box. Just click on the icon you want to use, and then click on Apply.

The Button Editor is like a very simple drawing program. Across the top are the tools to draw lines, circles, and points as well as an eraser. Along the right side, you see a color toolbar from which you can choose colors for you icon button. In the upper left, you see a preview of your button. The following describes the rest of the options:

Grid turns a grid on and off in the drawing area. This grid can be an aid in drawing your icon.

Clear erases the entire contents of the drawing area.

Open opens a .bmp file to import an icon. The .bmp file must be small enough to fit in the 16 x 16 pixel matrix provided for icons (24 x 24 for large format icons).

Save As   saves your icon as a .bmp file under a name you enter.

Save   saves your icon under a name that AutoCAD provides, usually a series of numbers and letters.

Close   exits the Button Editor.

Help   displays helpful information about the features of the Button Editor.

Undo   undoes the last operation you performed.

Now let's continue by creating a new icon.

3. Draw the door icon shown here. Don't worry if it's not perfect; you can always go back and fix it.

4. Click on Save, and then Close.

5. In the Button Properties dialog box, click on Apply. You'll see the icon appear in the button in your toolbar.

6. Now click on the Close button of the Toolbars dialog box.

WARNING   The Door drawing must be in the default directory or in the Acad search path before the door button will be inserted.

7. Click on the Door button of your new toolbar. The door appears in your drawing ready to be placed.

You can continue to add more buttons to your toolbar to build a toolbar of symbols. Of course, you're not limited to a symbols library. You can also incorporate your favorite macros or even AutoLISP routines that you may accumulate as you work with AutoCAD. The possibilities are endless.

Setting the Properties of Flyouts

Just as you added a new button to your toolbar, you can also add flyouts. Remember that flyouts are really just another form of a toolbar. This next example shows how you can add a copy of the Zoom toolbar to your custom toolbar, and then make adjustments to the properties of the flyout.

1. Right-click on the door button in the Toolbar you just finished. The Toolbar dialog box opens with My Toolbar already highlighted.

2. Click on Customize, and then at the Customize Toolbar dialog box, open the pull-down list and select Custom.

3. Click and drag the flyout button from the list box into the My Toolbar toolbar.

TIP   To delete a button from a toolbar, open the Toolbars dialog box, and then click on Customize.... When the Customize Toolbars dialog box appears, click and drag the button you want to delete out of the toolbar and into the drawing area.

You could have simply clicked and dragged an existing flyout from the Customize Toolbars dialog box. You now have a blank flyout to which you can add you own icon. Let's see what options are available for flyout buttons.

4. Close the Customize Toolbars dialog box, and then right-click on the new, blank flyout button you just added to your toolbar. The Flyout Properties dialog box appears.

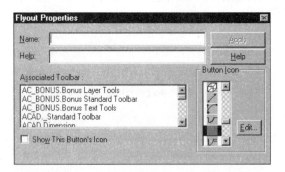

Notice how this dialog box resembles the Button Properties dialog box you used in the previous exercise. But instead of the Macro input box, you see a list of associated toolbars.

5. Scroll down the list of toolbar names until you find ACAD.Zoom. This is a predefined toolbar, though it can be a toolbar you define yourself.

6. Highlight ACAD.Zoom, and then enter **My Zoom Flyout** in the Name input box. Enter **My very own flyout** in the Help input box.

7. Locate an icon in the icon scroll box that looks like a magnifying glass, and click on it.

8. Click on the checkbox labeled Show This Button's Icon so that an x appears in the box.

9. Click on Apply. The flyout button in the My Toolbar toolbar shows the icon you selected.

10. Close the Toolbars dialog box, and then place the arrow cursor on the flyout to display its tool tip. Notice that your new tool tip and help message appear.

11. Click and drag the Zoom icon, and then select Zoom In from the flyout. Notice that even though you selected Zoom In, the original Zoom icon remains as the icon for the flyout.

Step 11 demonstrates that you can disable the feature that causes the last flyout to appear as the default on the toolbar. You disabled this feature in step 8 by checking the Show This Button's Icon checkbox.

Editing Existing Buttons

If you want to edit an existing button or flyout, you can go directly to either the Button Properties or the Flyout Properties dialog box by double-right-clicking on a button. Once one of these dialog boxes is open, you can make changes to any component of the button definition.

The Windows Menu Files

As you create and modify icon buttons and toolbars, you see a messages momentarily appear in the status line at the bottom of the AutoCAD window. These messages are telling you that AutoCAD is creating new menu files. The Windows version of AutoCAD creates several menu files it uses in the course of an editing session.

Here's a brief rundown of what those different menu files are:

Acad.mnu is the source text file that contains the information required to build the AutoCAD menu. If you are a programmer, you would use this file to do detailed customization of the AutoCAD menu. Here, you can edit the pull-downs, image tiles, buttons, etc. Most users won't have a need to edit this file.

Acad.mnc is AutoCAD's translation of the Acad.mnu file. AutoCAD translates, or "compiles," the Acad.mnu file so that it can read the menu faster.

Acad.mns is a text file created by AutoCAD containing the source information from the .mnu file plus additional comments. This file is rewritten whenever an .mnu file is loaded.

Acad.mnr is the menu resource file. It is a binary file that contains the bitmap images used for buttons and other graphics.

As you create or edit icon buttons and toolbars, AutoCAD first adds your custom items to the Acad.mns file. It then compiles this file into the Acad.mnc and Acad.mnr files for quicker access to the menus. If you reload the MNU version of your menu, AutoCAD recreates the MNS file thereby removing any toolbar customization you may have done.

Note that the Acad.mns file is the file you will want to copy to other computers to transfer your custom buttons and toolbars. Also, if you create your own pull-down menu files, as in the Mymenu.mnu example in this chapter, AutoCAD will create the source, compiled, and resource files for your custom menu file. You have the option to store new toolbars in your custom menu through the Menu Group pull-down list of the New Toolbar dialog box.

Adding Your Own Pull-Down Menu

In addition to adding buttons and toolbars, AutoCAD lets you add pull-down menu options. This sections looks at how you might add a custom pull-down menu to your AutoCAD environment.

Creating Your First Pull-Down Menu

Let's start by trying the following exercise to create a simple pull-down menu file called My Menu.

1. Using a text editor, like the Windows Notepad, create a file called **Mymenu.mnu**, containing the following lines:

```
***POP1
[My 1st Menu]
[Line]^c^c_line
[-]
[->More]
[Arc-SED]^c^c_arc \_e \_d
[<-Break At]^c^c(defun c:breakat ()+
(command "break" pause "f" pause "@")+
);breakat
[Fillet 0]^c^c_fillet r 0;;
[Point Style X]'pdmode 3
***POP2
[My 2nd Menu]
[door]^c^cInsert door
[Continue Line]^C^CLINE;;
```

2. Save this file, and be sure you place it in your \AutoCAD R14\support directory.

WARNING Pay special attention to the spaces between letters in the commands described in this chapter (though you need not worry much about whether to type upper- or lowercase letters).

Once you've stored the file, you've got your first custom pull-down menu. You may have noticed some familiar items among the lines you entered. The menu contains the Line and Arc commands. It also contains the Breakat macro you worked on in Chapter 19; this time, that macro is broken into shorter lines.

Now let's see how My Menu works in AutoCAD.

Loading a Menu

In the following exercise, you will load the menu you have just created and test it out. The procedure described here for loading menus is the same for all menus, regardless of their source.

1. Click on Tools ➤ Customize Menus…. The Menu Customization dialog box appears.

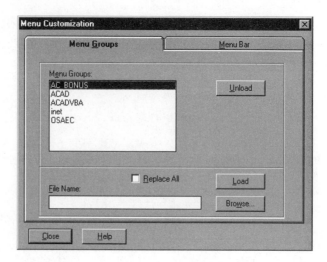

2. Click on Browse at the bottom of the dialog box. The Select Menu file dialog box appears.

3. Click on the Files of Type drop-down list, and then select Menu Template (*.mnu).

4. Locate the Mymenu.mnu file, highlight it, and then click on Open. You return to the Menu Customization dialog box.

5. Click Load. You see a warning message telling you that you will lose any toolbar customization you have made. This only refers to the specific menu you are loading. Since you haven't made any toolbar customization changes to your menu, you won't lose anything.

6. Click Yes. The warning dialog box closes and you see the name of your menu group listed in the Menu Group list box.

7. Highlight Mymenu.mnu in the list box, and then click on the Menu Bar tab at the top of the dialog box. The dialog box changes to show two lists.

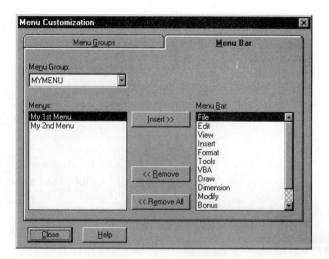

On the left is the name of the menus available in your menu file. The list on the right shows the currently available pull-down menus.

8. Highlight Help in the right-hand column. This tells AutoCAD you want to add your pull-down in front of the Help pull-down.

9. Highlight My 1st Menu from the list on the left, and then click on the Insert >> button. My 1st Menu moves into the right-hand column and it appears in the AutoCAD menu bar.

10. Highlight My 2nd Menu from the list on the left, and then click on Insert >> again. My 2nd Menu is copied to the right-hand column and it also appears in the menu bar.

11. Close the Menu Customization dialog box.

12. Draw a line on the screen, and then try the My 1st Menu ➤ More ➤ Break At option.

With just an 11-line menu file, you created a menu that contains virtually every tool used to build menus. Now let's take a more detailed look at how menu files work.

How the Pull-Down Menu Works

Let's take a closer look at the Mymenu.mns file. The first item in the file, ***POP1, identifies the beginning of a pull-down menu. The item just below this is the phrase My 1st Menu in square brackets. This is the title of the pull-down menu; it is what appears in the toolbar. Every pull-down menu must have this title element.

Following the title, each item on the list starts with a word enclosed in brackets; these words are the options that actually appear when you open the pull-down menu. If you were to remove everything else, you would have the menu as it appears on the screen. The text that follows the item in brackets conveys instructions to AutoCAD about the option.

Finally, in the My Menu sample, you see ***POP2. This is the beginning of a second pull-down menu. Again, you must follow this with a pull-down menu title in square brackets. Below the title, you can add other menu options.

Calling Commands

Now look at the Line option in the Mymenu.mnu listing. The two Ctrl + C (^C) elements that follow the square brackets will cancel any command that is currently operative. The Line command follows, written just as it would be entered through the keyboard. Two Cancels are issued in case you are in a command that has two levels, such as the Edit Vertex option of the Pedit command (Modify ➤ Object ➤ Polyline).

The underline that precedes the Line command tells AutoCAD that you are using the English-language version of this command. This feature lets you program non-English versions of AutoCAD using the English-language command names.

You may also notice that there is no space between the second ^C and the NEW command. A space in the line would be the same as a ↵. If there were a space between these two elements, a ↵ would be entered between the last Ctrl + C and the New command, causing the command sequence to misstep. Another way to indicate a ↵ is by using the semicolon, as in the following example:

```
[Continue Line]^C^CLINE;;
```

> **TIP**
>
> When you have many ↵s in a menu macro, using semicolons instead of spaces can help make your macro more readable.

In this sample menu option, the Line command is issued, and then an additional ↵ is added. The effect of choosing this option would be a line that continues from the last line entered into your drawing. The two semicolons following the word "LINE" tell AutoCAD to start the Line command, and then issue ↵ twice to begin a line from the endpoint of the last line entered. (AutoCAD automatically issues a single ↵ at the end of a menu line. In this case, however, you want two ↵s, so they must be represented as semicolons.)

Pausing for User Input

Another symbol used in the menu file is the backslash (\); it is used when a pause is required for user input. For example, when you selected the Arc-SED option in My Menu, it started the Arc command and then paused for your input.

```
[Arc-SED]^c^c_arc \_e \_d
```

> **NOTE**
>
> The underline that precedes the command name and option input tells AutoCAD that you are entering the English-language versions of these commands.

The space between ^c^c_arc and the backslash (\) represents the pressing of the spacebar. The backslash indicates a pause to allow you to select the starting endpoint for the arc. Once you have picked a point, the _e represents the selection of the Endpoint option under the Arc command. A second backslash allows another point selection. Finally, the _d represents the selection of the Direction option. Figure 21.1 illustrates this.

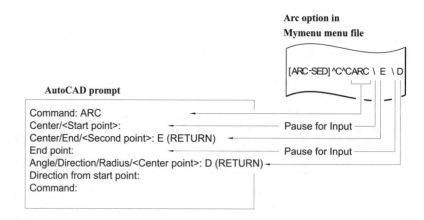

FIGURE 21.1:

The execution of the
Arc menu item

If you want the last character in a menu item to be a backslash, you must follow the backslash with a semicolon.

Using the Plus Sign for Long Lines

As you browse through the Acad.mnu file, you'll notice that many of the lines end with a plus sign (+). The length of each line in the menu file is limited to about 80 characters, but you can break a line into two or more lines by adding a plus sign at the end of the line that continues, like this:

```
[<-Break At]^c^c(defun c:breakat ()+
(command "break" pause "f" pause "@")+
);breakat
```

> **TIP**
>
> It's okay to break an AutoLISP program into smaller lines. In fact, it can help you read and understand the program more easily.

This example shows how you would include the Breakat AutoLISP macro in a menu. Everything in this segment is entered just as it would be with the keyboard. The plus sign is used to indicate the continuation of this long item to the subsequent lines, and the semicolon is used in place of ↵.

Creating a Cascading Menu

Look at the More option in the File pull-down menu group; it starts with these characters: ->. This is the way you indicate a menu item that opens a cascading menu. Everything that follows the [->More] menu item will appear in the cascading menu. To indicate the end of the cascading menu, you use the characters <-, as in the [<-Rotate90] menu item farther down. Anything beyond this <- item appears in the main part of the menu. If the last item in a cascading menu is also the last item in the menu group, you must use <-<-, as in [<-<-.XZ].

Placing Division Lines and Dimmed Text in Pull-Down Menus

Two symbols are used to place dividing lines in your pull-down menus. One is the *double-hyphen* symbol (--). This is used to divide groups of items in a menu; it will expand to fill the entire width of the pull-down menu with a line of hyphens. The other option is the *tilde* symbol (~). If the tilde precedes a bracketed option name, that option will be dimmed when displayed; when clicked on, it will have no effect. You have probably encountered these dimmed options on various pull-down menus in the programs you use. When you see a dimmed menu item, it usually means that the option is not valid under the current command.

Loading AutoLISP Macros with Your Submenu

As you become a more advanced AutoCAD user, you may find that you want to have many of your own AutoLISP macros load with your menus. This can be accomplished by combining all of your AutoLISP macros into a single file. Give this file the same name as your menu file with the .mnl file name extension. Such a file will be automatically loaded with its menu counterpart. For example, say you have a file called Mymenu.mnl containing the Breakat AutoLISP macro. Whenever you load the Mymenu.mns, Mymenu.mnl will automatically load along with it, giving you access to the Breakat Macro. This is a good way to manage and organize any AutoLISP program code you want to include with a menu.

Adding Help Messages to Pull-Down Menu Items

Earlier in this chapter, I showed you how you can include a help message with an icon button. The help message appears in the status bar of AutoCAD window when you highlight an option. You can also include a help message with a pull-down menu item.

First, you must give your pull-down menu file a menu group name. This helps AutoCAD isolate your file and its help messages from other menus that might be loaded along with yours. To give your menu file a group name, add the following line at the top of the file:

```
***MENUGROUP=MYMENU
```

where *MYMENU* is the name you want for your menu group name.

Next, you will have to add an ID name to each menu item that requires a help message. The following shows a sample of how this might be done for the My 1st Menu example you used earlier:

```
***MENUGROUP=MYMENU
***POP1
[My 1st Menu]
ID_1line       [Line]^c^c_line
[--]
[->More]
ID_1arc-sed  [Arc-SED]^c^c_arc \_e \_d
ID_1breakat  [<-Break At]^c^c(defun c:breakat ()+
(command "break" pause "f" pause "@")+
);breakat
ID_1fillet0  [Fillet 0]^c^c_fillet r 0;;
ID_1pointx   [Point Style X]'pdmode 3
***POP2
[My 2nd Menu]
[door]^c^cInsert door
[Continue Line]^C^CLINE;;
```

The ID name starts with the characters "ID" followed by an underline, and then the name for the menu item. Several spaces are added so the menu items align for clarity. Each menu item must have a unique ID name.

Finally, you add a section at the end of your file called ***HELPSTRINGS. For this example, it would look like the following code.

```
***HELPSTRINGS
```

```
ID_1line      [Draws a line]
ID_1arc-sed   [Draws an arc with start, end, direction]
ID_1breakat   [Breaks an object at a single point]
ID_1fillet0   [Sets the Fillet radius to zero]
ID_1pointx    [Sets the Point style to an X]
```

The menu item ID names are duplicated exactly, followed by several spaces, and then the actual text you want to have appear in the status line, enclosed in brackets. The spaces between the ID and the text are for clarity.

> **WARNING** The ID names are case sensitive, so make sure they match up in both the HELPSTRINGS section and in the menu section.

Once you've done this, and then loaded the menu file, you will see these same messages appear in the status bar when these menu options are highlighted. In fact, if you browse your Acad.mnu file, you will see similar ID names. If you prefer, you can use numbers in place of names.

Creating Accelerator Keys

Perhaps one of the more popular methods for customizing AutoCAD has been the keyboard accelerator keys. Accelerator keys are Ctrl or Shift key combinations that invoke commonly used commands or tools in AutoCAD. The Osnaps are a popular candidate for accelerator keys, as are the display commands.

To add accelerator key definitions to AutoCAD, you need to add some additional code to your menu file. The following is an example of what you can add to the Mymenu.mnu file to define a set of accelerator keys.

```
***ACCELERATORS
[CONTROL+SHIFT+"E"]endp
[CONTROL+SHIFT+"X"]int
ID_1breakat   [CONTROL+SHIFT+"B"]
```

The ***ACCELERATORS line at the top of the list is the group heading, similar to the ***HELPSTRINGS heading in that it defines the beginning of the section. This is followed by the Accelerator descriptions.

There are two methods shown above for defining an accelerator key. The first two bracketed follow the format you've already seen for the pull-down menu.

But instead of the menu text in square brackets, you see the keys required to invoke the action that follows the brackets. So in the first line:

```
[CONTROL+SHIFT+"E"]endp
```

the CONTROL+SHIFT+"E" tells AutoCAD to enter the Endpoint Osnap (endp) whenever the Ctrl + Shift + E key combination is pressed. Notice that the E is in quotation marks and that all the characters are uppercase. Follow this format for quotation marks and capitalization when you create your own accelerator keys.

A second method is shown in the third line:

```
ID_1breakat   [CONTROL+SHIFT+"B"]
```

Here, the ID_1breakat is used to associate a keystroke combination with a menu option not unlike the way it is used to associate a menu item with a helpstring. This line tells AutoCAD to issue the Breakat macro listed earlier in the menu whenever the Ctrl + Shift + B key combination is pressed.

You can use either Ctrl or Shift individually or together in combination with most keys on your keyboard, including the function keys. You can also assign keys without the Control or Shift options. Note that the function keys and the Esc key are already defined, so take care that you don't redefine them unless you really want to. Table 21.1 is a brief listing of some of the special keys you can define and how you need to specify them in the menu file.

T A B L E 21.1: Key names to use in your accelerator key definitions.

Key	Format used in AutoCAD Menu
Numeric keypad	"NUMPAD0" through "NUMPAD9"
Ins	"INSERT"
Del	"DELETE"
Function keys	"F2" through "F12"
Up arrow	"UP"
Down arrow	"DOWN"
Left arrow	"LEFT"
Right arrow	"RIGHT"

Although you can use the F1 and Esc keys for accelerator keys, their use is discouraged because they serve other functions for both Windows and AutoCAD.

Creating Custom Line Types and Hatch Patterns

As your drawing needs expand, you may find that the standard line types and hatch patterns are not adequate for your application. Fortunately, you can create your own. This section explains how to go about creating custom line types and patterns.

Viewing Available Line Types

Although AutoCAD provides the line types most commonly used in drafting (see Figure 21.2), the dashes and dots may not be spaced the way you would like, or you may want an entirely new line type.

NOTE AutoCAD stores the line types in a file called Acad.lin, which is in ASCII format. When you create a new line type, you are actually adding information to this file. Or, if you create a new file containing your own line-type definitions, it, too, will have the extension .lin. You can edit line types as described here, or you can edit them directly in these files.

To create a custom line type, you use the Linetype command. Let's see how this handy command works, by first listing the available line types.

1. Open a new AutoCAD file.

2. Enter **-Linetype** ↵ at the command prompt. (Don't forget the minus sign at the beginning of the word Linetype.)

3. At the ?/Create/Load/Set prompt, enter ? ↵.

4. In the File dialog box that appears, locate and double-click on ACAD in the listing of available line type files. You get the listing shown in the top and bottom images of Figure 21.3, which shows the line types available in the Acad.lin file along with a simple description of each line. The top image of Figure 21.3 shows the standard line types; the bottom image shows the ISO and complex line types.

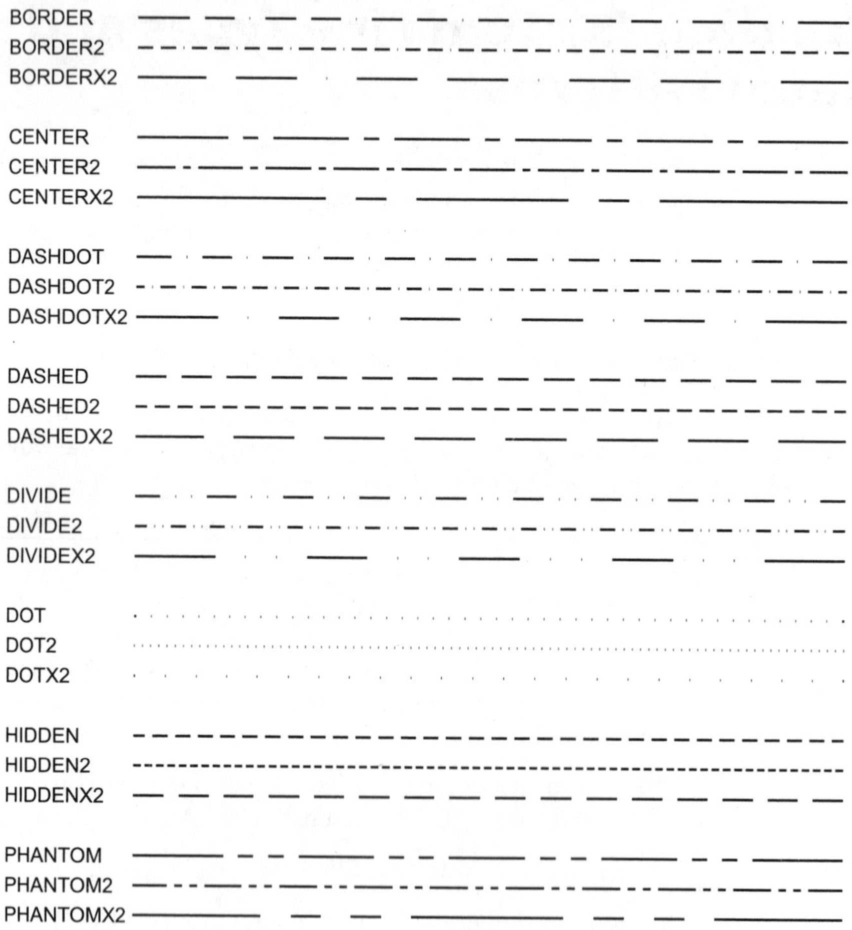

FIGURE 21.2:

The standard AutoCAD line types

BORDER
BORDER2
BORDERX2

CENTER
CENTER2
CENTERX2

DASHDOT
DASHDOT2
DASHDOTX2

DASHED
DASHED2
DASHEDX2

DIVIDE
DIVIDE2
DIVIDEX2

DOT
DOT2
DOTX2

HIDDEN
HIDDEN2
HIDDENX2

PHANTOM
PHANTOM2
PHANTOMX2

FIGURE 21.3:

The lines in this listing of standard line types were generated with the underline key and the period, and are only rough representations of the actual lines.

BORDER	Border	__ __ . __ __ . __ __ .
BORDER2	Border (.5x)	_._._._._._._._._._._._.
BORDERX2	Border (2x)	____ ____ . ____ ____ . ____
CENTER	Center	____ _ ____ _ ____ _ ____
CENTER2	Center (.5x)	___ _ ___ _ ___ _ ___ _ ___
CENTERX2	Center (2x)	_____ __ _____ __ _____
DASHDOT	Dash dot	__ . __ . __ . __ . __ .
DASHDOT2	Dash dot (.5x)	_._._._._._._._._._._._._.
DASHDOTX2	Dash dot (2x)	____ . ____ . ____ . ____
DASHED	Dashed	__ __ __ __ __ __ __ __ __
DASHED2	Dashed (.5x)	_ _ _ _ _ _ _ _ _ _ _ _ _
DASHEDX2	Dashed (2x)	____ ____ ____ ____ ____
DIVIDE	Divide	____ . . ____ . . ____ . . ____
DIVIDE2	Divide (.5x)	_.._.._.._.._.._.._..
DIVIDEX2	Divide (2x)	_____ . . _____ . . ____
DOT	Dot	. . . .
DOT2	Dot (.5x)	....
DOTX2	Dot (2x)	. . . .
HIDDEN	Hidden	__ __ __ __ __ __ __ __ __ __
HIDDEN2	Hidden (.5x)	_ _ _ _ _ _ _ _ _ _ _ _ _ _
HIDDENX2	Hidden (2x)	____ ____ ____ ____ ____
PHANTOM	Phantom	_____ __ __ _____ __ __ _____
PHANTOM2	Phantom (.5x)	____ _ _ ____ _ _ ____ _ _
PHANTOMX2	Phantom (2x)	_____ __ __ _____ __
ACAD_ISO02W100	ISO dash	__ __ __ __ __ __ __ __ __ __
ACAD_ISO03W100	ISO dash space	__ __ __ __ __
ACAD_ISO04W100	ISO long-dash dot	____ . ____ . ____ . ____ . .
ACAD_ISO05W100	ISO long-dash double-dot	____ . . ____ . . ____ .
ACAD_ISO06W100	ISO long-dash triple-dot	____ . . . ____ . . . ____
ACAD_ISO07W100	ISO dot	. . . .
ACAD_ISO08W100	ISO long-dash short-dash	____ __ ____ __ ____ __
ACAD_ISO09W100	ISO long-dash double-short-dash	____ __ __ ____ __ __
ACAD_ISO10W100	ISO dash dot	__ . __ . __ . __ . __ .
ACAD_ISO11W100	ISO double-dash dot	__ __ . __ __ . __ __ .
ACAD_ISO12W100	ISO dash double-dot	__ . . __ . . __ . . __ . .
ACAD_ISO13W100	ISO double-dash double-dot	__ __ . . __ __ . .
ACAD_ISO14W100	ISO dash triple-dot	__ . . . __ . . . __ .
ACAD_ISO15W100	ISO double-dash triple-dot	__ __ . . . __ __ .
FENCELINE1	Fenceline circle	----0-----0----0-----0----0---
FENCELINE2	Fenceline square	----[]-----[]----[]-----[]----
TRACKS	Tracks	-|-|-|-|-|-|-|-|-|-|-|-|-|-|-|-|-|
BATTING	Batting	SSSSSSSSSSSSSSSSSSSSSSSSSSSSSSSSSSSSSS
HOT_WATER_SUPPLY	Hot water supply	---- HW ---- HW ---- HW ----
GAS_LINE	Gas line	----GAS----GAS----GAS----GAS--
ZIGZAG	Zig zag	/\/\/\/\/\/\/\/\/\/\/\/\/\/\/\/\/

Creating a New Line Type

Next, try creating a new line type.

1. At the ?/Create/Load/Set prompt, enter **C** ↵.

2. At the `Name of linetype to create` prompt, enter **Custom** ↵ as the name of your new line type.

3. Notice that the File dialog box you see next is named Create or Append Linetype File. You need to enter the name of the line-type file you want to create or add to. If you pick the default line-type file, ACAD, your new line type will be added to the `Acad.lin` file. If you choose to create a new line-type file, AutoCAD will open a file containing the line type you create and add .lin to the file name you supply.

4. Let's assume you want to start a new line-type file; enter **Newline** ↵ at the File Name input box.

NOTE   If you had accepted the default line-type file, ACAD, the prompt in step 5 would say `Wait, checking if linetype already defined....` This protects you from inadvertently overwriting an existing line type you may want to keep.

---

5. At the `Creating new file... Descriptive text` prompt, enter a text description of your line type. You can use any keyboard character as part of your description, but the actual line type can be composed only of a series of lines, points, and blank spaces. For this exercise, enter:

    `Custom - My own center line _____ _ _____  ` ↵

    using the underline key to simulate the appearance of your line.

6. At the `Enter pattern (on next line)` prompt, enter the following numbers, known as the line-type code (after the a that appears automatically):

    `1.0,-.125,.25,-.125` ↵

WARNING   If you use the Set option of the -Linetype command to set a new default line type, you will get that line type no matter what layer you are on.

---

7. At the `New definition written to file. ?/Create/Load/Set` prompt, press ↵ to exit the -Linetype command.

Remember, once you've created a line type, you must load it in order to use it, as discussed in the *Assigning Line Types to Layers* section of Chapter 4.

TIP	You may also open the Acad.lin or other .lin file with the Windows Notepad and add the descriptive text and line-type code directly to the end of the file.

The Line-Type Code

In step 6 of the previous exercise you entered a series of numbers separated by commas. This is the line-type code, representing the different lengths of the components that make up the line type. The separate elements of the line-type code are explained as follows:

- The 1.0 following the a is the length of the first part of the line. (The a that begins the line-type definition is a code that is applied to all line types.)

- The first -.125 is the blank or broken part of the line. The minus sign tells AutoCAD that the line is *not* to be drawn for the specified length, which is 0.125 units in this example.

- Next comes the positive value of 0.25. This tells AutoCAD to draw a line segment 0.25 units long after the blank part of the line.

- Finally, the last negative value, -.125, again tells AutoCAD to skip drawing the line for the distance of 0.125 units.

This series of numbers represents the one segment that is repeated to form the line (see Figure 21.4). You could also create a very complex line type that looks like a random broken line, as in Figure 21.5.

FIGURE 21.4:

Line-type description with plotted line

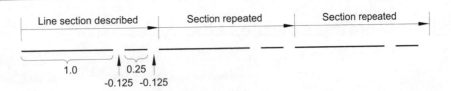

FIGURE 21.5:

Random broken line

You may be wondering what purpose the a serves at the beginning of the line-type code. A line type is composed of a series of line segments and points. The a, which is supplied by AutoCAD automatically, is a code that forces the line type to start and end on a line segment rather than a blank space in the series of lines. At times, AutoCAD stretches the last line segment to force this condition, as shown in Figure 21.6.

FIGURE 21.6:

AutoCAD stretches the beginning and end of the line as necessary

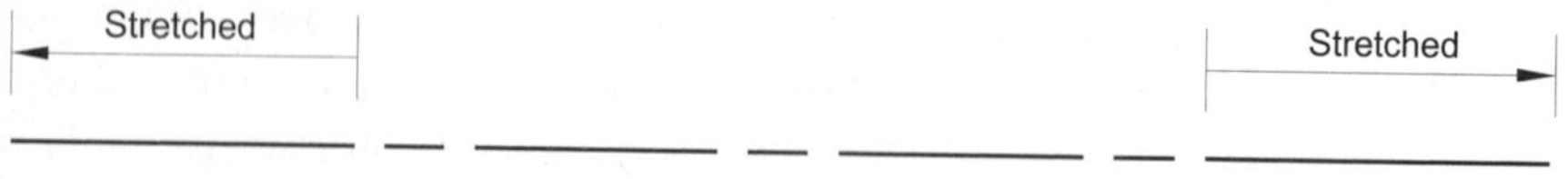

NOTE   The values you enter for the line-segment lengths are multiplied by the Ltscale factor, so be sure to enter values for the *plotted* lengths

As mentioned in the beginning of this section, you can also create line types outside AutoCAD by using a word processor or text editor such as Windows Notepad. The standard Acad.lin file looks like Figure 21.6. This is the same file you saw earlier, with the addition of the code used by AutoCAD to determine the line segment lengths.

Normally, to use a line type you have created, you have to load it, through either the Layer or the Linetype dialog box (Data ➤ Layers…, or Data ➤ Linetype…). If you use one of your own line types frequently, you may want to create an icon button macro, so it will be available as an option on a menu.

Creating Complex Line Types

A complex line type is one that incorporates text or special graphics. For example, if you want to show an underground gas line in a site plan, you normally show a line with an intermittent "G," as shown in Figure 21.7. Fences are often shown with an intermittent "X."

For the graphics needed to compose complex line types, you can use any of the symbols found in the AutoCAD font files discussed in Chapter 8. Just create a text style using these symbol fonts, and then specify the appropriate symbol by using its corresponding letter in the line-type description.

FIGURE 21.7:

Samples of complex
line types

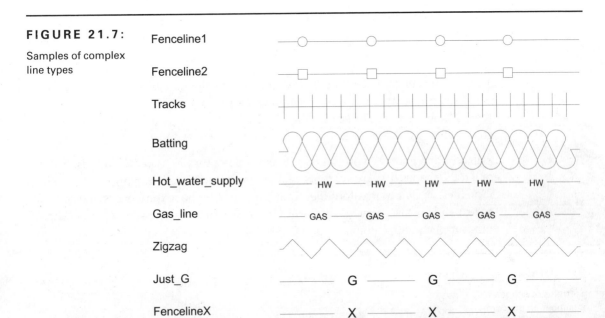

Fenceline1

Fenceline2

Tracks

Batting

Hot_water_supply

Gas_line

Zigzag

Just_G

FencelineX

To create a line type that includes text, you use the same line-type code
described earlier, with the addition of the necessary font file information in brackets. For example, say you want to create the line type for the underground gas
line mentioned above. You would add the following to your Acad.lin file:

```
*Gas line -- G -- G --
a,1.0,-0.25, ["G", standard, S=.2, R=0, X=-.1, Y=-.1], -0.25
```

The information in the square brackets describes the characteristics of the text.
The actual text that you want to appear in the line is surrounded by quotes. Next
are the text style, scale, rotation angle, x displacement, and y displacement.

WARNING You cannot use the -Linetype command to define complex line types.
Instead, you must open the Acad.lin file using a text editor, such as the
Windows Notepad, and add the line-type information to the end of the file.
Make sure you don't duplicate the name of an existing line type.

You can substitute the rotation angle (the R value) with an A, as in the following example:

```
a,1.0,-0.25, ["G", standard, S=.2 A=0, X=.1, Y=.1], -0.25
```

This has the effect of keeping the text at the same angle, regardless of the line's direction. Notice that in this sample, the X and Y values are a -.1; this will center the "G"s on the line. The scale value of .2 will cause the text to be .2 units high, so the -.1 is half the height.

In addition to fonts, you can also specify shapes for line-type definitions. Instead of letters, shapes display symbols. Shapes are stored not as drawings, but as definition files, similar to text-font files. In fact, shape files have the same .shx extension as text and are also defined similarly. Figure 21.8 shows some symbols from shape files supplied with the companion CD-ROM.

FIGURE 21.8:

Samples of shapes available on the companion CD-ROM

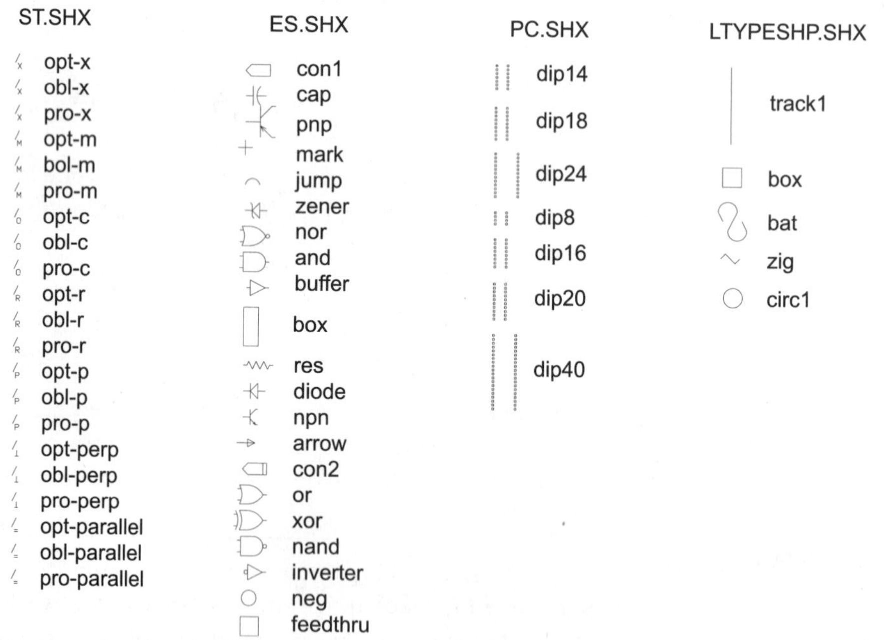

ST.SHX	ES.SHX	PC.SHX	LTYPESHP.SHX
opt-x	con1	dip14	track1
obl-x	cap	dip18	
pro-x	pnp		box
opt-m	mark	dip24	
bol-m	jump		bat
pro-m	zener	dip8	
opt-c	nor	dip16	zig
obl-c	and		
pro-c	buffer	dip20	circ1
opt-r			
obl-r	box	dip40	
pro-r			
opt-p	res		
obl-p	diode		
pro-p	npn		
opt-perp	arrow		
obl-perp	con2		
pro-perp	or		
opt-parallel	xor		
obl-parallel	nand		
pro-parallel	inverter		
	neg		
	feedthru		

To use a shape in a line-type code, you use the same format as shown previously for text. However, instead of using a letter and style name, you use the shape name and the shape file name, as in the following example:

```
*Capline, ====
a,1.0,-0.25,[CAP,ES.SHX,S=.2,R=0,X=-.1,Y=-.1],-0.25
```

This example uses the Cap symbol from the Es.shx shape file. The symbol is scaled to .2 units with 0 rotation and an X and Y displacement of -.1.

Creating Hatch Patterns

AutoCAD provides several predefined hatch patterns you can choose from (see Figure 21.9), but you can also create your own. This section demonstrates the basic elements of pattern definition.

FIGURE 21.9:

The standard hatch patterns

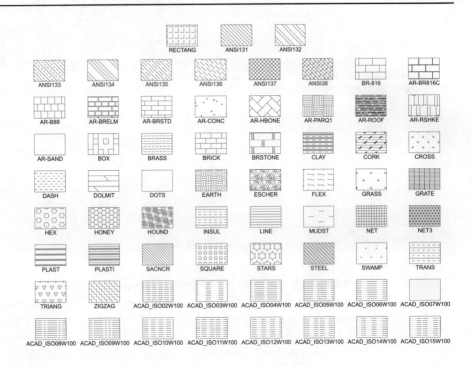

Unlike line types, hatch patterns cannot be created while you are in an AutoCAD file. The pattern definitions are contained in an external file named Acad.pat. This file can be opened and edited with a text editor that can handle ASCII files, such as the Windows Notepad. Here is one hatch pattern definition from that file:

```
*square,Small aligned squares
0, 0,0, 0,.125, .125,-.125
90, 0,0, 0,.125, .125,-.125
```

You can see some similarities between pattern descriptions and line-type descriptions. They both start with a line of descriptive text, and then give numeric values defining the pattern. However, the numbers in pattern descriptions have a different meaning. This example shows two lines of information. Each line represents a line in the pattern. The first line determines the horizontal line component of the pattern, and the second line represents the vertical component. Figure 21.10 shows the hatch pattern defined in the example.

FIGURE 21.10:

Square pattern

A pattern is made up of *line groups*. A line group is like a line type that is arrayed a specified distance to fill the area to be hatched. A line group is defined by a line of code, much as a line type is defined. In the square pattern, for instance, two lines— one horizontal and one vertical—are used. Each of these lines is duplicated in a fashion that makes the lines appear as boxes when they are combined. Figure 21.11 illustrates this point.

FIGURE 21.11:

The individual and combined line groups

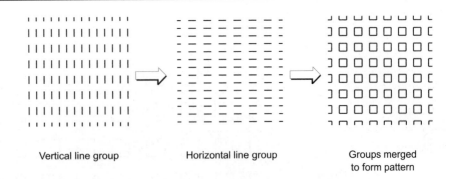

Vertical line group   Horizontal line group   Groups merged
                                                             to form pattern

Look at the first line in the definition:

```
0, 0,0, 0,.125, .125,-.125
```

This example shows a series of numbers separated by commas, and it represents one line group. It actually contains four sets of information, separated by blank spaces:

- The first component is the 0 at the beginning. This value indicates the angle of the line group, as determined by the line's orientation. In this case it is 0 for a horizontal line that runs from left to right.

- The next component is the origin of the line group, 0,0. This does not mean that the line actually begins at the drawing origin (see Figure 21.12). It gives you a reference point to determine the location of other line groups involved in generating the pattern.

NOTE If you have forgotten the numeric values for the various directions, refer back to Figure 2.4 in Chapter 2, which shows AutoCAD's system for specifying angles.

FIGURE 21.12:

The origin of the patterns

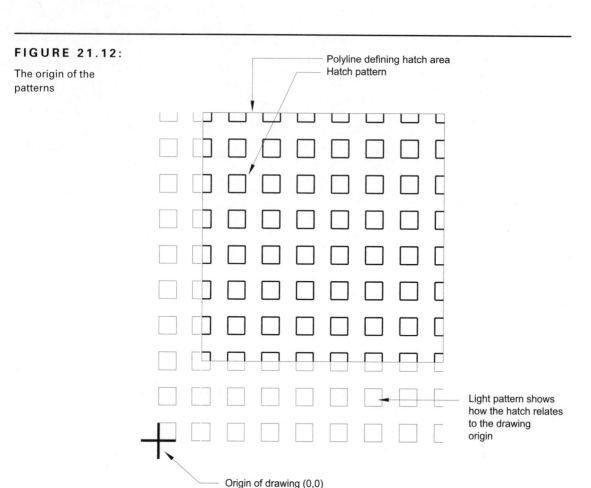

Polyline defining hatch area
Hatch pattern

Light pattern shows how the hatch relates to the drawing origin

Origin of drawing (0,0)

- The next component is 0,.125. This determines the distance for arraying the line and in what direction, as illustrated in Figure 21.13. This value is like a relative coordinate indicating x and y distances for a rectangular array. It is not based on the drawing coordinates, but on a coordinate system relative to the orientation of the line. For a line oriented at a 0° angle, the code 0,.125 indicates a precisely vertical direction. For a line oriented at a 45° angle, the code 0,.125 represents a 135~o direction. In this example, the duplication occurs 90° in relation to the line group, because the x value is 0. Figure 21.14 illustrates this point.

FIGURE 21.13:

The distance and direction of duplication

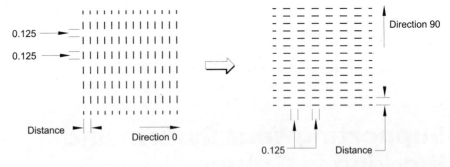

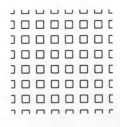

Result

FIGURE 21.14:

How the direction of the line group copy is determined

The X and Y coordinate values given for the array distance are based on the orientation of the line group.

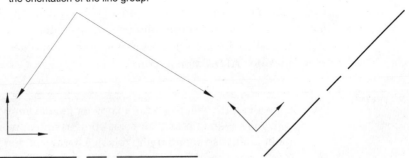

- The last component is the actual description of the line pattern. This value is equivalent to the value given when you create a line type. Positive values are line segments, and negative values are blank segments. This part of the line group definition works exactly as in the line-type definitions you studied in the previous section.

This system of defining hatch patterns may seem somewhat limiting, but you can actually do a lot with it. Autodesk managed to come up with 53 patterns—and that was really only scratching the surface.

Supporting Your System and Working in Groups

So far in this book you have worked with AutoCAD as an individual learning a program. However, chances are you are usually not alone when you use Auto-CAD on a project. Your success with AutoCAD may depend as much on the people you work with as on your knowledge of the program. In the last half of this chapter, we'll look at some of the issues you may face as a member of an interactive group: selecting a system and obtaining support for it; what happens once that system arrives in the office; and some ways you can manage your system.

Getting Outside Support

It helps to have knowledgeable people to consult when questions arise. Most often, the vendor who sells the CAD system is also the source for technical support. Another source is an independent CAD consultant. And don't overlook colleagues who have had some solid experience with AutoCAD. Most likely, you will tap all three of these sources at one point or another as you start to implement an AutoCAD system in your work.

TIP   It is well worth searching for a knowledgeable vendor. Your vendor can save you several times their sales commission in work hours your office might otherwise spend trying to solve hardware and software problems. Your vendor can also help you set up a system of file organization and management—something that can become a nightmare if left unattended.

It can be difficult to find a vendor who understands your special needs. This is because the vendor must have specialized knowledge of computers as well as design or production. A good vendor should offer training and phone support, both of which are crucial to productive use of a program with as much complexity as AutoCAD. Some vendors even offer user groups as a means of maintaining an active and open communication with their clients. Here are some further suggestions:

- In addition to your vendor, you may want to find an independent consultant who is familiar with AutoCAD. Although it may be harder to find a good CAD consultant than to find a good vendor, the consultant's view of your needs is unbiased by the motivation to make a sale. The consultant's main goal is to help you gain productivity from your CAD system, so he or she will be more helpful in these areas than your average vendor.

- Get references before you use anyone's services. Your own colleagues may be the best source of information on vendors, consultants, and even hardware. You can learn from their good fortune or mistakes.

- Don't rely on magazine reviews and product demonstrations at shows. These can often be misleading or offer incomplete information. If you see something you like, test it before you buy it. For some products this may be difficult, but because of the complex nature of computer-aided design and drafting, it is important to know exactly what you are getting.

Choosing In-House Experts

Perhaps even more important than a good vendor is an individual within your office who knows your CAD system thoroughly. Ideally, everyone closely involved in your drafting and design projects should be a proficient AutoCAD user, but it is impractical to expect everyone to give time to system management. Usually one individual is chosen for this task. It can often be a thankless one, but when the going gets rough, an in-house expert is indispensable.

NOTE   If you find that a task can be automated, a knowledgeable in-house person can create custom macros and commands on the spot, saving your design or production staff hundreds of work hours—especially if several people are performing that task. Your in-house authority can also train new personnel and answer users' questions.

In a smaller office, the in-house authority may need to be an expert on design, production, and computers—all rolled into one. The point is that to really take advantage of AutoCAD or any CAD system, you should provide some in-house expertise. AutoCAD is a powerful tool, but that power is wasted if you don't take advantage of it.

However, you must be aware that the role of the in-house expert will require significant time spent away from other tasks. Dealing with questions about the program's use can be disruptive to the expert's own work, and writing custom applications is often at least a part-time job in itself. Keep this under consideration when scheduling work or managing costs on a project. It also pays to keep the following in mind:

- The in-house expert should be a professional trained in your firm's field of specialization, rather than someone with a computer background. Every architect or engineer on your staff represents years of training, while learning AutoCAD can take a matter of weeks or months. The expert-to-be, however, should be willing to develop some computer expertise.

- Running a CAD system is not a simple clerical task. It takes not only clear thinking and good organizational skills, but good communication skills as well. The in-house authority should have some interest in teaching, and the ability to be patient when dealing with interruptions and "stupid" questions. He or she may well be a manager and will need access to the same information as any key player on your design team.

- If you have several computers, you may also want to obtain some general technical support. Especially if your company is implementing its first computer environment, many questions will arise that are not directly related to AutoCAD. The technical support person will be able to answer highly technical questions for which a computer background is required more so than familiarity with your professional specialty.

- Consider contracting with an outside consultant to occasionally provide additional support. This will allow development of custom applications without waiting for your staff to develop the necessary skills. A consultant can also help train your staff and even fill in from time to time when production schedules become too tight.

Acclimatizing the Staff

Once an AutoCAD system is installed and operational, the next step is to get the staff acquainted with that system. This can be the most difficult task of all. In nearly every office, there is at least one key person who resists the use of computers. This can be a tremendous obstacle, especially if that individual is at management level—though nearly anyone who is resisting the project goals can do damage. The human capacity to undermine the sincerest efforts is astounding, and when coupled with a complex computer system, the results can be disastrous. Unfortunately, there is no easy solution to this problem aside from fostering a positive attitude toward the CAD system's capabilities and its implementation.

AutoCAD has a way of adding force to everything you do, both good and bad. Because it is capable of reproducing work rapidly, it is very easy to unintentionally multiply errors until they are actually out of hand. This also holds true for project management. Poor management tends to be magnified when AutoCAD comes into the picture. You are managing yet another dimension of information—blocks, symbols, layers, and so on. If the users cannot manage and communicate this information, problems are sure to arise.

On the other hand, a smooth-running, well-organized project is reflective of the way AutoCAD enhances your productivity. In fact, good management is essential for realizing productivity gains with AutoCAD. A project on AutoCAD is only as good as the information you provide and the manner in which the system is administered. Open communication and good record keeping are essential to the development and integrity of a design or a set of drawings. The better managed a project is, the fewer problems arise, and the less time is required to get results.

Discussing CAD management procedures in your project kickoff meetings will help get people accustomed to the idea of using the system. Exchanging information with your consultants concerning your CAD system standards is also an important step in keeping a job running smoothly from the start, especially if they are also using AutoCAD.

Learning the System

Learning AutoCAD can be time consuming. If you are the one who is to operate the AutoCAD system, at first you won't be as productive as you were when you were doing everything manually, and don't expect to perform miracles overnight. Once you have a good working knowledge of the program, you still have to integrate it into your day-to-day work. It will take you a month or two, depending on how much time you spend studying AutoCAD, to get to a point where you are entering drawings with any proficiency. It also helps to have a real project you can work on while you are in training. Choose project that doesn't have a tight schedule, so that if anything goes wrong you have enough time to make corrections.

Remember that it is important to communicate to others what they can expect from you. Otherwise, you may find yourself in an awkward position because you haven't produced the results that someone anticipated.

Making AutoCAD Use Easier

Not everyone in your organization needs to be an AutoCAD expert, but in order for your firm to obtain maximum productivity from AutoCAD, almost everyone involved in design or production should be able to use the system. Designers especially should be involved, since AutoCAD can produce significant time savings in the design phase of a project.

You may want to consider an add-on software package to aid those who need to use AutoCAD but who are not likely to spend a lot of time learning it. These add-ons automate some of the typical functions of a particular application. They can also provide ready-made office standards for symbols and layers. Add-ons are available for architects, circuit board designers, electrical engineers, civil engineers, and mechanical designers, to name a few.

TIP   If you are serious about being productive with AutoCAD, you will want to develop custom applications. See Chapter 19 to find out more about customization and third-party software.

Add-ons shouldn't be viewed as the only means of using AutoCAD within your office, but rather as aids to casual users, and partners to your own custom applications. No two offices work alike and no two projects are exactly the same, so add-ons cannot be all things to all people. Remember, AutoCAD is really a graphics tool whose commands and interface can be manipulated to suit any project or office. And that is the way it should be.

Managing an AutoCAD Project

If you are managing a project that is to be put on AutoCAD, be sure you understand what it can and can't do. If your expectations are unreasonable, or if you don't communicate your requirements to the design or production team, friction and problems may occur. Open and clear communication is of the utmost importance, especially when using AutoCAD or any CAD program in a work group environment. Here are some further points to consider:

- If your office is just beginning to use AutoCAD, be sure you allow time for staff training. Generally, an individual can become independent on the program after 24 to 36 hours of training. ("Independent" means able to produce drawings without having to constantly refer to a manual or call in the trainer.) This book should provide enough guidance to accomplish this level of skill.

- Once at the point of independence, most individuals will take another month or so to reach a work rate comparable to hand drafting. After that, the individual's productivity will depend on his or her creativity and problem-solving ability. These are very rough estimates, but they should give you an idea of what to expect.

- If you are using a software add-on product, the training period may be shorter, but the user won't have the same depth of knowledge as someone who isn't using the enhancements. As mentioned earlier, this kind of education may be fine for casual users, but you will reach an artificial upper limit on productivity if you rely too heavily on add-ons.

As you or your staff members are learning AutoCAD, you will need to learn how to best utilize this new tool in the context of your office's operations. This may mean rethinking how you go about running a project. It may also mean training coworkers to operate differently.

For example, one of the most common production challenges is scheduling work so that check plots can be produced on a timely basis. Normally, project members have grown accustomed to looking at drawings at convenient times as they progress, even when there are scheduled review dates. With AutoCAD, you won't have that luxury. You will have to consider plotting time when scheduling drawing review dates. This means that the person doing the drawings must get accurate information in time to enter last-minute changes and to plot the drawings.

Establishing Office Standards

Communication is especially important when you are one of many people working on the same project on separate computers. A well-developed set of standards and procedures helps to minimize problems that might be caused by miscommunication. In this section, you'll find some suggestions on how to set up these standards.

Establishing Layering Conventions

You have seen how layers can be a useful tool. But they can easily get out of hand when you have free rein over their creation and naming. This can be especially troublesome when more than one person is working on the same set of drawings. The following scenario illustrates this point.

One day the drawing you are working on has twenty layers. Then the next day, you find that someone has added six more, with names that have no meaning to you whatsoever. You don't dare delete those layers, or modify the objects on them, for fear of retaliation from the individual who put them there. You ask around, but no one seems to know anything about these new layers. Finally, after spending an hour or two tracking down the culprit, you discover that the layers are not important at all.

With an appropriate layer-naming convention, you can minimize this type of problem (though you may not eliminate it entirely). A too-rigid naming convention can cause as many problems as no convention at all, so it is best to give general guidelines rather than force everyone to stay within narrow limits. As mentioned in Chapter 6, you can create layer names in a way that allows you to group them using wildcards. AutoCAD allows up to 31 characters in a layer name, so you can use descriptive names.

Line weights should be standardized in conjunction with colors. If you intend to use a service bureau for your plotting, check with them first; they may require that you conform to their color and line-weight standards.

TIP   If you are an architect, engineer, or in the construction business, check out some of the CAD layering standards set forth by the American Institute of Architects (AIA) and the Construction Standards Institute (CSI).

Maintaining Files

As you use your computer system, you will generate files rapidly. Some files will be garbage, some will be necessary but infrequently used, and others will be current job files or system files that are constantly used. In addition, AutoCAD automatically creates backup files (they have the file name extension .bak). If something is wrong with the most-recent version, you can restore the .bak file to a drawing file by simply changing the .bak extension to .dwg. You may or may not want to keep these backup files.

NOTE An AutoCAD backup file is a copy of the most recent version of the file before you issued the last Save or End command. If you save the .bak files, you will always have the next-to-most recent version of a file.

All these files take up valuable space, and you may end up with insufficient room for your working files. Because of this, you will want to regularly clear the unused files from the hard disk, by erasing unwanted files and archiving those that are used infrequently. You may even want to erase current files from your hard disk once they have been backed up on floppy disks. It's wise to do this at every editing session, so you don't confuse meaningful files with garbage. You may want to erase all your .bak files, as well, if you don't care to keep them.

TIP You can set up AutoCAD so the it does not create the .bak files. Open the Preferences dialog box, click on the General tab, and then remove the checkmark from the Create backup copy with each save option.

Backing Up Files

Besides keeping your hard disk clear of unused and inactive files, consider backing it up daily or at least once a week. This might be done by the in-house expert or the technical support staff. You needn't back up the entire hard disk, just those crucial drawing files you've been slaving over for the past several months. When you do back up your entire hard disk, you save the configuration of all your programs and the directory structure. In the event of a hard disk failure, you won't have to reinstall and reconfigure all your software. You just restore the backups once the problem with the hard disk is remedied.

NOTE
In the event that you do have a system failure and some files become corrupted, AutoCAD has a built-in file-recovery routine. Whenever it attempts to load a corrupted file, it will tell you the file is corrupted and proceed to fix the problem as best it can. See Appendix A for more on this feature.

A good policy to follow is to back up your entire hard disk every week, and your data files every day, as a compromise to backing up everything daily.

There are two methods for backing up a hard disk. One is through software, using your existing floppy-disk drive and removable disks as the backup media. DOS provides software for this purpose, but it is slow and difficult to use. Tape backup systems are the preferred backup method for a hard disk. These systems transfer the contents of your hard disk onto a tape cartridge or cassette. The software to operate the tape system is usually provided as part of the system.

Tape backup systems cost a bit more than the software-only alternative, but tape systems offer more flexibility and ease of use. For example, with backup software, you must constantly insert and remove disks from the computer as they are filled up. A tape backup system allows you to start the backup process and then walk away to do something else. Some systems offer timed backup so you don't even have to think about starting them—it simply happens at a predetermined time, usually in the evening.

Tape backup systems can back up a hard disk at the rate of about 8MB to 20MB per minute. The price of these systems ranges from $150 for a system installed inside your PC, to $2,000 for an external multiuser unit, depending on tape capacity. The cartridges or cassettes used for storage cost around $15. Although you initially spend more on a tape backup system, you can save time and pay less for storage media.

There are other, faster, more flexible options, such as rewritable optical drives that can store 500MB to 1GB of data. Such a system usually costs twice as much as a tape system. Rewritable optical drives can be invaluable, however, in situations where large amounts of data must be archived and readily retrieved. You might also consider Recordable CD-ROM drives as a backup tool. They can also double as a means to distribute drawings or other project files to clients and consultants.

Labeling Hard Copies

A problem you will run into once you start to generate files is keeping track of which AutoCAD file goes with which hard copy drawing. It's a good idea to place an identifying tag on the drawing (and that will plot with the drawing) in some inconspicuous place. As well as the file name, the tag should include such information as the date and time the drawing was last edited, who edited it, and what submission the plot was done for. All these bits of information can prove helpful in the progress of a design or production project (see Figure 21.15).

FIGURE 21.15:

You can promote good drawing management by using a small note identifying the file used to generate the drawing.

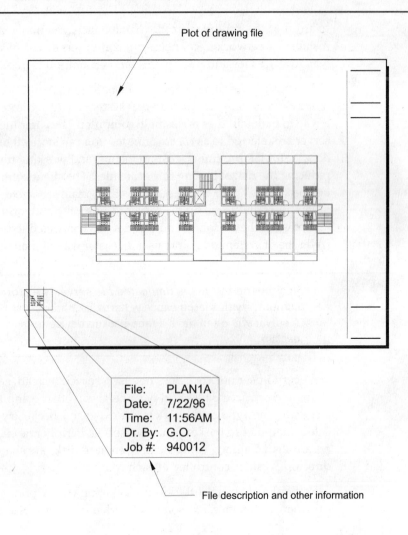

Plot of drawing file

File: PLAN1A
Date: 7/22/96
Time: 11:56AM
Dr. By: G.O.
Job #: 940012

File description and other information

TIP

> The Batch Plot utility described in Chapter 7 allows you to add a descriptive label to your drawings. Also, many of the modern ink jet plotters feature a plot-stamping function.

Using Networks with AutoCAD

In an effort to simplify your file maintenance, you may want to consider installing a network to connect your computers electronically. Networks offer a way to share files and peripherals among computers in different locations.

Two basic types of networks can be used with AutoCAD: *Dedicated file server/client* systems and *peer-to-peer* systems. The dedicated file server offers you a way to maintain files on a single computer. The computers connected to the server are referred to as *clients* or *nodes*. You can store all of your common symbols, AutoLISP programs, custom menus, and working files on the server, thus reducing the risk of having duplicate files. The client computers are simpler and less powerful. They use the server as their main storage device, accessing the programs and data stored on the server through the network. Networks with servers also have all the peripheral output devices connected to the server. This centralized type of system offers the user an easier way of managing files.

NOTE

> In simplified terms, a *dedicated file server* is a storage device, often a computer with a large-capacity hard disk, that acts as a repository of data. A server will often have a tape-backup device to facilitate regular system backup.

A peer-to-peer network does not use a server. Instead, each computer has equal status and can access files and peripherals on other computers on the network. Generally, this type of network is less expensive because you don't need to dedicate a computer to the single task of server. Peripherals such as plotters and printers are shared among computers. Even hard disks are shared, though access to directories can be controlled at each computer.

Networks can be useful tools in managing your work, but they can also introduce new difficulties. For some network users, file-version control becomes a major concern. Speed of file access can be another problem. No matter what form of network you have or install, you will need a system manager whose duties include backing up files in the server and making sure the network's output devices are operating as they should. Used properly, a network can save time by easing the flow of information between computer users; it must, however, be managed carefully.

Here are some tips on using AutoCAD on a network:

- If you can afford it, use a star topology for your network, with an active hub and a dedicated server.

- Configure AutoCAD to store temporary files on the client or node computer.

- Configure your network version of AutoCAD for multiple swap files and local code pages, and set the AutoCAD preferences to use the client or node computer for swap files (see Appendix A for more on these tasks).

Keeping Records

Computers are said to create "the paperless office." As you work more and more with them, however, you may find that quite the opposite is true. Although you can store more information on magnetic media, you will spend a good deal of time reviewing that information on hard copy because it is very difficult to spot errors on a computer monitor. When you use AutoCAD on large projects, another level of documentation must also exist: a way of keeping track of the many elements that go into the creation of drawings.

TIP   Your companion CD-ROM has AutoLISP utilities that will generate log files for you automatically. See the section on the AEC utilities in Appendix C for details.

Because job requirements vary, you may want to provide a layer log to keep track of layers and their intended uses for specific jobs, or better yet, use the Layer Manager bonus tool described in Chapter 19. Also, to manage blocks within files, a log of block names and their insertion values can help. Finally, plan to keep a log of symbols. You will probably have a library of symbols used in your work group, and this library will grow as your projects become more varied. Documenting these symbols will help to keep track of them.

Another activity that you may want to keep records for is plotting—especially if you bill your clients separately for computer time or for analyzing job costs. A plot log might contain such information as the time spent on plotting, the type of plot done, the purpose of the plot, and even a list of plotting errors and problems that arise with each drawing.

Although records may be the last thing on your mind when you are working to meet a deadline, in the long run they can save time and aggravation for you and the people you work with.

Understanding What AutoCAD Can Do for You

Many of us have only a vague idea of what AutoCAD can contribute to our work. We think it will make our drafting tasks go faster, but we're not sure exactly how. Or we may believe it will make us produce better-quality drawings. Some people expect AutoCAD will make them better designers or allow them to produce professional-quality drawings without having much drawing talent. All these things are true to an extent, and AutoCAD can help you in some ways that are less tangible than speed and quality.

Seeing the Hidden Advantages

We have discussed how AutoCAD can help you meet your drafting and design challenges by allowing you to visualize your ideas more clearly and by reducing the time it takes to do repetitive tasks. AutoCAD also forces you to organize your drawing process more efficiently. It changes your perception of problems and, though it may introduce new ones, the additional accuracy and information AutoCAD provides will minimize errors.

AutoCAD also provides drawing consistency. A set of drawings done on AutoCAD is more legible and consistent, reducing the possibility of errors caused by illegible handwriting or poor drafting. In our litigious culture, this is a significant feature.

Finally, because AutoCAD systems are becoming more prevalent, it is easier to find people who can use it proficiently. As this group of experts grows, training will become less of a burden to your company.

Taking a Project Off AutoCAD

As helpful as AutoCAD can be, there are times when making revisions on Auto-CAD is simply not worth the effort. Last minute changes that are minor but pervasive throughout a set of drawings are best made by hand on the most up-to-date hard copy. That way, you don't waste time and drawing media in plotting drawings.

Also, it is a good idea to have a label on every hard copy of a file so that users know which file to edit when the time comes to make changes.

TIP To keep your AutoCAD files up to date, once a project is done, you should go back and enter any final changes you made on the hard copy in the electronic version of the file.

Only your experience can help you determine the best time to stop using AutoCAD and start making changes by hand. Many factors will influence this decision: the size and complexity of the project, the people available to work on it, and the nature of the revisions—to name just a few.

As you have seen, AutoCAD is a powerful software tool, and like any powerful program, it is difficult to master. I hope this last chapter has given you the incentive to take advantage of AutoCAD's full potential. Remember: even after you've learned how to use AutoCAD, there are many other issues that you must confront while using AutoCAD in an office environment.

Unlike words, drawings have few restrictions. The process of writing requires adherence to the structures of our language. The process of drawing, on the other hand, has no fixed structure. For example, there are a million ways to draw a face or a building. For this reason, your use of AutoCAD is much less restricted, and there are certainly potential uses for it that are yet to be discovered. We encourage you to experiment with AutoCAD and explore the infinite possibilities it offers for solving your design problems and communicating your ideas.

I hope *Mastering AutoCAD 14 for Windows* has been of benefit to you and that you will continue to use it as a reference. If you have comments, criticisms, or ideas about how we can improve the next edition of this book, write to me at the address below. And thanks for choosing *Mastering AutoCAD 14.*

George Omura
Omura Illustration
P.O. Box 357
Albany, CA 94706-0357
E-Mail: gomura@sirius.com

PART VI

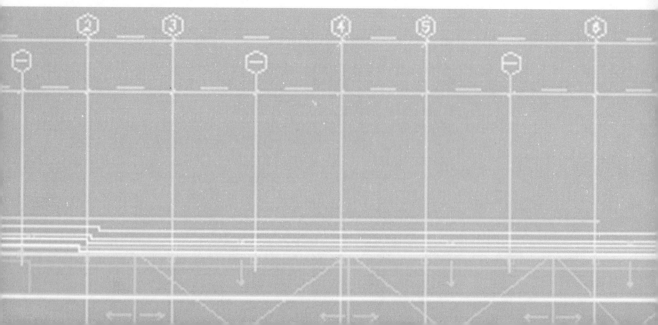

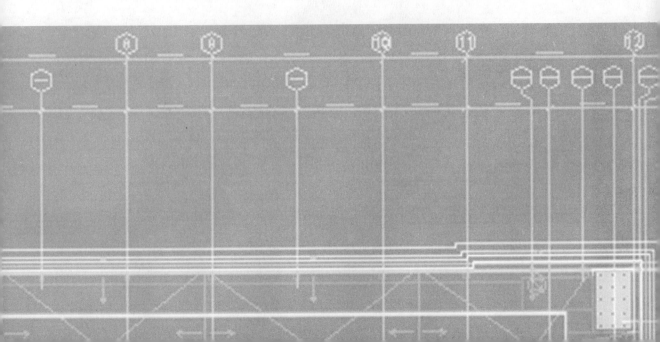

Appendices

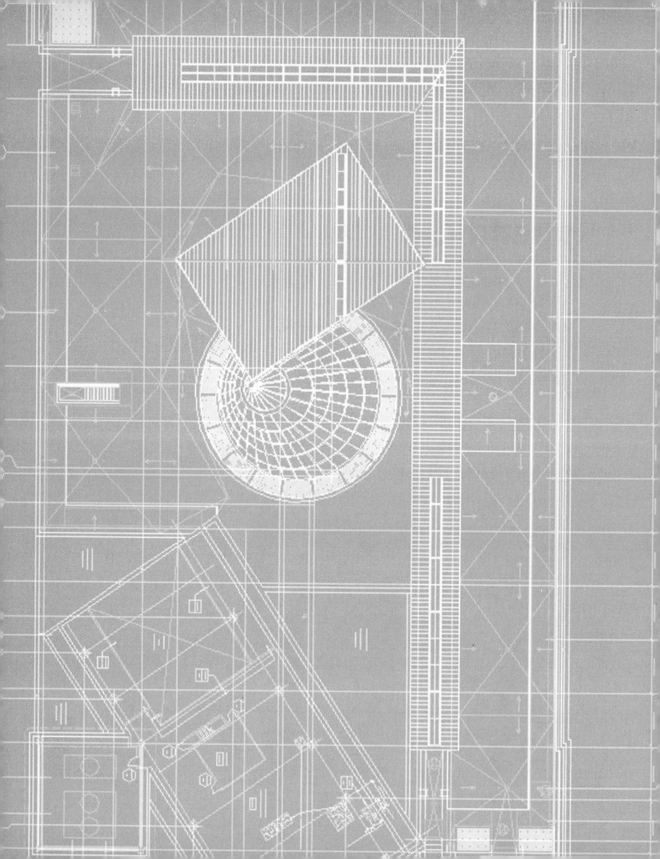

Hardware and Software Tips

Because some of the items that make up an AutoCAD system are not found on the typical desktop system, I have provided this appendix to help you understand some of the less common items you may need. This appendix also discusses ways you can improve AutoCAD's performance through software and hardware.

The Graphics Display

There are two issues to consider concerning the graphics display: *resolution* and *performance*.

If you are running Windows 95 or Windows NT 4 software, then in all probability you already have a high-resolution display card for your monitor. If you haven't set up your system yet, then a high-resolution display card and monitor is a must. SVGA display cards are inexpensive and offer high-quality display.

Graphics performance comes down to speed. To enhance graphics performance you need to consider the following resources.

PCI Bus   Contemporary motherboards use high-speed PCI expansion slots that offer the fastest video throughput available. Check that yours is a system of this type. If you are shopping for a graphics card, make sure that it is a plug-and-play–type card for ease of installation.

Video RAM   If you are shopping for a display system, you should also make sure that it has 2–8 megabytes of *video RAM*. Standard video cards typically have only two megabytes of video RAM. Greater amounts of up to eight megabytes will give you noticeably better performance with AutoCAD.

In earlier versions of AutoCAD it was advisable to obtain *display list* software to improve graphics performance. With Release 14 this is no longer necessary (though some third-party add-on video drivers may offer other features that enhance your use of AutoCAD). AutoCAD comes equipped with display list software. The display list gives you nearly instantaneous pans and zooms.

Pointing Devices

Our most basic means of communicating with computers is the keyboard and pointing device. Most likely, you will use a mouse, but if you are still in the market for a pointing device, choose an input device that generates smooth cursor movement. Some of the lesser-quality input devices cause erratic movement. When looking for an input device other than a mouse, choose one that provides positive feedback, such as a definitive button click when you pick an object on the screen. Many low-cost digitizers have a very poor button feel that can cause errors when you are selecting points or menu options.

In general, use a high-resolution mouse if you do not plan to do any tracing. If you must have the use of a tablet menu, or if you know you are going to trace drawings, then get a digitizer, but be sure it is of good quality.

The Digitizing Tablet

If you need to trace drawings, you should consider a digitizing tablet. It is usually a rectangular object with a penlike *stylus*, or a device called a *puck*, which resembles a mouse. It has a smooth surface on which to draw. The most popular size is 11"x11", but digitizing tablets are available in sizes up to 60"x70". The tablet gives a natural feel to drawing with the computer because the movement of the stylus or puck is directly translated into cursor movement. While many digitizers come with a stylus, you will want a multi-button puck to work with AutoCAD.

A digitizing tablet's puck often has *function buttons*. These buttons can be programmed through the AutoCAD menu file system to start your most frequently used commands, which is much faster than searching through an on-screen menu. You can also select commands from the tablet's surface if you install the *menu template* supplied with AutoCAD. A menu template is a flat sheet of plastic with the AutoCAD commands printed on it. You can select commands simply by pointing at them on the template. If you have a digitizing tablet, refer to Appendix B, which tells you how to install a template.

AutoCAD supports Wintab-compatible digitizers. If your digitizer has a Wintab driver, you can use your digitizer as both a *tracing device* (to trace drawings on a tablet) and as a *pointing device* (to choose AutoCAD or Windows 95 menu items).

Your Wintab digitizer must be installed and configured under Windows. Check that it is working in Windows before enabling it in AutoCAD, otherwise you will not be able to use the digitizer as a pointing device (mouse). To enable the digitizer in AutoCAD, choose Tools ➤ Preferences... Pointer tab. Then select the Digitizer or Digitizer & Mouse option in the Accept Input section.

Output Devices

Output options vary greatly in quality and price. Quality and paper size are the major considerations for both printers and plotters. Nearly all printers give accurate drawings, but some produce better line quality than others. Some plotters give merely acceptable results, while others are quite impressive in their speed and accuracy.

AutoCAD Release 14 can use the Windows 95 or NT *system printer*, so any device that Windows supports is also supported by AutoCAD. AutoCAD also gives you the option of plotting directly to an output device. By plotting directly to the output device, instead of going through Windows 95, AutoCAD can offer more control over the final output.

Printers

There are so many types of printers available these days that it has become more difficult to choose the right printer for your application. We are offering a description of the broad categories of printers available and how they relate to Auto-CAD. You will also want to consider the other uses for your printer, such as word-processing or color graphics. Here are a few printing options:

Laser Printers   produce high-quality line work output. The standard office laser printer is usually limited to 8½x11" paper; however, 11"x17" laser printers for graphics and CAD work are now becoming affordable, and are commonly used for proof plots. Resolution and speed are the major considerations if your are buying a laser printer. An output of 300 DPI (dots per inch) produces very acceptable plots, but 600 DPI is fast becoming the standard. You should look also for a laser printer with sufficient built-in memory to improve spooling and plotting speeds.

Ink Jet or Bubble Jet Printers   offer speed and quality output. Some ink jet printers even accept 17"x22" paper and offer PostScript emulation at up to 720 dots per inch. Since ink jet printers are competitively priced, they can offer the best solution for low-cost check plots. And the 17"x22" paper size is quite acceptable for half-size plots, a format that more architects and engineers are using.

PostScript Printers   If you want to use a PostScript device to output your drawings, the best method is to use File ➤ Export or the Psout command. These options convert your drawing into a true PostScript file. You can then send your file to a PostScript printer or typesetting machine. This can be especially useful for PCB layout where you require photo negatives for output. If you are an architect who needs presentation-quality drawings, you may want to consider using the Encapsulated PS (*.EPS) option in the Export Data dialog box. Often service bureaus who offer a raster plotter service can produce E-size PostScript output from a PostScript file. The uses of this option are really quite open-ended.

Plotters

A plotter is a mechanical drafting device used to draw a computer image on sheets of paper, vellum, or polyester film. In the early days of CAD, most plotters used ink pens. Now, ink-jet technology has taken over the plotter market. You can also find laser, thermal, or electrostatic plotters at a much higher price. Black and white ink jet plotters offer the best value; they are fast and fairly inexpensive compared to the older pen plotters they supersede. For a bit more expense, you can step up to a color plotter. Black and white plotters are capable of printing raster images in larger formats, and they can print patterns and screens for highlight effects.

If you need large plots but feel you can't afford a large plotter, many service bureaus (or blueprint companies) offer plotting as a service. This can be a very good alternative to purchasing your own plotter. Check with your local service bureau.

Fine-Tuning PostScript File Export

AutoCAD provides the PostScript user with a great deal of control over the formatting of the PostScript file that is output with the File ➤ Export and the Psout command. The options range from font-substitution mapping to custom Post-Script Prologue data.

However, AutoCAD does require you to master the PostScript programming language to take full advantage of AutoCAD PostScript output. Most of this control is offered through a file named Acad.psf. This is the master support file for the Psin and Psout commands. You can customize the PostScript file created by Psout by making changes in the Acad.psf file. Acad.psf is divided into sections that affect various parts of the PostScript output. Each section begins with a title preceded by an asterisk. The following briefly describes these sections:

*fonts   lets you control font substitution. You can assign a PostScript font to an AutoCAD font file or PostScript .pfb file used in the drawing.

*figureprologue   defines the procedures used for embedding figures included with Psin PostScript images.

*isofontprologue   defines the procedures used to re-encode fonts in order to be compatible with the ISO 8859 Latin/1 character set.

*fillprologue   defines the code used in the Psout file to describe area fills.

*fill   is a section where you can include your own custom fill patterns.

Most of these sections, with the exception of the *fonts section, will be of little use to the average user; but if you are a PostScript programmer, you can take advantage of these sections to customize your PostScript output.

You will also want to know about the *Psprolog* system variable. This system variable instructs Psout to include your custom prolog statement in its PostScript output. (See Chapter 14 for details on using Psout.) You add your custom prolog to the Acad.psf file using a text editor. The prolog should begin with a section heading that you devise. The heading can say anything, but it must begin with an asterisk like all the other section headings. Everything following the heading, up to the next heading or the end of the file, and excluding comments, will be included in the Psout output file. The following shows a sample prolog that converts color assignments to line widths in a way similar to pen plotters:

```
*widthprolog
/ACADLayer { pop } def
/ACADColor { pop pop pop dup 0.5 mul setlinewidth pop} def
/ACADLtype { pop
userdict /Linedict known not { /Linedict 100 dict def } if
1 index cvn Linedict exch known not {
```

```
mark 1 index { dup 0 eq { pop 1 72.0 div } if abs } forall
counttomark 2 add ~-1 roll astore exch pop
1 index cvn exch Linedict begin def end }
{ pop } ifelse
Linedict begin cvx exec 0 setdash end } bind def
/bd{bind def}bind def /m{moveto}bd /l{lineto}bd /s{stroke}bd
/a{arc}bd /an{arcn}bd /gs{gsave}bd /gr{grestore}bd
/cp{closepath}bd /tr{translate}bd /sc{scale}bd /co{concat}bd
/ff{findfont}bd /sf{setfont}bd /sh{show}bd /np{newpath}bd
/sw{setlinewidth}bd /sj{setlinejoin}bd /sm{setmiterlimit}bd /cl{clip}bd
/fi{fill}bd
%%EndProlog
```

A complete discussion of Psout and Psin's PostScript support is beyond the scope of this book. If you are interested in learning more, consult the PostScript section of the *AutoCAD Customization* manual. You can also learn a lot by looking at the PostScript files produced by Psout, browsing the `Acad.psf` file, and consulting the following publications:

- *Understanding PostScript* by David Holzgang (Sybex, 1992)

- *PostScript Language Program Design* by Adobe Systems Incorporated (Addison-Wesley Publishing Company, Inc., 1990)

- *PostScript Language Reference Manual* by Adobe Systems Incorporated (Addison-Wesley Publishing Company, Inc., 1991)

- *PostScript Language Tutorial and Cookbook* by Adobe Systems Incorporated (Addison-Wesley Publishing Company, Inc., 1989)

You can also add a PostScript plotter to the plotter configuration. When you do this, AutoCAD plots the drawing as a series of vectors, just like any other plotter. If you have any filled areas in your drawing and you are plotting to a PostScript file, the vectors that are used to plot those filled areas can greatly increase plot-file size and the time it takes to plot your PostScript file.

Memory and AutoCAD Performance

Next to your computer's CPU, memory has the greatest impact on AutoCAD's speed. How much you have, and how you use it, can make a big difference in whether you finish that rush job on schedule or work late nights trying. In this section I hope to clarify some basic points about memory and how AutoCAD uses it.

AutoCAD Release 14 is a virtual memory system. This means that when your RAM memory resources reach their limit, part of the data stored in RAM is temporarily moved to your hard disk to make more room in RAM. This temporary storage of RAM to your hard disk is called memory *paging*. Through memory paging, AutoCAD will continue to run, even though your work might exceed the capacity of your RAM.

AutoCAD uses memory in two ways. First, it stores its program code in RAM. The more programs you have open under Windows, the more RAM will be used. Windows controls the use of memory for program code, so if you start to reach the RAM limit, Windows will take care of memory paging. The second way AutoCAD uses memory is for storing drawing data. AutoCAD always attempts to store as much of your drawing in RAM as possible. Again, when the amount of RAM required for a drawing exceeds the actual RAM available, AutoCAD will page parts of the drawing data to the hard disk. The paging of drawing data is controlled strictly by AutoCAD. Since RAM is shared with both program code and drawing data, your drawing size and the number of programs you have open under Windows will affect how much RAM you have available. For this reason, if you find your AutoCAD editing session is slowing down, try closing other applications you might have open. This will free up more memory for AutoCAD and the drawing file.

AutoCAD and Your Hard Disk

You will notice that AutoCAD will slow down when paging occurs. If this happens frequently, the best thing you can do is add more RAM. But you can also improve the performance of AutoCAD under these conditions by ensuring that you have adequate hard-disk space and that any free hard-disk space has been *defragmented* or *optimized*. A defragmented disk will offer faster access, thereby improving paging speed.

With previous versions of Windows, you were recommended to set up a permanent swap file. With Windows 95 or NT 4, this is not necessary. Windows dynamically allocates swap-file space. However, you should make sure that there is enough free space on your hard disk to allow Windows to set up the space. A good guideline is to allow enough space for a swap file that is four times the size of your RAM capacity. If you have 32 megabytes of RAM you need to allow space for a 128 megabyte swap file (at a minimum). This will give your system 128 megabytes of virtual memory.

What to Do for "Out of RAM" and "Out of Page Space" Errors

After you have used AutoCAD for some time, you may find some odd-looking files with an .ac$ extension in the \Windows\Temp directory. These files are the temporary files for storing unused portions of a drawing. They often appear if AutoCAD has been terminated abnormally. You can usually erase these files without any adverse effect.

If you've discarded all the old swap files and your disk is still unusually full, there may be some lost file clusters filling up your hard disk. Lost clusters are pieces of files that are not actually assigned to a specific file. Often they crop up when a program has terminated abnormally. To eliminate them and free up the disk space they're using, exit AutoCAD and run Scandisk, which is a standard Windows accessory.

Finally, if you are not in the habit of emptying your Recycle bin, you should do so now. Every file that you "delete" using the Windows Explorer is actually passed to the Recycle bin. You need to clear this out regularly.

When Things Go Wrong

AutoCAD is a complex program, and at times things don't go exactly right. If you run into problems, chances are the problem is not insurmountable. Here are a few tips on what to do when things don't work.

Difficulty Starting Up or Opening a File

The most common reason why you'll have difficulty opening a file is the lack of free disk space. If you encounter errors attempting to open files, check to see if you have adequate free disk space on all your drives.

If you've recently installed AutoCAD but you cannot get it started, you may have a configuration problem. Before you panic, try reinstalling your AutoCAD from scratch. Particularly if you are installing the CD version, this does not take long (see Appendix B for installation instructions). Before you reinstall AutoCAD, use the Uninstall program to remove the current version of AutoCAD first. Also make sure you have your Authorization code, serial number, and CD-Key handy. Make sure that you've closed all other programs when you run the AutoCAD installation, and as a final measure, restart your computer when you've completed the installation.

Restoring Corrupted Files

Hardware failures can result in data files becoming corrupted. When this happens, AutoCAD is unable to open the drawing file. Fortunately, there is hope for damaged files. In most cases, AutoCAD will run through a file-recovery routine automatically when it attempts to load a corrupted file. If you have a file you know is corrupted, you can start the file-recovery utility by clicking on File ➤ Drawing Utilites ➤ Recover. This opens the Select File dialog box, allowing you to select the file you want to recover. Once you enter the name, AutoCAD goes to work. You get a series of messages, most of which have little meaning to the average user. Then the recovered file is opened. You may lose some data, but a partial file is better than no file at all, especially when the file represents several days of work.

Another possibility is to attempt to recover your drawing from the .bak file—the last saved version before your drawing was corrupted. Rename the drawing .bak file to a .dwg file with a different name, and then open it up. The drawing will contain only what was in your drawing when it was previously saved.

If you want to restore a file that you've just been working on, you can check the file named Auto.sv$. This is the file AutoCAD uses to store your drawing during automatic saves. Change the .sv$ file name extension to .dwg, and then open the file.

There may be situations when a file is so badly corrupted it cannot be restored. By backing up frequently, the inconvenience of such an occurrence can be minimized. You may also want to consider the Microsoft Office Plus package, which allows you to schedule backups and scan and defragment your drives during off hours. Programs such as Scandisk can spot problem areas on your hard disk before they cause trouble.

Troubleshooting

AutoCAD is a large, complex program, so you are bound to encounter some difficulties from time to time. This section covers a few of the more common problems experienced while using AutoCAD.

You can see but cannot select objects in a drawing someone else has worked on   This may be happening because you have a Paper Space view instead of a Model Space view. To make sure you're in Model Space, type **Tilemode** ↵, and then type **1** ↵. Or you can turn on the UCS icon (by typing **Ucsicon** ↵ **On** ↵, and if you see the triangular UCS icon in the lower-left corner, then you are in Paper Space. You must go to Model Space before you can edit the drawing.

Another item to check is the layer lock setting. If a layer is locked, you won't be able to edit objects on that layer.

Grips do not appear when objects are selected   Make sure the Grips feature is enabled (Tools ➤ Grips...). See Appendix B for details.

When you select objects, it doesn't work the way it appears in this book   Check the Selection settings to make sure they are set the same way as the exercise specifies (Tools ➤ Selection...). See Chapter 2 for details.

Text appears in the wrong font style, or an error message says AutoCAD cannot find font files   When you are working on files from another company, it's not uncommon that you will encounter a file that uses special third-party fonts that you do not have. You can usually substitute standard AutoCAD fonts for any fonts you don't have, without adverse effects. AutoCAD automatically presents a dialog box letting you select font files for the substitution. You can either choose a font file or press the Esc key to ignore the message (see Chapter 8 for more on font files). If you choose to ignore the error message, you may not see some of the text that would normally appear in the drawing.

.dxf files do not import   Various problems can occur during the DXF import, the most common of which is that you are trying to import a .dxf file into an existing drawing rather than a new drawing. Under some conditions, you can import a .dxf file into an existing drawing using the Dxfin command, but AutoCAD may not import the entire file.

To ensure that your entire .dxf file is safely imported, choose File ➢ Open and select *.DXF from the File Type pull-down list. Then import your .dxf file.

If you know the .dxf file you are trying to import is in the ASCII format and not a Binary DXF, take a look at the file with a text editor. If it contains odd-looking characters, chances are the file is damaged or contains extra data that AutoCAD cannot understand. Try deleting the odd-looking lines of characters, and then import the file again (make a backup copy of the file before you attempt this).

A file cannot be saved to disk Frequently, a hard drive will fill up quickly during an edit session. AutoCAD can generate temporary and swap files many times larger than the file you are editing. This can leave you with no room left to save your file. If this happens, you can empty the Recycle Bin to clear some space on your hard drive, or delete old AutoCAD .bak files you don't need. *Do not delete temporary AutoCAD files.*

AutoCAD does not display all the Paper Space viewports AutoCAD uses substantial memory to display Paper Space viewports. For this reason, it limits the number of viewports it will display at one time. Even though viewports don't display, they will still plot. Also, if you zoom in on a blank viewport while in Paper Space, you will be able to see its contents. The viewport regains visibility because you are reducing the number of viewports shown on the screen at one time.

You can increase the number of viewports AutoCAD will display at one time by resetting the *Maxactvp* system variable. (This is usually set to 48.) Be fore-warned, however, that increasing the Maxactvp setting will cause AutoCAD to use more memory. If you have limited memory on your system, this will slow down AutoCAD considerably.

AutoCAD becomes impossibly slow when adding more Paper Space viewports As mentioned for the preceding problem, AutoCAD consumes memory quickly when adding viewports. If your system resources are limited, you can reduce the *Maxactvp* system variable setting so that AutoCAD displays fewer viewports at one time. This will let you work on a file that has numerous viewports without causing a decrease in your computer's performance. Try reducing Maxactvp to 8, and then reduce or increase the setting until you find the optimum value for your situation. Alternatively, you can use the Mview OFF option to turn off viewports when you are not working in them.

AutoCAD won't open a large file, and displays a "Page File Full" message   AutoCAD will open drawing files larger than can fit into your system's RAM. In order to do this, however, AutoCAD attempts to store part of the drawing in a temporary file on your hard drive. If there isn't room on the hard drive, AutoCAD will give up. To remedy this problem, clear off some space on your hard drive. It is not uncommon for AutoCAD to require as much as 10MB of hard-disk space for every 1MB of a drawing file.

The keyboard shortcuts for commands are not working   If you are working on an unfamiliar computer, chances are the keyboard shortcuts (or command aliases) have been altered. The command aliases are stored in the Acad.pgp file. If you have installed the Release 14 Bonus Menu (see Appendix B for overall installation instructions), you can modify the keyboard shortcuts by using the Command Alias Editor option on the Bonus menu. Choose Bonus ➢ Tools ➢ Command Alias Editor, or type **aliasedit** at the command prompt. Then you may add, remove, or edit the keyboard shortcut codes. See Chapter 19 for more on the Alias Editor.

Plots come out blank   Check the scale factor you are using for your plot. Often, a blank plot means your scale factor is making the plot too large to fit on the sheet. Try plotting with the Scale to Fit option. If you get a plot, then you know your scale factor is incorrect. See Chapter 7 for more on plotting options. Check your output before you plot by using the Full Preview option in the Plot Configuration dialog box.

You cannot get your drawing to be properly oriented on the sheet If you want to change the orientation of your drawing on a plotted sheet, and the Plot Configuration orientation options don't seem to work, try rotating the UCS to align with your desired plot view, and then type **Plan** ↵. Adjust the view to display what you want to have plotted, and then use the View command (View ➢ Named Views...) to save this view. When you are ready to plot, use the View option in the Plot Configuration dialog box and plot the saved view, instead of rotating the plot.

Dimensions appear as lines and text and do not act   The Dimaso system variable is off, or was turned off when the dimension was created. Another possibility is that the dimension was reduced to its component objects using the Explode command. Make sure Dimaso is on by typing **Dimaso** ↵ **on** ↵. Unfortunately, an exploded dimension or one that was created with Dimaso turned off cannot be converted to a true dimension object. You must redraw the dimension.

A file containing Xref appears to be blank or parts are missing

AutoCAD cannot find the Xref file. Use the External Reference dialog box (Insert ➤ External Reference…) to reestablish connection with the Xref file. Once the External Reference dialog box is open, select the missing Xref from the list, and then click the Browse button and locate and select the file using the Browse dialog box.

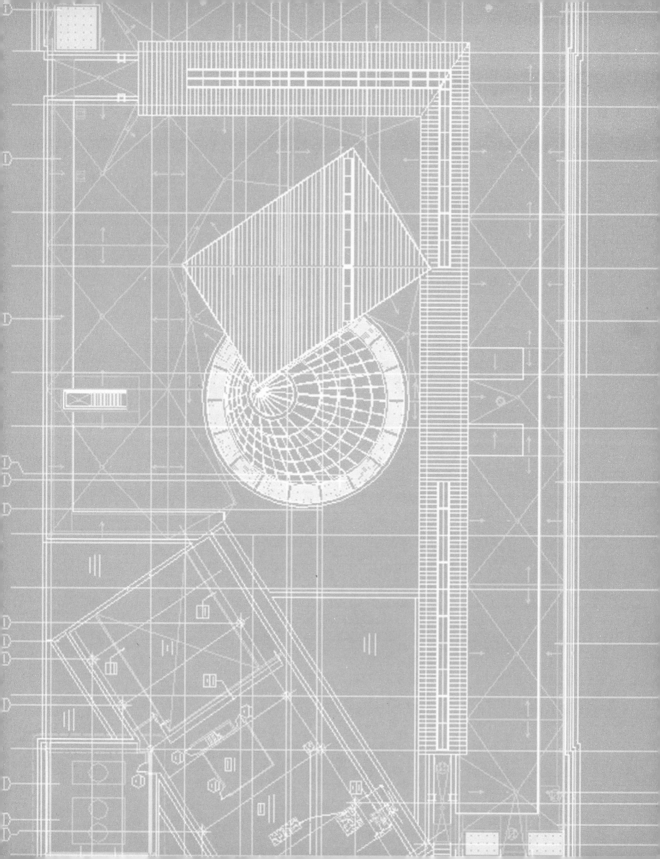

Installing and Setting Up AutoCAD

Before Installing AutoCAD

Before you begin the installation process, be sure you have a drive with at least 100MB of free disk space. In addition, you should know your AutoCAD vendor's name and phone number.

You will also want to have at least an additional 50MB of free disk space for AutoCAD *temporary files* and *swap files,* plus another 20MB for the tutorial files you will create. (Temporary and swap files are system files AutoCAD creates as it works. You don't have to deal with these files directly, but you do have to allow room for them. If you want to know more about these files, see Appendix A.) If you are installing AutoCAD on a drive other than the one on which Windows is installed, make sure you have about 20MB free on the Windows drive. AutoCAD also stores temporary files there.

Finally, have your AutoCAD vendor's name and phone number ready. You will be asked to enter this information during the installation. You will also want to have your network and single-user authorization code ready. These can be obtained by calling the toll-free number listed in your AutoCAD package. Single-user systems have a 30 day grace period, so you can install and use AutoCAD without having to enter your authorization code right away.

Installing the AutoCAD Software

After you've made sure you've enough disk space and you've closed all other programs, proceed with the following steps to install AutoCAD:

1. To begin your installation, be sure the AutoCAD CD is in your CD-ROM drive.

2. Click on the Windows Start button and choose Run.

3. At the Run dialog box, enter **D:setup** into the input box. Enter the drive letter of your CD-ROM in place of the *D* in this example. Click OK when you are ready. You see the Welcome dialog box warning you to make sure all other programs are closed. Click Next to continue.

4. The next dialog box is the Software License Agreement. Read it. If you accept the terms, click Accept.

5. In the Serial Number dialog box, enter the serial number and CD Key, and then click next.

6. Next, you see the Personal Information dialog box. To personalize Auto-CAD, you are asked for your name, company, and AutoCAD vendor's name and telephone number. This information will be displayed on the opening AutoCAD screen, so don't enter anything you'll regret later.

7. You are then asked to confirm the information you entered. If you changed your mind, you can go back and change the information in the previous dialog box. Otherwise, click Next.

8. Select the location for your AutoCAD files. The tutorial assumes you have AutoCAD on drive C and in a directory called \Program Files\AutoCAD R14 —these are the defaults during the installation. When you're done, click Next. If the installation location does not exist, you will see a message to this effect and asking if it is OK for the Installer to create it. Click OK.

9. In the next dialog box, choose the type of setup you want. You have the choice of Typical, Full, Compact, or Custom. We encourage you to choose the Full installation as this will enable you to take advantage of the Bonus utilities discussed in Chapter 19.

10. The installation will create a program folder with a set of AutoCAD related programs and documents. Enter a name for this folder in the next dialog box or choose to accept the default, AutoCAD R14.

11. You finally get a Setup confirmation dialog box showing you a listing of program components the Installation will install. Click Next to begin the actual file installation. This can take several minutes.

12. Once the installation is done, you see the Setup Complete dialog box. You can have the install program automatically open the AutoCAD R14 Readme document by checking the Yes I Want to View the Readme File. Click Finish to exit the installation.

13. Start AutoCAD by double-clicking on the AutoCAD R14 shortcut on the Windows Desktop.

14. You will then see a message telling you that you have 30 days to authorize your copy of AutoCAD. The message will also give you the phone numbers for obtaining your Authorization code. Enter your Authorization code and click Authorize, or click Defer to open AutoCAD without Authorization. If you don't enter an Authorization code, you will see this message each time you open AutoCAD—until you finally enter it.

The Program Files

In the \Program Files\AutoCAD 14 directory, you will see a number of subdirectories.

NOTE   This book's tutorial assumes you are working from the directory where the program files are stored. However, if you prefer to work from a different directory, be sure you have set a path for the AutoCAD directory; otherwise, AutoCAD will not start properly. Consult your DOS manual for more information on Path statements.

Here are brief descriptions of each subdirectory's contents:

Adsrx   contains sample ObjectARX code.

DRV   contains the drivers used by AutoCAD to control input and output devices. These drivers include the display drivers for VGA and SVGA.

Fonts   contains AutoCAD fonts.

Help   contains AutoCAD help documents.

Sample   contains the menu compiler and the SHROOM utility for creating a bigger shell.

Support   contains the files that define a variety of AutoCAD's functions that are specifically for the DOS version of AutoCAD.

Template   contains AutoCAD template files.

Textures   contains texture files for AutoCAD's rendering feature.

Vbakup   contains help files for AutoCAD VBA.

Vgasamp   contains sample AutoCAD VBA applications.

Bonus   contains the bonus utilities and samples described in Chapter 19. You won't see this directory unless you've installed the Bonus utilities or performed the Full AutoCAD installation.

Configuring AutoCAD

In this section, you will learn how to *configure* AutoCAD. By configure, we mean to set up AutoCAD to work with the particular hardware you have connected to your computer. AutoCAD often relies on it's own set of drivers to operate specialized equipment. By configuring AutoCAD, you tell it exactly what equipment it will be working with. With Release 14, you can configure AutoCAD at any time during an AutoCAD session through the Preferences dialog box.

The tutorials in this book assume that you are using the default Preference settings. As you become more familiar with the workings of AutoCAD, you may want to make adjustments to the way AutoCAD works throughout the Preferences dialog box.

This dialog box can be accessed by clicking on Tools ➢ Preferences.... It is further divided into sections shown as tabs across the top of the dialog box. The following describes the settings available on each of the tabs:

Files

The Files tab is where you tell AutoCAD where to place or find files it needs to operate. It uses a hierarchical list similar to the one presented by the Windows Explorer. You first see the general topics listed in the Search Path, File Names, and File Location list boxes. You can expand individual items in the list by clicking on the plus sign shown to the left of the item.

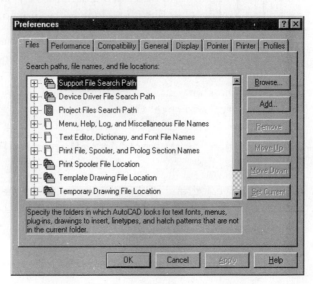

The following explains what each item in the list box is for. Chances are you won't have to use most of them, while others you may change occasionally.

Support File Search Path

AutoCAD relies on external files for many of its functions. Menus, text fonts, line types, and hatch patterns are a few examples of features that rely on external files. The Support File Search Path tells AutoCAD where to look for these files. You can add directory paths to this listing by clicking on the Add button and entering a new path or use the browse button. It's probably not a good idea to delete any of the existing items under this heading unless you really know what you are doing.

Device Driver File Search Path

This item locates the device drivers for AutoCAD. Device drivers are applications that allow AutoCAD to communicate directly with the printers, plotters, and input devices. In most cases, you do not have to do anything with this setting.

Project Files Search Path

Eventually, you will receive a set of files from a consultant or other AutoCAD user that is dependent on Xref or raster images. Often, such files will expect the Xref or raster image to be in a particular directory. When such files are moved to another location with a different directory system, Xref dependent files will not be able to find their Xrefs. The Support File Search Path allows you to specify a directory where Xrefs or other dependent files are stored. If AutoCAD is unable to find an Xref or other file, it will look in the directory you specify in this listing.

To set it, highlight Project File Search Path, and then click on the Add button. AutoCAD will suggest Project1 as the directory name. You can change the name if you prefer. Click on the plus sign next to Project1, and then click on Browse to select a location for your Project support path. The search path is stored in a system variable called Projectname.

Menu, Help, Log, and Miscellaneous File Names

This item lets you set the location of a variety of support files including menu, help, automatic save, log, and configuration files. It also lets you set the default Internet address for the Launch Browser button on the AutoCAD Standard toolbar. If you have a network installation, you may also set the License Manager location on your network.

Text Editor, Dictionary, and Font File Names

Use this item to set the location of the Text Editor, Custom and Standard dictionaries, and alternate font and font mapping files. See Chapter 8 for more on this item.

Print File, Spooler, and Prolog Section Names

You can specify a print file name other than the default that is supplied by AutoCAD whenever you plot to a file. The Spooler option lets you specify an application intended to read and plot a plot file. The Prolog option is intended for PostScript export. It lets you specify the Prolog section from the Acad.psf file that you want AutoCAD to include with exported Encapsulate PostScript files. See Appendix A and Chapter 14 for more on exporting PostScript files and the Acad.psf file. The prolog setting can also be controlled through the Psprolog system variable.

Print Spooler File Location

Print spooler applications will usually look in a specific directory for files that are to be plotted or printed. This item lets you set a directory location for print spool files.

Template Drawing File Location

When you select the Use a Template option in the Create New Drawing dialog box, AutoCAD looks at this setting for the location of template files. You can modify this setting, but chances are, you won't need to.

Temporary Drawing File Location

AutoCAD creates temporary files to store portions of your drawing as you work on them. You usually don't have to think about these temporary files until they start crowding your hard disk, or if you are working on a particularly large file on a system with little memory. This item lets you set the location for temporary files. The default location is the \Windows\Temp directory. If you have a hard drive that has lots of room and is very fast, you may want to change this setting to a location on that drive to improve performance.

Temporary External Reference File Location

If you are on a network, and you foresee a situation where another user will want to open an Xref file of a file you are working on, you can set the Demand Load setting in the Performance tab to Enable with Copy. This causes AutoCAD to make and use a copy of any Xref that is currently loaded. This way, the original file can be opened by others. The Temporary External Reference File Location lets you specify the directory where AutoCAD will store this copy of an Xref.

Texture Maps Search Path

This item specifies the location for AutoCAD Render texture maps. In most cases, you won't have to change this setting. You can, however, add a directory name to this item for your own texture maps as you acquire or create them.

Performance

The options found on this tab affect the performance of AutoCAD. Generally, you can leave these settings alone as they are tuned for a moderately powered computer. If you have a slow computer, you may want to change some of these settings. If you have a fast computer, you may alter some of these settings to improve display quality.

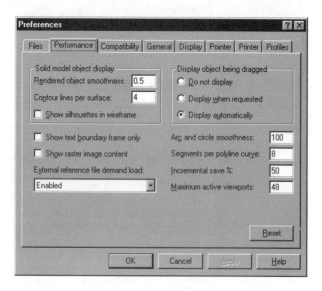

Solid Model Object Display

These settings affect the display of solid model wire frame views. See Chapter 18 for details. These setting are also controlled by the Facetres, Isolines, and Dispsilh system variables.

Display Objects Being Dragged

These radio button options determine how objects are dragged as they are moved, copied, or rotated. Normally, with Display Automatically selected, you see the objects move with the cursor. The Display When Requested setting lets you determine whether to drag objects as they are moving or not. When this option is selected, you will see a rubber-banding line indicating the move but you will not see an image of the object follow the cursor unless you type **Drag** ↵. Do Not Display turns off the dragging feature altogether. This setting is also controlled by the Dragmode system variable.

Show Text Boundary Frame Only

With this option selected, text will appear as a rectangle. See Chapter 8 for details. This setting is also controlled by the Qtextmode system variable.

Show Raster Image Content

With this option selected, AutoCAD will attempt to display the entire raster image as you perform pans and zooms; otherwise, only the bounding outline will be displayed. This setting is also controlled by the Rtdisplay system variable.

External Reference File Demand Load

Controls the Demand Load feature for external references. The Demand Load feature limits the amount of RAM used by an Xref, particularly if the Xref is clipped. See Chapter 12 for more on clipped Xrefs. This setting is also controlled by the Xloadctl system variable.

Arc and Circle Smoothness

This option controls the appearance of arcs and circles, particularly when you zoom in on them. In some instances, arc and circles will appear to be octagons, even though they will plot as smooth arcs and circles. If you want arcs and circles to appear smoother, you can increase this setting. An increase will also increase memory use. This setting is also controlled by the Viewres system variable.

Segments per Polyline Curve

This setting controls the smoothness of polyline curves. A higher number will make a curved polyline appear smoother. This setting is also controlled by the Splinesegs system variable.

Incremental Save %

When you issue a save, AutoCAD performs an incremental save until the file contains a 50 percent level of wasted space. When that level is reached, AutoCAD performs a full save, which takes more time. You can change the amount of wasted space allowed before a full save is performed. In general, you should leave this setting to 50 percent unless you are running into space limitations on your drive. This setting is also controlled by the Isavepercent system variable.

Maximum Active Viewports

AutoCAD limits the number of Paper Space viewports that display their contents to 48. This limit keeps AutoCAD's memory consumption down. You may decrease this number to improve memory use while in Paper Space. (Prior versions of AutoCAD were set to 16). This setting is also controlled by the Maxactvp system variable.

> **TIP**
>
> The Reset button resets the values on this tab to the default settings. You'll find this button on several of the tabs in the Preferences dialog box.

Compatibility

These settings allow you to adjust AutoCAD to be more compatible with earlier versions. If you find you just cannot get used to the new way AutoCAD R14 works, you can change these settings to make AutoCAD14 a more familiar environment.

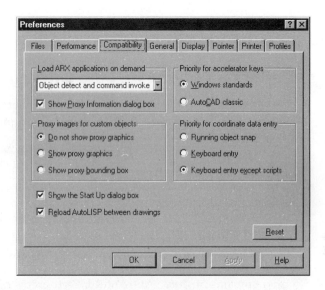

Load ARX Applications on Demand

AutoCAD R14 loads add-on applications, known as ARX applications, only when a command related to that application is invoked and a custom object associated with the application is detected. This is called *Demand Loading*. Two AutoCAD features, Render and Solids, are examples of such ARX add-on applications. With the settings in this group, you can control when Demand Loading is invoked. You usually don't have to change settings here as they are set to optimize AutoCAD performance. This setting is also controlled by the Demandload system variable.

Proxy Images for Custom Objects

Custom objects are objects that are created by third party add-on programs to AutoCAD. You can control the visibility of such objects through the options in this group. By default, the custom objects, called *proxy objects* when the add-on is not present, are represented as a wireframe. You have the option to not show them at all or to show them as a rectangle, known as a *bounding box*. This setting is also controlled by the Proxyshow system variable.

Priority for Accelerator Keys

Some keystroke combinations are reserved for Windows operations. Ctrl+C, for example, copies highlighted contents to the Clipboard. Older versions of AutoCAD, however, use these keystroke combinations differently. Ctrl+C executes the Cancel command in prior versions of AutoCAD. The settings in this group let you set which standard has priority: Windows or the prior AutoCAD versions.

Priority for Coordinate Data Entry

These options determine whether keyboard entry of coordinates overrides Running Object snaps. Options 1 and 2 override the running osnaps, with option 2 being the default.

Show the Start Up Dialog Box

This setting controls the appearance of the Start Up dialog box. When checked, you will see the Start Up dialog box whenever you create a new file or start AutoCAD.

Reload AutoLISP between Drawings

In prior versions of AutoCAD, AutoLISP programs had to be reloaded with each new file that was opened. This setting lets you maintain the prior method of handling AutoLISP programs or set AutoCAD to maintain the programs across file accesses. This setting is also controlled by the Lispinit system variable.

General

The options in this tab seem to control a handful of miscellaneous operations. For the most part, you won't want to change these settings, except perhaps the Automatic Save settings or the Log File feature.

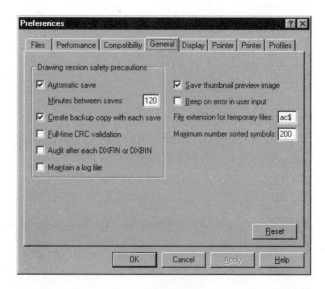

Drawing Session Safety Precaution

The settings in this group are concerned with file integrity. At the most basic level, you can turn the Automatic Save feature on or off and set the time interval between automatic saves. Other options affect whether or not files are checked as you work:

Automatic save   lets you turn the Automatic Save feature on or off. It is highly recommended that you leave this feature on.

Minutes between Save   lets you control the time interval at which AutoCAD performs automatic saves. This setting is also controlled by the Savetime system variable.

Create Backup Copy with Each Save   lets you determine whether Auto-CAD creates the .BAK backup file each time you perform a save. This setting is also controlled by the isavebak system variable.

Full-Time CRC Validation   checks the integrity of each object as it is created in AutoCAD. (CRC stands for Cyclic Redundancy Check). This can be used as a troubleshooting aid and can be turned on if you suspect there are problems with your hardware or AutoCAD.

Audit after Each DXFIN or DXBIN   performs an audit on a file after a DXFIN or DXBIN is performed. The Audit command performs the same function (File ➢ Drawing Utilities ➢ Audit). This can be a helpful tool if you are importing files from questionable sources.

Maintain a Log File   turns on the Log File feature discussed in Chapter 14. This setting is also controlled by the Logfilemode system variable.

Save Thumbnail Preview Image

When you open files, you see a preview of the file in a preview window. This preview image is a small bitmap file that is saved with the AutoCAD file. This setting lets you determine whether that thumbnail is created or not. If you turn this feature off, you won't see those preview images for the files that you save from now on. This setting is also controlled by the Rasterpreview system variable.

Beep on Error in User Input

This option is a holdover from the very early versions of AutoCAD. Just as the name implies, when you turn this option on, AutoCAD will beep whenever you do something AutoCAD doesn't understand. Chances are, you won't want to turn this on.

File Extension for Temporary Files

Whenever you open a file, particularly a large one, AutoCAD creates temporary files that it uses to store drawing data when it starts to run out of RAM. Typically, these files have the .ac$ extension that AutoCAD is famous for leaving around. If you are on a network, you may want to change this extension so it doesn't conflict with files from another user, or as a means to signal other users who may be opening a particular set of files.

Maximum Number Sorted Symbols

A few of AutoCAD's commands provide lists of items in text windows. This option determines how many items it will sort alphabetically in a list. If set to 0, listings are sorted by the order in which the item was created. This setting is also controlled by the Maxsort system variable.

Display

The settings on this tab let you control the appearance of AutoCAD. You can make AutoCAD look completely different with these settings if you choose. Scroll bars, fonts, and colors are all up for grabs.

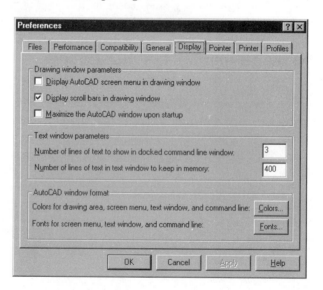

Drawing Window Parameters

These options control the general settings for the AutoCAD windows:

Display AutoCAD Screen Menu in Drawing Window turns on the old AutoCAD format screen menu that once appeared on the right side of the screen. If you really must have it, this is where you can turn it back on.

Display Scroll Bars in Drawing Window lets you turn the scroll bars on and off. If you've got a small monitor with low resolution, you may want to turn them off for a larger drawing area.

Maximize the AutoCAD Window upon Startup determines whether the AutoCAD screen is maximized when you open AutoCAD. Again, if you have a small monitor, you may want to turn this option on.

Text Window Parameters

These settings control the display of the Command window:

Number of Lines of Text to Show in Docked Command Line Window lets you increase or decrease the number of text lines displayed. If you feel comfortable with AutoCAD and don't need to refer to the prompt too often, you may want to decrease this value to get a larger drawing area.

Number of Lines of Text in Text Window to Keep in Memory determines how much of the text window is retained in memory before it is discarded. You will be able to scroll back in the text window to the number of lines indicated by this setting.

AutoCAD Window Format

Two buttons are offered here that open dialog boxes. These dialog boxes offer controls over the colors of the AutoCAD window and the fonts displayed on the menu bar, status bar, and screen menu.

Colors... opens a dialog box that lets you set the color for the various components of the AutoCAD window. This is where you can change the background color of the drawing area if you find that black doesn't work for you.

Fonts... opens a dialog box that lets you set the fonts of the AutoCAD window. You can select from the standard set of Windows fonts available in your system.

Pointer

There are two main functions on this tab. First, if you want to install a digitizing tablet, this is the place to install the AutoCAD drivers for it. Select the driver name from the list; then click on the Set Current button. You will be asked a series of questions regarding your hardware. When you are done, your tablet will be available for use with AutoCAD. You can always go back and change settings

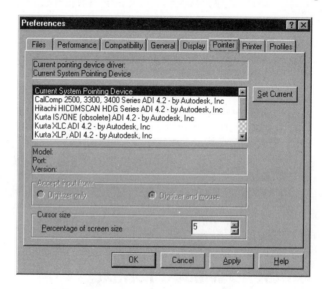

The other function is to allow control over the crosshair cursor in the AutoCAD drawing. Veteran AutoCAD users may prefer the larger cursor of previous versions. The Cursor Size input box can be set to 100 to restore the full screen cursor of previous versions.

Printer

The Printer tab lets you add, modify, or delete printers and plotters to your system. You can have multiple printers as well as raster file formats. See Chapter 14 for details on how to use this tab.

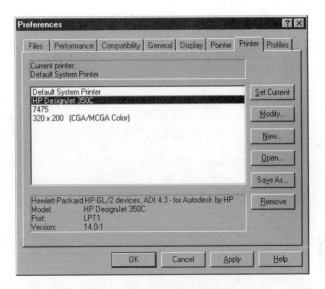

Profiles

If you are using Windows NT, you know that a user profile is saved for each log-in name. Depending on the log-in name you use, you will have a different Windows setup. The Profiles tab offers a similar function for AutoCAD users. You can store different Preferences settings and recall them at any time. You can also save them to a file with the .arg extension, then take that file to another system. It's a bit like being able to take your Preferences settings with you wherever you go.

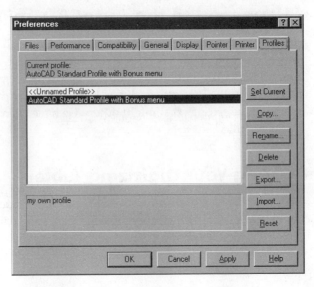

The main part of this tab displays a listing of profiles available. The default <<Unnamed Profile>> is the default profile. As you add more profiles, they will appear in the list.

To create a new profile, you highlight a profile name from the list, and then click Copy. A Copy Profile dialog box appears, allowing you to enter a profile name and a description of the profile. The description appears in the box below the list on the Profiles tab whenever that profile is selected.

Once you've created a new profile, you can modify the settings on the other tabs of the Preferences dialog box and the new settings will be associated with the new profile. Profiles will store the way menus are set up so they can be used as an aid to managing both your own customizations schemes and other third party software. Profiles can also be a way to manage multiple users on the same computer. Each user can maintain his or her own profile so they don't have to fight over how AutoCAD is set up. Here is a brief listing of the options on the Profiles tab:

Set Current installs the settings from the selected profile.

Copy... creates a new profile from an existing one.

Rename... allows you to rename a profile and change its description.

Delete removes the selected profile from the list.

Export... lets you save a profile to a file.

Import... imports a profile that has been saved to a file.

What Happened to the AutoCAD .ini File?

In prior Windows versions of AutoCAD, many of the AutoCAD settings were stored in the Acad.ini file. Release 14 now uses the Windows Registry to store information. Attempting to edit the Windows Registry is not recommended. Fortunately, the Preferences dialog box has been expanded to accommodate many of the settings that might otherwise have been accessed through the Acad.ini file.

Configuring Your Digitizing Tablet

If you are using a digitizer with AutoCAD for Windows, you will need to select some additional configuration options after you've installed the driver on the

Pointer tab of the Preferences dialog box. These other options allow you to add a menu template.

As an alternative, you may choose to configure your tablet as the Windows pointing device. You can then use the Wintab driver on the Pointer tab of the Preferences dialog box to make the appropriate changes to your table's configuration.

Configuring the Tablet Menu Area

If you own a digitizing tablet and you would like to use it with the AutoCAD tablet menu template, you must configure your tablet menu.

1. First, securely fasten your tablet menu template to the tablet. Be sure the area covered by the template is completely within the tablet's active drawing area.

2. Choose Options ➤ Tablet ➤ Configure. You will get this prompt:

   ```
   Digitize upper left corner of menu area 1:
   ```

   For the next series of prompts, you will be locating the four tablet menu areas, starting with menu area 1 (see Figure B.1).

3. Locate the position indicated in Figure B.1 as the upper-left corner of menu area 1. Place your puck or stylus to pick that point. The prompt will change to

   ```
   Digitize lower left corner of menu area 1:
   ```

4. Again, locate the position indicated in Figure B.1 as the lower-left corner of menu area 1.

5. Continue this process until you have selected three corners for four menu areas.

6. When you are done selecting the menu areas, you will get this prompt:

   ```
   Do you want to respecify the Fixed Screen Pointing Area:
   ```

   Type **Y** ⏎ and then pick the position indicated in Figure B.1.

7. Finally, you get this prompt:

   ```
   Digitize upper right corner of screen pointing area:
   ```

   Pick the position indicated in Figure B.1.

FIGURE B.1:

How to locate the tablet menu areas

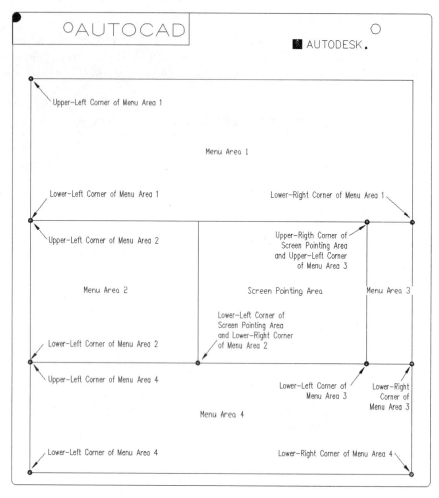

The three prompts that remain refer to a *Floating Screen Pointing Area*. This is an area on your tablet that allows you to select menu options and other areas on your screen outside the drawing area. This option is necessary because when you set up a digitizer for tracing, access to areas outside the drawing area is temporarily disabled. The floating screen pointing area lets you access pull-down menus and the status bar during tracing sessions (see Chapter 11).

8. If you never intend to trace drawings with your tablet, then answer **N** ↵ to all three prompts. Otherwise do the following three steps.

9. At the following prompt:

   ```
   Do you want to specify the Floating Screen Pointing Area? <N>:
   ```

   type **Y** ↵.

10. At the prompt:

    ```
    Do you want the Floating Screen Pointing Area to be the same size
    as the Fixed Screen Pointing Area? <Y>:
    ```

    type **Y** ↵ if you want the Floating Screen Pointing Area to be the same as the Fixed Screen Pointing area, the area you specified in steps 6 and 7. Type **N** ↵ if you want to use a separate area on your tablet for the Floating Screen Pointing Area.

11. The last prompt asks you if you want to use the F12 function key to toggle the Floating Screen Pointing Area on and off. (This is similar to the F10 key function of earlier releases of AutoCAD). Enter **Y** ↵ or **N** ↵, depending on whether you want to specify a different function key for the Floating Screen Pointing Area or not.

AutoCAD will remember this configuration until you change it again. Quit this file by selecting File ➢ Exit.

Turning on the Noun/Verb Option

If, for some reason, the Noun/Verb Selection method is not available, here are instructions on how to turn it back on.

1. Choose Tools ➢ Selection to display the Object Selection Settings dialog box.

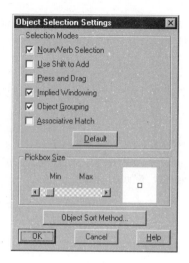

2. In the Selection Modes button group, find the Noun/Verb Selection setting. Click on the check box to turn this option on.

3. Click OK.

If it wasn't there before, you should now see a small square at the intersection of the crosshair cursor. This square is actually a pickbox superimposed on the cursor. It tells you that you can select objects, even while the command prompt appears at the bottom of the screen and no command is currently active. As you have seen earlier, the square will momentarily disappear when you are in a command that asks you to select points.

You can also turn on Noun/Verb Selection by entering **'Pickfirst** ↵ at the command prompt. When you are asked for New value for PICKFIRST <0>, enter **1** ↵ (entering **0** turns the Pickfirst function off). The Pickfirst system variable is stored in the AutoCAD configuration file. See Appendix D for more on system variables.

Other Selection Options

The Object Selection Settings dialog box lets you control the degree to which AutoCAD conforms to standard graphical user interface methods of operation. It also lets you adjust the size of the Object Selection pickbox.

In Chapter 2, you practiced selecting objects using the Noun/Verb Selection setting—one of several AutoCAD settings that make the program work more like other Windows programs. If you are used to working with other graphical environments, you may want to turn on some of the other options in the Selection

Settings dialog box. Here are descriptions of them; in brackets you'll find the names of the system variables that control these features.

Use Shift to Add [Pickadd]   With this option checked, you can use the standard GUI method of holding down the Shift key to pick multiple objects. When the Shift key is not held down, only the single object picked or the group of objects windowed will be selected. Previously selected objects are deselected, unless the Shift key is held down during selection. To turn this feature on using system variables, set Pickadd to 0.

Press and Drag [Pickdrag]   With this option checked, you can use the standard GUI method for placing windows: You first click and hold down the Pick button on the first corner of the window; then, while holding down the Pick button, you drag the other corner of the window into position. When the other corner is in place, you let go of the Pick button to finish the window. This setting applies to both Verb/Noun and Noun/Verb operations. In the system variables, set Pickadd to 1 for this option.

Implied Window [Pickauto]   When this option is checked, a window or crossing window will automatically start if no object is picked at the Select objects prompt. This setting has no effect on the Noun/Verb setting. In the system variables, set Pickadd to 1 for this option.

Turning on the Grips Feature

If for some reason the Grips feature is not available, here are instructions for turning it back on:

1. Choose Tools ➤ Grips…. The Grips dialog box appears.

2. At the top of the dialog box are the Select Settings check boxes. Click on the Enable Grips check box.

3. Click OK, and you are ready to proceed.

The Grips dialog box also lets you determine whether grips appear on objects that compose a block (see Chapter 4 for more on blocks), as well as set the grip color and size. These options can also be set using the system variables described in Appendix D.

You can also turn the Grips feature on and off by entering **'Grips** ⏎. At the prompt New value for GRIPS <0>:, enter a **1** to turn Grips on, or **0** to turn Grips off. Grips is a system variable that is stored in the AutoCAD configuration file.

Setting Up AutoCAD to Use ODBC

AutoCAD is capable of making use of the Open Database Connectivity or ODBC driver that allows you to view Microsoft Access files. Unfortunately, the path to establishing an ODBC link from AutoCAD is somewhat tortuous. This section is intended to give you the basic information you need to know to establish a connection between AutoCAD and your Access 7 files.

To connect to an ODBC file, you need both the database file you want to link to and another database file called the Reference file. In the following explanation, we will use a fictitious file named Mydb.mdb, which is located in the \AutoCAD R14\ samples directory.

Create a Reference Database File

First, you will need to create a reference table in Access to emulate Catalogs and Schemas as Access does not make use of Catalogs and Schemas directly. Take the following steps to create your reference file and tables:

1. Open Access and choose File ➤ New Database.

2. In the New dialog box, select the Blank Database icon from the General tab, and then click OK.

3. In the File New Database dialog box, enter a name for your new database file. For this example, use **acadlink**, though any name will work.

4. Save the file in a place you can remember easily. For this example, choose the \Acadr14 directory.

5. Click OK. Access will create a file called Acadlink.mdb.

6. At the Acadlink:Database dialog box, click on the New button.

7. At the New Table dialog box, click on Design View. A view of a new database table appears.

8. Click on the cell just below the Field Name column, then enter **CATALOG _NAME**.

9. Press the Tab key and the word "Text" appears under the Data Type column.

10. Click on the cell below CATALOG_NAME in the Field Name column and enter **SCHEMA_NAME**.

11. Press Tab to see Text in the Data Type column.

12. Click on the Close button in the upper-right corner of the Table1 window.

13. Click on Yes when the "Do you want to save changes" message appears.

14. In the Save As dialog box, enter **SCHEMATA** for the table name.

15. You will see a Primary Key warning message. Click No. You will return to the Acadlink:Database dialog box. The Schemata table now appears in the Tables tab.

16. Repeat steps 6 and 7.

17. Create the following four fields in the same way that you created the CATALOG_NAME and SCHEMA_NAME fields in steps 8 through 11. All fields should be of the Text data type:

    ```
    TABLE_CATALOG
    TABLE_SCHEMA
    TABLE_NAME
    TABLE_TYPE
    ```

18. Close the table window, click on Yes at the Save message, and enter the name **TABLES** in the Save As dialog box.

19. Click on No at the Primary Key warning message.

You've set up the tables. Now it's time to add some data to the tables. The data you add will be the name of the Access file to which you want to connect from AutoCAD, and the table names within that file.

1. At the Acadlink:Database dialog box, click on Schemata and click Open. The Schemata table appears.

2. Under the CATALOG_NAME field, enter **NULL**.

3. Under the SCHEMA_NAME field, enter **d:\acadr14\sample***mydb*, where *mydb* is the name of the actual database you want to access from AutoCAD (you needn't include the .mdb file name extension). You can replace the file location with any location where you plan to store your database files.

4. Close the table.

5. Highlight TABLES in the Acadlink:Database dialog box; then click Open.

6. Add a record for each table in your database that you wish to have access to. Under TABLE_CATALOG, enter **NULL**. Under TABLE_SCHEMA, enter the name of the database file including the directory path. Leave off the .mdb extension, however. Under TABLE_NAME, enter the name of the table in the database file. Finally, under TABLE_TYPE, enter **Base Table**. Table B.1 shows a sample of what might be entered for the Mydb example, assuming that Mydb contains three tables named computer, employee, and inventory.

TABLE B.1: What would be entered for the Mydb example

TABLE_CATALOG	TABLE_SCHEMA	TABLE_NAME	TABLE_TYPE
NULL	D:\ACADR14\SAMPLE\MYDB	computer	Base Table
NULL	D:\ACADR14\SAMPLE\MYDB	employee	Base Table
NULL	D:\ACADR14\SAMPLE\MYDB	inventory	Base Table

7. Close the table and save the file.

8. Exit Access.

Telling Windows Where the Reference File Resides

Next you need to tell Windows where to locate your database file. If you have Office 97 or Microsoft Access 97 installed, you should have an item in the

Windows 95/NT Control Panel called 32bit ODBC. Make sure you have this item in the Control Panel, then do the following:

1. Double click on 32bit ODBC.

2. At the ODBC Data Source Administrator, click on Add.

3. At the Create New Data Source dialog box, click on Microsoft Access Driver; then click Finish.

4. In the ODBC Microsoft Access 97 Setup dialog box, enter **AutoCAD_ODBC** in the Data Source Name input box.

5. Click the Select button in the Database button group.

6. In the Select Database dialog box, locate and select the Mydb.mdb file you created in the prior section.

7. In the ODBC Data Source Administrator dialog box, click OK.

Telling AutoCAD Where the Reference File Resides

Now you need to tell AutoCAD the location of the reference file. Here are the steps to follow:

1. From the Windows Start menu, choose Programs ➤ AutoCAD R14 ➤ External Database Configuration.

2. In the External Database Configuration dialog box, click Add.

3. For Select DBMS for New Environment, select ODBC; then enter **AutoCAD_ODBC** in the Environment Name input box. This is the same name you used when you configured the Windows Access driver. You may also enter a description in the Environment Description dialog box.

4. Click OK, and then in the Environment dialog box click on the Browse button and locate and select the reference database file. In our example we used the name Acadlink.

5. Make sure Not Supported is selected from the Set Schema drop down list.

6. Enter **NULL** in the Default Catalog input box.

7. Click OK; then click OK again at the External Database Configuration dialog box.

Now you are ready to access your database from within AutoCAD. When you open the Administration dialog box within AutoCAD, you will see AUTO-CAD_ODBC as one of the Environment options.

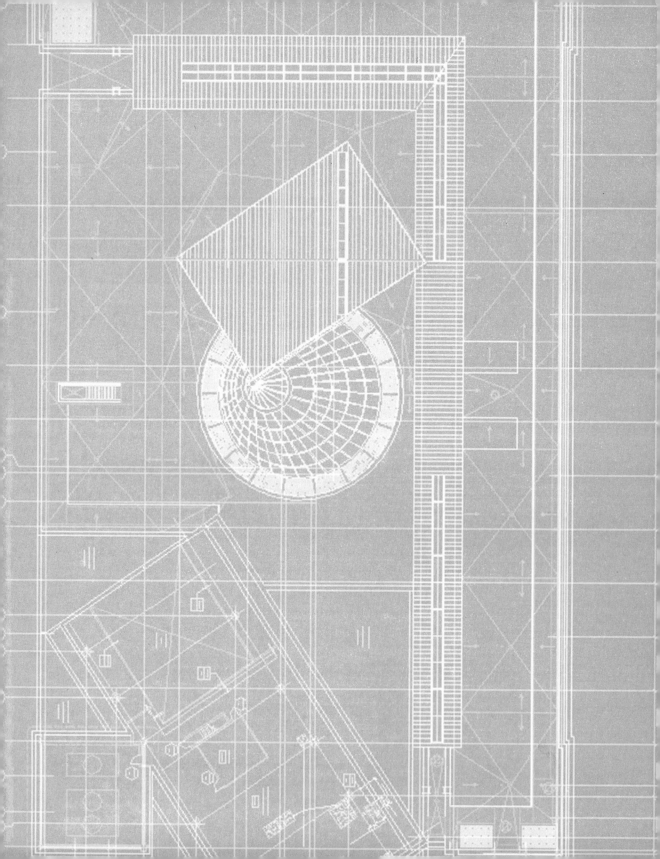

APPENDIX

C

What's on the Companion CD-ROM

This appendix describes the materials supplied on the companion CD-ROM that comes with this book. The CD-ROM contains a number of useful utilities and resources that you can load and run at any time. Before you use them, however, it's best to get familiar with AutoCAD. Many of these utilities work within Auto-CAD from the command line or from options from pull-down menus, and they offer prompts in a way similar to most other AutoCAD commands. Other utilities are stand-alone applications.

The Mastering AutoCAD Bonus Software

To help you get the most from AutoCAD and this book, I've included a set of programs and files. Once you load the CD, the Sybex interface will guide you to the following utilities:

Figures   is a directory of the drawings used in this book. If you follow the tutorial chapter by chapter, you'll create these figures yourself. If you want to do the exercises out of sequence, use these files as needed.

AEC   is a directory of the set of utilities described later in this appendix. These utilities are mostly aimed at the AEC environment but any Auto-CAD user will find them helpful.

Eye2eye   is a directory of the Eye2eye add-on to AutoCAD, described later in this appendix. Eye2eye makes perspective viewing of your 3D models a snap.

The *AutoCAD 14 Instant Reference*   is now an online book, and it's on the enclosed CD-ROM. This is the definitive companion to *Mastering AutoCAD 14* that is full of detailed descriptions of AutoCAD's commands and tools.

The *ABCs of AutoLISP*   is a complete tutorial and reference book for AutoLISP, the AutoCAD macro-programming language. This book has been a favorite of end users and developers alike, and it's now in an easy-to-use Web-browser format.

ActiveX samples   help you get started with Automation in AutoCAD. You can use these examples along with Chapter 20 to explore the newest customization feature of AutoCAD.

Whip2 Netscape Communicator plug-in allows you to view AutoCAD drawings over the Internet. It gives you full Pan and Zoom capabilities as well as access to Web links embedded in AutoCAD files.

Opening the Installation Program

The software discussed in this appendix can be easily installed using the interface and installation program on the CD-ROM. Take the following steps to open the installation program.

1. Insert the *Mastering AutoCAD 14* CD in your CD-ROM drive.

2. Open the Windows Explorer and view the contents of the CD.

3. Double-click on the Clickme file. This will start the installation application for the CD-ROM. You will first see the License Agreement screen.

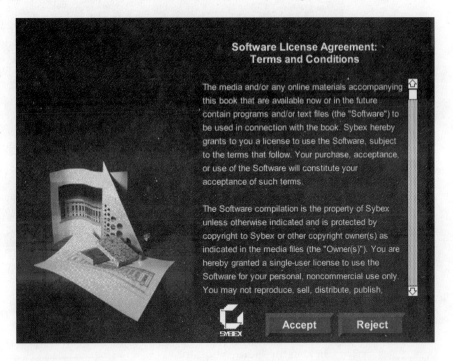

4. After you've read the agreement and accepted the terms, click Accept. You then see the *Mastering AutoCAD 14* software installation interface.

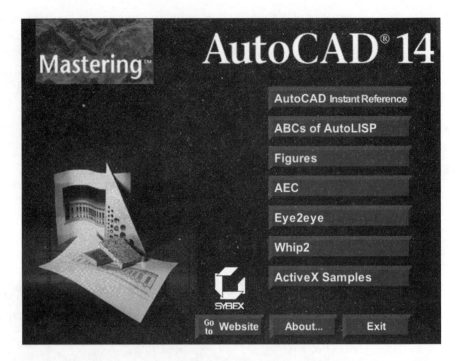

From here, you can select the software you wish to install. For details on each of these options, read the related sections that follow this one.

Installing and Using the Sample Drawing Files

The Figures directory contains sample drawing files for the exercises in this book. These drawings are provided for you in the event that you decide to skip some of the book's tutorial material. With these files, you can open the book to any chapter and start working, without having to construct the drawings from earlier chapters. An icon in each exercise, like the one shown here in the margin, lets you know when a file is available in the exercise sequence.

1. Start the *Mastering AutoCAD 14* software installation program, as described earlier in this appendix.

2. Click on the Figures button.

3. Click on Continue. You see the Winzip self-extractor dialog box. You have the option to accept the default directory shown in the input box, or you may enter a different location for the files.

4. When you've entered the location for the sample files, click Unzip. The files will be installed on your computer.

5. Click Close to return to the main installation program screen.

6. Proceed with another installation or click Exit.

Once you've installed the sample files, you have free access to them during the exercises.

Installing the Bonus Add-On Packages

The companion CD-ROM also includes two add-on packages called On-Screen AEC and Eye2eye. On-Screen AEC is a set of AutoLISP macros and architectural symbols, all integrated with a standard AutoCAD menu. This package offers the basic tools you'll need to start drawing architectural drawings. In addition, it contains many time-saving tools to aid all users, not just architects, in editing their drawings.

Eye2eye is a utility that replaces the AutoCAD Dview command with an easy-to-use method for creating perspective views. Eye2eye uses a camera-target metaphor to let you place viewpoints and view directions in a drawing.

Installing On-Screen AEC

Follow these steps to install On-Screen AEC:

1. Start the *Mastering AutoCAD 14* software installation program, as described earlier in this appendix.

2. Click on the AEC button.

3. Click on Continue. You see the Winzip self-extractor dialog box. You have the option to accept the default directory shown in the input box, or you may enter a different location for the files. We recommend that you install the AEC files in a subdirectory called AEC under the \Program Files\AutoCAD R14\ directory where AutoCAD is installed.

4. When you've entered the location for the AEC files, click Unzip. The files will be installed on your computer.

5. Click Close to return to the main installation program screen.

6. Click Exit, and then start AutoCAD.

7. Start AutoCAD and choose Tools ➤ Preferences....

8. Click on the Files tab at the top of the dialog box.

9. Click on Support Files Search Path.

10. Click on the Add button, and then click Browse.

11. Locate and select the \Program Files\AutoCAD R14\AEC directory, and then click OK.

12. Click OK in the Preferences dialog box.

On-Screen AEC is now installed and ready for use. The next section describes how to load the On-Screen AEC menu.

Loading the On-Screen AEC Menu

Now you are ready to load the On-Screen AEC menu to give you access to the symbols and utilities offered there. If you read through the section on custom menus in Chapter 21, this should be familiar ground. You will load a partial menu that will give you full access to all the AEC tools. Here's how it's done.

1. Once back in AutoCAD, choose Tools ➤ Customize Menu, or type **Menuload** ↵. The Menu Customization dialog box appears.

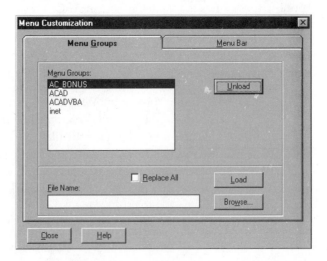

2. Click on the Browse button at the bottom of the dialog box. The Select Menu File dialog box appears.

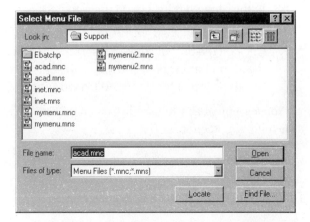

3. Locate the file name Osaec.mnu, and then double-click on it. You return to the Menu Customization dialog box and the Osaec.mnu file name appears in the File Name input box.

4. Click on the Load button just above the Browse button. AutoCAD takes a moment to load the menu. The AEC toolbar will appear on the screen.

5. In the Menu Groups list box in the upper portion of the dialog box, highlight OSAEC, and then click the Menu Bar tab at the top of the dialog box. The dialog box changes to reveal the Menu Bar tab options.

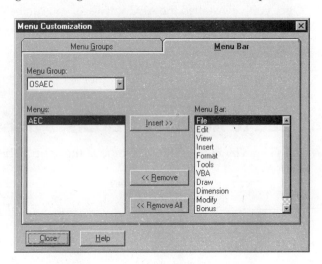

Notice that a menu called AEC appears in the Menu Groups list box to the left. This is a pull-down menu that is contained in the `Osaec.mnu` file.

6. In the Menu Bar list box to the right, click on Help to highlight it. This determines where the AEC pull-down menu will appear in the menu bar.

7. Click on the button labeled Insert >>. AEC will appear just above Help in the Menu Bar list box, and you will see AEC appear in the AutoCAD menu bar at the top of the AutoCAD Window.

You are now ready to use On-Screen AEC. Follow the instructions presented in the following section.

Using the AEC Utilities

On-Screen AEC is a basic architectural symbols library package. This package supplies utilities for creating doors, plumbing and electrical fixtures, wall patterns, and wall intersection clean-up. It also includes many time-saving utilities to help you work faster and more efficiently. Even if your application doesn't involve architecture, you may want to install On-Screen AEC just to take advantage of these utilities.

Getting Started with On-Screen AEC

Once you've installed the AEC software, you can begin to use On-Screen AEC. You may want to start by clicking on the Setup Drawing option in the AEC menu to bring up a dialog box you can use to set up your drawing. Once the setup is done, you will have a drawing area equivalent to your sheet size, with a grid representing 1" intervals on the final plot area.

Using AEC to Add Walls, Doors, Symbols, and Stairs

Let's begin by taking a look at some of the basic architectural features available with AEC.

Adding Walls

To draw walls, you could use AutoCAD's Multiline feature, but Multilines are a bit difficult to edit. Another alternative is to use the Walls option on the AEC menu. Here's how it works.

1. Choose AEC ➢ Walls, or click on Wall from the AEC palette.

2. At the `Enter width` prompt, enter a width for your wall in inches.

3. At the `Center/Up/Down of line <C>` prompt, enter the desired option. Center (the default) centers the wall along the points you pick. The Up and Down options place one side of the wall on the points you pick.

4. At the `Start relative to a position` prompt, you can press ↵ to start your wall anywhere, or type **Y** ↵ to place the beginning of the wall relative to another wall.

5. At the `Draw Centerline` prompt, you can enter ↵ to just draw a two-line representation of a wall, or enter **Y** ↵ to add a line along the points you pick.

6. At the `Pick beginning of parallel lines` prompt, start picking points for your wall. You will see the `Pick Next Point` prompt as you continue to pick points.

7. To stop picking points, press ↵.

8. At the `Close last corner` prompt, you can enter **Y** ↵ to close your wall, or **N** ↵ to exit the Walls utility without closing the wall.

Adding a Door

The door utility can be used only in the World Coordinate System. If you are in another UCS, switch back to the WCS temporarily to insert a door using this utility. Also, you must have drawn walls using the Wall utility to place doors.

1. Choose AEC ➢ Doors, and then select a door from the cascading menu. (To see what the door styles look like, select the Open Toolbar option at the bottom of the menu to open the Door Palette. You can then select a door type from the palette.)

2. Once you select a door, pick a reference point along the wall (see Figure C.1). This should be a known point, such as an interior corner or the midpoint of a wall. You will later enter a value to determine the distance from this point to the door hinge.

3. Pick a point on the opposite side of the wall, as shown in Figure C.1.

4. Again using Figure C.1 as your guide, pick a point along the wall indicating where the door opening will appear in relation to the last point selected.

5. When the command prompt asks you for a door width, enter a width or press ↵ to accept the default door width shown in the < > brackets.

6. Enter the distance from the reference point you picked earlier (step 3) that you want to place the door hinge. For example, if you picked the inside corner of a room for the reference point and you want the door to be 4" from that corner, enter **4**.

FIGURE C.1:

Select this sequence of points when adding a door.

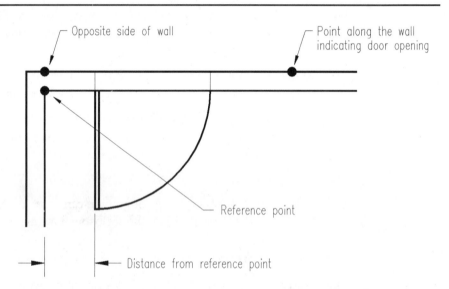

Notice the Settings option near the bottom of the menu; this lets you set the layers on which to place the door, door header, and door jamb. Once these layers are set, AutoCAD will remember them until you change them again. These layer settings affect newly inserted doors only, not previously inserted doors.

Adding a Wall Pattern

The following steps show you how to select and pick points for a wall pattern.

1. Choose AEC ➤ Wall Pattern.

2. From the cascading menu, select the wall pattern you want, or click on Open Toolbar to open the Wall Pattern palette.

3. At the `Pick wall at beginning of pattern` prompt, use the Osnap modes to select a point along the wall where the pattern is to start. For example, you can pick the intersection of two walls using the Intersect Osnap mode.

NOTE You must use an Osnap mode to select the beginning point of the pattern, or the pattern may not align properly with the wall.

4. At the `Pick the opposite side of the wall` prompt, pick any point on the opposite side of the wall from the last point you picked.

5. At the `Pick end of the wall pattern` prompt, pick a point indicating the end of the wall pattern. This point should be on the same side of the wall as the last point you picked.

The wall pattern appears between the first and last points you selected.

Adding Symbols

Here are the steps to add symbols to a drawing. If you would like to modify the AEC-supplied symbols to fit your own work environment, you can find them in the AEC subdirectory.

1. Pull down the AEC menu, and choose one of the three categories of symbols. A cascading menu appears which displays a list of symbols.

2. Choose the name of the symbol you want to use, or you can pick Open Toolbar from the menu to have better access to them (see Figure C.2).

3. Answer the Insertion point and rotation angle prompts on the command line. The symbol appears in the location you select.

Adding Stairs

The AEC menu also includes a stair-drawing option; the following steps show you how it works.

1. Click on AEC ➤ Draw Stairs.

2. At the Pick first corner of stair prompt, pick a point locating one corner of the first stair-tread nosing (see Figure C.3).

3. At the Pick second corner of stair prompt, pick the other corner of the nosing.

4. At the Pick third corner of stair prompt, pick the other end of the stair run.

5. Answer the following four prompts:

```
Enter minimum run of stair <10.00>:
Enter maximum rise of stair <7.50>:
Enter hand rail extension at top of stair <12.00>:
Enter hand rail extension at bottom of stair <12.00>:
```

The stairs appear within the three points you select, complete with handrails.

FIGURE C.2:

The toolbars available
on the AEC menu

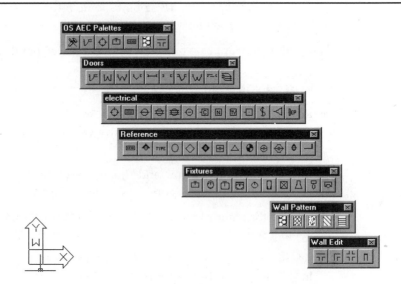

FIGURE C.3:

Adding stairs

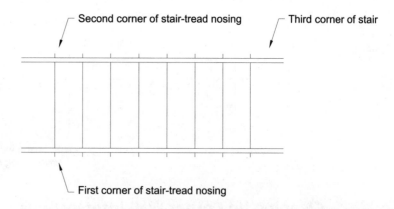

Second corner of stair-tread nosing

Third corner of stair

First corner of stair-tread nosing

Using the Wall Cleanup Utilities

The cleanup utilities will join double lines into tee, corner, and cross forma-tions. The lines joined must be simple lines, not polylines or Multilines. (To join Multilines, you use the Mledit command. To join Polylines, use the Join option of the Pedit command.)

Cleaning Up Tee Wall Intersections

To clean up tee wall intersection, do the following:

1. Click on AEC ➤ Wall Cleanup.

2. Select Tee from the cascading menu.

3. At the `Pick intersection with window` prompt, use a selection window to enclose the intersection of the walls forming the tee.

4. At the `Indicate leg of tee using axis` prompt, pick a point to one side of the leg of the tee. A rubber-banding line appears from the point you select.

5. Pick a second point so that the rubber-banding line crosses over the two lines of the leg of the tee. Take care not to cross over any lines other than those of the tee leg.

The tee intersection joins into a smooth tee intersection, as shown in Figure C.4.

FIGURE C.4:

Joining a tee
intersection

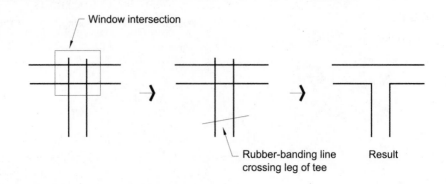

Cleaning Up Corner Wall Intersections

To clean up corner wall intersections, do the following:

1. Click on AEC ➤ Wall Cleanup and select Corner.

2. At the `Select intersection with window` prompt, window the intersection of the walls forming the corner.

3. At the `Pick inside of corner` prompt, a rubber-banding line appears. Pick a point on the inside of the corner. Try to pick this point so that the rubber-banding line divides the angle formed by the two walls exactly in half.

The walls first disappear and then reappear with the corner cleaned up, as shown in Figure C.5.

FIGURE C.5:

Joining a corner

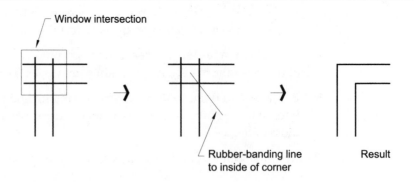

Cleaning Up Crossing Wall Intersections

This function only works if all the lines forming the walls are continuous through the intersection. If this is the case, do the following:

1. Click on AEC ➤ Wall Cleanup and choose Intersect.

2. At the `Select Intersection with Window` prompt, window the intersection of the walls.

3. At the `Pick Narrow Bisecting Angle of Intersection` prompt, pick a point between the intersecting walls, as close to midway between the two walls as possible. If the walls are not perpendicular, pick a point between the narrower angle between the walls.

The walls first disappear, and then reappear with the intersection cleaned up, as shown in Figure C.6.

FIGURE C.6:

Joining two intersecting walls

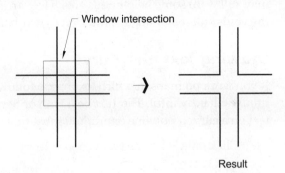

Window intersection

Result

Closing the End of a Wall

This function can be used on any two lines that need to be closed.

1. Click on AEC ➤ Wall Cleanup and choose Close End.

2. At the `Select end of wall with crossing line` prompt, indicate the end of the wall you want to close by picking two points that cross the end of the wall. The end of the wall closes.

Using the General Utilities

Along with the AEC utilities, the companion CD-ROM has several other general-purpose utilities to help you edit your drawings. These utilities are helpful no matter what your field of interest. Take a moment to read through the following descriptions and see if you haven't had a need for at least one or two of these tools.

If you want to use these utilities from a menu, check out the menu file called Master.mnu. This is a standard AutoCAD Release 14 menu, with these utilities added in a single pull-down menu. Use the MENU command to load the Master.mnu file, and then try the utilities out on a sample drawing.

Text-Related Utilities

AutoCAD has improved its text-handling capabilities over the years, but you may still want some help in this area. Here are some utilities that will fill many of the voids still remaining in AutoCAD's text-handling functions.

Drawing Text on a Curve

If you work on maps in which text has to follow some geographic feature, this utility will be helpful. The Text on a Path option on the AEC ➤ Text menu draws text on a curved polyline or arc. You must first draw the polyline or arc.

1. Click on AEC ➤ Text and choose Text on a Path.

2. At the Pick path for text prompt, click on the polyline you have created to define the path.

3. At the Enter text prompt, enter the text you want to follow the path, and press ↵.

4. At the Reverse Text? prompt, enter Y if you want the text to appear in a reverse direction. The text will appear momentarily.

Editing Several Single-Line Text Objects at Once

The Edit Dtext Block (Edsp) utility on the AEC ➤ Text menu allows you to use DOS Edit to make changes to a group of single-line text objects created using Dtext.

1. Click on AEC ➤ Text and choose Edit Dtext Block.

2. At the `Save to file/<Edit> ?` prompt, enter **S** ↵ to save text in a file for later retrieval. Enter **E** ↵ to edit the text in DOS Edit, and proceed to step 4.

3. If you entered **S** ↵, you are prompted with `Enter name of file to be saved <Filename.doc>`. You can enter a different file name, if you want, or press ↵ to accept the default.

4. The next prompt you see is:

   `Sort text by vertical location (this takes some time) ? <N>:`

   Here you have the option to have Edit Dtext Block sort text so it appears in the text file in the same order it appears in the drawing. This only applies to columns of text, so don't use this option unless you plan to select a column of text for editing.

5. At the `Select text:-EL Select objects` prompt, select the set of single-line text you want to edit.

NOTE   At this point, you also have the alternative of exiting AutoCAD entirely and making changes to your text file at a later time. If you choose to do this, be sure you save your file before exiting AutoCAD; otherwise, Edsp won't be able to update your text later. The next time you open the file, load Edsp, enter **(Sp_update)**, and the text in your drawing will be updated.

---

6. Next, using a word processor, open the file you just created, make your changes, and then return to the drawing.

7. Enter **(Sp_update)** ↵. The changes you made to your saved file are applied to your drawing.

8. If you chose to enter ↵ in step 2, AutoCAD loads a text editor and your selected text appears on the screen for you to edit. Once you've made your changes, choose File ➤ Exit. Be sure you answer Yes to save your changes. You will return to your drawing, and your text will be updated to reflect the changes you have made.

Quickly Changing Single Lines

You probably often run across the situation where you need to change several lines of text to make them all say the same thing. Instead of changing each line individually, use the Quick Text Edit utility on the AEC ➤ Text menu. It's a very simple utility that lets you select a set of text objects and change them all at once.

1. Click on AEC ➤ Text and choose Quick Text Edit.

2. At the `Pick text to be changed-EL Select objects` prompt, select the lines of text you want to change.

3. At the `Enter new string` prompt, enter the text you want to appear in place of the selected lines.

Changing Numeric Sequences

If one of your frequent chores is having to change the sequence of numbers—the numbering in parking stalls, for example, or sequential numbers in a table—Sequential Numbers (on the AEC ➤ Text ➤ menu) helps you do this quickly and easily. This utility lets you control the unit style of the numbers, as well as the increment of increase for each number in the sequence.

1. Click on AEC ➤ Text and choose Sequential Numbers.

2. At the `Pick numbers to be changed in order of increment` prompt, select the text objects that are to be converted into a new sequence of numbers. Select the objects in the order the numbers are to appear.

3. At the `Enter unit type Scientific/Decimal/Engin/Arch <D>` prompt, enter the unit style you want.

4. At the `Enter precision value` prompt, enter the decimal accuracy you want for the numbers.

5. At the `Enter increment value` prompt, enter the amount of increase for each number in the sequence.

6. At the `Enter new beginning value` prompt, enter the first number of the sequence. AutoCAD then proceeds to change the selected objects into sequential numbers.

Changing the Height of Text Objects

One of the more frequently requested utilities is one that will change text height. The Change Text Style utility on the AEC ➤ Text menu does this—and it also alters nearly any other property of a group of text objects. Unfortunately, it doesn't operate on Multiline text.

1. First, create a text style with the height you want.

2. Click on AEC ➤ Text and choose Change Text Style.

3. At the `Select Objects` prompt, select the text whose height you want to change.

Housekeeping Utilities

When you're working with a group of people, it is often helpful to keep a record of your layers and blocks. Your coworkers can then refer to these records to find out the assigned contents and purpose of existing layers and blocks. The two utilities described in this section create ASCII log files of your work.

Keeping a Log of Your Blocks

The Block Log utility on the AEC ➤ Blocks menu is a simple macro that creates a log file of blocks. You can specify a name for the file or use the default name, which is usually the drawing name with the .blk extension. The log file will contain the date and a space for remarks. You can edit the file using a text editor to add comments or view and print the file. Here's how it works.

1. Choose AEC ➤ Blocks ➤ Block Log.

2. At the `Enter name of block file <filename>` prompt, enter a block name or press ↵ to accept the default. If no file exists with the name you enter, a new file will be created; otherwise, the current block information will be appended to an existing file.

Keeping a Log of Your Layers

Layer Log does essentially the same thing as the Block Log utility described just above, except it creates an ASCII file log of your layers. This utility creates or appends to a file with the .LAY extension. The following steps show you how to use it.

1. Choose AEC ➤ Layers ➤ Layer Log.

2. At the `Enter name of layer file <filename>` prompt, enter a name or press ↵ to accept the default.

General Productivity Tools

The utilities in this section offer general help in drawing and editing.

Changing the Thickness of Lines

The Thicken utility on the AEC ➤ Drawing Aids menu changes the width of a set of lines, polylines, or arcs. This is useful if you like to control line thickness directly in your drawing, rather than relying on plotter pen settings.

1. Choose AEC ➤ Drawing Aids ➤ Thicken.

2. At the prompt, enter the thickness you want for your lines.

3. At the Select Objects prompt, select the lines, arcs, or polylines you want to change, and then press ↵.

NOTE If you want to change the width of circles, you must first turn them into 359° arcs by breaking them with a very small break.

Joining Broken Lines

It is considered bad form to leave disjointed lines in a CAD drawing. By the term "disjointed," I mean lines that appear to be continuous but are actually made up of several line segments. The Join Lines utility on the AEC ➤ Drawing Aids menu will help you clean up such lines, or just close a gap in any broken line except a polyline.

1. Choose AEC ➤ Drawing Aids ➤ Join Lines.

2. At the Select Two Lines to Be Joined prompt, pick the lines that are broken.

NOTE The Join Lines utility does not work on polylines. You can, however, use grips to first move a polyline endpoint to join the endpoint of the second polyline, and then use the Pedit command's Join option to connect them.

Attribute Template Files, Simplified

Creating and using attributes can be trying for the beginner and even the intermediate user. Extracting attribute data is even more difficult. The `Create Attrib` `.Templt.` option on the AEC ➤ Drawing Aids menu eases these chores by letting you easily create an attribute template file that tells AutoCAD what data to extract.

1. Choose AEC ➤ Drawing Aids ➤ Create Attrib.Templt.

2. At the `Name of attribute template file` prompt, enter the name you want for your template. Don't bother adding an extension; the utility will do that for you.

3. At the `?/Enter name of attribute tag` prompt, enter the name of the tag you wish to extract. You can also enter **?** ↵ to get a listing of existing tags.

4. At the `Is the attribute a Number or Character <C/N>?` prompt, enter **C** ↵ or **N** ↵ to specify the attribute as a character or number.

5. At the `Enter number of digits or characters` prompt, enter the number of characters or digits you want reserved for the attribute.

6. If you entered **N** ↵ in step 4, you'll see the `Enter number of decimal` `places wanted:` prompt next. Enter the number of decimal places you want to reserve for your number.

7. Repeat steps 3 through 5 for each attribute. These prompts will continue until you press ↵ at the `?/Enter name of attribute tag` prompt in step 3.

Cookie Cutter for Objects

There may be times when you want to export a portion of a drawing that is enmeshed in a larger set of objects. Cut Out on the AEC ➤ Drawing Aids menu offers a "cookie-cutter" tool for breaking out objects that are bound into a larger system of objects. The following steps show you how to use Cut Out.

1. Choose AEC ➤ Drawing Aids ➤ Cut Out.

2. At the `Pick first point of Fence/Select` prompt, pick a point to start a fence. This fence defines that area to be cut out.

3. At the `Next point` prompt, pick the next point of the fence.

4. At the Next point/Close prompt, continue to pick points defining the area you want to cut out.

5. At the last point of your fence, enter **C** ↵ to close the fence. The program will break each line, polyline, and circle that it encounters.

You can also predefine a fence by drawing a polyline in the shape of the area you want to cut out. Then, in step 2 you enter **S** ↵. At the prompt Pick line or Pline defining cut location prompt, select an object, and the fence will cut objects along the line or polyline.

There are a few restrictions when using Cut Out:

- You cannot use polyline arcs or splines for fence paths. If you want to cut an arc path, approximate the arc using a spline curve.

- The fence cannot cut blocks, text, arcs, or splines. Also, it will not reliably cut fitted polylines.

Counting Blocks

Is there a simple way to count the occurrences of blocks in a drawing? Yes. Perhaps the easiest method is to use the Selection Filters… option on the Assist menu to select the blocks you want. Then choose Assist ➤ Select Objects ➤ Previous to display the number of selected items. This is fine for counting individual block occurrences, but what if you want a quick count of several block definitions? The Count Blocks utility on the AEC ➤ Blocks menu gives you a listing of blocks and the number of times they occur in your drawing. It also saves the list as a file with the same name as your drawing and the .blk extension. Here's how it works.

1. Choose AEC ➤ Blocks ➤ Count Blocks.

2. At the Enter name(s) of blocks to count or RETURN for all prompt, enter the names of the blocks you want to count, separated by commas. Or you can press ↵ to count all the blocks in the drawing.

AutoCAD lists the blocks and their count. When the counting is done, an ASCII file is created to store the information displayed on the screen.

Creating Keyboard Macros

In Chapter 19, you learned how you can use AutoLISP to create a keyboard macro. I've included an AutoLISP program utility with On-Screen AEC that will do the work for you. This utility, Macro on the AEC ➤ Drawing Aids menu, allows you to record specific points in your drawing and also lets you insert pauses in your macro where you need them. To create a macro, follow these steps.

1. Choose AEC ➤ Drawing Aids ➤ Macro.

2. At the Enter keys to define prompt, enter the name of the macro. This is what you will enter at the command prompt to start your macro.

3. At the Will this macro require open ended object selection? prompt, enter **Y** ↵ if you want to be able to select objects without restrictions—this means you can use all the standard selection options whenever you run your macro. If you do enable this option, however, you must use the Previous setting (described at the end of this procedure) in the main part of your macro to indicate where you want the selected objects to be applied.

4. At the Previous/?=Pause/*=Point/#=done/<Keystroke> prompt, enter the keystrokes of your macro or enter one of the options, as described in the following list.

Here are descriptions of the options in the Previous/?=Pause/*=Point/#=done/<Keystroke> prompt:

Previous is used to indicate when the selected objects should be applied in your macro. Use this option where you anticipate a Select objects prompt. If you have enabled open-ended object selection (step 3 above), you must include this option.

? places a pause for input in the macro. Use this option when you want the macro to stop and wait for point or text input.

* lets you pick a point on the screen or enter a coordinate. This value becomes a fixed value in the macro.

ends the macro keystroke input and stores the macro in memory (or, optionally, on disk).

Eye2eye

Eye2eye is a set of AutoLISP utilities that aid the viewing of 3D models in AutoCAD. If you find you are struggling with the AutoCAD Dview command, these utilities will be of benefit to you.

Installing Eye2eye

Here's how to install Eye2eye:

1. Start the *Mastering AutoCAD 14* software installation program, as described earlier in this appendix.

2. Click on the Eye2eye button.

3. Click on Continue. You see the Winzip self-extractor dialog box. You have the option to accept the default directory shown in the input box, or you may enter a different location for the files. We recommend that you install the Eye2eye files in a subdirectory called Eye2eye under the \Program Files\AutoCAD R14\ directory where AutoCAD is installed.

4. When you've entered the location for the Eye2eye files, click Unzip. The files will be installed on your computer.

5. Click Close to return to the main installation program screen.

6. Click exit.

7. Start AutoCAD and choose Tools ➤ Preferences....

8. Click on the Files tab at the top of the dialog box.

9. Click on Support Files Search Path.

10. Click on the Add button, and then click Browse.

11. Locate and select the \Program Files\AutoCAD R14\Eye2eye directory, and then click OK.

12. Click OK in the Preferences dialog box.

Eye2eye is now available for loading and use. The next section describes how to access the Eye2eye features.

Using Eye2eye

Eye2eye is based on the idea of using a camera and target object to control your perspective views. I call the camera and target objects *eyes*, hence the name Eye2eye. To set up a view, you simply place the camera, or Eye2eye block (see Figure C.7), where you want your point of view. You then place the target, or Eyefrom block, where you want your center of attention. You then use Eye2eye's Showeye command to display the perspective.

FIGURE C.7:

The Eyeto block used with Eye2eye

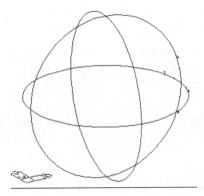

The following list gives a brief description of all of the Eye2eye commands:

Showeye   displays the current eye-target perspective view in the current viewport. Be sure to have the desired viewport active before using this command.

Findeye   draws a temporary vector between the camera and target points to help locate these points.

Crosseye   displays a view that reverses the camera and target locations.

Mtarg   moves the target location. You must be in an Orthagonal view for this command.

Meye   moves the camera location. You must be in an Orthagonal view for this command.

Seteye   allows you to turn the Perspective mode on or off, set camera "focal length," turn the camera and target objects on or off, pan the Perspective view, or set up multiple viewports for Eye2eye.

Paneye   lets you pan the Perspective view. This is useful for fine-tuning your Perspective view.

Matcheye   sets the camera and target objects to the current Perspective view. You must be in a Perspective viewport to use this command. This is useful when you've changed your view using methods outside of the Eye2eye command set, such as the Dview command.

Eye2eye assumes that you have a fairly good grasp of AutoCAD's 3D functions and the use of Paper Space viewports. It is best suited as a tool for viewing your model after you've created the basic massing.

Once you have a 3D model built, load the Eye2eye utilities by entering the following at the command prompt:

```
(load"eye2eye")
```

You can also use Tools ➤ Load Applications.... At the dialog box, click on the File button and locate and load the Eye2eye.lsp file in the \Program Files\ AutoCAD R14\Eye2eye directory.

After you've loaded Eye2eye, set up multiple viewports with the following steps.

1. Open a file containing a 3D model. Set up your display so that you can see all of the model plus some room for the camera location. Make sure this is a plan or top-down view.

2. Go to the World Coordinate System and enter **Eye2eye** ↵ at the command prompt.

3. Since this is the first time you are using Eye2eye, you are prompted to pick a camera point. Do so. Don't worry about the exact placement of your camera just yet, you will get a chance to adjust its location later. The camera object, a block called Eyeto, appears.

4. Next, you are prompted to select a target location. Do so. As with the camera location, it isn't important to place the target in an exact location at this time. You can easily adjust it later. Eye2eye will switch to Paper Space and set up four viewports: one large viewport (to the right) for your Perspective view and three smaller viewports (to the left) for your top, front, and left-side Orthogonal views. You will use the Orthogonal views to manipulate the camera and target points (see Figure C.8). You are now ready to use the Eye2eye utilities.

5. You'll also see the prompt:

```
Perspctv Off/ON/Focal lngth/Pan/cLose eyes/Show eyes/
fInd eyes/move Camera/move Target/Hide/Match prspctv/eXit:
```

FIGURE C.8:

A sample of the view-
port arrangement cre-
ated with Eye2eye's
Seteye command

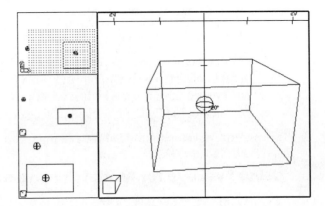

Because your views are in Paper Space, you can easily enlarge or resize a view
for easy editing. Just remember that while using the Eye2eye utilities, you must
be in tiled Model Space.

You are now ready to use the Eye2eye utilities. The options shown in the
Eye2eye prompt perform some of the same functions that are described in the
beginning of this section:

Perspctv Off/ON turns the Perspective mode off or on in the Perspective
viewport.

Focal length changes the focal length of the "camera."

Pan (Paneye) lets you pan the Perspective view. This is useful for fine-
tuning your Perspective view.

Close eyes turns off the layer on which the camera and target "eyes"
reside. This turns off the visibility of the eyes.

Show eyes turns on the layer on which the camera and target eyes
reside. This turns on the visibility of the eyes.

Find eyes helps you locate the camera and target eyes by zooming into
an area that just includes the eyes. You must be in a non-Perspective viewport before this option will take effect.

Move Camera (Meye) moves the camera location. You must be in an
Orthogonal view for this command.

Move Target (Mtarg) moves the target location. You must be in an Orthogonal view for this command.

Hide performs a hidden-line removal on the Perspective view.

Match prspctv (Matcheye) sets the camera and target objects to the current Perspective view. You must be in a Perspective viewport to use this command. This is useful when you've changed your view using methods outside of the Eye2eye command set, such as the Dview command.

Exit terminates the Eye2eye command.

Using Eye2eye for Model Construction

If you want to use Eye2eye as a tool to help you construct your 3D model, be sure you set up your Model Space work area *before* you proceed with the above steps. You can use the Ddsetup utility provided with Eye2eye to accomplish this. To use Ddsetup, enter

```
(load "ddsetup")↵
```

at the command prompt, and then enter **Ddsetup** ↵. A dialog box appears, from which you can choose a unit style, sheet size, and scale. Once you've selected the appropriate options, click OK. The drawing is then set up according to your selections. You will also see the grid dots. They are set to represent one inch intervals at your final plot size.

You can now setup Eye2eye as described above.

Setting the Eyes

Try moving the camera and target objects in the Orthogonal views. You can use the Meye and Mtarg commands to help you locate the camera and target objects. When you use these commands, a temporary red and green vector is drawn to show you the location of the camera and target. The red portion of the vector shows the direction of the camera while the green portion shows the direction of the target. Use the Redraw command to remove the vectors. They are not true AutoCAD objects and will not plot.

Mtarg and Meye work just like the Move command but you don't have to select an object; the camera (Meye) or target (Mtarg) is automatically selected. You only need to select the Base point and Second point for the move. You can also use the standard AutoCAD Move command to move the camera and target.

As you move the eye and target location with Mtarg and Meye, the Perspective viewport will automatically update to display the new eye-to-target orientation. If you happen to move the eye or target blocks using the move command, you can update the Perspective viewport by clicking on the Perspective viewport and entering **Showeye** ↵. A Perspective view based on the camera-target locations is displayed. You can then use the AutoCAD View command to save your view or go on to make minor adjustments. For example, you can use the Paneye command to adjust your perspective view before saving it.

Controlling the Eyes

You will notice some lines and numbers on the Perspective view. These are parts of the camera object showing you the angle below or above horizontal in 10-degree increments. You can turn off the display of camera and target objects by using the Hide Eyes option of the Seteye command. To turn them back on again, use the Show Eyes option. Alternately, you can simply turn the Eyes layer on or off. The Eyes layer is the layer on which the Eyeto and Eyefrom blocks were constructed.

The ActiveX Automation Samples

With AutoCAD Release 14, you now have a new way to create custom applications in AutoCAD. ActiveX Automation is a new feature that allows AutoCAD users to take control of AutoCAD either by creating Visual Basic applications or through other applications that support Automation.

Chapter 20 provides an introduction to ActiveX Automation as it relates to AutoCAD. There are some sample applications included on the CD-ROM that you can experiment with when you're reading Chapter 20. The following steps show you how to access those examples.

1. Start the *Mastering AutoCAD 14* software installation program, as described earlier in this appendix.

2. Click on the ActiveX Samples button.

3. Click on Continue. You see the Winzip self-extractor dialog box. You have the option to accept the default directory shown in the input box, or you may enter a different location for the files.

4. When you've entered the location for the ActiveX sample files, click Unzip. The files will be installed on your computer.

5. Click Close to return to the main installation program screen.

6. Proceed with another installation or click Exit.

The *AutoCAD Instant Reference*

Mastering AutoCAD was designed to help AutoCAD users by demonstrating commands in the context of everyday activities that you might encounter in your work. It shows you what commands to use in a given situation. As a result, I don't always show every option or permutation of a command. This is where the *AutoCAD 14 Instant Reference* comes in.

The *AutoCAD 14 Instant Reference* is the perfect companion to *Mastering AutoCAD 14*. You can think of it as a dictionary of AutoCAD commands that describes each command in detail, including all of the command options.

The CD-ROM contains a Modern Age Books electronic version of the *AutoCAD 14 Instant Reference*. You will need to install the Modern Age viewer to use this online book.

1. Start the *Mastering AutoCAD 14* software installation program, as described earlier in this appendix.

2. Click on the *AutoCAD Instant Reference* button. You'll see a message telling you that you are about to install the Modern Age Books viewer. You have the option to go back to the previous screen or install the view.

3. Click Install, and then follow the directions.

The *ABCs of AutoLISP*

In previous editions of this book, I included an introduction to AutoLISP in Chapter 20. In this edition of the book, I replaced the AutoLISP information with a chapter on ActiveX Automation. In place of the introduction to AutoLISP, I've included a complete AutoLISP tutorial and source book on the CD-ROM. The *ABCs of AutoLISP* offers a more detailed look at AutoCAD's macro-programming language.

The *ABCs of AutoLISP* is in a format that can be viewed using any Internet web browser, such as Netscape Communicator or Microsoft Internet Explorer. To use it, simply install it on to your hard drive and double-click on the Contents.HTM or `ABCs_of_AutoLISP.htm` file. The following steps show you how to install the *ABCs of AutoLISP*.

1. Start the *Mastering AutoCAD 14* software installation program, as described earlier in this appendix.

2. Click on the *ABCs of AutoLISP* button. You see a brief description of the *ABCs of AutoLISP* and the default location where it will be installed.

3. Click on Continue. You see the Winzip self-extractor dialog box. You have the option to accept the default directory shown in the input box, or you may enter a different location for the files.

4. When you've entered the location for the *ABCs of AutoLISP* files, click Unzip. The files will be installed on your computer.

5. Click Close to return to the main installation program screen.

6. Proceed with another installation or click Exit.

If you want to un-install the *ABCs of AutoLISP*, simply delete the folder containing the files.

The Whip2 Netscape Communicator Plug-In

In Chapter 19, I discuss how you can add drawings to a Web page. Before you can view such drawings, you need to install the Whip2 plug-in for your Web browser. You can obtain this plug-in from the AutoCAD Web site, but as a convenience, I've included it on the CD-ROM so you won't have to spend your time downloading this fairly large file.

WARNING   If you've installed the AutoCAD Internet Publishing Kit for Release 13, you will have to un-install it before installing the Whip2 plug-in. All of the Features of the Internet Publishing Kit are duplicated in Release 14, so you really won't be losing any features.

To install the Whip2 plug-in, first make sure that you have Netscape Navigator 3.0 or later or Netscape Communicator. Next, perform the following steps.

1. Make sure all other programs are closed.

2. Start the *Mastering AutoCAD 14* software installation program, as described earlier in this appendix.

3. Click on the Whip2 button. The Whip2 installation program will start.

4. Follow the instructions to complete the Whip2 installation.

If you are using Microsoft Internet Explorer, perform the following steps.

1. If your system requires that you log on to your Internet Service Provider before opening your Web browser, do so now.

2. Start the *Mastering AutoCAD 14* software installation program, as described earlier in this appendix.

3. Click on the Go To Website button. Your default Web browser will open a Web page with links to various other Web pages. If your default browser is Microsoft Internet Explorer, click on the word "here." This will take you to the Whip2 ActiveX Control automatic download page.

The Whip2 ActiveX Control software will take about 20 minutes to download. When it is done, your Internet Explorer will be able to view AutoCAD .dwf files online.

As an alternate, you may visit the Whip2 ActiveX Control Web site on your own. Here is the Web page address:

```
http://pilot1.autodesk.com/products/acadr14/features/whpdwnie.htm
```

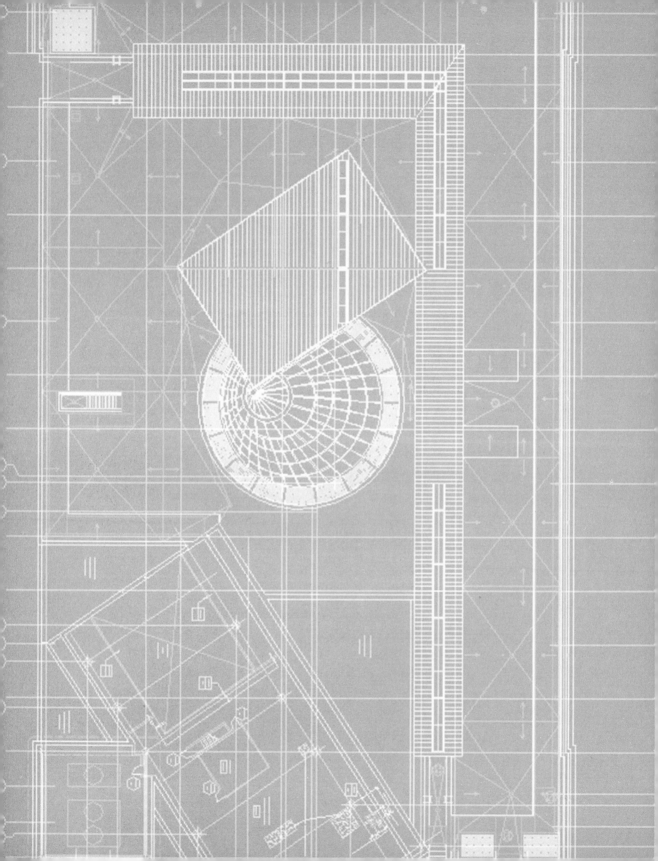

APPENDIX
D

System and Dimension Variables

This appendix discusses AutoCAD's system variables. It is divided into two sections: *system variables* and *dimension variables.* The general system variables let you fine-tune your AutoCAD environment. Dimension variables govern the specific dimensioning functions of AutoCAD.

System variables are accessible directly from the command prompt, and transparently (while in another command), by entering the variable name preceded by an apostrophe. These variables are also accessible through the AutoLISP interpreter by using the Getvar and Setvar functions.

We've divided this appendix into two main sections, Setting System Variables and Setting Dimension Variables. This division is somewhat artificial, because as far as AutoCAD is concerned, there is no difference between system variables and dimension variables—you use both types of variables the same way. But because the set of dimension variables is quite extensive, they are separated here for clarity.

Setting System Variables

Table D.1 lists the variables, and notes whether they are read-only or adjustable. Most of these variables have counterparts in other commands, as listed in the table. For example, Angdir and Angbase can be adjusted using the Ddunits command (Format ➢ Units). Many, such as Highlight and Expert, do not have equivalent commands. These must be adjusted at the command line (or through AutoLISP).

TABLE D.1: System variables

Variable Name	Associated Command	Where Saved	Use
Acadprefix	Preferences	*NA*	The ACAD environment setting.
Acadver	*NA*	*NA*	The AutoCAD version number.
Acisoutver	ACISOUT	With drawing	Controls ACIS version of SAT files.
Aflags	UNITS	*NA*	Controls attribute mode settings: 1 = invisible; 2 = constant; 4= verify; 8=preset.

TABLE D.1 CONTINUED: System variables

Variable Name	Associated Command	Where Saved	Use
Angbase	UNITS	With drawing	Controls direction of 0 angle, relative to the current UCS.
Angdir	UNITS	With drawing	Controls positive direction of angles: 0 = counterclockwise; 1 = clockwise.
Apbox	Draw and Edit commands	Registry	Displays Autosnap aperture box when autosnap is activated. 0=off, 1=on.
Aperture	Draw and Edit commands	Registry	Sets size of osnap cursor in pixels.
Area (read-only)	Area	*NA*	Displays last area calculation; use with Setvar or AutoLISP's Getvar function.
Attdia	INSERT/ Attribute	With drawing	Controls the Attribute dialog box: 0 = no dialog box; 1 = dialog box.
Attmode	Attdisp	With drawing	Controls attribute display mode: 0 = off; 1 = normal; 2 = on.
Attreq	Insert	With drawing	Controls the prompt for attributes: 0 = no prompt or dialog box for attributes (attributes use default values); 1 = normal prompt or dialog box upon attribute insertion.
Auditctl	Config	Registry	Controls whether an audit file is created: 0 = disable; 1 = enable creation of .ADT file.
Aunits	UNITS	With drawing	Controls angular units: 0 = decimal degrees; 1 = degrees-minutes-seconds; 2 = grads; 3 = radians; 4 = surveyor's units.
Auprec	UNITS	With drawing	Controls the precision of angular units determined by decimal place.
Autosnap	DRAW/EDIT	Registry	Controls autosnap display and features. 0 = everything off; 1 = marker on; 2 = snaptip on; 4 = magnet on.

TABLE D.1 CONTINUED: System variables

Variable Name	Associated Command	Where Saved	Use
Backz (read-only)	DVIEW	With drawing	Displays distance from DVIEW target to back clipping plane.
Blipmode	*NA*	With drawing	Controls appearance of blips: 0 = off; 1 = on.
Cdate (read-only)	TIME	*NA*	Displays calendar date/time read from system date (YYYY MMDD.HHMMSSMSEC).
Cecolor	COLOR	With drawing	Controls current default color assigned to new objects.
Celtscale	*NA*	With drawing	Controls current linetype scale for individual objects.
Celtype	LINETYPE	With drawing	Controls current default line type assigned to new objects.
Chamfera	CHAMFER	With drawing	Controls first chamfer distance.
Chamferb	CHAMFER	With drawing	Controls second chamfer distance.
Chamferc	CHAMFER	With drawing	Controls chamfer distance for Angle option.
Chamferd	CHAMFER	With drawing	Controls chamfer angle for Angle option.
Chammode	CHAMFER	*NA*	Controls method of chamfer: 0 = use 2 distances; 1 = use distance and angle.
Circlerad	CIRCLE	*NA*	Controls the default circle radius: 0 = no default.
Clayer	LAYER	With drawing	Sets the current layer.
Cmdactive (read-only)	*NA*	*NA*	Displays whether a command, script, or dialog box is active: 1 = command active; 2 = transparent command active; 4 = script active; 8 = dialog box active (values are cumulative, so 3 = command and transparent command are active).

TABLE D.1 CONTINUED: System variables

Variable Name	Associated Command	Where Saved	Use
Cmddia	*NA*	Registry	Controls use of dialog boxes for some commands: 0 = don't use dialog box; 1 = use dialog box.
Cmdecho	AutoLISP	*NA*	With AutoLISP, controls display of prompts from embedded AutoCAD commands: 0 = no display of prompt; 1 = display prompts.
Cmdnames (read-only)	*NA*	*NA*	Displays the English name of the currently active command.
Cmljust	MLINE	With drawing	Sets method of justification for Multilines: 0 = top; 1 = middle; 2 = bottom.
Cmlscale	MLINE	With drawing	Sets scale factor for Multiline widths: a 0 value collapes the Multiline to a single line; a negative value reverses the justification.
Cmlstyle (read-only)	MLINE	With drawing	Displays current Multiline style by name.
Coords	F6, Ctrl-D	With drawing	Controls coordinate readout: 0 = coordinates displayed only when points are picked; 1 = absolute coordinates dynamically displayed as cursor moves; 2 = distance and angle displayed during commands that accept relative distance input.
Cursorsize	*NA*	Registry	Determines size of crosshairs as a percentage of the screen size (1–100).
Cvport (read-only)	VPORTS	With drawing	Displays ID number of current viewport.
Date (read-only)	TIME	*NA*	Displays date and time in Julian format.

TABLE D.1 CONTINUED: System variables

Variable Name	Associated Command	Where Saved	Use
Dbmod (read-only)	*NA*	*NA*	Displays drawing modification status: 1 = object database modified; 2 = symbol table modified; 4 = database variable modified; 8 = window modified; 16 = view modified.
Dctcust	SPELL	Registry	Sets default custom spelling dictionary file name, including path.
Dctmain	SPELL	Registry	Sets default main spelling dictionary file name; requires specific keywords for each language. Use AutoCAD Help for complete list of keywords.
Delobj	*NA*	With drawing	Controls whether source objects used to create new objects are retained: 0 = delete objects; 1 = retain objects.
Demandload	*NA*	Registry	Controls loading of third party applications required for custom objects in drawing (0–3)
Diastat (read-only)	*NA*	*NA*	Displays how last dialog box was exited: 0 = Cancel; 1 = OK.
Dispsilh	All curved solids	With drawing	Controls silhouette display of curved 3D solids: 0 = no silhouette; 1 = silhouette curved solids.
Distance (read-only)	DIST	*NA*	Displays last distance calculated by DIST command.
Donutid	DONUT	*NA*	Controls default inside diameter of a donut.
Donutod	DONUT	*NA*	Controls default outside diameter of a donut.
Dragmode	*NA*	With drawing	Controls dragging: 0 = no dragging; 1 = if requested; 2 = automatic drag.
Dragp1	*NA*	Registry	Controls regeneration-drag input sampling rate.

TABLE D.1 CONTINUED: System variables

Variable Name	Associated Command	Where Saved	Use
Dragp2	*NA*	Registry	Controls fast-drag input sampling rate.
Dwgcodepage (read-only)	*NA*	With drawing	Displays code page of drawing (see Syscodepage).
Dwgname (read-only)	OPEN	*NA*	Displays drawing name and drive/directory, if specified by user.
Dwgprefix (read-only)	*NA*	*NA*	Displays drive and directory of current file.
Dwgtitled (read-only)	*NA*	*NA*	Displays whether a drawing has been named: 0 = untitled; 1 = named by user.
Edgemode	TRIM, EXTEND	Registry	Controls how trim and extend boundaries are determined: 0 = boundaries defined by object only; 1 = boundaries defined by objects and their extension.
Elevation	Elev	With drawing	Controls current 3D elevation relative to current UCS.
Expert	*NA*	*NA*	Controls prompts, depending on level of user's expertise: 0 = normal prompts; 1 = suppresses About to regen and Really want to turn the current layer off prompts; 2 = suppresses Block already defined and A drawing with this name already exists prompt for BLOCK command; 3 = suppresses An item with this name already exists prompt for the LINETYPE command; 4 = suppresses An item with this name already exists for the UCS/Save and VPORTS/Save options; 5 = suppresses An item with this name already exists for DIM/Save and DIM/Override commands.

TABLE D.1 CONTINUED: System variables

Variable Name	Associated Command	Where Saved	Use
Explmode	EXPLODE	With drawing	Controls whether blocks inserted with different X, Y, and Z values are exploded: 0 = blocks are not exploded; 1 = blocks are exploded.
Extmax (read-only)	ZOOM	With drawing	Displays upper-right corner coordinate of extents view
Extmin (read-only)	ZOOM	With drawing	Displays lower-left corner coordinate of extents view
Facetratio	SHADE, HIDE	*NA*	Controls aspect ratio of faceting of curved 3D surfaces. Value is zero or 1, where 1 increases the density of the mesh.
Facetres	SHADE, HIDE	With drawing	Controls appearance of smooth curved 3D surfaces when shaded or hidden. Value can be between 0.01 and 10. The higher the number, the more faceted (and smoother) the curved surface, and the longer the time needed for shade and hidden-line removal.
Filedia	Dialog box	Registry	Sets whether a file dialog box is used by default: 0 = don't use unless requested with a ~ (a tilde); 1 = use whenever possible.
Filletrad	FILLET	With drawing	Controls fillet radius.
Fillmode	FILL	With drawing	Controls fill status: 0 = off; 1 = on.
Fontalt	OPEN, DXFIN, other File ➤ Import options	Registry	Lets you specify an alternate font when AutoCAD cannot find the font associated with a file. If no font is specified for Fontalt, AutoCAD displays warning message and dialog box where you manually select a font.

TABLE D.1 CONTINUED: System variables

Variable Name	Associated Command	Where Saved	Use
Fontmap	OPEN, DXFIN, other import functions	Registry	Similar to Fontalt, but lets you designate a set of font substitutions through a font mapping file. Example line from mapping file: romans:c:\Program Files\ AutoCAD R14\fonts\times.ttf. This substitutes Romans font with Times TrueType font. Font mapping file can be any name, with extension .FMP.
Frontz (read-only)	DVIEW	With drawing	Controls front clipping plane for current viewport; use with View mode system variable.
Gridmode	GRID	With drawing	Controls grid: 0 = off; 1 = on.
Gridunit	GRID	With drawing	Controls grid spacing.
Gripblock	Grips	Registry	Controls display of grips in blocks: 0 = show insertion point grip only; 1 = show grips of all objects in block.
Gripcolor	Grips	Registry	Controls color of unselected grips. Choices are integers from 1 to 255; default is 5.
Griphot	Grips	Registry	Controls color of hot grips. Choices are integers from 1 to 255; default is 1.
Grips	Grips	Registry	Controls use of grips: 0 = grips disabled; 1 = grips enabled (default).
Gripsize	Grips	Registry	Controls grip size (in pixels), from 1 to 255 (default is 3).
Handles (read-only)	NA	With drawing	Displays status of object handles: 0 = off; 1 = on.
Hideprecision	HIDE, SHADE	NA	Controls the Hide/Shade precision accuracy: 0 = single level precision; 1 = double level precision.

TABLE D.1 CONTINUED: System variables

Variable Name	Associated Command	Where Saved	Use
Highlight	SELECT	*NA*	Controls whether objects are high-lighted when selected: 0 = none; 1 = highlighting.
Hpang	HATCH	*NA*	Sets default hatch pattern angle.
Hpbound	HATCH	Registry	Controls type of object created by HATCH and Boundary commands: 0 = region; 1 = Polyline.
Hpdouble	HATCH	*NA*	Sets default hatch doubling for user-defined hatch pattern: 0 = no doubling; 1 = doubling at 90°.
Hpname	HATCH	*NA*	Sets default hatch pattern name; use a period (.) to set to no default.
Hpscale	HATCH	*NA*	Sets default hatch pattern scale factor.
Hpspace	HATCH	*NA*	Sets default line spacing for user-defined hatch pattern; cannot be 0.
Indexctl	??????	With drawing	Controls whether layer and spatial indexes are created and saved in drawings: 0 = no index; 1 = layer index; 2 = spatial index; 3 = both.
Inetlocation	BROWSER	Registry	Stores the Internet location used by the BROWSER command.
Insbase	BASE	With drawing	Controls insertion base point of current drawing.
Insname	INSERT	*NA*	Sets default block or file name for INSERT command; enter a period (.) to set to no default.
Isavebak	SAVE	Registry	Controls the creation of BAK files: 0 = no BAK file created; 1 = BAK file created.
Isavepercent	SAVE	Registry	Determines whether to do a full or an incremental save based on the amount of wasted space tolerated in a drawing file: (0–100).

TABLE D.1 CONTINUED: System variables

Variable Name	Associated Command	Where Saved	Use
Isolines	Curved solids	With drawing	Specifies the number of lines on a Solid's surface to help visualize its shape.
Lastangle (read-only)	ARC	NA	Displays ending angle for last arc drawn.
Lastpoint	NA	NA	Sets or displays coordinate normally referenced by the @.
Lastprompt	NA	NA	Saves last string echoed to the command line.
Lenslength (read-only)	DVIEW	With drawing	Displays focal length of lens used for perspective display.
Limcheck	Limits	With drawing	Controls limit checking: 0 = no checking; 1 = checking.
Limmax	Limits	With drawing	Controls coordinate of drawing's upper-right limit.
Limmin	Limits	With drawing	Controls coordinate of drawing's lower-left limit.
Lispinit	LOAD		Preserves AutoLISP-defined functions and variables beyond current drawing session: 0 = AutoLISP variables preserved; 1 = AutoLISP functions valid for current session only.
Locale (read-only)	NA	NA	Displays ISO language code used by your version of AutoCAD.
Logfilemode	NA	Registry	Determines whether Logfile is recorded or not: 0 = logfile off 1 = Logfile on.
Logfilename	NA	Registry	Specifies name/path of Logfile.
Loginname (read-only)	NA	NA	Displays user's login name.
Ltscale	LTSCALE	With drawing	Controls the global line-type scale factor.

TABLE D.1 CONTINUED: System variables

Variable Name	Associated Command	Where Saved	Use
Lunits	UNITS	With drawing	Controls unit styles: 1 = scientific; 2 = decimal; 3 = engineering, 4 = architectural, 5 = fractional.
Luprec	UNITS	With drawing	Controls unit accuracy by decimal place or size of denominator.
Maxactvp	VIEWPORTS/ VPORTS	With drawing	Controls maximum number of viewports to regenerate at one time.
Maxobjmem	*NA*	*NA*	Specifies the amount of virtual memory that can be used before AutoCAD starts paging a drawing out to disk.
Maxsort	*NA*	Registry	Controls maximum number of items to be sorted when a command displays a list.
Measurement	BHATCH, Linetype	With drawing	Sets drawing units as English or metric: 0 = English; 1 = Metric.
Menuctl	*NA*	Registry	Controls whether side menu changes in response to a command name entered from the keyboard: 0 = no response; 1 = menu response.
Menuecho	*NA*	*NA*	Controls messages and command prompt display from commands embedded in menu: 0 = display all messages; 1 = suppress menu item name; 2 = suppress command prompts; 4 = Disable ^P toggle of menu echo; 8 = debugging aid for DEISEL expressions.
Menuname (read-only)	MENU	With drawing	Displays name of current menu file.
Mirrtext	MIRROR	With drawing	Controls mirroring of text: 0 = disabled; 1 = enabled.
Modemacro	*NA*	*NA*	Controls display of user-defined text in status line.

TABLE D.1 CONTINUED: System variables

Variable Name	Associated Command	Where Saved	Use
Mtexted	MTEXT	Registry	Controls name of program used for editing MTEXT objects.
Offsetdist	OFFSET	NA	Controls default offset distance.
Olehide	NA	Registry	Controls display of OLE objects.
Orthomode	F8, ORTHO	With drawing	Controls ortho mode: 0 = off; 1 = on.
Osmode	OSNAP	With drawing	Sets current default Osnap mode: 0 = none; 1 = endpoint; 2 = mid-point; 4 = center; 8 = node; 16 = quadrant; 32 = intersection; 64 = insert; 128 = perpendicular; 256 = nearest; 512 = quick. If more than one mode is required, enter the sum of those modes.
Osnapcoord	OSNAP	Registry	Controls whether coordinates entered at the command line use running object snaps. 0 = Running OSNAPS settings override; 1 = Keyboard entry overrides; 2 = Keyboard entry overrides except in scripts.
Pdmode	DDPTYPE	With drawing	Controls type of symbol used as a point during POINT command.
Pdsize	POINT	With drawing	Controls size of symbol set by PDMODE.
Pellipse	ELLIPSE	With drawing	Controls type of object created with ELLIPSE command: 0 = true NURBS ellipse; 1 = polyline repre-sentation of ellipse.
Perimeter (read-only)	AREA, LIST	NA	Displays last perimeter value derived from Area and List commands.
Pfacevmax (read-only)	PFACE	NA	Displays maximum number of vertices per face. (PFaces are 3D surfaces designed for use by third-party software producers and are not designed for end users.)

TABLE D.1 CONTINUED: System variables

Variable Name	Associated Command	Where Saved	Use
Pickadd	SELECT	Registry	Determines how items are added to a selection set: 0 = only most recently selected item(s) become selection set (to accumulate objects in a selection set, hold down Shift while selecting); 1 = selected objects accumulate in a selection set as you select them (hold down Shift while selecting items to remove those items from the selection set).
Pickauto	SELECT	Registry	Controls automatic window at Select objects prompt: 0 = window is enabled; 1 = window is disabled.
Pickbox	SELECT	Registry	Controls size of object-selection pickbox (in pixels).
Pickdrag	SELECT	Registry	Controls how selection windows are used: 0 = click on each corner of the window; 1 = Shift + click and hold on first corner, then drag and release for the second corner.
Pickfirst	SELECT	Registry	Controls whether you can pick object(s) before you select a command: 0 = disabled; 1 = enabled.
Pickstyle	GROUP, HATCH	With drawing	Controls whether groups and/or associative hatches are selectable: 0 = neither are selectable; 1 = groups only; 2 = associative hatches only; 3 = both groups and associative hatches.
Platform (read-only)	*NA*	*NA*	Identifies the version of AutoCAD being used.
Plinegen	PLINE/PEDIT	With drawing	Controls how polylines generate line types around vertices: 0 = line-type pattern begins and ends at vertices; 1 = line-type patterns ignore vertices and begin and end at polyline beginning and ending.

TABLE D.1 CONTINUED: System variables

Variable Name	Associated Command	Where Saved	Use
Plinetype	PLINE	Registry	Controls whether AutoCAD creates optimized 2D polylines and/or converts existing plines to optimized plines: 0 = plines in existing drawings are not converted , *and* new plines are not optimized; 1 = plines in existing drawings are not converted, *but* new plines are optimized; 2 = plines in existing drawings are not converted, *and* new plines are optimized.
Plinewid	PLINE	With drawing	Controls default polyline width.
Plotid	PLOT	Registry	Sets default plotter based on its description.
Plotrotmode	PLOT	Registry	Controls orientation of your plotter output.
Plotter	PLOT	Registry	Sets default plotter, based on its integer ID.
Polysides	POLYGON	*NA*	Controls default number of sides for a polygon.
Popups (read-only)	*NA*	*NA*	Displays whether the current system supports pull-down menus: 0 = no; 1 = yes.
Projectname	PREFERENCES	Registry	Assigns a project name to a drawing. The project name can be associated with one or more folders.
Projmode	TRIM, EXTEND	Registry	Controls how TRIM and EXTEND affect objects in 3D: 0 = objects must be coplanar; 1 = trims/extends based on a plane parallel to the current UCS; 2 = trims/extends based on a plane parallel to the current view plane.
Proxygraphics	*NA*	With drawing	Controls whther images of proxy objects are stored in a drawing: 0 = images not stored; 1 = images saved.

TABLE D.1 CONTINUED: System variables

Variable Name	Associated Command	Where Saved	Use
Proxynotice	*NA*	Registry	Issues a warning to the user when a proxy object is created, i.e., when user opens a drawing containing custom objects created using an application which is not loaded: 0 = no warning; 1 = warning displayed.
Proxyshow	*NA*	Registry	Specifies if and how proxy objects are displayed: 0 = No display; 1 = graphic display of all proxy objects; 2 = only bounding box shown.
Psltscale	PSPACE	With drawing	Controls Paper Space linetype scaling.
Psprolog	PSOUT	Registry	Controls what portion of the ACAD.PSF file is used for the prologue section of a PSOUT output file. Set this to the name of the section you want to use.
Psquality	PSIN	Registry	Controls how images are generated in AutoCAD with the PSIN command. Value is an integer: 0 = only bounding box is drawn; >0 = number of pixels per AutoCAD drawing unit; <0 = outline with no fills, and absolute value of setting determines pixels per drawing units.
Qtextmode	QTEXT	With drawing	Controls the quick text mode: 0 = off; 1 = on.
Rasterpreview	SAVE	Registry	Controls whether raster preview images are saved with the drawing and sets the format type: 0 = No preview image created; 1 = BMP preview image.
Regenmode	REGENAUTO	With drawing	Controls Regenauto mode: 0 = off; 1 = on.

TABLE D.1 CONTINUED: System variables

Variable Name	Associated Command	Where Saved	Use
Re-init	REINIT	*NA*	Reinitializes I/O ports, digitizers, display, plotter, and ACAD.PGP: 1 = digitizer port; 2 = Plotter port; 4 = digitizer; 8 = display; 16 = PGP file reload.
Rtdisplay	RTPAN, RTZOOM	Registry	Controls display of raster images during realtime Pan and Zoom
Savefile (read-only)	Autosave	Registry	Displays filename that is autosaved.
Savename (read-only)	SAVE	*NA*	Displays user filename under which file is saved.
Savetime	Autosave	Registry	Controls time interval between automatic saves, in minutes: 0 = disable automatic save.
Screenboxes (read-only)	Menu	Registry	Displays number of slots or boxes available in side menu.
Screenmode (read-only)	*NA*	Registry	Displays current display mode: 0 = text; 1 = graphics; 2 = dual screen.
Screensize (read-only)	*NA*	*NA*	Displays current viewport size in pixels.
Shadedge	SHADE	With drawing	Controls how drawing is shaded: 0 = faces shaded, no edge highlighting; 1 = faces shaded, edge highlighting; 2 = faces not filled, edges in object color; 3 = faces in object color, edges in background color.
Shadedif	SHADE	With drawing	Sets difference between diffuse reflective and ambient light. Value represents percentage of diffuse reflective light.
Shpname	SHAPE	*NA*	Controls default shape name.
Sketchinc	SKETCH	With drawing	Controls sketch record increment.
Skpoly	SKETCH	With drawing	Controls whether SKETCH uses regular lines or polylines: 0 = line; 1 = polyline.

1191

TABLE D.1 CONTINUED: System variables

Variable Name	Associated Command	Where Saved	Use
Snapang	SNAP	With drawing	Controls snap and grid angle.
Snapbase	SNAP	With drawing	Controls snap, grid, and hatch pattern origin.
Snapisopair	SNAP	With drawing	Controls isometric plane: 0 = left; 1 = top; 2 = right.
Snapmode	F9, SNAP	With drawing	Controls snap toggle: 0 = off; 1 = on.
Snapstyl	SNAP	With drawing	Controls snap style: 0 = standard; 1 = isometric.
Snapunit	SNAP	With drawing	Controls snap spacing given in x and y values.
Sortents	*NA*	Registry	Controls whether objects are sorted based on their order in database: 0 = disabled; 1 = sort for object selection; 2 = sort for object snap; 4 = sort for redraws; 8 = sort for MSLIDE; 16 = sort for regen; 32 = sort for plot; 64 = sort for PSOUT.
Splframe	PLINE, PEDIT, 3DFace	With drawing	Controls display of spline vertices, defining mesh of a surface-fit mesh, and display of "invisible" edges of 3DFaces: 0 = no display of spline vertices, display only fit surface of a smoothed 3DMesh, and no display of "invisible" edges of 3DFace; 1 = spline vertices are displayed, only defining mesh of a smoothed 3DMesh is displayed, "invisible" edges of 3DFace are displayed.
Splinesegs	PLINE, PEDIT	With drawing	Controls number of line segments used for each spline patch.
Splinetype	PLINE, PEDIT	With drawing	Controls type of spline curve generated by PEDIT spline: 5 = quadratic B-spline; 6 = cubic B-spline.

TABLE D.1 CONTINUED: System variables

Variable Name	Associated Command	Where Saved	Use
Surftab1	RULESURF, TABSURF, REVSURF, EDGESURF	With drawing	Controls number of facets in the m direction of meshes.
Surftab2	REVSURF, EDGESURF	With drawing	Controls number of facets in the n direction of meshes.
Surftype	PEDIT	With drawing	Controls type of surface fitting used by PEDIT's Smooth option: 5 = quadratic B-spline surface; 6 = cubic B-spline surface; 8 = Bezier surface.
Surfu	3DMESH	With drawing	Controls surface density in the m direction.
Surfv	3DMESH	With drawing	Controls surface density in the n direction.
Syscodepage (read-only)	*NA*	*NA*	Displays system code page specified in ACAD.XMX.
Tabmode	TABLET	*NA*	Controls tablet mode: 0 = off; 1 = on.
Target (read-only)	DVIEW	With drawing	Displays coordinate of perspective target point.
Tdcreate (read-only)	TIME	With drawing	Displays time and date of file creation in Julian format.
Tdindwg (read-only)	TIME	With drawing	Displays total editing time in days and decimal days.
Tdupdate (read-only)	TIME	With drawing	Displays time and date of last file update, in Julian format.
Tdusrtimer (read-only)	TIME	With drawing	Displays user-controlled elapsed time in days and decimal days.
Tempprefix (read-only)	*NA*	*NA*	Displays location for temporary files.

TABLE D.1 CONTINUED: System variables

Variable Name	Associated Command	Where Saved	Use
Texteval	*NA*	*NA*	Controls interpretation of text input: 0 = AutoCAD takes all text input literally; 1 = AutoCAD interprets "(" and "!" as part of an AutoLISP expression, unless either the TEXT or DTEXT command is active.
Textfill	TEXT	Registry	Controls display of Bitstream, TrueType, and PostScript Type 1 fonts: 0 = outlines; 1 = filled.
Textqlty	TEXT	With drawing	Controls resolution of Bitstream, TrueType, and PostScript Type 1 fonts: values from 1.0 to 100.0. The lower the value, the lower the output resolution. Higher resolutions improve font quality but decrease display and plot speeds.
Textsize	TEXT, DTEXT	With drawing	Controls default text height.
Textstyle	TEXT, DTEXT	With drawing	Controls default text style.
Thickness	ELEV	With drawing	Controls default 3D thickness of object being drawn.
Tilemode	MSPACE/ PSPACE	With drawing	Controls Paper Space and View port access: 0 = Paperspace and viewport objects enabled; 1 = strictly Modelspace.
Tooltips	Icon tool palettes	Registr	Controls display of ToolTips: 0 = off; 1 = on.
Tracewid	TRACE	With drawing	Controls trace width.
Treedepth	TREESTAT	With drawing	Controls depth of tree-structured spatial index affecting speed of AutoCAD database search. First two digits are for Modelspace nodes; second two digits are for Paperspace nodes. Use positive integers for 3D drawings and negative integers for 2D drawings. Negative values can improve speed of 2D operation.

TABLE D.1 CONTINUED: System variables

Variable Name	Associated Command	Where Saved	Use
Treemax	REGEN, TREEDEPTH	Registry	Limits memory use during regens by limiting maximum number of nodes in spatial index created with TREEDEPTH.
Trimmode	CHAMFER, FILLET	Registry	Controls whether lines are trimmed during CHAMFER and FILLET commands: 0 = no trim; 1 = trim (as with pre-Release 13 versions of AutoCAD).
Ucsfollow	UCS	With drawing	Controls whether AutoCAD automatically changes to plan view of UCS while in Model Space: 0 = UCS change does not affect view; 1 = UCS change causes view to change with UCS.
Ucsicon	UCSICON	With drawing	Controls UCS icon: 1 = on; 2 = UCS icon appears at origin.
Ucsname (read-only)	UCS	With drawing	Displays name of current UCS.
Ucsorg (read-only)	UCS	With drawing	Displays origin coordinate for current UCS relative to World Coordinate System.
Ucsxdir (read-only)	UCS	With drawing	Displays x direction of current UCS relative to world coordinate system.
Ucsydir (read-only)	UCS	With drawing	Displays y direction of current UCS relative to world coordinate system.
Undoctl (read-only)	Undo	NA	Displays current state of Undo feature: 1 = Undo enabled; 2 = only one command can be undone; 4 = Autogroup mode enabled; 8 = group is currently active.
Undomarks (read-only)	Undo	NA	Displays number of marks placed by Undo command.

TABLE D.1 CONTINUED: System variables

Variable Name	Associated Command	Where Saved	Use
Unitmode	UNITS	With drawing	Controls how AutoCAD displays fractional, foot-and-inch, and surveyors angles: 0 = industry standard; 1 = AutoCAD input format.
Useri1–Useri5	AutoLISP	With drawing	Five user variables capable of storing integer values.
Userr1–Userr5	AutoLISP	With drawing	Five user variables capable of storing real values.
Users1–Users5	AutoLISP	With drawing	Five user variables capable of storing string values.
Viewctr (read-only)	NA	With drawing	Displays center of current view in coordinates.
Viewdir (read-only)	DVIEW	With drawing	Displays camera viewing direction in coordinates.
Viewmode (read-only)	DVIEW	With drawing	Displays view-related settings for current viewport: 1 = perspective on; 2 = front clipping on; 4 = back clipping on; 8 = UCS follow on; 16 = front clip not at a point directly in front of the viewer's eye.
Viewsize (read-only)	NA	With drawing	Displays height of current view in drawing units.
Viewtwist (read-only)	DVIEW	With drawing	Displays twist angle for current viewport.
Visretain	LAYER	With drawing	Controls whether layer setting for Xrefs is retained: 0 = current layer color; line type and visibility settings retained when drawing is closed; 1 = layer settings of Xref drawing always renewed when file is opened.
Vsmax (read-only)	NA	With drawing	Displays coordinates of upper-right corner of virtual screen.
Vsmin (read-only)	NA	With drawing	Displays coordinates for lower-left corner of virtual screen.

TABLE D.1 CONTINUED: System variables

Variable Name	Associated Command	Where Saved	Use
Worlducs (read-only)	UCS	*NA*	Displays status of WCS: 0 = current UCS is not WCS; 1 = current UCS is WCS.
Worldview	DVIEW, VPOINT	With drawing	Controls whether DVIEW and VIEWPOINT operate relative to UCS or WCS: 0 = current UCS is used; 1 = WCS is used.
Writestat	*NA*	*NA*	Specifies whether current drawing is read-only or not: 0 = read-only; 1 = drawing can be written to.
Xclipframe	XREF	With drawing	Controls visibility of xref clipping boundaries: 0 = clipping boundary is not visible; 1 = boundary is visible.
Xloadctl	XREF, XCLIP	Registry	Controls xref demand loading, and creation of copies of original xref: 0 = No demand loading allowed, entire xref drawing is loaded; 1 = demand loading allowed, and original xref file is kept open; 2 = demand loading allowed, using a copy of xref file stored in AutoCAD temp files folder.
Xloadpath	XREF	Registry	Creates a path for storing temporary copies of demand-loaded xref files.
Xrefctl	XREF	Registry	Controls whether Xref log files are written: 0 = no log files; 1 = log files written.

Setting Dimension Variables

In Chapter 9, nearly all of the system variables related to dimensioning are shown with their associated options in the Dimension Styles dialog box. Later in the appendix you'll find a complete discussion of all elements of the Dimension Styles dialog box and how to use it.

This section provides further information about the dimension variables. For starters, Table D.2 lists the variables, their default status, and a brief description of what they do. You can get a similar listing by entering **Dimstyle** ⏎ at the command prompt, then typing **ST** to select the Status option. Alternatively, you can use the AutoCAD Help system. This section also discusses a few system variables that do not show up in the Dimension Styles dialog box.

TABLE D.2: The dimension variables

General Dimension Controls

Dimension Variable	Default Setting	Description
Dimaso	On	Turns associative dimension on and off.
Dimsho	On	Updates dimensions dynamically while dragging.
Dimstyle	Standard	Name of current dimension style.
Dimupt	Off	Controls user positioning of text during dimension input: 0 =automatic text positioning; 1 = user defined text positioning allowed.

Scale

Dimension Variable	Default Setting	Description
Dimscale	1.0000	Overall scale factor of dimensions.
Dimtxt	.18 (approx. 3/16")	Text height.
Dimasz	.18 (approx. 3/16")	Arrow size.
Dimtsz	0"	Tick size.
Dimcen	.09 (approx. 3/32")	Center mark size.
Dimlfac	1.0000	Multiplies measured distance by a specified scale factor.

TABLE D.2 CONTINUED: The dimension variables

Offsets

Dimension Variable	Default Setting	Description
Dimexo	.0625 or 1/16"	Extension line origin offset.
Dimexe	.18 (approx. 3/16")	Amount extension line extends beyond dimension line.
Dimdli	.38 (approx. 3/8")	Dimension line offset for continuation or base.
Dimdle	0"	Amount dimension line extends beyond extension line.

Tolerances

Dimension Variable	Default Setting	Description
Dimalttz	0	Controls zero suppression of tolerance values: 0 = leaves out zero feet and inches; 1 = includes zero feet and inches; 2 = includes zero feet; 3 = includes zero inches; 4 = suppresses leading zeroes in decimal dimensions; 8= suppresses leading zeroes in decimal dimensions.
Dimdec	4	Sets decimal place for primary tolerance values.
Dimtdec	4	Sets decimal place for tolerance values.
Dimtp	0"	Plus tolerance.
Dimtm	0"	Minus tolerance.
Dimtol	Off	When on, shows dimension tolerances.
Dimtolj	1	Controls vertical location of tolerance values relative to nominal dimension: 0 = bottom; 1 = middle; 2 = top.

TABLE D.2 CONTINUED: The dimension variables

Tolerances

Dimtzin	0	Controls zero suppression in tolerance values: 0 = leaves out zero feet and inches; 1 = includes zero feet and inches; 2 = includes zero feet; 3 = includes zero inches; 4 = suppresses leading zeroes in decimal dimensions; 8= suppresses leading zeroes in decimal dimensions; 12 = suppresses leading and trailing zeroes in decimal dimensions.
Dimlim	Off	When on, shows dimension limits.

Rounding

Dimension Variable	Default Setting	Description
Dimrnd	0"	Rounding value.
Dimzin	0	Controls zero suppression dimension text: 0 = leaves out zero feet and inches; 1 = includes zero feet and inches; 2 = includes zero feet; 3 = includes zero inches; 4 = suppresses leading zeroes in decimal dimensions; 8= suppresses leading zeroes in decimal dimensions; 12 = suppresses leading and trailing zeroes in decimal dimensions.

Dimension Arrow & Text Control

Dimension Variable	Default Setting	Description
Dimadec	-1	Controls the number of decimal places shown for angular dimension text: 1 = uses the value set by Dimdec dimension variable; 0-8 = Specifies the actual number of decimal places to be shown.
Dimaunit	0	Controls angle format for angular dimensions; settings are the same as for Aunits system variable.
Dimblk	" "	User-defined arrow block name.

TABLE D.2 CONTINUED: The dimension variables

Dimension Arrow & Text Control

Dimblk1	" "	User-defined arrow block name for first end of dimension line used with Dimsah.
Dimblk2	" "	User-defined arrow block name for second end of dimension line used with Dimsah.
Dimfit	3	Controls location of text and arrows for extension lines. If space is not available for both: 0 = text and arrows placed outside; 1 = text has priority, arrows are placed outside extension lines; 2 = arrows have priority; 3 = AutoCAD chooses between text and arrows, based on best fit; 4 = a leader is drawn from dimension line to dimension text when space for text not available; 5 = no leader.
Dimgap	1/16" or 0.09"	Controls distance between dimension text and dimension line.
Dimjust	0	Controls horizontal dimension text position: 0 = centered between extension lines; 1 = next to first extension line; 2 = next to second extension line; 3 = above and aligned with the first extension line; 4 = above and aligned with second extension line.
Dimsah	Off	Allows use of two different arrowheads on a dimension line. See Dimblk1 and Dimblk2.
Dimtfac	1.0"	Controls scale factor for dimension tolerance text.
Dimtih	On	When on, text inside extensions is horizontal.
Dimtoh	On	When on, text outside extensions is horizontal.
Dimtad	0	When on, places text above the dimension line.
Dimtix	Off	Forces text between extensions.

TABLE D.2 CONTINUED: The dimension variables

Dimension Arrow & Text Control

Dimtvp	0	Controls text's vertical position based on numeric value.
Dimtxsty	Standard	Controls text style for dimension text.
Dimunit	2	Controls unit style for all dimension style groups except angular. Settings are same as for Lunit system variable.

Dimension & Extension Line Control

Dimension Variable	Default Setting	Description
Dimsd1	Off	Suppresses the first dimension line.
Dimsd2	Off	Suppresses the second dimension line.
Dimse1	Off	When on, suppresses the first extension line.
Dimse2	Off	When on, suppresses the second extension line.
Dimtofl	Off	Forces a dimension line between extension lines.
Dimsoxd	Off	Suppresses dimension lines outside extension lines.

Alternate Dimension Options

Dimension Variable	Default Setting	Description
Dimalt	Off	When on, alternate units selected are shown.
Dimaltf	25.4000	Alternate unit scale factor.
Dimaltd	2	Alternate unit decimal places.
Dimalttd	2	Alternate unit tolerance decimal places.
Dimaltu	2	Alternate unit style. See Lunits system variable for values.

TABLE D.2 CONTINUED: The dimension variables

Alternate Dimension Options

Dimaltz	0	Controls the suppression zeroes for alternate dimension values.
Dimpost	" "	Adds suffix to dimension text.
Dimapost	" "	Adds suffix to alternate dimension text.

Colors

Dimension Variable	Default Setting	Description
Dimclrd	0 or *byblock*	Controls color of dimension lines and arrows.
Dimclre	0 or *byblock*	Controls color of dimension extension lines.
Dimclrt	0 or *byblock*	Controls color of dimension text.

Finally, for those of you who might want to write macros, scripts, or AutoLISP programs to control dimension styles, we'll talk about using two options of the DIMSTYLE command to set and recall dimension styles from the command line: **Dimstyle ⏎ S ⏎** and **Dimstyle ⏎ R ⏎**.

If you want to change a setting through the command line instead of through the Dimension Styles dialog box, you can enter the system variable name at the command prompt.

Controlling Associative Dimensioning

As discussed in Chapter 9, you can turn off AutoCAD's *associative dimensioning* by changing the Dimaso setting. The default for Dimaso is On.

The Dimsho setting controls whether the dimension value is dynamically updated while a dimension line is being dragged. The default for this setting is On.

Storing Dimension Styles through the Command Line

Once you have set the dimension variables as you like, you can save the settings by using the DIMSTYLE command. The Dimstyle/Save command records all of the current dimension variable settings (except Dimaso) with a name you specify.

1. At the command prompt, enter **Dimstyle** ↵

2. At the Save/Restore/Status/Variables/Apply/? prompt, type **S** ↵

3. When the ?/Name for new dimension style prompt appears, you can enter a question mark (**?**) to get a listing of any dimension styles currently saved, or you can enter a name under which you want the current settings saved.

For example, suppose you change some of your dimension settings through dimension variables instead of through the Dimension Styles dialog box, as shown in the following list:

Dimtsz   0.044

Dimtad   On

Dimtih   Off

Dimtoh   Off

These settings are typical for an architectural style of dimensioning; you might save them under the name Architect, as you did in an exercise Chapter 9. Then suppose you change other dimension settings for dimensions in another format—surveyor's dimensions on a site plan, for example. You might save them with the name Survey, again using the Save option of the DIMSTYLE command. When you want to return to the settings you used for your architectural drawing, you use the Restore option of the Dimstyle command, described in the next section.

Restoring a Dimension Style from the Command Line

To restore a dimension style you've saved using the Dimstyle Save option:

1. At the command prompt, enter **Dimstyle** ↵

2. At the Save/Restore/STatus/Variable/Apply/? prompt, type **R** ↵

3. At the following prompt:

    ?/Enter dimension style name or RETURN to select dimension:

    you have three options: Enter a question mark (**?**) to get a listing of saved dimension styles; or enter the name of a style, such as Arch, if you know the name of the style you want; or use the cursor to select a dimension on the screen whose style you want to match.

Notes on Metric Dimensioning

This book assumes you are using feet and inches as units of measure. The AutoCAD user community is worldwide, however, many of you may be using the metric system in your work. As long as you are not mixing U.S. (feet and inches) and metric measurements, using the English version of AutoCAD is fairly easy. With the Units command, set your measurement system to decimal, then draw distances in millimeters or centimeters. At plot time, select the MM radio button (millimeters) under Paper Size and Orientation in the Plot Configuration dialog box. Also, be sure you specify a scale that compensates for differences between millimeters (which are the AutoCAD base unit when you are using the metric system) and centimeters.

If your drawings are to be in both foot-and-inch and metric measurements, you will be concerned with several settings, as follows:

Dimlfac sets the scale factor for dimension values. The dimension value will be the measured distance in AutoCAD units times this scale factor. Set Dimlfac to 25.4 if you have drawn in inches but want to dimension in millimeters. The default is 1.00.

Dimalt turns the display of alternate dimensions on or off. Alternate dimensions are dimension text added to your drawing in addition to the standard dimension text.

Dimaltf sets the scale factor for alternate dimensions (i.e., metric). The default is 25.4, which is the millimeter equivalent of 1".

Dimaltd sets the number of decimal places displayed in the alternate dimensions.

Dimapost adds suffix to alternate dimensions, as in 4.5mm.

If you prefer, you can use the metric template drawing supplied by AutoCAD.

1. Start a New drawing.

2. In the Create New Drawing dialog box, select the Use a Template option.

3. Click on ACADISO.DWT, and press OK to open the template.

This drawing is set up for metric/ISO standard drawings.

A Closer Look at the Dimension Styles Dialog Box

As you saw in Chapter 9, you can control the appearance and format of dimensions through dimension styles. To get the Dimension Styles dialog box, you click on the Dimension Style button on the Dimensioning Toolbar, or enter **Ddim** ↵ at the command line.

The three buttons in the Dimension Styles dialog box—Geometry, Format, and Annotation—open related dialog boxes that control the variables associated with these three aspects of AutoCAD's dimensioning system. You'll get a closer look at these dialog boxes in the next section.

Within the Dimension Styles dialog box, dimensions are divided into "families" as a way of classifying the different types of dimensions available in AutoCAD. The dimension families are angular, diameter, linear, leader, ordinate, and radial. The Parent family affects all the dimension families globally. You can fine-tune your dimension styles by making settings to each family independently. If you don't set any of the families, their settings default to the Parent settings. To change the settings of a family, click on the family name's radio button before making changes in the Geometry, Format, or Annotation dialog boxes.

The following paragraphs describe the options in the Geometry, Format, and Annotation subdialogs. Each description specifies the dimension variables (in parentheses) that are related to the dialog box option. As you work through this appendix, you may want to refer back to Chapter 9's figures that illustrate these subdialogs.

The Geometry Dialog Box

This dialog box lets you control the placement and appearance of dimension lines, arrowheads, extension lines, and center marks. You can also set a scale factor for these dimension components.

The Dimension Line Group Refer to Figure D.1 for examples of the effects of these options.

> **Suppress (Dimsd1, Dimsd2)** suppresses the dimension line to the left or right of the dimension text.

Extension (Dimdle) sets the distance that dimension lines are drawn beyond extension lines, when using the standard AutoCAD dimension tick for arrows. This option is unavailable (grayed out) when the filled arrow is selected in the Arrowheads group.

Spacing (Dimdli) determines the distance between dimension lines from a common extension line generated by the Baseline Dimension or Continue Dimension options on the Dimensioning toolbar.

Color (Dimclrd) sets the color of dimension lines. The standard Auto-CAD Color dialog box appears, allowing you to visually select a color.

FIGURE D.1:

Examples of how the Dimension Line options affect dimensions

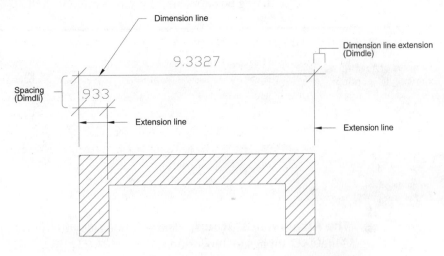

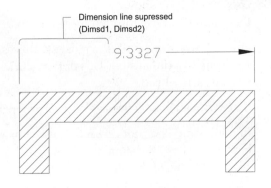

The Extension Line Group Refer to Figure D.2 for examples of the effects of these options.

Suppress (Dimse1, Dimse2) suppresses the first or second dimension extension line.

Extensions (Dimsexe) sets the distance that extension lines extend beyond the dimension line.

Origin Offset (Dimexo) sets the distance the extension line is offset from its point of origin on the object being dimensioned.

Color (Dimclre) sets the color of extension lines. The standard AutoCAD Color dialog box appears, allowing you to visually select a color.

FIGURE D.2:

Examples of how the Extension Line options affect extension lines

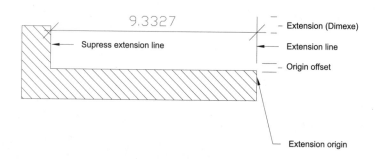

The Arrowheads Group These options let you control the type of arrowhead AutoCAD applies to dimensions.

1st shows you a pull-down list of choices to set the arrowheads at both ends of the dimension line. When you select an arrowhead, the graphic above the group shows you how the arrow will look. You can also click on the graphic to cycle through the selections.

2nd shows you a pull-down list of choices to set different arrowheads for each side of a dimension. This option works like the 1st option, but only sets one arrowhead.

Size (Dimasz) sets the size of the arrowhead.

In the 1st and 2nd pull-down lists is a choice called User; this lets you use a block in place of the standard arrows. A dialog box opens, in which you enter the name of the block you wish to use for the arrow. The block must already exist in the drawing before you can add it, and it must follow the guidelines described in the *Alternate Dimension Arrows* section of this appendix.

The Center Group   These options let you determine what center mark is drawn when using the Dimcenter command. Center marks are also drawn when dimension lines are placed outside a circle or arc using the Diameter or Dimradius commands. All these settings are controlled by the Dimcen system variable.

Mark   adds a center mark.

Line   creates a center mark and lines.

None   suppresses the creation of center marks and lines.

Size   controls the size of the center marks.

The Scale Group   These options let you control the overall scaling of dimensions.

Overall Scale (Dimscale)   sets the scale factor for the size of dimension components, text and arrow size, and text location. This setting has no effect on actual dimension text or the distances being dimensioned.

Scale to Paper Space   is meaningful only if you dimension objects in a Model Space viewport while you're in Paper Space. When this option is enabled, AutoCAD adjusts the scaling of dimension components to Paper Space.

The Format Dialog Box

This subdialog contains the following general settings:

User Defined (Dimupt)   overrides the dimension text location settings and lets you place the text manually when the dimensions are drawn.

Force Line Inside (Dimtofl)   forces a dimension line to be drawn between extension lines under all conditions.

Fit (Dimfit)   lets you determine how dimension text and arrows are placed between extension lines. In the pull-down list, Text and Arrows causes both arrows and text to be placed outside extensions if space isn't available. Text Only gives text priority, so that if space is available for text only, arrows will be placed outside extension lines. With the Best Fit option, AutoCAD determines whether text or arrows fit better, and draws the dimension accordingly. Leader draws a leader line from the dimension line to the dimension text when space for text is not available.

The settings in the Format subdialog control the location of dimension text. The **Text, Horizontal Justification, and Vertical Justification** groups include a graphic that demonstrates the effect of your selected option on the dimension text. You can also click on the graphic to scroll through the options.

The Text Group   These options let you control the text location.

Inside Horizontal (Dimtih)   orients text horizontally when it occurs between extension lines, regardless of the dimension lines' orientations.

Outside Horizontal (Dimtoh)   orients text horizontally when it occurs outside the extension lines, regardless of the dimension lines' orientations.

The Horizontal Justification Group   These settings can also be controlled using the Dimjust system variable.

Centered   centers the dimension text between the extension lines.

1st Extension Line   places the text next to the first extension line.

2nd Extension Line   places the text next to the second extension line.

Over 1st Extension   places the text over the first extension line, aligned with the extension line.

Over 2nd Extension   places the text over the second extension line, aligned with the extension line.

Vertical Justification   These options can also be set using the Dimtad system variable.

Centered   places the dimension text in line with the dimension line.

Above   places the text above the dimension line, as is typical for architectural dimensioning. The distance from the text to the dimension line can be set with the Gap option in the Annotation subdialog.

Outside places the text outside the dimension line at a point farthest away from the origin point of the first extension line. This effect is similar to the Above option, but is more apparent in circular dimensions.

JIS places text in conformance with the Japanese Industrial Standards.

The Annotation Dialog Box

This dialog box controls the dimension text. You can determine the style, color, and size of text, as well as the unit style, tolerance, and alternate dimensions.

Primary Units and Alternate Units These two groups offer the same options. The Primary Units options affect only the main dimension text, and the Alternate Units options control alternate units when they are enabled. (Alternate units are dimension values that are shown in brackets next to the standard dimension value, and are helpful when two unit systems, such as U.S. (feet and inches) and metric, are used in the same drawing.) The Enable Units check box turns on the alternate units (see Figure D.3).

FIGURE D.3:

An example of alternate units

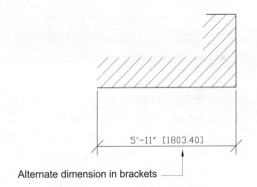

5'–11" [1803.40]

Alternate dimension in brackets

Prefix lets you include a prefix in dimension text, and **Suffix** lets you include a suffix in dimension text. For the primary dimension text, Prefix and Suffix are controlled by the same Dimpost system variable. For alternate dimension text, Prefix and Suffix share the Dimapost system variable. See Table D.2 for details on Dimpost and Dimapost.

Both the Primary Units and Alternate Units groups have a Units button, which you click to bring up the Primary Units and Alternate Units dialog boxes. These dialog boxes contain the same options; when enabled, the Primary Units options affect only the main dimension text, and the Alternate Units options affect only alternate dimension text. Here are descriptions of these options:

Units and **Angles**   let you select the unit and angle styles (which are the same styles as for the Units command described in Chapter 3). For Primary Units, the Units option is controlled by the Dimunit system variable, and the Angles option is controlled by the Dimaunit system variable. For Alternate Units, the Units option is controlled by the Dimaltu.

Dimension Precision and **Tolerance Precision** (Dimdec, Dimtdec, Dimaltd, Dimalttd)   set the number of decimal places you want to use for these values. Dimension precision can also be set using the Dimdec system variable, and tolerance precision using Dimtdec. For Alternate Units, dimension precision can be set using Dimaltd, and tolerance precision using Dimalttd.

Dimension Zero Suppression (Dimzin, Dimaltz)   controls how AutoCAD handles zeroes in dimensions. The Leading option suppresses leading zeroes in a decimal dimension (for example, 0.3000 becomes .3000). The Trailing option suppresses trailing zeroes (so that 8.8000 becomes 8.8, or 45.0000 becomes 45). The 0 Feet option suppresses zero feet values in an architectural dimension so that 0'–4" becomes 4".

0 Inches   suppresses zero inch values in an architectural dimension, so that 12' –0" becomes 12'. The Dimzin system variable controls this option for Primary Units; the Dimaltz system variable controls this option for Alternate Units.

Tolerance Zero Suppression (Dimtzin, Dimalttz)   controls how AutoCAD handles zeroes in tolerance dimensions. (See the description for Dimension Zero Suppression, just above.) The Dimtzin system variable controls this option for Primary Units; Dimalttz controls this option for Alternate Units.

Scale   lets you specify a scale factor to linear dimensions. This setting affects the dimension text value. For example, say you have drawn an object to one-half its actual size. To have your dimensions reflect the true size of the object, you would set the Linear input box to 2. When you place dimensions in the drawing, AutoCAD multiplies the drawing distances by 2 to derive the dimension text value. By checking the Paper Space Only check box, you tell AutoCAD to apply the scale factor only when dimensioning in Paper Space. These two options in Alternate Units perform the same function for alternate dimension text. In Primary Units, the Scale options are controlled by the Dimlfac system variable. When Paper Space Only is enabled, Dimlfac becomes a negative value. For Alternate Units, the scale options are controlled by the Dimaltf system variable.

The Tolerance Group   These options affect both primary and alternate units.

Method   sets the type of tolerance displayed in a dimension. Choose among the following: The Symmetrical option adds a single tolerance value with a plus-minus (±) sign; this is the same as Dimtol set to 1 and Dimlim set to 0. The Deviation option adds two stacked values, one a plus value and the other a minus value. The Limits option places two stacked dimension values, showing the allowable range for the dimension instead of the single dimension (this is the same as Dimtol set to 0 and Dimlim set to 1). The Basic option draws a box around the dimension text; the Dimgap system variable set to a negative value produces the same result.

Upper Value   sets the maximum tolerance limit. This is stored in the Dimtp system variable.

Lower Value   sets the minimum tolerance limit. This is stored in the Dimtm system variable.

Justification   sets the vertical location of stacked tolerance values.

Height   sets the height for tolerance values. This is stored in the Dimtfac system variable as a ratio of the tolerance height to the default text height used for dimension text.

The Text Group   These options let you control the appearance of text in a dimension.

Style (Dimtxsty)   sets the text style used for dimension text.

Height (Dimtxt)   sets the current text height for dimension text.

Gap (Dimgap)   sets a margin around the dimension text, within which margin the dimension line is broken.

Color (Dimclrt)   sets the color of the dimension text.

Round Off (Dimrnd)   sets the amount that dimensions are rounded off to the nearest value. This setting works in conjunction with the Dimtol system variable.

Importing Dimension Styles from Other Drawings

Dimension styles are saved within the current drawing file only. You don't have to recreate the dimension style for each new drawing, however. If you have loaded the Release 14 Bonus menu (see Appendix B for overall installation instructions), you can import a dimension style which you created in another drawing.

First, save the dimension style using the Bonus ➢ Tools ➢ Dimstyle Export option. The dimension style is saved to a user-specifed .dim file. For example, you might call it Standard.dim or mydim1.dim.

To restore an exported dimension style, choose Bonus ➢ Tools ➢ Dimstyle Import. The selected .dim file is loaded into your current drawing.

Drawing Blocks for Your Own Dimension Arrows and Tick Marks

If you don't want to use the arrowheads supplied by AutoCAD for your dimension lines, you can create a block of the arrowheads or tick marks you like, to be used in the Arrowheads group of the Dimension Styles/Geometry dialog box.

TIP   To get to the Arrowhead options, click on the Dimension Styles button on the Dimensioning toolbar, or type **Ddim** ↵. At the Dimension Styles dialog box, click on Geometry, and choose User from the pull-down list for the 1st arrowhead.

For example, say you want to have a tick mark that is thicker than the dimension lines and extensions. You can create a block of the tick mark on a layer you assign to a thick pen weight, and then assign that block to the Arrowhead setting. This is done by first opening the Geometry dialog box from the Dimension Styles dialog box (click on the Dimension Styles button on the Dimensioning toolbar to open the Dimension Styles dialog box.) Next, choose User Arrow from the first pull-down list in the Arrowheads group. At the User Arrow dialog box, enter the name of your arrow block.

When you draw the arrow block, make it one unit long. The block's insertion point will be used to determine the point of the arrow that meets the extension line, so make sure you place the insertion point at the tip of the arrow. Because the arrow on the right side of the dimension line will be inserted with a zero rotation value, create the arrow block so that it is pointing to the right (see Figure D.4). The arrow block is rotated 180° for the left side of the dimension line.

FIGURE D.4:

The orientation and size of a block used in place of the default arrow

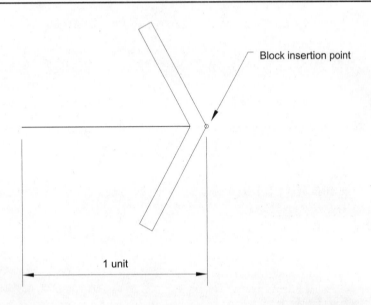

Block insertion point

1 unit

To have a different type of arrow at both ends of the dimension line, create a block for each arrow. Then, in the Dimension Styles/Geometry dialog box, choose User in the pull-down list for the 1st arrowhead, and enter the name of one block. Then choose User in the pull-down list for the second arrowhead, and enter the name of the other block.

INDEX

Note to the Reader: Throughout this index page numbers that appear in **boldface** indicate primary discussions of a topic. Page numbers that appear in *italics* indicate illustrations.

SYMBOLS

' (apostrophes), 491, 693

* (asterisks)

    in Acad.psf file, 1102

    with calculator, 625

    in layer filters, 183

@ (at signs) for last point, 51–52

\ (backslashes)

    in menus, 1059

    for spaces, 481

[] <> (brackets)

    with calculator, 624–625

    for default options, 59

    for line types, 1071

    for menu items, 1062, 1064

^ (carets), 625, 1059

, (commas)

    in Cartesian coordinates, 53

    in hatch patterns, 1075

    in line type patterns, 1068–1069

$ (dollar signs), 596

" (double quotes)

    as delimiters, 490–491

    in macros, 979

    in units, 97

= (equal signs) in filters, 619

! (exclamation points) in filters, 619

> (greater-than symbols)

    in filters, 619–620

    in pull-down menus, 1061

    for text, 423–424

< (less-than symbols). *See* less-than symbols (<)

- (minus signs)

    with calculator, 625

    for command prompt, 9

    in line type patterns, 1069

    in pull-down menus, 1061

    in units, 97

() parentheses

    for calculator, 625–626

    for functions, 978–979

% (percent signs), 394

. (periods), 670

+ (plus signs)

    with calculator, 625

    in menus, 1060

? (question marks)

    in layer filters, 183

    for system variables, 694

; (semicolons) in menus, 1060

' (single quotes), 491, 693

/ (slashes)

    with calculator, 625

    as delimiters, 491

    for options, 59

~ (tildes), 1061

_ (underlines), 394

| (vertical bars), 594, 596

NUMBERS

A

B

C

D

E

F

G

H

M

N

O

S

T

V

W

X

Y

What's on the CD

This CD-ROM is packed with valuable resources, including two electronic versions of Sybex books, add-ons, utilities, references, and drawing files from the exercises in this book. More specifically, the CD-ROM includes:

- *AutoCAD 14 Instant Reference*, a Sybex best seller, is now an electronic book. This is the definitive companion to *Mastering AutoCAD 14*, providing you with detailed descriptions of AutoCAD's commands and tools.

- **The** *ABC's of AutoLISP* is a complete tutorial and reference book for AutoLISP, the AutoCAD macro-programming language. This book has been a favorite of end users and developers alike, and it's now in an easy-to-use Web-browser format.

- **AEC On-Screen** is an architectural add-on that gives you the basic symbols library for drawing floor plans as well as utilities to simplify floor plan layout and drawing setup. It also includes general utilities to help make any drawing task easier.

- **Eye2eye** is an add-on utility that greatly simplifies the process for obtaining 3D perspective views of your 3D models. No more lost views and unwieldy commands. Set your views using an easy-to-use camera and target metaphor.

- **ActiveX samples** help you get started with Automation in AutoCAD. You can use these examples along with Chapter 20 to explore the newest customization feature of AutoCAD.

- **Whip2 Netscape Communicator plug-in** allows you to view AutoCAD drawings over the Internet. It gives you full Pan and Zoom capabilities as well as access to Web links embedded in AutoCAD files.

- **All the drawing files** from the exercises in the book are included so you can easily study any topic at any time. You can experiment with the files on your own without worrying about losing or corrupting them.